PORTRAITS IN AMERICAN ARCHAEOLOGY

PORTRAITS
IN
AMERICAN
ARCHAEOLOGY

REMEMBRANCES

OF SOME

DISTINGUISHED AMERICANISTS

Gordon Randolph Willey

UNIVERSITY OF NEW MEXICO PRESS

ALBUQUERQUE

Library of Congress Cataloging-in-Publication Data

Willey, Gordon Randolph, 1913–
Portraits in American archaeology : remembrances of some
distinguished Americanists / Gordon Randolph Willey.
p. cm.
Bibliography: p.
ISBN 0-8263-1133-4
ISBN 0-8263-1146-6 (pbk.)
1. Archaeologists—United States—Biography. 2. Americanists—
Biography. 3. America—Antiquities. 4. Indians—Antiquities.
I. Title.
E175.45.W55 1989
973.1'092'2—dc19
[B]
88-30442
CIP

TO KATHARINE

CONTENTS

Acknowledgments

The idea for this book originated with my wife, Katharine, who knew almost all of its subjects and who has read over all that I have written here about them. Her counsel, support, and love have been of utmost importance during its writing, as they have been for the past 50 years of my life. I dedicate the book to her.

A number of individuals have provided information about several of the subjects of my portraits. They are: Elizabeth Gibson, on Byron Cummings; Joanna Kelly Arline and Patricia Kelly, on Arthur Randolph Kelly; David T. W. McCord, on William Duncan Strong; Philip Phillips and F. L. Stagg, on George Clapp Vaillant; Heather Lechtman, on Junius Bouton Bird; Francis Lothrop and R. H. Ives Gammell, on Samuel Kirkland Lothrop; Marion Stirling Pugh, on Matthew Williams Stirling; Mary Ricketson Bullard, on William Rotch Bullard, Jr.; Katherine Winslow Pollock, on Harry Evelyn Dorr Pollock; and Betty Griggs Nichols Smith, on Augustus Ledyard Smith. I am indebted to all of them for their help.

Jeremy A. Sabloff, Patricia R. Anawalt, Elizabeth H. Boone, Richard M. Leventhal, Peter Guralnick, and Rosemary Sharp have read some of these portraits, and I am grateful to them for the encouragement they have given me to see such a work brought to completion.

My special thanks go to Elizabeth Hadas, Director of the University of New Mexico Press, for her interest in this work and for good advice in its preparation. Claire Sanderson's editing and Milenda Nan Ok Lee's design work put the finishing touches to the book, and I am most appreciative of their efforts.

G.R.W.
Cambridge, Massachusetts
24 March 1988

Introduction

This book is based upon the lives and careers of a number of American archaeologists, and upon my associations with them. One purpose in writing it has been for the sheer enjoyment of remembering. It is, for me, a series of "remembrances of things past"—going back for more than 50 years. At the same time, I also write for other archaeologists. Some few in such a potential audience will have been, like me, contemporaries, or partial contemporaries, of the people I talk about; but as these ranks are rapidly growing thinner, I suppose I am addressing myself mainly to a younger generation.

In this latter light, what I have to say could be considered a part of the history of American archaeology, that history we have become so self-conscious about in recent years. This sounds weightier than I mean it to. But history, of course, has many strands to it. Obviously, the main course of the history of American archaeology will be recorded by recounting its purposes, its procedures, its substantive results, and its interpretive statements, as all of these things have changed from one generation to the next. Still, archaeology is carried out by people, and a view of these people, as individuals and personalities, in the context of their times, is a part of history.

Clearly, one's professional colleagues play a large part in one's life. I think that this is particularly true of archaeology and, perhaps, especially of Americanist archaeology. The field used to be quite small. I can remember in 1937, when I was a beginner, that the annual meeting of the Society for American Archaeology, the principal official body of our profession, was held in a single room and with single sessions. Attendance was probably on the order of 30 or 40 of us, young and old. This smallness allowed for most of us to know each other personally, at least on the basis of face-to-face meetings and discussions. It promoted a kind of necessary in-group solidarity. We were terribly dependent upon each other. Today, the membership of the Society for American Archaeology is over 5,000 so that the old "in-group" quality does not exist to the degree that it once did; nevertheless, and compared to many other fields and disciplines, the relationships among archaeological colleagues are still close—close and gossipy, friendly and unfriendly, but charged with an interest in each other, as personalities as well as scholars.

In these memoirs, I have tried to give portraits of my subjects as people as well as archaeologists. Naturally, as an archaeologist writing about other archaeologists, some comments about their work, laudatory or critical, are a part of what I have to say, but I certainly have not attempted to write thoroughgoing intellectual evaluations of the individuals involved. Although I have made frequent bibliographic references to the works of my subjects, complete bibliographies have not been assembled for any of them. The remaining titles which I include in the book's bibliography are those by other authors which in some way relate to the lives and works of the individuals of the memoirs.

I have set no special criteria about whom to include in my "gallery of portraits". It is simply a highly personal and subjective selection. The list had to be limited, and it numbers sixteen individuals. I knew them all personally and was associated with them in social as well as professional contexts. Some, I would consider, were very close friends. All were people I liked. One might note that all of them are now dead. All, except one, were older than I although this varied from that true seniority of 30 years or more to as little as 2 years. While I did not set out with the idea of making this a list of the key figures in the development of Precolumbian archaeology, I know that many of the names I have chosen could be so regarded. Some of them are former professors, mentors, or bosses. Others were, I suppose, role models for a young, aspirant archaeologist; still others would be most accurately defined as side-by-side colleagues. At least at some stage in their careers all were "digging" archaeologists, although most of them can be said to have transcended this limitation—if it be one—by more general writings and researches. Two of these scholars, it will be seen, are more widely identified as social, cultural, or general anthropologists; however, both have done archaeology of high quality, and their contributions to the archaeological field are well recognized.

Finally, I should note that my arrangement of the portraits in this book follows the order in which I first came to know the people or at least to be closely associated with them. This autobiographical arrangement should help the reader put my reactions to my subjects in a proper perspective. As I grew older, I naturally brought my previous memories and experiences with me as I came to know each of these colleagues in turn. Such, of course, will have had a bearing on my impressions, my judgments, and my opinions. Although biographical in its primary intent, this book, perforce, has its autobiographical side.

Portraits in American Archaeology

BYRON CUMMINGS
In old age. Photo taken at Rainbow Natural Bridge in the summer
of 1935, by Tad Nichols.
Courtesy Arizona State Museum, University of Arizona, and Tad
Nichols.

BYRON CUMMINGS
(1860–1954)

Byron Cummings was one of the foremost pioneers in Southwestern archaeology. Indeed, he was the "Dean" of the field, a title which he justifiably carried by seniority and qualities of leadership. That he was always referred to as "Dean Cummings" at the University of Arizona, where he spent the last half of his academic career, also derived from the fact that he had served terms there as Dean of the Faculty of Letters, Arts, and Sciences and Dean of Men, and the title stuck even after he had relinquished these positions. I am uncomfortable in thinking about him with any form of address other than "Dean", and I am sure this applies to students who were my contemporaries, my predecessors, and my successors at Arizona.

Cummings was born in upstate New York. He graduated from Rutgers College, in New Jersey, and after this he went to Salt Lake City where he joined the faculty at the University of Utah in 1893. Those were still early days on the nation's western frontiers. The redoubtable Apache warrior, Geronimo, had only been subdued by the U.S. military in 1885, and the Wounded Knee uprising took place in 1890. States or Territories like Utah, Arizona, New Mexico, and Colorado were still thinly populated by white settlers. To be an archaeologist then was also to be an explorer. To understand Cummings' role in archaeology, it is necessary to view him in this context.

What later became the Southwestern United States had been made a part of the colony of New Spain, or Mexico, by the Spanish conquistadores in the 16th century. They left accounts of the living inhabitants as well as the archaeological Pueblo and Cliff-Dweller ruins of the area. More detailed descriptions of such ruins resulted from early United States government surveys of the latter half of the 19th century. A few archaeological reports also date to later in the 19th century, perhaps the most professional of these being the work of the Swedish archaeologist, Gustav von Nordenskiold (1893) on the cliff dwellings of Mesa Verde. Significant to this archaeological history of the Southwest, the universities of Utah, Arizona,

New Mexico, and Colorado were being founded in these late decades of the 19th century, and by the early 20th century scholars from these universities, as well as from Harvard and from the Smithsonian Institution, had entered the Southwestern archaeological field (Willey and Sabloff, 1974, pp. 59–60). Byron Cummings was one of these early archaeological scholars. He worked first from a base at the University of Utah, where he was a professor in the Classics Department, and, subsequently from the University of Arizona.

An early student of Cummings', Neil M. Judd, who was also his nephew, places Cummings' beginnings in Southwestern archaeological fieldwork with a summer trip made in 1906 through Nine-Mile Canyon in southern Utah (Judd, 1950, 1954a,b). The Southwest of the Four Corners region (the conjoining of the borders of Arizona, New Mexico, Utah, and Colorado) was wild country in those days. There was still occasional "trouble with the Indians", and U.S. Army units were posted in the area. On the 1906 trip, Cummings had a confrontation with a party of Ute Indians who insisted that he leave the Nine-Mile Canyon region immediately. In his firm but peaceful fashion, the Dean refused to turn around and go immediately but insisted on staying overnight. In the course of these negotiations, he invited the Indians for supper. They accepted, and all ended happily, with the Dean leaving the next morning, as he had promised.

This 1906 event was highly characteristic of the Dean. He was courageous and sure of himself; he respected others; but he would take no bullying from them. There was something of the young Theodore Roosevelt in his personality and even physical makeup. Both were small in stature, but both had developed muscular physiques. Both were men of indomitable will. As I write this, I recall that the Dean once told me that "he was a worshipper at the shrine of Theodore Roosevelt". Other Southwestern Indians—the Navajos—recognized the qualities of leadership in Byron Cummings. They called him "Natani Yazzie", or "Little Captain" (Tanner, 1954).

The basic themes of these early Southwestern expeditions were exploration and discovery, and these discoveries were not only archaeological ones. Thus, in 1909, Cummings and a small party of whites were the first non-Indians to see the spectacular Rainbow Natural Bridge in southern Utah. Word had come—through Indian sources—about such a "bridge", and this news eventually reached as far as Washington, D.C. There the president of the United States was anxious that the Rainbow Bridge, as well as some other similar natural "bridges" in the same territory, be explored and the region set aside as a National Area.

To this end, Cummings readied an expedition that was to be led into the Rainbow Bridge by a reliable Navajo Indian guide who had been recruited for him by the pioneer Wetherill family, the famous "Trader's to the Navajos". The expedition turned out to be not only an exciting but a rivalrous enterprise. I heard the Dean relate the story when he took a student group into Rainbow in 1935. It seems that in 1909, he had been asked, at the last minute, to hold up his trip to wait for a geologist who was being sent from Washington D.C. by the Geological Survey. When they were joined by this individual, relations did not develop altogether cordially. The newcomer took a superior attitude; he was, after all, the United States Government's official emissary on this important expedition; and, in his mind, he should have been the leader, or at least the chief personage, involved in the upcoming discovery. When the expedition finally neared Rainbow Bridge, and the Indian guide pointed it out, the Dean, who was riding ahead with the guide, turned in his saddle and relayed the information to the other members of the party. For a moment, the Washington "personage" appeared not to hear, or at least he refused to look in the direction indicated by the Dean. Then, quite suddenly, with a gesture and cry that would seem to signal an original and independent discovery, he spurred his horse ahead, apparently in a mad gallop to be the first to ride under the great natural arch and in so doing, claim it. But others in the Cummings party were unwilling to let this happen. It was one of the Wetherills, I believe the Dean said, who, not to be outdone, also put his horse into a gallop and beat the Washington interloper under the bridge. Whatever the trials of its discovery—and this was clearly a "white man's discovery"—the bridge is really quite a sight. I remember going to sleep beneath it on a moonlit night in the summer of 1935, just 26 years after Dean Cummings first set eyes upon it.

Cummings' archaeological discoveries in that 1906–1909 period were notable. He and his student assistants, led by Navajo guides, were taken to the now-famed cliff ruins of Betatakin, Inscription House, and Ladder House, among others. It is easy to sense the drama and excitement of these discoveries. The sheer beauty of some of these sites must have been a source of wonder for Cummings and his companions. In the summer of 1935, when our student party visited these ruins with the Dean, I was awestruck with the ruin of Betatakin. The canyon it was in had a lost, hidden quality. At its bottom it was filled with the lush greenery of summer vegetation. Above this, the ruin was magically nestled in its niche of the rock cliff face. When Cummings first visited it, one could walk into rooms which, centuries ago, had been abandoned by their former inhabitants, with pottery vessels and stone implements left where they had been last used on the floor.

Cummings' early work also involved excavations. One such excavation was at Alkali Ridge, in southern Utah, in 1908. Neil Judd was on this dig with him, as was A. V. Kidder. This work was partially financed by, and under the general aegis of, the School of American Research. Cummings' contemporary, Edgar Lee Hewett, was then director of the School, and there was a rivalry between Cummings and Hewett. These two pioneers might be said to have been competing for "first place" in Southwestern archaeology. Hewett assigned the then quite young (age 23) A. V. Kidder, a graduate student just out from Harvard, to be the director of the Alkali Ridge operation. Many years afterwards, Kidder told me that the situation had been an embarrassing one for him and would have been worse except for the Dean's gentlemanliness and amiability about the matter. They compromised by being "co-directors". Cummings continued with Southwestern fieldwork at Segazlin Mesa, Vandal Cave, and at various sites in the Flagstaff and Verde Valley regions. He also left the Southwest for his only foreign fieldwork, digging for two seasons at Cuicuilco (Cummings, 1933), in the Valley of Mexico, in 1924–1925. His major field project, however, was a Southwestern one, and it was also his last. This was at Kinishba (Cummings, 1940), a pueblo in the White Mountains of eastern Arizona, where he conducted excavations and restorations from 1931 until 1947.

Neil Judd (1954b), in appraising Cummings, said that the Dean had "adopted archaeology" in 1906, at a relatively late stage in his life (age 46), and that he was not a "trained archaeologist", but a self-taught one. This is true, in a sense, but in Cummings' college days there was little in the way of formal "training" in archaeology, especially in the United States, so that all of its leading practitioners of that time—Putnam, Brinton, Powell, Thomas—were essentially self-taught. Actually, Cummings did have an academic background related to archaeology in that his formal training was in classics. Combined with this, he had the humanistic and anthropological conviction that the human past of the North American Indian, although different from that of the Mediterranean Classical world, was of equal importance and that it should be recovered. He also realized the complexity and the difficulty of that task which lay before him and which would continue to confront those who followed him in Southwestern archaeological endeavors.

To give a more thorough account of Byron Cummings' background, let us note that he was born on 20 September 1860, in Westville, Franklin County, upstate New York, where his ancestors had lived since the time of the American Revolution. He was of a large family. His father was killed in the Civil War the year after his birth. As a boy, he had to work part time, or intermittently, to put himself through school so that he was 25 when he finally graduated from Oswego Normal School in 1885. From there he went to Rutgers College, taking an A.B. in 1889 and an A.M. in 1892. During part of his time at Rutgers he taught in the local preparatory school, giving instruction in Greek, Latin, and mathematics. Then, in 1893, he was offered a post at the new University of Utah. He accepted this, and after two years there he became Full Professor and the head of the Classics Department. In the summer of 1896 he took additional graduate work at the University of Chicago. This was also an important time for him in other ways as he married Isabell MacLaury that year. They were to have one son, Malcolm, who was to accompany his father on some of his early expeditions and who survived him. His wife, Isabell, died in 1929.

From 1905 to 1915, Cummings was Dean of the Faculty of Arts and Sciences at Utah, and, of course, it was during this period that he found time in a busy life to carry out the early archaeological explorations we have referred to. Always interested in learning more, he went to the University of Berlin to study archaeology on a sabbatical leave in the 1910–1911 academic year. Thus, while it is true that Byron Cummings "adopted" archaeology, and was "self-taught" within the context of the Southwestern field, he was also a firm believer in the formal academic aspects of the discipline.

In 1915 there were troubles at the University of Utah. A number of professors, including Cummings, were dissatisfied with the strong hand that the Mormon Church held over the university, and they resigned in protest. Cummings was immediately offered a position at the University of Arizona, in Tucson, which he accepted. Going there, he established a Department of Archaeology in that first year. At the same time, he reorganized the Arizona State Museum which, under his directorship, was turned more in the direction of archaeology and anthropology. In addition to his scholarship, his qualities as a leader and an administrator were very quickly recognized in his new setting. As I have already noted, he was Dean of the Faculty of Letters, Arts, and Sciences (from 1917 until 1921), and he also served as Dean of Men during much of this same (from 1918 until 1921). In the deadly influenza epidemic of 1918–1919, when many of the faculty were moved from the immediate campus area, the Dean insisted on staying to help in the nursing of the many sick students (Douglass, 1950). As I grew to know him during the few years I was at Arizona, I came to see how very much in character this would have been for the Dean.

My own first meeting with Byron Cummings was in 1931. As a high school student, at Woodrow Wilson High School, in Long Beach, California, I had decided that I wanted to become an archaeologist. I had had no particular encouragement in this direction other than that history had always been a favorite subject and this seemed like a powerfully romantic extension of it. Fortunately, in my last semester of high school, I had a teacher in Latin American history—a man for whom I had prepared book reports on Prescott's "Mexico" and "Peru"— who told me that if I really wanted to pursue an archaeological career I should seek out a Professor Byron Cummings at the University of Arizona. I also remember him adding the caution that I ought to consider it pretty seriously before going to "a place like the University of Arizona" (as opposed to what he considered to be the more prestigious University of California at Berkeley) and that I should consider even more seriously whether or not I wanted to go into "something like archaeology" (rather than a respectable field like history). But my mind was made up.

As I was ashamed of my penmanship, and had no typewriter, I had my father write to Professor Cummings for me, declaring my intentions to enter the University of Arizona. I should add that in those days awaiting college admission was not the terrifying ordeal that it is for the young today. If one—or one's parents—had the tuition and you had moderately respectable high school grades, there was nothing to it. Professor Cummings wrote back encouragingly, and I was duly admitted to Arizona and presented myself there in early February of 1931.

In those days, registration at the University of Arizona was held on the main floor of the men's gymnasium, with each department having a table at which were seated two or three faculty representatives. Prospective students lined up to speak to professors and to have their study cards signed. In 1931, Professor Cummings was 70. At that first meeting, I remember being shocked that this famous archaeologist was such an elderly man, indeed, grandfatherly. Subconsciously, I must have harboured an image of a famous archaeologist as an adventurous-looking figure, someone with a touch of gray at the temples, perhaps, but not really *old* old. It was cool in the gymnasium that morning, and Professor Cummings wore a black overcoat, cloakwise over his shoulders, as he sat behind the table. I had been told by someone that he was just recovering from a bout of flu, and he did look a little pale. I also thought he looked frail. This last was an erroneous impression.

When I presented myself to Cummings that morning, if I was surprised and, perhaps, a little disappointed, at his appearance, he may have been equally surprised and disappointed in mine. The letter that my father had written him, in a bold and flowing hand, must have impressed Professor Cummings as having been written by a mature person (as, indeed, it was). I remember that in his reply, he had referred to graduate work and an M.A. degree. I think he assumed that the writer was someone, perhaps, who wished to take up archaeology as an avocation or a second career. Anyhow, when Professor Cummings saw me in the gymnasium that morning, he commented upon my extremely youthful appearance and suggested that I begin my archaeological studies with just a single introductory anthropology course that would be offered by a comely young lady seated at his side, a Miss Fraps. That was fine, I replied, but couldn't I take a course with him as well? He looked at me very seriously—as he always did when addressing anyone—and said that "it might be a good idea if you put on a little muscle first." I guess he thought I looked frail, too.

For the first year at Arizona my anthropology and archaeology consisted of much needed and informative courses by the attractive Miss Fraps (better known afterwards as Mrs. Clara Lee Fraps Tanner), and my contacts with the Dean were limited to saying "good morning" as we passed each other in the stadium hallway from which the archaeology classrooms and offices opened. I should explain that in those days the Archaeology Department and the State Museum, the latter also in the Dean's charge, were housed in the football stadium, in effect, down beneath the stadium seats. I recall the Dean moving swiftly and purposefully down that hallway from office-to-office or office-to-classroom. I don't believe I ever saw him walk slowly or stroll casually there or anywhere else. He was for that period a remote authority figure for me. Indeed, he was always to remain an authority figure in my eyes, although eventually a much less remote one.

After the introductory anthropology courses of my freshman year at Arizona, I was allowed to take the Dean's "Southwestern Archaeology" course in the fall of 1932. In this course, Cummings pulled no punches. For the first time, I was given a taste of the details of archaeology—the specifics of basketry weaving and twining, the nature of stone implements and the probable ways of their manufacture and usages, and the multiplicity of pottery types and the importance of pottery in archaeology, especially Southwestern archaeology. It was with mixed feelings that I realized that this was what archaeology, or at least Southwestern archaeology, was going to be like. We had numerous papers to prepare. Usually these involved the collections in the Arizona State Museum. We had to draw objects as illustrations. I complainingly apologized to the Dean that I really couldn't draw, that I never could. "Well, Mr. Willey," he replied, "the only way to learn is just to do it. You may never be a professional artist, but by examining these artifacts and realizing what it is you want to show in your pictures, you'll be in a better position someday to instruct an artist in just what to look for and depict."

Gradually, as the semester went on, I began to see how the many detailed data of archaeology combined to give a larger picture. What was the purpose of this picture? At least one immediate purpose was some kind of culture-historical synthesis. This was some years after the first Pecos Conference of 1927 which had been held at the Pecos excavations in New Mexico, under the general direction of A. V. Kidder; but the Dean did not use the Pecos classification of Basketmaker I–III and Pueblo I–V. He preferred one of his own which, if I remember that classroom blackboard correctly, went something like this in its descending chronological order:

> Archaic
> > Early
> > Late
> Early Pueblo
> Great Pueblo
> Historic Pueblo

The Dean's Archaic Period referred to early cave and rock-shelter dwellers. This corresponded, at least in a general way, to the Pecos classification's hypothetical Basketmaker I Period, plus the definite preceramic Basketmaker II Period. Late

Archaic was the Cummings equivalent of Basketmaker III while Early Pueblo would have been about the same as the Pueblo I Period. The Cummings Great Pueblo Period subsumed the Pecos Pueblo II and III Periods, and the Historic Period bracketed Pueblo IV and V. In general, the Dean tried to be less rigid about period diagnostics than did the Pecos classification. Because of this, in the late 1920s and early 1930s, his scheme was considered less precise, "less-scientific", and more "old-fashioned" than the favored Pecos classification; however, it is interesting to note that by the latter half of the 1930s, as problems of trait time lags and differential rates of regional development began to become worrisome, one of the then younger leading Southwestern archaeologists, F. H. H. Roberts, Jr. (1935a, 1937; see also Kluckhohn in Kluckhohn and Reiter, eds. 1939), suggested revisions of the Pecos classification which moved back in the direction of Cummings' more loosely structured scheme.

It would be fair to say that the Dean never was fully comfortable with, nor sympathetic to, the push for chronological refinement that began to transform Southwestern archaeology in the second decade of the 20th century (Nelson, 1914, 1916; Kroeber, 1916; Spier, 1917; Kidder and Guernsey, 1919). Such systematics, of course, came to dominate the field in the 1920s and 1930s (Kidder, 1924, 1931; Schmidt, 1928; Gladwin, 1929; Gladwin *et al.* 1937; Roberts, 1932; see Willey and Sabloff, 1974). This is not to say that the Dean was oblivious to the importance of chronological or temporal-spatial controls, but it was not his first interest. While still an undergraduate, I remember that in a term paper I made the remark that "chronology was the primary goal of archaeology". The Dean marked this passage and questioned me about it. He looked at me in that patient but knowing way of his and said: "Do you really think so? Don't you think that there is something in archaeology that is more important than that." I reflected for a moment and then admitted that, "yes, a knowledge of the lives of the ancient people we were investigating was our prime responsibility." The Dean continued to look at me, nodded, and said: "Yes."

Dean Cummings was certainly not a cautious conservative

in many of his archaeological opinions. In fact, he often was an iconoclast, as in the question of the dating of Early Man in the Americas. On this, his discoveries and interpretations at the Double Adobe site in southern Arizona went against the main currents of established opinion in the early 1930s. The Dean held that his finds there were early, of Pleistocene date. This was before the archaeological community at large had accepted fully the dating of the Figgins discoveries at Folsom (Tanner, 1954). Now we know that he was correct. In other instances, hindsight now shows him to have been too daring. Thus, he wanted to date his Archaic ceramic strata at Cuicuilco to *ca.* 8000 B.C., taking the earliest end of a geological estimate of 2000 to 10,000 years ago that had been given to him on the Pedregal lava flows in the Valley of Mexico.

Although he voiced strong and independent opinions, the Dean tended to be uncomfortable with archaeological argument or disputation. He would occasionally discuss, in classes or seminars, his differences of opinion with other senior Southwestern archaeologists—Edgar Lee Hewett, O. S. Halseth, Earl Morris and H. S. Gladwin come immediately to mind in this connection. He left us with no doubt as to his convictions in these discussions and did not tarry long in considering adversarial explanations or interpretations. In graduate seminars, especially in Southwestern archaeology where some of my fellow students were much more knowledgeable in the subject than I, the Dean would listen to divergent opinions quite politely, but I don't think that he enjoyed doing so. He would then enunciate his position clearly, and go on to something else. In saying all this, I should remark that, in my more than 50 years in archaeology, I have not found this to be an unusual attitude among my many colleagues, and in his own time the Dean certainly was not alone in it.

I took an undergraduate course and, later, a graduate seminar with Cummings on the archaeology of Mexico, and I enjoyed these more than any others that I had at Arizona. They opened up another world in archaeology for me. As I think back, I am afraid I was a little snobbish about Southwestern archaeology. I wanted, instead, to study the "grand civilizations", places like Egypt and Mesopotamia. I had some introductory knowledge of these from courses with Miss Fraps, and I dreamed of going to these areas. I also realized that my chances of being able to do so were pretty slim. Mexico, obviously, was closer to home, and its prehistory offered a richness and complexity that at least approached those of Egypt or the Near East. Undoubtedly because of this, my student reports on Mexico were the best that I did for the Dean at Arizona. In my graduate year, after one such report, he told me that I should plan to go in this direction in archaeology rather than to long for Ur of the Chaldees or Abu Simbel. He thought that the American high cultures were exciting and romantic, and there was much to be done in areas like Mexico and Peru. He didn't strongly oppose my Old World ambitions, but he planted other ideas in my head. He was always very tolerant in such matters. He wasn't trying to live his students' lives for them; he expected industrious and decent behavior from them; but beyond that their course was their own.

As a student, I always felt that the Dean was well-disposed towards me. As I reflect back, I can see now that he was well-disposed towards all of his students, but that I should have thought of myself as favored in this regard at that time tells us something about the man and the charisma (how he would have detested that word!) that he exercised. I can see now that he recognized a high quotient of foolish romanticism in my attitudes about archaeology, but he overlooked this, with amusement, as the manner of the young. I was, of course, very young. In my graduate year at Arizona, most of my classmates were older in years than I and certainly older emotionally and in general experience. I can remember the Dean gently ridiculing me, on one occasion, for my youthful romantic posturings. A seminar group, of which I was a member, had been assembled to go out to what was known as the "University Ruin", a site owned by the university a few miles east of Tucson, for an afternoon's digging. As it happened, this was to be the first time for me to set spade into the ground in the interests of archaeology. I was prepared to do it in style. In some way or another, I had come into the possession of a very handsome pith helmet, an antique one, but beautifully silk-wrapped and in good condition. When I appeared with this fascinating item on my head, to set out for the University Ruin, the Dean, choking back laughter, could not refrain from observing that "Mr. Willey has appeared all set to play the part of an archaeologist in an H. Rider Haggard drama".

He was patient and long-suffering with me, more so than I deserved. For instance, in my first three years at Arizona, I failed to attend any of the summer field sessions at Kinishba; instead, I went back to Long Beach and spent my time on the beach and in other pleasures to be pursued by an idle youth. For someone who believed that fieldwork was the *sine qua non* of archaeology, this must have struck the Dean as pretty frivolous, especially on the part of a student who maintained such high aspirations for a career in archaeology. Yet, I guess he must have understood. I know that he did approve of some of the things that I did. I was on the track team at the university, and I used to see him in the stands at Saturday afternoon track meets. The following Monday, when I saw him in class, he always would congratulate me on my performance. He believed very firmly in such athletic activities and was a great supporter of them. The football field at the University of Utah, where he organized the athletic program many years ago, was named the Cummings Stadium in his honor (Tanner, 1954).

In June of 1935, a week after receiving my A.B. degree at Arizona, I went with Professor Cummings and a group of students to the dig at Kinishba. At long last, I must have decided that I had better forego my college-boy summer life on the beach in California and face up to the fact that I would soon be trying to be an archaeologist in the real world of graduate training and jobs. Kinishba, as mentioned, was in the White Mountains of eastern Arizona. It is on the Apache Indian Reservation, not far from the communities of Whiteriver Junction and Fort Apache. It is gorgeous country, green and lush with grass and small trees, or at least this fairly describes the environment around the Kinishba ruin in the summer time. I suppose the elevation at the site is about 5,000 feet. From the bowl-like valley in which it is situated, mountains can be viewed in all four directions. A dry ravine (more active in seasons other than the summer and flowing north-to-south) cuts through the valley, and the ancient pueblo town is situated on the two sides of the ravine, with its larger part on the east side. The east side was also the side where the University of Arizona field camp was located, at no great distance from the ruin. In 1935 (and all my descriptions shall be those of memory from that year for I have not seen Kinishba since) the men's camp was to the south of the main mounding of the ruin, the women's to the north. Down in the ravine was a cook shack and a building used both as a dining and lecture hall. This was sort of "headquarters" although the Dean maintained sleeping quarters and an office in two restored rooms at the south end of the pueblo.

We arrived at Kinishba—after the long drive from Tucson to Globe and then northward into the White Mountains—almost at dusk of a June evening. We had a supper by lantern light down in the dining hall and then set up our cots in the open near the ruin. This was the first time I had ever slept completely out in the open, with no tent or shelter, and it was my first time camping out in Arizona. All of my previous camp life had been in mosquito-infested terrain, and I remember being concerned at first about such a menace at Kinishba. I also wondered about possible rain—with no tent or awning over us. But, to my pleasant surprise, we had neither mosquitoes nor rain and passed a very good night. I began to be convinced that if one had to camp, Arizona was the place to do it. Years later, swathed in a mosquito net, in a hammock, in the Peten jungles, I would look back with longing on the cool, untroubled sleep of such Southwestern open-air camping.

The next morning, after breakfast, the Dean put us to work. A few of us, including my fellow student and best friend on the expedition, David Jones, a native of Gallup, New Mexico and a knowledgeable Southwestern archaeologist—who in later years was to become a National Park Service archaeologist—and I had come up a couple of days early with the Dean to set up camp and get things ready for the rest of our student colleagues. This we proceeded to do, pitching tents for both the men's and women's camps and doing a lot of other things. The Dean asked me if I was ready to do some excavating. I responded with an eager affirmative, inwardly enjoying the surprise that I had been the one to be singled out to begin the real archaeological work while my companions continued with the tents or enlarged the cook house. Could my pith helmet, which I still wore, I thought, with some panache, have at last worked its magic and given me a sudden status. But no, given my shovel, I was dispatched some distance up the ravine to dig a new latrine for the women's camp. Apparently, my skills as an excavator, as displayed at the University Ruin, still had not marked me out as the "point man" for serious archaeological digging.

That summer was a great time. I suppose many archaeological novices experience similar pleasures in their first sustained field stint: carefully recorded digging, the finding of artifacts, the tracing out room walls and floors—and, above all, the feeling of being an archaeologist, being a part of the group, of the team. We had lectures on some evenings down in the dining hall. There were a number of parties in the open. These were campfire circle affairs, with food, coffee, and talk. The Dean was an excellent raconteur on these occasions, telling stories of his explorations of a quarter-century earlier. The co-educational nature of the Kinishba operation was also very nice. I became romantically attached to one young lady. The two of us laid out a small nine-hole golf course not far from the ruin. By chance, someone on the dig, who had come in a private automobile, had some golf clubs in his car, and we borrowed these to play a round on our private course in the lovely sunset after supper. It soon became quite obvious that summer archaeology, in the White Mountains, was as pleasant, if not more so, than life on the beach back home in California.

Jones and I, who were tent-mates, were assigned a pueblo room together for excavation. Such assignments were made by simply placing the two of us in the rectangle made by the tops of the stone masonry walls of one of the pueblo rooms and telling us to go to it with pick and shovel. We made pretty good progress, taking out four or five feet of room fill in a week or so, locating the floor, and finding a couple of pottery vessels broken *in situ* upon it. We then made what I thought was an important discovery. Underneath our floor we came down upon the tops of masonry walls of rooms which were oriented slightly differently than ours. Here was clearly an earlier pueblo structure. I reported this with some excitement to the Dean, requesting permission to remove the walls of the upper, cleared room so that we could go on down and study this earlier architecture. Here, after all, was architectural stratigraphy—undoubtedly of some significance. But the Dean demurred. He told me, yes, that he was aware that the upper architectural levels were superimposed over earlier ones, that some sampling of this earlier building phase had been made in other parts of the site, but that here, in the Jones-Willey room, our objective was now to consolidate and restore the walls of that room, not to destroy those walls in a deeper search. We were disappointed, but we obeyed.

Kinishba had been laid up in a sort of roughly coursed ashlar-type masonry. We selected stones, which had fallen from the upper portions of the walls when these had collapsed, often shaped them a bit with geology hammers, and then fitted them into our wall constructions with mud mortar. I found that room wall restoration did not go as fast, nor was it nearly so much fun, as digging. Indeed, as I remember it, Jones and I spent the rest of June and all of July on this restoration duty. I have often wondered how our efforts have stood up, now that Kinishba is maintained by the Indian Service and is open to the public as a restored pueblo of the Pueblo III–IV, or Great Pueblo, Period. Hopefully, some of our masonry remains although I would surmise that a little cement mortar was subsequently applied.

We all stuck pretty much to our excavation or restoration duties during June, July, and into early August. We had weekly trips into the Indian School in Whiteriver Junction on Sundays, for a real shower bath and a chance to do some laundry. In that summer of 1935 the Dean was in his 75th year, but he was amazingly active. Our whole camp took the day off on the 4th of July to attend a fair in Whiteriver Junction. On this celebratory occasion, the Dean won the "senior" men's 100 yard dash with no trouble at all. I, too, contributed to the honor of the "Kinishba team" by winning the "junior" 100 yards, but then I was just a month or so off of the University of Arizona track team and a little more than 50 years younger than Dean. I remember showering at the Indian School on Sundays and marveling at the Dean's physique. He was of small stature, perhaps only 5 feet 4 inches in height, but he was solidly built and superbly muscled, without any fat whatsoever. My earlier impression of "frailness" had been wide of the mark. I remember thinking in Whiteriver then, wondering if in the far, far distant days when I would be as unbelievably old as the Dean was then, if I would be in as good a physical condition at 74 as he was. I am just that age as I write this, and I am afraid that the answer is no.

Other trips in the early months at Kinishba were to Apache dances, held at night, usually lasting from sundown to sunrise. These were celebrated at various points on the reservation. They always meant a night-long vigil so that one didn't feel up to much at the dig the next day. I realized then that I would never be an ethnologist. Our really big trip, however, was scheduled as a wind-up to the summer. This was to be in mid-to-late August and was to take us up to places like the Rainbow Bridge country, Betatakin, Keetsiel, and Chaco Canyon. A few days before we were due to depart, Jones and I, very serious minded, went to the Dean and asked if we couldn't stay behind at Kinishba and, with the Apache Indian crew, do some continued digging. We said we could appreciate the importance of the trip but that we thought that archaeological science would be better served if we went on with researches at Kinishba. I can't remember now what got into us to make such a fool request. It was probably my idea; Jones was always more sensible. But, luckily, the Dean said no. He went on to justify his refusal by telling me that if I was some day going to be associated with archaeologists in Mesopotamia, Egypt, or the Maya area it would be more than passing strange if I told my colleagues in these exotic settings that, despite the fact that I had studied archaeology at the University of Arizona, and had done fieldwork in the Southwest, I had never seen such places as Betatakin or Pueblo Bonito. Jones and I both went on the trip and had a first-rate time. In addition to some of the places already mentioned, we visited archaeological sites in Canyon de Chelly, met the Wetherills at their home base, and spent one day at the Hopi pueblos. The summer field group broke up in Holbrook, Arizona. Those with cars of their own departed in their respective home directions; those taking the train had the main line of the Santa Fe at hand. I stayed with the Dean and drove back to Kinishba for a final week or so of finishing up things for the season and breaking camp. This carried us into early September, when he and I returned to Tucson.

During the summer I had spoken with Dean about my desire to go to graduate school, either to the Oriental Institute at the University of Chicago, or, with Mesoamerican interests in mind, to Harvard. With his encouragement, as well as letters of support, I wrote to both Chicago and Harvard, but was successful in neither application. I then asked if he would accept me as a graduate student at Arizona, where I could acquire an A.M. degree in a year. The Dean very kindly assented to my request. I can think of many colleagues today who, if so selected as second or third choice by a prospective graduate student, would have told the applicant to forget it, but not Byron Cummings. With his blessing, I enrolled at Arizona as a graduate student.

In the graduate year of 1935–36, I continued to live at my fraternity house, but I did pursue a more scholarly and serious existence than had been my undergraduate custom. I took another Mexican-Central American seminar with the Dean, and I had courses in physical anthropology and social anthropology from John Provinse, an anthropologist out of the University of Chicago who had joined the faculty at Arizona a year or so earlier, as Cummings had moved to broaden what had been an archaeology department into an anthropological one. After my summer field season, I was curious about archaeological field methods or digging techniques. I told the Dean I wanted to do my A.M. thesis on this theme. He readily acceded to my request. I think others in the department, both faculty and fellow graduate students, were surprised that he had agreed to have me do this. A younger generation hardly considered "excavation methods" to be the Dean's forte. They were right; niceties of fine stratigraphy, seriation, or contextual associations had not been the Dean's primary interests in those days when he was making his explorations and discoveries or in the days which followed in which his central objective was to develop a public and a general academic interest in archaeology, and particularly Southwestern archaeology. But his critics underestimated him. He was a man of vision. He saw the direction I was pointing in, and he did not view it as a negative reflection upon him and his work but as an expansion of the field.

So, with the Dean's blessing, I wrote a Master's thesis on: "Methods and Problems in Archaeological Excavation, with Special Reference to the Southwestern United States." It was quite an undertaking for a tyro. The "Special Reference to the Southwestern United States" bit resulted from a compromise with the Graduate Dean of Letters, Arts, and Sciences who had wanted me to limit the thesis to the Southwest alone; but Dean Cummings backed me up in my broader approach. He was ready to let me look into how they dug anywhere in the world. I worked away on this thesis for much of the 1935–36 academic year, but especially during the spring semester. In addition, I was kept busy with the regular graduate course work. To supplement my income, I had a job coaching the freshman track team in the spring, and this took up what was left of my time. As May came around, and the thesis deadline neared, I slaved to finish up, and barely did. The thesis was accepted; the Dean was very pleased with it, and, naturally, I was gratified by his approval. I am also sure that he was well aware of its many limitations. I had tried to cover the world and had done so very feebly and sketchily. Local library facilities had not been ideal for the undertaking. Looking back on it now, I doubt if I would have found very much specific literature on archaeological "field methods" or "digging techniques" in any library. The subject had not yet been addressed in that way. Today, as we know, the field of archaeology is awash in "manuals" devoted to the subject, and every excavation or survey monograph devotes explicit pages to methods or procedures involved in that particular study.

I think that the Dean approved of my thesis effort, quixotic as it was, because it appealed to his adventurous and exploratory spirit. He knew I would learn by it even if I did, so to speak, "fall on my face" in the process. A copy of the thesis was duly deposited in the University of Arizona Library—where, presumably, it still sits. I have never seen it since; and, curiously, considering all the work I poured into it, I did not keep a copy.

All during my last year at Arizona, I was not only concerned about my thesis but about my future. I tried to find employment for the coming year, soliciting various museums and research institutions in the Southwest and in California. There was nothing to be had. I applied for admission to graduate schools where I could go on toward a Ph.D. degree—writing, again, to Chicago, Harvard, and also to other universities—but I had no luck. In order to continue with graduate training, substantial scholarship aid would have been necessary in my case, and I found none. Fortunately, I at last had a break, and the Dean was instrumental in this. Sometime early in the spring semester, he had called me into his office and shown me a notice of a Laboratory of Anthropology Summer Field Fellowship in archaeology. He suggested I apply. I did so, and that May, not long before my thesis was finished, I received word that I had been awarded the Fellowship for that summer of 1936. The future, that is a future in archaeology, was assured at least for the next few months. I have already commented upon my inner feelings that the Dean was always "well-disposed towards me". In this instance, he certainly must have been. Several others in the 1936 A.M. degree graduating group had also applied for the same fellowship, but the Dean's letter on my behalf must have been the strongest. I see no other way to explain it. My overall academic record was no better, if as good, as that of my classmates. For whatever reasons, he picked me, and I have always been immensely glad that he did.

I saw the Dean briefly after that 1936 graduation when I called at his office to say goodbye. As it happened, he was leaving Tucson before I was, getting ready for another summer's field session at Kinishba. Busy as ever, he sat and talked with me for a bit. No Polonius, he did not bore me with advice. He simply indicated that he thought I would do well and that I should let him know sometime how I was getting along. I was never to see him again. We did correspond, however, and on several occasions he wrote on my behalf to university graduate admissions offices until, in 1939, I finally was taken into a doctoral graduate program.

In 1938, Byron Cummings became *Emeritus*, retiring as a Professor of Archaeology and as Director of the Arizona State

Museum. It was to his satisfaction that he was replaced in both of these positions by a former student, Emil W. Haury, one of the coming leaders of Southwestern archaeology. But the Dean did not rest. Ever tireless in his mission of bringing archaeology to the attention of the public, he returned to Kinishba where, under the auspices of the Indian Service, he continued the restoration of that site as an archaeological monument and museum. In 1946, he returned to his home in Tucson, and there, in 1947, he married Miss Ann Chatham. In 1949, on his 89th birthday, a group of former students celebrated the occasion at his home by presenting him with a *festschrift* volume, entitled *For the Dean*, (Reed and King, eds., 1950). Although honored to have been one of those to contribute to this volume, I regret that I was not one of those present for this occasion.

Bothered by failing eyesight in his last years, the Dean still did not give up on archaeology. He was concerned about the backlog of notes and records that had accrued from his many years of field explorations and excavations. He realized that he had failed to write, and to publish, as substantially as he should have done. He belonged to an age that preceded academic "careerism". That is, he did not live by the dictum of "publish or perish". Such was not his view of archaeology or his role in it. Exploration and teaching had been his priorities. But now, conscientiously, in spite of his age and infirmities, he set to work trying to fulfill what he saw as his obligations by setting down on paper what he had seen, done, and thought. In so doing, he completed, and in 1953 published, a book entitled. *First Inhabitants of Arizona and the Southwest.* This was a general synthesis and semi-popular account of Southwestern prehistory, a distillation of his long experience in the field. After this, he moved on to other writing tasks. He was still working to the last. On 21 May 1954, Byron Cummings died in his 94th year.

How shall I conclude this memoir? I know now that in those long ago years of our association I was too young, too full of myself, to realize just what Byron Cummings meant to me and what he had done for me. What he had done—what he had given me—went far beyond those recommendations that led to a 1936 summer fellowship or, still later, to a 1939 graduate school admission. His gift to me is, I think, best summed up in a quotation. In that *festschrift,* to which I have just referred, and which was presented to him on his 89th birthday. An old friend and colleague wrote this about Byron Cummings (Douglass, 1950, p. 2):

> " . . . his fine feeling of companionship with his students and his influence on them conveyed those intangible forces of right and wrong that ordinary teaching does not necessarily give to the student."

I can only hope that in my own case this "conveyance" has had some small effect. But as one remembers the Dean, his important legacy was that he made you feel that he had confidence in you to do the right thing.

ARTHUR RANDOLPH KELLY
In middle age.
Courtesy Mrs. Joanna Arline and Miss Patricia Kelly.

ARTHUR RANDOLPH KELLY
(1900–1979)

Arthur Randolph Kelly was my first boss in archaeology. I feel attached to him, or to my memory of him, in much the same way that I feel attached to Byron Cummings, my first professor in the field. I met Kelly in the summer of 1936, in Macon, Georgia (Willey, n.d. 1), and we were closely associated there over the next two years. Following that, our paths crossed only occasionally. Consequently, the portrait I retain of him in my mind's eye dates mainly from those early years.

Arthur Kelly is remembered as a significant figure in the development of archaeology in the Southeastern United States. In 1933, when Kelly first came to Georgia, what was then considered "modern archaeology", with its concerns for formal typology, stratigraphy and seriation, and the definition of recurring artifact complexes or "cultures", was not yet in place in the Southeast. Kelly was a central figure in such modernizations in the crucial years from 1933 to 1937.

My acquaintance with Kelly came about as the result of my being chosen, at the close of graduate work at the University of Arizona, for the aforementioned Laboratory of Anthropology Summer Field Fellowship in 1936. The site of this Summer Fellowship was to be in Macon, Georgia, and it was to be integrated into a large, ongoing, Federal Relief archaeological project that, I learned, was to be under the direction of one, Dr. Arthur R. Kelly. I spent my last weeks in Arizona trying to bone up on Georgia archaeology. I had had no course work in Eastern United States prehistory and knew nothing about it. I read Shetrone's (1930) *The Mound Builders*, without much understanding; and, with Georgia specifically in mind, I found Moorehead's (1932) study on Etowah in the University library. From this limited research, I could see that Georgia was a different archaeological world from anything I had seen in the Southwest.

In the last week in June, I drove the Laboratory of Anthropology station wagon from Santa Fe, New Mexico back to Georgia. It took me six days to make the trip, and I arrived in Macon on a hot steamy Saturday night. My instructions were to go to the Macon Y.M.C.A. which was to be the Fellows housing facility. I was also instructed to report immediately to Dr. Kelly. I found my quarters at the "Y", but, as it was 10 PM, I judged it inadvisable to arouse Dr. Kelly at such an hour.

The following Sunday morning was hot but very quiet in Macon's downtown streets. I ventured out to find a restaurant for breakfast. Then I went about the business of finding Dr. Kelly. As this was a Sunday, I presumed (correctly as it turned out) that he would be at home. The telephone book gave only equivocal information. There was a listing for an "A. Kelly", but no "Arthur R. Kelly" or "A. R. Kelly". I rang "A. Kelly's" number. After a few rings, a woman's voice answered. I explained who I was and asked if Dr. Kelly were in. After some silence, the voice replied, "He's heah, but he ain't no doctuh." I apologized for my intrusion and hung up. I was almost resigned to having to wait until Monday morning and confront him at the excavations, when I remembered that I had with me some Laboratory of Anthropology correspondence. Checking through that, I found no telephone number, but I did find an address. It was on a Laurel Street, or a Laurel Avenue, and it was not the address of the belated "A. Kelly", who lacked the higher degree. The garage man, across the street from the "Y", where I had stored the station wagon the night before, quickly informed me how to find Laurel. It was some distance away on the other side of the river. Excitedly, I set out to find Dr. Kelly.

I remember that the Kelly Laurel Street residence was set back some distance from a shady residential street, on a hill-slope at some elevation above street-level so that it was approached by steep stairs. On that Sunday morning, I mounted these stairs in nervous anticipation. As I neared the top of the stairs, I could see a figure, or a part of a figure, seated in a porch swing. Only two very long legs and two large feet were visible from beneath a Sunday paper which this individual held before him and in which he was deeply engrossed. Perhaps, in my nervousness, I had climbed the stairs and advanced across the porch rather quietly for I had to shuffle around and clear my throat a couple of times before the newspaper came down and its reader eyed me gravely and, I thought, not altogether with satisfaction. Had I come at a bad time, intruding on a relaxed Sunday morning? Should I have waited for the next day before presenting myself? But it was too late for such second thoughts. I announced who I was, that I came with the blessing of the Laboratory of Anthropology, that I had their official vehicle in the street below—a testament to my authenticity—and that I was seeking Dr. Arthur R. Kelly. The man in the swing arose slowly from the position where he had been seated, or, more accurately, reclining on the back of his neck. Erect, he was about 6′ 2″. Still contemplating me in a serious manner, he announced, in a Texas drawl, that he was, indeed, Dr. Kelly, and that he had been expecting me and the other members of the Laboratory of Anthropology group. Dr. Kelly had a very formal style or address. It might even be said that he put on a bit of "side" with strangers, or until he came to know one better. A part of this was conveyed in a stance that, more than erect, was a trifle backward-leaning so that he seemed to be regarding you at some remove. It had nothing to do with attire. Elegance in dress was never a characteristic of Kelly.

Arthur Kelly was just 35 years of age at this time. Only 12 years separated us, but he seemed ages older. A high widow's-peak of straight brown hair rose above his forehead. He had large, and I think dark, eyes which protruded a bit. His features were by no means classically handsome. The nose was large and bulbous with a central indentation. The mouth was generous, and it held a Sherlock Holmes-style, underslung pipe. The pipe was as much a part of Kelly as it was of the great detective. After our introduction, Kelly walked over to the edge of the porch, took the pipe out of his mouth, and gave it a tremendous bang on the railing, scattering ashes and dottle in all directions. He returned to the swing with slow, smooth movements. I don't believe I ever saw him move quickly or swiftly anywhere, not even on the tennis court. In spite of his height and size—he was not heavy but not thin either—he had a feline grace. Later, I came to learn that he was very fond of cats, and I can still see him, in an armchair, pipe in mouth, slowly stroking a contented angora.

Still rather solemnly, on that long-ago Sunday morning in

June, Dr. Kelly invited me to take a porch chair. Having done so, I waited for him to start the conversation, but he seemed in no hurry to do so. He refilled his pipe, lit it slowly with a wooden match, which I thought burned down perilously close to his fingertips, and continued to regard me with the utmost gravity. It was going to be up to me. "Sir, how are the archaeological excavations going——?" That was all it took. I had no further cause to worry about embarrassing conversational pauses.

Dr. Kelly informed me, in that slow Texas speech, but in some detail and with great enthusiasm, that he was engaged on a new project—"chronimetric studies of flint patination" was the way he put it. I was somewhat at a loss to know what he meant and must have shown it although I tried to look knowledgable. He asked me if I was familiar with European Paleolithic studies. I confessed I was not. I was also ashamed that I didn't know what "patination" was. I guess I had heard of "patina" in connection with Classical bronzes, but I didn't make the flint connection. Besides, I was all prepared to hear about "Indian Mounds", and I was "blind-sided" by the Paleolithic. Kelly went on to tell me about lithics on the "Macon Plateau", the name for the main Macon site, and how these were proof of Early Man in this part of the country. Like any cautious, reasonably schooled young American archaeological student of that time, I was silently dubious. He said that many of the Macon flints were heavily patinated, or decomposed, and that the relative thicknesses of the patina, from flint to flint, might be a clue to relative chronological age. Thousands of such flints were being measured now in his WPA archaeological laboratory. I began to wonder if I would enjoy the summer as much as I had anticipated.

At my first opportunity, I switched the subject to "Indian Mounds". Dr. Kelly switched easily, without a pause, to this theme, acknowledging that the Macon site and region had many and that they were, indeed, the primary objectives of his enterprise. I felt relieved. To show I was not completely ignorant of the topic, I inquired if the Macon mounds were culturally related to those of "Ee-tow-wah". (I think this was the way I said it.) Dr. Kelly looked baffled for a moment and then said, yes, that there were some relationships between the central Georgia sites and "Et-o-wah", in the northern part of the state. (This was when I learned the correct way to pronounce Eto-wah.) He went on from this to tell me about "complicated stamped pottery", something else I had never heard of before. I was having all I could do to keep up with this when Mrs. Kelly, a charming lady, came out on the porch and said, "Arthur, stop talking for awhile and introduce us." She was accompanied by their three young daughters, Sheila, Joanna, and Patricia, then ages 8, 5, and 3, as I remember. After the introductions, Mrs. Kelly said they were having a picnic lunch that day, down along the banks of the Ocmulgee River nearby, and invited me to join them. I accepted with great pleasure.

After lunch, Kelly and I drove back into town to see if any others of our group had arrived. One by one, we met them at the railroad station: J. B. Birdsell and then Larry Angel, both physical anthropologists from Harvard; H. Y. ("Arf") Feng, a Chinese graduate student from the University of Pennsylvania, and Charles ("Chuck") Wagley, from Columbia, both ethnologists; and W. W. ("Walt") Taylor, from Yale, an archaeologist. That evening, Dr. Kelly introduced us to Roberts' Cafeteria, across the street corner from the "Y", where he had arranged for us to board during the summer. We were alerted to be ready early on the morrow to see Macon archaeology.

Archaeological digging at Macon had begun with Federal Relief funding in December of 1933—the pit of the economic depression. Its principal purpose was welfare, especially the employment of hundreds of workers who had lost their jobs in the Macon cotton mills. There was, of course, some intellectual and scholarly drive, as well, behind the Macon archaeological program. This was provided by three distinguished citizens of the city, General W. A. Harris, a lawyer, Dr. Charles C. Harold, a surgeon, and Mr. Linton M. Solomon, a retired businessman. They were all local history and archaeology enthusiasts; they were the founders and nucleus of the Society for Georgia Archaeology; and they were prominent persons with political "clout" who could, and did, arrange in Washington for Federal Relief funds to be assigned to Macon for this purpose. The Smithsonian Institution, however, was the first official scientific sponsor of the Macon project. In this role, the Smithsonian had hired Dr. Kelly, formerly of the Department of Anthropology of the University of Illinois, to be the director of the excavations. Kelly had had experience with mound digging at Cahokia in Illinois. He was provided with James A. Ford as his assistant. Ford was a youngster then, only 22, but he had done field archaeology with Henry Collins, of the Smithsonian, both in the Southeastern United States and Alaska.

When Kelly and Ford arrived in Macon, they were met by a vast army of WPA laborers. The numbers I have often heard cited vary from 700 to 1000 or more; no one seemed sure of the exact count; the Relief roll assignments tended to be changing and fluid. By any count, however, there were a lot of potential diggers—more, probably, than any archaeologist had ever been confronted with outside of the great digs of the Middle East or the classical world. Certainly, archaeologists in the American field—including Kelly and Ford—had had no experience in working with crews of this size. Today we say that there should be one archaeological supervisor to every 12 diggers; Kelly and Ford had a "one to 500 situation". They attempted to solve it as best they could by holding classes of instruction during the first few weeks. Selecting among the 700–to–1000 men who had been assigned to them, they sorted out former bank clerks, insurance agents, and other "white-collar" types and gave them cram courses on the fundamentals of archaeological field recording. Fortunately, they had a few civil engineers or surveyors in their group, two of whom were college-trained. They proved invaluable for the necessary mapping and surveying.

In those early operations of 1933–1934, the huge crew of diggers were largely concentrated on the "Macon Plateau" site. This was the name given to some red clay hills or high ground on the east side of the Ocmulgee River, the side opposite the modern city of Macon. The area had been occupied from very ancient times; indeed, some of those patinated flints which Kelly had told me about on my first morning in Macon were the scattered remains of Paleo-Indian and Archaic Period settlement. Subsequent occupations included Early and Middle Woodland villages which had been followed by a sizable Mississippian town. This last, which included the principal mound structures of the "Macon Plateau", was eventually designated by Kelly as the "Macon Plateau culture" (Kelly, 1938). Its largest mound, Mound A, was a huge, flat-topped pyramid, over 50 feet in height. Mound A, like comparable mounds in the Southeast or Mississippi Valley, was too daunting to tackle, but another Mound, "C", renamed the "Funeral Mound" (Fairbanks, 1956), had been cross-sectioned years previously by a railroad cut. Taking advantage of this, and by judicious stepping, Kelly cleaned and trimmed a spectacular profile, revealing a complicated layered construction of different colored clays and many elaborately prepared burials in the different strata.

Other parts of the crew were placed on other mounds. One of these, a low circular affair, turned out to be a collapsed "Ceremonial Earth Lodge" (Fairbanks, 1946). Careful excavation revealed the charred timbers of big upright support posts and numerous smaller logs that had formed the roof. The features modeled in clay on the floor—a series of 50 individual seats around the walls, an impressive eagle-shaped dais or altar, and a central fire pit—made this a wonderful Natural Park Service exhibition, as it eventually became. In addition to the mound digging, long test trenches were stretched across the flat ground of the Plateau. One of these was 2000 feet long. Its excavation had been carefully controlled in 5 x 10 foot sections. It was one of the easiest ways of keeping several hundred men with picks and shovels under supervision. Much of this digging on the Plateau had been completed before our Laboratory of Anthropology student group arrived in the summer of 1936, but we heard about it and saw some of the results.

On the Monday after our Sunday arrival, Kelly gave us a tour of all operations, past and current. On the Plateau, a couple of smaller mounds were being profiled, and some test trenches were still in process. I think we were all properly impressed with the numbers of men and the organization of the project. During our morning's walk, several excavation supervisors came up to Kelly to report or ask questions. They didn't quite salute, but I always felt they were going to. As these subordinates checked in, Kelly would listen very seriously and issue commands. I still don't quite understand it. Kelly was anything but a "military-type" personality, and Jim Ford had absolutely no leanings in this direction; yet, somehow, there was a military *esprit d' corps* about the whole works. I think that the fairly large cadre of supervisors that had been developed by 1936—the "white-collar types" that I have referred to—may have had something to do with this. Poor as their relief pittances were, they felt they were a part of an organized effort toward something that was very important, however little their understanding of the archaeological enterprise may have been. They were the sergeants and corporals of Kelly's army and proud of it. But the military theme also, in some mysterious way, emanated from Kelly. Perhaps, like many intellectuals he had some secret "Walter Mitty" desires along these lines.

We were also taken to other sites in the county. By law, Kelly had permission to deploy WPA labor for archaeology anywhere within that jurisdiction. We went down to the Lamar. This was on the river flats about a mile below the Macon Plateau. No work was going on there in 1936, but earlier Ford had carried out excavations there. The site, whose approximate 40 acres was later incorporated into Ocmulgee National Monument along with the Macon Plateau, had two large mounds of the temple type. The Lamar culture was proved to be later than the Macon Plateau culture and featured a distinctive complicated stamped pottery. We then went out to the Swift Creek site, a few miles from Macon, which was an ongoing operation with one of Kelly's locally trained foremen in charge of a crew of Black women diggers. Swift Creek has since been immortalized as the type site for a distinctive, pre-Lamar, and pre-Macon Plateau kind of complicated stamped pottery.

The day following our tour, Kelly put us all to work under the instruction of a Georgia Tech engineer on his staff, Joe Tamplin, who was an excellent teacher in the uses of the transit and alidade. We spent a week on training in mapping.

During this week, I talked with Dr. Kelly about the prospects of dendrochronology in the area. He knew I had been a student of Douglass', at Arizona, and he had asked me if the abundant charred timbers in the Ceremonial Earth Lodge might not be susceptible to such dating. I explained that they might, but that we would have a long period of research ahead of us with living and early historic wood in order to extend a tree-ring chronology back to a point where it might meet that of the archaeological specimens. But Kelly was not given to pessimism and spent a day with me going around to local sawmills on the outskirts of Macon so that I could look at freshly cut Georgia pines to see if ring patterns appeared "sensitive" enough to permit the development of a chronology. I wasn't altogether sure. I didn't have enough experience in dendrochronology to really make a judgment. The Georgia pine ring patterns were more "complacent" than those of the pines or pinons of the Southwest, with which I had some familiarity, but in the century of 1935 back to 1835 I noted that there were at least a half-dozen recognizable "checking rings". I, of course, wanted a chance at it, and Kelly agreed. I said that I thought that we should remove the charred wood specimens from the Ceremonial Earthlodge and properly preserve them in a kerosene and paraffin dip. My fellow Lab students and I were given the job which we accomplished in a week. I don't think my colleagues were as happy about this as I was. They wanted to do some real archaeology, but they put up with this "dendrochronological delay" until the burned timbers were removed, properly dunked in kerosene (which ruined them forever as C-14 specimens), and packed in cotton.

It had been Dr. Kelly's plan—and one which we were all very enthusiastic about—to let us do a mound excavation for the balance of the summer. Eventually, he selected one which appeared to be about the right size for tyros. This was known as the "Stubbs Mound", after the then current landowner. It was not a part of the Macon group but was located some distance away. One reached it by taking the main highway south out of the Macon for about 12 miles. Then one took a small dirt, or red clay, road off to the left. This road grew progressively narrower, and nastier (if wet), as one neared the site. At one point it traversed a very putrid swamp hole (in which we were frequently stuck) before emerging to go up a low hill into a cornfield. The cornfield sloped away toward another but larger patch of swamp, seen at a distance as a cypress forest. At the far end of the cornfield, and on the edge of this cypress swamp, was

Stubbs, or "Stubbs'es", Mound. It was a little round tumulus about 4 feet high and not over 100 feet in diameter. In mid-July the location was a hell-hole as far as breezeless heat, swamp odors, and mosquitoes went—and they went pretty far. We were to spend the next six weeks of our summer fellowship here at "Stubbs'es Mound".

The first day at Stubbs we went out in the station wagon, with Dr. Kelly, followed by a couple of broken down cars carrying our crew of a dozen WPA diggers. While the crew stood around or sought shade at the swamp's edge, the six students held a long discussion about just how we were going to tackle the excavation. Kelly was very patient and tolerant, letting us decide what staking and recording system we were going to use. Puffing on the Sherlock Holmes pipe which served as no mean defense against the ubiquitous mosquitoes, he put in an observation only now and then.

Dr. Kelly's tolerance, though, had limits. I have mentioned his air of formality. He was very strict in adhering to what he considered proper in interpersonal relationships, and he believed firmly in the structuring of these relationships. He had become quite easy and friendly with us; that was one thing; but he still had his standards. This came out at "Stubbs'es" on that first day. As we held our lengthy "conference" on field methods, one of the workmen, called "Popeye" by his comrades because he had a spectacularly undershot jaw and smoked a corn-cob pipe, was heard to say in loud and not uncertain terms, leaning upon his shovel and fanning mosquitoes, that "he wished Old Man Stubbs had this here mound" in a certain place. Dr. Kelly was not amused, but he didn't say anything. When the digging finally began and progressed, if but slowly in the late morning heat, "Popeye" was heard to make this observation again—and then again, undoubtedly a performer's response to an appreciative round of guffaws from the audience of his mates. It was at this point that Dr. Kelly intervened. As he explained to us later, bringing the "military motif" back into the picture, we, as "officers of the expedition", had an obligation to demand certain standards of behavior from what were, in effect, "enlisted ranks". The verbally rebellious "Popeye" obviously was not conforming to these standards. Thus, after his third reiteration of the offensive reference to the Stubbs Mound and its owner, Dr. Kelly issued "Popeye" a stern reprimand. When the errant "Popeye" attempted to explain—"Doctor Kelly, I didn't mean nuthin'. I just said I wished old Man Stubbs had this here mound up his ass!"—it only made things worse.

"Popeye" barely avoided being transferred to another Federal Relief fiefdom in the county, the dread "Malarial Drainage Project", the "Siberia", we were told, of local WPA endeavors. As we were all secretly sympathetic with "Popeye", agreeing, silently, that our swampside location was not exactly a dream spot, we put in a word for him with Dr. Kelly. Relenting, he fixed "Popeye's" punishment (reward?) at banishment from the Stubbs Mound crew; however, he was saved for archaeology, at least for then, by being sent back to the Macon Plateau. This Stubbs Mound incident, however, may have presaged a deep-seated indiscipline in "Popeye", for I am told, that although he remained loyal to prehistoric studies, and even continued on the Ocmulgee National Monument staff in post-WPA years, he was eventually cashiered for operating a still on the Macon Plateau, somewhere in the undergrowth down in back of Mound A. This practice, conforming to a well-known and ancient Georgia tradition, has also long been considered a Federal offense, and this offense was compounded by its occurrence on U.S. Government premises. After this, not even Dr. Kelly could save him.

As the summer wore on, we toiled each day at Stubbs. We got a break in that we had grumbled about the quality and monotony of the fare at Roberts' Cafeteria, our assigned mess hall, finally getting up the courage to petition to our commanding officer for a shift of venue in the "junior officer's mess" to the grill room of the Dempsey Hotel, then Macon's leading hostelry. Here we could dine luxuriously in air-conditioned comfort every evening. Never one to be unaware of the weaknesses of the flesh, Dr. Kelly acceded to our request, stating, with gravity, that such an arrangement would be fitting for his trainees.

A part of our training that summer was held at night, on the front porch of the Kelly residence. We would gather there after dinner, at about 8:00 o'clock. Dr. Kelly would hold forth on the meanings of all of the Macon research, attempting to put this into a larger setting of Southeastern archaeology. There were several difficulties in all this. The prime one was that none of us had enough knowledge of Southeastern or Eastern United States prehistory to be able to follow Kelly's presentations. We were all highly motivated in learning field techniques, and I think we were doing that, with Kelly's tutelage and by trial and error, in our stints at Stubbs. But we had no sense of problem or any conception of the outlines of the culture history of the Macon region. We didn't know one pottery type from another. It was not until over a year later, after I had begun to learn the local ceramics, that I realized that Stubbs might be a very important site in working out central Georgia culture sequences. Much of the ceramic chronology was right there in that little mound, as has been brought out in a report on it published almost 50 years after we dug it (Williams, 1975). In addition to our lack of background, we tended to get sleepy, after our long day in the sun, and our pleasant two hours at the dinner table in the Dempsey.

Kelly was very conscientious about our seeing something more of Georgia archaeology than the Macon and Bibb County sites. On weekends, he and the six of us took the station wagon on various excursions—to St. Simon's Island, where Preston Holder was doing some shell mound digging under Kelly's general supervision, to a project near Columbus, Georgia, where an engineer, Frank Lester, was similarly on detached duty in Kelly's domain, and then to Etowah and to Kolomoki, on separate trips, just to see these great mound sites.

On the first of September the Laboratory of Anthropology Summer Field School came to an end. My five graduate colleagues departed from the Macon railroad station, all returning to graduate work in academic settings in the north. I stayed behind. Very fortunately for me, Dr. Kelly had agreed to hire me to carry out the dendrochronological researches that I have mentioned. I was signed on as a "non-relief" employee of the WPA and given a salary like that of the two engineers. This "non-relief" status, similar to that enjoyed by Dr. Kelly, meant that one didn't have to give proof of indigency; but, in my case at least, this could have been a very finely shaded matter. In any event, I was employed at last, doing archaeology. The Laboratory people in Santa Fe, on hearing of my good fortune, very generously sent on someone else to Georgia to drive the station wagon back to New Mexico.

With the other students gone, I began to see more of Dr. Kelly on a day-to-day basis than I had before. He followed my tree-ring work with interest; I tried to keep up with what was going on in the various Macon digs; and we took a number of trips together to other parts of the state to visit archaeological sites or to collect tree-borings. I was a frequent recipient of the Kelly's hospitality in their home, where Mrs. Kelly and the children treated me like one of the family. As I grew to know Dr. Kelly better, I came to realize that he was an extraordinarily kind man. Now, years later, I would say that he was one of the kindest I have ever known. He was a great ego-builder for others, particularly young ones, as I was then. He was invariably considerate of me when distinguished dignitaries visited Macon, and a number of these came in and out in 1936 and 1937. Some were National Park Service officials visiting the Macon site after it became a National Monument in December of 1936; others were archaeologists interested in the Southeast, such as Philip Phillips of Harvard or Matthew W. Stirling of the Smithsonian. Kelly always introduced me as his "Assistant"—to my mind fully establishing my professional status— and he always included me in any parties or gatherings he might host for the visitors.

As I keep saying, Kelly had a "style" about him that set him apart. He maintained a decorum, almost an inner *hauteur*, that I found fascinating then and, in retrospect, still do. On one occasion, a millionaire, in another part of the state, invited Kelly to his palatial residence for lunch, and Kelly took me along. This man had called Kelly long-distance, telling him that he was very interested in archaeology and "would like to do something about it". Obviously, we were intrigued. After a long morning's drive, we were ushered into the presence of this magnate and handsomely treated to drinks and a fine lunch. Our host expressed his disgust at the way archaeologists had to grub about on Federal Relief. I could see Dr. Kelly's hopes swell—as did mine. Perhaps our research was about to be funded in some gold-plated private way. But, as the conversation wore along, it became increasingly clear that our host's disapproval over the WPA was not going to lead in the way we hoped it would. That he was expressing displeasure at the "relief" concept did not necessarily mean that he was going to supplant it.

The let down became definite, when it became clear that what was wanted was Kelly's advice on assembling a private collection of antiquities—pots, arrowheads, and the like. A large collection of Georgia and Southeastern antiquities was known to be available for sale somewhere. Should our host buy it? It was clear that he would be willing to pay generously for professional aid in helping him catalogue, authenticate, and document the collection. No, he did not want to give it to any university or museum. He wanted his own collection, right here in his own house, where he could enjoy it and show it to his friends. What did Dr. Kelly think? Kelly told him in no uncertain terms. This was not the way to go about archaeology. In an attempt to "civilize" this tycoon, he made a counterproposal. Why not establish a research foundation, an institution which could be named after its donor? Such a foundation could begin by hiring a young archaeologist. Kelly looked meaningfully over at me. (God bless his heart!) Survey could be carried out in this part of Georgia where little was known as yet about archaeology. But our host's attention had begun to flag with such a scenario. It was not what he had in mind. After the coffee, we were dismissed.

As we drove away from the baronial lodge, Kelly was silent for a long time. He took out his Sherlock Holmes pipe, rolled down the car window and absent-mindedly banged it hard a couple of times against the outside of the door (Ow! The paint!). He drew his arm back in, rolled the window back up, filled the pipe, lit it, and puffed a while, still in silence. "Well, Gordon," he finally said, "We musn't encourage that sort of thing. Archaeology is not to be commercialized. As officers of this expedition, it is our duty to adhere to professional standards."

Kelly had a wonderful way with words and phrases. His

names for things and places gave them a larger-than-life quality. So it was with that phenomenal excavation unit on the Macon Plateau, "The 2000 Foot Correlation Trench". This wasn't just any old trench. It was not only long; to hear it referred to in this way gave it a mystery and excitement. Another favorite of his, less majestic but more recondite, was "The Nine-Foot Level". I think it was some stratum that had been encountered deep down in the constructional filling between Mounds A and B, but when it was tossed out like that, in the middle of an argument, it carried an aura of indisputable antiquity. It scored one over his opponent by its deep esoteric implications. "Fossil Soils" was still another term of Kelly's. I think he was referring to old surface levels which had been covered with mound construction layers, but, as a phrase, it carried romantic connotations of great age. He had a "PR" flair for the impressive statement. Thus, in telling someone about the history of the Macon excavations, he would shun an off-hand remark like, "I've been working here for about three years" in favor of, "I've been conducting intensive research on the Macon Plateau for 34½ months." He could appreciate this side of himself, too, I remember once, shortly after I had been taken on as his assistant, we were driving along in the still borrowed Santa Fe vehicle. Dr. Kelly, incidentally, had never learned to drive a car so I was always the one at the wheel. He had been solemn, silent, and pipe-puffing for a long time. I wondered what was on his mind. Perhaps I was proving a disappointment to him in my new position. But finally, he broke the silence. "Lad," he said, just up the road here is a little restaurant and bar. I wonder if you would mind pulling in there and we'll have a beer. After 34½ months of intensive research a man needs a little relaxation." I had no hesitancy in doing so. After only 2½ months of intensive research, I wanted a beer, too.

By April of 1937, I had carried my dendrochronological research to a point where I published a master chart on central Georgia living pines that went back to about 1810 (Willey, 1937). Ahead of me, would have been still more work on living trees and then attempts to find Colonial era timbers in old houses that might have extended the ring record still further back in time. It looked to be a formidable task. But at about that time, the National Park Service moved into the picture at the Macon site, or Ocmulgee National Monument as it was now to be called, by establishing a CCC Camp there for its further development. By May, the camp was constructed, and Dr. Kelly was named as its Superintendent. Along with the two engineers from the WPA digging, I was made what was called a Senior Foreman, in my case deputized to archaeology. This called for archaeological fieldwork, in monument areas and, at Dr. Kelly's discretion, elsewhere in the county or even farther afield. I began this fieldwork in earnest, using the CCC crews and transportation, and continued it for over a year.

One of my main concerns was chronology-relative chronology as this would be carried by pottery stratigraphy and seriation. To this end, I had to learn something about central Georgia ceramics. Dr. Kelly knew them and had a good eye for them, being a very effective sherd-sorter if he wanted to tie himself down to the task. Unfortunately, he didn't very often although he did spend some Saturday afternoons instructing me at a little lab I had set up for this purpose in the CCC Camp.

Because Kelly had amassed thousands of pages of descriptive notes during his four years of Federal Relief digging, he was swamped with information that could not be swiftly reduced and communicated. From memory, and he had a very retentive memory, he prepared the short monograph, *A Preliminary Report on Archaeological Explorations at Macon, Georgia*, which was published by the Smithsonian in 1938. I remember him doing this in the CCC Camp office in the winter and spring months of 1937. He dictated a first draft, over a period of several days, to a secretary named Tidwell, a large, heavy, sleepy-eyed and silent man, who, I think, had been a court reporter before joining Federal Relief ranks in 1933. Tidwell not only took down this monograph manuscript in shorthand, but for the four previous years he had been the one who recorded and typed the vast mountain of field notes that accrued from the excavations. I learned from this the perils of crushing oneself beneath field and laboratory data that would take almost superhuman strength and patience to bring into a publishable form.

I think it was late in 1937 that Dr. Kelly was promoted from being the CCC Camp Superintendent to the position of Super-intendent of the Ocmulgee National Monument, becoming with this promotion a full-fledged member of the National Park Service. Then, very soon after that, he was elevated again, this time being made Chief Archaeologist of the National Park Service, and with this promotion the Kelly's moved to Wash-ington, D.C., where he was to have an office at the Park Service Headquarters in the Department of the Interior. These changes brought to a close my steady associations with A. R. Kelly. I was to see him again, but, as I have said, the memories I carry of him go back largely to this time—an important time in his life as an archaeologist and certainly a formative time in mine. Not long after Kelly's departure there were changes in my life, too. I married Katharine Whaley of Macon in September of 1938, and we left Macon immediately afterwards to live in New Orleans where I had taken a job with James Ford on his Federal Relief archaeological project.

To this point, I have viewed Arthur Randolph Kelly through my youthful eyes and by benefit of my aging memory. More objectively now, you should know that he was born on 27 October 1900, in Hubbard City, in east central Texas. He was the oldest of the seven children of Thomas Lucius Kelly and Mamye Lewis (Atwood) Kelly. Arthur graduated from high school in Hillsboro, Texas and then went to the University of Texas, at Austin, as his father had before him. His father wanted Arthur to follow him in the law, and the young Kelly began his undergraduate studies with this in mind. Among his pre-legal courses, however, was one on criminology, and this led, in the tradition of those times, to physical anthropology and a study of the physiognomy of the inmates of the Texas prisons. He had further courses at Texas with the noted anthro-pologist G. C. Engerrand who encouraged him to go to Harvard to study under Earnest Hooton. Before making this move, how-ever, Kelly married Rowena Whitman, of Conroe, Texas whom he had met at the University where she was also a graduate student.

Kelly entered Harvard sometime in the mid-1920s. As the records of the University show that he received a A.M. degree in Anthropology in 1926, it is probable that he matriculated at

Harvard in 1925. Hooton became his principal professor, and he remembered his old mentor with great fondness. In Macon, in 1936, he told me often how he and Rowena ("Rene") enjoyed their frequent visits to the Hootons for afternoon tea. One of his research activities at Harvard was measuring the Boston area prison populations as a part of Hooton's "Criminal Series" research. Kelly's doctoral dissertation topic, however, was the physical anthropology of the living Cherokee in North Carolina, and he received the Ph.D. from Harvard in 1929. Arthur and Rowena had their first child, Sheila, while they were in Cambridge, Massachusetts. Subsequently, they were to have three more daughters: Joanna and Patricia, whom I met, together with Sheila, on the Kelly front porch on that long ago Sunday morning in 1936, and Cora Lewis, who was born some years later.

In June of 1929, the depression had not yet struck the nation's economy; there were academic jobs available; and Kelly landed one of the these at the University of Illinois, in Urbana-Champaign. Although trained primarily as a physical anthropologist, he had had some course work in archaeology, both under Engerrand, in Texas, and with Hooton and others at Harvard. While he taught various courses in anthropology at Illinois, his research there was to be primarily archaeological. The university had been fortunate enough to receive a large private bequest to carry out local Illinois archaeology, and Kelly, in addition to his teaching during regular academic term times, was put in charge of summer archaeological field operations. In so doing, he was indoctrinated into Mississippi Valley archaeology in a big way. He began excavation in the American Bottom region near East St. Louis. The famed Cahokia site, with its Monk's Mound, the largest prehistoric tumulus in the United States, is located in the American Bottom. Originally, there were at least 200 other tumuli in the region. Kelly excavated at one of these, a sizable earthen pyramid known as the Powell Mound. As I remember his accounts of this, he worked there for two years, or two seasons, and in so doing gained some familiarity with a brand of Early Middle Mississippian culture that was related to the Macon Plateau complex which he was to deal with later in Georgia. By 1931, however, the Depression had set in solidly; the special research funds which had supported his fieldwork at the Powell Mound were exhausted; and the University of Illinois, in its retrenchments, eliminated Kelly from its Department of Anthropology. Unfortunately, he was never able to complete the reports on this research and publish it. Two difficult years followed in which the only employment he could obtain were research grants, for work in physical anthropology, which was provided via Hooton at Harvard. Then, in December 1933, Kelly was appointed Smithsonian representative in charge of the new Federal Relief archaeological program in Macon, Georgia.

I have recounted the 1933–1937 Macon years, the focus of my remembrances, ending with Kelly's appointment as the chief archaeologist of the National Park Service and his move, with his family, to Washington, D.C. He remained there for two years. I visited him on a couple of occasions. He seemed enormously happy in the job. But, in 1941, the Park Service eliminated the chief archaeologist's job, and Kelly was sent to the Custom's House National Monument in Salem, Massachusetts, as its superintendent. He did not enjoy it there. The echoes of Federalist New England life and the shades of Nathaniel Hawthorne hardly replaced the excitement of dirt archaeology. Then in 1943, he was transferred back to Ocmulgee, again as its superintendent. He told me later that he had requested it, that he had hoped in this way to get back to some digging. Unfortunately, with the war on, there was no chance of this.

In 1946, I had the opportunity to see him for several days. In February, I was on my way from Washington to Peru and stopped for a time in Macon. I drove out to Ocmulgee. Although Kelly by that time had been joined by Park Service archaeologist, Charles Fairbanks, Ocmulgee seemed a lonely place. Kelly was, justifiably, disconsolate. Although the war was over, it did not appear that he would be recalled to Washington to take up his former post of chief archaeologist again, and there were no provisions for further digging in the Monument area. Kelly and I drove back into town from the Monument and wound up in the bar of the Dempsey Hotel, much as we used to in the old days. It soon became apparent that Kelly had not lost all of the old fire. Over scotch and sodas, he told me what he had told me many times before—that Georgia archaeology was just opening up, that the vistas for research were unlimited. Not only were River Basin Survey funds becoming available throughout the Southeast, but the Georgia State Park Service was contemplating making both Kolomoki and Etowah State Parks, with attendant provisions for more archaeological work in both places. Why only tomorrow, he and Fairbanks were driving up to Cartersville to consult with local dignitaries about the Etowah project. Why didn't I come along.

I agreed to do so, and Kelly, Fairbanks, and I set out the next morning. We pulled into Cartersville, which was the town nearest the great Etowah Mound site, sometime in the afternoon. Reservations had been made for us at the local hotel. Kelly was at his expansive best with some of the town leaders who were anxious for the State Park to be established near their community. Of course Kelly didn't have to be sold on the idea. He was all for it from the start, but, as I recall, a State Park Service man, a more down-to-earth type, while not actually opposed, raised, from time to time, some practical objections. The leader of the progressive Cartersville citizenry then played his trump card. "Gentlemen, let me show you this." He brought forth a small box, carefully untied and unwrapped it, and poured out on the table before us a collection of perhaps 20 pottery figurines. With excitement, he said that his wife had picked these up on the surface of the Etowah Mounds just last summer. He also said that nothing like this had ever been found in Georgia or anywhere in the Southeast before. He was right. They were a mixed lot of Preclassic, Teotihuacan, and later figurines from the Valley of Mexico. It was an embarrassing moment, and I am afraid I didn't handle it very well. Revealing my great expertese on the higher cultures of the Americas, I identified them at some length. No one else said much of anything. Kelly walked over to the window and puffed his pipe. The State Park Service representative grinned. The gentleman with the figurines eyed me in a not altogether friendly way. I murmured something about how easy it was sometimes to get collections of old archaeological "things" mixed up and that his wife probably had done so with a box of Etowah "things". But after a little period of silence, everything seemed to get back on track. Kelly never remonstrated with me for my public relations gaffe. Not long afterward Etowah did become a State Park.

Later in 1946, Kelly was "rescued" from Ocmulgee by being invited by the University of Georgia to come there and develop a Department of Archaeology and Anthropology. He accepted, left Macon and the Park Service, and went to Athens and the University in 1947. Here he was able to pursue archaeological field research to his heart's content. From this base he promoted and carried out survey and excavations all over the state. This was done through various collaborations, but primarily with the aid of the newly formed River Basin Surveys program and the Georgia State Park Service. Kelly founded the Society for the Preservation of Early Georgia History, bringing in more public support. In 1950, Kelly was made archaeological consultant to the state of Georgia, and, a year later, he became a founding member of the Georgia Historical Commission. A number of younger archaeologists, whose names are now well-known in Southeastern research—J. B. Caldwell, W. H. Sears, and Lewis Larson—all worked with him.

I had a chance to see Kelly again in 1949. He was running a summer dig and field school in south Georgia, near Blakely. He very kindly invited me to come down and teach a course in connection with it. The prospect was a pleasing one. I could use the extra money. My wife and our daughters could stay with Katharine's parents in Macon, where I could also be on week-ends, and during the week I could be in Blakeley. And this would give me a chance to brush up on Southeastern archaeology. In the mornings, Kelly took his student group out for some digging on a minor site somewhere near Kolomoki. Bill Sears was digging a burial mound at Kolomoki proper. In the afternoons, I would lecture back at the field camp which was an old CCC barracks then owned by the State Park Service. As always, I was impressed by the way Kelly handled the local citizens, winning their admiration and support. He took me to a Blakeley Rotary Club lunch where he was the lion of the group. And Kolomoki, too, became a State Park.

At Athens, Kelly served as departmental chairman from 1947 until 1953, continuing as a professor there until 1967, when he became professor emeritus. In the field, he worked at Etowah (Kelly, 1954; Kelly and Larson, 1956), the Lake Douglas Mound, the Oliver and Walter F. George River Basin surveys, the Estatoe Mound (Kelly and De Baillou, 1960), the Chauga Mound (Kelly and Neitzel, 1961), and the Bell Field Mound (Kelly, 1970), to name only the more important places. His 1967 retirement did not slow him down on field research. Indeed, the Bell Field excavations were continued through most of his years of formal "retirement".

Arthur Kelly was one of the great promoters of archaeology. He was a spellbinder who spread the word with a zeal almost unsurpassed. He sold the subject to Federal, State, and university officials, and, above all, to the public at large. His mission in all of this was largely selfless. Like any of us in the field, he wanted a job to maintain himself and his family; but, above all, he wanted the job as a platform from which to "preach the gospel" about archaeology. He was doing this in talks and in interviews with the press right up until the time of his death, which came suddenly and quietly, of a heart attack, on 4 November 1979.

I think of him often now, in this role of a champion of archaeology. I remember him, too, in those more relaxed moments in which we raised a glass to ease the tension of the fatiguing months of intensive research out on the old Plateau and elsewhere. Sometimes we would play tennis together. The only concession he would make to suiting up for the game was to wear tennis shoes. He had to, or they wouldn't have let us on those clay courts on Buckingham Drive, not far from his house in Macon. Otherwise, he would only remove his suit jacket. With a fedora pulled down low over his eyes, and the under-slung pipe gripped firmly between his teeth, he would whale the hell out of any ball that came within his reach, and on these and on his serve he had quite a delivery. But if they didn't come in close he wouldn't run for them.

JAMES ALFRED FORD
In his youth.
Courtesy Stephen Williams.

James Alfred Ford
(1911–1968)

James Alfred Ford was one of America's most remarkable archaeologists, one of the very few, in my opinion, to whom that
controversial term "genius" might be applied. His intellectual
qualities and his contributions to the Americanist field are
well known and well documented (Webb, 1968; Evans, 1968;
Willey, 1969; Brown, 1978). "Jim" Ford became an important
figure in my life and my career quite early, when I was only 24.
Jim at the time was only two years older than I, by the calendar
that is, but he was infinitely more mature. We were closely
associated in archaeological research in the late 1930s and
early 1940s, and during this time we were also fellow graduate
students for a year at Columbia University. In 1946, we were
again collaborating in field research. Subsequently, we saw less
of each other but maintained some communication up until
the time of his death in 1968.

James Ford was a Mississippian, of hill country and small
farm—rather than delta and plantation—background. He was
born on 12 February 1911, in the little community of Water
Valley, Mississippi, the son of James Alfred and Janie David
(Johnson) Ford. The senior James Alfred, a engineer on the
Illinois Central Railroad, was killed in a rail accident when
young James was only three years of age. Thereafter, James and
a younger brother, David, were raised by their mother, an intelligent and forceful woman who had been a school teacher and
who returned to this profession after her husband's death. That
Jim was born on February the 12th, the same month and day as
Abraham Lincoln, has always caught my fancy. The two had
many things in common: the tall, rangy physique, the powerful personality and intellect, the Scots-Irish and English ancestry, the humble yeoman American background, and, above all,
the magnetic qualities of leadership.

The Ford's moved to the larger town of Clinton, Mississippi
in 1919, and Jim graduated from the public high school there in
1927. He entered Mississippi College in Clinton, where he had

an uncle who was a Classics professor and who became, to some extent, a father figure to him in these early years. I think it likely that this uncle may have guided Jim's early interests in the direction of archaeology.

These archaeological interests began when Jim, and a friend, Moreau B. Chambers, obtained jobs with the Mississippi Department of Archives and History in the state capitol at Jackson, immediately after their high school graduation. The director of that department put these two young men to work digging up and collecting "Indian relics" from the numerous mounds in the state. They did this for three summers. Jim has told me that they traveled around on what was his first archaeological survey in a team and wagon. They had no instruction or indoctrination in archaeological digging, yet Jim's innate sense of order and system led him to devise rough attempts at provenience controls by establishing bench marks on large trees near the mounds and noting positions of finds with reference to these bench marks.

It was during these summers of mound digging that Jim had the good fortune to meet Henry B. Collins, an archaeologist with the Bureau of American Ethnology at the Smithsonian Institution. Collins was also a Mississippian who had done some Southeastern archaeology, but at that time he was establishing himself as a leading Arctic archaeologist. He recognized Jim's youthful abilities and became his mentor in those early years, advising him on the local surveys and, even more importantly, taking Jim with him on archaeological expeditions to Alaska.

Jim had another stroke of luck during his Mississippi Archives and History connection. He met a nice young lady named Ethel Campbell, who was the director's secretary, and she became Mrs. James Ford in 1934.

In the late 1920s and early 1930s Jim's Mississippi College attendance was intermittent with periods of archaeological fieldwork in Alaska, where he accompanied Collins as his assistant. This was a very important indoctrination for Jim, educating him in such things as stratigraphy, artifact typology, and seriation. He was particularly impressed with the power of artifact seriation, and his seriational studies of Southeastern ceramics, in subsequent years, owe much to this Arctic experience.

Unlike that other southerner, Sam McGee, Jim adapted to the frozen north with no trouble at all. As one of the last great frontiers of America, Alaska had a romantic fascination for him. It provided a physical challenge which combined with and reinforced the intellectual challenge of archaeology. There is a recurrent motif here in this matter of "challenge". Jim was always one to "test himself". In so doing, he drove himself to the limit, and often others with him who, not surprisingly, often failed to enjoy the tests as much as he did.

After his second trip to Alaska, however, Jim turned back to his primary interests in Southeastern archaeology. To do this, he applied for and received a National Research Council grant in 1933, to carry out surveys and excavations of archaeological sites in Mississippi and Louisiana. The results of this work, together with much of the survey material from the earlier Ford-Chambers fieldwork, as well as data from earlier minor publications, were drawn together in a sizable monograph, *Analysis of Indian Village Site Collections from Louisiana and Mississippi* (1936), Ford's first major publication. It established the outlines of an archaeological chronology for this part of the Lower Mississippi Valley. When these surveys were over, he was selected by Frank Setzler, of the United States National Museum, and a Smithsonian colleague of Collins, to serve as assistant on a dig at Marksville, in east-central Louisiana. Here he saw, at first hand, the resemblances between southern Marksville and northern Hopewell cultures, a theme he would return to in later writings. After the Marksville project, Ford, on the Smithsonian's recommendation, joined A. R. Kelly at Macon, Georgia, in late 1933. He stayed there for several months—well into 1934—and, as I have indicated in my previous memoir, he played a part in helping Kelly set up the huge central Georgia Federal Relief archaeological operation. There was a restlessness about Jim, and, although I do not know the details of his leaving the Macon project, other than that they were quite amicable, I imagine that he got bored with the "factory-like" routine of the Macon set-up.

Upon leaving Macon, Jim did a job for the Georgia State Park

Service in the summer of 1934 by excavating some "tabby" constructions of the Georgia coast. The sponsors of this under-taking held the romantic hope that these "tabby" ruins were old 16th century Spanish missions. Jim demonstrated, beyond much doubt, that they were early 19th century sugar mills, a finding not well received by his employers; but Jim was never one to pull his punches or to suffer fools gladly. After this, he returned to the Lower Mississippi Valley, this time to Loui-siana State University and its Department of Geography where he was enrolled as a student and also employed as a Research Associate. In 1936, Ford received his A.B. from Louisiana State and began with some graduate courses there, while continuing with his Lower Mississippi archaeological surveys.

At sometime in the late spring of 1937, Jim made a trip to Macon. I had heard about him during the previous summer from Kelly and from others in Macon. He was often spoken of as a sort of Paul Bunyan—this with reference to both his achievements on the project and his physical size. I am not quite sure where I first saw him. As I have written elsewhere (Willey, 1969, p. 66):

> "The power of Ford's personality was overwhelming. One re-members the spare, 6 ft., 4 in., Lincolnesque frame, the wide, slightly hunched shoulders, the deep-set, intense eyes.
> Clearly, there was a quality of the messianic about him—as there may be in all innovators."

At that time, in his youth, Jim had jet black hair and very dark brown or black eyes. It was a face which in repose could be quite gentle and appealing; but, when alive with the fire of a new idea or an argument, its seriousness could be command-ing, to say the least.

From the first, I was impressed by Ford. He asked me nu-merous questions about the dendrochronological research I was conducting. We talked of the local archaeology. He asked my opinion as to how, if I had a large research fund, I would go about doing archaeology in some relatively unexplored region of Southeast. I was flattered at being drawn out on all of this, and I held forth at great length. But there was nothing superfi-

JAMES ALFRED FORD

cial in Jim's attention; he was by no means a "conversational flatterer". He was truly interested in your ideas, and he could be immediately critical of them, as well as agreeing with you on certain points. We had many arguments—in fact, conversations with Jim tended to be running arguments. On that first meeting, I made some observations about certain older archaeologists in the Southeastern field, those whose credentials I was apt to dismiss by considering them "amateurs", even "pot-hunters". Jim wouldn't take this, pointing out that these were men who had devoted large parts of their lives to the pursuit of archaeology. "Who was I", he asked, "an obvious novice in the field, to throw off on them, just because I had a couple of college degrees in the subject?" This little interchange showed a side of Jim that was to reemerge many times in our association. He had a kind of "frontiersman's" or "backwoodsman's" suspicion of the "formal establishment", especially as represented by those who were too willing to identify with it in order to be at one with the "in-group", to look snobbishly at "outsiders".

Jim was only around Macon for a few days on that visit, but later in the summer he returned to help with the restoration of the Ceremonial Earth Lodge or Council Chamber. The National Park Service had decided to make an impressive exhibit out of this excavated structure at the Macon Plateau site, which had now become Ocmulgee National Monument. A steel and concrete shell was to be constructed, dome-like, over the Earth Lodge's well-preserved clay floor, with its eagle-shaped altar, seats, and fire-pit. The architect, who designed this shell, needed someone who knew the archaeology but also had certain practical skills as a construction foreman to act as a constant on-the-job supervisor. Jim, who had had a hand in the original excavation of the Chamber, and who loved a practical challenge, was just the man for the job. He was hired and remained in Macon for several weeks during that summer of 1937. As a result, I had the opportunity to see a good bit of him in off-hours. He reviewed many of the potsherd collections that I was bringing in from my stratigraphic survey, and these formed a basis for long discussions of pottery typology.

Later in the summer, Jim and Ethel went out to Chaco Canyon and the University of New Mexico Field School for a six-week field study fellowship. He came back to Macon in September, full of ideas about pottery classification, in the wake of the Southwestern experience. I had, that summer, been travelling often down to St. Simon's Island to visit Preston Holder's WPA digs, and, in the course of these visits, had become acquainted with A. J. ("Tono") Waring, Jr. of Savannah, a young Yale medical student who also had a long-standing interest in Georgia archaeology. On Jim's return from New Mexico, I took him to St. Simon's to meet Holder and Waring. On one rainy fall day the four of us drove from St. Simon's to Savannah, stopping at various roadhouses as we went along in a kind of "moveable feast" or "moving seminar" on Southeastern ceramic typology.

Immediately after this, Jim invited me to drive back to Baton Rouge with him so that I could see the Louisiana pottery types at first hand. This is a good place to digress on cross-country traveling with Jim. We went from Macon to Louisiana in Jim's car. Shortly after we left, Jim suddenly came up with the idea that we should make a circuitous approach on Louisiana by way of Knoxville, Tennessee. This would enable us to stop off and visit Major W. S. Webb, then in charge of Tennessee Valley Authority archaeology in that state. After all, it wouldn't be time lost if we could have a look at some Tennessee pottery too. Then Jim informed me, once we were well on the road, that he really didn't believe in stopping overnight on these trips. It was a waste of time and money. One of us could grab a few winks in the backseat while the other drove, and then we could switch. I didn't like the idea but said nothing.

We had left Macon in the afternoon so it was not long before we were roaring through the night somewhere in north Georgia. I took the first "sleeping car accommodation" in the back seat. Even at my height, of 5' 10", it wasn't so satisfactory. I didn't sleep much. Somewhere at a filling station, at some time in the middle of the night, we switched. I wondered how Jim, at 6' 4", would make out in the back seat—but it was all his idea. With dawn coming on, we stopped somewhere outside of Knoxville for coffee and breakfast. Jim wasn't at all a good companion before that morning coffee. Feeling pretty worn out and seedy, at least I was, we paid our call on Major Webb, in some TVA office building in Knoxville, where Jim and the Major hashed things over for a couple of hours but we didn't see any pottery. We left Knoxville after lunch, but just when I was beginning to feel human again, we repeated "operation red-eye" on the drive to Baton Rouge which was twice as long as the trip just finished. I can't even remember when we pulled in there.

In Baton Rouge, after I had recovered from our second "night-owl" experience, a look at Jim's Louisiana State Laboratory and his pottery collections was most enlightening. I stayed for only a couple of days. It was getting well along into September, and Jim was departing shortly for a graduate year at the University of Michigan, to study with Griffin and Leslie White. I shuddered to think of his solitary "forced march" up the Mississippi Valley to Michigan, hunched over the wheel of his V-8, peering into the darkness, and thanked my lucky stars I wouldn't be along to trade off with the driving. Instead, I took the train back to Macon. Before we separated, however, Jim told me that after a year at Michigan he would return to Louisiana and set up a big WPA program of excavation in the state. In this connection, he planned a large, central laboratory, and he wanted me to take charge of it for him. In spite of the grueling highway discipline to which I had just been subjected, I was excited by the idea. Jim could outline and present a research program like a call to arms. No loyal archaeologist could refuse. Victory was just over the horizon. Together we would solve all kinds of problems as we envisaged them then: Hopewellian origins, the rise of Middle Mississippian, the role of the Caddoan cultures. That night, as I lay in the comforts of a Pullman birth, no longer under Jim's stern surveillance, I fell asleep and dreamt of archaeological glories to come.

Jim came back from Ann Arbor with sweeping visions of Southeastern prehistory. Under Griffin's stimulation, he now had a perspective on the whole of the Eastern United States, not just the Southeast. Together, they organized the "First Southeastern Archaeological Conference", which was held in Ann Arbor (Ford and Griffin, 1938). In retrospect, I think it can be said that the interaction, argument, and dialogue between

Ford and Griffin was to advance the prehistory of Eastern North America to a new, or perhaps we should say a first, level of synthesis (see Ford and Willey, 1941; Griffin, 1946). At Michigan, Jim was also profoundly influenced by Leslie White. I have often wondered about the degree to which Jim was already turned, consciously or subconsciously, in the direction of cultural evolution and "culturology" before he went to Michigan and listened to some of White's "evangelical" lectures. Certainly, evolutionary doctrine had an appeal to Jim that seemed to go beyond intellectual appreciation, to something akin to an emotional response.

I spent the 1937–38 year in Macon. The most important event of that year for me was getting married in September of 1938; however, on the professional side of things I continued with digging and classifying pottery. Jim was as good as his word about the Louisiana job. He came back to Baton Rouge from Michigan and organized his planned WPA archaeological survey, including the laboratory which was to be in New Orleans. I accepted his offer, and immediately after our marriage, Katharine and I left Macon to set up house in New Orleans.

There, before the end of September, Jim and I had the new laboratory in going order. We had 25 or 30 employees in the lab—washing and numbering sherds, restoring vessels, classifying sherds, making various charts, and drawing and photographing pottery and other artifacts. In the field, there were two digs going: one at the Crooks Mound, in LaSalle Parish, and the other at the Greenhouse site, near Marksville, in Avoyelles Parish. Bill Mulloy and Arden King were in charge at Crooks while Stuart Neitzel ran the dig at Greenhouse. They all kept a steady flow of materials coming into the lab. Jim, living in Baton Rouge, shuttled back and forth between us, bringing the sherds down to me as fast as they came out of the ground.

Jim was a driven leader, driven by those forces within himself that saw the digging, the sorting, the classifications, the tabulations, the correlations—as the enormous job to be gotten through before we could arrive at results. We must work unstintingly, passionately, to achieve the latter. He would come into the lab with those great loping strides, his eyes burning down upon me. There were never casual salutations; he would get right to the point. "Say", he would intone, in that deep voice, "why haven't those chaps in the restoration section moved along faster with the pots from the Crooks Mound? You'd better get them going. I'll be bringing in another big load of restorable vessels from there early next week."

Jim then might suddenly stride over to the photographic dark room in a corner of the lab to review the work of our photographer. The photographer was a sad little man who at one time had had some marginal association with Hollywood. One result of this former, and almost certainly more fascinating, employment were residual bits of slang retained in his speech, such as "douse the glims", which he used in reference to turning off his floodlights. His results were never quite up to snuff. For example, the edges of the projectile points in his photo prints, might all look a little furry—the unavoidable result, he assured me, of the vibrations caused by the movement of heavy trucks in the street below just as the shutter was snapped. I was unable to advise him how to cope with this deranging factor other than, perhaps, to wait cautiously until such tremors had stilled before pushing the button. Jim made no attempt to be so understanding, and, as a consequence, the photographer lived in awe and fear of this grimmer head boss. I can see him looking up beseechingly at Jim's towering figure for the word of praise which never came. Indeed, the offending photographic prints might be tossed down with the single word "worthless", and the poor man, near tears, could only reply, "Oh, Mr. Ford, I tried so hard!" He finally retired into his dark room one day with a bottle—not developing fluid—and, as the saying goes, was "invalided out".

On a couple of occasions, I went up country with Jim to visit the field operations, and we made another trip once to the little town of Hope, in southwestern Arkansas, to visit a collector. Jim and I made a rapid photographic record of his collection of Mississippian and Caddoan pots on 35 mm film. This was a good way for me to learn more about Lower Mississippi and Red River pottery, and Jim was a fine teacher in such a situation. We had good rapport on a task like this. We talked during our cross-country drives. This was mostly archaeology although now and then we touched on other matters. Generally, we got along well enough although we had our differences. These would most often be on personal matters or personal tastes. I know that I was quite taken by Louisiana French cooking. Sometimes I would hold forth on various dishes— ones I had eaten in New Orleans or, maybe, some that we had just finished in a restaurant in Marksville. On one occasion, I must have said too much, for Jim suddenly blurted out, "Gordon, for God's sake, stop talking about food, it embarrasses me." Years later, down in Peru, he told me the same thing, again, as I was verbalizing about the local Creole cuisine.

The 1938–1939 year wore along. Jim and I collaborated on the Crooks Mound site report (Ford and Willey, 1940) which was to appear the next year. Under his guidance I learned a lot of practical things such as the putting together of an archaeological report, including the selection and preparation of photographs, the making up of plates of illustrations, the designing of charts for various purposes. It was a good year, and Jim offered me another one on the project if I wanted it; but I at last had been successful in obtaining a scholarship to return to graduate school, and in early September of 1939, just as Hitler invaded Poland and World War II started, Katharine and I left New Orleans for New York and Columbia University.

While I was at Columbia that fall, I was invited by George Vaillant to present a paper on Eastern United States archaeological chronology in a symposium he had organized on New World chronologies for the annual meeting of the American Anthropological Association. I felt distinctly honored, but I also knew that much of what I knew or thought about the subject had come from James A. Ford and that it would be better if Jim and I did the paper jointly. So we composed our symposium piece via correspondence between New York and Baton Rouge, and we met in Chicago, the AAA meeting place, just after Christmas. Although Jim was the senior author, I delivered the paper; he didn't like public speaking. This paper was a first trial run of one that we were to do a year later and to publish under the title of "An Interpretation of the Prehistory of the Eastern United States" (Ford and Willey, 1941).

At that same Chicago meeting, Ford, Philip Phillips, and

James Griffin were talking about a major survey in eastern Arkansas and adjacent western Mississippi. One of the objectives was to bridge from Ford's Lower Mississippi Valley chronology into sequences farther north, and also, as we thought of it then, to seek out the origins of Middle Mississippian culture. They invited me to join them. I remember thinking about the offer on the train going from Chicago back to New York. The project sounded exciting; but I finally decided I would rather work on my own for a while. As a result, and funded from Columbia University, I went to northwest Florida. Phillips, Ford, and Griffin pursued the Mississippi program and eventually published a major monograph on it (Phillips, Ford, and Griffin, 1951), as I did on my work in Florida (Willey, 1949).

In the fall of 1940, Jim entered graduate school at Columbia, where I had already been in residence for a year. Openly, Jim had an immediate and strongly negative reaction to New York city life. I think that underneath he was fascinated by the intensity and variety of the great city even though he was repelled by what he thought of as its falseness and its glitter. Often, he strained too hard in his denunciations. For my part, I didn't feel that it was fair for him to lump The Metropolitan Museum of Art along with night clubs and Radio City Music Hall in his condemnations of "Babylon". Thinking back about it, Jim may have been a little afraid of some of the trappings of "civilization"—things like the paintings and sculptures one might see in a great museum such as the Metropolitan. He didn't like to be put in a position of awe or wonder. He had no use at all for a place like The Museum of Modern Art, which he considered a temple dedicated to snobbism and fakery. I suppose Jim was uncomfortable in a situation where he felt he was not in control or at least "on top" of things. If the fleshpots of New Orleans raised his hackles, New York magnified all of this unease and mistrust to the tenth power.

At Columbia, Jim adapted without any overt trouble. True, he didn't have much use for his courses in social anthropology. Ruth Benedict's outlook was not that of his former mentor, Leslie White, and Jim remained firmly in the camp of the latter. But he enjoyed his other courses, especially those in archaeology with Duncan Strong. For the coming summer, Strong had promised me departmental financial support, again, to continue digging in northwest Florida. Jim thought this the most errant nonsense. He said I should never have pulled out of the Lower Mississippi Valley enterprise with him, Phillips, and Griffin, and he argued vehemently that I should take my upcoming Columbia field stipend and join them that June. As he put it, "Gordon, you've got to have a scientific, systematic approach to this stuff! The Mississippi Valley is the "spine" for the whole East. If we can work that out there, the whole picture will fall into place. Don't waste your time on the edges in Florida!" But I would have none of it, and I held to my stubborn plans for the "Floridian periphery".

It was at about this time that George Vaillant, at the American Museum of Natural History, came up with his plan for a series of Latin American archaeological expeditions to be run through the Institute of Andean Research, with U.S. State Department Funds. Strong, as a member of the Institute, was to have one of these expeditions, and he asked me if I would like to go along as his assistant—if and when the money was secured. Thoughts of Florida vanished from my head with this opportunity looming, and thoughts of Mississippi and Arkansas vanished from Jim's. As someone older and more experienced in the field than I, Jim was a little miffed that I had been picked to go to Peru, despite the fact that I had been a student at Columbia a year longer. Strong, however, suggested to Jim that he apply to Wendell Bennett, at Yale, who was to be in charge of another of the expeditions, the one going to the Republic of Colombia. Jim did and was chosen to go. He and I were back on a good sound footing again—Florida, the Mississippi Valley, and any hint of rivalry about who was going to South America were all behind us. Vaillant received the funds from the State Department for our expeditions, and in early June of 1941, we all headed for South America.

After the Institute of Andean Research programs were completed, and we returned to the United States, Jim went into the U.S. Army Quartermaster Corps in the summer of 1942. Here he served as a civilian specialist in the development of Arctic clothing and gear for the armed forces. In this capacity, he spent a good part of his time in Alaska. Many have complained that their wartime years were spent doing something that they were not qualified for, or didn't like, to do; but for Jim, this definitely was not the case. His experience in, and love of, the Arctic made him the ideal person for such a job where he worked in close concert with the noted polar explorer, Sir Hubert Wilkins.

After the war, in the fall of 1945, Jim returned to graduate school at Columbia, and in the winter and spring of 1945–46 he became involved, as Duncan Strong's assistant, in the Viru Valley program. This was a scheme which Wendell Bennett, Julian Steward, and I originally concocted for intensive archaeological survey of a single Peruvian valley. We selected the Viru Valley on the north coast of that country where Bennett had done some previous work. This program was to be coordinated under the Institute of Andean Research and funded by several participating institutions—Yale, the Smithsonian, Columbia University, the American Museum of Natural History, the Field Museum of Natural History, and Cornell University. The Smithsonian and the Columbia University contingents took to the field in March of 1946.

This was the first time I had ever been with Jim in a Latin American country. My only previous experience in Latin America had been the above-mentioned Institute's 1941–1942 program, and this also had been Jim's only time there. Jim was very sensitive to his Latin American environment. He worked hard, much harder than I ever did, on his Spanish, which was ruggedly fluent (much more so than mine) although marked with a very definite "gringo" accent. Ethel spoke even better Spanish than Jim, and largely without his pronounced accent. Jim also went out of his way to try to adapt to Latin American social customs. In the provincial city of Trujillo, Peru, where we were based for the duration of the Viru Valley project, he once said to me that "when you are in a place like this it is important to blend in, to be one of them." Jim was well-liked by the natives although I would question his "blending in". In his physical appearance, and especially his great height, as well as in a good many other traits, Jim was doomed to be a "gringo" of "gringos" although I think the Trujillanos good-humoredly appreciated his attempts "to be one of them".

At the beginning of our Viru fieldwork, Jim had suggested that we operate together. His job was to be a surface survey and seriational treatment of Viru ceramics; mine was a study of site settlement patterns. Obviously, they should be closely linked investigations for Jim's dating would be essential to my interpretations. The other members of the expedition were to be engaged mostly in excavations. Jim, with his ingenuity and practicality, made a number of excellent suggestions for my work, especially ones concerning rapid techniques for mapping (see Willey, 1953). We traveled around the valley together in a Jeep with two workmen, one to collect potsherds and the other to help me in mapping and recording. We carried air photographs of the valley with us, and it was easiest to consult these if they were pinned out on a large drawing board. I wanted to keep the drawing board in the back of the Jeep and consult it periodically, but Jim didn't like this. He put the windshield down and fastened the drawing board on top of it. True, we could consult it more rapidly, but the driving through the low-hanging algorroba thickets, which were common on the edges of the valley, could often prove quite painful without the windshield for protection. As Wendell Bennett commented one evening when we drove into camp after a hard day in the field: "You can tell where you guys have been from the scars."

For a time, Jim and I drove the Jeep each day the 30 km from Trujillo to Viru and repeated this, the other way, in the evening. Strong and his other assistant, Clifford Evans, who were excavating, did the same. But Jim got fed up with this and decided we should camp in the Viru, returning to town only on weekends. This had both advantages and disadvantages. Ethel probably had the poorest time of it for she had to do all the camp cooking for us. Ethel gave us good meals, and after dinner we would sit around and talk—or argue.

Jim liked a constant dialectical interchange. I am afraid I was a poor foil. The ever-ready confrontational stance or address is not to my liking. After a few nights of it, I would tend to concede point after point. Jim would become exasperated at this. "God-damnit", he would say, "you won't argue about anything. Don't just sit there and agree with me!" One always had the feeling that Jim was "testing you out", either physically or intellectually.

JAMES ALFRED FORD

But our campside arguments went better than those Jim engaged in back at the hotel in Trujillo—or, given my dislike of controversy, one could say that they were less heated. Jim and Duncan Strong went at it pretty hot and heavy. For instance, Duncan, whose Peruvian archaeology began to take form for him with his study of Uhle's grave lot collections in the museum at the University of California, was not entranced by the idea of classifying the thousands of plain red, brown, or black sherds that came in from the Viru Valley surface collections or refuse digging. He wanted to rely only upon the fragments of Moche modelled or Tiahuanacoid painted types. Jim would listen to Duncan's ideas on this in smouldering silence. Then he would grumble, "Dunc, we've got to have a scientific method in this stuff. We're not collecting antiquities." That would tie it—and several libations of the best (or worst?) Peruvian rum would not help unloosen the knot. Jim was not a happy drinker. Alcohol, to him, was not a way to conviviality. I think that the savoring of liquor, like the gourmet discussions of fine foods, would have "embarrassed" him. Such giving in to the sins of the flesh would have stirred feelings of guilt. Drink was something that one turned to for relief from deep and dark brooding—and perhaps to fuel an argument.

If it had not been for Jim, I am afraid that my settlement sample of over 300 sites would not have been so heavily weighted on the side of the high rocky-crag fortifications, shrines, and other sites that occur on the hilltops bordering the valley. I think Jim used to delight in spotting these with the field glasses and then encouraging me in "mountain-climbing" exploration. This "testing" of me revealed Jim as the practical joker. Leading the way up these hill-crags, he would always manage to take me over a route where I felt I was hanging on by my fingernails. One site, in particular, was most memorable in this regard. I eventually tabulated it as V–61 (see Willey, 1953, Fig. 2, pp. 290–292) and always referred to it thereafter as "Cerro Jaimes Ford". It was on the north side of the valley, near the southwest corner of the Queneto Quebrada. Jim must have found it with the field glasses. It was on one of the highest and most inaccessible peaks that we scaled in our survey. Jim went up it alone first while I was attending to something else. He came back and reported that it was most impressive: a small mountaintop village, presumably put there because of its defensible position. The walls of several rooms were still standing, and in two of them roof timbers were exposed. From surface material, its dating appeared to be late, probably from the Tomaval (Tiahuanacoid), La Plata (Chimu) and Inca phases, but substantial piles of refuse indicated that some stratigraphic excavation was in order. His description of the place so intrigued Duncan Strong that the latter wanted to go see it so Jim took him up first. I didn't get an opportunity to talk with Dunc about it until some days later, but apparently their trip, at least from Dunc's standpoint, was something less than a success.

Meanwhile, though, Jim had told me that when I went up with him we should be prepared for a finely calibrated stratigraphic dig in one of the most promising middens of the site. I demurred at first. We had done virtually no digging on our survey, leaving that to the other members of the Viru group. Such an activity, I argued, would slow us down, and we would not be able to cover as many sites in the valley as I would like. Jim countered with an argument that was hard to refuse. He was having trouble differentiating between the household wares of the three late phases of the valley's prehistory, and he needed some good stratigraphy that would properly segregate these phases and set him on the right track. After all, I was depending on his ceramic dating for my settlement study, and this would be as much to my advantage as to his. I gave in. Jim then said that to do the kind of a stratigraphic job that we should do, we should have a screen constructed so that we wouldn't miss anything in the digging and our sherd samples from the midden would be as large as possible. Jim handled this question with no trouble. A great screen, measuring about 8 by 4 feet, was constructed with heavy timbers. It must have weighed over 100 pounds. On the following day, Jim and I and our two workmen had the hellish task of carrying this monstrous device up the perilous slopes of "Cerro Jaimes Ford". At one point, when I was ill-advised enough to look down, I had a view below my feet that kept me from looking down again. For me, it would have been a mountaineering achievement without the screen; with the screen it was a superhuman accomplishment. I protested at various junctures. Jim finally said, "Gordon, the trouble with you is, you don't like to punish your body." My unvoiced reply was, "Jim, old boy, you've never spoken a truer word."

Once the screen was in place beside our midden pile it proved an absolute "bust"—in more ways than one. The refuse pile, which did look to be about 2.00 m deep, consisted almost entirely of rock spalls. Presumably, these were from ancient stone dressing in the construction of the site. There were a few, but not many, sherds mixed in with the spalls. The spalls and the sherds were about the same size, and very few of either passed through the screen. It became overweighted and broke before long. We abandoned it there on the mountaintop where, given the nature of the preservation on the Peruvian coast, it may still be. I can think of no one save the ghosts of the ancient inhabitants who might come to take it away. Afterwards, as I reflected on Jim's overwhelming desire to screen rock on this particular mountaintop, I wondered if this had not been designed as a "character-building" exercise. Was it a practical joke—knowing as he did my disinclination to climb mountains even when unimpeded by special excavational gear? Surely, he must have realized that the "refuse pile" was relatively worthless for stratigraphic purposes. But one never knew for sure about Jim in a situation like this.

After Viru, Jim and Ethel returned to New York. He completed his doctoral dissertation (Ford, 1949), which was based on his Viru ceramic survey. Even before that, he was appointed to a curatorial position at the American Museum of Natural History. With his negative feelings about life in the "metropolis", Jim purchased a lot in the fairly distant suburb of Tarrytown, well up the Hudson, joining his friends and museum colleagues, Gordon Ekholm and Harry Tschopik, who already lived in that community. There the Fords built a house. This phrasing should be taken literally for Jim did most of the construction work on the house himself. He was pretty good at this sort of thing and had little patience with intellectuals who could do nothing practical with their hands. Of course, most of us can't although Jim found a sympathetic buddy in this regard at the museum—Junius Bird. The Fords were to remain in Tarrytown for 18 years, with Jim at the American Museum.

During this time at the American Museum of Natural History, Jim carried out substantial archaeological fieldwork in the Southeast, again in Peru, in Alaska once more, and in Mexico. The spate of publications resulting from this work is impressive: *The Jaketown Site in West-Central Mississippi* (Ford, Phillips and Haag, 1955); *Poverty Point* (Ford and Webb, 1956); *Menard Site* (Ford, 1961); *Hopewell Culture Burial Mounds near Helena, Arkansas* (Ford, 1963); and *Eskimo Prehistory in the Vicinity of Point Barrow, Alaska* (Ford, 1959). Jim was not one, as so many archaeologists are, to let the dust gather on his field notes and collections before writing them up. Besides this extremely high level of research production, Ford also managed to investigate early man sites in the Texas Panhandle, serve as a consultant to the Louisiana State Park Service in connection with their development program at the Marksville site, begin a study of alluvial valley changes and their relationships to aboriginal occupation in the Mississippi Valley, and help organize and participate in a symposium on archaeological field methods which was held in Barranquilla, Colombia for the benefit of young Latin American archaeologists. Jim's productiveness, energy, and leadership were recognized by the Society for American Archaeology which elected him its President in 1963–64. That Jim did not come into many other honors within the profession was due to his untimely death at the relatively early age of 57.

Before leaving the American Museum, Jim launched his last major field effort, an archaeological survey and excavation program on the Veracruz coast of Mexico. This was to follow out an old wish: to search this region for clues to Mesoamerican-Southeastern United States relationships. In the course of this project, Jim resigned from the American Museum of Natural History and took up a post at the Florida State Museum in Gainesville. He talked with me about his leaving New York, and in doing so he voiced various dissatisfactions with the American Museum. I think, though, that at heart it was his old restlessness that promoted the move. He just was not a man who could be happy for long within the confining structure of any institution. To me, that he stayed as long as he did in New York is more surprising than his leaving.

The Veracruz survey lasted until 1966 when, for reasons of

ill health, Jim had to abandon it. Within a few months he was diagnosed for cancer, but he didn't stop working. In fact, he galloped ahead, trying in a last great effort to demonstrate the grand historical design for which the Veracruz project was to have been just a segment. He sought to relate, historically, all of the "Formative" ceramic complexes of the Americas. It was to be his theme that all later New World Precolumbian agricultural and pottery-making societies could be traced back to a Nuclear American hearth—a hearth probably located somewhere in Ecuador. This concept of an "American Formative" can be seen as a revision, extension, and modernization of Spinden's "Archaic Hypothesis" (Willey, 1981). As in the old Southeastern archaeological days of 30 years before, Jim called for a conference of specialists to argue out and help him plot these diffusions of his "American Formative". A number of his archaeological colleagues responded and joined him in a meeting in Gainesville in the autumn of 1966. Most of these colleagues were sympathetic to Jim's diffusionist ideas; a few were not; but Jim looked upon the conference as a success. It had provided him, he thought, with sufficient data to finish his task. This was the completion of his last major work, *A Comparison of Formative Cultures in the Americas: Diffusion or the Psychic Unity of Man?* (Ford, 1969). He submitted the manuscript for publication a few days before his death on 25 February 1968.

As one looks back over the outlines of Jim Ford's career, his role in American archaeology emerges very clearly. In the early 1930s, archaeology in the Southeastern United States was ready for a major change. The way had been prepared by the numerous excavation projects that had been carried out through the Federal Relief programs, and the direction of the change had been signaled by the advances in chronology-building and systematic pottery typology in the Southwestern United States. Ford early on saw the significance of what had been done in the latter area. His own intensive and extensive earlier work with Louisiana and Mississippi pottery collections made him the best prepared and the most logical advocate of a systematic ceramic typology and nomenclature for the Southeast. In his drive for such a system, and for the full participation of his colleagues in it, he never took his eye off the ball. His single-mindedness paid off. In Peru he also made a similar contribution.

But Jim was never fully satisfied with this typological-chronological structuring in and of itself alone. He wanted to demonstrate the "flow of history" over as wide and deep a range, geographically and chronologically, as possible. He wanted to demonstrate it, and he wanted to explain it. He saw two fundamental explanations. One of these explanations was in the process of diffusion. His last book, treating of the "American Formative" and its spread throughout much of the two continents, was an attempt at such a great diffusionist "explanation". What did Jim mean by "diffusion"? The term can subsume a lot of different processes. Gradual "down-the-line" exchanges, more purposefully directed trading enterprises, invasions or migrations of peoples would be some of these. Yet Jim always seemed uninterested in such processual specifics. Perhaps he thought that he was doing first things first—that he was laying out the pattern of events in time and space and that the way of how the pattern came into being would be detailed later. We can only be sorry that he did not address such questions, that he made no attempt at explanations in terms of human behavior. How, for instance, was an "American Formative", or a New World Neolithic way of life, installed in a region where it had not existed before? What were the specific transformations, not only in basic economy, but in social and political structuring, and in inferred ideologies, that took place in these situations? And what happened after this? How divergent were the developments from place to place as societies rose from a "Village Formative" to a more complex level of development? We can only regret in not having Ford's ideas about such matters, speculative as they might have been.

Ford's other fundamental explanation of the flow of culture history was the theory of cultural evolution. For one who was so much a master of his own destiny, who prided himself on being equal to any situation, whether it be a philosophical debate or extracting the Jeep from a mudhole, it always struck me as contradictory that Ford found the inevitability of cultural determinism so compatible. I wonder if he really believed it? He seemed as little interested in examining the processual machinery of *in situ* culture growth and development as he was in examining the processual specifics of diffusion. For instance, he never addressed such questions as the relationships of population size to the rise of the centralized state, or the roles of the institutions of warfare or trade in political development. Instead, he moved swiftly away from evolution to a "catch-all" diffusionism which was not further explained. The closest he came to the specifics of the evolutionary process was in the uni-modal curves of his pottery-type life-history graphs; but here, again, he avoided the human dimension. The graphs, to him, were expressions of the "superorganic", the culture *geist*, and could only be understood as such. People were only the "carriers" of culture, not the causative agents of it. To attempt to look below the "culturological" level was to him reductionistic and futile. One wonders, did Jim also consider it dangerous? Might it not be disturbing to inquire too deeply into the human element, the force and power of personalities and passions in cultural and social change?

None of us is completely consistent within himself or herself, and an element of greatness may well lie in the ability of the individual to in some way reconcile or harmonize the opposing ideas one carries in one's head. Was Jim satisfied by simply quantifying the flow of culture history, of measuring it as it ran passionless through predetermined channels? I cannot believe it. For James Ford was a man of strong emotions, but these were emotions, I am sure, which he felt must be held in check. I have observed before (Willey, 1969), that "highfalutin'" literature, like similar art or music, made Jim uncomfortable; and, as I have said, he often told me that the only literary man he admired was Mark Twain. I must repeat that this is significant in understanding Jim. The two men had much in common. Both were peculiarly American geniuses, and both were southern Americans. The tragic fate of the South had left both without an appropriate heritage. Thus, each, in his own time, stood somewhat apart from the successful and "progressive" North, being attracted by its technological and scientific proficiency but also oppressed by the meretricious materialism of this image of the "future". Each, through his own genius, competed successfully with—indeed, might be said to have "conquered"—this adversarial North. Yet each had misgivings and bouts of withdrawal from their confrontations. They sought to escape to some purer vision of the American Dream and man's destiny—to Huck Finn and his Odyssey of the wilderness—or to archaeology and those ultimate truths of man's past, to an archaeology unfettered by petty institutional constraints. Like Twain, Ford was a romantic who scoffed bitterly at romanticism, proclaiming the practical. Like Twain, also, a courageous optimism and a dark pessimism warred in his nature. Out of these contradictions, these tensions came the singular creative drive of James Alfred Ford.

After saying this, I must conclude by also saying that Jim would have declared the above paragraph "ridiculous" and "embarrassing". "Why do you always have to carry on with some God-damned nonsense like that?" he would have said. "What's any of that got to do with archaeology?"

WILLIAM DUNCAN STRONG
In middle age.
Courtesy Mrs. W. D. Strong.

WILLIAM DUNCAN STRONG
(1899–1962)

In 1935 a book called *An Introduction to Nebraska Archaeology* had a revolutionary impact on both North American archaeology and ethnology. It laid out in detail the archaeological evidence for a culture history of the Great Plains, but this was not the culture history that had been anticipated for this homeland of the semi-nomadic Plains Indians with their horses and their flamboyant feather headdresses. Instead, the archaeological record showed that far from being the descendants of simple hunting and gathering foot nomads—the colorful horsemen of the Plains had sprung from sedentary riverine farmers of an Eastern Woodland tradition. The book was a telling demonstration of how archaeology could be an integral part of anthropology, providing us as it did a corrective for ethnological preconceptions. As such, *An Introduction to Nebraska Archaeology* was generally conceded to be the best archaeological monograph to appear on the North American scene since Kidder's (1924) "Introduction" to the Southwestern Area, and it established its author, William Duncan Strong, as a foremost New World archaeologist and, especially, an archaeologist who was also an anthropologist (see also Strong, 1933).

William Duncan Strong was a westerner, born on 30 January 1899, in Portland, Oregon, the son of Thomas Nelson and Mary Elizabeth (Stone) Strong. His ancestors were New Englanders, one of them being an early governor of Massachusetts. William Duncan grew up in Portland, attending the local schools there. Years later, an old Portland classmate, David T. W. McCord, the distinguished Boston poet, remembered him as the handsomest member of the high school class. Dave recalled how—in that earlier, innocent time—the romantic young Duncan, at high school parties, would regale his friends, and especially his girl friends, with dramatic recitations of the poetry of Robert Service.

Coming out of high school, Duncan enlisted in the Navy in World War I and was assigned to the USS *South Dakota* on convoy duty in the Atlantic. His memories of the service remained with him, and he often referred to his youthful experiences on the "Dakota", sometimes wryly, sometimes humorously—such as the time he ran into the Captain with a coal-filled wheelbarrow when the latter was all freshly decked out in his "going ashore whites". But, in spite of such mishaps, it would be fair to say that "Dunc" remained a devoted "Navy man" for the rest of his life. It is possible that family tradition had something to do with this loyalty for a much admired older brother was a career naval officer.

After the war, Strong entered the University of California at Berkeley, graduating from there with an A.B. in 1923. As a student, he was, at first, interested in the biological sciences, particularly in zoology and ornithology. One of his Navy stories related to such interests. He had been assigned to a gun turret where it was his duty to train the gun which moved mechanically in response to his telescopic sighting. During a set of routine maneuvers, he became so fascinated with a bird, which he had accidentally picked up in his telescopic field of vision, that he continued to follow it for some minutes. Meanwhile, this particular cannon was waving around crazily in the sky until a blast in his earphones, coming from the bridge, wanted to know "What the God-damned hell was going on in turret so-and-so!" But in spite of these early preoccupations with natural history, he became intrigued with anthropology, especially under the tutelage of A. L. Kroeber, so he finished at Berkeley with the Ph.D. in that field in 1926.

Strong's doctoral dissertation, "An Analysis of Southwestern Society" was published in the *American Anthropologist* a year later (Strong, 1927). Two years after this he brought out *The Aboriginal Society of Southern California* (Strong, 1929). Both of these works are ethnological classics, and both are strongly historical in theoretical orientation (Solecki and Wagley, 1963). While he was still a graduate student, he collaborated with Kroeber in the study of Uhle's Peruvian archaeological collections, classifying, analyzing, and seriating Uhle's grave lot collections from Peru which were stored in the museum at the University of California (Kroeber and Strong, 1924 a,b; Strong, 1925). This was important training for Strong in archaeological description and seriation, and it also instilled an interest in Peru which he would follow up a number of years later. While he was a post-doctoral assistant at Berkeley he also did his first extensive archaeological fieldwork. This was in the Dalles region on the Columbia River where he collaborated with Julian Steward and W. E. Schenck (Strong, Steward, and Schenck, 1930).

Strong's first major professional position was with the Field Museum of Natural History, in Chicago, where he was an Assistant Curator of North American Ethnology and Archaeology from 1926 until 1929, and it was under Field Museum aegis that he participated in the Rawson-MacMillan Subarctic Expedition in 1927–28. He had some memorable experiences on this trip, spending a winter with the Naskapi Indians in Labrador, and among his unpublished papers is a diary entitled "Indian Winter". To quote David McCord again, who has read the manuscript, this diary, aside from its ethnological value, is a literary gem. Dunc had a flair for writing which comes through in all of his works, even some of his most severely descriptive archaeological pieces.

The Naskapi interlude prompts a wonderful Duncan story which he told me once after describing some of the rigors of his "Indian Winter". Upon his return to Chicago, he was invited by the "Adventurer's Club", apparently at that time a kind of Chicago version of the New York Explorer's Club, to give a luncheon lecture on his Subarctic adventures. On arriving at the Drake Hotel, he was duly seated at the table on the dais, along with the president of the club; but he was surprised to find that there was another guest of honor seated next to him who was none other than the ruling Cowboy movie star of the 1920s, the one and only Tom Mix! As might be expected, Tom's introduction generated much more enthusiasm on the part of the audience than that accorded the assistant curator from the Field Museum. After the cheering for "good old Tom Mix" finally died down, the hero of the Westerns rose—resplendent in boots, white doeskin breeches, black shirt with little white arrowheads hemstitched on the pockets, and a colorful kerchief at his throat—and delivered a eulogy about his horse Tony who, it seems, had just passed away. As Mix then phrased it in his peroration, "A man is only half-a-man without his horse!" If his introduction had thrilled the "Adventurers", this climax to his speech brought down the house. When the tumult had died down, an enthusiastic member stood up in the audience and proposed that Tom Mix be made an honorary life-time member of the Adventurer's Club. This was carried by a voice vote of acclaim which lasted for another five minutes. Dunc queried the president as to who the other lifetime members of the Adventurer's Club were. He was told above the din that there were only two others, Theodore Roosevelt and William Howard Taft! Perhaps he was so unnerved by the thought of having to follow this "act", that Duncan, in getting up to speak, inadvertently knocked over his glass of "bootleg red" wine on Tom Mix's white doeskin breeches. Fortunately, the star of sage and sand was without his trusty side-arm (as well as his horse) for if looks had been followed by appropriate action, Dunc would have been shot dead.

Dunc remembers beginning his talk, as he stood before a projection screen showing the map of Labrador, with the exciting announcement that the "Naskapi Indians were the northernmost Algonkin-speaking people in the world". His audience, by this time thoroughly fired up by the emotional crisis of Tony's death, to say nothing of being well—charged with the "bootleg red", were indifferent to any such ethnolinguistic announcements, however well-grounded they may have been in fact. Ignoring the Naskapi's language affiliation, they cried out, instead, for an encore by their previous speaker. Shouts of "We want good old Tom Mix! Hooray for old Tom!" drowned out all attempts by Dunc to inform them of the customs of the "northernmost Algonquin-speaking peoples of the world". Dunc could only plow along through the tumult, an innocent victim of such a cruel double-billing. Needless to say, when he was finally finished, the name of William Duncan Strong was not inscribed upon the club's lifetime honorary membership rolls, following those of Theodore Roosevelt, William Howard Taft, and Thomas Mix.

To return to more serious biographical matters after this digression, Duncan Strong's time in Chicago and at the Field Museum brought him a number of new and important associations. A colleague there was Ralph Linton, who was later to be with him at Columbia. Another was Berthold Laufer, a distinguished Orientalist and a great scholar who had a definite intellectual influence on Strong. Also, it was while he was on the staff of the Field Museum that Duncan married Jean (Stevens) Strong whom he had known from his college days.

In 1929 Strong was offered a professorship at the University of Nebraska where he remained until 1931. In these two brief years he began his work in Plains archaeology, which was to climax in the *Introduction to Nebraska Archaeology*, and which was to continue for several years after he left Nebraska. In this Plains research, he was to train and encourage a number of colleagues and students. Some of the best known of these were John Champe, a Nebraska businessman who became a long-time friend and, with Dunc's encouragement, a professional archaeologist, Waldo Wedel, later an archaeologist with the Smithsonian Institution and a leader in Plains prehistory, and Albert Spaulding, a Columbia University student of Dunc's, whose name is well-known in Plains archaeology as well as in archaeological theory.

In 1931 Strong left Nebraska, moving to Washington, D.C. and taking up a position as Senior Anthropologist in the Bureau of American Ethnology, Smithsonian Institution. He stayed there for six years. These years in the Bureau were to be some of the most productive in his life. It was here that he completed his *Introduction to Nebraska Archaeology*, and between stints of writing, he branched out into Central American archaeology. This new interest was begun in 1933, when he went to the Bay Islands of Honduras as the Smithsonian's representative on an archaeological expedition. Strong was in the field for most of the first half of 1933, and he published the results of the expedition in a Smithsonian series in 1935 as *Archaeological Investigations in the Bay Islands, Spanish Honduras*. In this monograph, Strong brought together not only the collections and data from his own field trip but those from two earlier expeditions which had touched on the Bay Islands, one led by Junius Bird and the other by T. Mitchell-Hedges. Strong's archaeological results from the islands were essentially descriptive; however, he was able to define ceramic

complexes and to present an excellent summary of their ethnohistoric settings.

Best of all, the Bay Islands expedition engaged his interest in
Honduran archaeology, and he returned there in 1936, when he
joined with Alfred Kidder II and A. J. Drexel Paul, from the
Peabody Museum at Harvard, to launch the Smithsonian-Har-
vard University Expedition into northwestern Honduras. In
selecting this region, they were guided especially by some
digging that had been carried out a few years earlier by the then
recently deceased Dorothy Hughes Popenoe (1934). She had
found some quite early, or "Archaic-appearing", pottery at
Playa de los Muertos on the bank of the Ulua River. This was at
a time when the Mesoamerican "Archaic", "Formative", or
"Preclassic" was the focus of considerable controversy, following Spinden's (1917, 1928; Willey, 1981) formulations of the
subject and Lothrop's (1927) and Vaillant's (1934) "Q-Complex" critiques. Strong, Kidder, and Paul demonstrated the
clear Preclassic stratigraphic position of the Playa de los Muertos and other early Honduran complexes, and, in support of
Lothrop and Vaillant, showed the "Archaic" to be much more
complex and multi-rooted than Spinden's theories of Valley of
Mexico origins maintained. Beyond this, they were able to
clarify later ceramic complexes and occupations, including
those of the Late Classic "Ulua Mayoid" style and still later
Postclassic cultures. Their *Preliminary Report on the Smithsonian Institution-Harvard University Archaeological Expedition to Northwestern Honduras, 1936* (Strong, Kidder, and
Paul, 1938) brought this previously little known southern periphery of Mesoamerica into archaeological recognition, with
the beginnings of a substantial regional chronology.

Those who knew Dunc will remember the missing two fingers on his left hand. Although he used to speak of this minor
mutilation in jest—"I wore them off feeling for post-molds in
the Plains"—it was the result of a mishap that occurred on one
of these Honduran expeditions. As he told me the story, he and
a companion were wading in a shallow stream, duck-hunting.
He was carrying a double-barreled shotgun, and, as a duck rose
up from the stream some distance ahead of him, Dunc brought
his gun up quickly and fired. Unfortunately, in this swift mo-

ment, he had scooped up some water from the river into the gun barrel. As a result, the barrel burst, and the explosive charge literally stripped the flesh from the two lower joints of the two left-hand fingers that had held the barrel. The shock of seeing what had happened was worse than the pain at the time. Obviously, drastic measures were needed. They were two or three days mule ride from any competent medical help. His companion was in almost as great a shock as the patient and couldn't face up to performing the necessary surgery. As a consequence, Dunc had to saw off his own fingerbones with a hunting-knife. They then applied what first-aid they could, and made their way over the next two days to a United Fruit Company hospital. Luckily, blood-poisoning did not set in. Dunc tended to view tropical exploration romantically. I might add that of all the archaeologists I have ever known—and, by and large, they are a crowd of romanticists—Dunc viewed things in the most romantic perspective. But the episode of the shotgun and the fingers transcends jungle adventurism.

On his return to the States from Honduras, and in the last year of his Smithsonian career, 1936–37, Strong was loaned by the Bureau of American Ethnology to the United States Indian Service. This was during the Roosevelt administration's drastic reorganization of the Indian Service under John Collier, and, as I understood it from Dunc, he was one of several anthropologists who were called together to advise on new courses to be taken in Indian Service policy. This must have been an unsettling time for Duncan. His marriage to Jean was breaking up, eventually ending in divorce. Perhaps the temporary new job offered something of a relief from his personal troubles. It also must have been at about this time, if not earlier, that Strong was approached by Columbia University with an offer to join their anthropology faculty. As it transpired, both Strong and Ralph Linton, a former colleague of Duncan's at the Field Museum, came to Columbia at this time to fill the void left by Boas.

My foreknowledge of Strong came through a personal source in Georgia. Preston Holder, who was digging on the Georgia coast in 1937, while I was in Macon, referred to him on many occasions. Holder had known him at both the University of

Nebraska and the University of California, and he had also worked under Strong one summer on an excavation in California. Holder had been very impressed with Strong, and he indicated to me that when he returned to graduate school he would seek out Strong, as he did by going to Columbia in 1938.

At the end of 1937, I had the chance to meet Strong. This was in New Haven, at the meetings of the American Anthropological Association. He was a man of middle height, at that time giving the impression of stockiness. Later, in middle age, he slimmed down a bit. He held himself very erect, perhaps a residue of his youthful Navy training. There was a notable quickness, a nervous suddenness, to his movements which he retained all of his life. Among other things, this expressed itself in a rapid walking pace. At that time Strong was 38. He was beginning to go bald. Beneath an impressive brow, he had quite prominent light-blue eyes and a straight, well-proportioned nose. The jaw and chin were clear-cut. I remember him as extraordinarily gracious on introduction. I told him that I was then employed in archaeology at Macon and that I had heard of him through Preston Holder. We talked a bit about the possibilities of my entering the graduate school at Columbia. This conversation was resumed a few days later when I stopped off to see him in New York, on my way back to Georgia.

I did not go to graduate school in the fall of 1938, but I did get there in 1939, entering Columbia in mid-September. On the morning after my registration, I walked over to Schermerhorn, the building which then housed the Department of Anthropology, and seated myself on the well-known bench in the hall outside the offices of Strong, Benedict, Linton, Boas (emeritus), and others. Strong, I had been informed by the Departmental Secretary, was at that moment tied up in another student interview. While I sat there, musing on the fact that I was at last in one of the great centers of anthropological learning, the door to Strong's office opened. His visitor left, followed immediately by a brisk-walking Strong, who shook my hand and ushered me in. After a few preliminaries, he told me that he wanted to hold a seminar on Southeastern United States archaeology that fall and hoped that I would be in it. As this was just what I was wanting to hear, I responded with enthusiasm and set about telling him of all of the recent discoveries in Louisiana archaeology. I must have been hard to get rid of, but, then, Duncan Strong always had great patience with his students.

Katharine and I had taken a little apartment near Columbia. The next morning the phone rang there. It was Duncan Strong. He had to go downtown that day, to the American Museum of Natural History. Would I like to go along to meet some of the men there? I would indeed. We rode in on the subway together. At the museum we went first to George Vaillant's office and then stopped by to pick up Harry Shapiro. Vaillant said that he wanted to go to the bank after lunch so why didn't we go out somewhere rather than eating in the museum restaurant. I think we went to a Schraft's. I was considerably bowled over and obviously delighted to be in the company of three of my anthropological "heroes". At that time both Vaillant and Shapiro were offering courses at Columbia, and I had signed up for Vaillant's Middle American lectures and for Shapiro's introductory course in physical anthropology. Strong had made it possible for me to meet them both ahead of classes. Naturally, I was most grateful. As I was to learn, the gesture was very typical of him. He was the ideal graduate teacher—at least from the student's point of view—the "coach", as it were, who brought the aspirant into the fold and made him feel one of the "brotherhood".

Strong was also an inspired and inspiring seminar and classroom teacher for me that first year at Columbia. His seminar was held in his office, not a large room. There were seven or eight in the seminar on the Southeast. Al Spaulding, who had preceded me by a year at Columbia, and I were the only ones with Southeastern archaeological field experience although Carlyle Smith, a local Long Island man, had had direct experience in the Northeast so he was more or less "in the know". For the rest of the group, it was an introduction to the subject. After a preliminary session in which Strong lectured, I was scheduled to lead off on the Lower Mississippi Valley, the region from which I had just arrived. Strong cautioned me beforehand that archaeology was "pretty new" at Columbia and "to take it easy on the pottery type detail" and kindred matters. For my session, he had invited some of his colleagues in. I remember the presence of Ruth Benedict and Gene Welt-fish. I should have been more nervous about it all than I was, but I launched into the potsherds and the emerging Louisiana-Mississippi chronology with gusto and no trepidations. At some point, about two-thirds of the way through my two-hour harangue, Ruth Benedict, in an attempt to get a more anthro-pological perspective on the whole business, asked me if I had any idea of how the people behind the potsherds had lived. What was their life-style, their ethos? I was unable to address this question very effectively. Afterwards, Strong was kind enough to reassure me, again, by telling me that "archaeology was pretty new at Columbia". I suppose he could only hope that my vision of the archaeological past would broaden with my continued exposure to anthropology. To this end, I also took Strong's more general lecture course, "New World Origins and Continuities". At that time, it was probably the best gen-eral survey course on North and Middle American archaeology that was offered in any university. From listening to Strong in this course, I began to get an idea of how an archaeologist might talk about culture history.

Strong also offered a course in anthropological and archae-ological theory which I took during the second semester of that first year. Like many "theory" courses at that time and since, it was involved with the history of the development of the field, and, with Strong's urging, I researched the writings of Daniel Garrison Brinton, one of the founders of academic American anthropology in pre-Boasian days. Strong was always fasci-nated with the early pioneers of the field. They had a romantic glow for him which was very evident when he lectured about them.

Toward the close of the academic year, I learned that I was to be given significant fellowship aid for the coming year and that, in addition, funds were to be made available for me for summer fieldwork. I told Duncan that I would like to explore along the Florida Gulf Coast, following along the trail once blazed by C. B. Moore but with an approach geared toward establishing a regional archaeological chronology. Richard Woodbury (see Willey and Woodbury, 1942), a fellow student during that first year at Columbia, whose primary interest was Southwestern archaeology but who wanted to see another American area, was selected to go along as my junior colleague.

Strong, himself, went to Peru that summer of 1940 and began to involve himself, once more, in Peruvian archaeology. He had studied the Uhle collections as a student; now he wanted to become directly involved in fieldwork in the area. He came back full of enthusiasm about his trip. He had done no digging or collecting, but he had traveled widely in the country and had spent considerable time with Julio C. Tello, Peru's leading archaeologist. He announced, almost as soon as he got off the boat, that his seminar that fall was going to be on Peru. I had gone down to the dock to meet him, and I announced that I was going to take the seminar.

This Peruvian seminar was the only course I had with Strong during 1940–41. I did, though, serve as Strong's teaching assistant in a survey course on the American Indian. This particular course revealed him as an ethnologist as well as an archaeologist, but he had a way of viewing the two disciplines in concert, of wanting to see no barriers between them.

Strong's South American seminar, like the Southeastern archaeological one, had a small group of students; the only other one I now recall from it was Ned Hall, later to become the E. T. Hall, Jr. of "Proxemics" fame, but then completely dedicated to archaeology. None of us knew anything about Peruvian archaeology. I chose the north coastal region for my survey topic. Wendell Bennett's "North Coast" monograph (Bennett, 1939) had appeared only the year before, and it was my introductory guide to the mysteries of Early Chimu (Moche), Cupisnique, Gallinazo, and the Black-White-Red style. Strong was a good seminar leader. We were given considerable leeway in how we organized our presentations. He didn't talk too much himself, but he put in comments and points during the student presentations and kept the discussions moving along. On the day I came "to bat" on the north coast, who should he bring in as a distinguished visitor-participant but Bennett himself, who was passing through New York. At that time, Bennett was fresh from a series of important excavations and publications in Peru-Bolivian archaeology. He was, as Kroeber in a review had dubbed him not long before, "at the very forefront of Andean studies." I gave my digests and opinions on what I had read; Bennett expanded on or corrected these; and Strong cut in every so often to relate the north coast data to the Peruvian scene as a whole. That seminar and that day were great learning experiences for me. I was happy, excited, and stimulated to be a part of such archaeological discussions. I wanted to be a Peruvian archaeologist along with them. This, I think, is the result of good teaching.

As the spring of 1941 moved along, I heard the rumor of the Institute of Andean Research's grant from the State Department for archaeological Research in Latin America, and then one day Strong called me into his office, told me what he knew of the situation, and said that if the money came through he wanted me to go along to Peru as his assistant. A couple of weeks later, Vaillant, who was the principal organizer of the enterprise, received favorable word: the money would be made available. Strong assigned me the task of organizing a certain amount of equipment to bring down to Peru when I sailed. He took ship two weeks before I did. I scurried around for the next two weeks. Katharine, who had been in Georgia, joined me in New York, and a few days later we sailed for South America.

When Katharine and I arrived in Peru, we joined Duncan at the Gran Hotel Bolivar in Lima which we used as our base for the next two weeks. We purchased an automobile and made a number of excursions along the coast, some just for the day but on two occasions, a drive north to Pativilca and another south to Ica, for more extended periods (Strong and Willey, 1943). Junius Bird accompanied us on some of these trips, and we also added another member to our party, John M. Corbett. Duncan had met John in Lima during the time he was there prior to my arrival. Corbett had been a student of Edgar Lee Hewett's at the University of Southern California in Los Angeles. He had gone to Ecuador on an archaeological expedition with a fellow Southern California student, Edwin N. Ferdon, and they had excavated on the Ecuador coast. When this work was over, he, and his wife, Jackie, had come down to Peru for a look around before returning to the States. The Corbetts were great companions, both in the field and elsewhere. Jackie, Katharine, John, Dunc, and I went to restaurants in Lima frequently during those first two weeks in Lima, including the basement Grill Room of the Hotel Bolivar, the city's most fashionable after-hours bistro. Sam and Eleanor Lothrop (see Lothrop memoir) were also habitues of this nocturnal spa. Dunc was a real nightclub enthusiast. As a dancer, he had rhythm in his bones. The nervous abruptness or jerkiness in his ordinary movements was apparently allayed by the music. While I think he was fond of night spots at home, Peru seemed to have an exhilarating effect on him in this regard.

Duncan also responded very positively to other aspects of Peruvian life, including the cuisine. Unlike me, he must have had an iron stomach and intestinal tract. He rarely suffered from the "turista complaint", a definite advantage for a field archaeologist. He greatly enjoyed a day in the field with Tello. We would travel around from one archaeological site to another, stopping, usually well into the afternoon, at some very beaten-down-looking little place, either in the slums of Lima or in some small town. After two or three jolts of Pisco, a fierce white grape brandy and a specialty of the nation, we might move onto some *seviche* (raw fish in lime juice), a bowl of *chupe* (a tasty soup with everything in it), and a plate of fried guinea pig. All the while we were being regaled by Tello with anecdotes from his career in archaeology and politics. After one of these excursions, Dunc would insist on the importance of "living into the country", of being "Criolla", of being at one with his hosts. I was exhorted not to be such a cautious "gringo". Not surprisingly, these manic moods of Duncan's were inconstant, and "Criolla" life, which often had its share of frustrating moments, would be denounced in no uncertain terms.

For one thing, Dunc was a hopeless linguist. In passing this judgment, I would like to include myself in this category by pointing out that I, too, have little facility in this regard. But Dunc's Spanish even outdid mine, remaining always unique and virtually unintelligible. In that first season in Peru, we relied heavily on Junius (until he departed for Chile) and on John Corbett who was passably competent in the language. In moments of stress, Dunc's struggle with "Castellano", the name by which the Peruvians always liked to refer to their language, became a nerve-wracking ordeal for him and every-body else. After a bad night in a flea-infested hotel, equipped with mattresses and pillows that appeared to have been stuffed with damp cement, the necessity of having to settle the bill in his "second language" was just one thing too many. At such times, it was only natural that Dunc's desire "to live into the country" waned appreciably.

After Dunc and I had made our preliminary surveys along the coast, we left the Hotel Bolivar and rented a house in the Lima suburbs. It was a modest two-story, stucco dwelling whose gleaming white walls, fronting the street, proved irre-sistible to nocturnal scribblers of political statements. These usually called for a violent ousting of the President of the Republic. On more than one occasion, the police, calling by in the mornings, sternly instructed us to remove the seditious slogans before nightfall. The address, which Dunc and I even-tually mastered in the native tongue, still rings in my ears— "Once-Zero-Seis, La Avenida Lloque Yupanqui". This for-mula, if intoned loudly and clearly to a taxi-driver, usually, although not inevitably, brought us to our appointed destina-tion on this avenue named for an early and legendary Inca. The quarters, though, were quite adequate, and we had efficient laboratory and storage facilities for the archaeological collec-tions that we were soon to bring in from the field.

Our original field plans had called for a beginning at Ancon or Supe, in the shell mounds at these places where Uhle (1913) had found what appeared to be very early pottery and which had been studied by Kroeber (1925) and Strong (1925). But these plans were changed when Tello issued us an invitation to work at Pachacamac. Strong had been telling Tello of the pressing need for refuse-heap stratigraphy in Peruvian archaeology, and so finally the latter had countered with a request for a "com-mand performance" where he could observe just what we had been doing all the talking about. We were in no position to refuse. Tello took us out to Pachacamac, a great and imposing ruin about 20 km south of Lima, and showed us a real refuse heap, a black, shaggy-looking pile on the slope below the great Inca Temple of the Sun. He, Tello, was then excavating and restoring a complex of buildings on another part of the site, and he made a group of his workmen available to us for our efforts.

Duncan, John Corbett, and I began by cutting a great swath through the Pachacamac refuse pile—the "haystack" as we came to call it. With the remarkable preservation of the Peruvian coast, this Inca refuse consisted largely of only slightly decayed or dessicated vegetal matter—corn stalks, other plants, peanut shells, old rags, and so forth. There was, of course, an awfully lot of pottery in it, all apparently Inca and much of it polychrome, including fragments of the well-known "arybaloid jars" with their "fern-pattern" designs and numerous little plates with various life-form figures. The refuse was also dusty beyond belief. We and the workmen went around all the time with handkerchiefs or mufflers tied over our noses and mouths, and in the late afternoon, on our return to Lima, we had the appearance of Welsh miners after a long day in the pits. The midden was pretty odorous too. Luckily, we encountered only one burial in it which we deposited in Tello's field lab located about a half-mile from our dig. We transported it—a horrifically-smelling, brown-stained, and slightly sticky mummy-bundle—in the back seat of our Pontiac sedan, with Corbett and I on each side of it. Dunc wisely exercised seniority and road in front with Lucio, our trusty chauffeur, who was highly disapproving and afterwards had to work for two days to get the smell out of the car's upholstery.

The Inca "hay" was several meters deep in places, but toward the bottom of the slope we soon struck an underlying deposit of sandy, semi-consolidated soil which contained sherds of a non-Inca genre. With my limited Peruvian knowledge, the stuff was new to me. It had black and white lines and dots superimposed in geometric arrangements on a red slip. From this, I thought it might be the "Black-White-Red Geometric" pottery of the Epigonal Period (in modern parlance read "the latter part of the Middle Horizon), but Dunc said no; and that night, back at the house, he showed me an illustration of a sherd in Uhle's (1903) *Pachacamac* volume which was a dead ringer for what we were finding in our pre-Inca stratum. This was a fragment of the then so-called "Interlocking style" (later to be better known as the "Early Lima" style). It dated to pre-Tiahuanaco Horizon times, as Uhle had realized so many years before.

After we completed our initial Pachacamac excavation, and

had exposed a profile through the Inca "hay" and the underlying sandy stratum, on down to sterile soil, we set about with a more carefully controlled stratigraphic cut, in effect, a one meter-wide slice which we took back in from the profile face in a great many small stratigraphic provenience units. This took some time, and, in fact, was not finished until after Duncan had left to return to the States on the first of September. John Corbett and I completed it and closed our work at Pachacamac. Tello was not particularly dazzled by our "refuse heap stratigraphy". We had demonstrated Inca debris to be superimposed over an early style pottery, what we spoke of as the "Interlocking style". While the latter style was something he, Tello, had always called "Mantaro", in reference to his belief of its highland affiliations, he had already known that such Mantaro was earlier than Inca; our stratigraphy was hardly necessary to convince him. Indeed, everybody knew that Inca was later than everything else anyway, so why all this fuss about stratigraphy? I had to admit that in this instance his reasoning could hardly be faulted. Still, our Pachacamac stratigraphic dig did offer one chronological insight of a more subtle nature. Within the "Interlocking", or "Early Lima", deposit a two-color, black-and-orange, negative-painted, or resist-painted, pottery had its highest incidence of occurrence at the lowest depths. This was a clue which would prove useful to me later, in the Chancay Valley.

With Duncan gone, Corbett and I spent the months from September 1941 until March of 1942 digging at Chancay, Puerto de Supe, and Ancon. For much of this work we were joined by Marshall Newman who supervised our several burial excavations. He was a physical anthropologist who was working on the Institute of Andean Research "Paracas Mummy-Bundle" project with Sam Lothrop and Tello. The Chancay Valley digs were to form the basis for my doctoral dissertation at Columbia (Willey, 1943), and Corbett was to use the Supe and Ancon data for his thesis (Willey and Corbett, 1954). Corbett also collaborated with Duncan in the Pachacamac publication (Strong and Corbett, 1943). Duncan was always generous with his students about credit; more than just being generous, he pushed them along professionally.

World War II began while Corbett, Newman, and I were

digging at Puerto de Supe. We were living in an Italian Hotel in nearby Huacho; however, the proprietor displayed no pictures of "Il Duce" in the dining room, and the food remained un-poisoned. Katharine and I flew back to the States in May, and when I got to New York, and Columbia, I found that Duncan had plans for me. He had just been called to Washington, D.C., to work at the Smithsonian as the Director of the Ethnogeo-graphic Board, a new war-time agency. He asked if I would take over his teaching duties at Columbia in his absence, and I accepted. Needless to say, I was highly honored at being asked to fill in for one of the most distinguished Americanists. My teaching there, while a new experience for me and by no means easy, was expedited by the fact that Strong turned over all of his notes to me for the lecture course, "New World Origins and Continuities". The breadth of Strong's reading and his great ability to select out key facts and ideas from this reading and to combine them into a coherent whole were very evident in these notes. They showed me how such a synthesis could be achieved so that years later I was able to write *An Introduction to American Archaeology* (Willey, 1966–1971).

During 1942–43, I had several occasions to go to Washington and, on these visits, to see Dunc. He was ensconced in a cathe-dral-like office in the Old Smithsonian Building, across the Mall from the Museum. The Ethnogeographic Board was made up of Smithsonian and other scientists. Its principal function was to provide information for the Armed Services on foreign regions and their native peoples and cultures, especially those in the Pacific theatre. Its day-to-day working staff consisted of Strong, as Director, and Ethel Ford, Jim Ford's wife, as his loyal secretary. Strong was consulted regularly by liaison officers of the services, especially by those of the Navy. As he was over-age for direct military service, this Ethnogeographic Board duty came as a godsend to him. It put him into wartime com-munication with his old service, his beloved Navy. He thrived on this, and he continued in this position from mid-1942 until V-J day in 1945. In the summer of 1945, Duncan married Helen Richardson, whom he had met in Washington and who re-turned to New York and Columbia with him in the fall of 1945. Their marriage remained a very happy one throughout his life.

I had continued to see Dunc regularly after I joined the

Bureau of American Ethnology at the Smithsonian in 1943, and these close associations were to be maintained well into 1946. In the fall and winter of 1945–46, Julian Steward, my boss at the Smithsonian, and Wendell Bennett, who was often in Washington at that time, and I were frequent lunch companions. In these informal meetings, we planned the Viru Valley program for the north coast of Peru, an enterprise to which I have just referred in the preceding Ford memoir. Although he was back at Columbia, we brought Duncan into the scheme early on.

The Viru project was to be a cooperative venture, under the general aegis of the Institute of Andean Research; however, it was to have multi-institutional sponsorship with Yale (Bennett), the Smithsonian Institution (Willey), Columbia (Strong, Ford, and Clifford Evans), the American Museum of Natural History (Junius Bird), and the Field Museum of Natural History (Donald Collier). To these were later added Alan Holmberg, a social anthropologist, employed jointly by Cornell University and the Smithsonian, and F. W. MacBryde, a cultural geographer, then on the staff of the Smithsonian's Institute of Social Anthropology. Each of the participants was to be funded in his travel and subsistence by his own institution; but over and beyond this there was to be a common "service fund" from which all would benefit. The Wenner-Gren Foundation of New York generously provided this fund. It was to supply things like vehicles, vehicle maintenance, and air photos and maps. Such would be needed by all members of the program, at various times and in varying degrees. This "service fund" would be presided over and disbursed by an Institute of Andean Research committee.

As might have been anticipated, the complexity of the arrangement carried within it problems for coordinate action— especially smooth and happy coordinate action on the part of individualists like archaeologists. A certain amount of wrangling started even before we had left the States. Who was really to be the boss? Duncan was at that time the President of the Institute of Andean Research and felt that the mantle of "Head" should descend upon him, but the rest of us felt that the presidency of that rather pro-forma body did not automatically confer such a distinction. To our way of thinking, the Viru Committee, the *ad hoc* body which had conceived and set up the program, should constitute the directorate. This hydraheaded committee, consisting of Bennett, Strong, and myself, had a hard time sorting things out, and I found myself in a tough spot being called upon frequently to cast the deciding vote between my two senior colleagues. But easy collaboration was even more seriously jeopardized by Duncan bringing Jim Ford along as his assistant. I was wary of such a team-up. It seemed to me to contain the elements for built-in trouble. Jim had returned to Columbia to graduate school in the fall of 1945, and his Viru participation seemed the quickest way to a doctoral dissertation under Dunc's aegis. At the same time, the role of "assistant", for the brilliant and highly independent Jim, at age 35, looked like a mistake. He was too far advanced to play such a part. While Dunc liked and admired Jim, he didn't know him as well as I did—and, for that matter, Jim didn't know Dunc as well as I did.

We got off to a bad start in Panama City, an air stopover in those days between Miami and Lima. Dunc and Jim disagreed violently in a restaurant on the proper way for a "gringo" to behave "south of the border". Both were uneasy in a foreign country, as, indeed, most of us were. Both were deeply concerned with the necessity of "blending in", of "being a part of the culture", of not appearing like an unsure, boorish "gringo". But Dunc didn't want Jim to tell him how to behave. When Dunc and I had worked together in Peru in 1941, we were both rather inept about a lot of practical things—things like getting a car or a Jeep out of the sand when it was stuck—and we spoke our poor Spanish together. Probably because of this, we got along fine. But Jim was more adept at such matters than Dunc—and, to make matters worse, he rubbed it in. On one occasion, which involved the Jeep being stuck in a mudhole in the lower Viru Valley, and our related courtesies, or lack of courtesies, toward a local hacienda owner from whom we sought help, Jim, losing patience, told Dunc that the only way they could get along would be for "him to be a worse duffer at field operations than Dunc was." Dunc naturally remonstrated with vigor, invoking, as was his wont, an old Naval form of address to junior officers: "Mister, don't talk to me like that ever again!"

While the Viru relationships of Dunc and Jim, if taken incident by incident, might be said to have their aspects of comedy, my residual remembrance of them taken altogether is a sad one. Wendy Bennett and I tried to smooth things down, but it didn't work. Perhaps this all has a familiar ring to those who have been members of other large expeditions. What is called "camp fever" is not a rare disease in such contexts. But, in any event, whether the Viru experience was run-of-the-mill or exceptional, it is certain that Duncan didn't enjoy his 1946 Viru participation as he should have done.

Fortunately, with Cliff Evans' help, Dunc did some important stratigraphy in Viru, and this was published with relative promptness (Strong and Evans, 1952). They had been searching all the time we were there for a stratigraphic resolution to the question of the chronological relationships between the Gallinazo culture, with its ubiquitous negative-painted pottery, and the Moche culture, but this resolution eluded them until they excavated at a largish ruin in the very center of the valley, the Huaca de la Cruz. Here they found it. Pure Gallinazo refuse deposits were found underlying Moche levels and structures. Dunc also had the "end-of-season luck" to discover a spectacular Moche tomb on the last planned day of excavations. He published this in a preliminary way with the *National Geographic Magazine* (Strong, 1947). This was the tomb of the so-called "Warrior-God". It was a very old male of obviously high status. He was surrounded by pottery vessels and accompanied by some remarkable carved wooden staffs and a copper-shod war-club. It was the sort of discovery usually made—unfortunately—by the Peruvian professional grave-diggers or *huaqueros*. Here, at last, was an archaeological opportunity to record such a burial in great detail, which Strong and Evans did.

One of the highlights of the Viru season was the Chiclin Conference, held at the Hacienda Chiclin, in the Chicama Valley, at the invitation of the Larco family (Willey, 1946). Sr. Rafael Larco Hoyle was a devoted amateur archaeologist who had assembled a great collection in his private museum at

Chiclin. The conference was held after most of our fieldwork was over so we could report on our results. The idea of Peruvian archaeological chronological-developmental schemes was in the air, and these were expressed by several of those at the conference, including both Larco Hoyle and Strong. Duncan was to present his scheme in greater detail at a still later conference that was held in New York in the following year (Strong, 1948).

Duncan maintained his interest and productivity in the Peruvian field after Viru. In 1952, he went to Peru again, this time taking his graduate students, Rose Lilien and Robert Stigler, as his assistants. He chose the south coast for what was to be his final major archaeological expedition, with surveys and excavations being carried out in both the Ica and Nazca Valleys. After the fieldwork was over, Dunc was as reliable as ever in getting the results written and published. The monograph, *Paracas, Nazca, and Tiahuanacoid Cultural Relationships in South Coastal Peru*, appeared in 1957, and it constituted, as did his Viru work, a major contribution to Peruvian archaeological systematics. Relationships between Nazca style ceramics and those of the earlier Paracas and Necropolis were greatly clarified as a result of his diggings and analyses.

At Columbia, Duncan continued as a teacher, still being some years short of retirement age. I visited him in New York in the late 1940s and 1950s, and on two or three occasions he and Helen came up to Cambridge, Massachusetts to pay us return visits. We also ran into each other at meetings in those decades; but, as is so often the case in academic life, we drift apart from our old teachers, colleagues, and friends as a simple result of non-proximity. The last time I saw Duncan was in December of 1961, at an Institute of Andean Research meeting in the American Museum of Natural History in New York. He appeared in good health. He had those same quick movements and the swift walk that characterized him over 20 years before.

In addition to their apartment on Riverside Drive in the city, the Strongs had purchased a country home at Kent Cliffs, some miles up the Hudson. It was at this latter residence that he died, quite suddenly, on 29 January 1962.

As other biographers have written, Duncan Strong "was one

of the major figures in anthropology in the twentieth century" (Solecki and Wagley, 1963). If my personalized, "close-up" view of him here has tended to blur over this fact, let me reemphasize it here. Strong's early promise in the Californian monographs, was substantially validated by the Nebraskan and Honduran work of the early middle years. He continued to do research, write, and to teach throughout middle age. His Peruvian field reports on Pachacamac, Viru, and Ica-Nazca maintained his old high standards. Throughout his career, Strong was highly regarded by his colleagues and his students. He was advanced to the position of Loubat Professor of Archaeology during his tenure at Columbia. He served as President of both the American Ethnological Society (1941–42) and the Society for American Archaeology (1955–56). He held research associateships or fellowships at both the American Museum of Natural History and the University Museum in Philadelphia. In 1954 he was awarded the prestigious Viking Fund Medal for Archaeology. He was a distinguished scholar and a memorable man. I shall always remember him as one who had a major role in shaping my life.

GEORGE CLAPP VAILLANT
In early middle age.
Courtesy Mrs. Robert Hatt.

George Clapp Vaillant
(1901–1945)

Charm, consummate charm, is the quality that first comes to my mind in thinking about George Vaillant. The word sometimes carries with it a connotation of shallowness, or surface gloss, but with George it was a charm with depth, underlain by a richness of personality and backed by a strong intelligence. He was not exactly handsome, at least in the conventional sense of that term, but somehow one remembers him that way. The features were slightly heavy, but an attractive direct gaze, with just a cast of an "underlook" to it, overcame this heaviness. His hair was dark and thick, his complexion clear and healthfully ruddy. He was tall, perhaps a bit over six feet. I imagine that in his youth he had been gangling, even a bit awkward, but by the time I knew him, when he was in his middle thirties, he had filled out, and he moved with grace. He projected, even on first acquaintance, a sympathetic understanding. His Latin American colleagues sensed this for they invariably referred to him as "muy sympatico". While his manner was pleasant, he was nothing so crassly affable as a "hale fellow well met". Rather, there was always a hint of shyness, even a touch of naivete, about him. Such an air of modesty was very appealing in the light of his notable accomplishments. These accomplishments can be summed up very succinctly. While still in his thirties, George Vaillant had changed the course of Mexican archaeology and placed it on a new and professional footing.

As I reflect on this image of my mind's eye—which goes back to over forty years ago—I am well aware that these remembrances of George Vaillant are tinged with romanticism. After all, he was, *par excellence,* the American archaeological hero of his time,—intelligent, able, attractive, and fantastically successful at a very young age—the Fitzgeraldian protagonist who seemed to walk in a protective circle of magic. That, like Fitzgerald's Gatsby, he must have had his dark moments was not something that occurred to me in those days. But youth is not a time for such thoughts.

In writing this memoir of George Vaillant, I should make clear at the outset that my relationships with him were never as close as they were with many of the others that I include in this book. I did not have the student-to-professor closeness with him that I had with Cummings or Strong. He was not my professor or constant mentor in the ways that they were. Nor did I establish the kind of intimacy that I had with Bennett or Bird, although he was not a great deal older than these men. I was always a little too much in awe of Vaillant, of the glamorous remoteness that seemed to surround him. That I have included him in these "Portraits" is undoubtedly due to the singular—perhaps I should say charismatic-impression that he made upon me.

George Clapp Vaillant was born in Boston on 5 April 1901, the son of George Wightman and Alice Clapp Vaillant. He was the middle one of three children, with sisters both older and younger. A. V. Kidder (1945), who knew him well, has written that Vaillant's forbears were of old New England stock but that his great grandparents in the name line were French. Supporters of the royalist cause of Louis Phillipe, they had left France for this country after the revolution of 1848. Kidder went on to suggest that this French strain may have been responsible for Vaillant's "quickness and clarity of mind and his characteristic Gallic aversity to all forms of hypocrisy". The traits were certainly George's, whatever their ethnic line of descent. That some Gallic genes did stay in the family is suggested by an observation of another friend of George's, Frederick Stagg, who once told me that George's father was "intensely French" in appearance and manner. George's background, breeding, and schooling, however, were all firmly in a New England Anglo-Saxon mold. The name Vaillant, incidentally, had lost its French pronunciation, probably early on in Massachusetts, and was rendered as "Valiant".

George went to Noble and Greenough School in Boston and to Phillips Academy in Andover, Massachusetts. He completed preparatory school at the latter institution in 1918. He entered Harvard as a Freshman that year, had a brief enlistment in the U.S. Marines which was terminated by the Armistice, and then resumed his studies at Harvard.

GEORGE CLAPP VAILLANT

Archaeology entered George Vaillant's life while he was at Harvard. A classmate, from both Phillips Academy and Harvard, Singleton Moorehead, convinced him that he should go along on a summer archaeological expedition to Maine. The expedition was run by Warren K. Moorehead, the father of Singleton ("Sing"), who was then the Director of the R. S. Peabody Foundation and Museum at the Phillips Academy and a well-known archaeologist of his day. George, with nothing better to do for the summer, had taken his friend up on the offer, and they went with the elder Moorehead, plus some other students, to Waterville, Maine. Here they proceeded to dig up a "Red Paint Culture" cemetery, and in the course of this George had the good fortune to find a cache of slate spear points. The "Red Paint" people had a relatively simple society, but like many groups of this kind they excelled in some of their manufactures. Items which were made for utilitarian purposes were often fashioned as works of art. So it is with their slate points. Years later, "Sing" wrote Kidder (Ibid.) that this moment of discovery of the slate points marked George's decision to become an archaeologist. If so, I am sure that it wasn't merely the "success" of a good archaeological "find" that turned him in this direction. With George's kind of imagination, such a discovery would have opened up for him that infinitely romantic realization that here was something that had been fashioned with care and devotion by other men long ages ago. It was the sort of humanistic experience that would have appealed to him—the establishment of an empathy that could bridge centuries or millennia. He must have seen then— in a flash—that this was what archaeology was really all about. In any event, George Vaillant went on to make archaeology an important part of his life.

Up to that time, Vaillant had been an indifferent college student, but now he began to concentrate in anthropology and archaeology, both in the classroom and through other summer field expeditions. In 1921, between his junior and senior years at Harvard, he accompanied S. J. Guernsey to the cliff ruins of northeastern Arizona, and then he continued his interests in Southwestern archaeology by working under Kidder at Pecos. His field associations with Kidder extended into his graduate years, and the latter has written of Vaillant in this South-western context:

> "No one ever had a more loyal and capable assistant, or a more dependable, cheery companion. Even then he evinced the qualities that were to make him so effective in later life: keenness in observation, accuracy in recording, ability to grasp the wider implications of what he saw. To these attributes were added a readiness, exceptional in so young a man, to view himself and his work objectively, and a remarkable faculty for getting on with people of all ages and sorts" (Kidder, Ibid., pp. 589–591).

To this roll call of virtues, however, we must add a more critical view from Pecos. Once while I was visiting Dr. Kidder, and he was reminiscing about George, Mrs. Kidder, who had run the Pecos camp with a motherly eye on the younger student assistants, made the no-nonsense observation that George Vaillant, no matter how brilliant he may have been, was one of the untidiest young men they ever had in camp. Apparently, she had been after him one season about the necessity of airing out and remaking his bed at decent intervals, but to no avail. Finally, she took matters into her own hands and set about doing it herself. Mrs. Kidder always maintained that she had found a mouse-nest in the bedclothes, down at the foot of the bed! I wouldn't challenge her veracity in all this, but I can't help but wonder if one of George's camp-mates hadn't played a practical joke and "framed" him when they caught word of the forthcoming "bed-inspection".

Vaillant received the A.B. degree at Harvard in June of 1922, and he entered into graduate training there in the fall of the same year. He and his pal, "Sing" Moorehead, who was now going to Harvard's architectural school, took rooms together in Cambridge. It was through "Sing" that George first came to know Philip Phillips. The latter, before going into archaeology, a career switch he made at George's suggestion, was then an architectural classmate of "Sing's". Phil has told me a number of stories about George from these associations in the early and middle twenties. George and "Sing" shared bachelor's quarters, along with several others, in a house in a rather run-down part of Cambridge. Phil, being married, wasn't a roomer there, but he was regularly invited over by his friends. It was quite a crowd, according to Phil, including an eccentric Cambridge poet, an inventor of underwater gear, and a presiding figure who seems best remembered for his ritual detestation of the then Prince of Wales, always referred to in this household as "that so-and-so H. R. H." George, also, contributed to the colorful character of the establishment. Apparently, this had little to do with his chosen profession of archaeology. Instead, he distinguished himself by an extraordinary flair as a versifier and playwright. His productions in both media were quite bawdy. In them, he displayed that self-deprecatory quality that friends from later life would remember. He had a way of turning his satires against himself, of being the butt of his own jokes. George, too, was the house "liquor steward", an important officer in those prohibition days. He was in charge of two huge carboys. Both contained clear liquid, one gin, which George, as chief alchemist, prepared in the manner of those times. The other was grain alcohol, the reserve supply of the main ingredient for the former. Unfortunately, George had no sense of smell so often there was a confusion as to which of the identically-appearing white liquids was served.

Phil also remembers a more delicate side of George's piquant imagination than that displayed in the verses and playlets. There is a quality of child-like freshness and wonder about the incident. One day as they were walking through downtown Boston and were about to pass the entrance to a little side-street or alley, George suddenly put a hand on Phil's arm and stopped him. They stood there for a minute in silence, Phil waiting expectantly for whatever it was. Then George, eyes bright with the pleasure of memory, said: "You know, I once saw an elephant come out of here." That was all there was to it, but George had treasured the recollection. On questioning, it came out that the elephant must have had something to do with a circus that had been in town at the time, back in George's boyhood; but George did not want to go into the practical details of the matter. For him they destroyed the fascination of the memory, the magic of the appearance of this unlikely creature in such a setting that had now been transformed from the mundane to the bizarre.

As a graduate student, Vaillant came under Alfred Tozzer's influence, and the focus of his interests shifted from the North American Southwest to Mexican and Middle American archaeology. However, an important episode in Vaillant's archaeological education broke into his Middle American studies early on. In the winter of 1923–24, Professor George A. Reisner, the distinguished Egyptologist, who was then at Harvard and the Fogg Museum, agreed to take Vaillant with him for a field season in Egypt. This was done at both Tozzer's and Kidder's urgings. Tozzer felt that this visit to the great civilization of the ancient world would be very appropriate for someone whom he hoped would become a Mayanist; and Kidder, who, as a graduate student, had taken a course with Reisner, had great respect for the Egyptologist as an expert in field methods and techniques. This was looked upon as an unusual opportunity for Vaillant. George once told me that, indeed, he had learned a lot about stratigraphy and structural excavation with Reisner, but he also added that he was glad he didn't have to go through it again. He sorely recalled one occasion during his Egyptian sojourn when he had been assigned the task of mapping a recently excavated area. He had placed some building foundations and related features on his map with great accuracy, but for a large, open, paved floor section he had simply indicated the paving stones, which were pretty much of a uniform rectangular shape and size, with a standard symbol. Reisner would have none of this last. The great man made him map the paving over again by meticulously measuring and plotting out each individual brick. Apparently, George, perhaps not unreasonably, felt that this was carrying "accuracy in recording" over and beyond the call of duty. I don't know if George was ever tempted to forsake Americanist studies for ancient Egypt, but, if he had been, this may have turned him off.

Back to Middle America, Vaillant had his first serious digging in the area in 1926 when he went with the Carnegie Institution group to Chichen Itza. He did both architectural and refuse digging there that season, but it was the latter that most engaged his attention. He made some stratigraphic cuts in refuse beds behind the Temple of the Phalli. According to Kidder (Ibid.), this was the first potsherd stratigraphy and typological classification ever attempted in the Maya area, and it pointed the way for George Brainerd's (1958) later ceramic chronological studies in Yucatan. Vaillant followed this up a little later by digging a stratigraphic pit at another Lowland Maya Carnegie dig, this one at Uaxactun. This single small test at Uaxactun was to have great repercussions for Maya archaeology, and the background to it is worth recounting.

As Tozzer's graduate student, Vaillant had studied the then unpublished data and collections which R. E. Merwin (an earlier Tozzer student, by then deceased) had obtained in his 1910–1912 excavations at Holmul. Holmul is a Lowland Maya site on the Peten-British Honduras border, not far from Uaxactun and Tikal. The tomb stratigraphy from there, combined with the ceramic contents from these tombs, provided some of the most important leads for Lowland Maya ceramic chronology. As seriated by Vaillant, the Holmul sequence began with a Holmul I phase which was the first revelation of "Archaic" (Formative or Preclassic) pottery in the Maya Lowlands. The sequence then continued through what are now considered the Early Classic and Late Classic Periods. As the result of this research, Vaillant, utilizing Merwin's notes, wrote most of the Holmul site monograph. It was not to be published until a few years later (Merwin and Vaillant, 1932), but the knowledge he acquired from the Holmul collection led him into his doctoral dissertation. This dissertation, entitled "The Chronological Significance of Maya Ceramics", was submitted and accepted in 1927, and Vaillant was awarded the Ph.D. degree at Harvard in that year. Although never published, the thesis was made available in several copies, and it fast became the most frequently cited Ph.D. dissertation in the Maya field.

But to continue with sequent events, it was in the next year that Vaillant made his trip to Uaxactun and dug what was to become a famous test pit. What the pit demonstrated was that beneath the Classic Period plaza floors of Uaxactun were deep deposits of "Archaic" or Preclassic ceramic refuse (see Ricketson and Ricketson, 1937). Robert E. Smith (1936a,b, 1955) of the Carnegie would later define and describe these Preclassic ceramic phases, the earlier Mamom and the later Chicanel. Together with those of the subsequent post-plaza Early Classic (Tzakol) and Late Classic (Tepeu) phases, this sequence was to become the basic ceramic yardstick for the Maya Lowlands.

As a graduate student, I had read the Holmul and Uaxactun (Ricketson and Ricketson, 1937) reports, and, in the library down at the American Museum of Natural History, I had been through a copy of Vaillant's thesis. With this introductory knowledge of Maya ceramic chronology, I suppose it was only natural that I should ask Vaillant about his digging of the Uaxactun test pit. Of course, the way he told the story to me in 1939, a dozen years after the event, made it all sound very offhand and casual. He wouldn't place himself in any heroic light. Much of his account was a description of the trip into Uaxactun. In those days one went first to Belize City and from there upriver, for three days and three nights, on a little steamer. But I have a feeling that he left out some of the most interesting parts of that. Harry Pollock was on that 1928 trip, and Harry told me, many years later, that while some of them tried to sleep in hammocks on the little ship's deck, George simply stayed up all night and played cards with other "night-owl" passengers, mahogany contractors and other fairly rough business types who were headed for the interior of the bush. They were met in El Cayo, the head of navigation on the river, by one of the Uaxactun Carnegie staff, and from there they all began a four-day mule-back trip into the ruin. When they finally arrived at Uaxactun, they were dazzled by the newly excavated Temple E-VII-sub. I tried to get the subject back to the test pit, but I was never very successful in doing so. As far as George was concerned, it was one of those things that could have happened to anybody. It was luck. They dug a pit and struck it just right. I guess what I wanted was a rundown of how my archaeological hero had reasoned, from the Holmul study and from the research on his thesis, that there must be Preclassic levels at Uaxactun and the way he then proceeded to disclose them, but that just wasn't George Vaillant's way of telling a story.

Vaillant did not abandon his interest in the Maya after his

Uaxactun trip; a later article, "Chronology and Stratigraphy in the Maya Area" (Vaillant, 1935a), was a major contribution to Maya studies. Nevertheless, the year 1927 did mark a turning away from the Maya for Central Mexico. In that year, he was appointed Assistant Curator at the American Museum of Natural History in New York. There he became closely associated with Clarence L. Hay, a Trustee and a Research Associate of the Museum, who had long maintained an interest in Mexico and Mexican archaeology. Hay, who was the son of John Hay, Theodore Roosevelt's Secretary of State, was something of a father figure for George. He had been a student of Tozzer's at Harvard, a good many years before Vaillant's time, and had taken an A.M. degree in anthropology. While he never published, he was extremely knowledgeable in Mexican prehistory. At that time the most controversial idea in Mexican—and New World—archaeology was Spinden's (1917, 1928) "Archaic Hypothesis". It clearly needed further investigation, and Hay convinced Vaillant that the Valley of Mexico was the place to do this.

I have referred to the "Archaic hypothesis" in the previous Strong memoir, but to fill in more background on it one begins with Gamio's stratigraphic excavations in the Valley of Mexico in the years just before the First World War (Gamio, 1913). These had disclosed an early ceramic culture underlying the remains of the later Teotihuacan civilization. The revelation of these early levels had led Spinden to offer the theory that this ancient, or "Archaic", culture represented the beginnings of sedentary life, farming, and pottery for the Americas, traits which spread rapidly from central Mexico to other parts of the New World. While the hypothesis was important in making American archaeologists confront the basic questions of the nature and origins of such a "Neolithic-type base" for New World civilizations, it was to prove too simple a formulation to accommodate the archaeological data (Kidder, 1945; Willey, 1981). S. K. Lothrop (1921, 1926b, 1933) opposed Spinden's idea, and Vaillant, with his knowledge of the Holmul I complex and his test pit at Uaxactun, plus an analysis of the Playa de los Muertos pottery collections from Honduras (Vaillant, 1934a), joined him in this opposition. This was the "Archaic" versus the "Q-Complex" debate previously referred to. In brief, the Lothrop and Vaillant position was that certain pottery complexes in southern Mesoamerica, which were as early as the Valley of Mexico "Archaic", had traits and features that in no way could have been derived from the Central Mexican "Archaic". This implied multiple and probably more ancient origins for early New World agriculture and pottery than was allowed for by the Spinden hypothesis. Were any of these more ancient origins to be found in the Valley of Mexico?

To answer this question, Vaillant began by digging at Zacatenco, a sizable "Archaic" village midden not far from Mexico City. This was in 1927–28 and 1928–29. The report, *Excavations at Zacatenco*, appeared in 1930 in the American Museum of Natural History series. On a strictly factual level, Vaillant demonstrated that what Spinden had taken for the beginnings of farming and pottery-making life were relatively late manifestations of such a tradition. But, over and beyond this, *Excavations at Zacatenco* was both an innovative and a model archaeological report for that time, and to read it today is to comprehend the intellect and good sense that went into it. Its "Introduction" was an excellent statement on the aims of the archaeological discipline and the meanings and methods of stratigraphy. In it, Vaillant acknowledges his debt to the training he received from Kidder. The "Introduction" is followed by discussions of Zacatenco physical and cultural stratigraphy and by a presentation of the Zacatenco culture sequence. The last half of the report has the detailed descriptions of ceramics, pottery figurines, and other artifacts. In figurines, Vaillant was pursuing a graduate student interest which he had begun under Tozzer—a very elaborate typological classification of figurine specimens which were in the Peabody Museum but for which there were no provenience data. The Zacatenco and his other Valley of Mexico stratigraphic operations gave chronological meaning to many of his types.

Zacatenco was followed by *Excavations at Ticoman* (Vaillant, 1931), *Excavations at Gualupita* (S. B. and G. C. Vaillant, 1934), and *Excavations at El Arbolillo* (Vaillant, 1935b)—three additional basic site monographs devoted, to the "Archaic" cultures of Central Mexico (see also Vaillant, 1935c). Vaillant (1941) was soon to refer to the "Archaic" complexes as the

"Middle" cultures, a term by which he meant that they did not represent the first human habitations of Central Mexico but, instead, had an intermediate chronological position between earlier and as yet undiscovered remains and those of the later Mexican civilizations, such as the Teotihuacan, Toltec, and Aztec. Today, we refer to these "Archaic" or "Middle" cultures as those of the Preclassic Period or the Formative stage. With an additional 50 years of digging behind us, we can now place Vaillant's Zacatenco (or Copilco-Zacatenco) phase in what we call the Middle Preclassic Period. Gamio's and Spinden's "Archaic", or the Cuicuilco-Ticoman phase, is now dated as Late Preclassic.

While most of Vaillant's excavations were directed to the "Archaic", "Middle", or Preclassic cultures, he was well aware that chronological problems still beset the later cultures of the Valley of Mexico. To this end he excavated at a number of later sites, including Teotihuacan and Atzcapotzalco. His findings on these sites were never published in full, but he brought out an important paper, "A Correlation of Archaeological and Historical Sequences in the Valley of Mexico" (Vaillant, 1938; see also Vaillant, 1933), in which he made some of his results available. It is a scholarly and evidentially substantiated attempt to show how the archaeology of the Central Mexican potsherds correlated with ethnohistoric documents.

During his time in Mexico, George Vaillant met Suzannah Beck, the daughter of a prominent North American businessman, Eman Beck. The latter had been a longtime resident of Mexico and was a close friend of Clarence Hay. George and Suzannah Beck were married in 1930. Over the next decade they had three children, Joanna, George, and Henry. Suzannah Beck Vaillant aided George in both the field and laboratory and collaborated with him (as referenced above) on the Gualupita monograph.

It was at the end of the 1930s, after the close of over a decade of his field excavations in Mexico, that I first came to know George Vaillant. As I have recounted in the previous memoir, I met him through Duncan Strong in the fall of 1939, when I was a new and beginning graduate student at Columbia University, and when I took his Middle American course at Columbia. At that time, there was no good single library resource at Columbia for archaeological literature. An alternative, of which I often availed myself, was to go down to the American Museum of Natural History and use their very extensive library. It was in this way that I had the opportunity to read Vaillant's thesis on "The Chronological Significance of Maya Ceramics". On these trips, I had the opportunity to call on Vaillant in his office. On my first New York meeting with him—the day he, Strong, Shapiro, and I had lunch together—he had broached the subject of Precolumbian Mesoamerican influences into the areas to the north—specifically, the North American Southwest, about which he had published a paper (Vaillant, 1932), and the Southeast, about which he had then just read a paper by our mutual friend, Philip Phillips. This was the article which Phillips (1940) was to publish the next year in the Tozzer *festschrift* volume, *The Maya and Their Neighbors.* Vaillant was one of the organizers and editors of that volume. Vaillant asked me what I thought about the whole matter of Mesoamerican and Southeastern United States connections, and I wasn't bashful in opening up on the subject. He suggested I come by his office sometime and we would talk further. Such an invitation, to an audience-hungry graduate student, was a measure of George's kindness. Needless to say, I took him up on the offer.

Vaillant's office was on the fifth floor of the old wing (at the 77th Street end) of the American Museum building complex. The library was also on that floor. One walked down long, high-ceilinged corridors, between glassed-in and curtained storage shelves, to go from the library to the Vaillant office. Near the end of the corridor, you turned right, and it was the second door on the right. Like all of the fifth floor, the office ceiling was high, the room spacious in the late nineteenth century manner. Two old-fashioned roll-top desks stood back-to-back in the center of the room. One of these—the one on the right as you came in—was Vaillant's; the other was Clarence Hay's. A few years later, after Vaillant had left the American Museum, his successor Gordon Ekholm would sit at the Vaillant desk. On the fall day of 1939, when I paid my first visit, Vaillant was alone in the office that morning. He rose, graciously pulled out a chair by the desk, and invited me to sit down. The great charm was there—the arresting eyes, the feeling that he was absolutely delighted you had stopped by and that his attention was all yours. A cultivated manner? I suppose so, in part anyway. After all, who at age 38 does not have a cultivated manner of one kind or another? But few had one as nice as the one George Vaillant had. I told him a little of recent developments in Southeastern archaeology. He responded with questions that indicated that he knew something about them. I set forth some ideas of when and how I thought Mesoamerican traits and stimuli had entered the Southeast. I can't recall now just what some of these were. It was at a period in American archaeology when one tended to reach, almost automatically, for diffusionist explanations. The whole question of Mesoamerican-Southeastern relationships was a tough one then—as it still is. Vaillant, nevertheless, was very responsive to whatever thoughts I had on the matter. This doesn't mean that he was positive about all the things I set forth. Maybe he didn't want to discourage me by open disagreement. He had a way, though, of covertly developing counter-arguments that had delayed-action effects—intellectual "depth-charges" that you didn't react to when they were rather casually slipped overboard in the course of the conversations. These were never in any way "mean". The manner in which they were delivered was always interlaced with humor and that frequent sense of the ridiculous with which he sometimes seemed to view archaeology, and more often himself. While I remember little of the substantive details of these conversations, I know that after them I always felt buoyed up.

So I stopped by to see Vaillant a good many times. I believe that on the next occasion Clarence Hay was there—a very courtly-looking gentleman seated behind the other roll-top desk. George, on introducing me, said: "You know Clarence Hay, of course." Of course I didn't, anymore than on another occasion did I know Theodore Roosevelt, Jr., who had stopped in to see George when I was there—but Vaillant always had this very "inclusive" way of making a young outsider feel at home. On another visit, I met Gordon Ekholm, then a graduate student at Harvard and Vaillant's "understudy" in Mesoamerican archaeology. On still another, I happened to be there when Vaillant's wife, Suzannah, an extremely attractive woman, and his little daughter, Joanna, came in.

On a time or two, I had lunch with Vaillant and Shapiro, downstairs in the Museum Restaurant. George was very food conscious, but "gourmand" rather than "gourmet" would have been the term for him in this regard. Perhaps the defective sense of smell precluded the latter. (Did he really have such an infirmity or was this a George-type joke?) At one such lunch, George queried the waitress on a menu item described as a "Sardine Surprise". She assured him that it was "very nice", and he so placed his order. Harry Shapiro questioned George on his lunchtime asceticism, and the latter replied that he wanted to feel virtuous. But when this delicacy appeared it was a single slice of toast on a plate with two sardines forming a dainty St. Andrew's cross upon the toast. This was virtue well beyond his expectations. "My dear girl," George expostulated to the waitress, "I am 'surprised'! Why this is not enough for a bird to eat, a very small bird! Take it away and bring me something else!"

On one of my calls to the Museum, I brought in a lengthy outline of what I said could have been a future book, one dealing with the whole matter of Mesoamerican-Southeast ties. Rather than setting it aside, with a promise to look at it later, Vaillant read it immediately. Whether this was with true interest or politely feigned interest didn't really matter to me at that time. Then he told me, with enthusiasm, that I really had a grip on the whole business, that this was just the way to go about it, and that I should fill in the outline, write the book now, without further delay! Quite possibly he was getting a little fed up with the whole subject and thought this might be the best way to get me out of his hair. But, secretly pleased and flattered by his response, I nevertheless demurred. I was too young, I said. I was just starting out. I needed to know more before I launched into anything so momentous. "Nonsense", he retorted. "Now is just the time, while you're young and full of beans! Don't wait until you're old, and have a family, and are worrying about things like money and your career!" I never wrote such a book, but I suppose these conversations with him

led me to write a paper on Southeastern archaeological chronology. This was the one which Vaillant invited me, and Jim
Ford, to do for a symposium (see the Ford memoir).

At that time, in 1939 and 1940, George Vaillant was himself
at work on what was destined to be the climax of his research
and writing career, his splendid book, *Aztecs of Mexico* (Vaillant, 1941). Duncan Strong, who was both a colleague and a
close friend of George's, has told of the pains and care that
Vaillant took to make this volume the masterpiece that it was
(Strong, 1945). In it, Vaillant poured all of the knowledge that
he had acquired in the preceding decade. This, included all that
he had learned about the "Middle", or Preclassic, cultures from
his stratigraphic excavations in the Valley of Mexico. These
cultures were the foundations of later Aztec life. He also dealt
with Teotihuacan, or the "Classical Toltecs", the first great
civilization of Central Mexico, and from this he went on to
treat of what we now think of as the Early Postclassic—his
"Chichimec Period" and the "Dynastic Toltecs". The last part
of the book, well more than half, is then devoted to the Aztecs,
with a close and sensitive look at their economy, arts, craftsmanship, religion, and social life, especially as these could be
viewed in their spectacular capital city of Tenochtitlan. The
book closes with the denoument of that civilization, precipitated by the advent of Cortez and his Spanish army in 1519–21.
In all of this, of course, he was drawing upon much more than
the material remains of archaeology. He was telling a story in
human terms, and in doing so he drew upon archival resources
of Indian and Colonial documents. The volume, which was
handsomely produced and illustrated, was the finest synthesis
of Mexican archaeology to that date, and it remains a classic in
the field—despite the inevitable revisions in the archaeological record brought about by subsequent research. Above all, it
is a beautifully and perceptively written book. It sought to
understand the material remains of past cultures within the
contexts of the human aspirations and ideas that produced
them. On the flyleaf of the book there is a quotation from the
artist, Giorgio de Chirico, which gives us some sense of Vaillant's feelings about the ancient Aztec.

"One of the strangest feelings left to us by prehistory is the
sensation of omen. It will always exist. It is like an eternal
proof of the non-sequitur of the universe. The first man must
have seen omens everywhere, he must have shuddered at each
step."

Duncan Strong, in writing about George Vaillant's literary
interests of his formative years, has stated that:

"His literary lode stars, I am told, were then Thomas Hardy,
Dostoevsky, and Henry James, and his earlier writings on
Mayan and Mexican stratigraphy have at times puzzled his
contemporaries, perhaps for that reason. They are factual to
an almost unlimited extent but they are complex, for not only
were the facts complex but his was a complex and searching
mind. Gradually as one follows his work a clearer delineation
appears. Throughout the later record, the facts and their temporal placing still come first but, more and more, his penetrating interpretations in humanistic terms become simplified in
expression and easier to understand." (Strong, 1945, p. 113.)

Strong then goes on to say that "this significant progression"
reaches its best expression in *Aztecs of Mexico.* There is no
doubt that George Vaillant had very deep literary interests.
From things that I inferred from those few talks I had with him
and, indeed, from remarks that he made to me quite directly, I
think that he would have liked to have been a fiction writer.
This underlying desire made him impatient with archaeology.
I can remember him expressing to me his doubts and reservations about our abilities ever to understand the past. There
were so many constraints laid upon the archaeologist. He
wrote me once—it was in the summer of 1940 when he was
either at work upon or had just finished *Aztecs of Mexico*—
that we archaeologists were like the blind men in the fable of
their meeting with the elephant. Individually, they might discover the "truth of the tree" of the animal's trunk, the "wall" of
his sides, or the "rope" of the tail; but they could not conceive
of the "truth" of his total being. In a "Vaillantesque" and scato-
logical punchline to this, he added that he, no doubt, had been
the "blind man" with his hand in the droppings.

GEORGE CLAPP VAILLANT

I have often wondered what George Vaillant's ideas about archaeology would have been if he had lived longer. Some of the dissatisfactions he felt are probably those voiced by a later generation who have questioned the rigidity of the assumptions that archaeologists often make in their attempts to reconstruct the past. I doubt, though, that he would have embraced some of the social science and philosophical solutions that have been propounded. While articles on archaeological methodology were relatively rare in those days, the few that did appear made little impression on him. He referred to them as "shadow-boxing". He was unwilling to disassociate method from substance. Besides this, he would never have been comfortable in turning his back completely on the esthetic and the intuitive. Of one thing, I am sure. His dissatisfactions would not have been expressed polemically and epistemologically, as injunctions to others. They would have been internalized.

The literary, the esthetic, the intuitive, or whatever we want to call it found an expression in two of Vaillant's articles written early in his career: "A Bearded Mystery" (1931b) and "A Pre-Columbian Jade" (1932b). Both were published in the journal *Natural History*, probably to emphasize their "popular", non-scientific nature. In these articles, Vaillant, working from specimens for which there was little or no provenience information, recognized the presence of an as yet unheralded style in Mesoamerican Precolumbian art. He had also glimpsed the style in some of the "Archaic" or Preclassic figurines from the Valley of Mexico which he had studied assiduously over so many years. It was the Olmec style, and it was to be almost ten years before it would be more thoroughly revealed and documented by the systematic explorations and excavations of M. W. Stirling (1940a). Naturally, Vaillant was excited with Stirling's first Olmec work in Veracruz, and I remember a frequent visitor to Vaillant's office in 1939–40 was Clarence Weiant, who had worked as an assistant to Stirling, who was then doing a dissertation on some of the Tres Zapotes collections (Weiant, 1943), and who sought Vaillant's counsel. Other presentations of Precolumbian art objects which further attest to Vaillant's artistic and esthetic interests include, his "The Sculpture of Pre-Columbian Central America," (Vaillant

1934b), *Indian Arts in North America* (Vaillant, 1939a), and "By Their Arts You Shall Know Them" (Vaillant 1939b).

The academic year 1940–41 saw Vaillant engaged in a number of activities. At the American Museum, in recognition of his very successful renovation of the Mexican and Middle American Hall, the Trustees of the Museum appointed him the head of a special committee to review and study all of the other halls devoted to anthropological exhibits and develop plans for new installations that would make the collections more attractive to general viewers. In this new position, he was shifted from the comfortable old office on the fifth floor of the old wing of the Museum and installed in much grander quarters, replete with an outer-office secretarial staff, in the newer Roosevelt wing of the building. Because of I called on him a couple of times in these new quarters. On one of these occasions, I saw him for the purpose of taking my Spanish language reading exam for the doctoral candidate qualifications at Columbia. He still served as examiner for this duty. I had made an appointment—a necessity now in view of his new job—and when I arrived he had some museum display experts or advisors closeted with him in his inner office. He was pretty busy, but, eventually, he came out and we had the exam there in the outer office. It was a reading translation, from Spanish to English. He chose some journal with an article, I believe, by Alfonso Caso. I struggled along, leaping from nouns to nouns and papering over the verb tenses as best I could. Finally, Vaillant said, "All right, you can sweat it out if you have to. You'll do." And he gave me a pass.

The other occasion was a more comfortable one for both of us. It was after the State Department funds from the Office of the Coordinator of Interamerican Affairs had been made available for the Institute of Andean Research archaeological expeditions to Latin America in 1941–42. As I have recounted in the previous memoir, I had been chosen to accompany Duncan Strong on one of the Peruvian projects. The Institute of Andean Research had its "home office" at the American Museum—in fact, its "business office" was essentially the same as the business office of the Museum. I had to go down there to receive certain vouchers, advances, and instructions in connection with the forthcoming trip. This was in late April of 1941. One item of business needed Vaillant's signature so I went over to see him. He wished me luck in Peru. He had never been down there himself, but, in his capacity as the overall organizer of the Institute's program, he said he was making a quick trip down—in fact, sailing with Dunc Strong and Wendy Bennett. I remember him telling me that they wanted all of us younger participants, who were the ones who would be staying for the full year, to be happy and content. That's why he had seen to it that funds were available to take our wives along, and that he wanted us to do our best to establish "good cultural relations" with our hosts. He had assured his friend Nelson Rockefeller, the Coordinator of Inter-American Affairs in the State Department, that archaeologists would be good at this and we musn't let him down. I told him I would exude all the "good will" that I could. He gave me one of those large-mouthed grins that so characterized that very alive face, and said, "Swell!"

In this connection, Vaillant's role in the 1941–42 Institute of Andean Research program deserves a mention of acclaim. It was he who had sold the whole idea to the State Department. It was a bold conception for those days. This was before the time of NSF and NEH Grants and heavily funded, "big-swinging" projects. While quite a bit of money had been spent in Federal Relief archaeology, the vast bulk of this had gone for welfare rather than to the archaeologists. Here for the first time, ten field units, each consisting of two or three archaeologists, were going into foreign areas in a well-funded fashion. Vaillant deserves a lot of credit for putting it over.

A week or so after that I took my Ph.D. General Examinations at Columbia. The first section of these were written examinations, and Vaillant had contributed a set of questions on Middle America. The weekend after the exam I saw Vaillant at a cocktail party. I told him I had taken the exam, and asked if he had seen the papers yet. He said he hadn't, but went on to add that "if I couldn't pass that exam, I deserved to have my" ——kicked!" As I recall, it wasn't all that easy, but I did pass it.

During my year in Peru, I corresponded with Vaillant occasionally. We were supposed to report to him, as chief of our program, as to how things were going. These reports went in every two months, and I remember writing him the details of our various digs at Pachacamac, Chancay, and elsewhere. He would write back, more briefly, although always entertainingly. At sometime in 1941, in the last half of that year, Vaillant was offered the Directorship of the University Museum in Philadelphia, and he accepted it. I must have heard about it from Strong, but I know that when I returned to the States in May of 1942 he was by then installed in Philadelphia. I had looked forward to seeing him again in New York, but only did so on a couple of occasions when he was in town for meetings or to see his friend Strong. On one of these he thanked me very graciously for the "good job" I had done in Peru. We got to talking about Peruvian archaeology. He had driven around for a few days to look at coastal sites on his rapid trip there. He told me he didn't like it—the archaeology there, that is. As he put it, "there was such a horrible feeling of death" about it all. He painted a word picture of places such as Ancon or Chancay in the fog season, when he had been there. Above was the lowering cloud ceiling, as he phrased it, "about 10 feet up". Below the ceiling were "those awful birds"—the vultures—circling forlornly over the pock-marked landscape. Vaillant, then, slightly hunched, raised and lowered his elbows in avian simulation. What were "the birds" seeking, he wanted to know, as they settled down, now and then, among the sacked graves and the broken and scattered mummified remains that the *huaqueros* had left strewn around them? One dared not ask.

Toward the end of 1942, Vaillant stopped off one night with Strong, who was then in Washington, and the three of us, although perhaps Wendy Bennett was along, too, to make up a fourth, had dinner at the Cosmos Club. He seemed both restless and low in spirits. But as that evening went along, from drink to drink before dinner and with another one after, it became very evident from what he had to say that he was unhappy at being stuck in the Museum and not taking part in the war. Apparently, he had gone to his old service, the Marines, and asked if they had anything for him. They didn't. He similarly solicited the other services, with the same answer. They had told him, "Professor, you're a nice guy but you're just too old." George said he had something else in mind that might work out, but he didn't say then what it was, at least in my presence.

Thus, it wasn't too much of a surprise when I heard that Vaillant had accepted a wartime State Department post as the U.S. Cultural Attache to our embassy in Peru. I believe I am right in saying that this was the first time that our diplomatic service established such posts. Other countries may long have had missions of this type but not the United States. At least, I am certain that Vaillant was the first to be so designated to Peru.

George and his wife and family spent the years 1944–1945 in Lima. I think I had one letter from him in that time, and this was received in my capacity as the assistant editor of the *Handbook of South American Indians.* He had written in to referree a dispute between Julian Steward and myself, on one hand, and an irate Peruvian contributor on the other. With his wonderful choice of words, George said that he was in receipt of an "incandescent" letter from the gentleman in question, and could we not, in our editorial wisdom, smooth things over a bit—which we promptly did. This would seem to have been a positive score for cultural relations, however transient. I don't know whether George enjoyed the cultural relations job or not. Certainly, the record would indicate that he performed very well. He and Suzannah were honored at a special State Department luncheon at Blair House, on their return, and his formal biographers (Kidder, 1945; Strong, 1945) indicate that he established excellent relations with the Peruvians. Both he and his wife left many friends there among Peruvian intellectuals. But there was a vagueness about the duties of the post that I think bothered him. Some of this comes out in the article that he published after his return from Peru, "Shadow and Substance in Cultural Relations" (Vaillant, 1945). I don't think there was much doubt in George's mind that the "substance" was something that would develop in the context of real collaborative work and achievement, the kind of thing he had supported in the Institute of Andean Research program of archaeology. I also feel quite sure that the "public relations" aspects of cultural relations would have turned him off.

During his career George was the recipient of many honors. The one of these that he prized most highly was the title of "Honorary Professor" which was bestowed upon him by the National Museum of Mexico. It was given to him in special recognition of his book *Aztecs of Mexico*, which his Mexican colleagues considered as a tribute to their heritage. His considerable accomplishments were recognized by the American Philosophical Society which elected him to membership. He was a member of many professional societies both at home and abroad. He served as President of the American Ethnological Society from 1936 to 1939. Many of his honors were working honors. He did service for the National Research Council on its Committee on Latin-American Anthropology, and he did the same on the American Council of Learned Society's Fine Arts and Inter-American Arts Committees. He served the Government as Chairman of its Committee on Cultural Relations with Latin America from 1942 to 1945. He was an associate trustee of the University of Pennsylvania and a member of its Board of Fine Arts.

On his return from his stint as Cultural Attache in Peru, Vaillant resumed his duties at the University Museum in Philadelphia. Sometime, either in late 1944 or early 1945, he stopped by the Smithsonian for a visit with Matt Stirling, and I had the opportunity to say hello. To me, he seemed much the same as ever, genial and full of stories. I think it was the last time that I ever saw him. Not long after that, he was offered another State Department post. This time it was to be as his country's chief representative in Madrid at the Office of War Information. He accepted. I am sure he felt it was his duty and that he could not refuse. He set about making preparations to leave the country again, but this time it was not to be.

On 13 May 1945, at his home in Devon, Pennsylvania, at the height of a brilliant career and seemingly in the midst of plans for another phase of it, George Vaillant, for no apparent reason, took his own life.

WENDELL CLARK BENNETT
In early middle age.
Courtesy Mrs. Richard Bamberger.

WENDELL CLARK BENNETT
(1905–1953)

Wendell Bennett always exuded a captivating quality of self-assurance. This was neither an aggressive nor a defensive self-assurance, as it can sometimes be when an individual has doubts about himself, but a very positive assurance which seemed to have been come by easily; one sensed no inner doubts. It was an assurance that extended out to others and included them. It was as if he were signalling to you in some way that if you joined forces with him all would go well for both of you—you would be on top of things. Quite naturally, younger, aspirant archaeological colleagues responded to this and to him very positively. It was also an assurance that transcended archaeology. Indeed, of all of the archaeologists I write about in this book, I think Bennett would have been the best bet for success in almost any line of endeavor—say the business or legal world—if he had opted to go into something other than academic life. I have often wondered if Wendy had his self-confidence genetically, or at least from parental example. He once told me that his minister father had been an inspirational lecturer on the old Chataqua summer circuits.

You liked Bennett almost as soon as you met him. This certainly was my reaction when he visited Columbia and participated in Duncan Strong's South American archaeology seminar in the fall of 1940. While I had seen him before, at one or two anthropological gatherings, I had not had the opportunity to talk with him so our 1940 meeting was really the first. He was a man of about my height although more heavily set and ruggedly built than I. He had very sharp and lively blue eyes, heavy light brown hair, a sharply cut nose, a well-developed chin, and a broad jaw.

In writing and thinking about Bennett, I settle easily into the name "Wendy". So it was when I first knew him, and I was not usually one to use first names for my elders, at least on short acquaintance. He was only eight years older than I, and this may have been part of the reason for my ease with him, in spite of the prominence that he had already achieved, but all I can be certain of is that Bennett, in whatever indefinable way, very swiftly generated a feeling of comradeship. With equals or juniors he would move quickly to a familiarity of address. This would take the form of nicknames. Usually, these were personalizations of his own. Thus, his colleague at Yale, Ben Rouse, became "Benjo"; Junius Bird was always "Junio"; or Jim Ford, "Jimbo". Our similar backgrounds also could have had something to do with my quick rapport with Wendy. He was a middle westerner, as was I. In college he had been very much of a fraternity man, as had I. We had ways of looking at things that I did not share with Strong or Vaillant, or Ford.

Wendell Bennett came to the American Museum of Natural History in 1931. The year before he had been engaged in both archaeological and ethnological fieldwork in the Tarahumara region of northern Mexico—his first and only Latin American area experience up to that time. At the American Museum he succeeded Ronald L. Olson as assistant curator in Anthropology, with a particular mandate for archaeological research in Andean South America. After I came to know him better, I asked him once what it had been like to come into such a prestigious place as the American Museum of Natural History as a fledgling 26-year-old. He indicated that it was pretty sticky going around the AMNH at first. Junius (Bird) was all right, but George (Vaillant) and Harry (Shapiro), who were the two other young ones in the anthropology department, had been Harvard men together, and, while they were outwardly nice enough, they seemed to put up something of a wall against him. He tried lunching with them a few times, but he felt like an outsider. "Then," he said, "I got them one at a time for lunch. They must have said to each other afterwards that 'the new fellow wasn't such a bad guy'. Things were all right after that." The episode is revealing of Wendy and the way he went about things, and it is also revealing in that he had no inhibitions whatsoever in telling me about a matter of social manners that might have embarrassed some.

At the American Museum, Bennett lost no time in getting into the field. He went to Bolivia in 1932. His objectives were clear. As of that date, Peru-Bolivian archaeology had been given a systematic chronological framework by Max Uhle (1903), and by A. L. Kroeber (1927) working with Uhle's notes and collections. The relative chronology, from latest to earliest, began with an Inca horizon. This was underlain by an immediately pre-Incaic late period. A Tiahuanaco horizon was earlier than this; but this, in turn, had been preceded by a pre-Tiahuanaco "Early Period". J. C. Tello (1923, 1929) and P. A. Means (1931) had also contributed to this formulation although their views differed somewhat from the Uhle-Kroeber scheme and from each other. Thus, while the archaeology of the Central Andes was in its infancy and presented many problems, it was clear that one of these concerned the nature of the widespread Tiahuanaco horizon and the great site of Tiahuanaco where it was assumed to have originated. The art style seen in the famous sculptures and stone friezes at this site on the Bolivian altiplano (Stubel and Uhle, 1892) was often found reproduced in ceramics and textiles from other parts of the Central Andean area, especially on the Peruvian coast; but nothing was known of chronology at Tiahuanaco itself. It was Bennett's intention to remedy this.

He obtained permission to excavate from Arturo Posnansky, a former Prussian military man, who by 1932 was a Bolivian citizen and the country's head of antiquities. This permit was to allow him to dig 10 test pits, of a specified and uniform surface size, at Tiahuanaco. His approach was to be the metrical stratigraphy which Vaillant, his colleague at the American Museum, had employed so successfully in the Valley of Mexico only a few years before. Bennett was proceeding in a routine manner with his pits when, in one, he came down on the carved front face of one of the finest Tiahuanaco giant "warrior" stone sculptures. Posnansky and the Bolivians could not have been more elated, and they instructed him immediately to widen his pit in order to expose completely this sensational find. Bennett said he could hardly do this for such a lateral extension of this particular excavation would use up the "square meterage" that had been allotted to him for those stratigraphic pits still remaining to be dug. Needless to say, the original agreement was modified so that both the carved monolith could be uncovered and his quota of stratigraphic pits completed.

Bennett did all this, and, today, his name is memorialized by the "Monolito Bennett" now on public display in La Paz. In addition to this, he was awarded the Order of the Condor of the Andes by the Bolivian Government for his discovery of the "Monolito". This may have been an example of "Bennett luck" although I have often wondered. Wendy himself told me that he sank this particular pit near an old excavation that had been made by the French archaeologist, De Courty, a good many years before. One wall of the De Courty excavation was faced with what appeared to be a large plain stone slab. Digging a few feet away, Bennett uncovered the carved face of the "monolito" of which the "slab" of the De Courty pit turned out to be the monument's base. Indeed, the news story in the La Paz press, covering the event, quoted Posnansky to the effect "that De Courty had discovered the base, Bennett the front, and Posnansky the back." In spite of the international composition of the "discovery team", Bennett received the lion's share of the credit for the discovery, at least as such things seem to be awarded by posterity.

On the less spectacular "potsherd level" of archaeology, Bennett's pitting operations at Tiahuanaco enabled him to establish three ceramic periods for the site: Early, Classic, and Decadent. The prompt publication of these stratigraphic and typological results was a boost for Andean archaeology (Bennett, 1934). The sequence stood as such until it was subdivided and refined by the work of Carlos Ponce Sangines (1972) some years later. At the time, it established Bennett's reputation as an archaeologist both in Latin American circles and at home.

Bennett swiftly consolidated this reputation with other excavations made that same year in Venezuela. This was at the site of La Mata, in the Valencia region (Bennett, 1937). His opportunity to go to Venezuela to dig was a windfall of circumstances, and did not have the "problem orientation" that led him to Tiahuanaco. Nevertheless, the work at La Mata was an important archaeological beginning for Venezuela. One of his biographers, Alfred Kidder II (1954, p. 270), has described La Mata as "the first properly controlled excavation in that country."

Bennett returned to Bolivia in 1934 when he excavated at Chiripa, in the highlands to the southeast of the Tiahuanaco

WENDELL CLARK BENNETT

site, as well as in the Bolivian lowlands at several locations, including Arani. At Arani, he established a ceramic sequence that linked Tiahuanaco to the lowland Mojos region, still further to the east, where Nordenskiold (1913) had dug over two decades before. But Bennett was faced with special problems in the writing of the report on this Bolivian work. When it came time for him to depart from Bolivia, he found that his permit to export collections to New York for study had been revoked. Perhaps his fame as an archaeologist had increased too fast not to arouse some jealousies, but, for whatever reason, his Bolivian colleague, Posnansky, had changed his mind about the permit. Fortunately, Bennett had detailed field notes on the work and was able to prepare the final report from these, although to be sure a less well-illustrated one than it might have been otherwise (Bennett, 1936). The incident was a good measure of Wendy's character. In the face of such an adversity, he offered no excuses, but simply went right ahead in the best way that he could. The archaeological profession is littered with cases where such a crisis has resulted in at least the temporary "derailment" of a career, if not a permanent paranoia, but Bennett took it in stride and said little about it. He only told me about it years afterwards, as a casual story, to break the monotony of a New York-to-New Haven train ride.

Another sidelight on the 1934 Bolivian field season concerns the discovery of the Chiripa culture. At that time, Bennett thought it fell chronologically into a post-Classic, but pre-Decadent, Tiahuanaco interval. Some years later, when subsequent work in the region by others showed this not to be the case, Bennett (1948a) had no trouble in revising his ideas and accepting a pre-Early Tiahuanaco dating for the Chiripa complex. He was never one to feel any embarrassment about having to change his mind.

In 1936, Bennett shifted to the north coast of Peru, surveying from Paramonga to Lambayeque, with surface collecting and some test digging. When the monograph on this survey was written, Bennett was unsure of the position of Chavin in Peruvian sequences. Tello had long claimed it to be early, indeed to be the foundation of ancient Peruvian civilization, but Chavinoid stylistic "archaisms" imbedded in Moche ceramics led

Bennett (1939) to continue to question such an antiquity for a Chavin horizon. Bearing down on this problem, his next expedition to Peru, in 1938, was to the site of Chavin de Huantar in the north highlands. His digging there resolved the question in his mind (Bennett, 1943): the stratigraphic position of Chavin style pottery at the great type site was clearly primary and earlier than anything else he found there (Bennett, 1944a).

Certainly by 1940, when I first met Bennett, he was then the leading North American Andean archaeologist actively engaged in field research. He had three major monographs to his credit and a fourth one well on the way. He had accomplished all of this in less than a decade. What about his background before he came to the American Museum and set out on such a swift course into Andean archaeology?

Wendell Clark Bennett was born on 17 August 1905, in Marion, Indiana, the son of William Rainey Bennett, a Protestant minister, and his wife, Ethel (Clark) Bennett. He was raised in Oak Park, Illinois, and after attending high school there he went to the University of Chicago, graduating with a Ph.B. degree in 1927, an M.A. in 1929, and a Ph.D. in 1930. His doctoral thesis was on Polynesian religious structures (Bennett, 1932), and he had also published a monograph on the archaeology of Kauai (Bennett, 1931), in the Hawaiian Islands. The research for both of these Hawaiian projects was done under the auspices of the Bishop Museum of Honolulu where he had an appointment in 1928–29, prior to receiving the doctoral degree. After the degree, he was appointed a research instructor at Chicago and spent the 1930–31 year in northern Mexico where he collaborated with Robert M. Zingg in the aforementioned study of the Tarahumara Indians. Bennett's part of the monograph that resulted from this Tarahumara work (Bennett and Zingg, 1935) was in social anthropology rather than material culture. Thus, as one reviews this rapid early career rise, it is to be noted that Bennett published more ethnology and social anthropology at the beginning than he did archaeology; however, it should be mentioned that Bennett, before the Hawaiian studies, had had some archaeological field experience with F. C. Cole's University of Chicago summer excavation programs in Illinois. What is probably most impor-

tant in this connection is that Bennett was always firmly convinced that archaeology and ethnology were truly related and
should work in tandem wherever possible (Rouse, 1954a). Finally, in all of this, it may be seen that Bennett was, from the
very beginning, alert to the importance of publishing his field
results promptly, whether they were in archaeology or ethnology. After I came to know Wendy, I remember him saying once,
in reference to a long-awaited but still non-existent publication by a laggard colleague, that this was no way to do things.
"When you go out and dig a site," he muttered, "the other guys
(your colleagues) want to know what you found. They're not
interested in waiting around for the perfect report." The remark is reminiscent of an observation Kroeber made on more
than one occasion: "What isn't published doesn't exist."

Bennett went to the American Museum in 1931, immediately after the Tarahumara field study, and, as we have seen,
lost no time in launching into South American archaeology
and getting out the results. During his time at the Museum, he
met and married Hope Ranslow, a pretty girl from New Hampshire who had been a librarian at the Museum. She was to go on
subsequent field expeditions with him to Peru, and they were
to have two daughters, Lucy and Martha. Wendy and Hope
were actually in Peru when, in 1938, he was offered an associate professorship in the Department of Anthropology at the
University of Wisconsin, which he accepted. He was there
until 1940 when he went to Yale to join their Department of
Anthropology and to become a colleague of his old University
of Chicago fellow-student, Cornelius Osgood.

After our meeting in Strong's 1940 seminar, I saw Bennett
briefly before he sailed from New York for Colombia as a part
of the Institute of Andean Research program in 1941–42. In
June of 1942, when we had all returned from South America,
Hope and Wendy happened to be in New York on a short trip.
On learning of my Chancay Valley results (Willey, 1943), and of
the early chronological position there of what we then referred
to as "White-on-red Style" ceramics, Wendy insisted that I
return on the train with them to New Haven, spend a couple of
days at their house, and look over his collections from Chavin
de Huantar which he was then in process of studying for his

upcoming report on that site (Bennett, 1944a). I accepted the invitation with delight, and, on seeing his materials at the Yale 55 Hillhouse office and laboratory, was fascinated to note that he, too, had White-on-red pottery from Chavin where it had occurred immediately above the Chavin Style sherds in his stratigraphy.

On this trip to New Haven, as well as others that I made later, I went with Wendy and some other of his Yale colleagues to the famous "Morey's" where Wendy's tastes in martinis seemed to be especially catered to. To anyone who knew him, it would be superfluous to add that Wendy was a particular connoisseur of that cocktail. The "Morey's and martini" theme prompts a story from a Morey's lunch a few years later than that 1942 visit. On this second occasion, Ralph Linton, the distinguished ethnologist and social anthropologist, had by that time joined the Yale faculty, and he was in our lunch party. We started off with martinis. Linton had reached the dregs of his when he called the waiter over and pointed accusingly at a very small black speck adhering to the inside of the glass, demanding to know, a little huffily, just what this was. The waiter said, "Sorry, sir," took the glass with its offending speck and returned shortly with another full-up martini. Placing it before the aggrieved patron, he said, apologetically: "This one, sir, is on the house." The now placated Linton acknowledged this restitution with a dignified nod, and we drank in silence for a moment. Then Wendy's face suddenly took on an un-characteristically grave expression. He called the waiter back to the table. "There's something in mine, too," he said very seriously, pointing to the olive in the bottom of the glass. "How about another refill on the house?" Wendy had his "flip" side.

But Wendy's conversation was always a bit "flip" and cer-tainly scintillating. On that first Morey visit, he began by entertaining us with stories of personalities in South Ameri-can archaeology. He had a gift for comic mimicry that had a wonderful power to bring the people he was talking about to life. He carried you along with him until you began to feel that you, too, knew them—colleagues both foreign and domestic, government bureaucrats, hacienda owners, and laborers. All were evoked with a sense of place and event. He talked about his recent trip to Colombia. It had been a new place for him. As he said, you had to begin with a set of pottery types and styles that you had never seen before. He'd picked Colombia because he had been impressed with the width, length, and fertile appearance of the Cauca River valley as he had flown over it on previous trips. Had this long, north-south valley once been a major route for peoples and influences moving between Middle and South America? But his single season's work there, with Jim Ford had not been able to throw much light on such large questions. What they had found had not been in the fertile valley bottoms. Most of the sites they had come across had been in the bordering hills, and they were locations of deep-shaft tombs of the sort the Cauca Valley *huaqueros* had been looting for years. Ford, he said, would report on these Cauca surveys and excavations (see Ford, 1944). Wendy digressed for a bit to tell of his all-day horseback riding stints through the mountains of Colombia, urged on by the indefatigable Ford. I felt a bond of silent sympathy for someone else who didn't like to "punish himself".

Wendy's own published research following the 1941–42 season in Colombia was of a more general nature. It was a much needed inventory of Colombian archaeology, and was based upon his studies of the Colombian museum collections. He drew up a series of regional summaries, with chronological information and speculations added (Bennett, 1944b). It was a useful book which served as a basic reference for a long time. He was to do the same thing a few years later for Northwest Argentine archaeology (Bennett, Bleiler, and Sommer, 1948). Both of these summary monographs show that workman-like quality and that sense of the necessity of basic systematics that characterized Bennett's archaeology.

In the fall of 1943, when I moved to Washington to join Julian Steward on the staff of the *Handbook of South American Indians*, I saw Wendy several times on trips I made to Washington. He was active on Strong's Ethnogeographic Board at the Smithsonian and was frequently in the city. By that time, he had already prepared a number of major articles for the *Handbook*, including a long introduction to the Andean Highlands

(Bennett, 1946a) as well as the major Central Andean (Peru-Bolivian) archaeological essay (Bennett, 1946b). Before the *Handbook* was completed he would contribute still more articles, including ones on Colombian (Bennett, 1946c) and North Chilean (Bennett, 1946d) archaeology, plus various topical papers for later volumes (Bennett, 1949a,b,c).

Bennett went back into the field briefly in 1944, this time to Ecuador where he made some excavations in the south highlands, near Cuenca. Donald Collier and J. V. Murra had worked in the region a few years before as a part of the Institute of Andean Research program, and they had made a start on ceramic chronology at Cerro Narrio (Collier and Murra, 1943). Bennett (1946e) was able to add a little to what they had done by way of pottery descriptions and stratigraphy; but this was too early to be able to evaluate and place the Cerro Narrio or Monjashuaico complexes in any very understandable picture of Ecuadorian archaeology. It would be another decade or more before a working archaeological chronology for Ecuador became a reality.

As I have related elsewhere in this volume, it was during my Washington associations with Bennett that we began the planning of the Viru Valley project. I remember the restaurant lunch in Washington in the fall of 1945 when he raised the issue, with Julian Steward and myself, of a single valley survey in Peru. We talked for a while about which Peruvian Valley would be most suitable, and Wendy suggested Viru. It had featured in his Peruvian north coast report, he was familiar with it, and he knew it to be of a manageable size for a relatively short-term program. As Rouse (1954a) has stated, Bennett was the moving spirit in the Viru undertaking. Nevertheless, as was so characteristic with him, he enjoyed stimulating others and developing ideas in concert with them. There can be no doubt that Bennett always saw archaeology as a very cooperative venture; but, at the same time, he was strong for autonomy and independence in the pursuit of individual pieces of research. I know that in Viru his conception of the program was that of a concentration of scholars on the prehistory and ethnology of a single Valley. We would outline certain tasks or segments of the total research enterprise beforehand.

These tasks would focus on problems which were of interest to the various members of our group or team. Each scholar would then pursue his research task or problem in his own way, including the writing of his own report. Collaboration would come about in two ways: 1) practically, through the sharing of certain facilities and equipment, and 2) intellectually, through a sharing of the data of our results. But Wendy always felt that intellectual independence should be maintained by the collaborators.

As we continued with our Viru planning through 1945, Wendy began to have some misgivings about all this. As I have recounted in some of the previous memoirs, he, Julian, Duncan Strong, Jim Ford, and I all had our own ideas on just how things should progress, and some fairly spirited debates developed. The multi-institutional nature of what we were planning to do also furthered disagreements. University presidents and deans, museum directors, the officers of the Smithsonian—all such persons had made it clear that they expected "their man" to have a prominent role in whatever was done. In the face of all this, Wendy told me, early in 1946, that he was going to modify his plans. He said that he thought things might go more smoothly if he was not in Peru at the start of the Viru operations but joined us later. I was quite distressed at this. After all, I said, the idea had been his; we needed him there at the beginning. He was certainly the most knowledgeable of all of us about north coast Peruvian archaeology, and there could be no question that his local contacts would be invaluable. I became quite worked up about it. He listened for a while and then said: "Look, the thing I admire most is a quality of independence. Don't depend on me to run this thing for you. You have to look out for yourself." That was that.

The Strongs, the Fords, Cliff Evans, and I departed for Peru in early March of 1946. Wendy didn't go with us, but took off, instead, for Buenos Aires. He spent some weeks there. This didn't involve digging, but he studied the museum collections, talked with Argentine colleagues, and gave a conference which was a prelude to the already mentioned publication on Northwest Argentine archaeology (Bennett, Bleiler, and Summer, 1948). I also think he did this as "insurance", in case the Viru project did not work out. He was not deserting us, but he wasn't putting all of his eggs in one basket either, especially when there were too many hands trying to carry the basket.

Wendy eventually joined the rest of us in Viru in April. His wife, Hope, and their daughter Martha, were with him, and they all shared our Hotel Jacobs quarters with us in Trujillo. In the original Viru discussions, Wendy had opted for the theme of "architecture" as his research problem, but, after looking over the valley for a few days, he decided to modify this by concentrating on the architecture and the archaeology of the single large site, Gallinazo. His excavations there were interesting and productive. The site is a huge clustering of adobe-walled residence compounds grouped around the great Gallinazo pyramid. The last, rising 25 m above the valley floor, is, in sheer cubic bulk, the largest of the Precolumbian structures of the Viru Valley. The residential compounds appeared as great dun-colored mounds or hillocks, ranging anywhere from 3 to 8 m in height. It was only with Bennett's excavations that these hillocks were revealed to be honeycombed arrangements of adobe-walled rooms. Layers of such rooms had been frequently filled in and then built over by new layers of rooms. All rooms were of a dwelling size, but, curiously, they had no doorways. Wendy argued that they must have been entered from the roof. I have always been sorry that he was not able to excavate longer at Gallinazo and find out more about this fascinating apartment-type architecture. He dug there for only a few weeks. I am still somewhat unsatisfied with the "roof-entrance" interpretation although I admit that I can't see how else the inhabitants could have gotten into them.

I was interested to observe Wendy in the field. In those days, archaeologists were less encumbered with field gear than they are today, but, even then, Wendy "traveled light". A Brunton compass, a 30-meter tape, a few chaining pits and string, and an engineering notebook made up his equipment. He used neither transit nor plane table. He told me he had operated this way at Tiahuanaco and ever since. In saying this about his field procedures, it is to be remembered that he never really engaged in what one would call a "big dig", one where 50 to 100 workmen would be hired and where digging would continue over a period of years or at least for several seasons. What he was involved in was relatively small scale testing, and I think his procedures were adequate for it, at least in accordance with standards of his time.

During most of his stay at Gallinazo, Wendy, with Hope and Martha, resided at the Hacienda Carmelo, in the lower Viru. In 1946, Carmelo was one of the two functioning haciendas in the valley, the other being Hacienda Tomaval in the upper drainage. The hacienda house at Carmelo was a 19th century affair, large, two-storied, and rambling. Its occupant was a Sr. Roehder, of German background, as were many of the north coast hacienda families. He was a friendly man, tall and large and with a stentorian voice. He was an overseer rather than the owner—although perhaps he had some stock in the Carmelo operation. The Carmelo lands were planted in cotton. Roehder had known the Bennett's from their previous stay in Viru in the 1930's, and he had urged them to come and put up there with him this time. The interior of the hacienda house was now rather a ghost of its former glories; there was no Sra. Roehder to look after this side of things; however, the cook who was in charge of the dining room laid a good table. Jim Ford, Don Collier, and I were invited in for lunch on one occasion while the Bennetts were there. Roehder, like many hacienda owners or officials, was an ardent *huaquero,* and he had a great fund of stories about his field research. Wendy loved to get him started on them. Roehder's accounts were in Spanish, but as his delivery was not only loud but slow I could follow with no trouble.

An engaging tale surfaced that day at lunch when I inquired about a large looted cemetery just to the windward side of the great Purpur sand dune. This mammoth lunate sand pile is a Viru Valley landmark. Situated on the northern edge of the valley, just west of the Panamerican Highway, it is easily within sight of the Carmelo Hacienda. According to Roehder, some years previously, a rival *hacendado-huaquero,* from another valley, had arrived at the Purpur cemetery one day, with a squad of men, and they had begun digging. Roehder and his men had watched their work through field glasses for a couple of days. Finally, on the third day, the interlopers struck it rich.

One gold object after another was brought out of a tomb—plates, vessels, and a variety of ornaments. Included among the latter was something which our host described as "un pinion con nueve dientes" (in English, "a pinion with nine teeth or cogs"). By his way of thinking, it was a "pinion-gear" which had been an integral part of a machine that had been fashioned by the old Moche people to grind up gold ore. A kind of "gold-madness", no doubt stimulated by the presence of so much of the precious metal, must have influenced Roehder's "functional interpretation". I should add that the kind of object he described is more conventionally considered as an ear ornament, complete with shaft, disk, and nine ornamental gold balls welded to the rim of the disk. Such interpretive niceties aside, the climax of Roehder's story was his sudden descent with his "troops" who, pistols at the ready, hijacked all the golden loot from the invaders. My question, in my best Spanish, about what happened afterwards to all the golden artifacts, including the "pinion-gear" was lost in linguistic misunderstanding. Such had been, at least in the "bad old days", the nature of competitive archaeological research in the land of the Incas.

During this period, with the Bennetts at Carmelo and Jim and Ethel Ford and I in our camp near the Viru River delta, we would all take the weekends off and come back in to Trujillo and to the Hotel Jacobs where the Strongs and Cliff Evans were staying. On these weekends, we came to know a number of people in Trujillo. The Jacobs family, the owners of the Hotel Jacobs, were among these. Another was an archaeologist at the provincial university in the city, Professor Hans Horkheimer. Horkheimer had been a German refugee who had come to Peru in 1939. While not an archaeologist by original training, he had made himself knowledgeable in the field, and had established himself at the Universidad de La Libertad. He had also published a book on the archaeology of the north coast region (Horkheimer, 1944). Horkheimer had heard of Bennett, of course, and he had called on us in our quarters at the Hotel Jacobs. Afterwards, Wendy and I lunched with him at the other hotel, the Trujillo. As a result of our various contacts in the city and the university, the entire Viru contingent was invited to a special dinner one evening at the Club Trujillo. I think I have remembered the name of the club correctly; in any event, I can identify it by saying that in 1946 it was Trujillo's leading institution of this sort—the city's equivalent of a "Union Club". The dinner was a delightful affair. The club, in the old part of the city, was housed in a handsome building of the Colonial Period. The interior decor fitted the setting. The food and wines were delicious. We were lionized as guests of honor. Our hosts eulogized us in one toast after another—all in Spanish. Clearly, it was going to be a monolingual evening. Also, it was obvious that we needed a toastmaster to reply. Wendy rose to the occasion spectacularly. In that flawless Spanish of his, at least it always sounded flawless to me, he did the honors. He was superb in such a context, and I have seen him so perform on many ceremonial occasions.

An important feature of the Viru year was the Chiclin Conference (see also the Strong memoir). The Hacienda Chiclin was in the Chicama Valley, to the north of Trujillo. It was owned by the wealthy and powerful Larco family. They were originally from Corsica, and an ancestor had settled in the Chicama Valley in the mid-19th century. In 1946 Don Rafael Larco Herrera, a former Vice-President of Peru, was the head of the family. He had three sons Rafael Larco Hoyle, the eldest, and his two brothers, Constante and Javier. Rafael Larco Hoyle was a devotee of archaeology. He had established a large museum on the grounds of the hacienda, and had published substantially in the subject of north coast archaeology by the time of our arrival there (Larco Hoyle, 1938–40, 1941). Bennett had known the Larcos from his earlier north coastal surveys, when he had stayed at the hacienda, and the two younger brothers, who had attended Cornell, had been members of the same fraternity that Wendy had belonged to at Chicago. Seeing and hearing Wendy in their company, it was obvious that he was considered a very good friend. This didn't keep Wendy and Rafael ("Ray") from arguing about archaeology. Earlier, back in 1936, Ray had tried to convince Wendy that the Cupisnique style of the north coast, with its Chavinoid affiliations, was earlier than Moche. Wendy wasn't sure then. Later, after his own digging at Chavin de Huantar, he was won over. Ray enjoyed being right on that one, and let Wendy and the rest of us know it.

Our Viru contingent saw the Larcos frequently. One or the other of them came into Trujillo on business regularly. I remember, especially, some archaeological talk over lunches or dinner with Ray at an excellent "chifa", or Chinese restaurants, in the city. Besides these meetings in town, we had all been invited out to Chiclin for a lunch and a look around at his museum shortly after our arrival on the north coast. I had seen the museum once before, when the Grace Liner had stopped at Salaverry in 1941, but in the intervening few years the collections had grown enormously. One could pour over the Moche life-modelled vessels for hours so we didn't hesitate to take every opportunity to go out to Chiclin.

I remember once a *Time Magazine* reporter was scheduled to come up from Lima to see what all this "Viru archaeology business" was about. *Time, Inc.*, I found out later, had been alerted about Viru by my "home office", the Smithsonian in Washington. Wendy and I took one of the Jeeps out to the Trujillo airport, and while we were waiting around there for the arrival of our man, Wendy came up with the pleasant idea of taking him direct from the airport to Chiclin. "It'll be too hard to start in talking to this guy about settlement patterns, potsherd stratigraphy, and Gallinazo adobe-walled rooms out in Viru," he said. "Let's take him out where he can get some idea of what Peruvian archaeology is like on its flashier side. 'Big Ray' will love to meet him, and we can all have an excellent lunch." He had no argument from me. Wendy made the necessary telephone calls out to the hacienda, and Constante Larco, the middle brother, and incidentally Wendy's closest pal of the three, said, sure, they would be delighted. The *Time, Inc.* gentleman came in on the plane shortly after that, and the three of us set off for Chiclin. When we got there it all went very well except that the younger brother, Javier ("Johnny"), got Wendy and me aside and asked us not to say anything about our guest's affiliation with *Time Magazine* when we introduced him to their father, Don Rafael Larco Herrera. Johnny went on to explain that a few years back, *Time* had written a rather snide piece about the old gentleman when he was vice-president of the Republic and that it all still rankled. *Time Magazine* was not in his good books. Wendy delegated me to explain this to the reporter as quickly and surreptitiously as possible—and I did. The *Time* man said, "No strain. It happens all the time."

To get back to archaeology and the Larcos, Ray, was not only extremely well informed about Peruvian north coast prehistory, but he had many definite ideas about it—some sound, some bizarre—and he was a strong defender of these ideas. One of them was that the Chavin civilization had developed right there in the Cupisnique Quebrada of the Chicama Valley, and, most probably, on those lands that were a part of his hacienda. In passing, I might mention that Chavin origins are still somewhat moot, and Ray's "chauvinism", or particular brand of "Chavinism", may some day be shown to have a basis in fact. On the other hand, Ray's thesis about Moche "bean writing", or hieroglyphics which Larco believed had been inscribed on Lima beans, (see Larco Hoyle, 1946, p. 175) probably has a more doubtful future. What I want to tell about now, however, is what came to be known as the "Chiclin Conference". Like so many things relating to Viru, Wendy was the first to have the idea of the conference. He then planted it with Ray. The latter was enthusiastic and generously agreed to hold it at the Hacienda Chiclin. Furthermore, "he had some ideas of his own that he wanted us to hear". All of us in the Viru crowd were favorably disposed to the idea. Most of us were close to finishing up our work, and this would give us a first chance to think over our results and to present them in a formal fashion. The meeting was held on the 7th and 8th of August, 1946, in the pleasant Chiclin surroundings. Invitations were issued to a number of dignitaries in Peruvian archaeology, in Peru and abroad—Julio C. Tello, Luis E. Valcarcel, and A. L. Kroeber. None of these were able to attend; however we started off in style by electing Kroeber honorary chairman of the conference and so notified him by a cable sent immediately from the hacienda's telegraph office. The Larco family was represented by the two Don Rafaels, senior and junior, and by younger brother Javier; Constante who was not much for archaeology, despite his close friendship with Wendy, bowed out. The Viru archaeologists were all there: Bennett, Bird, Collier, Evans, Ford, Strong, and me; in addition, we brought along F. W. McBryde, the cultural geographer from the Smithsonian, who had given us some important assistance in Viru map-making.

The conference was a success (Willey, 1946). All of us in the Viru crowd came up with good summaries of our work to date. I think we were pleasantly surprised to hear just how much we had been doing in the months we had been there. Ray Larco made a number of useful observations about our work. I remember one of these concerned the "pukio" ("puqio", "mahamaes") crib irrigation plots which I had been surveying down near the beach. I was uncertain as to just what they were. Ray explained that they had been excavated in Precolumbian times to take advantage of subsurface water run-off for ancient cultivation. They were quite a new thing to me. Ray passed them off as a matter of course. He wasn't much interested in them. They were too commonplace. Everybody knew about them and knew what they were, he said, even the hacienda workmen. Perhaps, but they certainly were not widely known in academic archaeological circles. I referred to them in my Viru settlement monograph (Willey, 1953, pp. 16–17), but it was to be another 15 years or so before references to "pukios" or "mahamaes" became common in the archaeological literature (e.g., Parsons, 1968).

The conference was also Larco's opportunity to launch a general chronological-developmental classificatory scheme for North Peruvian prehistory (Larco Hoyle, 1948). These were the ideas that he especially wanted us to hear, and they did generate a lot of discussion. A number of us had been thinking along these lines for sometime, including Bennett. We differed in terminology and, to some extent, in stage or period criteria. But Larco should be given credit for formalizing his scheme as early as 1946. Other schemes were to be unveiled in the next few years, including some that would be presented back in the States at another Peruvian archaeological conference.

This second conference was very much Wendy's idea, and he took the lead in organizing it. While the Viru Valley work had prompted this one too, he conceived of it as being projected more broadly. It would be a stock-taking, a general "reappraisal", of the Peruvian archaeological field. Plans for it went ahead successfully, and it was held in New York City, on 17–19 July, 1947. The Viking Fund (Wenner-Gren Foundation), which had supported us with the Viru fieldwork, and the Institute of Andean Research were the co-sponsors. Attendance was larger than that at the Chiclin Conference. Perhaps 50 invitations were sent out. At least 30 persons attended, including the Viru group and a number of other Peruvianist colleagues in the States. This time A. L. Kroeber came in person. Wendy very definitely left his impress on the proceedings, editing the volume which emerged from the conference (Bennett, ed., 1948), and presenting two papers of his own (Bennett, 1948a,b). He also suggested the topic for my paper (Willey, 1948). He did this when he came down to Washington to the Smithsonian to tell me about his plans for the conference. I said I'd like to come, but I wasn't sure what I would have to say—over and above what I had already said about the Viru settlement survey at Chiclin. He said no, that I ought to come up with a more general paper for this one, and he reminded me that I had once published an article on Peruvian "Horizon Styles". It had been a strict descriptive-chronological treatment (Willey, 1945b). "Now," he suggested, "why didn't I try to explain just what these "Horizons" signified. What was their meaning in cultural and social terms?" I liked the idea and said I'd give it a try. As my 1945 paper had actually been on "Horizon Styles and Pottery Traditions", I asked if someone else was going to cover the "Traditions" part of it. He thought a minute and said, "Maybe I will".

I doubt if this conversation marked the moment Bennett conceived of the idea of the "Peruvian Co-Tradition". I think he had had the idea for that paper for some time. Certainly the "co-tradition" concept, as he defined and applied it, goes far beyond the limits of a specific pottery tradition. Paul Kirchhoff (1943), a few years earlier, had come up with something like the co-tradition formulation in his definition of "Mesoamerica". He was attempting to talk about a culture area with time depth. Bennett's definition was sharper and more abstract than Kirchhoff's. Although applied by him only to Peru, it obviously had the potential for application to other geographical-cultural areas (see Willey, 1953b; Rouse, 1954). I suppose Bennett will not be remembered as a "theorist" in archaeology. Most of his work seems too pragmatic, too strictly oriented to descriptive space-time particulars of the field work at hand. Yet the co-tradition concept is a major theoretical contribution. It is to archaeology what the culture area concept was to ethnography and ethnology. It establishes for the archaeologist a frame of reference—a geographical area, a range of time, and a condition of cultural interrelatedness in that space and time. In other words, it provides the context in which to examine both history and process. Bennett drew upon his knowledge of and detailed experience in Peruvian archaeology, ethnohistory, and ethnology in conceiving it. To his systematic mind it came as a logical and necessary step in the development of the field.

Wendy was to go on from the Peruvian "Reappraisal" conference and the "co-tradition" paper to his book with Junius Bird, *Andean Culture History* (Bennett and Bird, 1949). In doing this, he took time out from working on his Viru monograph. This was forced upon him as the various pottery collections from the Viru excavations were slow in reaching the United States for study. But *Andean Culture History* turned out to be a landmark work. It opens with a section by Bennett which is an overview of the Andean area and of all of South America. This is then followed by his second section which is a resume of the culture history of the Central Andean or Peru-Bolivian area, the area of the Peruvian Co-Tradition. This section is organized by period-stages. The third section of the book was Junius Bird's treatment of the ceramic, metallurgical, and, especially, textile techniques of the Peruvian Co-Tradition. The Bennett-Bird book preceded two other Peruvian handbooks which would follow it (Bushnell, 1956; Mason, 1957) by more than a half-dozen years. It broke new ground in its time and definitely advanced the field. Since then, John Rowe's (1960) chronological scheme, with its attempt to adhere to strict periods, as opposed to developmental stages, has found greater favor than Bennett's or the other developmentally-oriented schemes.

I saw a good bit of Bennett in the early 1950s. We were on the Executive Board of the American Anthropological Association at the same time. He was president in 1952, and I always marveled at his deft way of running a meeting. He was a master in the chair, beautifully organized and with an unusual facility for getting along with people. He could bring harmony out of some of the most potentially difficult situations. As I have said at the beginning, Bennett would have been a success in business as well as academic life. Of course, in academic life, his administrative abilities were widely recognized. He served on various Latin American study or area committees, including those of the National Research Council and the American Council of Learned Societies. He was a great promoter of academic "Area Studies". He represented the American Anthropological Association on the Social Science Research Council for several years, and he eventually became a member of the board of directors of that body. I can remember him telling me that this sort of thing was very important for the field, for anthropology basically, but for archaeology too. He felt that archaeology was to a large extent "hidden" from the big foundations which served the sciences and social sciences. Part of this was traditional in academic structuring. Much of archaeology was in the "houses" of Fine Arts or Classics; but he also thought that a part of the reason for our obscurity lay in the fact that we didn't try to make ourselves known in other circles. He encouraged me to become a AAA representative on the Social Science Research Council, which I did; but I never had his flair for such things, nor was I motivated by his concern that archaeology lacked recognition in the corridors of social science power.

This institutional or academic place for archaeology in the world of universities and the foundations seemed an especially persistent worry for Wendy in the early 1950s. We both attended the Wenner-Gren symposium in New York City in the summer of 1952—a conclave of anthropologists from all over the world whose purpose was to discuss "the state of the art". Archaeology was well represented. I have never totaled up the score from the roster, but I would have estimated that a fifth or a quarter of those attending were archaeologists. One afternoon chat with Wendy sticks in my mind. After the day's sessions, he and I walked around the corner from the Wenner-

Gren quarters to the Polo Bar, in the Westbury Hotel, for a drink. I was, for whatever reason, quite upbeat about the symposium at that point. I felt that the things said that day indicated a growing closeness between archaeology and the other disciplines of the field, that the reality of a "unified anthropology" was soon to be achieved. Wendy was more pessimistic. "Look," I argued, "I was talking to Kroeber at lunch, and he said 'he always came away from archaeology feeling encouraged". "Chico," Wendy replied, "the operative phrase is 'came away'. We're not getting any closer to the center of the field. We're getting farther away." Was Wendy losing his old optimism about archaeology? In the years since, I have often reflected on his remark.

But whatever his feelings about the future of archaeology within the social sciences, he stayed at it. In 1950, four years after his Viru dig, he went to Huari (Wari), in the central Peruvian highlands, and excavated there (Bennett, 1953). As with Tiahuanaco and Chavin de Huantar, he carried the flag right to what at that time seemed to be the center of research action. And in the spring of 1953 he was talking about going to Peru, again, for more fieldwork the following year.

I think that the last time I saw Wendy was in that spring of 1953. I was in New Haven on some other business that didn't involve Wendy, perhaps to see Ben Rouse about something. Wendy and Hope were having a cocktail party, and, hearing I was in town, they invited me over. They were in a new, spacious apartment, having recently sold their large, hard-to-heat New Haven house. Wendy was enthusiastic about the move. He was not one for cutting the grass, worrying about the boiler, or shoveling snow. At the party, I'd come out to the kitchen with him. He was mixing martinis. I thought back about the times he used to do this bartender's chore, elegantly and with care, in the old Viru days at the Hotel Jacobs in Trujillo. He and I had composed a song then. It was a simpleminded little ditty dedicated to those moments of severe camp fever. Its opening lines ran:

"Oh, Viru -
I hope I never see you."

WENDELL CLARK BENNETT

As I watched him there in his New Haven kitchen, I remembered him singing it back in Peru, in that good drinking-party tenor voice, while he applied the vermouth sparingly to the pitcher and stirred, as he was doing now.

Late in the summer of 1953, on 8 September, Wendy, Hope, and their daughter Martha were at Martha's Vineyard, where they had a beach cottage. They were on the beach at Chilmark that afternoon. Martha had gone into the surf which suddenly had begun to roll in heavily and threateningly. Wendy went in to bring Martha out, or to see that she was all right. He was a strong swimmer. He must have had a heart attack shortly after he hit the water. Those on the beach say the last they saw of him was when he emerged at the top of a large roller, at which point he suddenly appeared to faint or collapse. Fortunately, Martha emerged safely, but Wendy died in the sea.

JUNIUS BOUTON BIRD
In old age.
Courtesy Mrs. J. B. Bird

Junius Bouton Bird
(1907–1982)

In those exciting days in the spring of 1941, just before my departure for Peru, I first made the acquaintance of Junius Bird. As I have recounted in some of the preceding memoirs, I used to go down to the American Museum frequently when I was a graduate student at Columbia. I had seen Junius there often in the fifth floor halls—his office was near George Vaillant's—but we had never met. We finally did one day at lunch in the Museum restaurant. I had heard that he was to be a part of the Institute of Andean Research program that was just getting under way, and he had been informed that I was to be involved as well. Junius was to be the head of a Chilean expedition, and I was going along with Duncan Strong to Peru. As it came out in our lunch table conversation that day, the Birds and Katharine and I would be sailing on the same Grace Line ship.

Junius was a very outgoing sort. He asked me a string of questions about my interests and background. He exuded vitality, jumping from one subject to another, sprinkling jokes and wisecracks through his conversation. I remembered a talk he had given a few years before—that one at the annual meeting of the American Anthropological Association in New Haven in 1937, where I had first met or seen so many other archaeologists. It had been an after-dinner lecture, accompanied by a motion picture film, about his, and his wife Peggy's, field trip to the Straits of Magellan, and it had been delivered in the same informal and amusing manner as he was now using at the lunch table. This Magellan-Tierra del Fuegian expedition had been a great success. Junius Bird had demonstrated a respectable antiquity for man at that far end of the Americas (Bird, 1938) and, as a result, had established an archaeological reputation for himself by the age of 30.

In 1941 Junius was a lean, wiry man—a little shorter than I. He had a long narrow face, with something very mischievous and impish about it. His eyes were intense and sparkling blue. Baldish, he had a small toothbrush mustache which seemed to contribute to his impish quality. I don't know whether he was always in physical motion or not, but one remembers him that way. Certainly he projected restlessness, but a positive, happy restlessness. He was very much alive. He wanted to know if I had my passport yet and then said that when I did get it we might go down to the Peruvian consulate together for our visas. Although Chile was his main destination, he had planned to stop off for a couple of weeks in Peru, just to get a feel for the country there before catching the next Grace Liner to Valparaiso. I was grateful for his suggestion. I had never been out of the United States before, and I welcomed knowledgeable companionship in such matters as visas. This was sometime in the latter part of May. There were about two weeks to go before we sailed in early June. Strong had already departed on an earlier ship but had left me with the chore of buying, assembling, and packing certain items of equipment to bring on the boat with me. And Junius most generously gave me a hand with this.

At this time, Junius Bird was an assistant curator in the Department of Anthropology at the American Museum of Natural History. He had been promoted to this rank only two years before. Prior to that, his museum title was "field assistant". He had no academic degrees, not even an A.B., so he had not entered the museum from the "academic ladder". This always seemed strange to me as he had been born and raised in a well-to-do family of formal scientific traditions. His father, Henry, was an established entomologist; his mother, Harriet, was a descendant of Seymour Bouton, a well-known naturalist of his time; and his older brother, Roland, became a paleontologist. But Junius, as it were, simply came into the American Museum by "the back door"—as an "interested amateur".

Junius Bird was born 21 September 1907, in Rye, New York. He went to school in Rye, and it is reported that he was fascinated by archaeology as early as the age of nine. After high school, he quite properly entered Columbia University. This was in 1925; but then he dropped out, after only two years, to go with the noted explorer, Captain Bob Bartlett, to the Arctic. It was a major turning point in his life. After this adventurous journey to the frozen north, Junius was lost to academia. He never went back to college, except later when, as a well-known archaeologist, he was invited to lecture at a number of them. He made more trips to the Arctic, and in the course of one of these trips he did some archaeology in Labrador which he published many years later (Bird, 1945). In 1931, the American Museum gave him his "field assistant" title, probably feeling that with no academic degree whatsoever this was the best they could do. Actually, he had been using the Museum as a base sometime before that. In the next few years Junius pursued local archaeology—in New York, New Jersey, and Pennsylvania—and in 1931 he made a coastal archaeological survey of Caribbean Honduras and British Honduras. His story of sitting out the 1931 hurricane in a small boat in the Belize harbor was one of his best. He launched the southern Chilean work, to which I have referred, in 1934. Before his departure he married Margaret McKelvy, and he took Margaret (Peggy) along on an archaeological honeymoon to one of the far ends of the earth. Both the honeymoon and the expedition were great successes. Peggy was a formidable ally on both land and sea. Such, in brief, was Junius Bird's background up to the time when I first knew him (Willey, 1985).

Peggy, Junius, their sons Robert and Harry (aged about 4 and 2 respectively), and Katharine and I all duly embarked from New York, on 6 June, on the then new Grace Liner, S.S. *Santa Elena*. On that June morning in 1941, the *Elena* was a gorgeous and glistening vessel, inside and out, as we glided down the Hudson to sea. Passengers numbered over 200. A lot of rich and stylish Latin Americans were aboard, particularly Chileans, and these included a vice-admiral, the commander-in-chief of the Chilean Navy, who, naturally sat at the Captain's table. The Birds and ourselves had a table for four at a respectful distance from this center of social attention. Except for breakfast, this did not include the Birds' children, who may have been fed in some children's seating, or perhaps in their stateroom. Not being a parent at that time, I was not very conscious of, or interested in, such procedures for the young. On the third or fourth night out, when we were entering the waters of the Caribbean, a large section of the ceiling in the dining room was rolled back so (as the Grace Line then advertised) one could "dine under the stars". But it was rather impressive and very nice: the soft Caribbean breezes from above, not coming in very directly but just enough to flutter the dinner table candles in their glass containers, the fresh odor of the night air mingled with the perfumes of the beautifully dressed ladies, the excellent food, the handsome surroundings, the murmur of happy conversation. I remember thinking then that this, if not the way archaeology should be, was the kind of perquisite archaeology should have—at least every now and then.

I don't think, though, that Junius was ever as bemused or enchanted with such high life in the way that I was. Perhaps he'd had more of it and thought it a little boring. I think it was on one of those Caribbean nights under the stars that we were served, individually, as our main course, either a Cornish Rock Hen or maybe a very large squab. I was eating away, delicately removing the last morsels that could be detached with decorum with a fork, when I heard Peggy exclaim, "Oh!, Junius!" I looked up. Junius's plate was absolutely empty, and the only sign of the fowl that had been on it was a last little bone protruding from his mouth against his moustache. He was chewing away mightily, the imp grin on his face. After swallowing, he said that he always ate all the bones of fowl and small animals—"Awfully good for you!" Peggy was quite concerned about what the waiter and waitress would think. Junius replied that it would give them a little something to figure out. I'm still not sure if he stowed the bones away in a napkin and put them in his pocket, just to make a joke, or if he had really eaten them. But he loved to shock, especially on grand or ceremonial occasions, just as little kids like to shock. I was told that for another black-tie dinner, this one in New York some years later, Junius came in and sat down at a table for eight, with a large gold nose-pendant of Colombian native goldwork dangling from his septum. He played it absolutely deadpan. It was at a banquet in connection with the opening of an American Museum Precolumbian gold show which he had organized. I guess he thought he'd be as consistent as he could in carrying out the exhibition theme.

On our cruise down I became aware of another Junius characteristic. He was much interested in the ladies. As we sat in our deck chairs—on those times when Peggy and Katharine were not present—Junius rarely missed an opportunity to make an observation as some modish Señorita or Señora swished past. These were, of course, *sotto voce*, for my benefit alone. They were fairly earthy remarks but not too vulgar. On one occasion I reversed things by calling his attention to a trim and petite number, the wife of a rich Argentinian. She was a very expensive-looking lady, exquisitely dressed and given to peals of social laughter which were quite carrying, even on the open deck. I had chatted with her once at the Captain's cocktail party, or some similar shipboard affair, and I had admired her in the exercise gymnasium as she worked at keeping that glorious figure in shape. I suppose she was in her late twenties and much the flashiest beauty to grace the decks of the Grace Line's *Santa Elena* on that particular voyage. To my surprise, Junius had nothing but scorn for her. "What! That gaudy trinket! Can't you see she has none of the milk of human kindness about her. She'd be nothing but trouble! I wouldn't waste five minutes on her." I didn't argue, but it seemed to me that the question of character hardly entered into it. We were simply making basic observations about other qualities. Anyway, it was all very much of an academic discussion. The next morning, I came across Junius on the sun deck, leaning on the rail and in deep conversation with the waitress from our table, a very lively looking American girl, but in a different league from the elegant Argentinian. I mentioned this to Junius later, and he said that the waitress "was a peach, a real down-to-earth girl, the kind you like to spend time with." Later, in a retrospect on these analyses of the opposite sex, I had to concede that Junius may have been right in his characterological appraisal of "Madame Buenos Aires". On the night of the ship's fancy dress party, just before we docked in Lima on the following morning, the lady in question ended up in a gentleman's stateroom—not her husband's—and the enraged husband, revolver in hand, had to be restrained by the Captain from beating down the door and despatching his rival. It had been a fairly noisy episode, and the ship was buzzing with gossip the next morning. It did appear, as Junius had predicted, that the "goddess" I had admired at a respectful distance was, indeed, "trouble".

But the most amusing incident that happened on the voyage, at least from my point of view, concerned Junius's involvement with Holy Orders. There were two Roman Catholic priests on board, North Americans who were going to visit colleagues in either Peru or Chile. They had planned an early morning mass in the ship's lounge for our first Sunday out, and the furniture in the lounge had been rearranged the night before so that all would be in readiness for the early Sunday mass. We were going through the Caribbean then, and it was exceptionally hot, even at night. As I found out later, Junius, to escape the heat in his stateroom, had gone up on deck during the night and bedded himself down on one of the davenports in the lounge, as the lounge windows were open to the sea breezes. A little before 6:00 A.M., I, too, gave up trying to sleep below and came up on deck. I stood by the rail a bit, enjoying the early morning breeze. Then I turned around and saw through the open windows of the lounge that a religious mass was in progress inside. As dawn was only beginning to break, lights were on there. Prayers or chants were in progress. There was a cross set up on an improvised table-altar. The priests were in front of this, their small flock seated in lounge chairs in front of them. As it happened, Junius had chosen a davenport for his slumbers which was directly behind the table-altar although facing away from it, so that his sleeping figure had not been visible to the celebrants at the beginnings of the ceremonies. I watched sleepily, gradually feeling revived by the deck air. I suppose the open lounge windows were only 10 or 15 feet from me. Suddenly, a low groaning yawn came up from the davenport. It was quite audible as a kind of contrapuntal background to the priestly chants. Then tableau-like, the pajama-clad figure of Junius arose above the level of the back of the davenport and the altar. He continued to make yawning sounds, stretching out his arms, scratching his head and going through those traditional motions of waking up. He looked around grumpily, as though to determine whatever or whoever it was that was disturbing his morning slumbers—in this instance the priests. You could see the shock of recognition on his face when he realized his predicament. He dove back down on the davenport, out of sight. Apparently, Junius crawled off the davenport and then along the floor until, still on hands and knees, he made his way out of a lounge door at some point back of the altar, coming out on deck not very far from where I was standing by the rail. Indignant functionaries and members of the flock whose service had been so recently defamed looked angrily at us out of the lounge windows. I suggested a retreat to another part of the deck. For the rest of the voyage as the two Fathers took their swift daily walk, three times around the deck, they offered no salutations as they passed our deck chairs.

After going through the Panama Canal, the *Santa Elena* stopped at Buenaventura (Colombia) and Guayaquil (Ecuador). We didn't go ashore at Buenaventura, which was a grim looking place, at least from the sea, but Junius and I did debark at Guayaquil. We walked around Guayaquil a bit, Junius taking the lead. He avoided the city's "Gran Hotel" and the more impressive looking bars. We strayed into the outskirts, definitely not to the high rent districts but, instead, to the slums. Here, finally, Junius stopped and looked in the wide open door of a carpenter's or woodworker's shop. The craftsman was at his task, turning out pieces of furniture, several examples of which were on display. He was also a coffin-maker, and some of those rhomboidal symbols of mortality had been leaned up against the walls where they could be examined by prospective customers. We watched in silence for a while as the carpenter worked away with an adze and a draw-shave. The few other implements of his trade on a bench beside him were the basic ones, all obviously long-used but carefully cared for. Junius began to talk. It was casual, laconic, respectful. "*Maestro, digame, por favor. . . .* " And he went on to ask questions that revealed both an interest in and a knowledge of carpentry—of the woods being used, of the problems confronted and solved. Junius's Spanish was fluent and effective although he had told me before, with a characteristic if misleading modesty, that he couldn't speak it at all. But in a few minutes he had established a rapport with the man. They talked, perhaps, for half an hour. As best as I could follow the conversation, it rambled around all over the place, moving from the woodworker's art to the prices of wood, the value of the pieces of furniture, including the coffins, Ecuadorian politics, and the human condition in general. When we left, Junius and his new acquaintance parted like old friends although we had not made a purchase nor even hinted at doing so. As we strolled back to the dock, Junius spoke seriously about the man and the kind of work he was doing, of his evident skills. There was nothing condescending in any of this. We hadn't been "slumming". The carpenter might have been a colleague of ours.

It must have been the next day that we stopped off at Salaverry, the port facility in northern Peru, for the larger city of Trujillo. Landing here was by launches or lighters, and it provided some excitement for the tourists as the heavy seas made the descent into the small vessels a minor adventure. Still, a number of passengers got off. We were met by guides and taken to the great Chimu ruin of Chan Chan with its maze of giant adobe-walled enclosures, or "Ciudadelas". Junius immediately detached himself from the main tourist group and took off on his own into the Chan Chan labyrinth. I, of course, followed him. We ended up in the bad graces of the tour director when we delayed our bus departure from the ruin by about a half hour. After Chan Chan, we went on to the Hacienda Chiclin, in the Chicama Valley, and saw the museum which had been established there by the Larco family (see the previous memoir). Afterwards, there was a lavish picnic in the hacienda courtyard, replete with native dancers, but Junius took a dim view of this hokey tourist extravaganza.

In Lima, Katharine and I put up at the Gran Hotel Bolivar. Junius and Peggy went to Hope Morris's suburban pension, a more homey, comfortable place, run by an English lady, where life was easier for the children. As I have already recounted in my memoir about Strong, we very soon set about looking at archaeological sites. Junius went with us up the coast, as far as Pativilca, and, on a second trip, south to the mouth of the Ica Valley. One of his favorite enterprises on these excursions was searching for lithic remains. Chipped stone is almost unknown for the Peruvian coastal ceramic cultures, and in 1941 no one ever thought about looking for it. But as we walked over the coastal shell middens south of Lima, searching for the rare Early Ancon-type sherds, Junius picked up a number of black, percussion-chipped rocks which he maintained were artifacts (Strong and Willey, 1943). I used to think Junius did this just to annoy the rest of us. None of us—Dunc, myself, John Corbett, who had joined us in Lima, and certainly not Dr. Tello, who came along on some of our trips, showed any interest in such remains. Indeed, I didn't think they were even artifacts. It would be almost 20 years before Peruvian coastal preceramic periods were identified and the kinds of "rocks" Junius collected on these trips accepted as a part of an early lithic tradition.

Junius's field-collecting interests, however, spanned the archaeological spectrum, and he was not only an avid surface collector but a dedicated practical joker. One afternoon we visited Zapallan, or Zapallar, in the Chillon Valley (see Lothrop memoir). His collecting there that day, as I later found out, included portions of human remains, part of the vandalized detritus left behind by "huaqueros". Later, back at the Boliver Hotel, after I had gone up to our room, there was a rap on the door. Katharine, who had not been with us on our afternoon's jaunt, answered it and was presented by a bellboy with a carefully tied up little package. She unwrapped it to find, with dismay, a mummified human hand, part of Junius's loot of the afternoon. Later, Junius explained that he wanted the hand back; it bore a splendid example of tattooing. I was glad to oblige. I had felt a little uncertain about consigning it to one of the Hotel Bolivar's waste baskets. At the end of their two-week stay in Lima, the Birds took the next southbound Grace Liner and continued on down to Valparaiso and to what was to be an important new archaeological chapter in Junius's life.

But before turning to this new chaper, which will be a Chilean chapter, let's review Junius Bird's Straits of Magellan work mentioned earlier. In 1934, when Junius and Peggy went to far southern South America, the whole question of Early Man in the Americas was enjoying a revival. This began when J. D. Figgins (1927) established a strong claim for Pleistocene man and artifacts at Folsom, New Mexico, and on the heels of this came the discoveries of F. H. H. Roberts, Jr. (1935b) at Lindenmeier and E. B. Howard (1935) at Clovis. All of this was before radiocarbon dating, but the geological contexts of these several discoveries left little doubt of their great antiquity. In brief, the case was made for Early Man in North America. But how about South America? There the issue had long been clouded by a number of uncertain or hotly disputed claims (Lacerda, 1882; Ameghino, 1911; Outes, 1905; Uhle, 1919, 1922; Hrdlicka *et. al.* 1912). Bird wanted to go down to South America and see for himself. He picked the distant end of the continent. How early had man arrived in these ultimate reaches of the hemisphere? I am sure, too, that the physical difficulties involved in such an expedition and the romantic remoteness of the destination also had something to do with the choice of the Straits of Magellan and Tierra del Fuego. Junius, like Jim Ford, loved to test himself.

It was in the Straits of Magellan, on the mainland side, that Junius found some early cultural remains. The sites were old rock shelters. The people who had lived in them had been land hunters, pursuing the now extinct native horse and ground sloth as well as the still extant guanaco. In the lowest levels of both Palli Aike and Fell's shelters were bifacially flaked, chipped stone projectile points of a distinctive ovate-bladed, stemmed form in which the stem had a "fish-tail" appearance as well as some slight fluting on both faces. While by no means the same as the then newly recognized Folsom and Clovis points of the North American Early Man sites, the suggestive typology, the early position of the artifacts in deep stratified refuse, and the associated extinct fauna all implied antiquity. At that time, Bird was cautious in his age estimates, and he suggested no more than a date of 4000 B.C. for the early Fell's and Palli Aike complexes (Bird, 1938). Since then, the Straits of Magellan sites have given a radiocarbon date of ca. 9000 B.C., and points of the Fell's Cave or Magellan type have been found in other parts of South America in Pleistocene contexts. As is obvious, the Magellan Straits date is of utmost importance for New World culture history for we know that by that time man, the early hunter, had found his way down the whole length of the western hemisphere to its southern terminus. Bird's Straits of Magellan sequence has also had an importance beyond this.

In 1941, Junius had decided to keep on following the question of Early Man, but this time he was going to do it in

northern Chile, in the vicinity of Arica. The archaeology of
this part of Chile was then known mostly from the researches
of Max Uhle (1919, 1922) and his Chilean patron, Ricardo
Latcham (1928, 1936a,b). Uhle, the great German savant, had
gone to Chile from Peru at Latcham's invitation in 1908. It was
Latcham's wish that Uhle develop a Chilean chronology comparable to the one he had constructed for Peru. In this, Uhle
had been only partially successful. Through grave lot seriations, grave superpositions, and attempted typological cross-
ties to his Peruvian work, he fashioned a six-period sequence.
Junius felt that the sequence was flawed; he went to Arica to
test it.

For one thing, Uhle (1919, 1922) had begun his Chilean
chronology with a "Paleolithic Period". This was very clearly
modeled on Old World archaeology, and Junius was dubious of
Uhle's reasoning. His own careful north Chilean refuse stratigraphy certainly did not substantiate the Uhle scheme. Forty
or more years later, as the cumulative result of a number of
discoveries, we know that Early Man sites do occur at several
places in Chile; but the lower levels of the Arica shell mounds,
dubbed as "Paleolithic" by Uhle, are not part of this Early Man
occupation. What Junius's excavations demonstrated was that
Uhle's two oldest periods corresponded to early fishing cultures, identified by a variety of chipped points, ground stone
implements, cordage, textiles, and basketry. Bird also found
what Uhle had not—that these two periods were followed by a
time in which maize, but not pottery, was present, and by a
still later time with early plain pottery (Willey, 1971, Ch. 4).
Radiocarbon dating has since revealed that the pre-maize and
pre-pottery range of this early coastal sequence falls within
dates of about 4000 to 2000 B.C., respectably early but not
"Paleolithic", Paleo-Indian, or Early Man. The advent of maize
and pottery follows after that in a 1000 to 500 B.C. time span
(Nunez, 1978). Uhle had a third period in his sequence which
he attributed to Chavin influence although his data for this
were ambiguous, and neither Bird nor anyone else has ever
come up with such an occupation in north Chile. Uhle's fourth
period was referred to by him as Tiahuanaco-influenced, and
here he was on solid ground with certain grave lot artifacts

appearing which were definitely in a Tiahuanaco style. Uhle's fifth period was substantial enough. He called it "Chincha-Atacameno", again trying to make a Peruvian connection via the Peruvian south coastal cultures. Bird rejected the "Chincha" attribution as stylistically uncertain and simply called these late, pre-Inca, coastal polychromes the Arica I and II styles. Presumably, they are Atacameno in ethnic identification. Both Uhle and Bird found Inca materials in very late prehistoric graves and middens (see Bird, 1943).

I saw Junius back in New York in the fall of 1942, when he had returned to the American Museum and I was doing a year's teaching at Columbia University. I had finished my doctoral dissertation on the Peruvian Chancay Valley digs and was making some preliminary moves toward studying the rest of my Peruvian collections from the 1941 project. These were mainly from the Ancon and Puerto de Supe shell midden sites, and they were stored at the museum. At our first meeting at the museum, Junius had asked me if I had found anything interesting in the way of cloth materials. I said no, not really, just a few dirty old scraps which, usually, I had tucked into the sherd bags. I think Junius was alerted by my cavalier attitude toward such remains because he then volunteered to assist me in the unpacking of my collections.

A few days later, I went back to the American Museum and was confronted by both an indignant and elated Junius. "Good God, man," he exploded, "do you realize that two of those 'dirty textile scraps' of yours from Supe, which you never even bothered to look at, are the finest pieces of Chavin-style tapestry weaving that anybody has ever seen?" No, I had not realized it. These "two scraps" are now well-known pieces, with their fascinating interwoven condor/feline designs. The late Lila M. O'Neale, a Peruvian textile expert without peer in her time, enthused over them, described them, and illustrated them in the Ancon-Supe report (Willey and Corbett, 1954).

In late 1945, when we were planning the Viru Valley project, Wendy Bennett convinced Junius that he should come along. His Viru "assignment" was to be the early occupation of the valley. By Junius's way of thinking, this had to be a preceramic occupation, but, at that time, this was not a view shared by many. In 1941, I already had excavated a preceramic site at Puerto de Supe (Willey and Corbett, 1954), but had refused to be fully convinced of such a period. None of the Peruvian archaeologists, including Tello and Larco, had ever indicated any interest in the preceramic; indeed, Tello's chief assistant once proclaimed at a conference that she "did not believe in the preceramic". For Viru, all of the participants, save Junius, had their eyes fixed firmly on the ceramic horizons.

In 1946, Junius arrived in Peru a month or two later than the rest of us. He had Peggy and the children with him. They now had a third son, Thomas, in addition to Robert and Harry. Junius looked around for a few days on the north coast, and then he decided he would begin with a major excavation on a huge refuse hill in the Chicama Valley, the Huaca Prieta. This was not in Viru but two coastal valleys to the north. Actually, it all worked out for the best. Junius had picked Huaca Prieta because of its great size, its shore-line location, its surface appearance, and its surface refuse. Almost certainly it was not an adobe pyramid pertaining to the later periods. It was a refuse pile but one of enormous size so that its interior should reveal a long sequence of occupation. Its coastal situation, as well as its refuse, suggested that its builders may have been dependent upon marine foods. Finally, the surface collection Junius picked up there consisted of potsherds of the Cupisnique or Coastal Chavin style. If its upper levels so dated, might not the deeper strata of the mound go back earlier than the Chavin horizon, at that time the earliest definite period of Peruvian prehistory? Moreover, Junius reasoned, if he could bring up assemblages of lithic implements from non-ceramic contexts which were stratigraphically below ceramic layers, he could definitely pin down a preceramic period for the Peruvian coast. Junius's deep excavations confirmed just this. Below the Chavin horizon pottery he found pre-Chavin ceramics, now assigned to the then unheard of Initial Period of Peruvian chronology. Still deeper down were the preceramic strata. After the Huaca Prieta dig, Junius came down to Viru and repeated this stratigraphy for us in another, although much smaller, refuse heap known as the Cerro Prieto (Bird, 1948).

Huaca Prieta and Cerro Prieto were landmarks in Peruvian

archaeology, in much the same way that the Straits of Magellan digs and the excavations in northern Chile were for those regions of South America. The Peruvian chronological structure, that had been begun by Uhle and extended downward by others to include the Chavin horizon, was now shoved backward in time for another millennium or more, with the Initial Period and a Preceramic Period added to the bottom of the time chart. When radiocarbon datings became available, it was seen that ceramics went back to the beginnings of the second millennium B.C. Before this was an unplumbed preceramic era; Junius's excavation had penetrated only into its latest centuries of the third millennium B.C. Today, a well-dated preceramic sequence extends back to very early times, but Junius gets the credit for opening the door.

Huaca Prieta and Cerro Prieto not only gave us new information on ceramics and preceramic lithics, but with the desert conditions of preservation these sites afforded a wealth of data on food remains and textiles. Plant specimens found in the preceramic included cotton, domesticated lima beans, squash, jack beans, peppers, and gourds. Many of the cotton fabrics found had very intricate woven designs, and it was in studying the rich corpus of textile materials from Huaca Prieta that Junius was led into the complex world of textiles and weaving, a subject that was to interest him for the rest of his archaeological career. Still another line of investigation opened up by Bird's work at Huaca Prieta and Cerro Prieto was that of early architecture. Prior to this, we had all thought that adobe construction began with the Chavin horizon. The Huaca Prieta excavations disclosed both adobe and mud-and-stone structures dating to the Initial and Preceramic Periods. While no huge public constructions dating this early were found there, they have since been found at other coastal sites (Patterson, 1985; Feldman, 1985). Junius opened other archaeologist's eyes to the possibility.

The Straits of Magellan, northern Chile, and Huaca Prieta in northern Peru—these were the three great fieldwork centerpieces in Junius Bird's career. They have immeasurably widened and enriched our perspectives of New World prehistory. The distinguished British prehistorian Grahame Clark once said to me: "You know this man Junius Bird always seems to be digging at just the right time and in the right place to provide the answers for some of the most important questions." Clark, at this time, was preparing his book, *World Prehistory* (Clark, 1961), and he was hitting only the high and crucial spots in his survey.

After the Huaca Prieta excavations, Junius was made an associate curator at the American Museum, in late 1946; subsequently, in 1957, he became a full curator there. He never stopped fieldwork. The Early Man theme seems to have been uppermost in his mind in much of this research, as in Panama where the discovery of surface finds of fishtailed, Magellan-like points led him to initiate and continue surveys there. He also participated in Panamanian excavations which revealed a sequence spanning the post-Pleistocene millennia from 5000 B.C. to the beginnings of the Christian era, one in which early agriculture and ceramics made their first appearances in that part of the Americas. Late in life he returned once more to far southern South America.

One thinks of Junius primarily as a "field man", and he was that, *par excellence*, ready, literally and figuratively, to carry the archaeological banner to the far ends of the earth. Yet in the latter part of his career he turned, more and more, to the analyses of man's handicrafts, studies which opened to him, and to others, the abilities, the aspirations, and the mind of Precolumbian American craftsmen and craftswomen. These interests in technology were first signaled in print by his collaboration with Wendell C. Bennett in their general book on Andean and Peruvian prehistory, *Andean Culture History* (Bennett and Bird, 1949). Junius's part in this useful synthesis was a separately signed section on "Techniques". In it he dealt with ceramics, metallurgy, and textiles. His "ceramic" section was quite brief; one might assume that he felt that ceramics had already received so much attention in archaeology that other, less well-studied aspects of material culture now deserved intensive study. Actually, pottery in archaeology has received its greatest attention as a cultural "label" or "tag", in the working out chronologies and distributions. Ceramic techniques of manufacture are not generally well-known, and this is especially true of South America. As one reads over Junius's ceramic section in the book, it becomes obvious that the author had looked at a great deal of South American, and especially Peruvian, pottery and had examined it closely from a technological standpoint. He was particularly interested in mold-made wares and in the processes that the ancients had followed in their manufacture. This same interest was maintained when he turned to the negative- or resist-painting of vessel surfaces. Complexity in craftsmanship always fascinated Junius.

In the metallurgical section of the book, Junius realized how little he knew of this complex subject and, also, how little was really known at that time about the subject in its South American prehistoric setting. He dealt with casting, gilding, and alloying with caution. His discussions of smelting and of "lost-wax", or *cire perdue,* casting, reveal his ever present concern with the details of the way things were done. Thus, in describing a Peruvian gold beaker, he directed his main attention to the types of tools that were used in making such a vessel (Bird, 1967–68). In the scholarly context of Garcilaso's ethnohistoric descriptions of an Andean metalworker's kit, Junius explains how such polished stone anvils, hammers, and other utensils were employed, how the edges and surfaces of these implements imparted such-and-such effects to the final appearance of the gold beaker. This same interest in the craftsman's techniques, equipment, and quality of life comes through, again, in a paper he did (Bird, 1979a) on the "Copper Man", the mummy of a prehistoric Chilean miner killed in a cave-in in a mine shaft in the Atacama desert. The associated finds—the still-hafted wooden-handled stone hammers, the wedges, wooden spades, the baskets and rawhide llama-skin bags which the miner had with him for collecting and transporting the ore— give us an on-the-scene picture of Precolumbian copper mining. The article is not only a study in technology, but it carries a quality of empathy, an identification on the part of the archaeologist with the ancient miner—a feeling for his tasks and the dangers which confronted him, which in this case had proven fatal.

Junius also worked with chemists and geologists in his pursuit of Andean metallurgical knowledge (Friedman et al. 1972). He drew upon their analyses in a discussion of Moche copper pedestal cups, attempting to distinguish which vessels were made from "free" copper and which, apparently, from ores that had required smelting. His metallurgical interests also led him to an intuitive generalization which, as an hypothesis, is most intriguing. Junius observed that the very finest and most delicate lost-wax casting in native America came from Colombia and Lower Central America. He also noted that the stingless bee is native to these regions. This bee, which is not found farther south in the metallurgical regions of the Peruvian coast or Andes, produces the most suitable wax for fine-grained casting (1979b). This correlation has a very Junius-like quality about it—eminently sensible and grounded in his characteristic observations of the ordinary and the humble as well as the exotic and the spectacular.

This earthy kindredness, the ability and desire to empathize with the ordinary person in his or her ordinary tasks, was the quality, I am sure, which led the extraordinary Junius Bird into the study of textiles. Metallurgy and ceramics can eventually lead the investigator into highly specialized aspects of chemistry and the physical sciences; textiles, in contrast, while complex, do not normally demand such backgrounds. The ancient weaver was confronted with a task, and he or she went about solving it in a manner that literally could be unraveled and reduplicated by the investigator. As the ancient artist grew more skilled and more given to virtuoso performances so, too, could the diligent researcher become more knowledgeable and adept at understanding, recreating, and reliving the products and experiences of the original makers. In recent years I do not think I ever visited Junius's office at the museum when he did not fail to take me by the arm, lead me over to some textile fragments, and explain some technical twist or trick that he had just discovered. It was always phrased as: "Look at what the weaver did on this one; look at how ingeniously this problem was solved." Junius, eyes aglow, was right back there with the ancients, applauding their successes. I was reminded of that day, long ago, when he had made me stop and watch the furniture-maker in the little shop in Guayaquil. He was enormously interested in how things were made, the steps, the processes in craftsmanship. I know he was always somewhat disgusted with my lack of this kind of an interest. To Junius, it was at least half of what archaeology was all about.

When Junius Bird launched seriously into the study of Peruvian textiles, following his Huaca Prieta excavations and discoveries, he pretty much had that highly interesting and important field to himself. Lila O'Neale, to whom I have referred, had just died. Over the next 20 years, Junius, more than any other single person, was to train and inspire a host of coworkers in the study of archaeological textiles. And he did this by training himself at the same time; he had had no particular teacher. His attitude toward the Peruvian textile arts is revealed in a sentence in his *Andean Culture History* essay. There he states: "The fact that some of them (textiles) rank high among the finest fabrics ever produced should lead us, in all humility, to seek not only a knowledge of their origin and development, but also a better understanding of what they actually represent in terms of human accomplishment" (Bennett and Bird, 1949, p. 256). In another later essay, he said that he felt that textiles provided "a surprising range of information about the people who made them, probably more than can be derived from any other of the commonly associated artifacts" (Bird, 1951, p. 51). He went on to explain this by saying that such things as plant and animal domestication may be reflected in the fibers used, chemical knowledge detected in the dyes, mathematical calculations implied in the constructions, and even insights obtained into the individual personalities of weavers from a close inspection of their products.

Junius learned to weave himself; indeed, one would have to in order to pursue his Peruvian textile studies in the way he wished. The body of the Chicama-Viru cloth revealed things about Peruvian textiles that others had missed. Shreds and fragments that had appeared as plain revealed on closer inspection some amazing warp and weft designs. Such elements were plotted, strand by strand, on graph paper and the graph checked back against the textile (Bird, 1963). One result of all of this research, as Junius was to point out, was that much of Peruvian art with its characteristic rectilinearity—the ancient and

widespread interlocking-fish design would be an example—
was seen to have its beginnings in weaving technology, these
geometric designs and motifs later being transferred to other
media. How could one summarize Junius Bird's most important contributions to Peruvian textile studies? One might
draw up a list: his definition of the importance of the change-
over from twining to weaving in Peruvian coastal sequences
and all of the cultural implications of this; his pointing out of
the great step-up in cloth production with the appearance of
the loom; or his discoveries of numerous design and weaving
techniques. But all of his colleagues who have been interested
in Peruvian textiles have made repeatedly clear to me that
Junius's greatest impact on the field was that of an inspirational leader who trained, encouraged, and stimulated others.
These colleagues or students, however one might want to classify them, held him in high regard. A measure of this was seen
in the *Junius B. Bird Pre-Columbian Textile Conference* which
was held in his honor at the Textile Museum, in Washington,
D.C., and the published proceedings were dedicated to him
(Rowe et al. 1970).

In many ways, Junius was indifferent to "careerism" and
certainly to self-promotion. His bibliography, although containing some impressive and important writings, does not have
the monographic weight that it would have had if he had been
more dedicated to writing. For instance, the very important
Huaca Prieta final monograph did not come out until after his
death, and it was completed by colleagues who edited and
finished his manuscript (Bird, Hyslop, and Skinner, 1985). He
was, though, admired and honored by the profession in his
lifetime. He received the Viking Fund Medal for Archaeology
in 1956 and an honorary Doctor of Science degree from Wesley-
an University in 1958. In 1961 he was the president of the
Society for American Archaeology. The Peruvian government
honored him with the Order of Merit in 1962 and the Order of
"El Sol del Peru", that nation's highest award, in 1974. In New
York, in 1975, he was given the Explorer's Club Medal, and a
more popular sort of award was bestowed after that by the *New
York Magazine* which listed him among the metropolis' *One
Hundred Most Interesting New Yorkers*. Anyone who knew

Junius personally would certainly have gone along with this choice.

I have said that Junius was a great teacher, and this was especially true in the laboratory, surrounded by his textiles spread out upon every table. He did, though, give special seminars and lectures at a number of major universities: Yale, Columbia, Harvard, Berkeley, UCLA, and Rice Institute. At the American Museum he organized two major shows, "Art and Life in Old Peru" in 1961 and a Pre-Columbian gold show in 1970. He was a key participant in organizations and institutions other than his own, serving as one of the original Trustees of the Textile Museum in Washington, D.C., as a member of the Pre-Columbian Advisory Committee at Dumbarton Oaks, and as a president and long-time member of the Institute of Andean Research.

In this portrait of Junius Bird I have attempted to show him as an essentially happy and well-adjusted man, certainly one of the happiest and best adjusted of my colleagues. I know that appearances can sometimes be deceiving, but I don't think that this was so in Junius' case. For one thing, Junius was doing exactly what he wanted to be doing. He was not pining for something else; he was not driven by unbearable ambition; he had what he wanted. He was thoroughly "in character" in his work. Whether he was searching for caves in the Straits of Magellan, exploring the Arctic, digging coastal middens in South America, researching metallurgical techniques, or experimenting with weaving in his laboratory in the American Museum, he fitted the part. But there was absolutely no "staginess" about this; he wasn't acting out the role of an archaeologist; he was an archaeologist. I remember him for a number of personality traits which, I think, contributed to this "naturalness".

To begin with, he was, in his deepest nature, adventurous, questioning, and innovative. It led him to reject formal academic restraints and go off to the Arctic with Captain Bob Bartlett. But this adventurousness never became aimless or neurotic restlessness. There was a balance wheel, an inner quiet discipline. It was the discipline that organized and thought out the Magellanic expedition which, otherwise,

might have come a cropper. It was the discipline and the dedication that led him to learn how to weave and to pick out the
thousand threads in a textile design as he analyzed his Peruvian textiles. It was a discipline that was also combined with a
sense of practicality, a pragmatic approach to problems. This
discipline, in harness with common sense, is the quality that
makes adventurous, innovative vision pay off.

Junius was also a very modest man, but there was nothing
false about this modesty. He knew what he knew, and he was
not hesitant in letting you know it in no uncertain terms. But
he did not feel that he had the answer to everything, and it was
not necessary for him to put down others to justify himself.

Another most salient quality in Junius's makeup was his
generosity. All who knew him well remember this. It came
through in professional dealings. He shared his insights and his
information with anyone who evidenced an interest in what he
was doing, and he was not only willing to do this but was
excited and enthused by doing so. Enthusiasm, too, was a
Junius characteristic. It seemed boundless and was combined
with a sense of good humor, or, indeed, high humor. In a
discussion about the possible use of Veracruz stone yokes in
the Precolumbian ball game, I can remember Junius fitting one
around his waist (he maintained an admirable slimness all his
life) and galloping up and down the hall outside his office to
demonstrate to the rest of us that they were not too heavy to
have been worn by the players. Stories like this, and others of
the practical-jokester turn, are legend about Junius. When Jim
Ford joined the staff at the American Museum, the two made a
formidable team. Their impersonation of a bear walking
through the snow in the neighborhood of a colleague's house in
Sleepy Hollow, New York is well-known in the annals of anthropological practical jokes. I have always understood it was
Junius who donned the bear-paws (borrowed from the American Museum of Natural History) to make the requisite tracks.

Junius and Peggy maintained a happy home in Riverdale in
the Bronx. Their house was in a little sylvan setting not far
from the river and somehow sheltered from the noise and rush
of the great city which lay so close by. Junius's professional and
social generosity overflowed to their home which, on more

than one occasion, housed visiting archaeologists or provided a meeting place for late night archaeological discussions. The Birds gave freely of their time to community and civic affairs and were members of various clubs and associations. In sum, Junius was a citizen, a neighbor, and a family man—as well as a very distinguished scientist.

I am fond of something his friend, William Conklin, wrote about him at the time of the *Junius B. Bird Textile Conference:* "(Junius') special ability, to read artifacts the way mortals read books, was like the ability of the genius naturalists—of men like Darwin—who looked at the objects and life of our world and used that visual data to produce entirely new conclusions about the events and laws of the past" (Conklin in Rowe et al. 1979, p. 9).

For Junius was like the great naturalists of the past. He loved his chosen profession of archaeology, but he refused to be constrained and confined by it, especially when that profession became rigid from establishment doctrine. He also refused to be fenced in by topical or regional specializations. He believed in ranging widely. At the same time, he carried within himself that secret discipline of a scholar.

ALFRED LOUIS KROEBER
In late middle age.
Photo by Paul Bishop. Courtesy Mrs. A. L. Kroeber.

ALFRED LOUIS KROEBER
(1876–1960)

Alfred Louis Kroeber was a great general and theoretical anthropologist, the author of such well-known books as *Anthropology* (Kroeber, 1923, 1948a) and *Configurations of Culture
Growth* (Kroeber, 1944a); but he was also an archaeologist. By
this, I mean that he gave the discipline more than a passing
nod. Although many anthropologists do not realize it, he conducted field surveys, excavations, and laboratory studies of
specimens; and he also saw to the publication of his archaeological findings. Indeed, a large part of his extensive bibliography may be classified as archaeological. As to my temerity in
including Kroeber in such a personal gallery of portraits, let me
make clear that I advance no claims to a special friendship or
intimacy. I was not his student, at least in the formal sense, nor
was I old enough to have been a close colleague. In the field of
Peruvian archaeology, where I knew him best, I was an occasional professional associate. Most of these associations took
place in the 1940s although I was fortunate enough to see and
talk with him a good many times after this, up until the time of
his death in 1960.

Kroeber was an arresting figure. About 5' 8" in height, he was
compactly and strongly, although not heavily, built. There was
a quality of trimness and neatness about him. This physical
impression of self-contained compactness harmonized with an
emotional and intellectual containment. Julian Steward has
written about him:

> "... he always seemed a miraculously well-integrated,
> smoothly-functioning man. It was hard to imagine a person
> who evidenced fewer internal conflicts, worked with less lost
> motion, and managed more felicitously to combine an ex-
> tremely happy family life with monumental professional ac-
> complishments" (Steward, 1961, p. 1041).

When I first knew him, Kroeber was in his middle sixties. He
had ample but neat gray hair which lay close to his head and a

gray, full Van Dyke beard to match. Keen dark eyes were marked with rather noticeable "Nordic folds". The nose was smallish but well shaped, the mouth and chin slightly protruding. I have heard it said that he grew the beard because he didn't like the appearance of his mouth, but in his early, pre-bearded, photographs the lower part of his face is pleasant enough looking. I think it more likely that Kroeber grew the beard because it made him look older at a time when he had the responsibilities of establishing not only himself but the fledgling profession of anthropology. Later, in an era when beards were not common—at least in the United States—he kept it, quite justifiably to my mind, because it made him look very handsome and distinguished. In this connection, I remember a dinner we had in 1947 at New York's then very fashionable "Club 21". This was in connection with the Peruvianist archaeological conference referred to in a preceding memoir. As we arrived at the "21", either couple by couple, or singly, we were all immediately hustled upstairs, without any questions being asked, to the private dining room that had been reserved by us for the occasion; but when Kroeber and his wife came in it was quite different. The elegant head waiter went over to them and, bowing serenely, asked, "Sir, may I show you to a table?" At the time, I thought it strange. Kroeber certainly looked more like an archaeological savant than any of the rest of us. On reflection, however, I realized that Kroeber, with his distinguished, perhaps even Continental, appearance, was the type who would be given preferred treatment by a *maitre d'* long experienced in the *haute monde.*

In the fall of 1940, when I was a graduate student at Columbia, Kroeber stopped in at the Department of Anthropology on a visit to New York. Strong, who had been his student at Berkeley, had him as a guest, and he also paid calls on Ruth Benedict and on his former professor and the doyen of the anthropological field, Franz Boas. As might be imagined, Kroeber's presence created a small stir. I remember edging around the door into Strong's office in my attempt to meet this celebrated figure and finally being invited in and introduced. Kroeber was often clad in handsome tweeds of a light shade, as he was that day. He also wore a bright orange necktie which contrasted nicely with the tweeds and the gray hair and beard. He had a penchant for bright neckwear. At that time he would have been 64 and was in vigorous health. He was also most cordial. Strong had told him that I had been working in Southeastern United States archaeology and had just returned from a summer of digging in Florida. I had some potsherds in the lab next door. Kroeber looked at them, listened to my story of a potsherd sequence for the area, and commented that it was good that some archaeological chronology was at last beginning to come out of the Eastern United States. He wanted to see order, system, and chronology in the prehistory of the hemisphere and was very supportive of research designed to this end. Shortly after this, he voluntarily submitted a favorable and encouraging comment to *American Antiquity* (Kroeber, 1942a) on a general essay on Eastern United States prehistory which James Ford and I had published (Ford and Willey, 1941).

There are a great many biographies, obituaries, and appraisals of Alfred Louis Kroeber (see Steward, 1961, 1973; Rowe, 1962; Hymes, 1962 for a sampling). Besides these more strictly career accounts, there is also the portrait of the man, *Alfred Kroeber, A Personal Configuration*, by his wife, Theodora (T. Kroeber, 1970). Alfred Louis Kroeber was born on 11 June 1876 in Hoboken, New Jersey, the son of Florence Kroeber and Johanna Muller Kroeber. Both the Kroeber and Muller families were people of German background who had settled in New York City, and a few years after Alfred Kroeber's birth his immediate family moved back to Manhattan where he was brought up. He was the oldest of four children, which included two boys and two girls. His father was a prosperous importer of European *objets d'art*, including, especially, clocks. I remember that the first time Kroeber was in our house he commented upon a mantelpiece clock which had been in my wife's family for some years. It was a French clock in a glass case, and Kroeber said he wouldn't be surprised if it was one of those his father had brought into New York toward the end of the last century.

The Kroeber family was an upper-middle-class New York one of the period. They had a three-story residence which was located not far from Central Park, and Kroeber recalled playing in the park as a boy. The social and intellectual ambience in which he grew up was German-American, with friends both Protestant and Jewish and with little concern over this religious difference. Among his close boyhood friends were Carl Alsberg and Hans Zinsser, the latter to become the distinguished medical researcher of *Rats, Lice, and History* fame. While the Kroebers were Protestants—young Alfred had been baptized as a Lutheran—he and his siblings were educated in a tradition of secular "Ethical Culture" with a predominance of Jewish teachers and fellow students. In reading Theodora Kroeber's account of her husband's early years, both the home life and schooling sound happy, disciplined, and instructive. It was an ideal setting in which to bring up a liberal scholar, one with a middle class Central European respect for formal learning, yet one also imbued with that uniquely American, democratic sense of values.

I think back on my own father as I write this. He, too, like Kroeber, was born in 1876, that centennial year of the Republic. His Anglo, farm background in Iowa was different in so many ways from Kroeber's, and he was not a scholar; and yet, to me at least, they seemed to share many qualities. In wondering about this, I am reminded of Kroeber's insistence on the reality and validity of a "culture", even though the ways it becomes pervasive remain mysterious.

Kroeber enrolled at Columbia University in 1892, when he was 16. His academic interests were wide-ranging: the natural sciences, languages, art history, and English literature. In 1896, Franz Boas was appointed to the Faculty at Columbia, and Kroeber, who was then in his senior year, took a linguistics seminar with him. Kroeber, however, went on to an M.A. degree in English literature and even served as a teaching assistant in this subject from 1897 to 1899; however, in those same years he was becoming more engrossed in anthropological linguistics under Boas' guidance. He took more courses in anthropology. In 1899 Boas was made a full professor at Columbia, and a doctorate in this new and as yet unformulated discipline became possible. Kroeber decided to pursue it in earnest. He went into the field as an ethnologist and linguist in both 1899 and 1900, studying the Arapaho, Ute, and other western tribes.

His doctoral dissertation, "Decorative Symbolism of the Arapaho," was successfully defended at Columbia in 1901 and shortly thereafter published in the *American Anthropologist* (Kroeber, 1901). For better or for worse, he was now embarked professionally on the uncharted seas of anthropology. Clearly, an able and intelligent young scholar, such as Alfred Kroeber must have been, could have opted for what would have appeared at the turn of the century a more secure academic career. English literature, in which he had made a good beginning, or perhaps history would have been the more established options, but, instead, he chose anthropology. There can have been no other reasons for such a choice than sheer interest and intellectual curiosity.

In that same year, Kroeber accepted a position as an Instructor in anthropology at the University of California at Berkeley. The moving spirit, and the financial donor, behind this appointment was Mrs. Phoebe Hearst, the mother of the future press tycoon, William Randolph Hearst. A Department of Anthropology and a University Museum had been established at Berkeley at her urging. F. W. Putnam, the director of Harvard's Peabody Museum and one of the nation's great promoters of archaeological and ethnological museums, also became director of the new California Museum, traveling between the two coasts to hold down the two positions. Kroeber was to serve as Putnam's assistant director of the Museum and the assistant head of the Department of Anthropology. Owing to these somewhat unusual arrangements, and Putnam's poor health, Kroeber became *de facto* head of both; although throughout this collaboration he and Putnam maintained an amicable working relationship. As it turned out, the plans for a new museum building had to be set aside; indeed, it would be over 50 years before an anthropological museum was constructed on the Berkeley campus. From these not altogether auspicious beginnings, Kroeber launched and guided anthropology in California. Graduate students were relatively few; Julian Steward (1961) has stated that there were only two completed Ph.D.'s in the Department of Anthropology prior to 1926; but Kroeber persevered with teaching and research from this base that he was to build up into one of the primary centers of anthropology.

For Kroeber, the years up to the First World War were devoted primarily to ethnological and linguistic studies in California and the bordering western States. He published numerous short papers on this research, and much of it was brought together eventually in his famous, 995-page-long, *Handbook of the Indians of California* (Kroeber, 1925b). An incident, that turned into a five-year-long story, belongs to this period in Kroeber's life, and it is very revealing of his character. In 1911, the California newspapers reported that a "wild Indian" had been taken into custody by the authorities of Oroville, a town in the northern part of the state. This was the beginning of the story of Ishi. Ishi was a Yana Indian, the last of his people. Sick and half-starved, unable to communicate with any of the whites of Oroville, he had been placed in the county jail. Kroeber and his colleague at Berkeley, T. T. Waterman, went to Oroville and were able to talk with Ishi in his native tongue. With the permission of the Department of Indian Affairs, they had Ishi released in their care. He was settled in a room in the Museum in San Francisco, where he was nursed back to health, and where he was befriended by Kroeber, Waterman, and other colleagues. Ishi learned English, and, to some extent, he became accustomed to the White Man's ways. The poignancy and tragedy of the situation needs no elaboration. Theodora Kroeber (1961) has recounted his story in a moving book. Ishi was a man not only "without a country" but one without a society or a culture, except insofar as his memories could sustain him. He did serve his new foreign friends as an informant, but Kroeber was very protective of him and adamant that he should not be exploited. They became close friends. But civilization proved too much for Ishi. He became ill of tuberculosis, and after some years of struggling against the disease, died in 1916. After his death, there was talk in some circles that his remains should be preserved for anthropological study. Kroeber's response was magnificently unequivocal on the side of good taste and human decency. He was away from Berkeley at the time, but he wrote to a colleague (T. Kroeber, 1961, p. 92):

"If there is any talk of the interests of science, say for me that science can go to hell. We propose to stand by our friends."

As a result, Ishi's body was cremated, according to the customs of his people.

Although Kroeber's focus in these early California years was on ethnology, he was not indifferent to archaeology. He was aware of the Peruvian collections which Max Uhle had brought to the University's museum (Kroeber, 1904, 1906). He also offered a course in North American archaeology in 1905 and again in 1908; and he took an intellectual interest in the San Francisco Bay shell mound excavations that were being carried on nearby, under the Museum's aegis, by the geologist, J. C. Merriam. Both Max Uhle, who was in California for a time, and N. C. Nelson, one of Kroeber's students, were involved in this work and later published on it (Uhle, 1907; Nelson, 1909, 1910). It has an important place in the history of American archaeology for it was one of the first attempts at cultural stratigraphy in the United States (Rowe, 1962; Willey and Sabloff, 1974, pp. 63–64). Kroeber (1909), in reviewing Uhle's results, was not impressed with the stratigraphic evidence for culture change; to him, the minor artifactual changes from early to late strata seemed inconsequential, and native California culture was deemed amazingly conservative. Only a few years later, however, Kroeber took quite a different point of view about the importance of gradual time change in artifact development. Thus, at Zuni Pueblo and in its environs, he made archaeological surveys, gathering surface potsherds, separately, from modern, historic, and prehistoric pueblo sites, and then seriating them typologically and chronologically. He published a paper on these "Zuni potsherds" (Kroeber, 1916), his first important contribution to archaeology and a small classic.

Kroeber's personal life in California in the early years was for a time brightened by his marriage to a San Francisco girl, Henrietta Rothschild. This was in 1906, but after two years of marriage, Henrietta contracted tuberculosis. She lived for five years after this, her hopes and Kroeber's rising and falling with the course of the disease and its treatment. In 1913 she died. There were no children of the marriage.

The years of Henrietta's illness and death were obviously ones of strain for Kroeber. While he continued to work and to write, nothing seemed to stop him in this, he was emotionally exhausted. He continued without a break for three years after her death. He also had his commitments to his friend Ishi; but when Ishi died in 1916 he arranged for academic leave the next year. In 1917 he went to New York where he entered into psychoanalysis. Kroeber had long been interested in Freudian analysis and had studied psychology at Columbia under James Cattell. Some of his reasons for going into analysis were personal, and followed in the wake of Henrietta's death; others were intellectual. He told his second wife, Theodora, some years later, that he found the experience not only personally rewarding, one presumes he meant therapeutic, but didactically fascinating (T. Kroeber, 1970, pp. 101–104).

This latter response seems borne out by his own actions for, on his return to California, in 1918, Kroeber set himself up as a lay analyst. He practiced for over two years, with offices in the Stanford Clinic and, later, in downtown San Francisco. To do this, he obtained a leave from his teaching duties in Berkeley, but he continued as director of the museum. It is also to be noted that during this 1917–22 period, in which he was involved in psychoanalysis, his publications in anthropology did not lag. Among these were two items, both published in the *American Anthropologist,* which have become famous as essays in anthropological theory: "The Superorganic" (1917) and "On the Principles of Order in Civilization as Exemplified by Changes of Fashion" (1919). Rowe (1962) has listed these among the "Archaeological Publications of A. L. Kroeber". I suppose one could argue that they are not strictly so; they do not deal with "digging"; but they take an archaeological view of culture and culture change, and perhaps they presage a new phase in Kroeber's interests. For when Kroeber returned full-time to anthropology, after his interlude with psychoanalysis, he turned directly to archaeology. He went beyond its theoretical aspects, as these were addressed or implied in the "Superorganic" or "Principles of Order" papers, to archaeology as it might be more strictly defined, that is the archaeology of objects and the "dirt" in which they were found. He began with the Uhle Peruvian collections in the University Museum. He and his graduate students produced a spate of publications on these materials—all appearing during the mid-1920s. They include monographs on the collections from Chincha (Kroeber and Strong, 1924a); Ica (Kroeber and Strong, 1924b); Supe (Kroeber, 1925a); Moche (Kroeber, 1925c); Ancon (Strong, 1925); Chancay (Kroeber, 1926a); and Nazca (Gayton and Kroeber, 1927).

After these laboratory studies, Kroeber was anxious to go to Peru for fieldwork and to see the land and the sites Uhle had explored. He had hoped to go in 1924; but research funds at Berkeley were too limited for a Peruvian trip. He did have enough money, though, to take himself to Mexico—that other New World area of ancient high civilizations. Manuel Gamio, then Mexico's leading archaeologist—and the one who encouraged Byron Cummings to dig at Cuicuilco that same year—suggested that Kroeber make some stratigraphic tests in "Archaic", or Formative, stage sites in the Valley of Mexico. Kroeber did this at San Angel and Copilco. It was his first actual digging. In Mexico, he also made excavations at Teotihuacan and did some surface collecting at other sites in the Valley as well. He attempted seriations of the ceramics from all of this work (Kroeber, 1925d), but his chronological ordering of the materials seemed for him, then, inconclusive although George Vaillant's later stratigraphies would largely confirm it. Perhaps most importantly, this season in the field in Mexico gave Kroeber, with his extraordinary ability to grasp and to take in so much in such a short time, the beginnings of a "feel" for Mesoamerican archaeology. His ability to synthesize the Mesoamerican data, and to view it in the context of the Americas as a whole, including Peru, are seen in the excellent conference summaries he wrote later for *The Maya and Their Neighbors* (Kroeber, 1940) and *A Reappraisal of Peruvian Archaeology* (Kroeber, 1948b).

In 1925 and, again, in 1926, Kroeber did, at last, get to Peru. Both of these trips were under the sponsorship of the Field Museum of Natural History of Chicago. On the first expedition, he renewed an acquaintance with Julio C. Tello, whom he had met briefly before in the United States, and this acquaintanceship developed into a lifetime friendship. Their views on Peruvian archaeology were not always the same, and Kroeber did not shrink from disagreeing; but the relationship remained warm and amicable. Much later, in 1942, when Kroeber visited Peru for the last time, I remember Tello expressing to me his great admiration for his old colleague.

In 1925, Kroeber visited the North Coast of Peru, and, at Tello's suggestion, he made a number of excavations on the Central Coast, exploring Proto-Lima, or Interlocking culture, structures and burials. Following this, he worked in the South Coast Canete and Nazca Valleys. In looking at Nazca and related collections he discovered some textile fragments with embroidered designs which he recognized as being similar to the painted figures on the Nazca pottery. These were, of course, bits of the Paracas style textiles. Later that year, Tello and S. K. Lothrop went to the South Coast and discovered the famed Paracas cemeteries.

In 1926, Kroeber made a short trip into the Peruvian Highlands, exploring near Huancayo, but he spent most of his time on the South Coast, going, again, to the Nazca Valley. There he made the first refuse stratigraphic excavations carried out in Peru, though his test cuts turned out to be entirely within Late Period–post-Nazca or Ica style, debris. Notably, one of the discoveries of the 1926 Nazca sojourn were the famous "lines" or "markings" on the desert that have attracted so much attention since then. He finished up this season by another survey look at the North Coast.

As he was accustomed to do, Kroeber published promptly on these two seasons of Peruvian fieldwork, bringing out two monographs with the Field Museum on the North Coast (Kroeber, 1926b, 1930) within the next four years. Drawing on all of his Peruvian research, both with the Uhle collections and his own field experiences, he also published two important article-length syntheses (Kroeber, 1926c, 1927), the latter of these easily being the best summary statement on Peruvian prehistory up to that time. Over the next thirty years, Kroeber returned to his Peruvian collections and data from time to time, bringing out a Canete Valley monograph fairly soon (Kroeber, 1937) and later two others on his Central Coastal (Kroeber, 1954), and Nazca (Kroeber, 1956) excavations. In another monograph of the 1950s, *Paracas Cavernas and Chavin* (Kroeber, 1953), Kroeber took issue with me (Willey, 1951) over the degree of Chavin influence found on the South Coast in the early Paracas Period, and had the better of the argument. In brief, he remained actively involved with current findings and thinking in Peruvian archaeology to the very end of his life.

In 1926, Alfred Kroeber married Theodora Kracaw Brown, a young widow, with two young sons. Originally a University of California graduate (Class of 1919), Theodora had gone back to Graduate School in Berkeley two years after the death of her husband and was one of Kroeber's students. Theodora (or "Krakie", her nickname from her maiden name of Kracaw) was a warm and outgoing, person, happy in herself, and she made Kroeber very happy. Her two young sons, Clifton and Ted, became Kroeber's sons as well, and Theodora and Kroeber had two more children of their own, Karl and Ursula.

In the 1920s, the Kroebers bought a new house in Berkeley and were busy raising a family. Kroeber's research productivity in the late 1920s and the 1930s was prodigious. One of his feats was to contribute substantially to the *14th Edition of the Encyclopedia Britannica* (see Steward, 1961, pp. 1072–1073). He also wrote *Cultural and Natural Areas of Native North America* (Kroeber, 1939) and *Configurations of Culture Growth* (Kroeber, 1944a), both major works with archaeological dimensions. "Cultural and Natural Areas" dealt with the culture areas, with cultural adaptations to natural environment, and with the diachronic concept of "culture climax". "Configurations" is Kroeber's response to Spengler, Toynbee, and the other "philosophers of history". His approach was not an impressionistic one. He sought for some way to objectively identify "cultures" or "civilizations" and to plot their "life histories". He did this by plotting the clusterings of individual geniuses as a measure of civilizational climax. In the midst of all this, in 1936, Kroeber was honored with a *festschrift* volume, *Essays in Anthropology Presented to A. L. Kroeber in Celebration of His Sixtieth Birthday* (Lowie, ed., 1936).

With the coming of World War II, Kroeber restlessly wanted to be in some way involved. The Committee on Inter-American Artistic and Intellectual Relations, of which Nelson Rockefeller of the State Department was a member, and which was a sponsor of the Institute of Andean Research archaeological program in Latin America, invited Kroeber to come to Peru where four of the Institute's projects were operating. (I have referred to these projects in several of the previous memoirs.) Kroeber, after hesitating for awhile, finally replied to the letter of invitation with his characteristic candor as well as good judgment (T. Kroeber, 1970, p. 152):

> "If my presence in Peru were really considered of any mo-
> ment, I can see only one thing I might do which would per-
> haps have intrinsic significance: a visit to ruins, sites,
> collections, and results made accessible since I was last in the
> country in 1926, to enable me to interpret and advise and plan
> with the men who will be on the firing line of Peruvian ar-
> chaeology during the next generation. This will mean a mini-
> mum of time in Lima and a maximum touring the provinces
> by car."

As it turned out, it was a perfect statement of what he was to do. His monograph, *Peruvian Archaeology in 1942* (Kroeber, 1944b), resulting from his trip, was just such a synthesis and a guidebook for those of us who followed him.

Kroeber, accompanied by Theodora, arrived in Lima in January of 1942. At that time, I was finishing up my digging at Ancon and living in Lima; John Rowe was still in the South Highlands on his project; and Ted McCown, Kroeber's young colleague at Berkeley, was in Lima, having just completed his survey in the North Highlands. Ted brought Kroeber out to our house in Lima the night after he arrived. We went right to business. I had been looking forward to it. I was able to show him sherds, grave lot collections, and stratigraphic profiles from my excavations at Cerro de Trinidad in the Chancay Valley where I claimed that the White-on-red pottery style, defined by Uhle many years before, was earlier than the Inter-locking style, reversing Uhle's chronological order of the two (Willey, 1943). Kroeber was intimately familiar with the mate-rials, having published on Uhle's Chancay collections some years before (Kroeber, 1926a), and having dealt with Interlock-ing style pottery in his own Maranga excavations (Kroeber, 1954). He went over everything very carefully: the strata dia-grams, the nature of the digging, the percentages of the sherds by types per level. Finally, he bestowed the accolade: "Well", he said very seriously, "I think we can take that as proven. It's an important step in straightening out the Central Coastal chronology. Now how do you suppose this all fits into the Ancon sequence?"

It was one of my great moments as a young archaeologist. I think Kroeber knew it, too. He could be informal, off-hand, "down-to-earth", as he was with me and others on many occasions; but there are times, I think, that call for formality, for just a touch of "side", and this was one of them. Here I was, my first time in Peru, finishing up what had been a six-month stint of hard fieldwork, and presenting my offering to the "head of the Peruvianist archaeological establishment". He knew I deserved and needed a formal encomium, and he gave it to me.

The effect of Kroeber's visit was inspirational for all of the North American anthropologists in Peru at that time—for Ted McCown, John Rowe, Sam Lothrop, Harry Tschopik (whom he had seen in the highlands), and Marshall Newman, as well as myself. Kroeber's knowledge of the Peruvian field was staggering. With his fascination with style, he had a great visual memory. He could recall specimens from digs or museum tours of years back, comparing them, as we talked, with pieces we had seen a few hours previously in a tour of Lima museums. After his extended journey through the country by car, Kroeber came back to Lima brimming with enthusiasm, suggesting lines of investigation for the future, and giving us an insight on just how he meant to summarize his visit.

Kroeber's relationships with the Peruvians were equally inspiring. He spent a good many hours with his friend Tello, talking over old times. Kroeber also took time to explain to me some of Tello's ideas about Peruvian archaeology.

> "He looks at these things differently than you do, Gordon. You must remember that your backgrounds and training have been very different. He doesn't organize or use evidence the way you have been trained to do; but he has seen a lot and he knows a lot. He has ideas that it might be well for some of us to follow up. You'll do well to listen and learn from him."

Besides Tello, Kroeber also met and talked with some of the younger Peruvian archaeologists, and two of them traveled with the Kroebers on their trips through the country.

The high point of Kroeber's Peruvian tour was a lecture he gave near the end of his stay at the University of San Marcos. He spoke to a packed house on "Los Metodos de la Arqueologia Peruana" (Kroeber, 1942). His Spanish, while not fluent, was measured and impressive. Sitting there in the darkened, cathedral-like hall, of what the Limeños claim is the oldest university in the Americas, and looking at Kroeber, his distinguished bearded face illuminated by the small reading light on the speaker's lectern, I reflected on the fact that our country could not have been better represented in Peruvian academic circles.

The 1942 Peruvian trip may have tired Kroeber, and on his return to Berkeley he was pressed into service immediately in a campus foreign language training program for our armed services. The administrative duties for this proved onerous. In 1943, at the age of 67, he suffered a severe heart attack which almost ended his life. Gradually, the doctors and Theodora nursed him back to health. He also was a good patient. After that he took it easy. I remember him at meetings, taking care to put his feet up on a chair, moving slowly, carefully, taking stairs slowly. The great good sense that had seen him through earlier difficulties served him well again. He was to live to be 84, a remarkable record given the severity of the 1943 attack.

Gradually he went back to work. In 1945 the Kroebers went to London where he gave the Huxley Lecture at the Royal Anthropological Institute, the first American to be so honored. The title of his talk was *The Ancient Oikoumene as an Historic Culture Aggregate* (Kroeber, 1946). It is another famous scholarly paper. I find the idea of the "Oikoumene" a romantic, almost a poetic conception. Kroeber visualized the ancient Old World, with its roots in the Middle East and the Classical lands and its branches throughout Europe, as a vast "culture area with time depth", an entity of interlinked traditions and ideologies. Those within its embrace belonged to the "known world"; those outside were the barbarians beyond the pale. One readily recognizes it as a very "Kroeberian" idea.

Kroeber retired at Berkeley in 1946. In the summer of 1947, he and Theodora came east for the Institute of Andean Research-Wenner-Gren Foundation Peruvian archaeological conference in New York. This was the one which climaxed in the dinner at which the Kroebers were given the preferred treatment by the headwaiter at the "Club 21"—as I have related above. At those meetings, I gave what was for me, and I suppose for the times, a rather "far-out" paper (Willey, 1948). During the discussion which followed it, I asked Kroeber if he thought what I had said "ran too far ahead of the data". His somewhat offhand and pragmatic reply was that "it ran ahead of the data, but not too far". I was encouraged and emboldened.

In 1947–48 Kroeber taught at Harvard for a year, during which time he collaborated with his good friend Clyde Kluckhohn on their monograph, *Culture; A Critical Review of Concepts and Definitions* (Kroeber and Kluckhohn, 1952). Then, from 1948 to 1952 Duncan Strong and Julian Steward invited him to Columbia as a visiting professor. This period was particularly pleasant and gratifying for him. Back in 1931, Boas, his old mentor, had asked him to leave Berkeley and come to Columbia as his replacement. Kroeber agonized over his decision for a long time. He had a great affection for and a sense of loyalty to Boas; in addition, he had friends and family relations in New York which had been his original home; but the Californian and western roots which he had put down were too deep, and in the end he refused the offer. Now he had a chance to spend some time at his old university and in a city that he loved.

I saw him several times while he was at Columbia. George Foster, who was with me at the Smithsonian in the late 1940s, was a former student and great admirer of Kroeber's, and, together with Julian Steward, he arranged for Kroeber to preside over a series of free-discussion seminars on Saturday mornings. George and I would travel up from Washington the night before to come to these. They were well attended—a dozen or so colleagues, varying from meeting to meeting, some from New York, others from out of town. Clyde Kluckhohn came to one of them. The discussions would often boil down to arguments between Steward and Kroeber. They were conducted in a very friendly vein, but they brought into sharp relief the fundamental theoretical differences between the two. Steward (1961) has set these out in his obituary review of Kroeber and of Kroeber's theoretical position. I should add that our Saturday

morning seminars came along at about the time Julian's article, "Cultural Causality and Law: A Trial Formulation of the
Development of Early Civilizations (Steward, 1949) appeared
in the *American Anthropologist*. Kroeber, while interested in
the growth configurations of civilizations through time, after
all he had written a major book on the subject, was wary of
causality. He preferred to appreciate, almost to savor each individual civilizational growth for itself alone. He was not averse
to making comparisons between them, although he was not
very sanguine about "laws" emerging therefrom. I have a quotation of his, with which I dedicated an essay to his memory
(Willey, 1962), which nicely sums up his thoughts on the matter: "Experience has shown that it is hopeless to storm, by a
frontal attack, the great citadels of the causality underlying
highly complex groups of facts." But Julian was all for charging
the battlements. Kroeber, laughingly, accused Julian of wanting to be a "universalist". Julian countered by saying all right,
there is a place for some "universalism", that "laws of civilizational growth" enabled us to better face the future. Kroeber
would have none of that (see Wolf, 1981). In this connection, I
remember him at a symposium in Washington, D.C., in the fall
of 1948, where he presented a paper, "Have Civilizations a Life
History? (Kroeber, 1950)" Someone in the audience asked: Was
it not the task of the historian, archaeologist, or anthropologist
to help us predict the future by the study of the past? Kroeber
replied: "What's going to happen in the future? I don't know.
I'm not Nostradamus; that's not my game."

During that stay at Columbia, the Kroebers took an apartment on Riverside Drive. I visited him there sometime in 1951
or 1952. He was in fine form, relaxed and taking it easy. I had
some small matter of business, and when it was finished I got
up to leave; but Kroeber invited me to stay a while longer. We
got off onto Peruvian archaeology. His daughter, Ursula came
in. It was the first and only time I met her. She was an engaging
young lady. She is now, after her marriage, Ursula Le Guin, well
known as an author of popular science fiction. Then, in her
early twenties, I believe she was a graduate student at Columbia. After a bit, her father and I moved the conversation back to
archaeology. I was holding forth on my idea of a "pottery tradi-

tion", in brief, the regional persistence over long periods of time, and through different styles, of basic modes of vessel form, painting, modelling, or whatever. It was the sort of idea that Kroeber liked—a configuration in the archaeological or historical record, however small but nevertheless fascinating; explanation of it could wait. He contributed to the discussion by observing that there might be one interesting fundamental difference between North Coast and South Coast Peruvian pottery: the vessel bottoms. He thought that in the north they were essentially flat while in the south they were nearly always rounded. This carried us for about ten minutes as we each went over various periods, styles, and pottery types in the two regions checking on this interesting fact. Our conclusions were positive. Kroeber finally said, quite gravely, "Well, Gordon, I think we have a finding here. In the north they preferred flat bottoms, but in the south they liked round bottoms". Ursula, who had been sitting quietly through this weighty dialogue, suddenly began giggling hysterically jumped up and ran out of the room. Kroeber, in some puzzlement, watched her go, saying: "Now what's gotten into her?"

In the summer of 1952, Kroeber had a key role in the organizing and running of the two-week long international symposium in anthropology held at the Wenner-Gren Foundation in New York City. This resulted in the compendium, *Anthropology Today* (Kroeber and others, eds., 1953). His own commentaries and summaries, given in the course of that symposium, were memorable. I had a lunch table conversation with him one day during those sessions. It was a mixed seating at our table, of social anthropologists and archaeologists. The question arose as to what the other branches of anthropology wanted from archaeology. There were a number of desiderata put forward. I remember the late Robert Redfield, perhaps to needle the archaeologists, said that what the rest of the field wanted to know about were "the states of mind of primitive man". Kroeber didn't say anything for a while. I can see him now, turning his head to one side, as he did, perhaps to compensate for a deafness in one ear resulting from an infection of many years before. After a while, he said, quietly, to me alone: "What archaeologists should do is to get on with culture history. Don't be put off with this kind of thing. It just leads to piddling." I would hold neither Redfield nor Kroeber fully accountable for their off-the-cuff remarks at that time; both were overstating things. But I think I understood what they both were driving at. My sympathies were with Kroeber.

In later years, almost every time I met Kroeber, he gave me what might be called career advice, and it always made me feel very good when he did. For one thing, it was good advice, and, for another, I was quite flattered and pleased that he cared. In reflecting on this, I know I had a very benign and kindly father. Although I do not qualify as a Freudian psychologist, I seem to remember their doctrine that this makes for a son who, in later life, responds well and happily to authority figures, paying attention to what they tell him. I can remember one instance in the middle 1950s, when Kroeber and Theodora were in Cambridge for a time, while he was teaching out at Brandeis University. They dined with us and we with them. At that time, I was chairman of our department, and I remember telling Kroeber all about my new duties and new-found troubles in my first time in such a position. "Don't let it worry you too much, Gordon," he said. "You have to do a certain amount of this kind of thing in academic life, but don't become too engrossed in it. It's not your style. Stick to your archaeology."

Another occasion of advice was somewhat more amusing. In the summer of 1950, just before I was to come to Harvard, I was at the Smithsonian, filling in temporarily for George Foster as acting director of the Institute of Social Anthropology. I was not ideally suited for the job, but had agreed to do this for George while he was on leave in Spain. The Institute's activities were those of academic teaching in Latin American countries. Although hardly a social anthropologist, I did know something of Latin America, and the Smithsonian's administration felt that I could look after things for a while. That summer we received a notice to the effect that the Smithsonian's Institute of Social Anthropology should be represented at a forthcoming meeting of the Society for Applied Anthropology to be held at Vassar College. I was not terribly enthusiastic about going, but the Smithsonian administration said that I should. Accordingly, I traveled up to Poughkeepsie, New York and reported in at the Alumnae House of the college, which was to be the central meeting place. Surprisingly, one of the first persons I met there was Kroeber. In fact, he was one of the few people that I saw in my whole time there that I knew. He came up with a smile on his face and asked: "What's an archaeologist like you doing at a meeting like this?" I started to explain, but then he was pulled away into some other conversation so I didn't have a chance to finish my explanation.

The meeting lasted a couple of days. I dutifully went to several sessions where I noticed Kroeber in the audience, but I didn't have a chance to speak to him again. On the departure morning, however, I was down in the railroad station at Poughkeepsie, waiting for the train, when I saw Kroeber on the platform. At about the same time, a formidable looking lady, presumably an applied anthropologist, spied Kroeber and was bearing down on him—quite possibly for a more serious discussion than he wanted to undertake that morning. Anyway, Kroeber took my arm and turned away from his prospective conversational assailant. Putting that elegant gray head slightly to one side, he looked at me attentively and said: "Gordon, when I asked what an archaeologist like you was doing at a meeting like this, the other day, I didn't mean to be rude."

"Oh, that's all right, Dr. Kroeber," I replied. It's just that the Smithsonian made me come up here———."

"Don't say that," he whispered. "Don't let them hear you say that." He eyed me rather gravely for a moment and continued. "Gordon, you're going up to Harvard now, and you're going to take Alfred Tozzer's place there. You have an important position. This means you have to be something more than just an archaeologist." I think he caught the alarmed look on my face for he lightened his tone a bit, but went on: "That's all right, that's all right," he consoled. "It's just that it's a good idea for you to be seen at meetings like this now. Don't tell them you were sent. Let them think you came because you wanted to. You don't have to say anything. Just be here and look interested. That's the important thing, look interested." Meanwhile, our lady colleague could no longer countenance the great man wasting time on an unknown like me and moved in and took him over.

This was by far the most unusual career advice Kroeber had

ever given me. I wondered about it all the way back on the train to Washington, and a few nights later I even had a most colorful and disturbing dream about not being admitted to some kind of an anthropological heaven, presided over by a very disappointed but God-like Kroeber, because I was only an archaeologist. In thinking about it since, I suppose that Kroeber, at that time, was disturbed by the increasing fragmentation of the field, a condition even quite noticeable by 1950, and was trying to encourage his intellectual sons and grandsons to stay on top of things.

In 1959, I was invited to the Darwin Centennial celebration at the University of Chicago, and Kroeber, of course, had an important role in the proceedings. I went to see him in his suite in the Windermere Hotel before the formal sessions began. He said he had read my paper for the conference (Willey, 1960) and that he approved of it. We moved on to talk about archaeology. What was I doing now that I had shifted to Maya archaeology? He thought my settlement pattern emphases a good idea. He had told me so back when I had finished the Viru Valley study and had advised me to stay with it, even though I worked in areas other than Peru. It didn't hold the fascination for him that art styles did, but he recognized it as something that needed to be done in archaeology. In preparation for the public sessions at Chicago, we had some preliminary meetings of the panelists or discussants who were going to take the stage for the main events. Kroeber, Steward, Kluckhohn, Leslie White, Robert McCormick Adams, and I helped make up one such group, together with three or four scholars from other fields, plus, as moderator, Sir Julian Huxley. At one of the preliminary meetings, one of our group (not one of the anthropologists mentioned) began to badger Kroeber on a series of points. Kroeber contained himself for a good while. Finally, he got up, saying he was really too old to proceed further with the discussions, that he "would leave it with my [his] younger colleagues" (indicating Adams and myself) to argue it out, and left the room. I never saw him back off from a reasonable argument about any anthropological issue, but he would walk away from sniping.

The main Darwin event, before a large audience, went off

smoothly although I came away feeling that I had not been clear enough in my distinctions between "history" and "evolution", or had understood in all particulars just what others meant when they contrasted those terms. Kroeber told me not to worry, that he was never sure of the distinction either. It was the last time I was ever to see him.

In what I have said here, I have tried to indicate something of the enormously prestigious position Alfred Kroeber held in the field of anthropology, both at home and abroad. Looking at the formal record of honors, I can only sample from a long list. He was a founding member of the American Anthropological Association and one of its early presidents; he had similar roles in the Linguistic Society of America; and he was one of the founders of the Society for American Archaeology. He belonged to the three most prestigious learned societies or academies in the United States: the National Academy of Sciences, the American Philosophical Society, and the American Academy of Arts and Sciences. Abroad, he was an Honorary Fellow of the Royal Anthropological Institute of Great Britain and Ireland, a Corresponding Member of the Societe des Americanistes de Paris, and to the National Academy of Sciences of Denmark and Peru. I have mentioned the award of the Huxley Medal from the Royal Anthropological Institute. In the United States he received the Viking Fund Medal from the Wenner-Gren Foundation on the nomination of the American Anthropological Association. His honorary degrees were from the Universidad Nacional Mayor de San Marcos in Lima in 1942; from Yale in 1946; from California in 1951; from Harvard in 1952; from Columbia in 1953; and from Chicago in 1959.

In the late summer of 1960, I had a telephone call from Kroeber. He was calling from Berkeley; he had just heard of Clyde Kluckhohn's sudden death of a heart attack, and he wanted to know if I would take Clyde's place at a symposium that was to be held that September at the Burg Wartenstein in Austria. He and Clyde had planned it, and the Wenner-Gren Foundation had scheduled it for the Castle. It was to be on "Anthropological Horizons". Naturally, I was very pleased— almost "bowled over" would be the more appropriate term—to be invited and to be thought of as someone who could fill in for

Kluckhohn. I told Kroeber I hardly thought I would be a suitable substitute. Kroeber countered by saying that while I didn't have all of Clyde's interests, I could still contribute by bringing a broad New World archaeological and historical point of view to the meeting. But I had been at a Burg-Wartenstein conference just earlier that summer, and another trip there so soon seemed too much. I declined. I wish now I hadn't. It would have been my last chance to see and be with Kroeber.

The Burg-Wartenstein symposium went off successfully, and Kroeber and Theodora went from Austria to Paris to spend some time there as sightseers. On 4 October, back in their hotel after dinner, Kroeber told his wife of a new monograph he had just begun that morning. In her words (T. Kroeber, 1970, p. 285):

> " . . . it was about the new Europe in which he sensed a single and growing pan-Western culture, whose similarities of outlook and values—to each other and to America, greatly outweighed the national differences."

Kroeber's death, of a massive heart attack shortly after this, at a few minutes past midnight on 5 October 1960, blotted out this last exciting idea. Was it to be another "Oikoumene", another "configuration" to be delineated by the rich scientific and historical intellect of Alfred Louis Kroeber? Sadly, we shall never know.

SAMUEL KIRKLAND LOTHROP
In middle age.
Photo by Nikolas Muray. Courtesy Photo Archives, Peabody
Museum, Harvard University.

SAMUEL KIRKLAND LOTHROP
(1892–1965)

Samuel Kirkland Lothrop was a New England "Brahmin" in the full sense of that term—a caste that has been known to include those with a tendency for revolt against the constraints that this heritage has laid upon them. He was a gentleman and a scholar, a man of breeding and charm; he was also a *bon vivant* who enjoyed more than an occasional cup or a fling in a night club.

When I first met "Sam", as he was called by his peers, he was an internationally known archaeologist of considerable reputation and distinction. This was in 1941, just before we both departed for Peru to take part in the Institute of Andean Research archaeological program. Some of my clearest memories of him date from that 1941–1942 year; but a longer association came later, from after 1950 and my arrival at Harvard and the Peabody Museum, where he was a research associate and the curator of Andean Archaeology.

Samuel Kirkland Lothrop was born on 6 July 1892, in Milton, Massachusetts, the oldest son of William Sturgis Hooper Lothrop and Alice Putnam (Bacon) Lothrop. His great-grandfather, for whom Sam was named, was a well-known Unitarian minister of his time, the Reverend Samuel Kirkland Lothrop. If one goes to the Library of Congress card files, you will find that the great-grandfather has almost as many titles as the great-grandson, so Sam's was a distinguished intellectual lineage in the referred to Brahmin tradition. As a boy, he grew up in Massachusetts and Puerto Rico. His father had sugar plantation interests in Puerto Rico at the turn of the century, and this Puerto Rican experience at an early age may have provided some of the incentive that eventually turned Sam to Latin American archaeology. Indeed, in later years, he carried out some archaeological researches on the island. However, his younger brother, Francis, once told me that it was more likely that the father of a Groton classmate, a man named William Crocker, who was a collector of antiquities of all kinds, was the source of Sam's archaeological inspiration.

In a proper Bostonian manner, Sam attended Groton School where he played end on the football team and stroked the crew. He also must have performed respectably in the classroom for he was chosen as Senior Prefect, an honor he looked back on with pride. Still, it seems not to have been his scholarly achievements for which Sam was best remembered by his Groton classmates. After his death, I showed the late R. H. Ives Gammell, a distinguished Boston artist, who had been at Groton with Sam, a biography I had prepared on Samuel Kirkland Lothrop for the National Academy of Sciences (Willey, 1976). In this memoir I had stressed, naturally, the subject's preeminence as one of the world's leading archaeologists. Ives, who had not seen much of Sam in the intervening 50 years, and was no follower of the careers of archaeologists, was unbelieving. "Lothie", he exclaimed, "A great scholar? My God! I don't believe it! He must have changed since I knew him! I would never have predicted it. He was anything but that in those days."

But, to get back to the course of my biographical narrative, Sam, having successfully negotiated Groton, quite properly and expectably entered Harvard in 1911, where he eventually graduated with the Class of 1915. It was during these undergraduate years that Samuel Lothrop's professional archaeological career may be said to have begun. He came under the influence of that remarkable teacher of Mexican and Central American archaeology and ethnology, Alfred M. Tozzer, and from then on he had no doubts about what he wanted to do. Many years later, Tozzer told me that Sam was a favored pupil of his from the first and that he had always held him in the highest regard. With Tozzer's encouragement, Sam went to Pecos, New Mexico, to do his first archaeological fieldwork. This was with A. V. Kidder, in the summer of 1915, and Kidder, along with Tozzer, was to be another important figure in the development of Sam's career.

After that summer, Sam returned to Harvard and to graduate studies with Tozzer. During these graduate years, he traveled extensively in Central America and Puerto Rico, visiting archaeological sites, doing some minor digging, and, especially, examining museum collections. From the outset, I believe, this research was pointed toward the doctoral dissertation he eventually completed on Central American ceramics. World War I intervened, and Lothrop served as a Second Lieutenant with U.S. Army Military Intelligence. He was assigned to Central America, and I suspect that he made those years, in such an out of the way military billet as Central America must have been, count for something archaeologically.

Sam returned to Harvard in 1919 to resume his Central American research full time. He published his first scientific paper, an article on Panamanian goldwork, in 1919. He also continued his study of Central American ceramics by making a tour of the European museums where such collections existed. During these trips he made the acquaintance of the British Museum's great Americanist, Thomas Joyce. This was a significant meeting for him. Joyce was a man with a vast knowledge of New World archaeology, gleaned from years of museum and library study of the kind which Lothrop was then carrying out. They hit it off famously, the Britisher encouraging and aiding the young Harvard scholar in the kind of study that he, too, loved so well. By the time I came to know Sam Lothrop, he was the closest thing to a "Thomas Joyce" on this side of the Atlantic in his mastery of the details of Latin American archaeological data.

Sam submitted the thesis, *Pottery of Costa Rica and Nicaragua*, in 1921, and received his doctoral degree that year. The thesis was published in 1926. Today, more than 60 years after, it still remains the most valuable descriptive compendium on the subject. At the time, it established Lothrop, still in his early thirties, as the leading archaeologist working in the Lower Central American area. In 1921, Sam was employed by the Carnegie Institution of Washington, and he did for them what was to be his only Lowland Maya field research, at the site of Tulum, in Yucatan (Lothrop, 1924).

After this, between 1924 and 1930, Sam was on the staff of the Museum of the American Indian, Heye Foundation, in New York City. That institution had, and still has, some of the finest specimens of Precolumbian art from Central and South America that are to be found in any museum in the world. This was the result of the aggressive acquisition policy of its founder, patron, and long-time director, George Gustav Heye. In the second and third decades of the 20th century, the Heye Foundation also distinguished itself in archaeological field research. Marshall H. Saville, the former Loubat Professor at Columbia University, who worked for the Heye Foundation both in Mexico and in Ecuador, was a member of their research staff and became an esteemed colleague of Lothrop's when the latter joined them in 1924. In his years at the Museum of the American Indian, Sam carried out archaeological and ethnographical explorations in Puerto Rico, the Guatemalan Highlands, El Salvador, Peru, Argentina, and even distant Tierra del Fuego. In addition to this fieldwork, it should be stressed that, from the beginnings of his career, Sam was devoted to the literature, especially the ethnohistoric background literature pertinent to any region in which he carried out research; and he continued to develop this knowledge of the literature during his years with the Heye Foundation.

Unfortunately, this highly productive and happy association with the Museum of the American Indian ended for Sam with the dissolution of the Heye Foundation's research interests in 1930. After the stock market crash of the fall before, George Heye felt that retrenchment was necessary; and faced with the necessity of giving up either the purchasing of specimens or his research staff he chose to dispense with the latter. Both Marshall Saville and Sam Lothrop were let go. Sam, quite justifiably, was enraged by this decision, especially for what it did to Saville. He, Lothrop, was a man with an independent income, and although Heye's decision put a crimp in his research activities, the abrupt termination of his employment caused no financial hardship. Regrettably, the same was not true for the then aging Marshall Saville who had left Columbia to join the Heye Foundation staff and was now left without an income. Sam never forgave Heye for this. Years later, the Lothrop (1957a) obituary statement on Heye is the only one I can think of in the American archaeological literature in which the deceased is given a "bad press".

Lothrop had brought out some studies in the Heye Foundation publication series while he was on their staff, but the curtailment of their operations in 1930, left him with many manuscripts and projects hanging fire. Always highly conscientious about prompt publication of fieldwork, he turned to other scientific series for publishing these manuscripts. One of the outstanding examples of this was his *Indians of the Parana Delta* which was brought out by the New York Academy of Sciences (Lothrop, 1932a). The archaeological excavations behind this Parana Delta publication had been made possible through his friendships with Argentine archaeologists—particularly Fernando Marquez Miranda, a contemporary of Sam's and, like him, a man of considerable personal charm and a taste for life's pleasures. In 1950, almost 20 years afterwards, I dined one evening with Marquez Miranda in Buenos Aires, and he expressed to me his great admiration for Sam, as a scholar and a gentleman. Through such relationships, Sam was one of the very few North Americans, of that time or since, who was ever invited to conduct archaeological explorations on Argentine soil. For a long time, this "Parana" field study remained the very best published work on the archaeology of the Buenos Aires region.

After the Museum of the American Indian job folded, Lothrop came back to the Peabody Museum at Harvard where he was made a research associate and a curator of Andean Archaeology, positions which he held until 1958. After this he continued as a curator emeritus, with research and writing from this base. Sam was intensely loyal to the Peabody and to Harvard. His salary during his active years in these positions was a nominal pittance; he contributed more to subsidizing his own research in Panama and Costa Rica, than he received in salary. Nevertheless, he prized his official status at and association with the museum. This was demonstrated in his will in which he left his splendid library of Americana—perhaps the finest private library of Latin American area archaeology and ethnology in the world at that time—to the Peabody.

To break off from career and archaeological matters and to turn briefly to personal ones, I should note that Sam had married Rachel Warren, of Boston, in 1914, shortly before his Harvard College graduation, when he was only 22. They had three children, Samuel K., Jr., Joan, and John Warren. They were divorced, however, in the late 1920's, and he married a second

time, to Eleanor Bachman, of Philadelphia, in 1929, just before
his ties were severed with the Heye Foundation. Sam and his
new wife continued to live in New York City, however, even
though Sam's professional base was now at the Peabody Museum in Cambridge.

It was from the Peabody and Harvard that Sam launched
what was to be his best known field program—the work on the
Cocle culture at Sitio Conte in central Panama which was
carried out in the early 1930's. In 1930, Professor Tozzer heard
from an amateur archaeological enthusiast of some amazing
archaeological gold finds in the Cocle Province of Panama. The
discoveries had been made on the property of the Conte family.
Apparently, the Cocle River, during a seasonal flood, had cut
into deep archaeological deposits, exposing and washing out
ceramics, gold, and other artifacts. Panamanian, and for that
matter most Lower Central American, regions are not characterized by spectacular above-ground archaeological features,
such as large mounds, platforms, or other imposing constructions. The Sitio Conte, in surface appearance, looked like
nothing more than a cow pasture. Thus, if it had not been for
the washout, knowledge of the Cocle culture would not have
come about when it did. After these windfall discoveries,
Tozzer and others from Peabody went down to see the situation on the ground. Arrangements were made with the Conte
family for permission to excavate and for a sharing of the
materials from the dig.

Sam directed the Sitio Conte excavations, and in many ways
they were a model for archaeological digging, just as the ensuing publications were to be models of fine quality archaeological reporting (Lothrop, 1937–1942). A section of the site proved
to be the cemetery for rich chiefs. Large group burials included
the principal, presumably the chief or king, himself, who was
surrounded by several others who appeared to be immolated
retainers—probably wives, slaves, and persons of lower status.
The grave goods were absolutely fabulous, fully coming up to
the expectations that had been raised by the washouts of gold
objects prior to the excavations. Handsomely painted luxury
ceramics, carved bone and stone objects, and gold ornaments,
the latter sometimes set with emeralds, abounded in the

graves. A perusal of the photographs and drawings in the reports will reveal the great care with which the masses of grave objects were uncovered and left for a time *in situ* while the detailed recording went on. A two-period sequence of Early and Late Cocle was established on the bases of grave superpositions and stylistic seriations. Finally, the Sitio Conte operation was placed in an early 16th century ethnohistorical context— or in the setting of Spanish descriptions of the actual burial ceremonies of powerful rulers of the several territorially small, but extraordinarily rich, chiefdoms that existed in this part of Panama. The graves and their contents, and in general the record in the ground, corresponded amazingly closely with the Spanish accounts. Since the time of Lothrop's excavations and analyses at Sitio Conte we have found that the Cocle culture dated to some centuries before the Spanish *entradas;* however, the burial traditions appear to have changed but little in those late Precolumbian centuries.

If *Pottery of Costa Rica and Nicaragua* (1926) had established Lothrop as the leading archaeologist of Lower Central America a dozen or so years before, *Cocle; an Archaeological Study of Central Panama* (1937–1942) consolidated the author's position in the very front rank of Americanists.

It was at about this time that I first met Sam Lothrop. This occurred at the American Museum of Natural History. Sam, who continued to live in New York, and who was a close friend of George Vaillant, was often there at the museum, either examining collections or gossiping with George. In my memoirs of Strong and Vaillant, I have related how I, as a graduate student at Columbia, tended to haunt the museum. In the Spring of that year, when Vaillant's Institute of Andean Research program with U.S. State Department's Office of the Coordinator of Interamerican Affairs was being planned, I attended some of the planning sessions for the program at the museum, along with Duncan Strong who had designated me as his assistant-to-be for a Peruvian "chapter" of that program.

My first opportunities to talk with Sam were not very successful. While in many ways quite informal, and maintaining a "joking relationship" attitude with the others of the American Museum crowd, he seemed pretty stiff with me. Of course, the others in these meetings were either senior people, or, if younger, like Junius Bird and Gordon Ekholm, were friends of long-standing. I was the most junior and had only just met him. This was undoubtedly part of the problem, but I thought then that it was something more than this. I was, to Sam, a kind of "outsider". Central American or South American archaeology was, I am sure, quite firmly established in his mind as a Harvard-Peabody Museum, or at least a Harvard-American Museum of Natural History, bailliwick. Some, like Wendell Bennett had overcome this disadvantage by a series of outstanding field performances and publications, but I was an unknown quantity. Moreover, I was a Columbia University product, and Columbia had not been an institution known for its archaeological research in Latin America. With Duncan Strong there, it was just beginning to go in this direction. I do not mean to overemphasize my feelings about this, and, as a young man, I was probably more sensitive about such things than I am now; but this was how I felt at the time, and it undoubtedly conditioned my attitudes toward and opinions about Sam Lothrop in those earlier years of our acquaintance.

I have mentioned Sam's personal charm. Part of this was in his impeccable manners. Although, in those first years of our acquaintance, I thought him standoffish and cool, he was never rude. Part of the charm was also his physical appearance, he was a man of middle height—perhaps about 5' 10". His shoulders and chest were well developed, presumably from those Groton crew and football days. In 1941–1942, he reminded one a bit of the actor, Clark Gable. Although not quite that handsome, he had a rugged, beetle-browed masculinity. He was very attractive to women and was attracted to them.

In talking about this personal side of Sam, I should note that he was a great sports fan. I remember—from a later time than those Peruvian days, and when we were somewhat better friends and easier with each other—that Sam took me to watch a swift and violent game of ice hockey at the Boston arena, the first game of that very "physical" sport that I had ever witnessed. His sense of identification with and enthusiasm for what was going on was most evident. His own participation in sports in later years was in yachting, and for a long time he maintained a Summer residence on the shore, in Mattapoisett, Massachusetts. As an archaeological footnote, one might add that these sailing interests overlapped to a degree with his professional researches, as evidenced by an important article which he wrote, "Aboriginal Navigation off the West Coast of South America" (Lothrop, 1932b).

Sam was, as are many archaeologists, a romantic. With him it was never hidden. In Lima, in the months between June and December of 1941, or just prior to Pearl Harbor, Sam reveled in what I am sure he thought of as fascinating international intrigue. Maybe it was. I never knew for certain. He was an habitue of the Gran Hotel Bolivar, Lima's leading "Grand Hotel", in the continental European sense of that "Grand" designation. There, at 6:00 PM, every evening except Sunday, the city's elite convened for cocktails and intensive social interaction. This was known as the "vermouth hour" in Lima society. It should be explained that upper class Limeños adhered to a very fashionable late dinner hour. For instance, 8:00 or 9:00 PM was painfully early and considered a deplorable "gringo" time to dine. Hence, the "vermouth hour" might well last until after 10:00 PM, when it was socially acceptable to enter the dining room. By some cynical observers, the room where the "vermouth hour" rituals took place, the Grand Rotunda, on the ground floor of the hotel, was, for these "vermouth" occasions, referred to as the "snake-pit". At the height of the "snake-pit" festivities, the chatter which rose from the many tables in the room competed with chamber music which was provided by musicians stationed at two places on mezzanine balconies above the elegant gathering. The latter included rich Peruvians, the sort who, in seeking refuge from the boredom of their country haciendas, might have been in Paris or on the Riviera, except for the war. The *Corps Diplomatique* was also well-represented. In those early months of World War II, when things looked perilous for the Allies and when America's possible entry into the hostilities was still uncertain, Lima still had its large contingents of German and Italian Embassy people. In addition, the Axis also had its sympathizers among the Peruvians. Sam would point the diplomats and their associates out to Bud Newman, John Corbett, or to me, whispering,

"Do you see that guy over there, talking to the blond? He's in the Italian military attache's office and someone to be wary of." Or, "That woman in the red dress, with the figure. Don't be taken in by her. She's the mistress of the Rumanian Ambassador who is a confirmed Nazi." It was all pretty heady stuff.

Sam may have been some kind of a U.S. agent, or he may have been just a patriotic amateur helping out. I never knew, and didn't want to know. He showed up one day with a bad limp and reported that the night before, in the Bolivar Bar, which was situated just off the Grand Rotunda room, a Nazi agent had stamped on his toe in what was obviously a definite attempt to put old "007" out of action. Maybe so. I suppose warring adversaries had to restrict themselves to relatively limited mayhem in the bar of the leading hotel of a neutral country.

During the day, Sam frequently maintained himself at a central window table in this same bar. It was a key position. Entrance to the bar, from either the hotel Rotunda room or a door leading to outside the hotel, could be monitored effectively from the window table. In addition, one could keep a pretty good eye on passersby rounding the corner into the Colmena from the Plaza San Martin. Just who and what to look for, always struck me as more of a problem, but then I wasn't in the know. Armed with a Manhattan (that wonderful drink, sadly no longer popular) or a double-scotch old fashioned (with no fruit or sugar), Sam remained faithfully at his post during the long pre-lunch cocktail hour. Newman, Corbett, and I used to call this strategically placed table "the office"; but, I should add, that in spite of such smart-aleck wisecracks among ourselves, we all enjoyed "reporting in" at the "office" and never refused to raise an arm ourselves when invited to by the generous Sam. I remember after one such pre-prandial indulgence, and the Bolivar lunch which followed, Sam asked Duncan Strong, Junius Bird and me if we wanted to see some archaeological sites in the Rimac and the nearby Lurin Valley. This was just before Strong and I had started our digging at Pachacamac, and we were at loose ends for a couple of days. I was delighted by the invitation.

Sam gave us a great tour. In those days, the Panamerican highway, which stretched north up through the Lurin Valley, to Ancon, and beyond, was a two-laned paved road, not terribly well engineered or banked on the curves. We piled into Sam's sedan and, once outside the limits of Lima, set off at a great rate. The sensation of speed was increased for me, psychologically, by the fact that the speedomcter in Sam's car was set for kilometers, rather than miles. I was beside him in the front seat. I watched the speedometer hand creep up to 100, 110. My God! As I realized later, this was only about 65 or 70 in "real" speed, but this misconception added to the terror then. This was especially so because I knew that Sam had one bad eye, due to a childhood injury, with only 25% vision on this side. As we roared along through the Lurin, under the coastal winter fog ceiling of June, which hung about 20 feet above our heads, Sam would frequently turn around to speak to our colleagues in the back seat and, with one hand on the wheel, would point out features of archaeological interests on roadside hills that flicked past with great rapidity. I prayed to the gods, both ancient Andean and Christian.

We visited two or three sites on the way through the Rimac and Lurin, eventually ending up at Ancon. I have described the appearance of coastal Peruvian sites in some of the previous memoirs. Evidences of looting, some of it of recent appearance, characterized the sites. One of the Lurin sites was Zapallan. Sam said he came to this one frequently and that "huaqueros" had been fairly active at the location in recent months. These grave robbers operate nocturnally because what they do was at least nominally against the law. In the daytime, large pieces of textiles, wooden artifacts, and huge sherds or partial vessels could be gleaned from the edges of their excavations. We helped Sam in making such a surface collection on his Zapallan "call" that day. Some years later, Sam and his third wife, Joy Mahler Lothrop, published on the Zapallan collections (Lothrop and Mahler, 1957).

On that particular trip we continued through the huge graveyard, or "Necropolis", of Ancon, which is situated on the high ground back from the shore of that little port town. The graveyard or "necropolis" has been mercilessly looted through the years. Huge collections were taken out—ceramics, textiles, and mummy bundles—in the 19th century (Reiss and Stubel, 1880–1887); and since then digging has continued there, most of it of a "huaquero" nature. When we drove through it in 1941, many evidences of this looting could be seen on both sides of the highway. Besides this, the Panamerican Highway roadway also had sliced through many of the archaeological deposits. A long time after this, when I went back to Ancon in 1971, the cemetery area still looked much the same.

Ancon was the town where the treaty ending the "War of the Pacific", between Chile and Peru, was signed in 1879. After that, in the late 19th and early 20th century it became a popular seaside resort, with several hotels and *pensiones* that catered to such trade. Those hotels were mostly wooden affairs, with the scroll-work ornamentation on the porches that is so characteristic of this period. On that late afternoon in early June of 1941, Sam and I, and our colleagues, repaired to the then principal old wooden hotel, with its turn-of-the-century ambience and well-stocked bar, and refreshed ourselves after our tiring field reconnaissance. Sadly, in recent years, since World War II, this Victorian atmosphere has been swept away by mid-20th century apartment house and hotel buildings of concrete.

Sam's archaeology of that year in Peru was largely confined to such collecting trips. He did no digging himself. He was in charge of the Paracas textile publication project, in collaboration with Dr. Tello. This was the same project to which Newman was to serve as the physical anthropologist studying the skeletons from the mummy bundles, and I have referred to it before. It didn't take up much of Sam's time. In addition to his collecting trips, and with Tello's permission, Sam also made frequent purchases of archaeological artifacts from various "huaqueros", or possibly, "middle men" acting for "huaqueros" who would call at his house with such goods. Sam would then show his purchases to Tello, and the latter would select whatever he wanted for the National Peruvian collections; the remainder, along with Sam's scavenged surface collections, were eventually shipped to the Peabody Museum. Sam was a great friend and favorite of Tello's. In fact, he was the only North American archaeologist who was on a first name—"Sam" and "Julio"—basis with Tello. Some of the others of our party attempted this familiarity with "Julio" during that year only to be brought up short by Peru's "First Archaeologist" with a sternly formal counter-address of "Doctor" or "Mister".

As the 1941–1942 year wore on, I had more opportunity to discuss archaeology with Sam. He visited our house in Lima and looked over my excavation collections from Pachacamac, Chancay, Puerto de Supe, and Ancon. In turn, I was invited to the Lothrop residence in San Isidro, a suburb of Lima, to look at the many objects that he had been collecting or purchasing. Besides this, Sam and Eleanor became the sort of official hosts for our Andean Institute group, entertaining us at lunches, dinners, and cocktail parties. Through those months, my relationships with Sam warmed up considerably. Our archaeological interests, however, were different. I was all steamed up about detailing chronological sequences, especially with the aid of refuse heap ceramic stratigraphy; Sam was more interested in the objects and their technological and esthetic properties. These differences would lead to problems between us in the future.

My wife and I left Lima in May of 1942. Sam and Eleanor Lothrop were still there at the time, and I can't remember now just when they did leave. In the years after the war, preceding 1950, I saw Sam on various occasions, usually in New York or, occasionally in Washington, where I was at the Smithsonian. In the latter context, it should be mentioned that he was a diligent, faithful, and dependable contributor to the *Handbook of South American Indians*, Julian Steward's enterprise on which I served as an assistant. But it was not until after 1950, when I came to the Peabody Museum and to Harvard, that we were again more frequently associated.

In the late 1940s and early 1950s, Sam and Eleanor Lothrop were still living in New York. In addition to their residential apartment, Sam also maintained a small separate apartment in that city which he used as a library and study. I think it was somewhere between the sixties and the eighties on the East side although I am not certain. As I remember, the apartment had a large living room, which had been turned into a library and study, a bedroom and bath, and a little kitchenette which served largely as a bar. The library-study was a scholar's dream. Books filled the walls from floor to ceiling, there may also have been some additional stack-type shelving. As I have said, this library was a great study resource. Here, surrounded by his books, journals, and thousands of reprints, an active storehouse of Americana, in archaeology, ethnohistory, and ethnography, Sam did the actual writing of his monographs, reports, and articles. Needless to say, it was a set-up of which any research archaeologist would have been jealous.

At some time after the 1941–1942 Peruvian trip, but prior to the time when I came to Harvard, I was made a member of the Institute of Andean Research. For one barely turned 30, I considered this quite an honor. The membership then was small, perhaps no more than a dozen. It was not until the late 1950s that it suddenly grew to 25 or so, and its "elite" glamor began to fade. In the late 1940s and early 1950s, Sam frequently hosted the Institute meetings in this wonderful private apartment and library—a sort of archaeological "holy of holies". This, in itself, would make the meetings worth coming up from Washington to attend. We would usually lunch out somewhere; return to Sam's; dispense with our business, which was never very onerous; and then settle down to some splendid late afternoon drinking from that well-supplied kitchenette-bar. Living in Washington, I had four hours to recover on the train trip home. I believe we continued with meetings of this sort until the early 1950s, when I was at Harvard. The only difference was that then I took the train home going the other way.

When I came to Harvard in the fall of 1950, Sam was in the habit of making frequent trips up from New York to the Peabody Museum. He maintained laboratory space there, rather than a formal office. His mode of work was of interest. I have observed Sam while he was studying a large collection, such as that from the Diquis region of Costa Rica, looking at pottery, goldwork, and artifacts of all kinds, which were spread out over every inch of table space as well as distributed around on the floor. He would spend days doing this, checking back on excavation notes, picking up objects and looking at them, and directing with utmost patience the efforts of the artists and photographers who were illustrating this material. Weeks, even months, would pass in this manner. He did not seem to be taking voluminous descriptive notes as he went along, but at some point he must have; otherwise, I don't see how he could have remembered the detail which characterizes his finished reports. Finally, at the end of such a laboratory session, or series of sessions, Sam would take the numerous photographs, pen-and-ink drawings, the original field notes, and whatever notes he may have taken during this long laboratory period, back to the library in New York. Here, surrounded by all of the pertinent literature, and deeply immersed in it, he would prepare the final report, a report that would not only be a finished descriptive document but one that would be very carefully compared and related to the extant body of scientific writings that could in any way bear upon the subject. The comparative work, obviously, was done from the illustrations that he brought from the laboratory to the library and that would, eventually, end up as the illustrations in his monograph.

At Harvard, I felt a kind of recurrence of my problem of making contact with Sam. I felt that a certain amount of the rapport I had developed with Sam in Peru, and afterwards in Institute of Andean Research contexts, had gone. I could only hope that any reserve toward me on Sam's part would gradually fade away. But then a couple of little things happened that didn't help in this regard.

The first of these was quite ridiculous as one looks back on it. In a basement laboratory of the Peabody, when I arrived there in 1950, was a collection of pottery vessels spread out on some tables which had been shipped by Lothrop from Peru to the States at some time in the 1940s and which he had only recently unpacked. Sam's shipments had been cleared through Tello's museum in Magdalena Vieja, and, I suppose, in some way or another, several crates of material from the Cerro Trinidad site in the Chancay Valley, which I had excavated in 1941, were sent to the Peabody by mistake. These were not the crates which I had been permitted by Tello to take when I left Peru and which were consigned to the American Museum of Natural History, via Columbia University, as a part of our share of the materials which I had excavated under the Institute of Andean Research permit. Those crates had arrived safely in New York back in 1942. They were, instead, the crates which contained the Peruvian's share of the Cerro Trinidad material. When I got to Harvard and the Peabody, I came across this material one day and was quite surprised to see some very familiar looking pots of the type which I had designated as Chancay White-on-red. On closer inspection, I saw that they bore the india ink catalogue numbers which I had put on them back in Peru. Without any question, they were pieces I had dug up at Cerro Trinidad. Each vessel, however, had a piece of paper stuck in it with the designation, "white-on-red pottery from Ancon". I mentioned the matter to Sam when I saw him some days later—not in any urgency but as something to be taken care of in the interests of accuracy. These vessels were, I said from my dig at Chancay. They must have been sent by Tello or his staff by mistake, and they were definitely from the Chancay Valley, not Ancon. Sam said nothing at first, but he didn't like it. Chancay and Ancon are adjacent valleys on the Peruvian coast; the White-on-red pottery was known from both; his mistake in identifying these as being from Ancon was a readily understandable one, lacking, as he did, any provenience information with the shipment; but he didn't like my proffered correction. Later, he said that he trusted "Julio" completely, that "Julio" had said the material was from Ancon, and that "Julio" obviously knew more about Peruvian archaeology than I did. I thought I'd better retire from the confrontation and did so.

A second disagreement was more serious. Although I had been brought to Harvard and the Peabody to continue the Mayan tradition there, a tradition that had been both Bowditch's and Tozzer's main concern, I made my first field expedition from my new institution a Panamanian one. This was by way of following up what I had begun with Stirling, at Monagrillo, in 1948. This was all right, as far as it went, but I don't think Sam much liked it. He was, after all, the Lower Central American expert at the museum and, beyond all odds, the leading Panamanian archaeological specialist in the world. I had gone to Panama, and Monagrillo, in 1952, without consulting him. Also, Monagrillo and its archaeology was not to his liking. In 1949, I had presented some preliminary results from the site at the New York International Congress of Americanists (Willey, 1951). Sam didn't think much of what I had found. He doubted the antiquity I wanted to assign to the Monagrillo complex, and he thought it was pretty grubby-looking stuff. Indeed, Monagrillo inciscd and punctated pottery is esthetically unsatisfactory, especially when compared with something like Cocle polychrome. I think Sam felt that I was sort of lowering the standards of Panamanian archaeology.

But the worst was still in the offing. In 1948, Stirling and I had excavated a number of sites in the Panamanian Parita-Santa Maria region, most of which were not on the early Monagrillo level but, instead, pertained to the general polychrome pottery horizon. Stirling had turned our collections from these sites over to me for publication. I had not finished this task before going to Harvard and had taken this material with me. Now, with my attention shifting to the Maya, I turned these polychrome horizon collections, plus other polychrome collections which I had made in my 1952 trip, over to a Harvard graduate student of mine, Jack Ladd. Ladd eventually completed a doctoral dissertation on all of this material and it was later published by the Smithsonian (Ladd, 1964). But while Ladd was preparing the thesis, I suggested to him that, as a related side project, it might be useful for him to review the old Lothrop Sitio Conte pottery collections. In going over Sam's publication on that site, I had noticed sherd illustrations of some material that did not fit the Cocle polychrome definitions. This was pottery painted in a geometric style which corresponded to ceramics which I had found in the lower levels of a deep midden site, the Giron site, on the Santa Maria River. I had published on this (Willey and Stoddard, 1954), designating the lower level pottery at Giron as the Santa Maria complex and noting that it stratigraphically preceded Cocle-type polychrome levels.

Ladd followed my suggestion and brought the Sitio Conte sherd collections down from the Peabody attic and analyzed or classified these according to Cocle and Santa Maria typologies. Sure enough, the Santa Maria material was most heavily distributed toward the bottom of a large trench that Lothrop had excavated for stratigraphic purposes; however, it had been Sam's contention that the trench showed no conclusive stratigraphic change. Jack, with my encouragement, published a short note in *American Antiquity*, "A Stratigraphic Trench at Sitio Conte, Panama", in which he clearly demonstrated the case for the Santa Maria complex chronological priority (Ladd, 1957).

I had done all of this without informing Sam before Ladd's note appeared. It was an omission I regret in looking back on it. Sam was furious. Shortly afterwards, he gave a symposium talk at the Peabody in which he counter-attacked. He blamed Jack Ladd as the immediate miscreant although he made it clear that "Ladd was Willey's student" and that I had misled him with a lot of nonsense about a non-existent Santa Maria complex. I defended myself. It was not the kind of shouting match that often has been known to characterize heated Americanist archaeological discourse. Both of us were too reserved for that sort of thing. Sam said afterwards that "there was no reason why we should not disagree about such matters", so keeping it all on the level of archaeological science. But it was not a thing to cement good personal relationships, and I have always been sorry that the incident developed as it did.

In Sam's later years at the Peabody, his research and writing did not flag. Ill health—an inner ear problem which made him somewhat unsteady on his feet—did preclude more fieldwork after his Diquis and Venado Beach excavations of the early 1950's; however, he brought out the Diquis report (1963), and was at work on the Venado Beach collections at the time of his death. In addition to these two projects, he wrote and published a masterly study on the *Metals from the Cenote of Sacrifice, Chichen Itza, Yucatan,* (Lothrop, 1952), in which he collaborated with the metallurgist, W. C. Root, and he also published numerous articles of synthesis on Central and South American topics (*eg.* Lothrop, 1959, 1961, 1966).

Sam was intensely interested in technological details and craftsmanship, and he believed in the most thoroughgoing descriptions and analyses of the archaeological remains from these standpoints. The Chichen Itza Cenote gold study is a case in point. Dudley Easby (1965) has written about Sam:

"He wrote with brilliance and clarity on pottery, lapidary work, fine metalwork, navigation, and, together with Rivet and Nordenskiold, was one of the first to consult technical specialists instead of dreaming up technological phantasies."

Sam was as intrigued by Precolumbian art as he was by its technology. He had an all-encompassing visual memory for specimens and for the details of these and a rare good taste. He demonstrated this connoisseurship in two famous "art books", one on the Robert Woods Bliss Collection from Dumbarton Oaks (Lothrop, 1957b) and another brought out by the Skira publishers of Geneva (Lothrop, 1964). He was working on a third at the time of his death in 1965.

To sum up Sam Lothrop's great contributions to American archaeology, we can note that they were heavily substantive and extended over a long period, from 1919 to a posthumously published article of 1966. He was a pioneer and explorer, appraising, describing, and laying out the groundwork for the archaeology of previously little known regions in Central and South America; but, at the same time, the work that he did within the scope of these explorations was in no way superficial. On the theoretical side, Lothrop's outstanding contributions were in the linking of archaeology and ethnohistory-ethnography. In this he was a most exacting documentary scholar, and his studies of this kind have not yet been duplicated for the Nicaraguan, Costa Rican, and Panamanian regions. I am sure that Sam would not have thought of this as "theoretical". To him, it was straightforward archaeology and history, and in many ways he did not distinguish between these two. Today, younger workers may question some of his archaeologic-to-ethnographic "continuities" and his "ethnographic analogies". I know I had misgivings about some of them as much as 30 years ago. He was often too willing to assume such "continuities"; but we must admit that Lothrop had the great advantage of knowing his particular areas of work in intimate detail so that the major guidelines of many of his reconstructions, such as those dealing with Panamanian chief-doms, are probably sound.

Sam showed little interest in such matters as *in situ* pro-cessual development of socio-political institutions. Indeed, even on a broader scale he did not appear to be much interested in evolutionary or broadly diffusionistic interpretations. Along with Vaillant, he opposed H. J. Spinden's imaginative "Archaic Hypothesis" for the development of New World high cultures and agricultural societies. On a specific diffusionistic level, he and Vaillant were right; on a more general evolutionary one, Spinden was more nearly correct. In retrospect, one sees Sam-uel Lothrop as a very "catholic" archaeologist for his time. Fittingly, for his generation, he bridged from the earlier great scholars, such as Eduard Seler, to a later somewhat more an-thropologically and "social-science-minded" group.

Lothrop received wide recognition during his career. He was the winner of the A. V. Kidder Medal for Archaeology in 1957, was awarded the Huxley Medal of the Royal Anthropological Institute in 1960, and the Wenner-Gren Medal for archaeology in 1961. He was elected to the United States National Acad-emy of Sciences in 1951, and he was honored by being made an Honorary, or Corresponding, Member of the Royal Anthropo-logical Institute some years after that.

Although Sam had no formal students, his influence on a number of younger colleagues was great. Doris Zemurray Stone, a distinguished Central American archaeologist and ethnologist, might very well be considered as his star "pupil". In 1961, Stone and other colleagues brought out a *festschrift*, *Essays in Pre-Columbioan Art and Archaeology* (Lothrop and others, eds., 1961), in which the Lothrop, himself, was invited to submit an article and also to be listed as the senior editor of the volume. Some years later, under the auspices of the School of American Research, in Santa Fe, New Mexico, another vol-ume, *Lower Central American Archaeology* (Lange and Stone, eds., 1984), was dedicated to the memory of the man who had pioneered the way in that field.

In 1958, Sam and Eleanor Lothrop were divorced, and he married Joy Mahler Lothrop, an archaeologist and colleague at the Peabody Museum. They established a residence in Belmont, Massachusetts, where he transferred his famous library from New York. In the last seven years of his life he continued, as I have already recounted, with research and writing at the Peabody and also abroad, the latter travels being undertaken for the purpose of visiting museums in Latin America and in Europe in connection with the preparation of his 1964 book on Precolumbian art.

In the summer of 1964, Ledyard Smith, who was a very old and close friend of Sam's, and I were in Madrid for a few days to attend sessions of that year's International Congress of Americanists which was being held in Spain. We had been told that Sam was not well, and one afternoon we went to pay a call on him. The address we had was in one of Madrid's newer apartment buildings, a modern-looking edifice that had been constructed after the Spanish Civil War. We entered the downstairs lobby and were looking for a listing of tenants when an elderly woman, apparently a building caretaker, or the wife of a caretaker, appeared and asked if she could help. We explained that we were looking for "Dr. Lothrop". The name is not one that comes easily to Spanish speakers, and for a moment she seemed at a loss trying to understand us. Then suddenly she beamed forth with a great smile. *"Ah, Don Sam-well! Don Sam-well! Si! si!"* Of course he was here. While a moment ago we had been examined, I thought, with some suspicion, this was all gone now. Clearly, if we were "Don Sam-well's" friends, we were proper people! I thought then of other times, back in Peru. Sam had always been much respected and loved by servants in his home, by familiar waiters in restaurants and hotels, by people like this *Mayordoma.* Some of it, undoubtedly, resulted from the fact that he tipped well, but it was also a kind of upwelling of good feeling, of affection for the man— and for the gentleman.

The woman in the lobby rode up in the elevator with us and rapped on the door of an apartment. When Sam appeared she excitedly told him that he had visitors, "extranjeros". Sam thanked her graciously. *"Por nada, Don Sam-well, por nada"*, and she was gone. Sam was glad to see us. He and Ledyard went back a long time together, in various associations, archaeological and otherwise. We exchanged gossip about the Congress meetings that we were attending. He was sorry he had not been able to come to any of the sessions, but he was being plagued by some sort of a fever that came up every evening. The doctors weren't quite sure what it was, something like flu perhaps. It had interrupted the work on his newest project for another compendium of Precolumbian art, but, all in all, he had enjoyed himself in Spain and had accomplished a lot. He prepared us drinks and grumbled a bit about not being able to take much himself. It was a nice visit, that last one we were ever to have, although we had no idea then that he was seriously ill. We left, going back down in the elevator in the beginning dusk.

A few months after this, at the end of the year, Sam Lothrop returned to Massachusetts, going directly to the hospital. He had continued to fail in health after Ledyard and I saw him, and had returned home for treatment. He died on 10 January 1965—a gentleman, a scholar, and an absolutely first-rate archaeologist.

JULIAN H. STEWARD
In middle age.
Courtesy Mrs. J. H. Steward.

JULIAN HAYNES STEWARD
(1902–1972)

Julian Steward was not primarily an archaeologist but an ethnologist-social anthropologist. Like Kroeber, he was also distinguished as an anthropological theorist. Early in his career Steward did do some "dirt" archaeology, but it is of greater significance that later on he was to have an influence on the development of our discipline in the Americas. He carried out most of his fieldwork—both archaeological and ethnological—in the North American west, especially in the Great Basin and the Interior Plateau country. Like Strong, Steward was a Kroeber student, at Berkeley, coming from there in the 1920s; and he followed Strong to the Bureau of American Ethnology at the Smithsonian. In 1946, Steward left the Bureau to join Strong as a member of the Department of Anthropology at Columbia University. Later, he went from Columbia to the University of Illinois where he remained for the rest of his career. Thinking back, I know now that Julian Steward was my last teacher, in the sense that Cummings, Kelly, Ford, and Strong had been my teachers, and I still feel very close to him.

While Steward was at the Smithsonian, he hired me to work with him on the *Handbook of South American Indians* (Steward, ed., 1946–1959). I became his assistant editor on the project, and I served in this capacity from the fall of 1943 until February of 1946. At that latter date, I left for an eight-month stay in Peru, in connection with the Viru Valley archaeological survey. Steward went to New York and Columbia University in the summer of the same year. While I saw him on a number of occasions after 1946, our last visit being in 1959, most of my memories of him derive from the 1943–1946 "*Handbook* period" in Washington.

Julian Steward was a tall man of medium-slender build and bone-structure. He had sloping shoulders and a long-neck which made him look even taller than his 6' 1". George Vaillant once wrote to Julian, thanking him for speaking at some sort of a function at the University Museum in Philadelphia, and closed his letter with the remark: "Julian, has anyone ever told you that you look like a lewd De Gaulle." The observation—incidentally, a very "Vaillant-esque" one—had some appropriateness. While I don't quite understand George's "lewd" characterization, it is true that Julian, with his long neck, long face, large straight nose, dominating deep-set dark eyes, and sometimes rather lugubrious expression, did have a resemblance to the World War II "Savior of France", whose pictures were then much in the news. But to continue with my description of Julian, he had, at that time, quite thick dark brown hair, which grew back from his forehead in a sharp "widows-peak", very heavy dark eyebrows, and a small dark mustache.

Steward had known me only slightly prior to 1943, but he took me on as his assistant for the *Handbook* upon the recommendations of Strong and of Matthew Stirling, the latter then Chief of the Bureau of American Ethnology. When Steward hired me, I was in Macon, Georgia, with Katharine. This was in the early fall of 1943, and I came up to Washington that October. Julian was kind enough to meet me at the railroad station, and he took me out to his house, across the Potomac in Virginia, where he and his hospitable wife, Jane, put me up for the first few days while I sought lodgings of my own in crowded, wartime Washington.

Driving out from the railroad station to Virginia on that night of my arrival, Julian immediately launched into *South American Handbook* matters: the purpose, the substance, and the trials and tribulations of the project. It was already well under way at that time. This new *Handbook* was to be an undertaking on a much larger scale, and of a quite different nature, than the Bureau of American Ethnology's old *Handbook of American Indians North of Mexico* (F. W. Hodge, ed., 1907–1910). That earlier *Handbook* had been organized as a vast series of alphabetized tribal or topical entries; in contrast, most of the volumes of the *South American Handbook* would follow a geographical and culture area and subarea organization. Each of these geographical divisions and subdivisions would have its tribal articles on modern tribes or tribes of the "historic present", as well as its archaeological articles. There would also be topical volumes, with articles pertaining to things like "ceramics", "architecture", or "weapons", and these would cross-cut both archaeology and ethnology. Archaeology would be well represented; that was the main reason I had been brought on board. Julian told me all this in a very serious, even morose, manner. While I was later to find out that he had a very engaging sense of humor, under the right conditions, and especially if he were warmed up with a couple of drinks, Julian never had what could be called the "light touch", say in the style of Wendy Bennett.

Julian also filled me in on the background of the project. The *Handbook* had its initial sponsorship in the National Research Council. Then he and the Smithsonian had successfully solicited the funds for it from the Office of the Coordinator of Interamerican Affairs of the United States State Department— the same office, I may note, which had made possible the Institute of Andean Research Latin American archaeological program.

Before going further with this personal narrative, let me pause to set down a few biographical facts about Julian Haynes Steward (see Shimkin, 1964; Manners, 1973; Murphy, 1981). Julian was 41 years old at the time of that Washington, D.C. meeting in 1943. Interestingly, he was an old Washingtonian so in coming to the Bureau of American Ethnology job he had, in a sense, "returned home". He had been born in that city on 31 January 1902, the son of Thomas Gifford Steward and Grace (Garriott) Steward. His father was chief of the Board of Examiners of the United States Patent Office. He had been self-trained in this work, and Julian once referred to him as a man of considerable intellectual potential who, had he been given the advantages of a university education, would have gone much farther. On his mother's side, an uncle, Edward Garriott, was the chief forecaster of the U.S. Weather Bureau. Thus, the Steward family, or the extended Steward-Garriott family, were part of that respectable and conservative middle class of Washingtonians whose members made up the Civil Service of the nation's capital in those pre-World War I days. Julian, in his own reminiscences (Manners, 1973, p. 888), saw little in this background that would account for his own career and his interests in anthropology. As far as anthropology was concerned, he was probably right; however, the familial ambience strikes one as favorable for the instilling of intellectual work habits and a sense of duty and dependability. Julian, in conversations with me, remembered his childhood as a happy one. In those days, Washington had many of the qualities of a small town, with its nearby woodlands and ravines as playgrounds for a small boy.

The young Steward must have shown early promise as a student for when he was 16 he was selected to attend what was then a very special and "progressive" school, Deep Springs, located in the mountains near Death Valley, California. Only 20 students, all young men, were enrolled in Deep Springs. In this remote and isolated setting, they were subjected to the austerities of an outdoor life combined with a high-quality and disciplined education. Although I never heard Julian say much about it in later years, the experience must have been a good one for him, and there can be little doubt that it transformed him into a "Westerner", with a love for the mountains and deserts. It was also significant in that it gave him his first view of Indian tribes—the local Shoshone and Paiute.

After Deep Springs, Steward entered the University of California at Berkeley, remaining there for his freshman year of 1921–22. At that time, he had his first course in anthropology, one taught jointly by Kroeber, Lowie, and Gifford. There was a tradition, however, for Deep Springs graduates to go to Cornell so Julian transferred from Berkeley to Ithaca for the completion of his undergraduate years. At that time, Cornell had no anthropological curriculum so he majored in geology and zoology. He was fortunate, though, in being given some special tutorial instruction in anthropology by Livingston Farrand, the President of the University and an anthropologist (Manners, 1973, p. 889). After completing the A.B. degree at Cornell, he immediately returned to Berkeley and entered into graduate anthropology. In so doing, he joined a graduate student group there which included Duncan Strong, Lloyd Warner, and Ralph Beals.

Julian taught anthropology at the University of Michigan from 1928 to 1930, and during this time he received his Ph.D. from California, with a doctoral dissertation on *The Cere-*

monial Buffoon of the American Indian. Both Kroeber and Lowie were his thesis advisors. In 1930 he joined the faculty at the University of Utah, which provided a base for his Great Basin ethnological and archaeological researches. He stayed at Utah for three years. Then, in 1933, he returned to Berkeley as a lecturer in the Anthropology Department for a year. In 1934 he married Jane Cannon. This was a very good marriage. The happy, down-to-earth Jane was the perfect counterpoise to the intense and temperamental Julian. They were to have two sons, Gary and Michael, to make up the Steward family that I first met on that night of my arrival in Washington in 1943.

After his marriage to Jane, the two of them spent more than a year in ethnographic field research in Great Basin-Plateau country. In 1935, Julian was appointed to the Bureau of American Ethnology in the Smithsonian. Once established there, he had the time to write and to publish a series of reports on these 1934–1935 Basin-Plateau investigations. The outstanding monograph, *Basin-Plateau Aboriginal Sociopolitical Groups* (Steward, 1938), was one of these. It is a brilliant treatment of subsistence practices and their socio-political correlates. In these early years at the Bureau, he also did ethnographic fieldwork in the Ecuadorian and Peruvian Highlands, and this experience in South America was to lead, eventually, to his roles in organizing and editing the South American *Handbook.* Such was Julian Steward's background, in sketchiest form, up to the time of my arrival in Washington to work with him.

To return to my narrative, on the day after my arrival, and after my preliminaries with the Smithsonian Personnel Office were completed, Julian installed me in an office in the "Old" Smithsonian building. This "Old Building" is the one tourists recognize by its Gothic towers. Julian's domain was in the large, block-like, lower tower at the eastern end of the building. Here, in a low-ceilinged, garret-like but nonetheless attractive office, he had a three-windowed view of the Washington Mall. A Miss Ethelwyn Carter, Julian's secretary and devoted *Handbook* helper, also had a desk in this office. I was put in a large, high-ceilinged, and bare-looking room across the hall from them. The other member of the *Handbook* staff, its associate director, the distinguished South Americanist, Dr.

Alfred Metraux, formerly had been in the room assigned to me, but he was now in cosier quarters on the floor below us.

A few words are in order about the "Old" Smithsonian. I speak of both the building and the institution. In those days of the 1940s, the Institution was just beginning to emerge from what can best be described as an "earlier tradition". For instance, when I entered on duty in 1943, a regulation, which had been in effect for about three years, prohibited any new staff member from maintaining a spitoon in his office. Those who had entered into service earlier, and who had been customary spitoon-users, were permitted to retain these receptacles, but no new ones were to be issued. I thought of Mrs. Trollope, mother of the great novelist, who, in touring America a hundred years before, had reported that the young Republic was virtually awash in tobacco juice. She would have been pleased at this progressive step taken by the Smithsonian authorities. Obviously, as the newest of the new, I was denied a spitoon, but I bore up under this deprivation manfully. After all, Julian, who had been there well ahead of me, had foregone this nicety.

The interior decor of the "Old" building was very Victorian but at the same time quite appealing. The third floor of the east wing, which was right beneath us, had comfortable and old-fashioned-looking offices opening off two sides of a long hallway. Matthew Stirling was in one of these, and F. H. H. Roberts, the well-known Southwestern archaeologist, was in another. At the far eastern end of the hallway was a large, handsomely carpeted office with a functioning fireplace which glowed enticingly on cold days. These were the quarters of W. P. True, the Smithsonian's chief editor. Three other Bureau of American Ethnology anthropologists—Henry B. Collins, William N. Fenton, and Homer Barnett, the latter quite new, like me—were housed more distantly from us in other parts of the building. If one descended to the second floor, things were much more grand. Here the old hardwood floors glistened handsomely for the offices of the central administration—the secretary, the assistant secretary, and their aides—opened off this hall. The entire building was served by a cadre of Black male employees. Some of these were responsible for the gleaming floors; others, of higher rank, were sedately black-suited and black-tied and served as receptionists or messengers attached to the secretary's office. All were soft-spoken and moved with grave decorum. Such was the physical setting of the Bureau of American Ethnology and its new "child", the *Handbook of South American Indians* project. Julian never seemed particularly sensitive—either through expressions of praise or complaint—to this ambience. As I think about it, Julian was always singularly indifferent to offices, furniture, clothes, or even most personal possessions.

On that first day, Julian showed me the great stack of received *Handbook* manuscripts. Well over half of those assigned had been submitted. He told me that the *Handbook* necessarily would be a multi-volumed enterprise and that he intended to group the articles into large geographic-culture area volumes. It was his intent then that there should be three of these volumes and that they would follow John M. Cooper's (1925, 1941) South American areal classification of Andean, Tropical Forest, and Southern Marginal Tribes. One of the first things he wanted me to do was to make up the tables-of-contents lists for these three volumes. He went back to his editing and left me to it. I felt a bit lost and overwhelmed. I knew about Peruvian archaeology, but now it was my task to group such tribes as the Cocama, the Witoto, the Bororo, and a great many others that I had never heard of before, into their proper geographical slots. At that time we still didn't have a completed master map of South American tribal locations.

Fortunately, I got some valuable assists from Alfred Metraux—whom I met for the first time—and with his help and some reading I sweated through it. For me, those first few days on the job served as an introductory "crash course" on South American ethnography, but I finally came up with the tables-of-contents lists. Julian went over my lists and tribal arrangements and made some changes. Then he pointed to places where we still lacked manuscripts, and told me to get busy on one that I should be able to do with no great difficulty. This was to be on the archaeology of the Argentine Pampa. Apparently, the Argentine archaeologist who had been asked to do this particular piece had not come through, and it didn't look like he would, so we would have to improvise. I had heard of the Pampas and the Puelche tribe, but I had no inkling of what Pampean archaeology was like or really how to begin looking to find out. Julian said that this would be another opportunity for me to further my education and that I would find Sam Lothrop's monograph on *The Indians of the Parana Delta, Argentina* (Lothrop, 1932a) a useful starting point. I could also profit by checking the bibliographies of other *Handbook* manuscripts from surrounding areas. I did these things, involving a month or so of library work, and produced an article (Willey, 1946b). It was characteristic of Julian to be seemingly offhand about such matters as the tables-of-contents or my assigned article. As a teacher, he obviously wasn't a "spoon-feeder", and, although I never studied under him in a formal classroom situation, I am sure he must have handled his students this way. Julian was also a patient boss. He was not a perfectionist; if he had been, the *Handbook* project would never have been completed; but he had high standards of practical scholarship. For the *Handbook*, he was its great driving force, an intellectual leader who led by example, encouragement, and well-timed advice.

In those first months on the job, I was so busy and so involved with settling into the situation, that I didn't really have much exchange with Julian on a serious intellectual level. Pampean potsherds and stone types, while perfectly respectable and serious archaeological concerns, do not, at least on the levels of recognition and description, lead immediately to higher theoretical discourse. I remember Julian being amused at my apparent love of potsherds. This came up after I had begun to prepare illustrations for my own Pampean archaeological article. I had set up one plate which was a fine photographic blow-up of a single sherd of what I called "drag-and-jab incised-punctated pottery". "Now, Gordon," he explained, "we want to have a reasonably thorough archaeological coverage of all areas, but we can't go in for 'sherd portraits', especially ones that look like that." I admitted that perhaps I should restrain myself, and we compromised on no less than four sherds to a plate (see Willey, 1946b, Pl. 16). Similarly, in illustrating Peruvian archaeology, I had tended to overextend us. As Julian put it, "I don't think it's necessary to illustrate every pottery type from every cultural complex." I began to get things into better perspective after a while.

We used to lunch together at a grubby little restaurant on Seventh Street, located somewhere off to the southeast of the Smithsonian buildings. This gave us a chance to talk in a more relaxed fashion, away from the pressures of the job in the office, and I began to appreciate the original qualities of Julian's mind. Not that these came as a surprise to me. As a graduate student, I had read some of his more strictly archaeological papers—"Archaeological Problems of the Northern Periphery of the Southwest" (Steward, 1933) and *Ancient Caves of the Great Salt Lake Region* (Steward, 1937a)—and Duncan Strong, in his lectures at Columbia, had emphasized that Steward was an ethnologist who was also an archaeologist and who synthesized the two disciplines in an imaginative way. I had then been introduced to this kind of synthesis in what have become two famous Steward papers: "The Economic and Social Basis of Primitive Bands" (Steward, 1936) and "Ecological Aspects of Southwestern Society" (Steward, 1937b). The latter has been described as "the first archaeological study of settlement patterns in the New World" (Shimkin, 1964, p. 4), as indeed it is. In it Steward demonstrated the evolution of Anasazi settlement forms, linking the settlement changes through time to subsistence, population growth, population concentration, and socio-political centralization. I remembered the satisfaction I felt in reading this paper and realizing that what I thought of as "functional interpretation" in archaeology need not be limited to figuring out how certain tools or implements were used but could also range over into the more exciting possibilities of understanding social and political organization.

Our first interesting theoretical discussions did, in fact, start out from what seemed to be routine *Handbook* editorial problems. Volume 1, *The Marginal Tribes*, (including Southern South America, The Chaco, and Eastern Brazil) was, by early 1944, pretty well wrapped up as far as editing and illustrations were concerned, and the same was true for Volume 2, *The Andean Civilizations*, (including the Central, Southern, and Northern Andes). With both of these volumes almost ready for the printer, we were working on Volume 3 which had been designated by the title, *Tropical Forest Tribes*. Its original geographical coverage was essentially all of the South American tropical lowlands. One day at lunch we got to talking about how this projected Volume 3 had grown too bulky for a single bound volume of a size comparable to Volumes 1 and 2. I passed this off by saying something to the effect that we would have to split it into two separately bound parts, but Julian had obviously been doing some more serious thinking about the matter. He acknowledged our printing and binding difficulties, but he went beyond these mere practicalities.

He began by saying that our difficulty with the oversized Volume 3 might be resolved by taking a somewhat different look at our material. In his editing of the manuscripts for that volume, he had been impressed by a difference between what he referred to as two basic "culture types". One of these "types" might be considered as truly representative of what we had been thinking of as a "Tropical Forest Tribe". This type was characterized by sedentary village communities with an egalitarian social order. Such societies were larger and more complex than the simple, hunting and gathering band societies of *The Marginal Tribes* of Volume 1, but they were less complex socio-politically than what he now wanted to consider as the next "type" in an ascending order of complexity. Julian wanted to call this new "type" the "Circum-Caribbean Tribe". It was characterized by a more diversified settlement pattern than that of the "Tropical Forest Tribe". Thus, some Circum-Caribbean communities were larger than others and served as social, political, and religious centers for sizable territories. These "capital" towns were the seats of an hereditary ruling elite. In brief, the social order was no longer egalitarian. Julian proposed taking all such "Circum-Caribbean" societies and cultures out of Volume 3 and putting them in a new and separate Volume 4, under the title of *The Circum-Caribbean Tribes*. Looking back on this discussion—or what might better be called Julian's lunch table presentation, as I had added little to any dialogue up to that point—it is evident, from our present perspectives, that Julian was then anticipating a definition of what were to be called "chiefdoms" a few years later (Fried, 1960; Service, 1962).

I was impressed and fascinated by what Julian had said, but then I began to argue with him. I came up on the question from a culture-historical point of view rather than one of social typology. Julian had proposed grouping together the cultures and regions of Lower Central America, Caribbean Colombia and Venezuela, and the West Indies into this new Volume 4. I thought this too much of a violation of culture history. I knew that Caribbean South America and the West Indies had been demonstrated, through archaeology, to be closely related, but I balked at including Lower Central America in this Caribbean-Antillean package. I held that what we knew of the archaeology of Panama, Costa Rica, Nicaragua, and eastern Honduras suggested a whole different set of origins and relationships—one that had little to do with Venezuela and the West Indies.

Julian admitted this but said that he was now speaking of "culture types" rather than culture areas or cultural traditions.

All right, I countered, I appreciated that difference, but went on to say that it seemed to me that a *Handbook* should be organized on culture area and culture-historical principles and not by inferred social typology. I also pointed out that he was shifting the basis of the *Handbook* volume organization in mid-stream. Wouldn't this be inconsistent with what we had already done? I recognized that Volume I, which had a certain geographical cohesion, was also conveniently defined by a single socio-political "type", presumably the simple band society. But what about Volume 2, the volume on "Andean Civilizations"? Were all the cultures and societies in Volume 2 to be typologically classed as "Civilizations"?

No, Julian said. He realized that probably only those of the Central Andes (Peru-Bolivia) would so qualify; those of the North Andes (Ecuador and Colombia) and the South Andes (Northwestern Argentina and Northern Chile) were, to be sure, structurally more like the Circum-Caribbean (or Chiefdom-level) societies.

Well, then, I wanted to know, if we were going to pull what had been planned as Volume 3 apart, on the basis of a social structural typology, shouldn't we do the same for Volume 2?

Julian saw the problem; indeed, he had seen it a long time before I did. We didn't take Volume 2 apart. Things had gone too far along for that. The *Handbook* eventually came out as a

compromise between "culture area" and "culture type" principles of organization. Years later, Steward, along with Louis
Faron, produced a book that was more to his liking in that it
followed a consistent "culture type" presentation—*Native
Peoples of South America* (Steward and Faron, 1959).

Steward's cultural typology, which he devised in the course
of editing the *Handbook,* seems a clear outgrowth of the ideas
he had developed in working with North American Great Basin and Southwestern archaeological and ethnological data.
The typology is obviously evolutionary. This gives it a certain
power for useful descriptive generalizations, and it arranges
the data nicely for some processual interpretations. But the
typology has the potential to mislead in culture-historical reconstructions. I remember that in the *Handbook* days Julian
saw the culture "types"—or levels, or stages, or however one
may wish to designate them—as essentially radiating out of
the Central Andes and spreading to other parts of South America. According to him, they had done this in a sequential
evolutionary fashion. Thus, the Circum-Caribbean groups,
with their "capital" towns and their hereditary rulers, were
territorially marginal reflections of a social and political stage
through which the Central Andean peoples had passed in some
earlier period. He could see little in the way of "advanced"
traits moving in the other direction. For this reason, he was
inclined to dismiss as ill-founded Tello's theories of Peruvian
Chavin origins lying, ultimately, in the Peruvian montana or
the Amazon Basin. There was a problem here, of course, in just
what traits were being considered. Were we talking of such
things as agriculture, basic food plants, pottery, and early settled village life? Or were we considering only social and political structures? For instance, settled village farming communities (quite probably based on maize as well as root-crops) and
pottery now appear to be earlier in the tropical forest and
montana country than they do in the Peruvian highlands or on
the Peruvian coast.

As of the mid-1940's, when Julian wrote two overviews or
interpretive summaries for the *Handbook* (Steward, 1948a,
1949b)—pieces which, by the way, were among his finest generalizing and synthesizing statements—he was inclined to see

the South American montana and tropical forest developments as essentially derivative. Whether he would have held to
these interpretations as steadfastly in later years, I am not sure.
His book with Faron would suggest that he would have modified his original views. Unfortunately, I never had occasion to
discuss these problems with him after the *Handbook* days.
Certainly, we know now, from more recent archaeological research (Lathrap, 1970, 1971, 1973), that the situation is much
more complicated than Steward first conceived it.

Julian, of course, did modify his opinions about cultural and
social evolution with his concept of "multilinear evolution"
(Steward, 1953), and I think that his experiences in trying to
handle culture history and cultural development for all of
South America must have been important in these modifica-
tions. With his deep understanding of cultural ecology, he saw
that the four-fold evolutionary model of the *Handbook*—in
effect: 1) Simple Bands; 2) Sedentary Agricultural Villages; 3)
Chiefdoms; and 4) Civilizations or States—could not be employed in simplistic unilinear fashion.

Julian did a tremendous amount of work on the *Handbook*.
Much of this work was done at home. He would put two or
three hefty manuscripts for editing in his briefcase every evening and bring them back the next morning, marked up and
ready for the printer. He usually wouldn't appear until about
10:00 or 10:30 in the morning. Official Smithsonian Civil
Service starting time was 8:45 AM. I once heard Julian say that
he was too busy to keep "Civil Service hours"; they were "a
luxury he could not afford". Happily, Matt Stirling, the Chief of
the Bureau of American Ethnology, and Julian's nominal boss,
was easy about such matters. I know that some more strict
"Civil Service types" within the organization frowned on
Julian's cavalier attitudes toward "punching the clock"—although nothing was ever said about it, at least on the upper
administrative levels. Not only Stirling, but Alexander Wetmore, the Secretary of the Smithsonian, and the Assistant
Secretary, John E. Graf, were highly supportive of Julian. As
new as I was around the place, even I could sense that there was
a recognition of Steward's fantastic productiveness, of the genius of the man. He got special handling, but he deserved it.

Julian was a great worrier—or at least he carried on like that at times. Some of it was undoubtedly put on; he couldn't have accomplished as much as he did if he had really agonized about all the things he claimed to be worrying about. Gloomily, he would sometimes give voice to dire predictions—the State Department would withdraw its support for the *Handbook*. This would come about through bureaucratic red tape and insensitivity. Everything he had worked for would go down the drain. I don't think he ever really believed any of this. He offered it as a kind of "protective magic", to ward off the evils before such imagined fates could overtake him. Another manifestation of what I came to think of as his "ceremonial worrying"—and also a way to make others worry as well—was to come into the office and announce that at 11 AM that morning he had a very important appointment over at the Office of Inter-American Affairs in the State Department. "Don't let me forget it," he would caution us. He would then get busy on some *Handbook* matter and, inevitably, find some horrible snarl-up. He'd work away frantically, checking back and forth from galley proof to galley proof, muttering away to himself. The clock would work its way around to 10:30, then to 10:40. A nervous Ethelwyn would be telling him that he must get off, that he'd barely have time to get there if he left that very minute. Julian would sigh and say that he "really couldn't afford the luxury of keeping appointments" if *Handbook* contributors, the Government Printing Office, and other incompetents kept putting roadblocks in his way. Eleven O'Clock would come and go with Julian still there in his chair. Ethelwyn would have to telephone the expectant functionaries at the State Department and make excuses.

Another expression of Julian's neuroses was his hypochondria—or at least what I thought at the time was hypochondria. Some of it had its comic aspects. Thus, there were times, during those war years, when steam heat was in short supply, or fed through the Smithsonian's pipes infrequently or sparingly. Julian had a great fur coat. It might have been a genuine coonskin garment of the sort that sporty undergraduates wore to football games in the 1920s—perhaps a relic of Cornell days. It was of ankle-length and had a huge collar. I can still see him sitting there at his desk on slightly chill afternoons, wearing the coat, with the collar turned up around his ears, and with a fever thermometer protruding from his mouth. After a while, he would take the thermometer out, look at it, groan, and resume his work. I could never get him to give me a reading on what the thermometer said. After a while, he'd pack up the briefcase and slouch out of the office, saying to Ethelwyn, or to me, that we might never see him again. But he'd be back the next morning, briefcase in hand and ready for the day's work. When I'd ask him about the fever, or whatever, he'd say something like: "My boy, I haven't time to be sick; it's a luxury I can't afford." Julian did have his share of colds, flus, and so forth, like the rest of us, but during our time together there at the Smithsonian I always thought that he was really pretty healthy. As someone who suffered from a spot of hypochondria myself, I thought I could recognize its symptoms in others. I may have been wrong about Julian. I know he was prone to intestinal disorders. He had come back from fieldwork in Highland Ecuador and Peru, in the late 1930s, with what was probably an amoebic infection. His eventual serious illnesses of much later life—those that led to his death—could very well have had their beginnings at that time.

The Bureau of American Ethnology had a number of new or temporary anthropologists in it, in addition to myself. All of these, in some way, were there as a result of Julian's enterprises, either directly or indirectly. Alfred Metraux and I belonged to the *Handbook* sector of Julian's activities. Metraux was about Julian's age. He was generally conceded to be one of the world's authorities on South American ethnography and ethnology. He was also quite volatile, excitable, and sometimes irascible. He and Julian used to have some flaming rows about *Handbook* particulars. As these proceeded, Metraux would become more volcanic, Julian more muted but equally determined. They often concerned Metraux's corrections on the galley proofs of his numerous articles for the *Handbook*. Metraux would take a nice clean set of galleys that had come back from the Government Printing Office, attack it, and bring it back to Julian with so many slips of text addenda glued to both margins that it looked like a centipede. Julian would remind him that he had already done that to at least two copies of typed manuscript of the piece under question and that Alfred had promised that everything was now in order. Alfred would expostulate, arms waving, that the *Handbook*, with his articles in it, was going to be the last word on many South American ethnographic matters for a very long time to come, and that it was his, Alfred Metraux's, duty to make his contributions just as correct and complete as they could possibly be, even if he had to go over to the Government Printing Office and stop the presses. Sometimes Julian would give in; sometimes he wouldn't. But these were "flash" storms. The next day Metraux, as well as Steward, would appear to have forgotten all about it. Metraux's articles in the *Handbook* are too many to list here, but a glance through Volume 1 will give some idea of the magnitude of his contribution (see, for example, his long article on "Ethnography of the Chaco", Metraux, 1946).

Homer Barnett, whom I have also already mentioned, was in the Bureau then as a replacement for Julian. That is, when Julian went on the State Department grant payroll, his old regular salary was made available for someone else; and Homer, taking leave from the University of Oregon, was appointed on this basis. That is, he was an "indirect" result of Julian's entrepreneurial behavior. More directly, Ralph Beals was with us for a time. He was engaged in founding a new Interamerican journal, another of Julian's "Cultural Relations" ideas which the State Department had bought. The journal, which made its debut in 1943, was *Acta Americana*, in whose first issue Paul Kirchhoff's famous article on "Mesoamerica" appeared.

Julian's founding of the Institute of Social Anthropology in 1943, again a State Department-funded organization, also brought other anthropologists to the Bureau. Some of them were there for only brief periods before they were assigned to field stations; but others, such as George Foster, who was to go to Mexico to set up the Institute's program there, had offices in the Smithsonian for an extended period. The purpose of the Institute of Social Anthropology was to send North American scholars into Latin America to teach social anthropology in existing Latin American institutions. Programs were eventually made operable in Mexico, Colombia, Peru, and Brazil, and these teaching programs engaged the services not only of North Americans but of local scholars. The Institute of Social Anthropology was to continue into the 1950s, and it was very successful—both in its teaching and publication efforts.

And just to keep busy, Julian launched a couple of more things. One of these was to become the nation's River Basins Archaeological Surveys program. He came into my office one morning with a small newsclipping in his hand. It was an announcement that the U.S. Army Corps of Engineers had received a large sum to build a series of flood control dams throughout the nation. Most of these would result in impounding huge reservoirs or lakes and, thereby, inundating large tracts of land. "Here," Julian said, "you're an archaeologist. Don't you think something should be done about this? Or, will you guys sit around until it's too late?" His address to me on the subject was rhetorical; but he went on to badger Frank Roberts about it, and the result was the formation of "The Committee for the Recovery of Archaeological Remains" which led, through a number of steps, to salvage archaeology being funded by the Federal Government throughout the country.

The other "alarm" that Julian sounded was the one that resulted in the reorganization of the American Anthropological Association. A biographer has stated: "He (Julian) was appointed chairman of a committee to plan the reorganization of the American Anthropological Association from a loose scientific forum into a cohesive professional body" (Shimkin, 1964, p. 5). This was quite true, and it occurred at the Annual Meeting of the Association held in Philadelphia toward the end of 1945. But it doesn't say that this happened after several previous months of agitation and a long, and at times fairly fiery, debate, about whether a reorganization was needed and, if it was, how it should be done. Julian was in the midst of the debate, battling down the opposition, right and left. As a matter of fact, he irritated so many colleagues that he lost the election for president of the eventually newly organized body. But that was never an important consideration for him. He wanted the organization changed in what seemed to him to be a needed direction for change.

For me, the most rewarding aspect of my relations with Julian came near the end of our association. This concerned the Viru Valley project and the concept of "settlement patterns". As I have indicated in some of the previous memoirs, planning for the Viru Valley program began in a rather casual way, over lunches in Washington. Wendell Bennett brought up the idea of a single valley study in Peru in which a number of archaeologists and other anthropologists could collaborate. Julian was most enthusiastic about the idea. From the beginning, he was insistent that I join the enterprise. By that time, most of my *Handbook* duties were over, and I was free to participate. Julian went to Stirling, and to Graf and Wetmore, to obtain permission for me to go and to arrange for funds so that I could do so. He gave help through his recently founded Institute of Social Anthropology by making it possible for Webster McBryde, a cultural geographer who was the Institute's representative in Peru, to collaborate with us; and later he sent the social anthropologist, Allan Holmberg, to study the modern Viru community.

When Wendy Bennett, Julian, and I began to talk about just how the archaeologists would share out the chores, I said I wanted to do a test-pitting program for dating sites in the valley and, in so doing, build up a cultural chronology. Julian replied that what I did was up to me but that he thought I could do something more original and more valuable than that. He pointed out that several of the other intended Viru archaeological collaborators were already talking about the joys of test-pitting and stratigraphic digging. Why didn't I, instead, concentrate on overall settlement patterns in the valley, with particular reference to when and how these patterns changed through time and what the changes implied? He reminded me of his 1937 article on "Ecological Aspects of Southwestern Society" and how he had done this in the Southwest. No one, he complained, had ever followed up on this sort of thing. We (the archaeologists) were all too busy running around classifying potsherds. Julian, need I add, had a rather critical eye for much of the archaeological—or for that matter, the anthropological—profession. He thought we were "set in concrete" in what we considered to be legitimate problems and ways of going about attacking them. He went on to tell me that the aforesaid 1937 article—which he then referred to, half in jest, as his "most famous theoretical paper"—had been rejected by the *American Anthropologist* for publication before *Anthropos* accepted it. I followed Julian's advice.

The Viru project came and went in 1946, and I returned to Washington and the Smithsonian that fall. Julian, as I have related, had moved to Columbia and New York in the summer of that year. The *Handbook* was essentially completed, and he had picked George Foster as his replacement as director of the Institute of Social Anthropology. I saw Julian shortly after my return, when he came down to Washington to consult with George. He didn't like the way George was running the Institute. I suppose this was inevitable. Julian wanted to go to Columbia and to enter into academic life, with the training of graduate students there; at the same time, he still wanted to run the Institute. George Foster was an able anthropologist and a sensible man, and he felt, quite rightly, that now that he had taken over the job he should be the one that made the decisions. It was all rather sad, but it was a part of Julian's worrying habit. It was a habit that sometimes led him on to creative efforts, such as those that I have described; but sometimes, as in this instance, it was wasted worry.

Julian and I kept in touch by correspondence, and we met occasionally in New York. He attended the symposium, *A Reappraisal of Peruvian Archaeology,* held there in the summer of 1947, and presented a very brief paper, "A Functional-Developmental Classification of American High Cultures" (Steward, 1948b). It was a kind of "warm-up" for his much more ambitious, "Cultural Causality and Law: A Trial Formulation of the Development of Early Civilizations" (Steward, 1949a). I was very much stimulated by, and enthusiastic about, these two articles. In late 1946, after the Viru survey, I had written a paper comparing the rise of civilizations in Mesoamerica to those of Peru. This had been done in the context of my many discussions with Julian over the previous two years. My paper, which was published five years later (Willey, 1950), was much less ambitious than Julian's "causality" essay. It not only lacked the worldwide scope, but I didn't attempt to face up to "causality". I was more set in a culture-historical out-look, in a word, much closer to Kroeber's approach about such things that I was to Steward's.

Julian and I participated in discussions about what might be called "the rise of civilizations and kindred matters" when I came up to Columbia for the Saturday morning "Kroeber seminars" that I have already described in the Kroeber memoir. In the course of these, I began to appreciate the differences between Julian's views and those of his old mentor. They were intellectual differences, of course, but I thought then, as I do now, that they derived out of very striking personality differences. Julian was, in the best sense of the term, a progressive activist. If he had not gone into anthropology and scholarly pursuits, he might very well have been a liberal, or even a radical, political leader. Kroeber was conservative, cautious, and he abhorred politics.

At Columbia University, Julian launched into a long-term study of Puerto Rico—its social and political history, its demography, economics, race relations, and ideology. He worked closely with his graduate students in this. They had preparatory seminar sessions and research assignments in pertinent literature. The field studies of Puerto Rican communities lasted a year-and-a-half, with writing and analyses of data going on for an extended period after that. Begun in 1947, it was essentially complete by 1951 although the major report did not appear until 1956 (Steward and others, 1956). It stands as one of the most thorough-going social anthropological studies of a nation and its institutions that has ever been carried out.

At the Wenner-Gren symposium, *Anthropology Today*, which Kroeber organized and chaired in the summer of 1952, Julian presented his views on multilinear evolution (Steward, 1953) and had some extended debates with Leslie White who looked upon Julian as something of an heretic who had strayed from the true paths of evolutionary doctrine. I had the opportunity to talk with Julian at some length—over dinners on a couple of evenings. He was much the same as the Julian of the *Handbook*. That is, he was full of fire and ideas. He was also secretly filled with joy and optimism; but, just as in the old days there in the Smithsonian fourth floor office, he tried to cover this up with that pessimistic "protective magic" that I have referred to—a kind of incantation to the gods that would forestall evil. He told me he was leaving Columbia to take up a research professorship at the University of Illinois. He had been promised exceptionally free research time and funding there and was looking forward to it.

At Illinois, Julian drew together and reworked some of his earlier papers which came out in his book, *Theory of Culture Change* (Steward, 1955). This was an important codification of a lifetime of anthropological thinking. I recall that earlier he had once told a colleague and mutual friend, in my presence: "You've got to plan your life. You can't just go along drifting into one kind of research, one kind of teaching, one kind of writing. It has to be a coherent whole." Our mutual friend, who rather enjoyed the unexpected in life, took violent issue with Julian on this pronouncement. I wondered at the time how much of a reconstruction after the fact this opinion of Julian's was. But as one goes through *Theory of Culture Change,* you begin to think that Julian had a case as far as his own professional life was concerned. His fieldwork, his accumulated theoretical writings—these add up to a very coherent, consistent body of opinion or world view. This case for coherence and consistency is borne but even more so in the last great project which Julian conceived of and carried out. In 1956 he obtained a Ford Foundation grant to carry out what he was to call "Studies of Cultural Regularities". It resulted in a three-volume work, *Contemporary Change in Traditional Societies* (Steward, ed., 1967). African, Asian, and Latin American societies and cultures are all treated in this cross-cultural analysis of change brought about through Western-derived modernization. A biographer has said of it:

> " . . . Steward attempted in this program to combine most of
> the major theoretical and research interests that had occupied
> virtually all of his professional career: causal factors in
> change, evolution, cultural ecology, convergence, moderniza-
> tion, levels of socio-cultural integration, and the 'larger con-
> text' or the influence of outside factors on the local culture."
> (Manners, 1973, p. 895)

These themes, all of which are treated in Julian Steward's writings in a way that makes their interrelationships clearly convincing, do make a case for the "planned life."

In 1959, I went to the Darwin Centennial at Chicago. Julian and I were to be on a discussion panel together—the same one I have referred to in my Kroeber memoir. Julian had prepared a paper for the Centennial volume (Steward, 1960). He seemed in good form—good combative form—on the day before the panel was to appear on the stage. He attended the preliminary sessions. But early the following morning, Jane called me from their hotel room and said Julian would like to see me. I went over. He was still in bed, and he told me that he was suffering from a detached retina in one eye and that he had to take it very easy and wouldn't be able to come to the panel. Naturally, he was down in spirits. We talked for awhile. I promised to stop in and see him after the panel session—which I did. The visit that evening was our last.

Julian Steward received appropriate honors in his middle and later years. He was given the Viking Fund Medal in General Anthropology in 1952, and two years after this he was elected to the National Academy of Sciences. On his 60th birthday, his colleagues and former students presented him with a *festschrift, Process and Pattern in Culture: Essays in Honor of Julian H. Steward* (Manners, ed., 1964). The graduate students at Illinois have named a semi-annual anthropological journal after him. He was a Fellow of both the Center for Advanced Study at Palo Alto and a similar center at the University of Illinois. His international reputation was such as to bring him an offer from the Japanese Government to serve as director of the Kyoto American Studies Seminar in 1956–1957. Julian appreciated honors, as does anyone, yet I would say that he was more indifferent—inattentive might be a better word—to them than most of the anthropologists or archaeologists that I have known. He would have preferred an enthusiastic reception of his last great work, *Contemporary Change in Traditional Societies,* to any number of medals. Or, even more to the point, he would have preferred for the messages in this three-volume work to have had an influence on the thinking and actions of other scholars and of government administrators.

That its reception was "lukewarm" (Manners, 1973, p. 895) undoubtedly saddened him; but maybe what he had to say will be better received by an anthropological generation to come.

In the last decade of Julian's life he was plagued by ill health and bad eyesight. In spite of this, and with Jane's good care, he kept working and writing up to the last. All of my portraits are of men committed to anthropology. Julian Steward was second to none in this. He died in Urbana, Illinois on 6 February 1972.

MATTHEW WILLIAMS STIRLING
In old age.
Courtesy Mrs. John Pugh.

MATTHEW WILLIAMS STIRLING
(1896–1975)

Matthew Williams Stirling was an "old Californian"—or an "old Anglo-Californian" would probably be the better way to put it. He once told me that his grandfather Williams had walked all the way out to California from somewhere in the East during the gold rush days. But this adventurous ancestor must soon have forsaken such financially uncertain pursuits as panning for gold dust for he became, instead, a prosperous rancher and one of the largest landowners in the Salinas Valley. The Salinas soon developed into one of the principal truck-gardening districts of the state, and today it is known especially for its lettuce. According to Matt, John Steinbeck, also from that neighborhood and a boyhood friend of his, fixed upon one of his grandfather Williams' ranches as the setting for the novel, "Of Mice and Men". Although Matt followed a quite different career than that of his land owning and ranching grandfather, one can't help but feel that the spirit of adventure which motivated grandfather Williams to walk halfway across the American continent was passed on to his grandson, Matthew Stirling. We shall see some evidence of this farther along.

I came to know Matt Stirling very well in those years, from 1943 to 1950, that I spent at the Bureau of American Ethnology. Matt was chief of the Bureau and had been since 1928. At some time during his tenure, and pursuant to some Government regulation, they were to change the title of his position from "chief" to "director". I always felt that this was much less romantic and preferred the old "Indian" designation; after all, it was more in keeping with our pursuits. During those seven years that I was there, Matt and I saw each other on almost a daily basis. Previous to this, we had met only occasionally. The first time had been in Macon, Georgia when he and his wife, Marion, visited the archaeological excavations there, in the fall of 1936. After that, I called on him in his office in the Smithsonian a few times. I specifically recall a visit I made in 1940. I was a graduate student at Columbia University then, and I had just spent the summer digging on the Florida Gulf Coast. Matt had been engaged in Florida archaeology back as early as the mid-1920s and, again, more extensively, with the Federal Relief-sponsored research there in the 1930s. On that visit, he was kind enough to read over some preliminary writings of mine on the subject. I told him that I wanted to do a Ph.D. dissertation on Florida prehistory, and he very generously responded by telling me that I could have all of the materials and notes from his Florida Federal Relief excavations of the 1930s to incorporate into such an exercise. This generosity was characteristic of him.

In addition to Florida archaeology, and right from the first, Matt and I had sports, as well as archaeology, to talk about. We were both old track men. I remember that in June of 1943, when I was still at Columbia, he called me from Washington and said he was coming up to New York to see that year's N.C.A.A. Track and Field Games and wanted me to go along. He had "lettered" in track at the University of California at Berkeley. He had been a respectable pole-vaulter although he always said his younger—and considerably bigger—brother Gene had far outstripped him in this event. Matt was better in the broad jump (now called the long jump) and the hop, step, and jump (now the triple jump). He had an astounding knowledge of track history, remembering meets, who won what, times, and distances—some of this going back to before World War I. I recall that in his office in the Smithsonian he kept a *World Almanac of Sports* on his desk. When we would disagree over who won the 200 meters in, say, the 1924 Olympics, whether it was Charley Paddock or Jackson Scholz, Matt would take down the *Almanac* and settle the dispute. He was invariably right about things like this.

Physically, Matt was not a large man. I remember him as being about 5' 8" in height and trim and slender in build, but he gave the impression of wiryness and physical toughness; and anyone who had been in the field with him would realize that this impression was correct. He always walked rapidly, albeit with a slight limp in later years, the result of a broken leg from a field accident in Mexico. His hair was grayish and sparse from the time I first knew him, and he had a small gray-white mustache. He had a very open, engaging countenance. The eyes were large and radiated a friendliness and good humor; the nose was quite prominent and high-bridged. He was extraordinarily good and congenial company. When the two of us would set out from the Old Smithsonian building on our way to lunch in one or the other of the restaurants we patronized, Matt would always regale me with a feast of anecdotes about almost anything—archaeology, sports, politics, all in a most amusing manner. He liked to talk about personalities, too. He could appreciate the foibles of his fellow anthropologists and other associates, but his was a kind humor with no mean edge to it. I cannot think of another colleague—at least none who held the kind of position that Matt did—who displayed less formal "side" than Matt. Any weightiness in manner, any hint of pomposity, were completely foreign to his nature.

More precise biographical accounts (see Collins, 1976; Coe, 1976) of Matthew Williams Stirling inform us that he was born on 28 August 1896, in Salinas, California, the son of John William and Ariana (Williams) Stirling. His father had a managerial position with the Southern Pacific Milling Company and was in charge of establishing warehouses throughout the Salinas Valley so that the family had moved about among a series of small towns in the region while Matt was a boy. The young Stirling also spent considerable time on the large ranches belonging to his grandfather Williams. To these facts, I might add that W. W. ("Nibs") Hill, later to be known as a leading anthropologist and ethnologist at the University of New Mexico, was a first cousin of Matt's and a member of this well-established Williams-Stirling-Hill "extended family". The young Matthew proved to be of a scholarly bent. Reading and arrowhead collecting were his favorite boyhood pastimes. He very definitely didn't want to be a rancher or a warehouse operator but planned on going to the university.

Matt entered the University of California on schedule, at age 18, in 1914. The First World War interrupted his studies, and for two years he was a junior officer in the United States Navy. As I remember his stories about his Naval Service, it was all done out in the Pacific. One of his first assignments, when he was still pretty green about nautical matters, was to take a small ship—of whatever kind a twenty-one-year-old Ensign would be put in charge of at that time—down along the coast to Mexican waters, presumably just to "show the flag" in Mexican ports. Afterwards, he was to return to San Francisco. He was the only officer on the ship and the only navigator. It was an intimidating experience. As Matt put it, he was able to "lampost" his way all down and then back up the Baja California coast by taking sightings on landmarks; fortunately, the weather remained clear. Navy life behind him, he went back to the University of California, graduating in 1920. His favorite courses were in anthropology, with Waterman, Kroeber, and Gifford, and his B.A. degree was with them.

The Stirling family went to Europe right after his 1920 graduation, and Michael Coe (1976), his biographer and fellow Olmec-enthusiast, reports that a view of an Olmec-style "baby-face" masquette in a Berlin museum made an impression on the young Stirling that was to remain with him ever-afterwards. But Matt's more immediate introduction to a salaried anthropological career came about in a less romantic manner. In 1921, he and some old college friends were going into San Francisco for a night on the town. One of the friends had to stop somewhere in the city to take a Civil Service examination for the post of assistant curator of Ethnology, then advertised at the U.S. National Museum, a part of the Smithsonian Institution in Washington. Matt went along to the place of examination, and, although he hadn't intended it, he thought he might as well take the exam in preference to just sitting around doing nothing for three hours. When the results of the exam eventually were posted, Matthew W. Stirling's name led all the rest. All of this, by the way, was a story Matt had related to me one time as we walked up Tenth Street to our favorite Chinese restaurant. He said he had been of two minds about taking the job. It sounded as though it might be pretty confining, but then he thought he might as well see what it was like to live in Washington, D.C. Even discounting this a bit as a "vintage Stirling" yarn, Matt could be just this casual and offhand about things many others took quite seriously. The fact that he combined this casualness with a truly deep modesty, led some people in the field to underrate him. The fact of the matter was, he had an absolutely first-class brain.

After he took the job, Stirling did a lot of curatorial and exhibit work at the U.S. National Museum during those first few years in Washington. In the evenings he took classes at George Washington University under Truman Michelson, which resulted in an M.A. degree in anthropology in 1922. But he also found time for travel. As a matter of fact, he always found time for travel, right up to the end of his life. In 1922, he and a friend, Perry Patton, spent a vacation touring southern France and northern Spain. They took in the famous Paleolithic caves in that part of Europe. Matt also told me about an experience he had on that sojourn while crossing through the Republic of Andorra, that small nation in the Pyrenees, between France and Spain. In those days, passports and visas were not the necessity for the traveler that they were to become later. He and Patton had moved through France and Spain without these documents; but at the Andorran frontier they were challenged by a stern guardsman to produce official papers. Matt's ingenuity came to the rescue. It happened that he had a receipt in his wallet from a firm known as the "United States Transfer and Storage Company, Washington, D.C." It was for some personal belongings that he had stored with them while on this journey. Emblazoned, as it was, with an eagle and the large initials, "U.S.", the receipt saw our hero and his companion safely across the border.

Back at the Smithsonian, Matt did one summer's digging out in South Dakota. Then his fieldwork shifted to Florida where he worked as assistant to J. W. Fewkes, who was at that time chief of the Bureau of American Ethnology. Fewkes, who had a long-time interest in West Indian archaeology, was much interested in the possibility of West Indian-Floridian Precolumbian connections. To investigate this problem, he had selected for excavation a mound on Weeden Island, in the Tampa Bay region of the Gulf Coast (Fewkes, 1924). While the Weeden Island site did not prove to be a "key" in any hoped for Antillean-North American connection, it was to become the type-site for the Floridian Weeden Island culture. Stirling carried out most of the excavations there.

It was during this stay at Weeden Island that he became acquainted with some real estate promoters who were plying that part of the state at the beginning of the Florida land boom.

As a diversion for their prospective customers, who were ferried about on a yacht, they frequently put in at Weeden Island where Matt would tell them about the local archaeology. Apparently, he held forth so engagingly in these talks that the real estate people offered him a remunerative job. He was to travel around with them and their clientele as a kind of "dragoman", pointing out Florida sites of interest. As he told it to me, the salary offer was so good he couldn't turn it down; and, in addition to the salary, he was to be given an opportunity to buy and sell some Florida real estate on his own. He took them up on the offer and resigned his Smithsonian position in the spring of 1924.

Before taking up his new job—which would not begin in earnest until the early winter months of 1924—he and his friend Patton again set off on another pleasure tour of their own, this time to Peru. They went from Lima up into the Peruvian highlands and then moved down, by stages, into the montana country and onto the Amazonian tributaries. They traveled most of the way by foot or in small canoes. One recalls grandfather Williams' foot-trek across the United States to California. On one occasion, Matt and Patton were left on a riverbank by one canoeman who had assured them that another would be along shortly to take them on to their next destination. After a long wait, they suddenly heard a torrent of cries from the nearby jungle and saw a horde of Indians—feather headdresses, nose-bones, and all—emerging from the bush and running towards them. The natives were brandishing spears in what appeared to be a very threatening manner. Were they to have the central roles in a cannibalistic feast? As it turned out, the natives were simply giving them a polite but joyous welcome. A few days thereafter they reached Iquitos where they took a Brazilian steamer all the way down to the mouth of the Amazon, a 3000 mile journey in which tedium was relieved only by five meals a day—all fish and manioc.

Back home, Matt's year in the Florida real estate business passed swiftly. He said he did little all of that time except ride around in the yacht and do a little talking. But he also must have found the time to do some real estate buying and selling of his own. In recounting how it all came to an end, he told me that one day in 1925—the climax as well as the year of denoument of the Florida land boom—he was advised that a lot in St. Petersburg had just been sold for one million dollars. When he heard this, he said to himself that "no damned sandbar in St. Petersburg was worth that much" and that the time had come to get out of the business. He did, selling his properties at the top of the market, just before the collapse. In so doing, he emerged with the money to fund a major anthropological expedition of his own.

Matt wanted to go to Dutch New Guinea. Just why he picked that part of the world is not altogether clear, and I don't believe I ever asked him. I think he wanted a look at the real anthropological unknown, a part of the world even more remote and unexplored than the upper Amazon. Anyhow, between 1925 and 1927, he organized and led a Smithsonian Institution-Dutch Colonial Government expedition, although it was financed largely by himself. This was an "Expedition" with a capital "E". It totaled more than 800 people, including canoemen, carriers, and a military escort. Matt brought back ethnological field notes and films on what were, in effect, Stone Age peoples and cultures. He also returned with a very large and splendid collection of material objects which today make up an important part of the Smithsonian's collections. All in all, the very young Matt Stirling had "brought it off" in New Guinea. Given the difficult circumstances which must have beset so complex an operation it was quite an achievement for a 31-year-old.

In addition to anthropological data and specimens, Matt, as might be expected of him, brought back a rich fund of New Guinea stories. Among other things, his expedition had had an airplane attached to it. In 1927, these were very rare in that part of the world; and, as can be imagined, this great soaring "bird" created quite an impression among of natives who had never seen a white man before, let alone one of his flying-machines. One of Matt's anecdotes was about taking a Melanesian chief aloft in it. The chief was asked by the pilot if he wanted to go up. In front of his people he could not refuse without serious loss of face. Gallantly, he got into the plane—that unbelievable monster in the entourage of the strangers—and comported himself nobly under these intimidating circumstances. He was rewarded for his bravery for, when he descended again to earth, he was received by his people as almost a demi-god. Touchingly, secretly, he confessed to Matt, through an interpreter, that he had been "afraid"—but he didn't want anyone else to know it and would appreciate it if Matt didn't tell anybody.

Another of Matt's New Guinea stories reflected his ever-present desire to amuse. He had taken with him into the field a child's "chemistry set". With its ingredients he was able to do things like turning a bowl of clear water into a bright red liquid by dropping into it only the merest pinch of a white powder. Whereas the airplane had been almost too much for them, this quiet, small-scale trick completely captivated the natives. One day, in response to eager demands by his intrigued audience for repeat performances, he dropped some other kind of chemical powder into the bowl and it changed miraculously from red back to a clear color. Matt, whose knowledge of chemistry was anything but profound, said he was more surprised than the Melanesians. Years later, when we were together in Panama, he would perform small sleight-of-hand tricks to captivate the sherd washers or the houseboys around the camp. I think Matt just wanted the people around him to be happy. It made him feel good, too.

Matt took his work seriously, but he refused to take himself seriously. He had an easy address to matters that others might become more uptight about. Sometimes this paid off in unexpected ways. I am reminded of a story he told me about an encounter he had shortly after he became chief of the Bureau of American Ethnology. He was at a dinner given for the Regents of the Smithsonian and found that he had been seated next to none other than the Vice-President of the United States, the eminent Charles G. Dawes, who held that position under Calvin Coolidge. In the course of the dinner, Vice-President Dawes, having learned that Matt was an authority on Precolumbian civilizations, spoke to him about a problem which he, Dawes, felt had been neglected in such studies. This was the matter of the "Lost Continent of Atlantis". Indeed, Dawes felt so strongly about this that he said he would like to contribute in the funding of research that would throw light on this ancient land mass which had disappeared so mysteriously beneath the sea, along with its inhabitants. Could he, Stirling, be of any assistance in this? Matt was not at a loss. He replied that, yes, he knew of a distinguished archival scholar, one Charles Upson Clark, who was seeking financial support to spend a year in the Archives of the Indies, in Sevilla, Spain. The Archives were a vast treasury of uncatalogued manuscripts, and who could say that among them there would not be one to throw light on this perplexing question. Intrigued, Mr. Dawes promised to send Stirling a check to support such work. He was as good as his word, and so was Matt. With the vice-president's generous gift in hand, Matt was able to despatch Clark to Sevilla. As it turned out, Clark found no traces of Atlantis in his archival searchings, but he did come up with the remarkable *Compendium and Description of the West Indies*, by Antonio Vasquez de Espinosa. This hitherto unknown document was translated and edited by Clark and eventually published by the Smithsonian (Vasquez de Espinosa, 1942). It remains a major source on early Spanish Colonial America. A more severe scholar than Matt would surely have let this Dawes windfall escape.

After New Guinea, Matt was to have other expeditionary achievements—ones that would establish his reputation not only as an explorer but as a pioneer in archaeological ideas and scholarship. But to tell about these, it is first necessary to take him back to the Smithsonian Institution.

In 1928, not long after the New Guinea trip, the Smithsonian Institution, for the second time, offered Matthew Stirling a job. This time, in contrast to the Assistant Curatorship of seven years before, it was the post of Chief of the Bureau of American Ethnology. His old Weeden Island mentor, J. W. Fewkes, was retiring. After a due and proper search, a Smithsonian committee selected Stirling, the leader of the publicized New Guinea expedition, to be Fewkes' successor. As such, Matt would follow a distinguished line of earlier chiefs—J. W. Powell, W. H. Holmes, F. W. Hodge, and Fewkes. The offer came as a complete surprise to Matt. He was both awed and honored. He was only 32 at the time.

Over the next ten years, Matt, as the new Chief, brought some distinguished talent to the Bureau by making a number of new appointments. With Frank H. H. Roberts, Jr. already on the staff, Matt added, among others, Henry B. Collins, William Duncan Strong, Julian H. Steward, and William N. Fenton. His own research in this period included an ethnological study of the Jivaro Indians of Ecuador (Stirling, 1938), a trip to Guatemala and Honduras, and, especially, his work in Florida archaeology. The results from these Florida digs, as I have recounted, were those which were turned over to me for final study and publication (Willey, 1949). Matt did, however, write one very important short article as a by-product of all of his Florida field experience. It was entitled, "Florida Cultural Affiliations in Relation to Adjacent Areas" (Stirling, 1936). In it, he not only placed the Florida cultures in the larger Southeastern archaeological picture—insofar as this could be done at that time—but he mapped out the cultural subregions of Florida and presented the beginnings of an archaeological chronology for the Gulf Coast as a guide for those who were to follow him (see Goggin, 1947, 1949).

But Matthew Stirlings's reputation in archaeology will rest on what he did next. This was to put Olmec archaeology on the map. It has already been noted that Matt was enchanted by an Olmec mask seen in a European museum early in his life. Like George Vaillant, Matt had a great sensitivity or "feeling" for art styles. He has described the almost uncanny fascination Olmec art had for him, as well as for Vaillant, Covarrubias, and many others (Stirling, 1968). Michael Coe and David Grove are two of the better known present-day Olmec "addicts" (see Coe, Grove, and Benson, eds. 1981), and most of us in Mesoamerican archaeology were certainly susceptible to the appeal of one of the New World's greatest art styles (see also Willey, 1962). By the early 1930's, Matt had read what little had been written about the Olmec style (see Stirling, 1968). It had first come to archaeological attention in the 19th century when one of the famed "great stone heads", was described by Jose Melgar (1869, 1871). This was the one at Hueyapan (or Tres Zapotes), in Veracruz. After that, it had been forgotten. Then, in the 1920s, Frans Blom and Oliver La Farge (1926) discovered and illustrated other similar heads, one of which was at the site of La Venta, in Tabasco. Hermann Beyer (1927), in reviewing the Blom-La Farge report, gave the name "Olmec" to the heads and the style they represented. The name was then applied by Marshall Saville (1929) to smaller carvings, especially jadeite figurines and axes. In 1932 Albert Weyerstall addressed the Olmec issue again, with special reference to the Hueyapan, or Tres Zapotes, head.

Matt's interest in Olmec art was also related to his dissatisfaction with the hypothesis that civilization in Mesoamerica arose with the Maya. He had noted that the well-known Tuxtla statuette, with its Long Count bar-and-dot hieroglyphic date, was a carving in the Olmec style. It came from Veracruz, and its date was earlier than any of the Maya Lowland Initial Series dates. Could it be, he asked himself, that Mesoamerican time-counting and calendrics had origins elsewhere than the Maya Lowlands and with peoples other than the Maya? Could these origins have been somewhere along the southern Gulf Coast of Mexico, in Veracruz and Tabasco—the territory which lay immediately to the west of the Classic Maya? This was Olmec country, so was the Olmec archaeological culture in some way involved in these origins? That the beginnings of Mesoamerican civilization might be found in areas adjacent to the Maya Lowlands, rather than in the Maya area proper, was an old idea with Matt. In an attempt to pursue it, he had encouraged Duncan Strong to work on the eastern, or Honduran, edge of the Maya domain. While Strong's work had revealed some interesting Preclassic developments on this eastern margin, it had not conclusively settled the question of the beginnings of "high cultures" (Strong, Kidder, and Paul, 1938). Why not address the problem now on the western margins, particularly in view of the Olmec presence there? This was the course of reasoning that led Stirling into southern Veracruz and Tabasco.

Before seeing Matt off to the Mexican Gulf Coastal country, we should record an important change in his life and, in so doing, introduce someone who was to be a companion and colleague in all of his subsequent expeditions. In 1933, he married Marion (Illig) Stirling. Eventually, they were to have two children, a son, Matthew Jr., and a daughter, Ariana. Mar-

ion had been his secretary in his early days as chief of the
Bureau of American Ethnology. She was a tall, dark-haired, and
attractive girl. She was also an intelligent young lady who was
interested in Matt's work. Marion had accompanied him on his
trips into the Southeastern United States, such as the one
when I first met them in Georgia. In 1938 she went with Matt
on his first exploratory trip to Veracruz. As a result, she too
became an Olmec enthusiast (see Pugh, 1981).

On the 1938 Veracruz trip, no digging was planned or carried
out. Matt simply wanted to see for himself the "great stone
head" of Hueyapan which had attracted the attention of Melgar and Weyerstall. What was its setting? No one had described
this. He reasoned that it must be an archaeological site and
that this would be a place to excavate and to learn something
about the ephemeral Olmec. Hueyapan, or Tres Zapotes, was
difficult of access, requiring an eight-hour horseback ride from
the town of Tlacotalpan, but the ride was worth it. The giant
head, buried up to its eyes, was situated in the center of a large
complex of earth mounds. Pottery was abundant at the site.
This was a place for a serious dig. Photography of the semi-
buried great stone head immediately captured the imagination
of the officials of the National Geographic Society, and they
offered a grant for this first Olmec work.

With National Geographic funding, Matt and Marion returned to Tres Zapotes for two seasons of work, in 1939 and
1940. During the first season, Clarence W. Weiant served as
Matt's assistant while Philip Drucker had this position in the
second season. Both were encouraged by Matt to publish significant reports on the ceramics and ceramic sequence at the
site (Weiant, 1943; Drucker, 1943a). A highpoint of the first
season was discovery of Stela C, a fragment of a monument
with a partial bar-and-dot date which the Stirlings interpreted
as pertaining to Cycle 7, with a reading at 31 B.C. in the 11. 16.
0. 0. 0 Correlation (Stirling, 1939, 1940a). This was about 350
years earlier than the then earliest known Maya Initial Series
inscription from the Maya Lowlands. Thus, it looked like Stirling might be right with his hypothesis of an early civilization
on the western borders of the Maya area. Here was a Long
Count carving that antedated those of the Classic Maya, and it

was obviously related to the mysterious Olmec. How would the "high priests" of the closed circle of Maya scholarship take this?

Stirling was not a Maya scholar nor a hieroglyphic expert nor, at that time, even a recognized authority on any aspect of Mesoamerican archaeology. How dare he meddle in such sacred matters as Maya calendrics and epigraphy? In 1941, J. Eric S. Thompson, the acknowledged "Dean" of Maya studies, and certainly one of the world's foremost authorities on the Maya Calendar, published an article (Thompson, 1941) rejecting the early date on Stela C. It should be explained that when it was first discovered Stela C was a fragment. The upper part of the monument, with the number for the cycle or baktun, was missing. Because of this, the Stirling's placement of the date in the 7th Cycle was a reconstruction based upon the remainder of the inscription. Thompson doubted this placement. Moreover, Thompson demanded, how could the Stirlings assume that the Tres Zapotes date, occurring as it did in a non-Maya site, was in the same system as the Maya Long Count dates? After considering the matter thoroughly, in all of its aspects, Thompson concluded that Stela C more probably should be assigned to the Early Postclassic Period (ca. 1000–1300 A.D.)— or well after the time the Classic Maya had ceased carving Initial Series dates. It was well-known, he said, that this southern Mexican Gulf Coast country was the homeland of various Postclassic Nahua-speaking tribes, including the Olmec. Thus, it was quite reasonable, thought Thompson, that these Olmec were the authors of the stone sculptures at Tres Zapotes. But this did not mean that any great antiquity was involved—certainly not an antiquity that would put such a monument in the 7th Cycle. Parenthetically, it should be explained here that the use of the ethnic name "Olmec" for the style of the Tres Zapotes stone monuments did not enlighten the argument. This was an ethnic attribution which can be blamed on Hermann Beyer. It was to plague "Olmec" archaeological studies for years, or until the ethnic implications were finally rinsed out of the name by its common usage as an archaeological term.

Matt didn't become very exercised about the rejection of his claims by the Maya establishment. He just quietly stuck to his position and went about doing more archaeology in the area. In 1941, he, Marion, and Philip Drucker shifted operations to Cerro de las Mesas, also in Veracruz. For the most part, this proved to be a later site, and the monuments there clearly dated to the Maya Classic Period; however, their inscribed dates left little doubt but that the peoples of the Olmec tradition were familiar with, and operating in, the Maya Long Count calendrical system. With his usual luck for discoveries, Matt found a splendid cache of Olmec style jades—presumably an "heirloom cache"—in the Cerro de las Mesas digging. The ceramics of Cerro de las Mesas were promptly published by Drucker (1943b). Stirling and his party also visited and worked at La Venta, a major Olmec sculptural center in Tabasco. He was to return there for more excavation, but prior to this he continued a survey of sites in southern Mexico, going to Piedra Parada, San Lorenzo, and south to Izapa, near the Pacific coast. He wrote and published descriptions of monuments from Tres Zapotes, Cerro de las Mesas, La Venta, and Izapa in his *Stone Monuments of Southern Mexico* report which appeared with admirable swiftness (Stirling, 1943); and he was to follow this with two other short survey reports on other southern Mexican sites (Stirling, 1955, 1957). After World War II, Drucker (1952) brought out the first monograph on the La Venta site.

When I first came to the Bureau, Matt was still involved in his Olmec and southern Mexican fieldwork, and he would continue with it through 1946—a total of eight seasons. I was unconvinced of the early dating of Tres Zapotes and, by implication, of La Venta. I remember arguing with him and expressing the view that the earliest ceramics at the two sites were probably Formative or Preclassic but that the great stone heads and the other sculptures were more likely on the Classic Period level. I felt that Olmec was neither a "mother culture" for the Maya nor a Postclassic manifestation but an essentially Classic Period development. Matt said he admitted there was some ambiguity in the Olmec ceramics and the ceramic sequences; we just didn't know enough yet about Gulf Coast pottery developments. Possibly I was right about Olmec great art being of Classic date, but he couldn't reconcile this with Stela C and the Cycle 7 Long Count date. He remained convinced that the date he had placed on it was the correct one.

Olmec dating was not to be resolved until more than a decade later. For a time, Drucker (1947, 1952) was hesitant about just how La Venta and its various levels and periods dated, and he, too, left the door open for a Middle La Venta phase, the one associated with the big sculptures, being as late as the Early Classic Period. Radiocarbon dates finally were to settle the question. They turned out to be overwhelmingly in favor of an Early-to-Middle Preclassic dating of Olmec sculptures (ca. 1200–600 B.C.) (Drucker, Heizer, and Squier, 1957, 1959). This was subsequently to be confirmed by Coe (1968) and Coe and Diehl (1980) at the San Lorenzo site. Tres Zapotes Stela C, dating at only 31 B.C., was then seen as an "Epi-Olmec" monument, pertaining to the Late Preclassic Period. A final justification for the Stirlings' 31 B.C. date on this stela came when, in 1972, a local farmer found the upper portion of the column with its Cycle 7 number.

Matt was never one to crow over being right anymore than he was one to become furiously embattled when someone accused him of being wrong. When I talked with him about it, after the radiocarbon results had come in, he just lit another cigar and looked up at me with that twinkle in his eye and said, "Well, archaeology's funny stuff; there are always a lot of surprises in it." He did, though, take great satisfaction in his whole Olmec venture. He realized it was a significant contribution and that it had advanced Mesoamerican prehistory. He was also happy that he had become a beloved figure down in the Veracruz and Tabasco country. As Michael Coe (1976) has related, he and Marion were "Don Mateo" and "Dona Mariana" to the country people there, dignitaries worthy of a special celebration, when they visited the region a quarter of a century after the period of their excavations.

In the years following the fieldwork, Matt wrote and published an important paper on Olmec jades (Stirling, 1961), and he also did a summary essay on Olmec sculptures for the *Handbook of Middle American Indians* (Stirling, 1965). His Olmec valedictory was his little paper on "Early History of the

Olmec Problem" for the Dumbarton Oaks symposium. It is a characteristically straightforward piece. He does not put himself or his ideas to the forefront. Instead, he gives credit to the Mexican archaeologist, Alfonso Caso, who was one of the few to support him in his argument for Olmec antiquity and its importance as Mesoamerica's "first civilization" (see Caso, 1953).

In 1946, when Matt was on his last Olmec season, I was in the Viru Valley in Peru. I returned to Washington somewhat later than he did that year. Julian had gone now, to Columbia, so I saw more of Matt then than of anyone else around the Smithsonian. Matt, as I believe I mentioned in the Steward memoir, had an office on the third floor of the old Smithsonian building. I would stop by there most days to see if he wanted to go out to lunch.

This office, at least as it was then, deserves some attention. One entered from the hall into a very large room. It was light and airy—the floors polished to a perilously glossy slickness—and with a bank of windows in the opposite wall which opened out onto the Mall. Besides various file cases and cabinets, and the famous Smithsonian paintings of 18th century Indian chiefs hanging on the walls, there were two desks in the room, both facing toward the outer door from which you entered. Behind the larger one on the left, was a sedate and serious male secretary, a man with years of seniority and rank in the secretarial hierarchy of the Civil Service. A female secretary, clearly of lesser rank, was at the smaller desk on the right. Strange visitors were always confronted by the former, who usually rose from his desk with an inquiring but impeccably polite, "Yes?" After one had identified oneself and put one's business, this slightly austere secretarial gentleman would inform you that Dr. Stirling was, indeed, in, and, if you had an appointment, that he was expecting you. This was always a little disconcerting for the first-time visitor for, as you looked around, there was no Dr. Stirling in the room nor any obvious door that might lead to where he was sequestered. But the secretary would then go over to the far left-hand corner of the room which, you then noticed for the first time, had a deepset aperture in it. He would announce your presence, then stand back and motion for you to come forward and enter. This aperture, you discovered when you got to that corner of the room, was low and vaulted; a tall visitor would have had to duck to pass through it. You stepped down two steps, between medievally thick walls, and were in Matt's office. It was a tiny hideaway, probably not more than eight or nine feet square. Tall windows, from floor to ceiling, were on both sides. Matt was to be found sitting there behind a desk, with a bookcase at his back, and, usually, a cigar in hand. There was room for an extra chair for visitors and that was about all.

Matt was never one to pay too much attention to Civil Service routine. He let it all flow around or over him. I was fascinated by one aspect of this routine in his office. The male secretary, who was highly adept at shorthand, would take dictation from Matt in the inner room. He would then take his stenographer's notebook over to the lady assistant at the other side of the room in the outer office and re-dictate the letter to her. It was her responsibility, then, to type it up. After which she returned it to her male colleague who then took it into the sanctum for the Chief's signature. I'm sure Matt never thought this up; as a matter of fact, answering letters was a great bore for him; but, seeing as this extraordinary routine was well-established, I suppose he just went along with it.

I looked forward to my lunches with Matt. He always had something to relate. Perhaps an irate anthropologist from a Latin American republic had called in that morning to present an indignant protest over not having been invited to submit an article to the *Handbook of South American Indians*. Julian, of course, would have been the proper one to have borne this expostulation, but he was gone now so Matt had soothed the injured feelings. Or, maybe a wild-eyed visitor from Montana or Idaho had arrived with a story of a golden treasure located in a remote place in his state and had demanded to know why the government's archaeologists could not come out and help him, a taxpayer, find it. Whatever it was, Matt took it in stride.

Sometimes at those lunches, after reviewing the fortunes of the "Redskins" and the "Senators" (the baseball ones, not those on Capitol Hill), we might get off onto archaeology. It was at one such lunch that Matt said he thought he'd let the Olmec rest for a while and go somewhere else on his next dig. I wanted to know where. Would he be interested in shifting to Peru? Well, he thought both Peru and Mesoamerica had seen a lot of archaeologists—not that there wasn't still a lot to do in both areas—but why not launch into some place "new"? How about somewhere in between? The very general problem of Meso-american-Peruvian relationships loomed, and would very likely "loom" for a long time, but so why not make a beginning, he asked? If someone were going to do this, I responded, wouldn't it be better to work out from the "edges" of either southern Mesoamerica or northern Peru? That way we would be working from the more or less known to the definitely unknown. Matt admitted the logic of this, but then he said it might be more interesting to leap right out in the middle. In other words, why not Panama?

This is how we worked our way around to going to Panama. By now it was sometime in 1947. As we had sort of planned this together—if, indeed, our rambling lunchtime discussions could have been dignified by that name—Matt asked me if I wanted to go, and I assented immediately. This called for some more serious planning. I read over the extant Panamanian archaeological literature: Lothrop's (1937–1942) Cocle volumes, Linne's (1929) Darien study, and Holmes (1888) and MacCurdy (1911) on the Chiriqui region. Just where in Panama were we going to go? Matt said we better stay away from the Atlantic side of the country; it rained over there all the time. I wondered if there were any shell mounds reported from the Panamanian coasts; such sites might lead us to earlier materials than Lothrop's Cocle polychromes. We asked Sam Lothrop about that possibility, but he had no information. Matt suggested that we go into the general region where Lothrop had worked—on the Pacific side of the Isthmus, north of the Canal, somewhere in the vicinity of the Azuero Peninsula. Were we too hit-and-miss, too randomly casual in our approach to just where we were going to dig? I suppose that you could say that we were. Other than our very general idea of working somewhere between Mesoamerica and Peru, we had no problem. We wanted to gather descriptive archaeological information reinforced, where it could be, by distributional and chronological data.

Did it really matter all that much just where we began? Matt obviously didn't think so. I think he would have thought it faking if we had claimed we were going to such-and-such specific region and site to attack a very particular problem—and he would have been right. I don't say this to decry problem-oriented archaeology or to imply that Matt had no appreciation of such. His Olmec work was certainly problem-oriented, right from the first, and it became more so as he went along in it. We just didn't know enough about Panama to be problem-oriented.

If we were going to follow in Lothrop's footsteps, we thought it might be a good idea to go up to Harvard and talk further with him and to review his collections which were stored in the Peabody Museum. We did this in November of 1947. Sam suggested that we go right back to Sitio Conte where he had found his spectacular burials with the polychrome ceramics and goldwork. Matt didn't say anything then but told me later that we might be broadening Panamanian archaeology a bit more if we went somewhere else—somewhere previously unexplored. After all, both Sam and Alden Mason had had a crack at Sitio Conte. I fully agreed. In December, Matt very sensibly flew down to Panama to make arrangements for our trip. These were successfully concluded with Alejandro Mendez, long-time Panamanian educator and then head of the National Museum in that country. In so doing, Matt had gotten us off to a good start before we had even left Washington.

The full expedition—Matt, Marion, Richard Stewart, the National Geographic photographer, and myself—left by ship for Panama the day after New Years' of 1948. One of our key contacts in Panama was Karl P. Curtis. Originally a Massachusetts man, and a retired Canal Zone employee, he was the one who had alerted Professor Tozzer to the Sitio Conte gold finds which led to Lothrop's excavations there. Matt had been in communication with Curtis, and the latter met us at the boat in Colon. A day or so later, Curtis and our party drove north (or actually west) from Balboa to the Cocle region and beyond, ending up in Chitre, the capital city of Herrera Province. We looked at a number of sites in the vicinity which Curtis knew about, but we couldn't tell much from such a quick survey.

These were all known as cemetery locations to Curtis, who had dug in some of them or knew of collections that had been obtained from them. All were grown over and showed no surface features, not even visible sherds.

We liked the looks of the little town or Parita, a short distance to the northwest of the larger and busier Chitre. On a hilltop just above the Parita River, about a kilometer from the town, we also saw a site that appeared as a promising place for excavation. A modern farm on the location had resulted in the removal of the heavy grass cover, and the ground was littered with sherds, including many polychromes of a general Cocle, or Cocle-like, genre. We had to begin somewhere and this seemed a favorable spot. After arranging for the rental of a house in the town, and with the help of a member of the Pinilla family, we made arrangements to dig at what came to be known as the Sixto Pinilla Place. This turned out to be a site, like many others in the region, which had been both a village and a cemetery. There was no great depth to the refuse, but we found a number of pit burials, most of which were accompanied by polychrome pottery. Matt told me, during the first few days, that he wanted me to be the one to study the collections and prepare the report on this and any other sites we might excavate during the season. As it eventually devolved, our 1948 work at Sixto Pinilla and other sites, plus some others which I was to excavate later, in 1952, was to result in publications by myself and my graduate students at Harvard in the following years (Willey and McGimsey, 1954; Willey and Stoddard, 1954; Ladd, 1964).

We worked a five-day week at Sixto Pinilla, and on the weekends we traveled around, with the alcalde of Parita as our guide, to look at a number of other sites. I remember, particularly, one Sunday trip when we left the highway in our pickup truck and drove for quite a distance over a nearly impassable road to a small finca. Near here, our guide told us, was a place where some remarkable burials had been found. The exact location was not far away. We set out on a hike through the bush that soon became a nightmare jungle operation as we clawed our way through an endless tangle of vines and undergrowth. After a good two hours of this, in the sweltering heat, we emerged, scarred, torn, and exhausted, into a little clearing. This was it, the place where the burials had been exhumed. There was, of course, nothing unusual to see—until I looked up in the direction of a roaring noise, and there, less than 100 yards away was the Panamanian Highway, with a truck grinding by. Clearly, under the leadership of our guide, we had done this one the "hard way". Matt always took a "character-building experience" like this in much better part than I did.

Later in the season, Matt, surveying on his own, found two other sites of considerable interest. One of these was Monagrillo, a shell mound, near the Rio Parita delta. It proved to be very early, and has become the type site for the earliest ceramic horizon of Central Panama (2500–1000 B.C.) (Willey and McGimsey, 1954). The other site was El Hatillo, about five miles west of the town of Parita (Ladd., 1964). It was distinguished by nine small mounds. When we dug there, the owner, had three domiciles, located individually on three separate mounds. In each was a separate wife and family. It remains a matter of speculation as to what degree this replicated ancient settlement arrangements under the site's Precolumbian seigneur. The El Hatillo occupation and ceramic style was found to bridge the local chronology from the end of the Late Cocle Period virtually to the Spanish *entradas* to the region. We finished that season's digging at El Hatillo sometime in April—the hottest and dryest month of the dry season in Pacific Panama. At lunchtime on our last day, after the completion of our excavations, and in order to close things down as swiftly as possible, we went to the owner and asked him how long it would take for our crew to backfill all of our excavations as we had promised to do. That polygamous gentleman contemplated this question for a while and said that it would take about one week. Accordingly, Matt gave him the money to pay the crew for that period of such intensive labor—to be undertaken under the owner's direction and to his satisfaction after our departure. We were later informed that the boys had finished it all up that same afternoon although we never did find out just how the funds were disbursed.

On our last night in Parita, the townspeople, including all of the men of our crew (numbering about 20) plus their womenfolk and offspring, as well as several town dignitaries, converged on our residence and honored us with a "despedida". Singing, dancing to the beat of the wooden drums or "tambores" and general merrymaking went on to midnight. We had been forewarned sufficiently so that we had a good supply of cane rum and Coca Cola on hand to carry everyone through the evening. We were all properly toasted, especially "Don Mateo" and "Dona Mariana".

After that 1948 season, Matt and Marion went in the three successive years to other regions of Panama (Stirling, 1950, 1953a,b, 1955) and then, still continuing with Intermediate Area cultures, to Ecuador (Stirling, 1963; Stirling and Stirling, 1963) and Costa Rica (1969). Matt retired from the Bureau of American Ethnology in 1958 but, as the above dates indicate, he continued traveling and digging almost up to the end of his life. He continued his Smithsonian affiliation as a research associate of that Institution, and he became an active member of the National Geographic Society's Committee on Research and Exploration.

Matt died at his home, in Washington, D.C., on 23 January 1975, just short of his 80th birthday. While those of us who worked with him appreciated his keen intelligence, always sparked by liveliness and wit, I don't think that the profession at large became aware of the magnitude of his contributions until after he was gone. These were commemorated in the volume, *The Olmec and Their Neighbors* (Coe, Grove, and Benson, eds., 1981), in which all of the leading Olmec scholars of the time dedicated articles to his memory. They, as well as many others who knew him, remembered his leadership, his unruffled perseverance, his many kindnesses, and that quiet greatness which underlay his modesty.

ALFRED MARSTON TOZZER
In middle age.
Courtesy Photo Archives, Peabody Museum, Harvard University.

Alfred Marston Tozzer
(1877–1954)

In those first years after I came to Harvard, in the early 1950s, the door to my office, Room 37 in the Peabody Museum, would frequently be flung open of a morning, and my distinguished predecessor, Mr. Alfred Marston Tozzer, coming from just across the hall in Room 36, would purposefully stride in, with the admonition, "Now look here. . . ." So alerted, I would then be briefed, with varying degrees of sternness, depending on the issue or infraction at hand, as to how I might better, or best, deploy or comport myself in my new environment at Harvard University. The advice, although often critical, was always well-intended—and most of the time I think it was good. Anyhow, I always followed it. For Tozzer knew his Harvard: he knew about its administration, its professors, its students, and most aspects of its academic and social life. I always felt "good", if sometimes chastened, after one of these morning confrontations—"good" in the sense of "secure". I was being "looked after" by this senior and great colleague, by the knowledge that he had my welfare at heart. It was an honor to me that he cared and that he looked upon me as a kind of continuation of himself. I was the "new man", and I could do with some guidance. Indeed, there hadn't been many other professorial appointees around the Department of Anthropology or the Peabody Museum for some time who had been quite so "new". I had never been a Harvard student, undergraduate or graduate, and had only visited the place once before coming there as Bowditch Professor in 1950. Tozzer saw to my academic well-being, and he kept me up to the mark for four years, from 1950 until his death in 1954. I am forever in his debt.

It is from this brief period that I have my memories of Alfred Marston Tozzer. As a child often does in remembering a parent, I look back upon that time now and wish that I could in some way recapture it, or at least some "Tozzerian" essence of it, for it went by so fast when it happened that I didn't properly appreciate it. Around Harvard in the 1950s, Tozzer was "Mr."

Tozzer. There was a kind of ritualistic reverse snobbery in this appellation, this subtle title which seems now to have disappeared from the Harvard scene. In those days, an undergraduate or a graduate student, was, naturally, a "Mr.", or, sometimes, a "Miss". A young, or sometimes a not so young, Ph.D. was a "Dr." The title "Professor", was obviously the generally desired one among the faculty, and, although there were Assistant and Associate Professors, there was a tendency, at least within the closed Harvard context, to restrict this title to Full Professors. But beyond and above that, and bestowed in some indefinable way, there was the special, elevated title of "Mr." It carried with it a kind of "seniority with distinction." Not all senior professors made it. It took something more than just years of tenure to receive that accolade—perhaps committee work over and beyond the call of duty or various honors within one's profession. The criteria were never quite clear. But "Mr. Tozzer" very definitely had made it. He was one of the "Mr. Harvards", and he was loyally and fiercely dedicated to his old college and university.

Needless to say, Tozzer had also "made it" in the great world beyond Harvard University. He was an anthropologist and archaeologist of national standing. By 1950, he had been a member of the National Academy and other prestigious bodies for a good many years, and he was truly one of the eminent figures of our profession. I had heard about him for a long time before I moved to Cambridge. I had met him once, quite briefly, when he stopped by the Bureau of American Ethnology in Washington. But my real meeting with him was a more important and extended one. It took place in the early winter of 1949 when I was invited to come up to Harvard to be interviewed as one of the candidates for the Bowditch Professorship.

On that snowy weekend, Philip Phillips, a friend of long-standing and a member of the Peabody Museum staff, had put me up in his apartment at the old Continental Hotel; and on the morning of my arrival he and Jo Brew, the then Director of the Peabody Museum, had come by to brief me on my upcoming interview with Tozzer. I think both Phil and Jo may have been a little tense about the impression I might make. After a chat with the two of them, Phil and I were scheduled to have

Sunday lunch with the Tozzers. We drove over from the Hotel to the Tozzer house on Bryant Street. This impressive brick-and-timbered residence, Norman French in style and a small mansion in its elegance, had been built by the Tozzers in 1913. We pulled up to the house a little before 1:00 P.M., our appointed time, so we sat outside in the car for a few minutes. We had arrived there a little too early, but, as Phil explained, it wouldn't do for us to be too late. Tozzer didn't like for his guests to straggle in 15, 10, or even 5 minutes after the hour for which they had been invited. Phil also told me that we must be careful not to overstay our time; 3:00 P.M. was a strict departure hour for a Sunday lunch and he would give me the signal when it was time for us to leave. With all of these forewarnings, I was beginning to grow just a little apprehensive when, as the clock on the distant tower of Memorial Hall tolled 1:00 PM, we synchronized it with the doorbell at 7 Bryant Street.

We were met immediately by an aproned-and-capped maid who ushered us in. There were two such live-in servants in the household. She informed us that Mr. Tozzer was awaiting us in the study. The entrance hall to the Tozzer residence was a handsome two-storied room. A stairway rose to a landing before turning again to go on up to the second floor. The door to the study, which was on this landing, opened and Tozzer appeared up there to greet us, smiling down cordially. My apprehensiveness vanished; Tozzer could radiate charm as well as authority. We went on up, and I was introduced. Our host ushered us into study. It was obvious that he was very fond of Phil. The first thing he said to me was: "You're here because of Phil Phillips. He has told me about you." I took it—quite correctly—that he meant not only was I there to lunch, through Phil's good offices, but that Phil had been instrumental in bringing me to Cambridge for the interview.

Tozzer was of medium to smallish stature, perhaps about 5' 8" in height, and fine-boned, with a neat, trim quality about him. He stood ramrod-straight, in spite of his 71 years. Originally, he must have been quite slender, but in later years he had a modest embonpoint covered with a well-tailored vest crossed by a gold watch chain. His movements were brisk as was his speech, and he liked to walk about while he talked. His voice was clear and carrying, and when he became excited, as he often did, it always went up an octave or two. He had well-defined, small features, and wore metal-rimmed glasses. The chin and jawline would definitely have been characterized as "strong"—and his was a strong personality. When I knew him his hair was iron-gray, reasonably abundant, straight, and lay close to his head. A small gray mustache contrasted with his ruddy complexion.

The Tozzer study at 7 Bryant Street, into which we had been shown, was at an intermediate elevation in the structure of the house—between the first and second floors. Except for windows and a fireplace, the walls were lined with floor-to-ceiling bookshelves, all well-stocked. Above the fireplace a woodcarving of the Aztec Calendar Stone was set into the panelling. Tozzer had had it carved especially and installed there when the house was built. This room, as I was to learn later, was something of a legend in Mesoamerican archaeological circles. It was, after all, the *sanctum sanctorum* of the "Dean" of the field. In one corner of the room, on the side opposite the fireplace, there was a small stairwell and stair which led down to a door that opened into one end of the very large living room on the first floor of the house. Tozzer often held after-dinner colloquia at his residence. He, with other senior faculty members and the speaker of the evening, would remain in the study while junior faculty and students, who made up the larger audience, took their chairs in the living room below. Then, the group in the study would descend by the little corner stair, and their descent onto the "stage" in this way would signal the beginning of the evening's proceedings. Old Tozzer students remember, with a slight quality of awe, this almost "high church" appearance of the dignitaries.

On that winter day in 1949, the study was darkish, but a multicolored, glass-shaded lamp—a true "Art Nouveau" fixture—placed on a large flat-topped desk, cast a warm glow over the room. There was a very big and comfortable black leather sofa with its back against the desk, facing the fireplace. On that Sunday Phil and I sat there as Tozzer, back to the fire with its replica of the Calendar Stone above it, stood or paced up and down before us. A maid had brought in a tray with a martini shaker and glasses. A word is in order about these special Tozzer martinis. He always prepared them himself, well ahead of time, and stored the shaker in the deep freeze. Thus, no ice whatsoever was allowed to dilute their contents. Made with sweet, rather than dry, vermouth, they were dark brown in color and unusually ferocious. They were well-known in Harvard archaeological circles for having had a near-lethal effect on more than one guest. I had been warned of them and sipped warily. Was this my first test?

Tozzer got right down to business. "Tell me about yourself," he began. I gave a brief career summary. "I know, I know," he cut in impatiently, "I've read all about that in your resume. But how about the rest of your background?" I complied with this request by reciting a few vital statistics. He asked me if I had any money. I answered no, that I didn't, that I would be entirely dependent on my salary. He said briskly that that didn't make any difference to him, that there were some people who felt that virtue resided only with the wealthy, but that he wasn't one of them. I wondered just who these "people" might be. Were they here at Harvard, those who would levy such a stern judgment on the poor?

"Well," Tozzer continued, "I've been looking at your record and your bibliography, and I like it. You've published quite a lot of stuff. A lot of it doesn't amount to much, but it shows you're alive, you're trying. I like that!" There wasn't much I could say at that point; but Tozzer went on: "Tell me," he asked, "if you should come here as the Bowditch Professor what kind of research would you do?" I replied without any hesitation. Maybe I had assumed that such a question was coming and was prepared for it, maybe I really believed all that I would say, or maybe it was the dark brown martinis. Anyhow, I launched into a long statement about how I had been working in Panama, how I would like to continue there, and that it would be my intention to "dig" my way northward from there to the Maya frontier. In this manner, I maintained, I would eventually attack the mysteries of the Maya from this southern or Lower Central American side, and by so doing we would come to know more about this ancient civilization by appreciating it in a more comprehensive setting. It all must have sounded pretty foolish. While such a strategy could probably be defended from a long-range, theoretical standpoint, it was absurd from a practical, short-term perspective. One would have needed several lifetimes. I don't know just what Tozzer thought of it at the time although events of two or three years later would lead me to believe that he never took it very seriously. For that moment, however, he nodded vigorously, paced up an down a bit, and said: "Good, good! I like to hear people who know their own minds! I get tired of always having to tell people around here what to do!" Phil must have wondered about this personality change that had suddenly overtaken his old mentor.

Shortly after this, Mrs. Tozzer came into the study. She was a tall, gracious lady. She sat for a moment but did not imbibe one of her husband's cocktails. We all talked of more general matters. Then she announced that lunch was ready, and we went down to the dining room.

Such was my introduction to Alfred Marston Tozzer—always to be "Mr. Tozzer" to me, except when I might forget and call him "Dr. Tozzer". As is well-appreciated by all who knew him, he always spoke his mind. As I think back about it, I think the only "punch" he ever "pulled" with me was on that Sunday when he let me get away with all that nonsense about "working my way up to the Maya from Panama." But, as I have indicated, he was to correct that later.

Alfred Marston Tozzer was born on the nation's 101st birthday—4 July 1877—in the manufacturing town of Lynn, Massachusetts, a few miles north of Boston. He was the older son of Samuel Clarence and Caroline Blanchard (Marston) Tozzer, who also had a younger son, Arthur. Samuel was a pharmacist and the owner of a drug store in Lynn. Young Alfred went to the Classical High School in Lynn, and, after graduation there, he entered Harvard, receiving the A.B. degree in 1900 (Spinden, 1957; Kluckhohn, 1956; Phillips, 1955; Lothrop, 1955).

Just what first turned Alfred Tozzer in the direction of a career in anthropology is unclear. I regret that I never thought to ask him this question in the years that I knew him. But whatever it was that originally and specifically motivated Tozzer to pursue anthropology, we know that F. W. Putnam, then Director of the Museum and Peabody Professor at Harvard, and

Charles P. Bowditch, the Museum's principal financial patron, were the ones who played important encouraging roles in the formative years of Tozzer's career. Tozzer had studied with Putnam as an undergraduate, and it is from Putnam that we first hear of Tozzer. The circumstances are somewhat involved, but they are interesting in what they reveal, not only about the character of Tozzer, but about these early beginnings in the formation and institutionalization of American archaeological research.

We can begin with Bowditch's desire to establish a program of Maya research at Harvard. Bowditch, after a trip to the Maya area in 1888, had become an enthusiast for Maya archaeology. Following that trip, he commissioned E. H. Thompson and Teobert Maler to carry out explorations of Maya ruins for the Peabody Museum, and he arranged with the Government of Honduras for the Museum to excavate at Copan. Bowditch was no simple amateur looking for archaeological treasures. He was deeply interested in Maya calendrics, astronomy, and hieroglyphics; he was later to publish in the field himself (Bowditch, 1910). At that time he was anxious, above all, that the hieroglyphs that Maudslay (1889–1902), Maler (1901), and others had found carved on the Maya monuments be translated. Bowditch reasoned that perhaps among the living descendants of the Maya there were some who still retained a knowledge of their ancient writing system. The basic approach therefore should be a linguistic-ethnographic one and should be carried out by someone who knew, or would learn, the Maya language and who would be willing to spend the necessary years in the field seeking out and living with unacculturated Maya groups. The logic was sound. One must credit Bowditch with designing a "problem-oriented research strategy" in archaeology more than ninety years ago. The thing he had to do was to find the right person to head up this research. Such an individual, then, would be the one to lead and develope Maya studies at Harvard.

But Bowditch had extremely bad luck for a while in finding that person. John Owens was an early choice, but while Owens was directing the Peabody Museum excavations at Copan he died of fever, in 1893. The modern historian of American archaeology, C. M. Hinsley (1984), has described Bowditch's further search for the right scholar. A linguist of repute, a gentleman named Curtin, was engaged by Bowditch after Owens' untimely death. Curtin assured Bowditch that there would be nothing to it; the translation of Maya hieroglyphic writing would be—to put it in the parlance of today's younger generation—"a piece of cake". It is surprising that this over-confidence about anything so formidably esoteric-appearing as the Maya hieroglyphs did not arouse suspicion in the usually tough-minded Bowditch. But, instead, Bowditch advanced the cocksure Curtin five-thousand dollars, a staggeringly large research grant for the 1890's. It can only be put down as a testimony to Bowditch's unbridled enthusiasm for translating the glyphs. Curtin went to Mexico and points south, but never managed to spring himself free from the leading hotels in the capital cities. After the five-thousand was exhausted, Bowditch cut his losses and cut Curtin off. E. H. Thompson, Teobert Maler, Byron Gordon, and others were all considered as the possible "white knight" to lead Harvard's Maya hieroglyphic program, but all were eventually rejected as unsuitable for one reason or another. For a while it appeared that Bowditch and the Peabody might be able to secure the services of a rising young linguistic and ethnological star, Alfred Kroeber; but Kroeber turned them down in favor of going to California to found the Department of Anthropology and the Museum at Berkeley.

Then Putnam, who had been helping Bowditch in this hunt for the suitable candidate, came up with the name of Alfred Tozzer, a recent Harvard graduate. Bowditch was not terribly enthusiastic. Tozzer, as described to him by Putnam, seemed too young and too inexperienced. Finally, however, Bowditch was persuaded that Tozzer should be given the Peabody Museum's Winthrop Fellowship to study Californian Indian languages during the summer of 1900. This, Bowditch and Putnam agreed, would be a way of "testing out" the tyro. Tozzer acquitted himself well on this assignment among the California tribes, but Bowditch was still hesitant in committing himself, and something so important as the future of Maya studies, to one so young. He wanted to interview the prospect. So

Putnam instructed Tozzer to call upon Bowditch. This was their first meeting. It was in June of 1901. After the interview, Bowditch wrote to Putnam:

> "He (Tozzer) strikes me on the whole as . . . very well intentioned, not overly strong intellectually, (although) probably capable of acquiring all the information which a student holding the scholarship, which we are talking about, would need to acquire, but whether he has got the stamina to hold his own with the uncivilized races, and whether he is going to be one who will do honor to the work with which we propose to entrust him, I hardly like to venture an opinion of him. . . . He does not impress me, however, as if he would be *sure* to accomplish this work." (Hinsley, 1984, pp. 64F–64G.)

In retrospect, this evaluation, of the man who did more than any other to establish Maya archaeology in the early years of the 20th century, cannot help but be amusing. At the time, though, Bowditch remained cautious; he had been badly burned before. Tozzer was to be further "tested", this time in New Mexico, with Navajo linguistics and ethnology, during the summer of 1901. Again, Tozzer performed ably. He enjoyed his work in the Navajo country, and three of his early publications are addressed to Navajo ethnology (Tozzer, 1905, 1906, 1909).

At last, late in 1901, Tozzer was awarded a traveling fellowship from the Archaeological Institute of America for linguistic and ethnological study in Yucatan. The "well intentioned young man" was now going to be given his chance to show, in Bowditch's further words, ". . . if he had the stamina to hold his own with the uncivilized races", this time those "races" south of the border. In Yucatan Tozzer went first to Chichen Itza where E. H. Thompson, Bowditch's "man in Yucatan", and also the American Consul in Merida, owned a hacienda. Tozzer learned Maya in the native households in the neighborhood. He also pushed into the Yucatecan back country on several trips in search of the "less-acculturated" Maya groups whose location was the next step in the Bowditch research plan for the solution of the mysteries of the Maya glyphs.

While at Chichen Itza, Tozzer was also introduced to Maya archaeology in the field. He spent several days going over the site with Thompson, studying its architecture, and he learned about Maya art and iconography from Adele Bretton, the British artist and archaeologist, who was at Chichen then, copying the monumental reliefs.

After Tozzer successfully completed this 1901–02 season in the field, Bowditch must have been reasonably satisfied with the way his neophyte had performed for he saw to it that the Institute's fellowhip funds were continued for 1902–03. The search for the elusive unacculturated Maya tribes continued. Tozzer decided to go to the Usumacinta country where Teobert Maler, the German scholar, explorer, and adventurer—and another protege of Bowditch—had been exploring in the territory of the Lacandon Maya tribes. Traveling by river and by horseback, Tozzer finally arrived at Lake Petha where he was to spend a good many months. He lived with the remote and un-Christianized Lacandones, establishing that they spoke an understandable Maya dialect and that their rituals were reminiscent of those described by the 16th century Bishop Landa in his *Relacion.* This was rugged field duty, and Tozzer no doubt felt isolated. At one point, he wrote to Bowditch proposing that he come home, write up his Central American notes to date, and complete his Ph.D. degree. Staying here in the jungle, he felt that all of his contemporaries in anthropology were passing him by and that he would be forgotten. But Bowditch replied that Tozzer had not been in the field with the Lacandones long enough to do a proper job, and that he should stay longer. In his words:

> "Several working maxims have always been before me from my boyhood. Among these are, 'What you do, do with all your might,'" and 'When you enter into an agreement, carry it out to the letter.'

And, further along:

> " . . . I feel sure you ought not to leave your work next year. The material, which you have collected, can wait. Your degree

can wait. . . . I write to you as I should to my own son, and I
hope you will believe me when I say that my advice is given
as much for your ultimate good as for that of the undertaking,
which you have entered into." (Hinsley, 1964, p. 64G.)

Anyone of my generation who has had graduate students of
his own must fight back a smile when reading this 19th century "fatherly" advice; but Tozzer took it, finishing out the
1903 season and returning, again, in 1904 to complete the
Lacandon linguistic and ethnological study. The work formed
the basis of his doctoral dissertation, and he received the Ph.D.
degree from Harvard in 1904. The thesis was eventually to be
published as *A Comparative Study of the Mayas and the Lacandones* (Tozzer, 1907), and it established Tozzer's reputation
as Maya ethnographer and linguist. In the latter field, he is also
known for his *Maya Grammar* (Tozzer, 1921a) which he began
to compile at this time. Perhaps even more importantly for his
career, Bowditch remained his firm supporter for ever after.
Unfortunately, Bowditch's prime desideratum, a discovery of a
knowledge of Maya hieroglyphics among the Lacandones, was
not realized. As we now know—and know largely from Tozzer's exploratory researches—these descendants of the Classic
Maya no longer retained such an intellectual heritage.

In 1905, Tozzer became a full-fledged member of the faculty
of the Department of Anthropology at Harvard, and he offered
for the first time Anthropology 9, the famous Maya seminar
which he was to give more or less steadily throughout his
career and in which virtually all of the Mayanists of the next
several archaeological generations were to participate. I recall
that in my first week on the job Tozzer called me over to his
office and showed me two wooden file drawers, each filled with
5 x 8 cards. They were the notes for Anthropology 9 (The Maya)
and the companion seminar, Anthropology 10 (Mexico). Here,
he told me, was everything I needed, all laid out for me. With
these notes I could continue giving the seminars where he had
left off. I never took him up on it. Maybe I should have, but I
thought I'd better sweat things out for myself. The notes,
however, were useful in guiding me into and through the literature. In addition to them, Tozzer had four large metal file

drawers in his office in which he had a valuable collection of photographs as well as illustrations and text sections cut from many books and monographs. He had no compunctions about taking the scissors and cutting the latter up; of course, he did have other complete copies on his shelves, either in the Museum office or at home. The materials in the files all dealt with Mesoamerica—mainly the Maya. The pictures and the text sections were arranged under sites (Tikal, Uaxactun, etc.) or topics (Architecture, Obsidians, etc.). Needless to say, they had been, and continued to be, of great use in seminar teaching.

But to get back to Alfred Tozzer's history and career, the next dozen years, following 1905, were divided between teaching duties at Harvard and fieldwork. In 1907, as a rest from the Maya, he took part in a Southwestern field expedition, at Rito de los Frijoles, in New Mexico. This was with Kidder, Hewett, and others. He returned to the Maya, though, in the 1909–10 period, heading field parties into Tikal, Nakum, Holmul, and other sites in the northeastern Peten, and promptly publishing on this work (Tozzer, 1911a, 1912, 1913). His advancement at Harvard was marked by his appointment to assistant professor in Anthropology and to curator of Middle American Archaeology and Ethnology in the Peabody Museum in 1913.

1913 was also very important to Alfred Tozzer in another way. The previous summer he had taken a North Cape vacation cruise to Scandinavia with his mother. On shipboard he had met Margaret Castle of Honululu, who was traveling with her mother. In April of 1913 they were married. The young Mr. and Mrs. Tozzer built a new home in Cambridge—the one at 7 Bryant Street. They were to have two daughters, Ann and Joan. Sadly, Ann died as a child; but Joan lived to become a leading figure skater of national reknown. Rightfully, Tozzer was immensely proud of her. He once asked me if I were superstitious. This came in the middle of a conversation we were having about Joan as a skater, and I was puzzled for a moment. He then went on to say that when Joan was competing he was always terribly careful not to step on a crack in the sidewalk and, by so doing, bring her bad luck. His propitiatory behavior must have paid off; Joan won the United States National Championship on two different years.

At Harvard, Tozzer broadened his teaching interests, offering, in addition to his Maya and Mexican seminars, a course in primitive society. It was to lead to a textbook, *Social Origins and Social Continuities* (Tozzer, 1925). He had leave from Harvard in 1913–14 to take over, for a year, the directorship of the International School of Archaeology and Ethnology in Mexico. This was the organization of which Franz Boas was also a member and which was instrumental in supporting the Mexican archaeologist, Manuel Gamio, in his early stratigraphic excavations in the Valley of Mexico (Gamio, 1913). Tozzer took his bride with him. It was her introduction to Mexico, and it turned out to be a rather rough experience. Mexico was in the midst of its revolution, which lasted from 1910 to 1920. The Tozzers and Clarence Hay were in a hotel in Veracruz when the United States Navy shelled the city. Years later, Mrs. Tozzer told my wife about waking up in the morning and looking out the window into the hotel courtyard where a U.S. Marine was on patrol. The Marine demanded to know who she was and was told, with that dignified composure which Mrs. Tozzer could muster on necessary occasions, that he "was addressing a United States citizen." I think she returned to the States soon after this Veracruz incident, but Tozzer stayed on and went up to Mexico City from where he started a dig at Santiago Ahuitzotla. This was to be his last fieldwork in Mesoamerica (Tozzer, 1921b).

With the United States entrance into World War I, Tozzer was commissioned a Captain in the Air Service, and the Tozzers went to Denver and, later, to San Francisco. His job was to be in charge of Air Service Examining Boards for the duration. To jump ahead in the Tozzer narrative, he was again very active in World War II. At the time of Pearl Harbor, Tozzer was making what was to be his last tour of Middle America. Accompanied by Phil Phillips, he was visiting at Copan when the news of the Japanese attack came in. He couldn't wait to get back home and then to go to Hawaii. After his marriage to Margaret Castle, the Tozzers had made almost annual trips to the islands to visit his wife's family. With the coming of the war in the Pacific, he became head of the Office of Strategic Services in Honolulu and served in this post for the duration. One important anthropological by-product of this service was his government-sponsored monograph on the peoples of Okinawa (Tozzer, 1944).

But it was in the years between the two wars that Tozzer was at the height of his powers and influence. He rapidly ascended the academic ladder at Harvard to full professor. Charles P. Bowditch died in 1920 and left the Peabody Museum well-endowed for the future. Actually, Tozzer was never the Bowditch Professor as the money for the Chair did not become available until 1946, or late in his career, and then Tozzer chose to let the funds accumulate rather than drawing this specially earmarked salary. In 1945, however, he was named the John E. Hudson Professor of Archaeology, a title bestowed by the University at large and usually held, as it was before and since, by a scholar in Classics or Fine Arts. This was unusual recognition for an Americanist, and he was very gratified by it. Some years later he was to indicate to me that "the Classical people" were very "snooty" about American archaeology, something, he said, "which you should be aware of".

The unofficial "Mr. Tozzer" status, to which I have referred earlier, was thoroughly consolidated during the 1920s and 1930s by conscientious and outstanding service to the Harvard community. In 1922 he became a member of the Academic Board of Radcliffe College, and ten years later he became the Secretary of the Board and a member of the Trustees and of the Council of the College. He served as a faculty representative of the Harvard Alumni Association during these years. Above all, in prestigeful Harvard duty, he was a permanent member of the Administrative Board of Harvard College from 1928 until his retirement. Retirement came in 1948, when he was 71, five years past the usual retirement age for Harvard's tenured professors at that time.

In addition to these internal Harvard honors, Tozzer was honored by his elections to the American Academy of Arts and Sciences (1911), the American Philosophical Society (1937), and the National Academy of Sciences (1942). He was sensitive to and appreciative of these "Academy distinctions" although at the same time he was very matter-of-fact about them and recognized their "political dimensions". I remember in 1952, two years after I arrived on the Harvard scene, he told me very curtly during one of our brisk morning interviews: "The American Academy of Arts and Sciences is one of three such organizations to which you should belong. I have just proposed you, for it. You'll have to get into the American Philosophical Society and the National Academy of Sciences on your own." Honors of this sort continued to come to Tozzer even past his retirement. In 1950 he was named by the American Anthropological Association as the first recipient of the Alfred Vincent Kidder Award for distinction in American Archaeology.

In his writing and publishing Tozzer showed a variety interests over and beyond those works of his already referred to. His article, "The Value of Ancient Mexican Manuscripts in the Study of the General Development of Writing" (Tozzer 1911b), is one such example, as is a short monograph, *Animal Figures in the Maya Codices* (Tozzer and Allen, 1910), which he prepared in collaboration with a zoologist. His "The Domain of the Aztecs and Their Relation to the Prehistoric Cultures of Mexico" (Tozzer, 1916) revealed his awareness of Middle America or Mesoamerica as a sphere of cultural interaction, or "a culture area-with-time depth", well before it would be so formally recognized by others (Kirchhoff, 1943). In 1927, he published "Time and American Archaeology," emphasizing the then new American preoccupation with archaeological chronology, and its pertinence to Middle America. A little after this, his "Maya and Toltec Figures at Chichen Itza" (Tozzer, 1930) struck the keynote of what was to be his last major work, his two volume opus on Chichen, its famed Cenote, and the wider relationships of the Postclassic Maya, not to be brought out until after his death (Tozzer, 1957). And all during the 1930's, of course, he was toiling away on another labor of love, his great edition of *Landa's Relacion de Las Cosas de Yucatan* (Tozzer, ed., 1941).

Tozzer's *Landa* typefies his great strengths as a scholar. It is extraordinarily thorough. As others have noted, it has in its annotations, which are far longer than the original Landa text, a compendium of all that was known of Maya ethnohistory when Tozzer prepared it. He has been accused by some of "not being able to see the forest for the trees", and it is true that the

Landa edition does describe every known "tree" in exhaustive detail; but he was not unaware of, or averse to, more general perspectives, as the above-cited general articles show. He did not have the flair for synthesis that characterized Kroeber or Kidder. His was a different type of mind. But as one views all of his writings, Tozzer's work can only be described as impressive.

Perhaps Tozzer's greatest contribution—and I think that he himself felt this—was as a teacher. All of his former students that I have talked with are in agreement on his unusual abilities to awaken, stimulate, and inspire. His intense enthusiasm for his subject was part of it. He bubbled over with excitement, and it was catching. As they have been described to me, there often appeared to be no tight organization in his lectures or seminar presentations. Illustrative materials, documents, sometimes objects—all were passed around a table with Tozzer, all the while, talking at a furious rate and setting things down on a blackboard in a fine hand (Phillips, 1955, p. 74). Somehow, though, it all came together—or it certainly came together for a great many. Their names and their articles are to be seen in the volume, *The Maya and Their Neighbors* (Hay and others, eds., 1940). Tozzer had always insisted that he did not want a formal *festschrift*. His students respected his wish only in the sense that they did not call it a *festschrift*, but on the dedication page of *The Maya and Their Neighbors*, they wrote:

> To Alfred Marston Tozzer
> His students and colleagues dedicate this
> volume, in recognition of his services
> to Middle American Research and in
> appreciation of their debt to him as
> teacher, counsellor, and friendly critic.

A total of 34 scholars are presented in that volume; 25 of these were Tozzer's students in the full sense of the term, and of the remaining nine at least three had taken some course instruction from him. Kidder, Morley, Spinden, Lothrop, Ricketson, Vaillant, Guthe, Pollock, Ruppert, Robert and Ledyard

Smith, Wauchope, Andrews, and many others are included in the table of contents. The list is a virtual roll call of Mayanists up to that time. I have always thought that the diversity among these Tozzer students was a great tribute to an exacting but liberal teacher: Morley, with his dogged persistence in recording all of the known Maya hieroglyphic texts of his time, Lothrop, with the erudition that wove together the strands of archaeology with those of ethnohistory; Kidder, with his great grasp and comprehension of New World culture history; or Vaillant, with that poetic, intuitive quality which contrasted with, and at the same time informed, his careful archaeological fieldwork and writings. Tozzer was never one to insist on students conforming to any pattern of his own. He didn't want disciples made over in his own image who would then set about their master's bidding. He would have been offended at the idea of such intellectual cloning.

Tozzer is not remembered for any particular theoretical position in anthropology. I suppose he could best be summed up as a Boasian historical particularist. In this connection, it should be noted that Tozzer had spent some time at Columbia, with Boas, in 1905, working on Maya linguistics and his *Maya Grammar* manuscript. Later, he was to invite Boas to Harvard to teach for a term. I know that Boas held Tozzer in high regard. Kluckhohn (1956, p. 131) quotes a letter that Boas wrote to Tozzer on the occasion of the 1940 presentation of *The Maya and Their Neighbors*. To this I can add that, as a student in the Department of Anthropology at Columbia, I was once in Professor Boas' office. On the walls there were many portraits of the anthropological great—Tylor, Bogoras, Von den Steinen, and a dozen more. All were European scholars except one. That one was Alfred Tozzer.

To return to Tozzer as a "theorist", or a "non-theorist", I think he thought of anthropology as essentially straightforward culture history and the faithful recording of the data that would pertain thereto. The things that Tozzer demanded of his students were hard work, intellectual honesty, and, above all, dedication. This was quite a bit, of course, and, according to the things I've heard, the learning process was sometimes painful; but once you had come through the fire you were free to go your own way. And you went with the affection and blessing of your old teacher, albeit, now and then, a scolding, no matter how long you had been out of the nest or how great you had become, if he felt you needed it. Tozzer was still turning out students, and students of high quality, right up to the time he retired. I was fortunate enough to inheirit some of these. Men as able as William Sanders, Michael Coe, and David Kelley were among some of his later undergraduates. To those familiar with the nature of the work of these men (see, e.g., Sanders, 1981; Coe, 1981; Kelley, 1976), it is clear that they were not formed in a single mold. Tozzer coached you in fundamentals and then let you go your own way.

There were times in my early days at Harvard when I rather wished that I had been a Tozzer student, and I will admit that I sometimes felt "a bit left out" when I observed the close relationships Tozzer maintained with students and former students. Although Tozzer, in many ways, looked after me as he might have looked after a student, there was a difference. I had been "raised" as an archaeologist as someone else's student. I was a 37 year old professional and his successor. He couldn't feel the same way about me as he did about them.

I think his "emeritus" status rankled Tozzer ever so slightly; it must have with anyone so intensely active as he had been. He got it off his chest by needling his successor every so often. I had come to Cambridge "ballyhooed" as "the settlement pattern archaeologist". This was then looked upon as a "new approach", but Tozzer got a little tired of hearing about it. He said to me one day—putting his head back with his nose in the air, and sniffing a bit, as he did when he was feeling argumentative—"Settlement patterns! I think that's what we used to call 'mapping the site'! Now it's all the rage!" He was a little suspicious of what might be termed "the social dimensions" of the settlement pattern concept. "Prehistoric sociology!", he used to call it, scoffingly. He liked to get a rise out of people, and I may have disappointed him in this regard, as being too passive. I know he was pleased, though, when my Viru settlement volume (Willey, 1953a) came out, and I presented him with a copy. His "new man" was at least active, even if only in some peculiar pursuit like "settlement patterns" and in an area too far outside of Middle America to be fully respectable. I was secretly gratified when I found out that it was one of the few archaeological site reports, other than those on Mesoamerican sites, that he kept in the study at 7 Bryant.

It was great fun having an office across the hall from Alfred Tozzer. There was rarely a dull moment. Those daily morning interviews were not all devoted to "straightening me out" on Harvardiana. Or,.perhaps, things could start out that way but would veer off into the ridiculous. During my first months in Cambridge, I had an old wooden desk in my office. It was some kind of a Peabody Museum heirloom; it may even have been one of Putnam's. Bowditch, I know, had had his own desk, and absolute mammoth, built to his specifications. Mine was of very ordinary size and appearance except that it was terribly delapidated. The drawers wouldn't open and the top was warped. My chair, too, was of a similar antique vintage, with one coaster wheel that kept dropping off every so often. After a further search of the Museum attic, and finding nothing better, Jo Brew suggested that I buy a new desk and chair from Bowditch funds. I did this without consulting Tozzer so that when he came into my office the morning after my new furniture had been delivered, he was taken aback by seeing me ensconced behind a modern-looking gray metal desk and a matching swivel chair replete with green leather upholstery. "Great Scott," he exploded. "Where have these horrors come from? It doesn't look like the Peabody Museum! It's not the sort of thing we have here!" Explaining that I had purchased it with Bowditch money didn't make things any better. "You spent Bowditch funds for that! Why it's the kind of desk that ought to be downtown in some brokerage office where they can afford to waste their money on unessentials! And a *green* chair, good God!"

"Well, Mr. Tozzer," I stammered, beginning to feel my guilt at such spendthrift behavior, "I really needed a new desk and chair. My old chair was falling apart!"

"You should have told me!", he shot back. "I could have found you a chair over at my house. We have got a lot of extra ones up in the attic." He turned on his heel and strode out. After a little while, his sense of humor must have gotten the better of him, for he stuck his head around the door and said mischievously and in that very carrying voice: "You know, Gordon, when you were appointed to the "Bowditch Chair", that was something you should have taken *figuratively*, not *literally*. It didn't mean you were going to be given a 'chair'! You were supposed to have your own 'chair'!" With that, I heard him going down the hall, chuckling.

Tozzer enjoyed visitors, and a lot of them came to see him. He preferred old students and some old colleagues. I was in his office one morning when Alfred Kroeber walked in. They were good friends and very congenial. Pretty soon John R. Swanton, then in his eighties and some years retired from the Bureau of American Ethnology, stopped by. He lived in a nearby suburb and rarely came around although he did that day, quite coincidentally with Kroeber's arrival. They all had a long chat, and I was a most interested junior auditor. Kroeber and Swanton finally departed. Tozzer said to me, "I'm going home now for lunch. When you go home you can tell your wife that you spent the morning with the world's three oldest living anthropologists!" Some visitors Tozzer may have found wearing. On more than one occasion, after I had heard talk for some time across the hall, Tozzer would come in my office, close the door, and in a behind-the-hand stage whisper would say to me: "So and so's in my office now. Get rid of him for me! Take him to lunch!" He'd then hand me a $20 bill. "Take this. Wait a few minutes, them come over. I'll introduce you and tell him that you two will have lunch together on me! I'll explain that I've got a very pressing engagement! There's no reason why at my age I have to be bored to death!" I had lunch with quite a few unusual persons in this manner. Frequently, the next day, I would hear some interesting gossip from Tozzer about the guest.

Of course, Tozzer liked to visit, and one of the almost daily things he did, usually after our morning discussions, was to go across the alley from the Peabody Museum, to 10 Frisbie Place, where the Carnegie Institution archaeologists had their offices. He liked to go especially to see Tatiana Proskouriakoff to talk with her about Chichen Itza iconography and the big monograph he was preparing. Harry Pollock, who had succeeded A. V. Kidder as Director of the Carnegie Archaeological

Division, was a great favorite of Tozzer's and a conversation and gossip companion. He also enjoyed a more or less running archaeological fight, of a good-natured kind, with Eric Thompson who was one of the Carnegie group. Eric, in a book review, had compared Tozzer's heavily annotated *Landa* to a similarly massively footnoted work brought out by an elderly antiquary in Norman Douglas' novel, *South Wind*. I don't know if Tozzer had ever read *South Wind*. I rather doubt that he had. He wasn't a reader of novels. But I think he suspected that Eric was secretly lampooning him. In any event, they continued to disagree about all kinds of things, including the identity of the Itza. A morning's "crossing of swords" with Eric always left Tozzer in fine fettle.

Tozzer was a very generous man. It was legend that he had helped a great many students financially, with gifts rather than loans. This was always done quietly, and it would come out only much later, and indirectly from others, if at all. The generosity extended to old colleagues as well. He came into my office one morning, carrying a rather strange looking, large and hollow figurine, presumably of some Mesoamerican genre. "Do you see this? Well, it's a fake. I know it's a fake. I just paid 'X' (and old friend and colleague) the sum of $1500 for it. He needed the money; he needed it very badly. Now I want you to take this thing down to the Catalogue Department and have it catalogued, as a *fake*, and I don't want to hear another damned thing about it!" So saying, he turned and strode briskly and very firmly out of the office. I could tell he was provoked. He didn't like doing what he had done, but he felt he had to help his friend.

I didn't go into the field in 1951, but I did in 1952. I returned to Panama. As I had indicated to Tozzer, in our first meeting in Cambridge, this was what I wanted to do. It conformed to the "research plan" I had outlined to him. I think he was satisfied that I was going somewhere, that I wasn't just vegetating on the job, but I know now that he wasn't overjoyed about the selection of Panama. Still, that country did evoke a few favorable memories with him. Sam Lothrop had worked there, and, in connection with this, Tozzer had made a trip to Panama when Karl Curtis had notified him of the Sitio Conte gold finds. But I don't think Tozzer had expected just what I brought back from this 1952 trip—a shipment largely of potsherds, and rather grim-looking Monagrillo potsherds at that. I remember going over the Monagrillo materials with him when McGimsey, the graduate student who had gone to Panama with me, and I had them spread out in a Museum lab. Tozzer didn't say much of anything although I recall that he sniffed rather scornfully.

The Tozzers were always extremely generous and cordial to my wife and to me, and Mrs. Tozzer and Katharine had a temperamental affinity which developed into a close friendship. In the summer of 1952, they invited us and our daughters to visit them in Tamworth, New Hampshire. This was a lovely summer residence of theirs which they had built shortly after the Cambridge house at 7 Bryant Street. Tamworth, incidentally, was where Bowditch had spent his summers. We had enjoyed ourselves immensely on this trip, staying for two or three days. On the last evening, Tozzer took me aside from the ladies, and over the dark brown martinis, which were also replicated in this New Hampshire household, asked me what my field plans were for the spring of 1953. Pursuant to my "Lower Central American plan", that I had outlined to him back in 1949, I began to tell him about my next projected trip to Panama. This time I would edge a bit north in that country, all the while keeping in mind my eventual arrival at the Maya frontier. I noticed Tozzer's face turning very red—or perhaps magenta would be a more accurate description—as I detailed my long-term research strategies. Then he blew up. "Gordon," he exclaimed, "you just can't do that! It defeats entirely the purpose of Mr. Bowditch's intentions and his will! You just can't continue to fool around in Panama with things like this shell mound culture of yours and neglect the Maya!"

Referring back to our pre-prandial conversation of that 1949 Sunday, I said, "But Mr. Tozzer, I thought you had agreed to all of this—this work in Central America south of the Maya! We're breaking new ground! Besides Mr. Bowditch's will says, specifically, 'Mexico and Central America'. Panama is in Central America!'"

Tozzer was not mollified. He came back: "You don't have to

tell me where Panama is! And you don't have to tell me what the will says! I know what the will says! I know, too, that when Mr. Bowditch said 'Central America' he meant the Maya! And you better get to them! You'll waste your life in some god forsaken place like Panama! Your job here at Harvard is to go into Maya archaeology!" This was the only real "fight" we ever had, and I am glad to say that he "won it". A career of digging in Lower Central America would have been an honorable and useful way to contribute to New World culture history, but I am glad I switched to the Maya. Certainly, if I had continued with my original plan, I think retirement would have overtaken me about halfway through Costa Rica, on my mole-like progress toward the Maya frontier. I conceded and leapt into the Maya area directly.

My Maya fieldwork began at Barton Ramie, in the Belize River Valley, and I selected the place with an eye on Maya settlement pattern studies (Willey *et al.* 1965). Tozzer, although he may not have been thrilled by my "settlement pattern approach", was content that whatever it was I was going to do, I was going to do it in the Maya area. After a survey season in 1953, I returned to the Belize Valley for some serious digging in 1954. I saw him briefly when I returned to Cambridge in early May. That summer we did not visit the Tozzers in Tamworth, as we had in the two summers before. He wasn't feeling very well. I had one letter and Phil Phillips had another which hinted at this.

That summer of 1954 we were "house-sitting" for the Tozzers at 7 Bryant Street. One morning in late August the phone rang. It was Tozzer. They had come down from Tamworth for just overnight and, not wanting to bother us, were staying in a hotel. He had come he said, to see the doctor. He wouldn't go into it, but when I had answered the phone he had said, "Gordon, this is Alfred. I thought we might get together for a little talk." I was alarmed. Not only had the old ginger gone out of his voice, but he had never before referred to himself, to me, as "Alfred". He came over to 7 Bryant, and while Mrs. Tozzer discussed some things with my wife, we had a talk in the study—that study where we had had our first conversation five years before. He was obviously not well, but he didn't say anything about it and clearly did not want to talk about it. We talked about the Museum, Maya archaeology, how I was doing. After a little while, the Tozzers went out to their car, and the chauffeur drove them away. I was not to see him again. Alfred Marston Tozzer died shortly after this on 5 October 1954.

ALFRED VINCENT KIDDER
In old age.
Courtesy Mrs. A. V. Kidder.

ALFRED VINCENT KIDDER
(1885–1963)

In 1950, when I first came to Harvard, I had known A. V. Kidder only slightly. Shortly after my arrival, I inquired about him and was told that he was at home but that he was not well. In his last official year with the Carnegie Institution, he had taken some leave during the spring period in response to an invitation from the University of California, at Berkeley, to come there and teach a seminar. He had enjoyed it immensely—as did the students, as I was later informed by some of them—and he and Mrs. Kidder had had a thoroughly good time. But on his return to Cambridge, in the summer, he had begun to ail. I should have called upon him when I first came to town, but, with the beginnings of classes and in a completely new environment, I put it off. I must confess, too, that there was another reason. His son, Alfred II, who had long been on the faculty at Harvard, had been one of the candidates for the Bowditch Professorship which had been awarded to me. I suppose I felt some embarrassment vis-a-vis Dr. Kidder because of this. I needn't have. He was the last one to have borne any resentment or negative feelings toward me because of such a circumstance. One day in my office the phone rang. It was Kidder. He simply said: "Gordon, why don't you come over and see me. I've been laid up, or I would have called by to see you. Just drop in any afternoon at cocktail time."

The Kidders lived on Holden Street, near Holden Green. This was only a short distance from Harvard University and the Peabody Museum. As I walked over there on the afternoon following my telephone invitation, I thought back about my previous associations with A. V. Kidder. I remembered the first time I saw him—although this could hardly be classed as an "association". It was at Kinishba, in eastern Arizona, in the summer of 1935. We were working on the ruin one day when three men drove up in a expensive-looking vehicle—perhaps a Stutz, Pierce-Arrow, or even a Rolls. They got out and shortly thereafter were met by Dean Cummings. The Dean and the three of them stood for a time on the highest point of the ruin, with the Dean pointing out various features of the work. One or two of my more forward student colleagues chose this very time to go to the Dean, undoubtedly to consult him on some pressing matter pertaining to the archaeology of Kinishba. They were rewarded by being introduced to the distinguished visitors. I was not so bold, but I was informed by my excavation companion, Davy Jones, that one of the strangers was A. V. Kidder, none other than *the* A. V. Kidder". The other two, I learned later, were Donald Scott, the then Director of the Peabody Museum at Harvard, and Harold Gladwin, Director of the Gila Pueblo Foundation at Globe, Arizona, and the owner of the elegant automobile. They had driven up from Globe, were on their way to northern New Mexico, and had stopped by to pay their respects to the Dean.

I had a better look at Dr. Kidder again, in New Haven, at the meetings of the American Anthropological Association in 1937. At that time, Kidder was in his early fifties. He was an impressive-looking man. Six feet, or just under he was heavily built, although not fat. He had strong, chiseled features—an aquiline nose, a clefted chin, and a square jaw. His complexion was very ruddy, and this, combined with hair which was beginning to go white, as well as a guardsman's mustache of the same shade, gave him a distinguished "British Colonel-appearance". I was told, later, that around the Peabody Museum at about that time the graduate students referred to him as "Handsome Al" although I don't suppose they used this address to his face. I saw Kidder again at a subsequent annual meeting of the AAA, this one held in Chicago, in 1939. He gave a most entertaining after-dinner talk there on doing archaeology in the Andover, Massachusetts town dump—a kind of early version of W. L. Rathje's "Garbage Archaeology" of the 1970s and 80s. On neither of these two occasions, however, did I have the pleasure of meeting him.

This did not occur until 1945, when the Society for American Archaeology meetings were held in Washington, D.C. Near the end of World War II, the sessions were only sparsely attended, and it was easy to meet and talk with everyone. Dr. Kidder was accompanied by his son, "Alfie" (Alfred Kidder II), also an archaeologist, whom I had known in Peru at the time of the Institute Andean Research expeditions, and who introduced me to his father. The younger Kidder was living in Washington then, and after sessions he invited a group of us out to his house where I had the chance to talk to Kidder senior. As I was to learn later, Dr. Kidder was always a very gracious listener, especially to young archaeological aspirants. I should mention that an article of mine on the "Weeden Island culture" of Florida had come out earlier that year in *American Antiquity* (Willey, 1945), and shortly after its appearance Kidder had written me a most encouraging letter, telling me how much he had enjoyed and been informed by the piece. That I was almost tempted to frame this letter and hang it on my wall is a measure of the prestige that Kidder carried at that time in the American archaeological profession.

After that first Washington meeting, Kidder stopped by the Bureau of American Ethnology on several occasions, to visit my boss, Matt Stirling. I should explain that the head offices of the Carnegie Institution were in Washington so that he came there often, from his home in Massachusetts. In the late 1940s, I sometimes had lunch with Stirling, Kidder, and others at the Cosmos Club. It was at about this time that I was fascinated with the parallels in the trajectories of Precolumbian Mesoamerican and Andean cultural developments. I mentioned this interest to Kidder when I saw him on one of his Washington visits, and I told him that I had prepared a manuscript on the subject and that I thought he would be interested in it. With his characteristic courtesy, he asked me to send him a copy. I did, but he wasn't very favorably impressed. I was puzzled by this at the time for Kidder had evinced an interest in such broad culture-historical and developmental problems (see especially, Kidder, 1936). The article I had prepared was by no means a first-rate attempt on such a sweeping and difficult subject, but I feel that its quality, alone, was not his primary objection to what I had written. I gathered, from his reply to me that it was more that he didn't approve of the theme, or of taking archaeology off in this direction. Perhaps with his background of experience, he realized how difficult such questions were and thought that they were not suited to the young and relatively uninitiated. Concerns such as the rise of the state and the expansion of empires might better be left to senior scholars with long experience, and even in their case—as I think his reasoning may have gone—these were concerns suitable for rare musings or speculations, rather than something to be addressed as research problems which would lead to a definite course of research action.

This notion about Kidder's intellectual conservatism, at least at that time and in that context, seemed to be confirmed a little later when I published a paper which attempted to explain the "functions" of horizon style phenomena in ancient Peru (Willey, 1948). Kidder definitely didn't like it. He told me that it "reminded him too much of Walter Taylor". I should explain that this was at the time that Taylor's controversial book, *A Study of Archaeology* (Taylor, 1948) had just appeared. In it Taylor had advocated, at least in a general way, some of the things I was trying to do in my "horizons' paper; but Taylor's book was also highly critical of Kidder, and this combination of what then was considered as "far out" archaeology and criticism may have been too much for the latter.

I was turning all of this over in my head as I made my way along Holden Street. The Kidder's house was a medium-sized, multi gabled, gray, two-story, frame structure which, I suppose, had been built near the turn of the century. It was set back some distance from Holden Street and surrounded by a large, tree-shaded lawn which was enclosed with a high, wire fence. By 1950, Dr. and Mrs. Kidder lived there alone. All of the five children were by now married and had gone elsewhere. That first visit was on a warm late September day. The front door of the house was closed only by a screen. Dr. Kidder, who had heard me come up the front steps or had seen me from the living room window, called out to come right on in. I did so and found him comfortably ensconced in a big leather easy chair at one end of the living room. He looked as I as I had seen him last, a handsome, ruddy-featured, healthy man, younger in appearance than his 65 years. He apologized for not rising when I came in. He explained that he didn't know what his illness was. He "just didn't feel any good", was the way he put it. The doctors couldn't seem to find out what it was, but ever since he had returned from California he had felt worn out—for "no good reason". Mrs. Kidder came into the room at about that time, and, after being introduced to me (this was the first time we had met), she voiced the opinion that there was a "good reason", that "Teddy" (as she always referred to him) had worn himself out driving all the way across the United States on their trip back from Berkeley. But she said he was getting better, and he gave ever appearance of it.

We had a good talk. Mrs. Kidder brought us in a couple of bourbons-on-the-rocks. We went over various new discoveries in archaeology—Southwestern, Mesoamerican, Peruvian. These led to rememberances and stories on his part—about past digs, the various archaeologists involved, amusing incidents. Kidder was a marvelous story teller. He never appeared at the heroic center of his tales but was, instead, positioned off to one side, frequently the embarrassed or bemused spectator. He told me that he expected to be back in the office shortly. This office was still over in the Carnegie quarters at 10 Frisbie Place, across the alley from the Peabody Museum, but he wanted to give his Carnegie colleagues more room there in their cramped lodgings so he was asking Jo Brew, the Director of the Peabody, for an office with us. Before I left, Kidder said, "It's bully to see you." He was fond of this Theodore Roose-veltian expletive of his youth. He made it graciously clear that he would like me to come back—any day at cocktail time.

Shortly after this, Kidder took an office in the Peabody, a small one on the fifth floor. He brought over a few books, not many, and he spent some time there. He seemed and looked well and apparently was much improved from his illness. Quite frequently, he put in an appearance at the Harvard Faculty Club for lunch, joining the Harvard and Carnegie archaeologists at a table where we frequented. Times and dates now telescope or rearrange themselves in my memory, but I think it was within a year or so, when I was giving a graduate seminar, that I invited Kidder to come and sit in. Needless to say, the presence of A.V.K. tended to enhance things for the students. As I had done with Kroeber, I enjoyed bringing him in, unannounced until the last minute, to the surprise and delight of the students, albeit with some consternation on the part of the one or ones scheduled to give their reports on that day. Kidder enjoyed it too, and, as might be expected, entered into the seminar discussions with enthusiasm.

My visits to Holden Street continued. As Dr. Kidder was old enough to have been my father, I was hesitant to address him by his first name and would not have thought of doing so except that he finally aske me to. He simply told me one day that he would like it if I called him "Ted", rather than "Dr. Kidder", and Mrs. Kidder, also, insisted that Katharine and I address her as "Madeline". Indeed, in those years, the Kidders did everything possible to make us feel "at home" in Cambridge and in the Harvard community in general. We were invited there to dinner on several occasions, and they, in turn, dined with us at our house.

In the course of our many cocktail hour conversations, I brought up questions that would draw Kidder out on archaeological "method and theory". I wanted to get him to talk about Mesoamerican and Peruvian developments—their parallels and divergences, the connections or lack of connections of the two areas. Perhaps now that he had come to know me better, I thought, he might divulge to me his objections to my paper of some years before. Although by no means a strong diffusionist, Kidder seemed to prefer to discuss these questions of Mesoamerican-Peruvian relationships solely within a diffusionist frame of reference. As I also felt there were some linkages of this nature—domesticated plants, early ceramics, late metallurgical connections—we would go along together up to a point; but when I turned to the larger and more difficult matter of institutional parallels—the rise of ceremonial centers, the beginnings of state-type government, urbanism, large-scale militarism—Kidder's interest was more difficult to hold. It wasn't that he disagreed about the existence of such parallels. He simply shied away from either agreements or arguments about the causal processes that might have been operative to produce the parallels. I recalled some of Walter Taylor's (1946) criticisms of Kidder, to the effect that while he spoke out in general for the need to understand the ways in which the various civilizations of the world had developed or decayed, he never did much about it. That is, he did not appear to be

concerned with "why" and "how" questions in his own research, or in that under his direction in the Carnegie Mesoamerican programs.

Kidder and I discussed the Taylor critique on more than one
of our late afternoon sessions on Holden Street. In the course of
these discussions I tried, without success, to get him to see
Taylor's point of view in the light of the kinds of questions I
have just referred to. One difficulty was that he had been
deeply hurt by Taylor's attack. He saw it as more personal than
it was. Kidder, as the major figure of the Americanist archaeological establishment, had taken the brunt of what had been a
more general criticism of traditional "ceramic chronology"
archaeology. I told him that he was taking the criticisms too
hard. Archaeology and the archaeological profession were
changing. The number of professionals was increasing; argument and debate was going to become ever more frequent; and
some of it was going to be pretty acrimonious. I pleaded that
Taylor had a point. A search for cause did have a place in
prehistory. True, historians had been arguing since time immemorial about "cause" in history, and it remained to be seen
how much agreement we might come to on the issue in archaeology. Still, in my opinion, I felt that it was a part of the human
condition to ask "how" and "why" questions and that it would
be foolish to ask archaeologists to refrain from doing so indefinitely. He, Kidder, my argument went, had "carried the ball"
pretty effectively in American archaeology for the past 30
years. If Taylor now wants to pick it up and run with it, in a
new direction, let's see how he does. I said then, what I have
always thought, that archaeology, like many of the depositions
and structures that it explores, is cumulative. No one will ever
have the final say, and no one, save through the edicts of
totalitarian states, will ever be able to ignore entirely what has
been done by archaeologists before them. But, sadly, Kidder
was not mollified. To him, it was as though the edifice of his
life's work had been declared unfit for habitation by a younger
and ungrateful generation.

At sometime toward the end of the early 1950s, Kidder had a
sudden heart attack. He was confined to bed and to home for a
time. It was not a violently severe illness. Very likely it had

been presaged by his vague tiredness or his feelings of not being "up to snuff" in the fall of 1950. He was still able to have visitors, and I continued to see him on afternoons. Others—Jo Brew and members of the Carnegie staff, Harry Pollock, the Smith brothers, Eric Thompson, Karl Ruppert, and Tania Proskouriakoff—also stopped by. He was back on his feet in a month or two, and he still came into the museum although not as much as before. He was working some, primarily upon his Pecos architectural data, which he eventually completed (Kidder, 1958), and he also was doing some writing on Kaminaljuyu, some of which came out as the last articles he was to publish (Kidder, 1961a,b). We continued our dialogue on archaeology. Philip Phillips and I (Phillips and Willey, 1953; Willey and Phillips, 1955) brought out our two articles which, with revisions and additions, were to compose our book on Method and Theory in *American Archaeology* (Willey and Phillips, 1958) so the discussions I had started with Kidder about New World culture history and cultural evolution went along. Kidder was not very enthusiastic about what we had written, especially our projections of American "culture stages", but we didn't argue much. Neither of us really liked to.

In late 1956 or early 1957, Kidder suffered a stroke. Again, as with the heart attack, it was not severe. After a brief hospitalization, he was home—in bed for a while but then getting up and going out some. His mind and speech were unimpaired. He had been made somewhat lame on one side of his body, but he was still able to walk short distances. He was, naturally, depressed, and he needed something to do to occupy himself. Early in the summer of 1957, Madeline suggested to me that it might be a good thing for Teddy if he consciously set about writing his memoirs. Why couldn't our frequent afternoon conversations be recorded as a working manuscript that he could then revise as a more finished text? It seemed like a fine idea to me. I applied to the Wenner-Gren Foundation for a small grant to pay for the rental of a tape-recorder (such machines were bulkier and more costly in those days than they are now). So equipped, I set the recorder up in the Kidder's living room, and during that summer and fall made more frequent visits there to draw Alfred Vincent Kidder out in talking about his life and times.

I had no very formal plan. Ted and I agreed that we should proceed chronologically but with as many digressions and detours as we went along as suited his fancy. It went wonderfully for a good many sessions. His remembrances about his early life and childhood were presented with vividness and charm. Indeed, we lingered so long over those years that Madeline, who used to come in to serve us drinks and sit by and listen, finally said: "My goodness, I think we've had enough of this. Why don't you two get to some archaeology? Teddy thinks he had such a wonderful childhood! I had a wonderful childhood, too. There's nothing so great about that!" So I asked questions that moved up in time. What were his undergraduate days like? How about the first Southwestern fieldwork? Kidder's answers came flooding out in a splendid reverie. He subsequently published a part of this segment in a piece entitled "Reminiscences in Southwest Archaeology: I" (Kidder, 1960). In this he begins with his undergraduate pre-med courses, his difficulties with these, and his escape from this boredom into the more romantic intellectual luxury of archaeology and the 1907 summer in the Southwest. He tells of his train trip west, of the nature of the country and the people. He is especially fascinated by the handsome waitresses in the midwestern hotels—"countesses", he calls them, with their high pompadours emphasizing their hauteur. As he goes farther west, the "countesses" become gradually less elegant until they are replaced by the simpler, wholesome "Harvey Girl" beauties who served one when the Santa Fe train stopped, at mealtimes, at small stations along the line. They are a young man's remembrances. Much of what he wrote did not come directly from the tape but from a diary which he had kept at the time.

The tape recorder worried Ted a bit. He was a little uncomfortable with it in the same way that I, now, in the 1980s, am uncomfortable with that "new-fangled gadget", the computer. I remember I came in one afternoon and he seemed down in the dumps. He had misgivings about our whole project. I asked why. He told me that he had just been listening to a playback of some of the tape, and that it depressed him no end. Again, I asked why. He said he sounded "absolutely terrible". I explained that this was everyone's reaction to the sound of his own voice reproduced electronically but that I thought that he sounded great. Besides, we weren't going on the air with this. This was to provide him with a draft—once it was all typed up—that would be a big help in the actual writing of the autobiography. We had never discussed this final outcome of our exercise very specifically, but I had always hoped that such would be the result. Well, he didn't know. He just couldn't stand to listen to it. But this depression was passing. On the next visit he was in better spirits, and we went ahead with no problems.

As I prompted Kidder, chronologically, from the early Southwestern days, through World War I, and into the completion of the Pecos enterprise, his reminiscences remained detailed and spiced with anecdotes—as much so as in the earlier childhood and college sections. He didn't avoid his war experiences although he related them in a humorous vein which, I am sure, may have been his way of talking about something that had been pretty horrible. I have heard from others—not Ted—that he saw some very bloody action on the Western Front. Pecos came through clearly. Some of it was reminiscent and anecdotal—and Madeline joined in some good stories of Pecos camp life that went into the record. Some of what Ted had to say was also strictly archaeological—his views of the dig and his interpretations of his findings, both then and now. Some of his retrospective reflections were very frank, and it was from these that I got the idea for a book which I brought out years later. I called it *Archaeological Researches in Retrospect* (Willey, ed., 1974), and in it I had asked various archaeologists to look back upon their field research and comment upon it from the benefit of hindsight, much as Kidder had done. I only wish I could have had Kidder's self-appraisal of Pecos for the book.

When we moved closer to the present in our sessions, beginning with his 1929 appointment as the head of the Carnegie Institution's Division of Historical Research, Ted's narrative became more telescoped. Some of this telescoping or shortening probably derived from that well-known phenomenon about memory or reminiscences: those things far back in time stay vivid or emerge with the clarity of only yesterday while others that happened much later in time are often dimmer. With Kidder, a part of the Carnegie story came through well enough. He had both easy reminiscences and archaeological opinions about the work at Chichen Itza and Uaxactun, or that at Kaminaljuyu, in which he had been more personally involved. While, as in all archaeology, one regrets the things left undone, I think Kidder had a healthy appreciation of, and pride in, these several excavations which had been carried out by him and his subordinates. But there was also depression in his Carnegie remembrances. He had a sense of failure—to my mind unjustified—about his great Maya area multidisciplinary scheme. He felt that archaeology, ethnohistory, and modern ethnography had not been hooked up as they should have been. This was even more the case, in his mind, with reference to biological and natural science researches. A number of practitioners, including some of great talent, had done their work, seemingly in creditable fashion; but the kind of synthesis of it all that he had been hoping for had not emerged—and, of course, because he was a synthesizer, *par excellence*, he blamed himself.

This mood of self-blame was exacerbated by a sad institutional circumstance. The head of the Carnegie Institution of Washington, succeeding Kidder's good friend Merriam, was Vannevar Bush. Bush was a chemist of world stature, one of the nation's best-known scientists who had been a key figure in American science during World War II. His prestige in scientific-academic and scientific-foundational circles was enormous. As it developed, he was to be the nemesis of Maya archaeology in the Carnegie Institution. Although the original founders of the Institution had included archaeology, history, and the humanities within its purview—in addition to the physical and natural sciences, Bush was of the opinion that these "soft" disciplines had no place within the organization. While he often said that he appreciated archaeology, and enjoyed the idea of finding ancient places and treasures as much as the next person, he didn't feel that it was a fit subject for the Carnegie Institution of Washington, at least as he wished to restructure that body. The only part of archaeology that he could conceive of as "science" was the laboratory microscope work that Anna Shepard was doing with pottery. The claim of archaeology that enraged Bush the most was just the sort of thing that Kidder had been saying—that archaeology had a place in discovering the ways in which civilizations rose and fell and the reasons behind these happenings. To put a stop to such "social science nonsense", Bush called the Carnegie archaeological staff together in the late 1940s and informed them that he was closing out the Division of Historical Research. Those who wished to leave now and go elsewhere should feel free to do so; others could remain and continue with whatever projects they chose to pursue; but all activities and salaries of the Division, except for pensions, were to be terminated by the year 1958. With this announcement, Bush also made clear that anyone who attempted to "go over his head" with an appeal to the Trustees would be peremptorily dismissed.

Quite understandably, Kidder was deeply hurt by what had happened. It added to this sense of failure that beset him at times—to my mind a neurosis of his that was quite unjustifiable in the light of his great gifts and many extraordinary achievments. Thus, it is, perhaps, no wonder that Kidder cut short his autobiographical narrative as we moved into these last years of disappointment with the Carnegie. In fact, he refused to talk about this termination of the Division of Historical Research; what I have related here I learned from others, not from Kidder himself.

By the end of that summer of 1957, I had everything that we had recorded typed up, and presented the manuscript to Ted and Madeline. Presumably, much of it has since been lost for a recent biographer of Kidder's has found only a fragment of it in the family files (Givens, 1986). I still do not know whether Kidder ever seriously planned a full-length autobiography. That he titled the one published piece of it, "Reminiscences in Southwest Archaeology: I" (Kidder, 1960), with the Roman Numeral "I", suggests that he did, or, at least, that he anticipated subsequent Southwestern "chapters". Sadly, he did not leave his colleagues any more than this first chapter.

Kidder's life and career is, of course, well-known. He was the leading American archaeologist of his time. A number of obituary statements have appeared since his death, including those in the leading American archaeological (Wauchope, 1965) and anthropological (Greengo, 1968) journals, and in the *Memoirs* of the National Academy of Science (Willey, 1967). A book-length biography is also available (Woodbury, 1973), and, as I write this, another has been prepared (Givens, 1986).

Alfred Vincent Kidder was essentially a New Englander—a New Englander of old Anglo-Saxon stock. His father was from Massachusetts but had gone west, temporarily, to the iron ore fields of Michigan's Upper Peninsula, as a mining engineer and a mining entrepreneur. Young Alfred Vincent was born there, in Marquette, Michigan, on 29 October 1885. His father was also an Alfred, although not an "Alfred Vincent", and his mother was Kate (Dalliba) Kidder, from Chicago, Illinois. When Alfred Vincent was still a small boy, the family left Michigan and returned to New England, to settle in Cambridge, Massachusetts. Here, he attended the Browne and Nichols School for a time, but in 1901, he entered the La Villa School, in Ouchy, Switzerland for two years. On his return to the States, he was sent to another New England preparatory school, Noble and Greenough, for a final year before going to Harvard in 1904.

At Harvard, it was Kidder's first intention to become a physician, or perhaps this was a family intention for the young Kidder seems to have had no very strong commitment in this direction. His experiences with premedical courses—in chemistry, physics, and mathematics—dampened whatever ardor he may have had for medicine. As he told me, years afterwards, he "thoroughly disliked" such disciplines, preferring, instead, history, languages, and the natural sciences. It was in seeking these alternative paths to learning that Kidder had an introductory anthropology course with Professor Roland B. Dixon. He enjoyed it and went on to take other courses in the Anthropology Department, with F. W. Putnam, Alfred M. Tozzer, and W. C. Farabee. At the end of his Junior year, in 1907, Tozzer arranged for him to go that summer to the Southwestern United States for archaeological fieldwork, and this seems to have been the deciding factor in his choice of a profession. It was this first season in the Southwest that generated many of his most interesting reminiscences that he related to me over the tape-recorder. He completed his A.B. degree in anthropology in 1908. After that, and after more Southwestern archaeological fieldwork, he entered the Harvard graduate school where he eventually received both his A.M. (1912) and Ph.D. (1914) degrees in anthropology. He was primarily Tozzer's student, but he also recalled, in talking about these graduate years at Harvard, a course with Franz Boas, who was there for a year as a Visiting Professor, and another with Professor George A. Reisner, the Egyptologist at the Fogg Museum. It was from the latter, a man who has gone down in archaeological history as the modernizer of Egyptian field methods, that Kidder learned many of the digging principles and techniques that he was to put into practice in the Americas.

In 1908–1909 Kidder was taken by his parents for a vacation in Greece and Egypt. Not only did this experience strengthen his interests in archaeology, but the Kidders were joined on this excursion by the Appleton family of Boston, whose daughter Madeline became engaged to young Alfred Kidder as they cruised up the Nile. They were married in 1910, and over the next dozen years they had three sons (Alfred II, Randolph, and James) and two daughters (Barbara and Faith). Madeline became a devotee of archaeology and was a constant companion and aid in his subsequent archaeological fieldwork, especially at Pecos, New Mexico, where she presided over a field camp that became famous. The several archaeological summers at Pecos were very important also to another member of the family, Alfred Kidder II, who, as noted, followed his father in the profession of archaeology.

During his graduate years and after, until 1915, Kidder continued his Southwestern explorations, especially those in Arizona. These were carried out under the aegis of the Peabody Museum at Harvard. His work in the "Basketmaker" caves of northeastern Arizona, which was done in collaboration with S. J. Guernsey, brought to attention and defined the early horticultural Basketmaker horizon of the Southwest (Kidder and Guernsey, 1919). Dating from this same period in his career is his doctoral dissertation: *Southwestern Ceramics: Their Value in Reconstructing the History of the Ancient Cliff Dwelling and Pueblo Tribes. An Exposition from the Point of View of Type Distinction* (Kidder, 1914, unpublished). It is less well known than the Kidder and Guernsey publication, but it may have been more important in the development of Kidder's thinking. From the title, it is obvious that Kidder was laying the groundwork for his later archaeological triumphs at Pecos—and, indeed, laying the chronological and typological groundwork for Southwestern archaeological systematics.

The Pecos excavations began in 1915, the year after Kidder had completed the Ph.D. He was now employed by the R. S. Peabody Foundation, at Andover, Massachusetts, which supported the Pecos work. The big pueblo ruin of Pecos is in the Rio Grande drainage of north-central New Mexico. It was selected by Kidder because of its great size, the depth of its refuse accumulations, and its sampling of pottery which indicated that the site spanned much of the then known time range of Southwestern prehistory. That it was at the eastern edge of the Southwestern archaeological culture area was another attraction. Although Plains archaeology was, as yet, an unknown quantity, Kidder was alert to the possibilities of eventually correlating the Southwestern relative chronology, to be worked out at Pecos, to regions to the east. Kidder also told me, in the course of our tape-recorded conversations, that he had in mind, as well, the possibilities of discovering relationships with Mesoamerica as these might possibly be traced via the Rio Grande Valley. Since then, the Plains connections have been established, the Mesoamerican ones have not, at least through a Rio Grande Valley route; but the fact that Kidder was thinking in these terms as early as 1915 shows the breadth of his culture-historical vision and his realization of the kinds of problems that American archaeologists would have to confront.

The Pecos excavations were the first large-scale systematic stratigraphic excavations in New World archaeology. Potsherd stratigraphy, of course, had Old World beginnings, and even within the Southwestern United States it had been employed by others in a limited way prior to the Pecos work (see Nelson, 1914); but Kidder used the method intensively, recovering massive amounts of pottery and eventually presenting his data in great detail. He also made explicit the methodological differences between metrical and physical stratigraphy and their theoretical implications.

Kidder worked the 1915 and 1916 seasons at Pecos, but operations there were interrupted by World War I. He went to France with the A.E.F., serving as a lieutenant, and later as a captain. His war record was a distinguished one. He took part in the St. Mihiel, Argonne-Meuse, and Ypres-Lys actions and was made a Chevalier of the Legion of Honor by the French Government. In the 1919 season he resumed work at Pecos, and this continued until 1929.

Kidder published the first Pecos results in a remarkable book that was to extend the knowledge and order derived from his stratigraphy at that site to much of the Southwestern area. This was his *An Introduction to the Study of Southwestern Archaeology, with a Preliminary Account of the Excavations at Pecos* (Kidder, 1924). It is a rarity in that it introduces systematics to a field previously unsystematized while being, at the same time, a vitally alive and unpedantic account. As such, it has stood as an American archaeological classic—one of the few works that could be said to belong to that genre. Later, as a basic monographic follow-up to this *Introduction*, Kidder brought out the large report, *The Pottery of Pecos, Vol. I* (Kidder, 1931). This is where he laid out the Pecos stratigraphy and ceramic typology in chapter and verse. Much later, after formal retirement, he conscientiously completed his Pecos excavation reporting with a monograph on kivas and architecture (Kidder, 1958).

An important by-product of the Pecos work was the First Pecos Conference in Southwestern Archaeology. It was called and organized by Kidder and held in 1927. As the name implies, the conferees met at the Pecos field camp, with A.V.K. and Madeline as host and hostess. Cultural and ceramic classification and chronology were at the top of the agenda, and the conference was attended by virtually all Southwestern archaeologists then practicing in the field. Out of it was to come the "Pecos Classification". These Pecos conferences continued in later years, becoming annual events, first under Kidder's leadership but, later, passing on to younger Southwestern archaeologists. Their subject matter and research emphases have changed with the times, but they have remained a vital force in the professionalization and advancement of the discipline in the Southwestern area.

ALFRED VINCENT KIDDER

Still another Pecos benefit to American archaeology was the training of students in field methods. Except for duty as a Teaching Fellow while a graduate student, and a semester at the University of California late in his career, Kidder was never a formal teacher; but the informal field training at Pecos was well remembered by such archaeologists as Carl E. Guthe, Samuel K. Lothrop, and George C. Vaillant. The latter was especially impressed by what he had learned with Kidder on and in the refuse dumps of Pecos and was to put these stratigraphic lessons to work in the Valley of Mexico a few years later.

While Kidder continued at Pecos until 1929, he was already involved in other archaeological interests in the latter half of the 1920s. These gradually took up more and more of his time, and one of them, Maya archaeology, eventually became the main focus of his research career. This involved the Carnegie Institution Washington, but let me digress a bit for a little background to this.

In 1902 the Carnegie Institution of Washington was founded as a research organization in the sciences, humanities, and social sciences, with anthropology and archaeology definitely included in its initial charter. Pumpelly's archaeological excavations at Anau, in Turkistan, in 1903 and 1904, were sponsored by the new institution, and the whole Pumpelly enterprise was path-breaking in that it combined archaeology with related earth and environmental sciences in the sort of research approach that someday would be called "interdisciplinary". The Carnegie Institution also carried out archaeological excavations in Greece and Rome. More immediately pertinent to Kidder's future was another Carnegie plan of survey and excavations, this one for the Maya ruins of Yucatan and Guatemala. It was initiated in 1914 by S. G. Morley, an old Harvard fellow graduate student of Kidder's, who in that year had been appointed a Research Associate to the Institution. Under Morley's guidance, Carnegie's Maya archaeological program had grown sufficiently by 1921 to require substantial annual appropriations. Long-term arrangements were underway with the goverments of Mexico and Guatemala for the continuance of the Institution's archaeological field operations in those countries. Archaeology had become a major part of the Carnegie. In 1926 Kidder, who had earlier been retained in the capacity of adviser on the archaeological work of the Institution, was also appointed as a Research Associate. The following year he was placed in charge of all of the archaeological activities of the Carnegie. Ultimately, in 1929, he became head of the Institution's Divison of Historical Research. This Division, which was the administrative grouping of humanistic studies, included such fields as United States History, the History of Greek Thought, and the History of Science, as well as Archaeology. Kidder was to remain its head until his retirement in 1950 (Pollock, 1958).

Kidder brought to his new job not only his long experience in the Southwest but a considerable knowledge of Middle American archaeology. It will be remembered he had been a student of Tozzer. He also had made an archaeological tour around Mexico as early as 1922, in company with Clarence L. Hay. In his several years as a consultant to the Carnegie group he had acquired a familiarity with the archaeological problems of the area. In assuming command of Carnegie's archaeological work, he also had in his favor the personal friendship of J. C. Merriam, an historian and humanist, then the President of the Carnegie Institution of Washington. Further, Kidder found his new position a very compatible one because he would be allied in it with his old friend, Sylvanus G. Morley, as well as with other Mayanists who were former students of Tozzer's.

Together with Morley, Kidder began to plan the future of archaeological research in the Maya region. This was a specialized program, but, in carrying it out, Kidder wanted to keep in mind that the course of human history in this one particular area was but a part of the much more embracing story of man and society in the world at large. What he set out to do was, in his own words, "based on the obvious fact that the knowledge of man was lagging dangerously behind that of the physical world. Such knowledge can only be gained by clearer understanding of the world's present civilizations: the conditions under which they have arisen, their careers, their present likenesses and differences, weaknesses and strengths. A necessary first step toward such ends is to learn what we can of the prehistoric developments which gave them birth" (Willey, 1967, p. 302). While conceding that the Precolumbian Maya civilization has had no full continuity to the present, Kidder argued that it could be considered one of man's great achievments of whatever time and place. Its accomplishments, trials, and downfall deserved scholarly attention in any comprehensive comparative examination of the ways of mankind. Thus, Kidder's ambitions for the Carnegie archaeological research program had a sweep and a sophistication to them. He was at that time in his early forties. Did he later come to feel that these goals were too ambitious? I was never sure in my talks with him. Perhaps he was only discouraged that he had not been able to achieve these very lofty goals.

As Pumpelly had at Anau, Kidder envisaged the proper attack on the Maya area as a "pan-scientific" one. Along with the ongoing program of traditional archaeological excavations and hieroglyphic studies—as these had been guided by Morley and which continued with Morley and others—Kidder opened up investigations into physical anthropology, medicine, social anthropology, ethnology, linguistics, Maya aboriginal documentary history, Colonial history, environmental studies involving plant and animal biology, ceramic technology, geography, geology, and agronomy. All of these investigations, carried out by Carnegie staff members and by colleagues from various universities and other institutions, were concerned with the Maya, living or dead, and with their environmental habitats in southern Mexico and adjacent Guatemala. It was Kidder's retrospective opinion, as we talked about all of this during the late 1950s, that this conception of an overall approach to Maya culture history was his most significant contribution to anthropology. It is difficult not to agree with this evaluation. No one had ever envisioned an American archaeological program of quite such scope and depth. Important beginnings were made which set the course of future Maya research, and that research still goes on.

Even if Kidder's "pan-scientific" dreams were not realized for the Maya area in his lifetime, we cannot deny the great substantive achievments of his program. They include the extensive and intensive excavations at Chichen Itza and Uaxactun,

and to these we can add the equally thorough Mayapan surveys
and excavations. The Mayapan work was carried out under
Pollock's direction, after Kidder's retirement; however, it followed in Kidder's larger plan to excavate strategic sites that,
taken together, would span the chronological range of Lowland
Maya culture. Besides these major excavation projects, a great
many other sites were partially explored, surveyed, and
mapped, throughout both the southern and northern Maya
Lowlands. In all of this digging, the Preclassic beginnings of
Maya civilization were disclosed; an important start was made
in Maya ceramic and artifactual analyses; detailed architectural studies were made; the hieroglyphic corpus was greatly
expanded; traditional studies of art and iconography were pursued and refined; and, within a wider frame of reference, the
Carnegie Institution's work in the Maya Highlands of
Guatemala gave a new perspective on the matter of Maya
Lowland origins.

In this account of the Carnegie's archaeological and historical achievments under Kidder's direction, we must take note
of his associates and colleagues. All attained scholarly distinction. They included, in addition to Morley, such people as
J. E. S. Thompson, Tatiana Proskouriakoff, O. G. Ricketson, Jr.,
H. E. D. Pollock, A. Ledyard and Robert E. Smith, E. M. Shook,
Ralph Roys, and Anna M. Shepard. Kidder was a good boss, and
he ran a "happy ship". His errors as a "commander" were on the
side of leniency rather than the reverse, but it has always been
my opinion that he realized the best way to treat researchers,
including some who were very strong-minded individuals, was
to let them have as much freedom as possible.

Although the administrative head of the Carnegie endeavor,
Kidder, himself, continued to write and publish. Notable in
this regard was his big monograph on excavations at Kaminaljuyu, the great Maya Highland site on the outskirts of the
present-day Guatemala City. Written in collaboration with
J. D. Jennings and E. M. Shook (Kidder, Jennings, and Shook,
1946), it served to introduce Maya Highland archaeology to
Mayanists and to Mesoamericanists at large. It placed special
emphasis on the Classic Period, and, in this connection, was
the first major work to lay out the data for Maya Classic-

Teotihuacan Classic contemporaneity. A second work on Kaminaljuyu, co-authored with Shook, revealed the depth and
complexity of the Preclassic Period in the Maya Highlands
(Shook and Kidder, 1952). In an interesting short paper, written
at the time he was doing some of the first Kaminaljuyu digging,
Kidder (1936) moved farther afield, examining the probabilities
and possibilities of Mesoamerican-Andean relationships. He
suggested a rehabilitation and revision of Herbert J. Spinden's
famous "Archaic Hypothesis" by pointing out that there was
steadily emerging evidence to support the idea of a substratum
of interrelated early agricultural societies underlying the more
specialized later developments in Mexico, Guatemala, and
Peru. Spinden, Kidder argued, rather than being wholly wrong,
had merely mistaken a relatively late Central Mexican manifestation of "Archaic", "Preclassic", or "Formative" culture as
the type example of the basic understratum. In this, and in a
1946 plan for future Carnegie research—which, unfortunately,
was never carried out—Kidder foresaw the importance of examining the evidence for inter-areal relationships within the
American high culture sphere, even though he was less sanguine about results than I was at the time I showed him my
1945 paper.

Kidder was outgoing in his professional relationships, and,
given his distinction, he was drawn into many services other
than his duties with the Carnegie. He served on various museum boards—the Peabody at Harvard, the Peabody at Yale, the
Southwest Museum in Los Angeles, and the Laboratory of
Anthropology in Santa Fe, New Mexico. He had a two-year
term on the National Research Council, as Chairman of its
Division of Anthropology and Psychology (1926–1927). He
was a principal founder of the Institute of Andean Research in
the 1930s.

He was the recipient of many honors, being elected President
of the Society for American Archaeology (1937) and of the
American Anthropological Association (1942), as well as being
a member of the National Academy of Sciences, the American
Academy of Arts and Sciences, and the American Philosophical Society. Honorary degrees were conferred upon him by the
University of New Mexico (1934), the University of Michigan

(1949), the National University of Mexico (1951), and San Carlos University of Guatemala (1955). In 1946 he was awarded the Viking Fund Medal for Archaeology, being the first recipient of this honor. In 1950 the American Anthropological Association established an Alfred V. Kidder Medal for excellence in the fields of Southwestern or Mesoamerican Archaeology. In 1955 the Guatemalan Government awarded him the Order of the Quetzal in appreciation of his many years of research in that country. And in 1958, the University Museum at the University of Pennsylvania bestowed the Drexel Medal for Archaeology on him. Thus, by the 1950s, when I had those many long afternoon conversations with Kidder, he had attained a pinnacle of success and recognition in the American archaeological field that was unsurpassed.

I continued to see Ted after our tape-recording sessions, which had ended in the early fall of 1957. While not robust, he, nevertheless, enjoyed reasonable health and looked hearty. As always, he was fun to talk with, about archaeology or a variety of subjects. In his late years he made a trip to Guatemala City, to visit his daughter Barbara and her family, and on this occasion he went out to Kaminaljuyu and was given a rousing welcome by many of his old workmen who were still engaged in archaeology at the site under Guatemalan Government auspices. I recall, too, that he and Madeline attended at least one Pecos summer conference where, quite properly, he was the beloved father figure. Katharine and I and our daughters had planned to spend the 1962–1963 year in England. Before we sailed, Ted and Madeline stopped by to see us. It was my last glimpse of him. He died on 11 June 1963, seated at his desk at his home in Cambridge.

WILLIAM ROTCH BULLARD, JR.
In early middle age.
Courtesy Mrs. W. R. Bullard, Jr.

WILLIAM ROTCH BULLARD, JR.
(1926–1972)

Bill Bullard was a colleague in Maya archaeology, dating back to my early days at Harvard and my entrance into the Maya field. He was also one of my first graduate students there. I had then, and have had since, many outstanding students in Meso-american and Maya archaeology, but I don't believe I have ever had one with whom I was more congenial. Let me say at the beginning that although Bill Bullard had a top-quality mind, he had none of the self-conscious awareness of this that so many bright people have. He didn't think about things like that. He remained singularly non-competitive in a graduate student atmosphere which fostered competitiveness.

In 1953, after I had reoriented my Central American research priorities under Mr. Tozzer's firm guidance (see the Tozzer memoir), I cast around for a way to go directly into the Maya field. I had made up my mind that it would be wise to do this by following a "settlement pattern" research theme. For one thing, it was obvious that overall settlement exploration was much needed in Maya studies; for another, I was going into a new area where many things would be strange and where I could serve archaeology and myself best by selecting a line of investigation with which I had some familiarity. I had discussed the matter with Linton Satterthwaite, Jr., then the leading Mayanist at the University of Pennsylvania, and he had encouraged me by suggesting that I make a beginning in British Honduras. He was going down there in the early winter of that year, to dig at Caracol, a major site in the southern part of the Colony. He told me that in the previous season he had worked near El Cayo (now San Ignacio), in west-central British Honduras. In his opinion, the small ceremonial center of Cahal Pech, a kilometer or so outside of the town of El Cayo, might be a suitable, as well as a logistically convenient, place to begin a settlement pattern survey. He said that if I wished, he would be glad to introduce me to El Cayo and Cahal Pech before he continued on to Caracol for his own work. His generous offer was very appealing, and I accepted it.

As I wanted to take someone along on this trip who would then continue with me on a Maya settlement pattern enterprise, and as, preferably, this should be one of my Harvard graduate students, I selected William Bullard to accompany me. Bullard had been in a lecture course on Middle American Archaeology which I had given in the fall semester of 1951–52. After that, I had recommended him to Harry Pollock to be one of the student assistants for the Carnegie dig at Mayapan in 1952. Bullard spent that winter and spring at Mayapan. Bill's task had been one of survey and mapping, especially of individual house mound "boundary" or "property walls" within the great Mayapan enclosure (Bullard, 1952a,b, 1953a). It seemed good field preparation for the residential unit settlement survey that I had in mind. He had also been one of the students in my South American Archaeological seminar (Anthropology 206) and had produced a very creditable paper there (Bullard, 1953b). It was obvious that he was as effective at the desk and in the library as he was in the field. He appeared to be the ideal junior colleague for my British Honduras settlement pattern venture—and this judgment turned out to be correct.

Bill, as a young man then, and later into early middle age, was a well-put-together, lean, wiry-looking specimen. He was a tough and rugged field man, one of those who loved the field, who truly liked to sleep in a hammock under a mosquito net and who actually enjoyed traveling light in the jungle and living on rice and beans. People like that always amaze me, but they are the ones who really make Maya field archaeology possible. About six feet in height and long-legged, Bill moved fast with a sturdy, slightly rolling gait. I can see him striding along ahead of me on the jungle trails or pushing his way through the bush, effectively swinging a machete at the vines and undergrowth, completely happy and at ease in his adopted tropical setting. Bill had a round, open countenance which was usually split with a grin. He had dark hair and eyes, and, although basically fair-complexioned, he tanned easily and evenly to a nut-brown color that stayed with him most of the year. Bill wore glasses much of the time—both in the field and otherwise. These were in keeping with his down-to-earth, conservative personality. They had small eye-pieces and steel frames. When he put them on, I always thought of the old-fashioned word "spectacles"; he wouldn't have tolerated fancier eye-wear. A straight-stemmed briar pipe was another facial fixture with Bill. Like any respectable pipe-smoker, he burned a lot of wooden matches and paid a good bit of attention to the cleaning, scraping, filling, tamping and general fiddling with the instrument.

Bill had a taciturn side. I recall it from the field. In the evenings when a group of us would sit around camp and discuss the days work or tomorrow's plans, Bill would often sit silent for a long time, pipe-puffing but following the discussion. But then, suddenly, he would break forth with considerable force and passion of conviction. This was usually by way of disagreement with the preceding speaker, myself or anyone else. He was the same way in seminars. In any seminar group of eight or ten, there will always be two or three students who do a lot of talking. The rest have to be drawn out. Bill was one of the latter. I would try to get him into the discussion. Often, this was like pulling teeth, but then he might cut loose, again in disagreement with what had been said by a previous speaker. He hated any kind of "jargonized" dialogue. He wanted to reduce things to simple English. He had a way of saying everything twice, sentence by sentence, as though he were guarding against any possible misunderstanding of his position. When it came to fieldwork, Bill was similarly direct, simple, and sensible. He could avoid or cut through unessentials.

One thinks of this directness, this simplicity, both in conversation and in action, as a New England trait, and, if it is, Bill Bullard came by it honestly. He was born in Boston, Massachusetts on 4 June 1926, the second of three sons of William Rotch and Hilda (Greenleaf) Bullard. The family was deeply rooted in both Boston and New Bedford. Bill once told me that one of his ancestors, on the eve of the American Revolution, gave his approval to those revolutionary-minded parties who were the instigators of the "Boston Tea Party". However, this Bullard forbear cautioned the militants that in the act of throwing the tea overboard they should be very careful not to damage the ships. After all, the ships were his property. Another ancestor, a little time after this, was the captain of a New

Bedford sailing vessel. Like Melville's mad, sad, Ahab, he was unfortunate enought to lose a leg in an encounter with a whale. Unlike Ahab, though, this doughty New Englander was neither mad nor sad and lived to tell about it (Willey, 1973a).

Young William Bullard, Jr. went to the Berkeley Preparatory School, in Sheffield, Massachusetts. Following this, he entered Harvard in the Class of 1947; but military service with the U.S. Army in Japan and Korea interrupted his college years so that he did not graduate until 1950, when he received his B.A. degree, *cum laude*. After that, Bill continued with graduate work at Harvard, in anthropology. During his graduate student period he interspersed classroom and seminar attendance with as much archaeological fieldwork as he could. Before I knew him, Bill had managed to get in a season in the North American Plains and another in Alaska. Later, while he was working with me in British Honduras, he also spent two summers (1953 and 1954) in the Southwestern United States as Jo Brew's assistant. The results of this Southwestern fieldwork were developed as a doctoral dissertation at the same time he was concerning himself with Maya settlement patterns.

To go back to 1953, at the point at which I began this story of Bill Bullard, he was then all set to return to Yucatan and spend the winter-spring season with Pollock and the Carnegie group at Mayapan. I asked why not precede this with a month with me in British Honduras? We could look things over down there, and make plans for long-term settlement pattern research. Pollock gave his approval, and Bill didn't need any further urging. So Bullard and I, along with Satterthwaite and Jerry Epstein, the latter a student of Satterthwaite's, departed for Belize, by way of Merida, Yucatan, in early February.

In Belize, guided by Satterthwaite, we put up at the new Fort George Hotel and were shown around the city by him. We called on the Governor of the colony, Sir Patrick Rennison, who received us graciously and listened to our archaeological proposals. Sir Patrick assured us of his support, relating that he had "read" archaeology as a student at Cambridge, before going into the Colonial Service, and that he was "keen" on the subject. A. H. Anderson, or Hamilton Anderson as we came to know him, was called in at some point in these discussions.

Anderson, among several other duties, was also Archaeological Commissioner of the Colony, and he could then have been described as "very keen" on Maya archaeology, as well as very well-informed about it. He agreed to join us at El Cayo, in the interior, in a few days.

I should, at this point, explain that archaeology was a very familiar activity in British Honduras. Ever since Morley's first expedition into the Peten, in 1914, Maya archaeologists had come first to Belize City—in the earlier years by boat, after World War II by plane—on their way into the Maya bush. The purchase of supplies and the final outfitting of the expeditions took place there. Around the city in 1953, there were still a good many "old-timers" who remembered the early days of the Carnegie and the Peabody Museum explorations. I recall one gentleman, a long-time British Civil Servant, who had been head of the police in the Colony at the time of the first Morley trip, when Morley's companion, Lafleur, was shot by an ambushing party of Guatemalan soldiers somewhere near the British Honduras-Guatemalan border (Carpenter, 1950). This same man also remembered the young Alfred Tozzer, who had passed through the city on his way into Tikal and Holmul.

There were some very famous bars in Belize City in 1953, and in saying this I do not refer to the then quite "posh" bar in the new Fort George Hotel. This exceedingly modern-looking "cocktail-lounge" had no real cachet among what we might have called "the good old boys" of Belize. Their favorite bar was the Palace, in the old hotel of the same name. This had been "the place" in Morley's and Tozzer's day, and it still was. The Palace was an ancient, three-storied, wooden structure near the center of the city. It was partially constructed on pilings, out over the water where patrons could enjoy the Caribbean breezes. The situation was also advantageous to the hotel's sanitary facilities. Again, following Satterthwaite's experienced guidance, we all repaired there in the late afternoon of our first day in town. Official visits were over; we could now turn to other matters.

But Bullard was unable to relax completely in the Palace atmosphere, being nagged by an official concern which he insisted he should take care of without undue delay. He tended to worry about such things. On this occasion, his problem was to obtain a visa in the Colony that would see him back across the border into Mexico so that he could return to Mayapan after our projected survey of the Cayo region. In some conversation at the bar with other parties, Bill made known his worry. We were assured by our newly met acquaintances at the Palace that this would be no problem at all, that if we would extend our stay only a little longer the man who could take care of this minor bureaucratic detail, none other than the Mexican Consul himself, one Don Carlos, would appear there to partake of a small apertif, as was his evening custom. All such arrangements as Bullard had in mind could be, forthwith, consummated, and we, gentlemen and archaeologists, would not be deflected from other, more serious pursuits.

So encouraged, we lingered at the Palace, ordering new drinks for ourselves and for our comforting companions. The tropical night came down like a black curtain at 6:15 PM—give or take a minute or two—but the good Don Carlos did not appear. Someone suggested that he had, perhaps, stopped off a short distance up the street, at another bar with which he was known to divide his custom. Suddenly, a small boy appeared and, with eagerness, told the by now restive Bullard, that for a very small sum—50 cents in British Honduras coin (then 35 cents U.S.)—he would produce his Honor, the Mexican Consul, in the winking of an eye. It seemed like a very trifling cost to me and one that we could easily justify in our expense account so I urged Bill to take the young man up on his offer and circumvent needless bureaucratic red tape. But Bullard was not to be persuaded. Something in his New England upbringing could not countenance this kind of an irregularity. No, he replied, it did not seem fitting that he should have to pay 50 cents (even if only 35 cents U.S.), to an obviously non-official intermediary, in order to see the Consular representative of a sovereign nation about a matter of official business. Moreover, the ambience for such a proposed confrontation was highly inappropriate. He repeated this opinion twice, that certain indication that the Bullard mind was made up. So we all gave up and went back to the Fort George for dinner.

The next day, at what seemed the suitable business hours of

WILLIAM ROTCH BULLARD, JR.

11 AM, 3 PM, and, again, 4 PM, Bullard paid official visits to the Mexican Consulate. Each time he was told by a frightened-looking female servant, who peeked out from behind a narrowly cracked door, that *"Don Carlos no esta!"* On the day following, results were much the same. A passerby in the street told him, again, that the place to find the elusive foreign emissary was the bar of the Palace Hotel. This informant suggested a later hour for the rendezvous than the routine cocktail hour. Somewhere nearer midnight, we were advised, would be best. Once more, a "finder's fee" on Don Carlos was suggested—this time of a dollar (70 cents U.S.). But Bullard remained adamant. Again, I advised Bill that maybe he better. Otherwise, he might have to return to New Orleans and make a second run on Mexico from the United States. Nevertheless, Bill, in his indignation, could not be swayed.

Fortunately, the dilemna of the visa was to be resolved in another way. On the morning following these last encounters, we all paid our respects to the American Consul at his residence in Belize. After some polite conversation with our countryman, Bill, with only a slight undertone of outrage in his voice, related the story of his failed Mexican visa search and kindred matters. "Our man in Belize" didn't say anything, but looked at us a little owlishly for a moment from behind thick glasses. Then he picked up the phone and asked for the Mexican Consulate. When there was an answer he identified himself and asked to speak to his opposite number in the Diplomatic Corps. After a short wait, this dignitary must have come on the line for a friendly telephone consversation in Spanish ensued. From what we heard from our end of it, it became obvious that things were at last on the right track. Putting down the phone, our host turned to Bill and told him that an appointment had been made for him to obtain his visa at the Mexican Consulate at 4:00 that afternoon.

By this time, I had become so intrigued by the whole business that I went with Bullard when he presented himself at the Consulate, promptly on the appointed hour. Everything went smoothly, formally, and without a hitch. It was clear that official channels had been properly opened. We were shown into a study by the heretofore furtive maidservant who now seemed quite composed. Don Carlos, elegant in a white linen suit, arose from his desk, bowed, and shook hands with us both. He bore a notable, although somewhat haggard resemblance to the late Rudolph Valentino. He dutifully stamped the visa in Bill's passport, and then prepared to sign it. This latter action was to be no trivial undertaking. Starting with the pen held high in his hand, about two feet above the desk, Don Carlos began circling motions reminiscent of the excessive arm movements of the old "Palmer Penmanship Method" of my childhood. Gradually the circling hand and pen descended toward the awaiting open page of the passport. Finally, contact was made, like an airplane coming to a swift landing, and signing was effected, quite audibly and with a fine flourish. The Consul arose, bowed, and handed the passport to Bill. We all shook hands again, and that was it. Bullard, with honor assuaged and a Mayapan arrival secure, was ready for our trek on the morrow into the British Honduran hinterlands in search of house mounds.

We went to El Cayo in a hired car the next day. It should be added that in so doing we had it easy compared to the way the same journey was made in the 1920s and 30s. Then there was no auto road, and cargo and passengers moved only by a river steamer. That trip took three days and three nights. (I have referred to it in the Vaillant memoir.) In El Cayo we were met by Leocadio E. Hopun, the agent who worked in concert with Melhado & Cia., our agents in Belize City. He had, for many years, so serviced the Carnegie expeditions when they came in to El Cayo to change to a mule-train for the further journey to Uaxactun. Hopun also acted for Satterthwaite, and he informed us that he would be delighted to serve in this capacity to me. Hopun was a most interesting man (A. L. Smith, *et al.* 1961). He had been born in the Colony of a Chinese father and a Mexican mother. Extremely knowledgeable about all local matters, I associate him in my mind with admonitory advice, which he later was to give me on many occasions.

El Cayo lacked a hostelry in those days, so we bedded down in the Church of England Rectory, which was then vacant. The next morning we breakfasted at a restaurant downtown. While so doing, a member of the Black Colonial Constabulary appeared at an open window of the dining room, calling a fulsome welcome to Linton Satterthwaite. After going over to the window for an amiable exchange with this representative of the law, Linton returned to the table with the remark: "Swell fellow! It's always good to keep in with these boys. It's something for you to remember if you're going to work around here." Ten minutes or so passed, as we worked our way through the eggs, frijoles refritos, and tortillas. Then, once more, Satterthwaite's policeman friend came to the window. "Doctor," he said, addressing Satterthwaite, as he pulled a small slip of paper from his shirt pocket, "this is a parking violation ticket from last year when you left your Jeep in an unauthorized zone here in El Cayo. It's a two dollar fine, Doctor. You can take it over to the Police Station to pay it, but I thought it would be more convenient for you just to pay me."

I mused then upon El Cayo's parking and traffic problems. In the short time we had been there, I didn't think I had seen more than one other vehicle, in addition to Satterthwaite's Jeep, in what might be called the "downtown business district"—at least at any given moment. Nevertheless, it was a lesson to me that parking violations would not be tolerated if we should decide to base ourselves here in the capital of the Western District. I don't know what Bullard thought, but it looked like he was having a hard time keeping a straight face through all this.

Breakfast over, we all piled into the Jeep and drove out of town, up the hill, to Cahal Pech. This small Maya ceremonial center was on the hilltop which overlooked El Cayo and the Macal branch of the Belize River. As I recall, it numbered two or three plazas, had a sizable pyramid, and a single plain stela. Linton was of the opinion that, as a center, it probably had drawn upon a sustaining area several kilometers in length, along the river. It was smaller and less grand than Benque Viejo, or Xunantunich, (Thompson, 1940) which was located nine kilometers to the west, on the Mopan branch of the Belize. Later, in preparing our final report of our Belize Valley surveys and excavations, we would devote some pages to a discussion of the probable relationships of these two, and other, sites in a site hierarchy (Willey et al. 1965, pp. 571–581).

In 1953, it was sufficient to recognize that Cahal Pech was certainly a suitable place from which one might start settlement pattern surveys.

Two workmen, armed with machetes, awaited us, by appointment, at Cahal Pech. Satterthwaite outlined his plan of action. We would begin on the lower slopes of the Cahal Pech hill and cut a *breccia,* or path, through the bush in an easterly direction from the center, down towards the river, which was about a kilometer away. In this way we would begin to get some idea of how densely or sparsely residential mounds were grouped around a center and, eventually, how far out they extended. Did they, for example, continue right along until we came to another ceremonial center? So we set to our task. It was about 8:00 in the morning, and the fog had not yet burned off when we began. Satterthwaite had not only arranged for the workmen, but he had also borrowed machetes for the four of us. The use of the machete, Linton advised, was absolutely essential for anyone aspiring to be a Maya archaeologist, and this was especially so in my case given my "settlement pattern" ambitions. How else would one find all the little mounds, and so comprehend "total settlement", except by its use? I had been in jungle before, but I had never confronted it with "sword in hand", so to speak. But I took my turns on the *breccia* and swung away uneasily with my unfamiliar weapon. I must confess that even after several seasons in the Maya bush I was never comfortable with the machete; I was always afraid that with an excessive swing I might cut my foot off. Bullard, though, enjoyed it thoroughly, with a display of swordsmanship that alternated between low, close-to-the-ground sweeps and overhead slashes. Jerry Epstein's style, like mine, was more cautious. The sun came out. We continued to whack away. Satterthwaite, although more experienced that I, was also a good bit older. The two of us began to spend more time at the rear of the column rather than on the front line. By about 11:00 o'clock, we had progressed a couple hundred meters or so into the thicket that seemed to grow more overwhelming as we penetrated it. By this time, we had discovered only two little mounds. I wondered aloud if maybe we shouldn't stop and reflect on all of this for a bit. After all, we didn't want to discover everything on the first day. Bullard was for going on, but Lint and I overruled him. The latter suggested we might go back in town for a little while. We could have a beer at a friendly place he knew and talk over the whole question of Maya settlement survey; besides Hamilton Anderson should be coming in shortly, and we should be on hand to meet him. So, breaking off this initial confrontation with the jungle, we retreated to city life in El Cayo.

Linton took us to a bar known as the "Western Club". In El Cayo one didn't just patronize a bar; one "belonged" to a "Club". Satterthwaite assured us that he was a member in good-standing at the "Western", that we would be welcome as his guests, and that there would be no trouble in "putting us for for membership", if we so desired. The "Western" was located at one end of the main thoroughfare, actually not far from the restaurant where we had breakfasted a few hours before. The other "Club" in town was the "Stork". It was situated at the opposite end of the same street, about a block away from the "Western". Despite the more fashionable associations of the "Stork's" name, we were given to understand that the "Western" was the really "in" place. The "Western's" interior was quite dark. Window-glass—in those days anyhow—was relatively rare in El Cayo. Light came in only from two open windows at the front whose wooden coverings had been raised and propped up by sticks. A bar ran along the back of the room. In the row of bottles behind the bar, I saw one with a sign on it which read: "Have a Drink on Dr. Satterthwaite". Lint told me, yes, that he was indeed the "sponsor" of this particular bottle and that it dated from his previous season at Cahal Pech. It was a good "public relations" idea, he said. I noticed the bottle was empty so his "public image" must have benefitted for a time, however brief.

There were some tables and chairs in front of the bar, and we found our way through the gloom to one of these. The bartender or proprietor—or perhaps as the principal functionaire of the "Club" he was known as the "Steward"—exchanged greetings with Satterthwaite that were as hearty as those that had passed that morning between the latter and his lawman friend. They first had some conversation about replenishing the "Have a Drink on Dr. Satterthwaite" bottle; then the bartender took our order for four cold beers and went back behind the bar. Not long after that, we heard the patter of bare feet on the floor, and magically four beers were placed before us, one by one, by a little black hand that came up from the dark below the table. The waiter, whom the bartender had dispatched to serve us, was a very efficient and courteous Black dwarf but one who, because of his height, was thus hidden in the obscurity below the table tops. It was a little unnerving for one only newly initiated into the "Club", but the beer turned out to be excellent.

As we sat there discussing the future of cutting *breccias* through the undergrowth of the Maya Lowlands in a search for house mounds and the mysteries of old Maya settlement, two other "members" of the Club showed up and took a table next to ours. They were English and very amiable fellows, one a labor foreman and the other an accountant, from the Barton Ramie Estate Project of the Colonial Development Corporation. The Barton Ramie Estate was a few kilometers down river, or to the east of El Cayo. It was then, I think, in its third year of operation. We were told that ramie was a tropical fibre plant, of southeast Asian origins. The fibres were used for making such things as fire-hoses or fishing lines. The ramie had been planted on the extensive alluvial flats near the Barton Creek tributary of the Belize River, and the hope was that it would be a factor in vitalizing the British Honduran economy, especially since plastics had replaced chicle as the base for chewing gum. We kept the conversation going on our side by identifying ourselves as archaeologists. We went on to specify our interests of the moment. We were not so much concerned with big pyramids or fancy sculptures, we said; instead, what we were really looking for were the small, simple mounds that marked the residences of the Maya common man. We thought that such must be around in great numbers although because of the jungle they were difficult to see. Our new Club-mates assured us that if that was what we were looking for we had better come back to Barton Ramie with them, where "there were more bloody little mounds than you could count". At about that time, Hamilton Anderson showed up at the "Western"; he had just arrived in town. He, too, knew of the Barton Ramie mounds so we all went outside to our Jeep and the Barton Ramie Estate Land-Rover which were parked—apparently legally, this tine—in front of the "Club", and, with the Land-Rover leading the way, we drove out to Barton Ramie.

At Barton Ramie, we were met by the manager, Mr. Marcus Chambers who was our courteous host then and, as it turned out, for the following season. The Barton Ramie mounds were truly impressive in their numbers. The agricultural clearing was at least 2 sq. kilometers in extent. The mounds could be seen everywhere in the open cultivated area. They were located, perhaps 50 to 60 meters apart. Eventually, we were to map and count 264 of them in the cleared area. Most averaged about 2.00 m in height and 20 to 30 m in diameter. There were a few larger ones, and one unit, in particular, consisted of a little plaza group which included a pyramid about 12 m in height. This unit, thus, had the appearance of a ceremonial center of a minor sort, but one much smaller than, say, Cahal Pech.

After this view of Barton Ramie, we spent the rest of the week looking around in the Belize Valley. We saw Xunantunich, where Anderson had been doing some excavation-restoration work, and we looked at other, smaller ceremonial centers in the region. One of these was Baking Pot, where Ricketson (1929) had dug before going into Uaxactun. It was about three kilometers west of, or upriver from, Barton Ramie, and it, too, was surrounded by numerous small residential-type mounds although the clearing here was not as large as the Barton Ramie one. We ranged in our survey all the way from the Guatemalan frontier to a site called Banana Bank, well to the east of Barton Ramie. In our stay, Bill and I even took the time to make some small scale excavations in a little house mound group called the "Melhado site" (Willey and Bullard, 1956), a very short distance to the north of El Cayo.

Before leaving El Cayo, I had an argument with Satterthwaite about my plans for subsequent seasons. I had made up my mind, I said, that I would begin with mapping and excavations at Barton Ramie. Linton thought this was a grave mistake, a setting off down the wrong path in settlement pattern studies. "If you do that," he said, "you won't know where you are." Warming to his theme, he continued. "Now if you start with a known, sizable ceremonial center, like Cahal Pech, as I suggested, and work out radially from this center, you'll have something around which you can define a 'sustaining area'".

I countered by saying that Maya settlement pattern studies at present were so little developed that none of us knew where he was anyhow. "What did it matter," I questioned, "where in the settlement scale we began. What was wrong with beginning somewhere near the lower end of that scale, if that was what the field of Barton Ramie small mounds represented, and working up from there to larger territorial assemblages?"

But Lint would have none of it. "The trouble with you," he said, "is that you're afraid of the bush! You don't like to cut *breccias!* You want it already cleared off for you!" I admitted as to how that had certain advantages. Our argument ended there, with me firmly committed to beginning at Barton Ramie.

Bill hadn't said much during all of this debate so when we got back to the hotel in Belize City, I asked him what he really thought. Was he content to start work at Barton Ramie? Or did he feel that what Satterthwaite had had to say ruled this out? Bill would always come out with a clean-cut opinion, but quite a bit of pipe-puffing, walking around, looking out of the hotel window, and tapping his foot on the floor went on before he answered me on this one. He finally said—and said most of it twice in Bullard fashion—that he thought Satterthwaite was logically correct, that conceptually, anyway, we had to work, and to think, "from centers outward"; otherwise, we could never get a grasp of Maya Lowland settlement. At the same time, we had to take advantage of opportunities and that it would be foolish to pass up the opportunity that the Barton Ramie clearing offered. In a very few years that clearing would probably all be grown over. I was happy to be confirmed in my thinking and to have some small exoneration from Satterthwaite's charge that "I was afraid of the bush"—but Bill would get back on the subject again before we had finished at Barton Ramie.

So we began at Barton Ramie in the early winter of 1954, with a National Science Foundation grant, and Bill and I continued there through 1956. In the 1954 season, John Glass was with us; in 1955, Glass and Philip D. Orcutt made up the party; and in the concluding season of 1956, John Ladd was the additional staff member. Bill was a mainstay in the operations for all three seasons. He was always good about taking orders, but his role was much more than that. He took charge when I wasn't there, and, eventually, he was to be one of the principal authors of our monograph on our Barton Ramie and Belize Valley work (Willey et al. 1965). We excavated several Barton Ramie mounds in detail. Bullard could dig swiftly but still maintain a good field record. He had a sense for structures and the stratigraphic complexities of structures plus refuse.

After a time, though, Bill began to be beset by the doubts sown by Satterthwaite's arguments. Where were we in the larger settlement picture in the Belize Valley? He argued that we should travel around more, see more of the country. I acceded to his request, and we began to use week-ends, when we weren't digging, for these trips. From them we did get the beginnings of a "macro-settlement" perspective (see Chang, 1968; Willey, 1981b). We revisited the Belize Valley sites which we had seen briefly in our short stay in 1953 (see Willey *et al.* 1965, Fig. 2). We also made a number of random checks through the bush at various points along the river's course. We did not explore to any extent in the hill country away from the valley. Bullard always maintained that this was a mistake not to do so. I didn't disagree, but we had time to do just so much. The way that time was allotted, and the priorities I established, are reflected in the Belize Valley monograph. Very recent settlement research in the Valley, which takes in hill country as well as alluvial bottomlands, has, indeed, revealed just how much settlement we didn't see (A. Ford, 1985).

Bullard was to survey on his own, after he finished the Barton Ramie work with me. He took off into the northeastern Peten, in Guatemala, with a small mule train, a guide, and a couple of machete men, and followed the old mahogany and chicle trails. Years before, P. W. Schufeldt (1950), a chicle contractor and a good friend of Morley's, had ridden through this same country and had commented that small ruin mounds of the Maya were literally everywhere, an observation that Tozzer also had made at about the same time (Tozzer, 1913). Bill simply rode along on mule-back, noting such mounds and their arrangements and groupings, particularly with reference to ceremonial centers of various sizes. Unfortunately, he was traveling too light and too swiftly to make detailed large-scale mappings, but he did emerge with a schematic hierarchical model for Lowland Maya settlement. His lowest rung in the hierarchy was what he designated as a *Cluster. Clusters* were composed of perhaps a half-dozen mounds, or little mound-and-plazuela units, distributed over an area 200–300 m in diameter. Above this, his *Zone* consisted of a dozen or so such *Clusters*, found within an area of perhaps a sq. km. Somewhere within the *Zone* would be a minor ceremonial center. The top level of his hierarchy was the *District*, an area of about 100 sq. km which subsumed several *Zones* and had somewhere within it a major ceremonial center. Although an idealized model, it was a first important step in Maya Lowland settlement macro-pattern determination (Bullard, 1960).

In listening to Bill talk about this Peten survey trip, it was obvious that this was the kind of Maya archaeology that was closest to his heart. He liked the free-roaming life in the bush, the independence it offered, and the self-reliance it engendered. He was a great admirer of his Maya Indian workmen. I remember that this was so in our Belize Valley time together. He told me once that they were "self-contained", fully self-reliant. Each man had his well-sharpened machete and his file to keep it sharp. Each had his native waterproof cloth bag to carry his few possessions, his gourd of cool water, his own *posole*, or ground maize dough, to mix with the water. The Maya Indian knew the forest, and he was not afraid to wander around in it alone or to sleep in it overnight. In sum, the Maya were Bill's jungle role models, clearly appealing to something in his disciplined New England soul. As he put it, "they were not looking for a hand-out. They did not expect the boss or the government to look after their every need". I used to take issue with him on this, pointing out that ancient, and even contemporary, Maya culture was not really all that "ruggedly individualistic" and "Republican". Indeed, I argued that in many of its aspects Maya society and culture might be looked upon as even "dangerously communal", let alone "New Deal Democratic". But Bill wasn't to be dissuaded by such sophistry.

Bullard joined Ledyard Smith and myself at Altar de Sacrificios for our first two seasons there, in 1959 and 1960. In 1959, he made the instrument survey for the site map (see Willey and Bullard, 1960). This was no mean task. Altar de Sacrificios was on what was really a swamp island, formed by the cutting off of an old river ox-bow. It was extremely low-lying and, except for the higher portions of its biggest platforms and pyramids, was frequently flooded in the rainy seasons. The vegetation was particularly nasty, featuring a lot of thorny bamboo thickets that made cutting lines of sight unpleasant work; but Bill enjoyed the job. He had special prestige with the workmen. They knew that Ledyard and I were the "bosses", the ultimate sources of their pay; however, we were addressed only as "Meester" while Bill was always saluted as "Ingeniero" ("Engineer"). I asked one of our crew once how they distinguished between an "Ingeniero" and an "Arqueologo". It was easy, he explained: " 'El Ingeniero' tiene sus instrumentos (transit, alidade, stadia rods), pero 'El Arqueologo' tiene solamente su camera, como un turista." After being reduced to the level of a "tourist", I was sorry I'd asked the question.

At Altar de Sacrificios, I envied Bill for more reasons than this. The site, in its swampside location, was a mosquito haven without parallel. In the 1959 season, before our screened houses were constructed, we slept in the open under palm-covered "lean-tos" or *champas*, protected only by our mosquito nets, or *pabellones*. We "dined", if that term can be used, in the open. Every evening, Ledyard, John Graham, and I would have to jump up from the table every so often and spray ourselves with insect repellent to keep the mosquitos at bay until we finished the meal. Bill, on the other hand, could continue his eating uninterrupted by these pests. After dinner, all of us except Bill would have to go to bed at nightfall (6:15 PM) to keep from being eaten alive. He could sit out, puffing his pipe, and enjoy the sunset. Maybe it was the pipe, but I began to be convinced he was just one of those people mosquitos didn't bite.

In 1960, Bill stayed at the Altar de Sacrificios camp for a

shorter time. I think maybe the screened houses and dining hall, together with the kerosene refrigerator, were too effete for his tastes. Anyway, he took off up the Lacantun River (see Bullard, 1965a) on an exploring trip in a canoe, accompanied only by a couple of workmen.

At the end of the 1960 field season, Bill then went to Guatemala City to join his fiance, Mary Ricketson, and they were married there. The Ricketson family, like the Bullards, had New Bedford connections, and Mary's father and Bill's father had been old friends and club-mates at Harvard and later. Mary's parents, it should be added, were Oliver G. Ricketson, Jr. and Edith (Bayles) Ricketson, Carnegie Institution archaeologists of Uaxactun fame. With this heritage, Mary, one might say, had been born into the Maya archaeological field. She had been working with Maya ceramic collections in the Peabody Museum at Harvard in the year before her marriage to Bill.

Shortly after their marriage, Bill accepted a job at the Royal Ontario Museum in Toronto, for the express purpose of leading that institution's Maya work in British Honduras. The new job took Bill into the field for several months each year, and Mary accompanied him on these expeditions. Among several sites, they dug at Baking Pot (Bullard, 1965b), where Mary's father, Oliver Ricketson ("Rick", to his Carnegie Institution colleagues) had excavated many years before and where Bill and I had made some tests during the 1956 season of our stay at Barton Ramie. Another excavation of this period was at San Estevan (Bullard, 1965c). In these and related studies Bill still had settlement objectives in mind, but he was also concerned with major site excavation in the region.

In 1963, Bullard left the Royal Ontario Museum to return to the Peabody at Harvard where he had been invited to serve as assistant director to J. O. Brew. He proved to be a conscientious and effective assistant director. He liked curatorial work and was good at it. He promoted orderliness in the Museum's collection storage, and he also set up some small exhibits. By more recent museology standards, Bill would be called pretty conservative when it came to display installations. I know he would have been appalled by the sizes of Federal grants that are now awarded to museums to plan and install large-scale displays. I can recall that his frugal nature was often offended when the old-style upright or table-top mahogany-and-glass cases, dating back to the pre-World War I days of the Peabody, were retired from use or sometimes even dismantled in favor or more modern facilities. Bill's idea of an appropriate exhibition was one with plenty of specimens and a few simple cards of cultural and chronological identification for the objects. In this dislike of painted composition board constructions and fancy labelling, he followed in the tradition of Alfred Tozzer.

Before going on with Bill's Maya career, I should turn back for a moment and say something about his Southwestern archaeology. His doctoral thesis, which was largely complete prior to his departure for Toronto, is entitled, *The Cerro Colorado Site and Pithouse Architecture in the Southwestern United Prior to A.D. 900* (Bullard, 1962). It resulted from his two summer seasons of Southwestern fieldwork in the 1950s. As might be expected of Bill, it is a lucid field account; but it goes beyond this in a section entitled "A Review and Critique of Anasazi, Mogollon, and Hohokam Chronology Prior to A.D. 900." In this, he displays that very clear writing which flowed from his clear thinking. He tackled, and I think he successfully answered, many of the questions that were then besetting Southwestern archaeologists about the nature and ancestry of Mogollon culture.

To return to the Maya, I think Bill's best theoretical paper was one written as a follow-up to the previously mentioned 1960 essay on "Maya Settlement Patterns in Northeastern Peten, Guatemala". He called the new paper, "Settlement Pattern and Social Structure in the Southern Maya Lowlands During the Classic Period" (Bullard, 1964). This was prepared for a Congress of Americanist symposium held in Mexico City in 1962. It is fair to call it a small landmark in Maya settlement archaeology. The social dimensions and correlates of settlement are, of course, subjects that have been addressed by many of us (see Ashmore, ed., 1981); but, given the information available to Bullard at that time, I don't think anyone has ever done better in writing sensible social interpretation from archaeological settlement data. It was by working from these

1960 and 1964 papers, that Bill and I wrote the Maya Lowland settlement pattern article for the *Handbook of Middle American Indians* (Willey and Bullard, 1965).

In his position as assistant director at the Peabody, Bullard had some time available for field work, and he and Mary returned to the Maya Lowlands to work at the Postclassic site of Topoxte. Bill published the Topoxte monograph in a Peabody Museum volume, *Monographs and Papers in Maya Archaeology,* which he and I planned together as a *festschrift* honoring Ledyard and Robert Smith, and which Bill edited (Bullard, ed., 1970). The Topoxte dig and the monograph deriving from it can be credited with helping start up an interest in the much neglected Postclassic Period in the Maya Lowlands. Bill's interest in the period had begun with our work at Barton Ramie where we felt we had evidence for a post-Tepeu 3 occupation on many of the residential mounds. With Gifford's ceramic analyses (Willey et al. 1965; Gifford, 1976), this late Barton Ramie occupation was assigned to what we called the New Town phase, and it was clear evidence that some Maya occupation had continued in the Peten Lowlands after the phenomenon of the "Classic Maya Collapse" (Culbert, ed., 1973). Gifford's New Town pottery type definitions and descriptions allowed Bullard to make comparisons with his Central Peten collections from Topoxte and elsewhere in the Peten Lakes region. From this research, he constructed a three-phase Postclassic chronology for the southern Lowlands (Bullard, 1973). This was an important pioneering systematic attempt at ordering Postclassic archaeology for the Maya Lowlands, and I consider it a major contribution. The subsequent field and laboratory work on the Lowlands Postclassic, by younger scholars such as Donald and Prudence Rice and Arlen and Diane Chase (see Sabloff and Andrews V, eds., 1985; Chase and Rice, eds., 1985), built on the foundations Bullard laid down.

Bill Bullard left the post of assistant director of the Peabody Museum at Harvard in 1968. For a part of that year, he taught as a part-time lecturer in anthropology at Franklin Pierce College in New Hampshire. Then he accepted a position as associate curator and chairman of the Department of Social Studies at the Florida State Museum (University of Florida), in Gainesville. While he was at the Florida State Museum he carried out still another, and larger Maya Posclassic site excavation, this time at Macanche Island, in the Peten. It was to be his last dig, and he did not live to complete the full study of the collections nor the preparation of the manuscript. This has been done by Prudence Rice (1987) who worked with Bullard's notes and collections, and the good condition of these data, left behind by the conscientious Bill, aided her in this task.

I saw Bill in the fall of 1970 when a group of us convened at Santa Fe, New Mexico, at the invitation of the School of American Research, to consider the problem of the "Classic Maya Collapse". This was the seminar for which his posthumous paper, just referred to, was prepared and in which he took an important part in the discussions. I had not seen him for some months prior to this. He seemed the same—or so I thought at first, but then, perhaps, he didn't. I suppose he didn't have all of his old bounce and good humor. Then, at some time during the next year, I heard that he was taking sick leave from Florida and that he and Mary were coming up to Boston. He was to enter the hospital here for a very serious operation. I had a hard time taking it in. I had always thought of Bill as tough and as stalwart as an oak tree. We saw each other a couple of times after the operation, and he and Mary spent time in New Hampshire that summer while he was recuperating. At the end of the summer, he looked well again, and we all had hopes. That fall they returned to Gainesville and his job there. But the illness returned, and he came back to Boston where he was operated on for a second time. After this second operation, there was little hope.

Bill retired to the old Ricketson cottage in South Dartmouth, Massachusetts, in the general New Bedford region, the home ground of his, as well as Mary's, forbears. It was here, he said, that he wanted to end up, to see another spring come in over his favorite marshes. Always a man of "form", of doing things the "proper way", Bill asked to see an Episcopalian minister two days before his death. He put things "right" with him and said he was ready to go. William Rotch Bullard, Jr. died on 21 May 1972.

The loss of an old friend is always sad, and it is doubly so when this friend is a colleague, a former student, to some extent a kind of "intellectual son". And it is tragic when he is only 45 years of age. Bill had more plans for Maya archaeology. He wanted to pursue the whole complex question of Postclassic culture in the Maya Lowlands. For in learning about it, he correctly reasoned, we would be better informed about the whole gamut of Maya culture, the forces involved in its rise as well as those that made for its curious failures or declines. He was unable to follow these plans. He would have done a great job if he had been allowed to do so. The record of his achievements in the relatively short time Bill Bullard had as a Maya archaeologist is indisputable testimony for that.

HARRY EVELYN DORR POLLOCK
In late middle age.
Courtesy Mrs. H. E. D. Pollock.

HARRY EVELYN DORR POLLOCK
(1900–1982)

When I remember Harry Pollock, I often do so in association with memories of Bill Bullard and Ledyard Smith, and I think of all three of them in our old familiar context of Maya archaeology in the bush—the ruins, the jungle, the field camps, the good times, the bad times. In addition to their dedication to the Maya field, Harry, Ledyard, and Bill shared other things in common. To begin with, their backgrounds were similar. Although Harry was a westerner, Ledyard a midwesterner, and Bill a native of Massachusetts, they had all gone to Eastern preparatory schools at the appropriate and formative periods in their lives. After that, Harry and Ledyard, being almost of an age, were at Harvard together. Bill went there too, but, appreciably younger than they, he wasn't on the Harvard scene until sometime later. While at Harvard, all three were members of the Fly Club, where, incidentally, Bill's father had been a member. It is perhaps not out of place, in detailing these background similarities and relationships, to add that all three came from moneyed families. Not surprisingly, all were quite conservative although in saying this I refer not only to politics but to basic disposition. Finally, from my point of view, it is even more important to note that all three were gentlemen and honest and straightforward scholars. It was my good fortune to have been their colleague. They were a pleasure to be with, and now that they are gone, I can only say that I sorely miss them.

In spite of their many likenesses, the three were strikingly different as personalities. I have already told you something about Bullard in the previous memoir and shall do so for Smith in the one which follows. Let me now talk about Pollock.

Harry Evelyn Dorr Pollock was born on 24 June 1900, in Salt Lake City, Utah. His father, James Albert Pollock, was a mining engineer and mine owner who had gone to the western states some years before and who had developed successful mining interests there. Harry's mother was Evelyn Prince (Dorr) Pollock. Harry had a brother 10 years older but no other siblings. Harry's early years were spent in Utah, then Missouri, and, finally, Pasadena, California. While living in California, he attended the Thatcher School at Ojai. After that he was sent east, to Hill School, in Pottstown, Pennsylvania, and from there he entered Harvard, graduating in the Class of 1923 (Willey, 1983).

When he left Harvard, Harry went into the brokerage business in New York City. He had not had formal "Business" training at Harvard, concentrating instead in Liberal Arts and Literature, but for one of his upbringing a Wall Street brokerage career must have seemed proper, suitable, and an even inevitable climax to prep school and Harvard. The only trouble was, Harry found that he didn't like being a stock and bond broker; indeed, he discovered that his feelings were quite the opposite. He told me once that he "hated every minute of it", that he chafed to get out of it. This presented a problem because he didn't know just what it was that he wanted to do with his life. Fate or luck intervened, and an opportunity for escape presented itself. He recalled that on one warm June evening in 1927, after a routine day of boredom in the financial district, he walked up town, as was his custom, to the Harvard Club for dinner. There he met his old Fly Club buddy, Ledyard Smith. Ledyard was just back from a season at Uaxactun, in Guatemala. He was a newly enrolled archaeologist who had just spent his first season in the field with a Carnegie Institution archaeological group. He had been working with another Fly Club mate of theirs, Oliver Ricketson, who was then in charge of the dig there, and had enjoyed himself enormously. It was a great life. Why didn't Harry come along next year and give archaeology a try if he was fed up with Wall Street? Ledyard was sure there would be no trouble in arranging it.

Knowing Harry, as I came to in later years, this seemingly casual offer must have presented him with a very agonizing decision. For one of his conservative nature, a sudden switch from the staid respectability of a New York brokerage career, even if he didn't like it, to something as seemingly bizarre as archaeology, would have demanded considerable soul-searching on his part. That he opted for archaeology, besides being a testament to his dislike of watching the ticker tape, tells us something of the inner romanticism which burned beneath that very proper and formal Pollock exterior.

For Harry did have a formal exterior. Part of this was his quite dignified, evenly stately, physical appearance. I didn't know him until he was in his early fifties, but earlier pictures taken of him even back in his undergraduate days reveal this formality of manner. He was a tall man—6' 2"—and rather slender-boned. When he was young—judging again from those college pictures—his must have been something of a "bean-pole" physique. Later, he filled out, although one always thought of him as tall and thin. He had a quite handsome and imposing countenance. The face was long, with a well-developed chin, a pleasant although firm mouth, and a medium-large straight nose. His eyes were deep-set and dark, the eyebrows heavy and dark. He had a brow that would have to be described as "noble", both in front view and in profile. I often thought that if one were casting Shakespeare's *Julius Caesar* Harry would have been ideal as a Roman Senator, in a flowing toga and, perhaps, with a wreath encircling that brow. His hair, originally quite dark, was graying when I first knew him, and it gradually whitened in the dignified aging of his seventies. He moved with decorum, with a long, usually slow, stride and with arm and body movements that were slow and deliberate.

This appearance was fully in keeping with Harry's serious manner. He could not be called glum; to the contrary, he almost always displayed a pleasant and equable disposition. But in spite of this, I think his overall demeanor would have to be described as "grave". In saying this, I want to emphasize that he was not one of those who could be accused of "taking himself too seriously". On the contrary, he had a ready, and at times even frivolous, sense of humor, which he was never hesitant to apply to himself. It was just that he was basically a serious man. He projected this seriousness in an unmistakable way, and others took him seriously. Around the dig at Mayapan, when I visited there for a few days in 1953 on my way to British Honduras, I observed that there was no question about who was boss. He didn't "throw his weight around" and was in no way overbearing; but he seemed to radiate a quite authority. As an example, truck drivers who were sent into Merida on errands, and who might be tempted to have a few drinks too many while in town, and to be late in returning, were very careful not to do this when they knew Dr. Pollock was in camp. Those who did it were known to have done it only once. I never heard him bawl anybody out. Maybe he did when I wasn't around, but he didn't seem to need to. The workers sensed his steady sternness, respected it, and were quite happy with it. He was eminently fair but always a bit remote.

Underneath this outward composure, however, Harry did his share of worrying. He was very conscientious about what he considered to be his duty—in whatever context he thought this duty might lie. Indeed, if we had to come up with a key word about Harry, it would be "conscientiousness". When he was director of the Carnegie Institution's Department of Archaeology, I can remember seeing the light burning late on many evenings in Harry's office at 10 Frisbie Place. Everyone else had departed in the winter's dark after 5:00 PM, but Harry was still at it at his desk, working on the annual reports that made up the Carnegie Institution's *Year Books*. These were the current summaries of field activities, his own and those of others. He was both a master of English prose and a very meticulous editor. His wife, Katy, used to say that he worked so hard on these reports, and, in general, worried so much about the Carnegie's archaeological program, that he developed ulcers. I remember that Harry had just had a stomach ulcer attack the year before I arrived in Cambridge, and he was to have an operation for ulcers in later years. Harry had been unlucky in the time that he took over the directorship of the Carnegie's Department of Archaeology. He became head in 1950, but just two years before that, as I have related in the Kidder memoir, the Carnegie Institution of Washington had decided to eliminate archaeology from its programs. Thus, Harry, from 1950 until 1958, the terminal date set for his Department, was forced into being the skipper of a doomed ship. In spite of this, he performed admirably right up to the end of the organization's lifetime; but it was a severe strain on a man of his painfully conscientious temperament. It would have been enough to produce ulcers.

In reading over what I have written, in this attempt to be

objective in describing a close friend, I may have made Harry Pollock sound a little cold. If so, let me say that I never found him that way. Our friendship developed gradually through the 1950s, but as I think back about him I realize that I came to feel closer to him and temperamentally more compatible with him, than with any of the other friends, colleagues, or associates remembered in this book.

But let us go back to the young Pollock who, on that June evening in 1927, made up his mind to go into Maya archaeology. In the following early winter of 1928, Harry Pollock resigned from his New York brokerage firm and subsequently sailed from New Orleans to British Honduras, on his way to joining the Carnegie team at Uaxactun. He went into the British Honduras interior on the same river steamer in which George Vaillant made his first trip (see the Vaillant and Bullard memoirs). Unlike George, Harry didn't stay up all night and play poker but slept, instead, in one of the hammocks that were slung on the deck of the little steamer. Harry's romanticism was nicely revealed in what he has told me of that trip and his first morning's awakening. He said, "It was like something out of Conrad." He "had felt like the young man in the story, 'Youth'", awakening into the soft dawn light of the tropics. The dark river was canopied over with trees. He heard the calls of strange birds and was aware of the brooding presence of the jungle. From the way Harry related it, the experience must have been just what he was seeking as the antidote for those years in the brokerage office. Its realization was as wonderful as what his mind's eye had conjured up back there in New York during his Harvard Club conversation with Ledyard. From that time on, he was captured for Maya archaeology.

Harry did some work at Uaxactun (Pollock, 1937); but, right from the first, he was given the opportunity by Morley, and later by Kidder, to explore new sites and new territory. And this was to become his favorite kind of field archaeology. He wasn't averse to digging, but I don't think he liked it as much as he did exploration. I can remember traveling around with him in Yucatan years later. We were going to sites that he had visited back in the 1930s on his Puuc architectural survey. He liked to prowl around quietly, in and about the buildings, making notes on structural and masonry details. He didn't like to talk too much when he was doing this. He was thoroughly absorbed in a solo way.

In that first 1928 season, Harry had the opportunity to go to both Chichen Itza (Pollock, 1929a), where Carnegie operations were still going forward, and, more excitingly from an exploratory standpoint, to Coba, (Pollock, 1929b), in northern Quintana Roo. His first major publication, written in collaboration with Eric Thompson and Jean Charlot, was on the latter site (Thompson, Pollock, and Charlot, 1932). It was in these earliest years in the field, from 1928 through 1930 that Harry began his interests in architecture (Pollock, 1931; see also Pollock, 1936a and 1937). This was to be his specialty as a Mayanist, and at the close of his career he had few peers in it.

In the fall semesters, when he was not in the field, Harry took up residence in Cambridge, Massachusetts and enrolled at Harvard again, this time as a graduate student in Maya archaeology and anthropology under Alfred Tozzer. Apparently, he had decided that if he was going to make Maya archaeology a central part of his life, then he better go about it in the right way and conscientiously. He systematically pushed on to an A.M degree in anthropology in 1930 and to a Ph.D. degree in 1936. Not surprisingly, Harry, with his devotion to duty, his probity, and his gentlemanliness, was always a great favorite with Tozzer. In return, it is not far off the mark to say that Alfred Tozzer was his role model as a scholar.

Harry's doctoral dissertation was on Maya architecture, *Round Structures of Aboriginal Middle America*, published by the Carnegie Institution in the same year he was awarded the doctorate (Pollock, 1936b). It is notable for its descriptive excellence and its thoroughness in drawing together what was known on the subject. In its preparation, he researched both archaeological and ethnohistorical sources. He had first become interested in round buildings at Chichen Itza, where he had been assigned to study the "Casa Redonda" (Pollock, 1936c). Zelia Nuttall (1930) had brought out a brief popular essay on round buildings a few years before, but no one had gone into the subject in serious detail. Harry began where Nuttall had left off, reviewing the pre-and post-Conquest sources, such as the Borgia Codex and the Codex Telleriano-Remensis for pictorial and written information. Round structures were associated in native symbolism with the Wind-God aspects of Quetzalcoatl. The archaeological literature afforded examples from several Mesoamerican regions. Round buildings of various kinds had been found in the Nahua territory of Central Mexico, in the Tarascan, Zapotecan, Totonacan, and Huastecan zones, in the Maya area, and even as far south as Nicaragua. It was Pollock's conclusion that within the Mesoamerican orbit he was looking at an historically interrelated phenomenon involving architecture and religion. He argued that this complex of ideas had come into the Maya area with "Mexican influences", that round buildings were not originally a Maya trait. Chronologically, he placed round buildings over a time range that included three major horizons: Late Teotihuacan; Post-Teotihuacan and Pre-Aztec; and Aztec. In the light of accrued knowledge of the past 40 years, this is all old hat now, but at the time *Round Structures* was a significant work of synthesis, and in it Harry revealed his interests in and abilities for culture-historical generalization. The monograph established him as a first-rank scholar in Mesoamerican archaeology, and in the Maya field he was now the clearly recognized authority on architecture (Pollock, 1940a). Not long after, he wrote the paper, "Sources and Methods in the Study of Maya Architecture," published in *The Maya and Their Neighbors* (Pollock, 1940b). Years later, he was the one to be selected, to prepare the definitive statement on Lowland Maya architecture for the *Handbook of Middle American Indians* (Pollock, 1965).

An important and happy change in Harry's life was his marriage, in 1940, to Katherine (Winslow) Pollock of Boston. They were to have one son, Harry, Jr. His new marriage was interrupted, however, by World War II. Harry served in the U.S. Army Air Corps in the European theatre from 1942 until 1945, before being discharged with the rank of Major.

After the War, Harry returned to his home and family in Cambridge and to his job with the Carnegie Institution. It was shortly after this that I met him for the first time. He had come to Washington with Ted Kidder, either in 1947 or 1948, and the two of them came over to the Smithsonian one day to pay a call on Matt Stirling. I remember it particularly because when Kidder introduced him, he explained that Pollock was to succeed him as director of the Carnegie's Department of Archaeology in 1950.

In the late 1940s, before taking over the directorship, Harry continued with a Puuc regional survey in Yucatan, which he had begun in the 1930s and pursued until the beginning of the War (Pollock, 1946, 1948). For those unfamiliar with Maya archaeology, it should be explained that the name "Puuc" comes from a hill region in the northwestern and northern part of the Yucatan Peninsula, and it is used to designate a distinctive architectural style of the region. The style is characterized by its ornate friezes on the upper moldings or panels of buildings. These friezes are composed of monster masks and other elements that are constructed, mosaic-fashion, of individual carved stone masonry blocks. Some of the best-developed and most famous Puuc-style architecture is to be found at the sites of Uxmal, Kabah, Labna, and Sayil. Puuc-type buildings also occur farther east, as of the site of Chichen Itza where they were traditionally considered to antedate Chichen's Mexicanized or "Toltec" style architecture (see Tozzer, 1957).

Although it takes us ahead in the story of Harry's career, this is a suitable place to point out that as early as the 1950s he was skeptical of this chronological placement of Mexicanized Chichen Itza with relation to the Puuc style and Puuc sites in general. It seemed to him unlikely that Chichen Itza was the only major site extant in Yucatan during the Early Postclassic Period. While the question continues to be argued in the 1980s (see various essays in Chase and Rice, eds., 1985; Sabloff and Andrews V, eds., 1985), the prevailing opinion now is that there was an appreciable chronological overlap between the so-called "Toltec" occupation at Chichen and such Puuc sites as Uxmal or Labna. To my mind, Harry was too reticent about putting forward his ideas on such interpretations, and in this case he should have done so earlier. I never felt that he held back because of fear of criticism. It was rather that he conceived of his Puuc survey as being primarily a job of scrupulous descriptive recording and presentation of the basic archaeological data. Fortunately, his big Puuc monograph, published near the end of his life (Pollock, 1980), contains such interpretive information.

Toward the close of the 1940s, when the fate of archaeology within the Carnegie Institution was sealed by Vannevar Bush's decision to eliminate it from the Carnegie's research programs, Harry designed what was to be their last major project in the Maya field. The Carnegie had fielded two major single-site projects in the Maya Lowlands during the existence of its archaeological section. In addition, of course, there were many other shorter-term site operations as well as such long-term survey endeavors as Morley's hieroglyphic studies (Morley, 1920, 1937–1938) and Pollock's architectural reconnaissances. The two major single-site efforts had been Chichen Itza (Morris, Charlot, and Morris, 1931) and Uaxactun (Ricketson and Ricketson, 1937; A. L. Smith, 1950). The first of these had involved the Late Classic-Early Postclassic Periods; the second had produced a vast amount of information on the Preclassic and Classic Periods. While all of this was going on, Kidder had engaged the efforts of historians and ethnohistorians, such as Roys (1933), Scholes (Scholes and Roys, 1938), and Chamberlain (1948), to study the Contact Period and the 16th century history of the Spanish Conquest of the Maya in Yucatan. One piece remained to be filled in, in this long chronological story—the Late Postclassic Period, from *ca.* A.D. 1250 to the arrival of the Spanish. The site to fill this gap was obviously Mayapan, known only cursorily by the archaeologists but well-documented from native accounts in the Books of Chilam Balam.

Pollock, with his orderly sense of completion and closure, organized and directed this long-term archaeological program at Mayapan. An excellent topographic map of the ruin (Jones, 1952) was prepared. Intensive survey, mapping, and digging then began in 1951 and continued through 1955. Additional stratigraphic digging at Uxmal and Kabah was carried out in 1956 to supplement the ceramic information from Mayapan. Following a large series of preliminary reports in the *Year Books* or *Current Reports*, by various authors, (*e.g.*, Pollock, 1954a,b, 1955, 1956; Smith and Ruppert, 1952, 1956; Proskouriakoff, 1954; Shook, 1952), the monograph, *Mayapan, Yucatan, Mexico*, authored by Pollock, R. L. Roys, Tatiana Proskouriakoff, and Ledyard Smith, appeared in 1962. Subsequently, R. E. Smith's (1971) very substantial *The Pottery of Mayapan* made the site one of the best known in Maya archaeology. In the 1962 report, Harry's actual text is limited to only an 18 page "Introduction"; however, this "Introduction" is much more than that. It is a beautifully written little essay on the place of Mayapan in late Maya culture history. Roys contributes a definitive section on the sources for the history of the site; Proskouriakoff has parts on the major architecture and on the artifacts found in the digging; and Ledyard Smith deals with the extensive residential architecture. Mayapan was, to be sure, a joint effort, but the guiding hand was Harry Pollock's.

With the Mayapan field operations behind him, Harry had some free time in 1957, as did I. I had finished the Barton Ramie and Belize Valley fieldwork in 1956. Before I launched into any new fieldwork venture, I thought it might be a good idea to use part of the spring semester of 1957 to travel around in Mesoamerica and look at regions and sites which I had never seen before. I asked Harry if he would like to go along. He fell in with the plan easily. He had to go down to Merida sometime during that spring to check on the Carnegie office and laboratory they still maintained there. He could take a trip through Mexico with me on his way down. At the same time, we brought Phil Phillips into the plan. He hadn't been in Middle America since he had taken a survey trip with Tozzer in 1941, and the idea of another look around appealed to him. We discussed transportation. Phil had a station wagon which we decided to take. This was in the dead of winter and none of us relished the idea of driving all the way out to El Paso, Texas, our decided upon point of entry into Mexico. We resolved this by shipping the station wagon to El Paso on a freight car and going out on the train to pick it up at its destination. At the last minute Phil was held up for a day so Harry and I went out on a train ahead. This was a long train journey, of a couple of days and nights, so Harry and I had a lot of time to talk in the Pullman cars going out.

Previous to then, my Cambridge associations with Harry had been frequent, quite friendly, but not very serious in the sense of discussing archaeology. It was on that train trip to El Paso that we finally did exchange views about such matters. Harry had led our discussions around to what, for that time, have been called the "new trends" in archaeology. They were obviously bothering him. In 1957, Lewis Binford was still to come so I think Walter Taylor's (1948) monograph of a decade before and Clyde Kluckhohn's (1940) even earlier critical article on Maya archaeology and its conceptual grounding were probably the take-off points for the argument which ensued. The Kluckhohn piece, appearing in *The Maya and Their Neighbors* as the only critical note in that general acclaim to Tozzer and the achievements of Maya archaeology, had long been a particularly sore point with Carnegie archaeologists (see the Kidder memoir). Harry thought it was "hollow", an unjustifiable complaint. I took another view by saying that while there was nothing wrong with culture history and our attempts to define its outlines as best we could, there were other things that archaeologists, and especially Maya archaeologists, should address. Kidder had been pointing to these in some general statements—the forces or the causes that led to the rise and fall of civilizations. Why, then, were the Carnegie archaeologists loath to pursue such questions in a more specific way? That, to me, was the crux of both Kluckhohn's and Taylor's criticism of the Carnegie Maya program, and I thought it justified. But Harry remained unconvinced.

I was not quite sure what it was at the time, but there had been something in the way he had opened and pursued this particular discussion that made me feel he was trying to tell me something. So I asked him. Did he feel I had been too much of a "new trender" in the way I pursued archaeology, and especially Maya archaeology since I had been in that field? Harry responded rather gravely by saying yes, he thought I was a little too "far out". Now Harry wasn't one to be openly critical of a friend, and this must have been difficult for him to say, but I had asked for it so he let me have it. It was as though, in spite of our congenial relations of the past seven years, he was beginning to have misgivings about me as a "proper Maya archaeologist". I then asked him for a specific example of what he had in mind. He told me that all the emphasis I was giving "settlement patterns" was a case in point.

I remembered then that I had picked up some criticism from some of my Carnegie colleagues at 10 Frisbie Place when I had begun the settlement pattern work in British Honduras. Both Tatiana Proskouriakoff and Eric Thompson felt I was "wasting my time", that "everyone already knew all about settlement in Maya archaeology." After all, Ricketson (Ricketson and Ricketson, 1937) had made a house mound survey at Uaxactun— something that nobody was ever very interested in; Wauchope (1934, 1938) had pursued the question; and Eric, himself (Thompson, 1931), had devoted a season to digging "small Maya sites". I had known all this but certainly differed with Tania's and Eric's assessment that Maya settlement pattern research "was all behind us"; but I was surprised to hear Harry imply that looking for settlement information was in some way "far out" or "trendy" archaeology. I reminded him that if this was so his Mayapan work could also be so classified. The mapping of over 2000 structures there was, in effect, a major settlement pattern study. But Harry felt that it was not quite the same thing. At Mayapan, he, or his trusty surveyor Morris Jones, had simply been mapping the site, as any conscientious archaeologist would do prior to excavations. I think Harry felt that because most of the Mayapan mapping was done within the encircling wall of the site, it was a single site operation and not a "settlement pattern study". Or maybe he was put off by my arguments (Willey, 1956) that settlement research would lead to a better understanding of ancient socio-political structure. Basically, though, I think the root of Harry's criticism during that train ride in 1957 was that he was deeply conservative in his archaeological thinking, and he didn't like to be "chivvied" around or pushed into anything just because it was "new". I should point out, though, that years later, in a statement made in his Preface to the Puuc architectural monograph (Polloc, 1980, p. xxiii), Harry had come to accept settlement pattern studies as a perfectly standard and respectable strategy in Maya research.

In El Paso, Harry and I put up at the old Paso del Norte Hotel.

Phil showed up the next day, and we set about getting the station wagon off the flat-car at the freight-yard and attending to tourist cards and auto insurance. I had known El Paso before, but it was the first time there for Harry and Phil. I think they may have had their reservations about the "Pass of the North". A tall stranger in a ten-gallon hat broke in on a conversation we were having in the hotel elevator, declaring to Harry, "You ah British, ahn't you, Suh? Ah kin always tell by the accent!" This certainly took me off-guard. I hadn't anticipated that we would be marked down as foreigners until we crossed the Rio Grande the next day. Was Harry's prep school and Harvard heritage to blame for this trans-Atlantic identification? In any event, Harry wasn't to be drawn out and maintained a grave silence; but Phil hastened to reassure the native phonologist: "He certainly is! You've got a mighty fine ear!"

On our trip through Mexico, we looked at archaeological sites in Durango and Zacatecas (see Kelley, 1971). We were all astounded by the size and architectural complexity of La Quemada. Harry felt that it, alone, justified the trip. We'd all been in central Mexico previously, but, even so, we spent some days there. We did the same, too, in Oaxaca, where we took in Monte Alban and Mitla once more; however, the most memorable part of the trip was a drive through the Tabasco lowlands and the Olmec country which none of us had seen before. At La Venta, we found that the famous sculptures had been carted away to the museum in Villahermosa. We got into the latter place late in the afternoon to find most of the hotels jammed although we were finally able to get accomodations at a "1 Star" hostelry (the lowest rung in luxury-and-comfort rating on a descending scale of 4 to 1). After a pretty noisy night, there was an hour or two of quiet just before dawn, but at about 6:00 AM this was shattered by an absolutely earth-shaking blast from somewhere within the town. Successive cannonading or explosions followed, and these went on for some time although they seemed to be occurring farther and farther away. No one seemed to pay much attention to all this racket as we went out to breakfast although there did seem to be an air of tension as we walked through the plaza. People were gossiping in small groups and, I thought, looked at us suspiciously.

After breakfast, we found the Tabasco State Museum unaccountably closed although we were able to see some of the Olmec sculptures which were outside in the grounds. Following this, we went to an arcaded sidewalk cafe for a drink, and it was while we were there that explosions and cannonading, like those at dawn, began again, furiously, at a far corner of the plaza. Soldiers appeared in the street, firing at each other. Cries of *"Viva los Revolucionarios!"* rang out. There was a lot of such cheering in the cafe, although everyone seemed happily excited rather than fearful. Still, I began to think that we really had been caught in some sort of a provincial revolutionary outbreak, and I think Harry's reaction was the same. He and I were always a little uneasy in Latin America; Phil, who had spent much less time down there than either of us, was more relaxed—even in a "revolutionary" situation. Just about then, though, we noticed that many of the soldiers involved in the street fighting wore uniforms that would have been more at home in the era of Napoleon III or Maximillian. What we were witnessing was a reenactment of a skirmish of 1867—one in which the "revolucionarios" had thoroughly routed the "French". The skirmish was pretty realistic. The two sides were firing blank cartridges at each other at what looked to me to be "powder-burn" range. Bayonet-duels were going on all over the place. The "climax", or perhaps "denoument", of the engagement came when the "revolutionary forces" bodily threw some of the "French interventionists" into the river at the end of one street. Phil, meanwhile, had left Harry and me at the cafe, and we next caught a glimpse of him taking close-range Leica shots of the action, kneeling down for better camera angles while the "minions of French Imperialism" were being "slaughtered" by the "patriotic republicans". After the heat of battle had died down, Harry said that henceforth we should refer to Phil as "Matthew Brady Phillips, intrepid photographer of the end of French adventurism in the Americas" (see S. Williams, ed., 1970).

During the course of that 1957 trip—especially in the latter parts of it when we got down to the Maya area—I talked with Harry about an appropriate site or region for my own future research. Although Harry was anything but an opinionated man, he had no hesitancy in giving me a quick and strong answer on this question. Altar de Sacrificios, he told me, was the place to go. I hadn't heard of it, or if I had it was only another Maya site on the map, but he explained it was at the confluence of the Pasion and the upper tributaries of the Usumacinta system, in the southwestern sector of the Peten, in Guatemala. He had been there back in 1937, accompanied by Ledyard Smith and Ed Shook, and they had spent a day or so, making a map and having a look around. The site's location, Harry said, at the juncture of the Pasion with a major river descending from the Guatemalan Highlands, suggested that it might be a crucial spot for picking up clues to Maya Highland-Lowland interactions. I asked Harry how it also might be for settlement exploration. He wasn't very sanguine about this, explaining that Altar de Sacrificios was really located in a swamp and that he had no idea about how house mounds might be distributed around it. Nevertheless, I decided to follow his advice, and Ledyard Smith and I made an exploratory trip into Altar in 1958. As the result of that trip, we launched a long-term excavation program there, beginning in 1959 and extending through 1964.

During this period, Harry visited us at the site. He came down during a period when Altar de Sacrificios was caught up in what might be called "international tensions". The Guatemalan and Mexican Governments were having a dispute in Pacific Coastal waters over what the press had inflated into the "Shrimp War". These "tensions" were felt even on the remote Usumacinta frontier between the two countries. There, the Guatemalans had "secured" this boundary by "fortifying" the environs of Altar de Sacrificios. A lieutenant and a squad of soldiers were stationed on the opposite bank of the Pasion from us. The soldiers, bored and mosquito bitten in their godforsaken outpost, used to come across the river for a little gossip with our workmen. This went on for several weeks. Then one afternoon, the Seventh-Day Adventist Missionary, from Sayaxche, appeared at their camp in a canoe powered by an outboard motor. He landed, conferred with the lieutenant and the men, and, from our side of the river, we heard a chorus of cheers from the soldiers. Shortly after that, the lieutenant was brought across the river by the missionary, and they requested an audience with Mr. Smith. We convened in the dining hall of our camp, Harry and I joining Ledyard to see what it was all about. The lieutenant, a middle-aged man and somewhat the worse for wear after his two-month stint in the Pasion River bush, put his case very succinctly. The good Reverend, he said, indicating the missionary, had just brought a telegraphic message downriver. Sayaxche had been notified that the "international crisis" with Mexico was over and that the troops could now be withdrawn. Needless to say the men were overjoyed. There was a problem, however, in that the Reverend, while generously offering his canoe and motor for their trip back to Sayaxche, was low on gasoline; indeed, he had used his last few gallons coming down and did not have enough to make the trip back. Could Mr. Smith loan them the necessary gallons for a return journey?

Ledyard's immediate reaction to all this was not altogether positive. Our gasoline, he explained, had to be flown into Sayaxche from Guatemala City and then brought by our canoes from there to Altar de Sacrificios. We didn't have a large supply on hand. When could the loan of the gas be repaid in kind? The lieutenant confessed that there might be some bureaucratic delay in this; bills and vouchers would have to be filed; it might take some time. Well, how much time, Ledyard wanted to know? Oh, perhaps two weeks, three weeks—three weeks at the outside. Ledyard thought for a minute and then asked: "How can I depend on that?" The lieutenant rose to his feet, stood stiffly to attention, raised his right hand palm outward, and, with a far-away look in his eye, intoned" *"Palabra Militar, Señor Smith!"* At this point, Harry disgraced us all by laughing. Indeed, he laughed so hard that I was a little nervous. But gasoline was uppermost in the lieutenant's mind, and, when Ledyard conceded that, the interview was brought to a swift and happy end. Any possible impugnment of the "military word" and military honor was forgotten. The lieutenant and the missionary departed with the gasoline. Across the river the men embarked in the canoe, and the outboard motor roared into action. As a salute to us, the cheering squad fired their rifles into the air as they departed upriver. This, happily, was the only time that we heard them in use during the period of our "military occupation".

In 1959, Harry and I also made a trip to Nicaragua. It came about this way. After Ledyard and I began our camp construction at Altar de Sacrificios, I wanted to get a graduate student, Albert Norweb, started on a season of survey and test-pitting in Nicaragua. I suggested to Harry that he might like to see what the country was like so why didn't he come along? He accepted the invitation, and the three of us flew on to Managua from Guatemala City.

The Somoza brothers were in power in Nicaragua in those days, but there was a semblance of a political opposition as represented by the well-known newspaper, *La Prensa*. The paper's staff made up the intellectual core of the capital city. When Harry, Norweb, and I arrived we saw a good bit of this group. I can remember being puzzled by the fact that it appeared to include individuals of both strong left-wing and right-wing persuasions, at least judging from their conversations. When I asked about this, one of them told me that in Nicaragua there were so few intellectuals you had to include both sides to have someone to talk to. Anyhow, they took us around to look at archaeological sites, and we were invited to a "conferencia", or lecture, given by one of their number before the local archaeological and historical society. Some of these lectures, we were told, could get pretty lively. At this one, the speaker of the evening was a Coronel Laszlo Pataky, a former professional soldier and man about Managua, who had befriended us and been kind enough to guide us to several archaeological sites. He was a large impressive man. When he ascended the platform the first thing he did was to take a giant .45 caliber revolver out of his waistband and put it in the drawer of a little table on the platform. Was he preparing for a "lively" discussion or ensuring that there wouldn't be one? A good crowd was in attendance that night. They seemed indifferent to the Coronel's display of "hardware". Patakay then gave a competent presentation, with slides, of the Nicaraguan eastern slopes and lowlands, that most thinly settled and "wildest" part of the country. There was some archaeology in his remarks although more ethnology. He had been with some of the Mosquito Indian groups. Afterwards, there was no end of "hot" discussion, but none of it was about archaeology or ethnology. Instead, it focused on labor relations in the gold mines of those districts. Pataky was accused of ignoring the plight of the workers to talk about inessentials. Finally, after about an hour of "discussion", the meeting ended. The speaker opened the drawer of the little table, took out the revolver, and stuck it back in his waistband. We were never quite sure of the significance or symbolism of all of this, but we didn't like to ask.

Pataky took us down to the Isthmus of Rivas on one trip I remember best. I had heard that there were some archaeological sites near the town of Brito. Brito, on the Pacific shore, turned out to be an extremely small hamlet. Pataky, who liked to think in military terms, outlined to us how a small invading party might take over Brito with neglible loss of life. One of the first things to do, he assured us, would be to cut the telephone lines—in other words, isolate the defenders. After that, with a minimum of surprise gunfire, there would be nothing to it. The defending garrison would surrender. After inspecting an archaeological site, we went into Brito's only bar, and ordered a round of drinks. Pataky said that he must call *La Prensa*, in Managua, to give them a news release on the archaeological site we had discovered. He asked the bartender if he could use the telephone, but the bartender told him the telephone lines were down. Harry couldn't refrain from pointing out to the Coronel that Brito's capture would have been even easier than had been outlined to us.

On the way back from Brito we stopped in the much larger town of Rivas for lunch. We went to a restaurant highly recommended by Pataky. It looked all right, but it turned out to be unscreened. Flies, which began to assemble in vast numbers with our arrival, and perhaps in anticipation of the forthcoming meal, became unbearable. We complained to the waitress. A no-nonsense sort of a person, she didn't seem surprised or alarmed but went out and came back shortly with an old-fashioned metal flit-gun. A candle was tied to it at the spraying end. She lit the candle and began to pump. A three-foot flame roared out across the tablecloth at each individual stroke. After about a minute of this, at least 200 flies lay dead on the slightly scorched-looking cloth. When the debris of battle had been swept away, we were able to eat our lunch—a pretty good one—in peace. Word must have gone out on the fly grapevine that it was really hell in there. Pataky (perhaps because of his military background) was as dazzled by this flame-throwing exhibition as we were. He confessed he'd never seen anything like it. I wondered about the fuel in the flamethrower (kerosene, or even gasoline/perhaps), and I even toyed with the idea of fixing up such a device; but Harry, while equally impressed, cautioned me against doing so.

Harry became a curator of Maya Archaeology at the Peabody Museum in 1958, at the closing of the Carnegie Institution's Department of Archaeology. He held the position and occupied a Museum office until 1968. During the late 1950s and early 1960s he was busy with the writing and editing of the Mayapan report. After that, he started the long writing job on his Puuc architectural monograph, but we managed another trip in 1971.

I had never seen the Rio Bec sites in Campeche so I suggested to Harry that we go down to Mexico and have a look. After that, we could move north, and he could review some of the Puuc sites. Then I got more expansive in my plans, and we began by visiting Gareth Lowe in Chiapas. Down there, after seeing the marvelous site of Izapa, I came down with something close to pneumonia. We went back to Mexico City for me to recuperate, but by this time Harry had picked up the bug from me. We were, in effect, "hospitalized" in adjoining rooms in one of Mexico City's elite hotels in the Zona Rosada. We were attended by a young *medico* on the hotel's staff, but we got no better fast. As it happened, we read in the newspaper that a very distinguished Boston physician, and a friend of Harry's, happened to be in Mexico City for a medical meeting. Now, we thought, we can get some expert attention, perhaps the right prescriptions, and resume our Rio Bec-Puuc part of the planned excursion. Harry at last made contact with this medical gentleman by telephone. There was a long conversation while Harry described our symptoms. Our hoped-for rescuer listened to all of this but commented very briefly—to the effect: "That you guys don't need me; there is nothing I can do for you." And he hung up. Harry opined that "the S-O-B was afraid he'd catch whatever it is we've got!" There was nothing for it but to spring ourselves out of the hotel, get on a plane, and come home. Our malady was never diagnosed, but Harry, inspired by an Associated Press story emanating out of Mexico, was sure that what we had was "Equine Encephalitis"—usually fatal to horses and sometimes to men.

We finally did see the Rio Bec and Puuc sites, taking another shot at it in the winter of 1972. This time we were successful and stayed healthy. I remember, particularly, one afternoon, when Harry was checking on some architectural detail at a major Puuc site. We were standing in front of a building, and, in response to some questions of mine, he had been telling me about a decorative frieze. At about that time, a small American tourist group wandered up. Harry immediately clammed up. Then one of the ladies in the group began asking aloud, to no one in particular, what such and such motifs signified in the frieze. She then said that she wished there was someone who could tell her. I couldn't resist. "Madame," I said, "you're in luck. It so happens that this gentleman, Dr. Harry Pollock, is a foremost authority on just this subject." I turned to Harry, just in time to see him disappearing around the corner of the building. It took him the rest of the day to forgive me. Harry's modesty and reclusiveness about his work in professional circles was notorious; on a popular level it was obsessive.

Harry was never one to attend many archaeological meetings or conferences. In fact, the only one I ever saw him at was one of the *Mesa Redondas* in Mexico. He did make an exception for a special conference on Puuc architecture that was held at Pella, Iowa, in 1977. As one thinks about it, it is hard to see how such a conference could have been held without him. Harry attended, and, although he did not contribute a paper to the proceedings (see Mills, ed., 1979), he did, uncharacteristically, contribute substantially to the discussions.

Harry intended the Puuc monograph to be his last work and his major contribution, and these intentions were to be satisfied. The weighty volume, *The Puuc, an Architectural Survey of the Hill Country of Yucatan and Northern Campeche, Mex-*

ico (Pollock, 1980) totals 600 quarto-size pages and includes 934 illustrations (drawings and photographs). All the major sites—Uxmal, Labna, Sayil, Oxxkintok, Xculoc, Xcalumkin— are described in detail, and well over 100 others are substantially treated. The author closes with a Summary Review which includes a very important subsection on "Architectural Style and Chronology". Harry wrote the whole thing in longhand. After a typist had produced a first typewritten draft, Harry went over this slowly and carefully. He did this in an office at home, in Cambridge, and at his summer place, "Pinecroft", in New Hampshire. Harry and Katy used to invite Katharine and me and our daughters to this latter place in the summers. This was especially pleasant, for tennis, swimming, and all such nice things. Harry would participate in them, but he also insisted on a certain amount of time each day for work on the "Puuc". He did this in a small, telephone-less cabin he had constructed in the woods, at some distance from the main house. When he was in this woodland study, he was not to be bothered. He completed the Puuc manuscript sometime in 1978, and he saw it through its editing over the next two years. As anyone who has read it, or even read parts of it, it is obvious that Harry wrote very well. He was always very resistant to editorial changes that he didn't think were necessary. Finally, in 1980, the monograph appeared.

The Puuc monograph was too staid and solid to create much of a stir in a field which currently tends to look for the "exciting" new idea, but Harry, who lived for only a short time after its appearance, did not mind this. He knew he had done his duty. He had put down on record, in a very conscientious and professional way, his years of survey and observations upon a complex body of data. He had produced a work which will have a long life in Maya archaeology. It is a permanent part of the "edifice" of our archaeological knowledge of the ancient Maya.

Harry had no formal students although his influence was important in the lives of many younger archaeologists whom he knew in the context of the Carnegie excavations and, later, at the Peabody Museum. To them, he was a model of "a scholar and a gentleman". In his retiring way, he did not seek honors nor push himself forward; his behavior was, instead, quite the reverse. His abilities, however, were recognized by those "in the know" in Maya archaeology, and his achievements were noted by such an organization as the American Academy of Arts and Sciences which elected him to membership.

I attended Harry's eightieth birthday celebration in June of 1980. He was in fine fettle then, surrounded by family and friends. A little more than a year later, I also attended his son's wedding. This was a particularly happy occasion for him. Shortly after that, he was taken ill, and he died on 15 March 1982 in Boston, Massachusetts.

As I remember Harry Pollock, I can only say that his Maya colleagues were fortunate to have counted him as one of them. One never knows for sure about such things, but I like to feel that he was happier with us than he would have been if he had opted to stay on Wall street way back in 1927.

Augustus Ledyard Smith
In late middle age.
Courtesy A. L. Smith, Jr.

AUGUSTUS LEDYARD SMITH
(1901–1985)

I can't remember the exact first time I saw or met Ledyard Smith, but it must have been shortly after I came to Harvard in 1950. I had known his brother Bob before, and I sometimes went over to the 10 Frisbie Place offices to see him or Harry Pollock, so in the course of these visits I must have run into Ledyard. He was easy to meet and to talk with—the sort of man you feel you have known for a long time even after short acquaintance. He was about my height and of medium build. He projected a quality of physical activeness and good conditioning. He moved and walked swiftly and carried himself with a certain panache expressed in a jauntiness of head movement. He had grown bald early. When I first knew him he would have been just short of fifty but by then he had only a fringe of hair. His face had an open, sunny quality, especially when he was wearing his customary smile.

My first association with Ledyard was in the winter of 1953 while he was working in Mayapan. I was on my way to British Honduras, accompanied by Bill Bullard and Linton Satterthwaite, and we stopped off in Yucatan to see Mayapan. Before making the trip into the ruins we stayed a night in Merida. Ledyard had come in from the site for the weekend, and he and his wife, Kitty, joined our group for dinner at the Hotel Merida. Afterwards, Ledyard was insistent that we all go to his favorite Merida night club. I can't remember the name of it, but it was housed in the basement of a building located near the Hotel. Its subterranean setting helped give it that airless, slightly illicit quality that one of my generation tends to associate with night clubs; but in putting it this way I suppose I reveal my lack of enthusiasm for such after-hours bistros. Ledyard was much more favorably disposed toward such institutions. In fact, he loved them—as I was to find out in our subsequent years of association. We didn't leave the Merida "dungeon" that night until well after 2 AM. I faced the following day with a hangover, but the ineffable Ledyard was as bright and chipper as a song bird.

Out at Mayapan, Ledyard and Karl Ruppert were engaged in their residential mound survey, and I spent most of my time there going around the site with them, on their systematic rounds. What they were doing was a next-stage follow-up to the Jones (1952) map. Both were highly professional in their knowledge of that kind of small architecture. They moved from one residence unit to another with extraordinary speed—plotting wall foundations on their map sections and jotting notes, gathering the information that would help them sort out units by sizes and types, with an eye to excavation sampling. They were Maya archaeological veterans, old colleagues who had begun with the Carnegie in Sylvanus Morley's time, a quarter-of-a-century before. Ruppert was known for his Chichen Itza Caracol monograph (Ruppert, 1935); Ledyard had recently brought out his classic *Uaxactun, Guatemala: Excavations of 1931–1937* (A. L. Smith, 1950; see also A. L. Smith, 1937).

I thought then of what I knew of Ledyard's career. He had been with the Carnegie Institution since 1927. The first ten years of that time had been spent at Uaxactun, first as Ricketson's assistant and then, from 1931 to 1937, as the director of excavations, himself. I knew that he had lived for several years after this in Guatemala City. Kidder had maintained a Carnegie Institution Guatemalan office there for an extended period, while he, Ledyard, Ed Shook, and others had been digging out at Kaminal juyu. Ledyard also had conducted surveys in the Motagua Valley and in the Guatemalan Highlands in this post-Uaxactun period. Jointly with Kidder, he had a Motagua survey monograph to his credit (A. L. Smith and Kidder, 1943), as well as an excavation report on the Highland site of Nebaj (A. L. Smith and Kidder, 1951). It had been my pleasure to review this latter work and to see something of Ledyard's skills as an excavator of big structures and as a recorder of these excavations (Willey, 1953c). After Ledyard had completed these Highland investigations he had joined Pollock and the others at Mayapan.

It was not until later, of course, that I came to know the vital statistics on Ledyard and the details of his background (Willey, n.d. 2). He was born in Milwaukee on 18 October 1901, the second son of Mary (Eliot) and Franklin Taylor Smith. Robert E. Smith, destined to become the leading Maya ceramic specialist of his time, was his older brother by two years, and the boys had an older sister. Ledyard once told me that his father had been a professor although I don't believe he ever went on to say just what his field was or where he was employed. In any event, his father's professorial duties must not have been too arduous, for the family traveled a good bit and were as much at home on the Eastern seaboard, or in Europe, as they were in the Middle West and Milwaukee. There was, though, a business in Milwaukee which was a source of family wealth. I believe I remember Ledyard and Bob describing it as being involved with lumber, woodworking, or sash-and-door manufacturing. After college, both of them were employed in it for a while, Bob for a longer time than Ledyard.

In their early years, Ledyard and Bob were taught by governesses. Later, while their parents traveled extensively in Europe, they were placed in the La Villa School, in Ouchy, Switzerland, where, as I've noted, A. V. Kidder was also enrolled in his boyhood. Bob and Ledyard were quite young then, especially Ledyard, and Bob once told me that Ledyard cried all the time for the first six months. Later, they were transferred back to the States and entered St. Paul's School, in Concord, New Hampshire, circumstances which were probably more to their liking. After finishing at St. Paul's, they entered Harvard where they were graduated, respectively, in the Classes of 1923 and 1925. Given their ages, this was a bit late for college graduation. Ledyard once explained to me that after the governesses and school in Switzerland, they had a little trouble settling into a St. Paul's-Harvard education.

After his 1925 graduation, Ledyard spent some months in Europe. This time, it sounds like it was more fun than at La Villa School. He was in Paris for much of his stay, and he entered into the night life with gusto. He once described a night out in a well-known Parisian cafe where he and his party met up with another group of temporary expatriates which included none other than F. Scott and Zelda Fitzgerald. Before the evening was over—or, more properly, before the dawn came—he and F. Scott engaged in some fisticuffs. Ledyard could not remember just how the altercation started, but he claimed that he won. On another occasion, in another bar, Ledyard had the temerity to insult none other than the later famed Hollywood restaurateur, "Mike" Romanoff, insisting that "Mike's" imperial pedigree would not stand up under close genealogical scrutiny. This time Ledyard was not so fortunate as in the Fitzgerald-Smith encounter; instead, the heir to the Romanoffs had "floored" him with a "lucky punch".

When this continental *wunderjahr* was over, Ledyard returned to Milwaukee and went into the aforementioned family woodworking business although I never heard him talk about this. Quite probably, he felt about it as Harry Pollock did about the bond business, that is, "he hated every minute of it". I infer this from the fact that it took him only about a year to get out of it. He was rescued by Oliver Ricketson, Jr., whom he had known at Harvard when they were in the Fly Club together. "Rick" was doing archaeology with Morley and the Carnegie and was starting a major new dig at Uaxactun. He invited Ledyard to join him, which Ledyard did for the 1927 season, just a year before he, Ledyard, was to bring Harry Pollock into the Maya archaeological fold. Ledyard's brother Bob, always more conservative by nature than Ledyard, wasn't to join them for another few years.

It was at this time in his life that Ledyard married Sandra Falk. They were to have two children, Ledyard, Jr. and Sandra. Their marriage ended in divorce in the war years while Ledyard was in Guatemala City. In 1948 Ledyard was married a second time, to Katharine Moss Mellon, the "Kitty" whom I met in Merida in 1953. They had a daughter, Camilla. Kitty, sadly, died of cancer in the mid-1950s.

At Mayapan, Ledyard and Karl Ruppert published a number of brief preliminary statements on their house mound surveys (*e.g.*, A. L. Smith and Ruppert, 1952, 1956), but it was left to Ledyard to do the final account of this work which was brought out in the compendium Mayapan volume (Pollock, Roys, Proskouriakoff, and A. L. Smith, 1962). It was when Ledyard was finishing up this Mayapan writing that our collaboration began. This was 1958, the year of the dissolution of the Carnegie's Department of Archaeology. At that time, some of the staff, including Eric Thompson, Karl Ruppert, Gus Stromsvik, and Ed Shook, either retired or accepted employment elsewhere. Harry Pollock, Tatiana Proskouriakoff, and Ledyard Smith all joined us at the Peabody Museum. Harry and Tania had writing projects of their own to continue with, but Ledyard, once his Mayapan report was completed, was left at a loose end. He was made an assistant curator of Middle American Archaeology and was assigned to work as an assistant to me. It could have been a sticky situation. Here was one of the most experienced and established Maya archaeologists in the field, a man twelve years my senior, placed under my supervision. How would he take to it? I confess to having worried over it, but I don't think Ledyard ever gave it a thought. I can only report that we got along fine right from the first and in over 20 years of collaboration. I guess some credit goes to both of us, but Ledyard deserves the larger share as he was placed in the more difficult situation. This is a good place to say that he was a man secure in himself. He knew what he knew, and he knew that he was very competent at it. He was not one to worry about status.

We began to work together almost at once; in fact, we went into the field together in 1958, actually prior to the Carnegie's closing. As I've recounted in the previous memoir, Harry Pollock, in response to my request for advice as to where to dig in the Maya Lowlands, suggested we have a look at Altar de Sacrificios in the Peten. When I decided to do this, Harry detached Ledyard from official Carnegie duties so that he could make the trip with me to Altar de Sacrificios. The two of us went down to Guatemala City in February.

Here I must begin by saying that Guatemala City was a place in which Ledyard was always happy. He had innumerable friends there. Many of these were from the coffee finca families—Guatemalan, German, British, and American—and it was obvious from the time that we stepped off the plane that these old friends were truly glad to see him. On that first trip, we were in the city for more than a week, and we dined out every night. One particular friend was Don Gustavo Stahl. Slightly older than Ledyard, he was a descendant of an old German-Guatemalan family from Quetzaltenango. But he had gone to the University of California at Berkeley, graduating from there in the 1920s, and in this process of Americanization he had acquired a wife, Janet, in San Francisco. Gus and Janet were to be our gracious hosts time and again over our ten years of fieldwork in Guatemala, entertaining us on our way "in" and "out" of the Peten. Gus had lots of "Ledyard stories" from the 1930s and 40s. Not surprisingly, I learned from Gus that my new colleague had been a most popular and indefatigable party-goer in the Guatemala City "international set". One story I got from Don Gustavo was perhaps a match for some of Ledyard's Parisian night-club adventures. It concerned how Ledyard, at the height of festivities at one particular and very gala cocktail party, had sat down on a cocktail glass and was, thereby, retired from the party in great pain and consternation, being subsequently hospitalized for necessary stitching and convalescence. By 1958, however, both Ledyard and Gustavo were older and nothing so untoward happened on any of our pre-or post-Peten stays in the city.

During the days of our week in Guatemala City, we attended to our official permit for archaeological reconnaissance, bought a few supplies for our journey, and arranged with an oil exploration company in the Peten to give us transport into a location which would be reasonably close to Altar de Sacrificios. The location in question was called "Sohio" (Standard Oil of Ohio), and it was their exploration field base, situated some distance south of the little town of La Libertad. I say this was "reasonably close" to Altar de Sacrificios, but the phrase is relative. The airline distance wasn't great, but ground and water movement in the Peten can be slow and difficult. When Pollock, Smith, and Shook had gone into Altar de Sacrificios in the 1930s, they had done it by paddle-powered dug-out canoes. Then it was a three day trip from Sayache, a small river-port town on the Pasion River. By the 1950s, with the availability of gasoline and outboard motors, a large dug-out canoe, with a powerful motor, could make the Sayaxche-to-Altar de Sacrificios trip in six to eight hours, at least if there were no emergencies and delays; but then there were always emergencies and delays. In fact, I don't think I ever made a trip anywhere in the Peten without some hold-ups and hitches, and our 1958 "rediscovery" of Altar de Sacrificios was to be no exception.

We were taken by the oil company people in one of their planes from Guatemala City to the Sohio camp one late afternoon in mid-February. It was a flight of only a couple of hours. We spent the night in a comfortable guest cabin at Sohio. The next morning we and a crew of five, who had been detached from the Sohio camp to help us, were taken in a camp truck for a few miles to a point on the banks of the Subin River. The Subin, I should explain, is a small tributary which flows into the Pasion from the north, joining the latter stream at Sayaxche. It was barely light when we started, but before long we could see enough to realize that the Subin, in the dry season at least, wasn't much of a river. In most places it was only about a dozen feet wide. It was also swift and perilously shallow. Much of our descent in it was spent in pushing the canoe off the rocks—an exercise in which the archaeologists as well as the crew took part. Therefore, it was not until much later in the morning than we anticipated that we reached the confluence with the Pasion, opposite Sayaxche. Here there was another considerable delay while we arranged for a larger and somewhat more "seaworthy" canoe and waited for an additional experienced boatman, "an old Peten hand who knew the river", to come aboard. So it was noon before we got going down the Pasion for our destination at Altar de Sacrificios. The Pasion is a sizable river, in most places being as much as 100 to 150 m from bank to bank. On its lower course, from Sayaxche to the Pasion confluence with the Chixoy-Usumacinta system, it flows slowly so even though the current was in our favor, and the outboard motor churned along steadily, the trip seemed to go on forever. I began to realize that all day in a canoe in the Peten, under cloudless skys, can be a tedious experience. The novelty wore off very rapidly. There wasn't much to see. Part of the time, I was told, we were passing through savanna country, and part of the time the surrounding vegetation was said to be big forest; but from the canoe you really couldn't tell where you were because of the gallery of trees that lined both banks of the stream. While the river shores were largely deserted of human habitation, we did come to a few tiny hamlets or farmsteads as we made our way along the seemingly endless bends of the river. These little communities consisted of three or four thatched huts on spots of high riverbank ground. A few forlorn-looking inhabitants would come out of the houses as we passed and exchange salutations with our crew. We stopped at a couple of them where our Sayaxche special boatmen wanted to deliver a message or, maybe, say hello to a girl friend. Most such places, we were to find out later, also had been occupied in the past by the ancient Maya. Nearly all of them had small house mounds, frequently serving as the bases for the modern huts.

On the way down it turned out that this special boatman, or "motorista", had been on the trip with Pollock, Shook, and Ledyard when they had visited Altar de Sacrificios in the 1930s. In his talks with Ledyard, it came up that this worthy had taken three "gringos" to the ruins some 20 years before. He had been a young paddleman then; now, in his maturity, he had gone with the times and was operating an outboard motor. I was reassured by this conversational exchange, especially when this pilot-navigator told us that everything was *"muy bueno"* at Altar de Sacrificios and that he could make a landfall there "with his eyes closed". A short few hours after this, in the dark, I felt that this extrasensory perception might come in handy.

The day wore on. The sun became less fierce, but it also began to get alarmingly low on the horizon. I asked Ledyard if it looked like we were getting anywhere near Altar. He asked the "motorista" who replied, with confidence, *"Si, esta cercita"*. But the delay in our departure from Sayaxche had been just a little too much for a daylight arrival. At just about 6:15 PM, as the light was fading fast, I noticed that the dark tree-shrouded riverbank on our left, or south, side loomed higher than it had. Were these mounds? Was this Altar de Sacrificios, at long last? Ledyard wasn't sure. It had been a long time since he had been there. In the fast-approaching dark, our pilot now seemed less confident. It had been a long time since he had been there, too—probably not since that long ago voyage with the "three gringos". Ledyard finally told him he better turn into the shore here. He complied, and we bumped against the bank. There wasn't any "beach" or a landing area at the point where we put in. The water lapped up against an eroding clay bank. We managed to grab hold of some exposed tree roots and pull in closer. In the fast dying light we could see piles of potsherds at the water's edge. This was some kind of an archaeological site, but where could we get ashore and unload the canoe? Our guide was not sure. *"Todo esta cambiado aqui Doctor"*, he told me. (All is changed here, Doctor.) At just about then the last light disappeared. We couldn't see a damn thing. The mosquitos buzzed in our ears. Then it began to rain. The "dry season" in the Peten, I was to learn, doesn't mean it doesn't rain.

We had a hurried council. Should we try to scale the bank in the rain and the dark, with all our camp gear? Our guide advised against it. He had a better idea. On the north bank, opposite the ruins, there was an abandoned house he knew about. It would keep the rain off. We could sling our hammocks inside of it, and cook supper there. We said lead on. We crossed the river and landed at a spot where we could get up the bank with only a moderate amount of slipping around in the mud. Sure enough, our flashlights showed us a delapidated house hidden away in the bush. It looked pretty dismal, but it was still standing. After we had lit our kerosene lanterns, we saw it was a two room affair, with a semi-open front room. The men built a fire in this part. I wondered about setting the thatch on fire, but they didn't seem concerned. The house posts and rafters appeared solid enough, and hammocks and *pabellones* were slung from these. The men said they didn't want to sleep in the back room so Ledyard and I took that accomodation. It certainly looked to be the driest and most secure part of the house. But it had another occupant—or former occupant. Directly beneath my hammock was the mound of a grave marked with a wooden cross that bore the name of the former owner of the house. It was a woman, the men told us, who, with her children, had been abandoned here by her husband. One day she was washing clothes in the river when she was attacked by a crocodile. She managed to escape but was mauled and bitten by the beast so that she died of these wounds. The errant husband came back, gave the lady a Christian burial in the dirt floor of the house, took the children, and was now living in Sayaxche.

This sad tale—how true or how fabricated it may have been I

never found out—did nothing to jolly up the evening. Altar de Sacrificios and its environs began to take on a sombre, even macabre, quality that made me wonder if I really wanted to spend the next three or four seasons there. The rewarmed beans, rice, and tortillas that made up our nocturnal repast on that rainy night did little to revive my sagging spirits. But then good old Ledyard called me into our back room, sepulchural sanctuary. He had that Ledyard grin on his face as he broke out his flask and handed it to me. And so it was that we toasted the success of our enterprise on that first night in the proximity of the ruins of Altar de Sacrificios.

We were all up before dawn the next day, breakfasting on the same fare that we had had the night before. The rain had stopped. As soon as it was light, we packed up, loaded the canoe, and took off. We had reached a point in the middle of the river, when the junior boatman, the "boga"—the one who stood in the prow with a long pole to test the river's depth— gave an excited cry and pointed back toward the shore from which we had just come. The "motorista", his eyes agleam with excitement, responded immediately, turning our craft full speed back toward the bank below the deserted house where we had spent the night. The other men in the boat took up the "boga's" cry and began to point in the same direction. As we drew nearer the shore, the "boga" grabbed up one of the picks we had brought along with us for our excavations. I was seated directly behind him and Ledyard behind me. My Spanish is slow on the "uptake" so it took me a couple of seconds to comprehend that the word the men were shouting was "largar-to" and another second after that to translate "lagarto" into "crocodile"! Good god! The nemesis of the unfortunate aban-doned wife! Had it returned for new victims? There it was on the bank ahead of us! It looked about the size of a telephone pole, but it increased in size as we drew nearer And we were going straight for it, engine at full speed. Ledyard, by now, had realized the situation. He told me later he was all braced for receiving a twelve-foot crocodile as a passenger in the canoe with us! Not slowing, we plowed directly into the mud bank. The "boga", his pick held overhead to deliver a killing blow to the great beast, went over on his head into the mud. The crocodile—I have never seen anything so big move so fast—leaped under the canoe and into the river in a great, silent, curving dive. We didn't see him again although we didn't look very hard.

We had a little disciplinary talk with the men after that. We couldn't tolerate, we said, their taking things into their own hands and setting off on such a dangerous exercise without our permission. They didn't seem much impressed, explaining that in circumstances like that one has to move fast, that there is no time for consultation. Ledyard instructed them that it was against Guatemlanan law to kill crocodiles. They said they knew that, but that a crocodile hide would bring in lots of money. Although they were said to frequent the Pasion delta, I saw only one other "lagarto" in all the time we were at Altar de Sacrificios. Maybe it was the same one of our first morning there, but it looked smaller. One of the workmen on the dig shot at it with a .22 rifle. We heard the bullet plunk against the hide and ricochet off with a whine. I don't know how a blow with a pick would have done. The "largarto" was undoubtedly formidable prey.

To continue with that same day in 1958, after our saurian adventure, we turned the boat around and, in the daylight, found a convenient landing on the south, or Altar de Sacrificios, bank with little trouble. The site loomed over the river which had, at some time in the past, cut a large piece out of one of the biggest mounds in what we were to designate as Group A. It was at the foot of this washout that we had come across all the potsherds on the night before. Once ashore, it took only a little machete work to locate Group B with its Early Classic stelae which Morley (1938–1939) had recorded there years before. We set up a camp and stayed at Altar for two nights. Ledyard did some digging along the river bank to get a pottery sample, and I put down a test in the plaza area of Group B. In our short time there we had enough pottery information to indicate a site occupation running from Middle Preclassic to Late Classic, and we also located some new monuments. It was enough to convince us that Altar de Sacrificios was worth more intensive study.

A National Science Foundation grant was obtained for this

purpose and in 1959 we began in earnest, establishing a large camp at the site, doing extensive clearing, and opening major cuts in the structures of Group B. Ledyard and I collaborated on several preliminary reports on Altar de Sacrificios (A. L. Smith and Willey, 1962; A. L. Smith, Willey, and Adams, 1962; Willey and A. L. Smith, 1963), as well as on the final reports (Willey and A. L. Smith, 1969; A. L. Smith, 1972; Willey, 1972, 1973b). In this collaboration, we were also joined by graduate students who developed and eventually published doctoral dissertations on various aspects of the work (Adams, 1971; Saul, 1972; J. A. Graham, 1972). During our time there, Ledyard was in the field for the full three-month field season each year, from 1959 through 1964. I was there for only a part of each season. As a consequence, the responsibility for the camp, the day-to-day digging, and the guidance and instruction of the graduate students was largely his.

After that initial 1958 survey trip to Altar de Sacrificios, we returned to Guatemala City. There we hired a car, and Ledyard showed me around the Pacific slopes where we looked at El Baul and other locations of the Santa Lucia Cotzumalhuapa style stone sculpture (Thompson, 1948). Subsequently, we were joined by Ledyard's older daughter, Sandra, who accompanied us on a trip through the Guatemalan Highlands, visiting Lake Atitlan, Chichicastenango, and the numerous sites which Ledyard had surveyed and described in a Guatemalan Highland monograph (A. L. Smith, 1955).

Back, again, in Guatemala City, and before our return to the States, I had another glimpse of Ledyard as a night-clubber. One of his favorite Guatemala City night spots was a dive called "El Gallito", famous, according to Ledyard, for the biggest (?), best (?), but certainly the loudest, marimba band "north of the Panama canal". He, Sandra, and I went there one night, and I've rarely seen anyone enjoy himself more thoroughly than Ledyard. After exchanging embraces with the proprietor (clearly Ledyard was well-known there from the old days), we were shown to a table. He and I alternated dancing with Sandra. After a time, Sandra and I got pretty tired of it all, but we couldn't get Ledyard to go. We must stay, he insisted, for the special salute, given nightly at 2:00 AM. This, we were assured, would be a surprise we would remember. It was. At the appointed hour, four trumpeters were stationed, respectively, at the four corners of the dance floor. On signal, and with the marimbas going full tilt, the horns cut loose. The blast and the general noise would have been memorable even by more modern standards. Only after this exhibition were we allowed to leave.

Ledyard's tirelessness in social activities covered all kinds of things. I can remember one time when we had had a long and difficult day flying up from the Peten to Guatemala City. We had started well before dawn, at about 5:00 AM. We'd gone downriver, this time from our Seibal field camp, to Sayaxche. After which, we got into a truck for a long, bumpy ride across the savanna to Flores, the capital of the Peten and its principal airport. After hanging around Flores for about five hours, we boarded one of Aviateca's DC–3's for a harrowing take-off and an hour's unsteady flight to the Guatemala City airport. As soon as we got into town and to the hotel, Ledyard was on the phone making dinner arrangements for us for that night. In this instance, our prospective host had just purchased a new airplane. He wanted us to go for a ride in it that very afternoon. There was plenty of time, he said, before dinner. I could hardly think of anything I wanted to do less, but Ledyard was all for it. Out he went again to the airport. I took a nap.

The 1964 field season was the last one at Altar de Sacrificios and the first one at Seibal. A couple of years before, during the Altar field season, Dick Adams and John Graham had gone up to Seibal for a preliminary look (Adams, 1963), and, later, Ledyard and I visited the site. These preliminaries led us to want to work there. The heavy occurrences of 9th century Fine Orange wares at Seibal related to the final occupations at Altar. What were the other relationships between the two sites? Also, the fact that Seibal appeared to have been going strong in the early 10th Cycle, when most Classic sites of the southern Lowlands had ceased monumental and building activities, made it a very interesting place. From this perspective, what light might Seibal throw on the phenomenon of the "Classic Collapse"? Again supported by a National Sceince grant, a Seibal camp was constructed in 1964, Ian Graham and Gair Tourtellot began a detailed map of the ruins.

Seibal is a much more pleasant site than Altar de Sacrificios.

It is located on some high hills at the "Great Bend" of the Pasion River. At 100 m or more above the level of the river, the site enjoys pleasant breezes and is relatively mosquito free, in striking contrast to Altar de Sacrificios. Seibal is also a much bigger site than Altar. Its pyramids and platforms are larger, more numerous, and cover a much larger area, and beyond the central religious and civic buildings at Seibal there is a densely settled residential zone far larger than any comparable zone at the other site. Our excavations would show that Seibal was occupied over the same span of time as Altar de Sacrificios, or from the Middle Preclassic through the Late Classic Period; however, it was a much larger place than Altar during the Late Preclassic, and in the Terminal Classic (A.D. 800–900) it was clearly the major political center of the Pasion drainage. The stelae record at Seibal does not begin until the Late Classic, but many of its late monuments are of a spectacular size and beauty, such as those associated with Temple A–3 (Maler, 1908; Morley, 1937–38), all with 10.1.0.0.0 Period Ending dates (A.D. 849). Seibal continued with stelae dedications until 10.3.0.0.0 (A.D. 889).

Our research at Seibal has been, or will be, reported upon in various articles and monographs. These include papers which Ledyard and I have presented at International Congresses (A. L. Smith and Willey, 1966, 1969) or otherwise published (Willey and A. L. Smith, 1967). The final Seibal reports consist of: a jointly authored (Willey et al. 1975) introductory volume, which contains Ian Graham's splendid maps; Ledyard's (A. L. Smith, 1982) monograph on the major architecture; J. A. Sabloff's (1975) publication on the ceramics; my own on the other artifacts (Willey, 1978); J. A. Graham's (n.d.) on monuments and hieroglyphics; Mary Pohl's (n.d.) on faunal remains; Gair Tourtellot's on peripheral settlement (1988) and on burials (n.d.); and my summary and conclusions of the project as a whole (Willey, n.d. 3).

No small factor in the Seibal work was Ledyard's maintenance of the field camp. He was an absolute past master at this kind of thing. Our Seibal camp, located just at the edge of the ruins, consisted of a main house or dining room, three identical cottages or dormitories, neatly arranged in a row, and, farther away, a large pottery and artifacts laboratory. The dining room and the three dormitories were trim pole-and-wattle structures, with white-washed walls and thatch roofs. Each building was tightly screened at window height on all four sides, and the screening had then been extended, ceiling-like, across the top. In effect, the inhabitants of such houses were protected in large screen-boxes which were set beneath thatch roofs. The pottery and artifact lab had no lower white-washed walls but was, simply, a giant screened box beneath a thatch roof. The camp grounds, perhaps 100 by 75 m in extent, had been carefully cleared of all trees and bush and planted in Kentucky blue grass, a plant which, amazingly, keeps tropical second growth from reappearing—or at least it did in the five years we were there. One of the household servants kept it mowed with a hand-pushed lawnmower, probably the only one in the Peten and ever a source of wonder to our machete-wielding workmen.

Ledyard was the steward par-excellence. Each year, during the winter back in Cambridge, he would order and organize supplies. These were S.S. *Pierce* canned goods which that firm would carefully pack for us in wooden boxes for the sea voyage to Guatemala and the trip by truck and canoe to our camp. At Seibal the cocktail hour was the prime time of the day. Every evening at 6:00 PM we'd gather in the dining room as the Coleman lanterns were lighted against the rapidly descending dark. There the key liquid supplies were available. Our kerosene-powered refrigerator—next to screened sleeping quarters the most indispensable amenity for Peten-life—provided the ice cubes. Boiled river water was properly charged in our soda-siphons. The *hor d'oeuvres* would be brought in by Tranquilino, our white-jacketed messboy. In these delicacies, Ledyard's fine hand was evident in such items as the tinned S.S. *Pierce* smoked oysters. These were consumed along with fresh hearts-of-palm chunks dashed with juice from our own Seibal-grown limes. The fresh hearts-of-palm bits, far superior to the pickled variety, were a "windfall" from archaeology. Every day or so we would have to cut down a palm tree from one of the mounds. Deep within the basal trunk of the tree would be the fresh growing core, the pale yellow-green, edible heart. Salad, thus, would be brought in from the field "yule log" fashion, over someone's shoulder. The cocktail hour would be succeeded by the soup course, again courtesy of S.S. *Pierce*. Then, if we were lucky, we might have catfish or turtle from the river or wild boar meat, as the entree; however, when fishing and hunting could not offer such provender, we fell back on some S.S. *Pierce* special, such as lobster newburg or duck a la orange.

Ledyard led us in a disciplined life, though. Breakfast was at 5:30 AM. After that, he paid his daily call on the cook and the kitchen to see that all was in order there. Work on the dig began at 6:00, with Ledyard making the rounds of the various excavations soon after, and stopping in the course of these to pay a call on the workmen's camp to check on their kitchen, sleeping quarters, and sanitary facilities.

We employed about 35 diggers. They had their own cooks and kitchens and were all under the charge of a responsible foreman. Ledyard was an admired and well-liked boss, both fair and solicitous. Every evening, after work stopped at 5:00, he maintained a kind of clinic or surgery where he attended to all kinds of lesser ills—those that were aspirin or bandage-and-adhesive-tape-treatable. For anything worse, he would always despatch the patient in the outboard motor boat to Sayaxche which was only an hour-and-a-half downriver from Seibal. Ledyard also patiently adjudicated disputes among the men. Our labor force was made up of off-season *milperos*, mahogany cutters, former oil exploration workmen, and river fishermen. Such a crew contained not a few rough-and-ready types. Ledyard not only dealt with them with great fairness but with a man-to-man openness that had within it no hint of distrust or suspicion. I was frequently surprised by what seemed to me a transformation in personalities when they treated with Ledyard. He, on the other hand, took that goodness which he seemed to bring forth from them for granted. As I write this, I recall that this was, essentially, what I said about Byron Cummings in the first memoir in this volume. Certainly, Cummings and Ledyard were strikingly different personalities, but they shared this admirable quality.

I was always careful not to interfere in Ledyard's various "labor relations". In the camp, "Mr. Smith" was the acknowledged top boss. My input into digging operations, which were largely in our excavation strategies and procedures, were always channeled through him.

On the dig, Ledyard's long experience showed to advantage. He had certain amateur engineering skills which were an aid in architectural excavation. He liked restoration work, as did most of our best workmen. His careful and faithful rebuilding of Seibal's Temple A−3 or the Round Structure are prime examples of this. He summed up these efforts in an article he wrote for the journal *Monumentum* at the close of the project (A. L. Smith, 1968). Daily, Ledyard moved around from one operation to another. I can see him walking briskly along the trails, usually in sneakers. I rarely saw him in field boots. As a matter of fact, Ledyard was not very fond of bush survey where boots were needed. He liked the "big digging"—clearing and restoring vaulted architecture, unearthing burials, caches.

Did Ledyard and I ever talk much archaeology with each other? As I think back about it, I realize that we didn't very much, at least not in the way that I did with Bill Bullard, Harry Pollock, or some my graduate students. What Ledyard and I discussed was apt to be the day-to-day practicalities of the digging operations—how many buildings we should sample in Seibal Group C, or how we should treat the broken fragments of the painted plaster frieze that had fallen from the facade of Temple A−3. This doesn't mean that Ledyard was not aware of the importance of such things as the appearance of Fine Orange sherds within the fill of Temple A−3, or of the Early Classic "gap" at Seibal and its relationship to the larger pattern of the "hiatus" in the southern Maya Lowlands. He was "hep" to all of this, but he just didn't seem as interested in such things as in keeping a good record of building levels in an excavation. When he did turn his hand to something other than excavation recording, he would produce a short paper on the significance of the "patolli-game" markings on one of the A-3 stela altars (A. L. Smith, 1977) or, more broadly oriented, a survey of ballcourt forms in the Guatemalan Highlands, which he did for a *festschrift* dedicated to his old colleague and friend. Sam Lothrop (A. L. Smith, 1961).

Some of the best times I had with Ledyard were in the course of our attendance at three International Congress of Americanist meetings. He enjoyed meetings although I don't think he had been to many of them during his career. In 1964 we went to the ICA meeting in Spain. This turned out to be a prolonged affair. It began in Barcelona, where Ledyard and I spent as much time in the art museum at Montjuich as we did in the sessions. While I don't think Ledyard could have been called a connoisseur of 16th or 17th century Spanish painting, he knew something about it, as he did about museum paintings in general. He was a cultivated man although he never made a fuss about being one. On the last afternoon of the Barcelona sessions, we dined at a restaurant in the city and got to discussing the plans for the morrow. The "laid-on" drill for the Congress was that everyone should board a train for a ten-hour ride to Madrid, where the second round of papers was scheduled. Ledyard pointed out that this wouldn't be much fun. We would, of course, "see a lot of the countryside" from such a perspective, but we would get a lot of the "countryside" in our eyes, too. Spanish trains then were apt to go rather slowly across the dusty plains and to do this with the windows open. Why did we not, he proposed, take the plane for a short hop to Madrid, arrive early in that city, and spend the afternoon in the Prado Museum? This seemed like a good suggestion so we did. We put up at the Ritz. The Prado was just across the street. We had an afternoon looking at the Goyas and were back in the hotel for one of those late Spanish dinners, at 10 PM. We were dining on pheasant and grapes when our dusty and travel-weary colleagues made their appearance. A civilized man, Ledyard. The next stop on the Spanish three-ring circus was Sevilla. It is a great city but a hot one in August. I had stayed at the Alfonso XIII the year before with my family, and I had been telling Ledyard what a great hotel it was. He agreed. Are chilled dry sherry and cold gazpacho Moorish inventions for dealing with long, hot evenings? Ledyard became quite a fan of such fare before we headed for home.

In 1966, the ICA was held in Argentina. It was a long ten-hour flight from New York to Buenos Aires. From the capital we then flew on down to Mar del Plata, a summer seaside resort, but, unfortunately, this was Argentina's winter time.

We narrowly escaped frostbite in a huge, ghostly, semi-inhabited hotel. The "heat" generated by the Congress's intellectual sessions was never able to overcome the chill. Ledyard and I went out to dinner one night, acquiring a North American colleague as an additional companion as we set out. The three of us finally found our way through dark and windy streets to a restaurant that had been highly recommended at our hotel. It too was forsaken and gloomy, and the menu was printed in Spanish and German. I had visions of former U-Boat commanders, turtle-necked sweaters under their brass-buttoned navy jackets, putting in there from cold south Atlantic duty for a glass of schnapps and, perhaps, a Heil Hitler salute. We ate our way through an uninspired plate of sauerbraten and potato cakes. Our new dinner companion and colleague gave the evening its eccentric touch. I had not known him before although I was aware of some of his archaeological writings. Ledyard was familiar with neither the man nor his work. When the dessert came—Vanilla ice cream—he took the cap off the pepper shaker and poured the entire contents on his portion, devouring this unusual "sundae" with relish, but making no comment. I could see that Ledyard was shaken by the incident. Musing about it afterward, it came to me that Ledyard had never really been exposed to many archaeologists, outside of his Carnegie colleagues. He never attended those annual meetings of the American Anthropological Association, for instance, with their late night informal and bibulous gatherings in hotel rooms. His life in the discipline had been sheltered. He had gone, literally, from the Fly Club to the Carnegie Institution's Department of Archaeology, places where deportment, if not exactly alcohol-free, tended to be predictable.

Our last ICA, and perhaps the best, was the one in Stuttgart and Munich, in 1968. I had purchased an automobile for delivery in Stuttgart—or in Sindelfingen, the location of the Mercedes-Benz works just outside of the larger city. After the Stuttgard sessions, we picked up the car and drove on to Munich. Ledyard spelled me on the driving and was more undaunted than I was at the 80-miles-an-hour-plus speeds on the autobahn. After the Munich meetings, where we each held forth on Seibal and kindred matters, he agreed to accompany me back through Germany, France and the Low Countries on my way to England, where I was going to spend the coming academic year. Neither of us had a word of German except for something that sounded like "ful-op" when we pulled into a filling station for gasoline. Ledyard, though, controlled enough French, as a residue of childhood instruction or those halcyon days of 1925 in Paris, to expedite our passage across the border into that country. He also saw that we got the wines we wanted as we made our way through France and Belgium. In Ostend, we had quite a conference with a hotel clerk about a bill, but Ledyard adjudicated it with the same even-handed aplomb that he used with the "troops" back at Seibal. Eventually, we got the car across the Channel to England without mishap. We parted there. I stayed in Cambridge, where I was joined shortly by my family; Ledyard returned to the United States.

The next I heard, and not long afterwards, Ledyard had married Betty Griggs Nichols, an attractive and intelligent widow who had been a near neighbor of his in Needham, Massachusetts. It was to be an excellent marriage; he was lucky; but then such a nice guy deserved to be. Betty's large family of children and grandchildren were united with Ledyard's. I remember attending a party—perhaps a wedding anniversary celebration after ten years—at which a happy throng of kin of all ages filled a country club dining room.

With the fieldwork at Seibal finished, Ledyard's time was given over to the preparation of his monograph. He only came into the museum on one day a week, and when he did he usually turned over to me the week's pages, neatly handwritten in pencil on legal-sized paper. I passed them on to a typist, and the manuscript grew. He was faithful to the task. Betty told me that he worked on it everyday. It took him a while. The dig was closed in 1968, and I think it was about 1978 before the long manuscript was complete. Still, it's not a bad record for a field archaeologist in his seventies. I used to use Ledyard's example of fidelity and diligence in completing an obligation of writing to shame some of my graduate student colleagues. He produced a very solid report. It lays out the "anatomy" of the site as revealed by our excavations. It provided a data bank from which others could go forward with some new interpretations. For instance, since we dug Seibal, we have come to realize that much of the major architecture dates to the Late Preclassic Period. At the time we were digging, we assumed that it was largely Late Classic. Ledyard's excellent field accounts and diagrams have allowed for this change in interpretation, in advance of the writing of the final summary monograph (Willey, n.d. 3).

Ledyard was not a formal teacher or professor, and because of this he did not have the graduate student cohorts that some of us have. As I have said, he was not one to frequent professional gatherings or meetings, nor would he have been readily or easily articulate in such assemblies. As a consequence of these circumstances, he is, perhaps, not as well known as he should have been. He has, though, received honors. He and his brother Bob were feted at a dinner in 1970, at which time they were presented with a *festschrift* volume, *Monographs and Papers in Maya Archaeology* (Bullard, ed., 1970). It contained contributions of high quality by old colleagues, such as Harry Pollock, Eric Thompson, Tatiana Proskouriakoff, and Robert Wauchope, and by younger student colleagues, including Bill Bullard, Dick Adams, Jerry Sabloff, and Gair Tourtellot. Ledyard felt very complimented by it. Another important recognition was an invitation to prepare a short essay or module on Uaxactun, as a classic example of a Maya "big dig". It was an indication that he had produced a "landmark" work in archaeology. Ledyard was pleased by the invitation, and he did a good job in preparing the module (A. L. Smith, 1973). I think, though, that the honor that pleased him most was the Order of the Quetzal, bestowed on him by the Government of Guatemala for what amounted to a lifetime of service in the development of the archaeology of that nation. Fittingly, the award was made at Seibal, at the very close of the 1968 field season, and at what was also the close of Ledyard's long, active, and honorable career as a field archaeologist.

In the long view, however, I am confident that Ledyard's reputation is not only secure but that it will become enhanced as time goes on. Fundamental to this reputation are his field reports: the Motagua Valley (1943); Uaxactun (1950); the Central Highlands of Guatemala (1955); Altar de Sacrificios (1972); and the crowning work at Seibal (1982).

While Ledyard technically had been retired, from his seventieth birthday onward, I certainly didn't think of him that way during those years he was working on his Seibal monograph. Jerry Sabloff, Gair Tourtellot, and I, as we were preparing manuscripts of our own, had questions for him all the time. He, himself, was busy writing. After the monograph finally came out in 1982, he did retire, giving up his office in Room 36—Tozzer's old quarters across the hall from me in the Peabody Museum. He came in once a month to attend Peabody Museum luncheons at the Harvard Faculty Club. I saw him more often than this socially, at his house or ours, or elsewhere. He was always in bounding good spirits—the brisk walk, the broad grin. Some of the last things he told me about were of letters he had received from old associates in Guatemala, and this included not only his friends in Guatemala City but those from the Peten, such as our former cook, the labor foreman, or the houseboy and waiter, Tranquilino.

It was as a surprise and shock, then, as it always is with a dear friend, to learn that Ledyard had been stricken with a heart attack on the early morning of 5 December 1985. He was rushed to the hospital, and for a few hours he seemed to be recovering, but he died later that day. I'll remember him, though—at Altar de Sacrificios, the crocodiles, the subterranean night clubs, those great evening cocktails at Seibal, or a sedate glass of sherry on the terrace at the Alfonso XIII. Ledyard was a man and a companion for all seasons and places.

Bibliography

ADAMS, R. E. W.
> 1963 "Seibal, Peten: Una Secuencia Ceramica Preliminar y un Nuevo Mapa," *Estudios Cultura Maya,* Vol. 3, pp. 85–96, Universidad Autonomo de Mexico, Mexico, D.F.
>
> 1971 *The Ceramics of Altar de Sacrificios,* Papers, Vol. 63, No. 1, Peabody Museum, Harvard University, Cambridge, Mass.

AMEGHINO, FLORENTINO
> 1911 "Une nouvelle industrie lithique. L'industrie de la pierre fendue dans le Tertiare de la region littorale au sud de Mar del Plata," *Anales del Museo Nacional de Buenos Aires,* Vol. 20, pp. 189–204.

ASHMORE, WENDY, ED.
> 1981 *Lowland Maya Settlement Patterns,* University of New Mexico Press, Albuquerque, N. Mex.

BENNETT, W. C.
> 1931 *Archaeology of Kauai,* Bishop Museum, Bulletin No. 80, Honolulu.
>
> 1932 "Hawaiian Heiaus and Comparative Religious Structures Throughout Polynesia," Doctoral Dissertation, University of Chicago, Chicago, Ill.
>
> 1934 *Excavations at Tiahuanaco,* Anthropological Papers, Vol. 34, Pt. 3, American Museum of Natural History, New York.
>
> 1936 *Excavations in Bolivia,* Anthropological Papers, Vol. 35, Pt. 4, American Museum of Natural History, New York.
>
> 1937 *Excavations at La Mata, Maracay, Venezuela,* Anthropological Papers, Vol. 36, Pt. 2, American Museum of Natural History, New York.
>
> 1939 *Archaeology of the North Coast of Peru,* Anthropological Papers, Vol. 37, Pt. 1, American Museum of Natural History, New York.
>
> 1944a *The North Highlands of Peru: Excavations in the Callejon de Huaylas and at Chavin de Huantar,* Anthropological Papers, American Museum of Natural History, Vol. 39, Pt. 1, New York.

BIBLIOGRAPHY

1944b   *Archaeological Regions of Colombia: A Ceramic Survey*, Yale University Publications in Anthropology, No. 30, New Haven, Conn.

1946a   "The Andean Highlands: An Introduction," *Handbook of South American Indians*, J. H. Steward, ed., Vol. 2, pp. 1–60, Bulletin 143, Bureau of American Ethnology, Smithsonian Institution, Washington, D.C.

1946b   "The Archaeology of the Central Andes," *Handbook of South American Indians*, J. H. Steward, ed., Vol. 2, pp. 61–147, Bulletin 143, Bureau of American Ethnology, Smithsonian Institution, Washington, D.C.

1946c   "The Archaeology of Colombia," *Handbook of South American Indians*, J. H. Steward, ed., Vol. 2, pp. 823–850, Bulletin 143, Bureau of American Ethnology, Smithsonian Institution, Washington, D.C.

1946d   "The Atacameño," *Handbook of South American Indians*, J. H. Steward, ed., Vol. 2, pp. 599–618, Bulletin 143, Bureau of American Ethnology, Smithsonian Institution, Washington, D.C.

1946e   *Excavations in the Cuenca Region, Ecuador*, Yale University Publications in Anthropology, No. 35, New Haven, Conn.

1948a   "A Revised Sequence for the South Titicaca Basin," *A Reappraisal of Peruvian Archaeology*, W. C. Bennett, ed., pp. 90–92, Society for American Archaeology, Memoir No. 4.

1948b   "The Peruvian Co-Tradition", *A Reappraisal of Peruvian Archaeology*, W. C. Bennett, ed., pp. 1–7, Society for American Archaeology, Memoir No. 4.

1949a   "Habitations, Household Furniture, Religious Structures, Engineering," *Handbook of South American Indians*, J. H. Steward, ed., Vol. 5, pp. 1–65, Bulletin 143, Bureau of American Ethnology, Smithsonian Institution, Washington, D.C.

1949b   "Mnemonic and Recording Devices," *Handbook of South American Indians*, J. H. Steward, ed., Vol. 5, pp. 611–619, Bulletin 143, Bureau of American Ethnology, Smithsonian Institution, Washington, D.C.

1949c   "Numbers, Measures, Weights, and Calendars," *Handbook of South American Indians*, J. H. Steward, ed., Vol. 5, pp. 601–610, Bulletin 143, Bureau of American Ethnology, Smithsonian Institution, Washington, D.C.

1950 *The Gallinazo Group, Viru Valley, Peru,* Yale University
       Publications in Anthropology, No. 43, New Haven, Conn.
1953 *Excavations at Wari, Ayacucho, Peru,* Yale University
       Publications in Anthropology, No. 49, New Haven, Conn.

BENNETT, W. C., ED.
1948A *Reappraisal of Peruvian Archaeology,* Society for Ameri-
       can Archaeology, Memoir No. 4.

BENNETT, W. C. AND J. B. BIRD
1949 *Andean Culture History,* American Museum of Natural
       History, Handbook Series No. 15, New York.

BENNETT, W. C., E. F. BLEILER, AND E. H. SOMMER
1948 *Northwest Argentine Archaeology,* Yale University Pub-
       lications in Anthropology, No. 38, New Haven, Conn.

BENNETT, W. C. AND R. M. ZINGG
1935 *The Tarahumara: An Indian Tribe of Northern Mexico,*
       University of Chicago Press, Chicago, Ill.

BEYER, HERMANN
1927 "Bibliografia: (Frans Blom and Oliver La Farge) Tribes and
       Temples," *El Mexico Antiguo,* Vol. 2, pp. 305–313, Mex-
       ico, D.F.

BIRD, J. B.
1938 "Antiquity and Migrations of the Early Inhabitants of
       Patagonia," *Geographical Review,* Vol. 28, No. 2, pp. 250–
       275, New York.
1943 *Excavations in Northern Chile,* Anthropological Papers,
       American Museum of Natural History, Vol. 38, No. 4,
       New York.
1945 *Archaeology of the Hopedale Area, Labrador,* Anthropo-
       logical Papers, American Museum of Natural History,
       Vol. 39, No. 2, New York.
1948 "Preceramic Cultures in Chicama and Viru," in *A Reap-
       praisal of Peruvian Archaeology,* W. C. Bennett, ed., pp.
       21–29, Memoir 4, Society for American Archaeology.
1951 "Recent Developments in the Treatment of Archaeologi-
       cal Textiles," in *Essays on Archaeological Methods: Pro-
       ceedings of a Conference Held Under the Auspices of the
       Viking Fund,* J. B. Griffin, ed., pp. 51–58, Anthropological
       Papers, Museum of Anthropology, University of Michi-
       gan, No. 8, Ann Arbor, Mich.
1963 "Pre-Ceramic Art from Huaca Prieta, Chicama Valley,"
       Nawpa Pacha, Vol. I, pp. 29–34, Berkeley, Calif.

1967–68   "Treasures from the Land of Gold," *Arts in Virginia*, Vol. 8, Nos. 1–2, pp. 20–23, Virginia Museum of Fine Arts, Richmond, Va.

1979a   "The 'Copper Man': A Prehistoric Miner and His Tools from Northern Chile," *Pre-Columbian Metallurgy of South America*, E. P. Benson, ed., pp. 105–132, Dumbarton Oaks, Washington, D.C.

1979b   "Legacy of the Stingless Bee," *Natural History*, Vol. 88, No. 9, pp. 49–51, American Museum of Natural History, New York.

BIRD, J. B., JOHN HYSLOP. AND M. D. SKINNER
   1985   *The Preceramic Excavations at Huaca Prieta, Chicama Valley, Peru*, Anthropological Papers, Vol. 62, American Museum of Natural History, New York.

BLOM, FRANS AND OLIVER LA FARGE
   1926   *Tribes and Temples*, Vol. 1, New Orleans, La.

BRAINERD, G. W.
   1958   *The Archaeological Ceramics of Yucatan*, Anthropological Records, No. 19, University of California Press, Berkeley and Los Angeles, Calif.

BROWN, IAN W.
   1978   *James Alfred Ford, the Man and His Works*. Southeastern Archaeological Conference, Special Publication No. 4.

BULLARD, W. R., JR.
   1952a   "Boundary Walls of Mayapan," *Year Book 51*, Carnegie Institution of Washington, Washington, D.C.

   1952b   "Residential Property Walls at Mayapan," *Current Reports*, No. 3, Vol. 1, pp. 35–45, Carnegie Institution of Washington, Washington, D.C.

   1953a   "Property Walls at Mayapan," *Year Book 52*, Carnegie Institution of Washington, Washington, D.C.

   1953b   "Archaeology of the South Highlands of Ecuador," Seminar Paper in *South American Archaeology, Anthropology 206*, G. R. Willey, ed., Tozzer Library, Harvard University, Cambridge, Mass.

   1960   "Maya Settlement Patterns in Northeastern Peten, Guatemala." *American Antiquity*, Vol. 25, pp. 355–372.

   1962   *The Cerro Colorado Site and Pithouse Architecture in the Southwestern United States Prior to A.D. 900*, Papers, Vol. 44, No. 2, Peabody Museum, Harvard University, Cambridge, Mass.

   1964   "Settlement Pattern and Social Structure in the Southern Maya Lowlands During the Classic Period, "*Actas y*

Memorias, 35th International Congress of Americanists,
Vol. 1, pp. 279–287, Mexico City.

1965a "Ruinas Ceremoniales Mayas en el Curso Inferior del
Rio Lacantun," *Estudios de Cultura Maya,* Vol. 5, pp. 41–
51, Mexico, D.F.

1965b *Late Classic Finds at Baking Pot, British Honduras,*
Occasional Paper 8, Art and Archaeology, Royal Ontario
Museum, Toronto, Canada.

1965c *Stratigraphic Excavations at San Estevan, British Honduras,* Occasional Paper 9, Art and Archaeology, Royal
Ontario Museum, Toronot, Canada.

1970 "Topoxte, A Postclassic Site in Peten, Guatemala,"
Monographs and Papers in Maya Archaeology, W. R. Bullard, Jr., ed., Papers, Vol. 61, pp. 245–307, Peabody Museum, Harvard University, Cambridge, Mass.

1973 "Postclassic Culture in Peten and Adjacent British Honduras," *the Classic Maya Collapse,* T. P. Culbert, ed., pp.
221–242, University of New Mexico Press, Albuquerque,
N. Mex.

BULLARD, W. R., JR., ED.

1970 *Monographs and Papers in Maya Archaeology,* Papers,
Vol. 61, Peabody Museum, Harvard University, Cambridge, Mass.

BUSHNELL, G. H. S.

1956 *Peru,* Thames and Hudson, London, U.K.

CARPENTER, ARTHUR

1950 "The Death of Lafleur: Two Letters from Morley," *Morleyana,* Boaz Long, ed., pp. 21–48, Museum of New Mexico and the School of American Research, Santa Fe, N.
Mex.

CASO, ALFONSO

1953 "New World Culture History: Middle America," *Anthropology Today,* A. L. Kroeber and others, eds., pp. 226–232,
University of Chicago Press, Chicago, Ill.

CHAMBERLAIN, R. S.

1948 *The Conquest and Colonization of Yucatan, 1517–1550,*
Publication 582, Carnegie Institution of Washington,
Washington, D.C.

CHANG, K. C.

1968 "Toward a Science of Prehistoric Society, *Settlement Archaeology,* K. C. Chang, ed., National Press, Palo Alto,
Calif.

CHASE, A. F. AND P. M. RICE, EDS.
1985   *The Lowland Maya Postclassic,* University of Texas Press, Austin, Tex.

CLARK, J. G. D.
1961   *World Prehistory,* Cambridge University Press, London, U.K.

COE, M. D.
La Victoria, an Early Site on the Pacific Coast of Guatemala, Papers, Vol. 53, Peabody Museum, Harvard University, Cambridge, Mass.
1976   "Matthew Williams Stirling, 1896–1975," *American Antiquity,* Vol. 41, No. 1, pp. 67–73.
1968   "San Lorenzo and the Olmec Civilization," *Dumbarton Oaks Conference on the Olmec,* E. P. Benson, ed., pp. 41–78, Dumbarton Oaks, Washington, D.C.
1981   "Religion and the Rise of Mesoamerican States," *The Transition to Statehood in the New World,* G. D. Jones and R. R. Kautz, eds., pp. 157–171, Cambridge University Press, Cambridge, U.K.

COE, M. D. AND R. A. DIEHL
1980   *In the Land of the Olmec,* 2 vols., University of Texas Press, Austin, Tex.

COE, M. D., DAVID GROVE, AND E. P. BENSON, EDS.
1981   *The Olmec and Their Neighbors, Essays in Memory of Matthew W. Stirling,* Dumbarton Oaks, Washington, D.C.

COLLIER, DONALD AND J. V. MURRA
1943   *Survey and Excavations in South Ecuador,* Anthropological Series, Vol. 35, Field Museum of Natural History, Chicago, Ill.

COLLINS, H. B.
1976   "Matthew Williams Stirling, 1896–1975," *American Anthropologist,* Vol. 78, No. 4, pp. 886–888.

COOPER, J. M.
1925   "Culture Diffusion and Culture Areas in Southern South America," *Proceedings, 21st International Congress of Americanists,* Vol. 1, pp. 406–421, Goteborg, Sweden.
1941   "Temporal Sequence and the Marginal Cultures," *Anthropological Series,* No. 10, Catholic University of America, Washington, D.C.

CULBERT, T. P., ED.
1973   *The Classic Maya Collapse,* University of New Mexico Press, Albuquerque, N. Mex.

CUMMINGS, BYRON

1933   *Cuicuilco and the Archaic Culture of Mexico*, Social Science Bulletin No. 4, University of Arizona, Tucson, Ariz.

1940   *Kinishba, A Prehistoric Pueblo of the Great Pueblo Period*, Hohokam Museums Association and the University of Arizona, Tucson, Ariz.

1953   *First Inhabitants of Arizona and the Southwest*, Cummings Publication Council, Tucson, Ariz.

DOUGLASS, A. E.

1950   "Our Friend, Byron Cummings," *For the Dean, Essays in Anthropology in Honor of Byron Cummings*, E. K. Reed and D. S. King, eds., pp. 1–3, Hohokam Museums Association and Southwestern Monuments Association, Tucson Ariz. and Santa Fe, N. Mex.

DRUCKER, PHILIP

1943a   *Ceramic Sequence at Tres Zapotes, Veracruz, Mexico*, Bulletin 140, Bureau of American Ethnology, Smithsonian Institution, Washington, D.C.

1943b   *Ceramic Stratigraphy at Cerro de las Mesas, Veracruz, Mexico*, Bulletin 141, Bureau of American Ethnology, Smithsonian Institution, Washington, D.C.

1947   *Some Implications of the Ceramic Complex of La Venta*, Smithsonian Miscellaneous Collections, Vol. 107, No. 8, Smithsonian Institution, Washington, D.C.

1952   La Venta, Tabasco: A Study of Olmec Ceramics and Art, Bulletin 153, Bureau of American Ethnology, Smithsonian Institution, Washington, D.C.

DRUCKER, PHILIP, R. F. HEIZER, AND R. J. SQUIER

1957   "Radiocarbon Dates from La Venta, Tabasco," *Science*, Vol. 126, pp. 72–73.

1959   *Excavations at La Venta, Tabasco, 1955*, Bulletin 170, Bureau of American Ethnology, Smithsonian Institution, Washington, D.C.

EASBY, DUDLEY, JR.

1965   "Samuel Kirkland Lothrop, 1892–1965," *American Antiquity*, Vol. 31, pp. 256–261.

EVANS, CLIFFORD, JR.

1968   "James Alfred Ford, 1911–1968," *American Anthropologist*, Vol. 70, No. 6, pp. 1161–1167.

FAIRBANKS, C. H.

1946   "The Macon Earthlodge," *American Antiquity*, Vol. 12, No. 2, pp. 94–108.

1956   *Archaeology of the Funeral Mound, Ocmulgee National Monument, Georgia,* Archaeological Research Series, No. 3, National Park Service, U.S. Department of Interior, Washington, D.C.

FELDMAN, R. A.

1985   "Preceramic Corporate Architecture Evidence for the Development of Non-Egalitarian Social Systems in Peru," in *Early Ceremonial Architecture in the Andes,* C. B. Donnan, ed., pp. 71–92, Dumbarton Oaks, Washington, D.C.

FEWKES, J. W.

1924   *Preliminary Archaeological Explorations at Weeden Island, Florida,* Smithsonian Miscellaneous Collections, Vol. 76, No. 13, Smithsonian Institution, Washington, D.C.

FIGGINS, J. D.

1927   "The Antiquity of Man in America," *Natural History,* Vol. 27, No. 3, pp. 229–239, American Museum of Natural History, New York.

FORD, ANABEL

1985   "Maya Settlement Pattern Chronology in the Belize River Area and the Implications for the Development of the Central Maya Lowlands," *Belcast Journal of Belizean Affairs,* Vol. 2, pp. 13–31, Belize.

FORD, J. A.

1936   *Analysis of Indian Village Site Collections from Louisiana and Mississippi,* Anthropological Study No. 2, Department of Conservation, Louisiana Geological Survey.

1944   *Excavations in the Vicinity of Cali, Colombia,* Yale University Publications in Anthropology, No. 31, New Haven.

1949   *Surface Survey of the Viru Valley, Peru. 2. Cultural Dating of Prehistoric Sites in Viru Valley, Peru,* Vol. 43, Pt. 1, Anthropological Papers, American Museum of Natural History, New York.

1959   *Eskimo Prehistory in the Vicinity of Point Barrow, Alaska,* Vol. 47, Pt. 1, Anthropological Papers, American Museum of Natural History, New York.

1961   *Menard Site the Quapaw Village of Osotouy on the Arkansas River,* Vol. 48, Pt. 2, Anthropological Papers, American Museum of Natural History, New York.

1963   *Hopewell Culture Burial Mounds near Helena, Arkansas,* Anthropological Papers, Vol. 50, Pt. 1, American Museum of Natural History, New York.

1969 *A Comparison of Formative Cultures in the Americas: Diffusion or the Psychic Unity of Man,* Smithsonian Institution Contributions to Anthropology, Vol. 11, Washington, D.C.

FORD, J. A. AND J. B. GRIFFIN
1938 "Report of the Conference on Southeastern Pottery Typology," *Proceedings of the First Southeastern Archaeological Conference,* Ann Arbor, Mich.

FORD, J. A., PHILIP PHILLIPS, AND W. G. HAAG
1955 *The Jaketown Site, in West-Central Mississippi,* Vol. 45, Pt. 1, Anthropological Papers, American Museum of Natural History, New York.

FORD, J. A. AND C. H. WEBB
1956 *Poverty Point, A Late Archaic Site in Louisiana,* Vol. 46, Pt. 1, Anthropological Papers, American Museum of Natural History, New York.

FORD, J. A. AND G. R. WILLEY
1940 *Crooks Site, A Marksville Period Burial Mound in La-Salle Parrish, Louisiana,* Louisiana Department of Conservation, Anthropological Study No. 3, Louisiana Geological Survey, New Orleans, La.
1941 "An Interpretation of the Prehistory of the Eastern United States," *American Anthropologist,* Vol. 43, No. 3, pp. 325–363.

FRIED, M. H.
1960 "On the Evolution of Social Stratification and the State," *Culture in History Essays in Honor of Paul Radin,* S. Diamond, ed., pp. 713–731, Columbia University Press, New York.

FRIEDMAN, A. M., EDWARD OLSEN, AND J. B. BIRD
1972 "Moche Copper Analysis: Early New World Metal Technology," *American Antiquity,* Vol. 37, pp. 254–258.

GAMIO, MANUEL
1913 "Arqueologia de Atzcapotzalco, D.F., Mexico," *Proceedings, 18th International Congress of Americanists,* pp. 180–187, London, U.K.

GAYTON, A. H. AND A. L. KROEBER
1927 *The Uhle Pottery Collections from Nazca,* University of California Publications in American Archaeology and Ethnology, Vol. 24, No. 1, Berkeley, Calif.

GIFFORD, J. C.
1976 *Prehistoric Pottery Analysis and the Ceramics of Barton*

Ramie in the Belize Valley, Memoirs, Vol. 18, Peabody Museum, Harvard University, Cambridge, Mass.

GIVENS, D. R.

1986   *Alfred Vincent Kidder and the Development of Americanist Archaeology*, Unpublished dissertation, Washington University, St. Louis, Mo.

GLADWIN, WINIFRED AND H. S.

1929   *The Red-on-Buff Culture of the Gila Basin*, Medallion Papers, No. 3, Globe, Ariz.

GLADWIN, H. S. *et al.*

1937   *Excavations at Snaketown: Material Culture*, Medallion Papers, No. 25, Vol. 1, Globe, Ariz.

GRAHAM, J. A.

1972   *The Hieroglyphic Inscriptions and Monumental Art of Altar de Sacrificios*, Papers, Vol. 64, No. 2, Peabody Museum, Harvard University, Cambridge, Mass.

n.d.   *Excavations at Seibal, Department of Peten, Guatemala: Monumental Sculpture and Hieroglyphic Inscriptions*, Memoirs, Vol. 17, No. 10, Peabody Museum, Harvard University, Cambridge, Mass.

GREENGO, R. E.

1968   "Alfred Vincent Kidder, 1885–1963," *American Anthropologist*, Vol. 70, No. 2, pp. 52–525.

GRIFFIN, J. B.

1946   "Cultural Change and Continuity in Eastern United States Archaeology," *Man in Northeastern North America*, F. Johnson, ed., pp. 37–95, Papers of the R. S. Peabody Foundation for Archaeology, Vol. 33, Andover, Mass.

GOGGIN, J. M.

1947   "A Preliminary Definition of Archaeological Areas and Periods in Florida," *American Antiquity*, Vol. 13, pp. 114–127.

1949   "Cultural Traditions in Florida Prehistory," *The Florida Indian and His Neighbors*, J. W. Griffin, ed., pp. 13–44, Rollins College, Winter Park, Fla.

HAY, C. L. AND OTHERS, EDS.

1940   *The Maya and Their Neighbors*, D. Appleton-Century Co., New York.

HINSLEY, C. M., JR.

1984   "Wanted: One Good Man to Discover Central American History," *Harvard Magazine*, November-December 1984, pp. 64A–H, Harvard University, Cambridge, Mass.

HODGE, F. W., ED.
   1907–10   *Handbook of American Indians North of Mexico,*
             Parts 1 and 2, Bulletin 30, Bureau of American Ethnology,
             Smithsonian Institution, Washington, D.C.

HOLMES, W. H.
   1888   *Ancient Art of the Province of Chiriqui, Colombia,* 6th
          Annual Report of the Bureau of American Ethnology,
          Smithsonian Institution, Washington, D.C.

HORKHEIMER, HANS
   1944   *Vistas Arqueologicas del Noroeste del Peru,* Libreria e
          Imprenta Moreno, Trujillo,

HOWARD, E. B.
   1935   "Occurrence of Flints and Extinct Animals in Pluvial
          Deposits near Clovis, New Mexico, Pt. 1. Introduction,"
          Prooceedings, Philadelphia Academy of Sciences, Vol.
          87, pp. 299–303.

HYMES, DELL
   1961   "Alfred Louis Kroeber," *Language,* Vol. 37, No. 1, pp. 1–
          28.

JONES, M. R.
   1952   "Map of the Ruins of Mayapan, Yucatan, Mexico," *Current Reports,* No. 1, Carnegie Institution of Washington,
          Cambridge, Mass.

JUDD, N. M.
   1950   "Pioneering in Southwestern Archaeology," *For the
          Dean, Essays in Anthropology in Honor of Byron Cummings,* E. K. Reed and D. S. King, eds., pp. 11–27, Hohokam Museums Association and the Southwestern Monuments Association, Tucson, Ariz. and Santa Fe, N. Mex.
   1954a "Byron Cummings, 1860–1954," *American Anthropologist,* Vol. 56, pp. 871–872.
   1954b "Byron Cummings—1860–1954," *American Antiquity,*
          Vol. 20, pp. 154–157.

KELLEY, D. H.
   1976   *Deciphering the Maya Script,* University of Texas Press,
          Austin, Tex.

KELLEY, J. C.
   1971   "Archaeology of the Northern Frontier: Zacatecas and
          Durango," *Handbook of Middle American Indians,* R.
          Wauchope, ed., Vol. 11, pp. 768–801, University of Texas
          Press, Austin, Tex.

KELLY, A. R.
1938 *A Preliminary Report on Archaeological Explorations at Macon, Georgia,* Anthropological Papers, No. 1, Bulletin 119, Bureau of American Ethnology, Smithsonian Institution, Washington, D.C.
1939 "The Macon Trading Post—An Historical Foundling," *American Antiquity,* Vol. 4, pp. 328–333.
1954 "Etowah, an Ancient Cult Center in Georgia," *Archaeology,* Vol. 7, No. 1, pp. 22–27.
1970 "Excavations at the Bell Field Mound, Carter's Dam: 1970 Season," *Southeastern Archaeological Conference,* Bulletin 13, pp. 118–120, Morgantown, W. Va.

KELLEY, A. R. AND CLEMENS DE BAILLOU
1960 "Excavation of the Presumptive Site of Estatoe," *Southern Indian Studies,* Vol. 12, pp. 3–30.

KELLY, A. R. AND L. H. LARSON, JR.
1956 "Explorations at Etowah Indian Mounds near Cartersville, Georgia Seasons 1954, 1955, 1956," *Archaeology,* Vol. 10, No. 1, pp. 1–10.

KELLY, A. R. AND R. S. NEITZEL
1961 *The Chauga Site in Oconee County, South Carolina,* University of Georgia, Laboratory of Archaeology Series, Report 3, Athens, Ga.

KIDDER, A. V.
1914 *Southwestern Ceramics: Their Value in Reconstructing the History of the Ancient Cliff Dwelling and Pueblo Tribes,* Unpublished doctoral dissertation, Harvard University, Cambridge, Mass.
1924 *An Introduction to the Study of Southwestern Archaeology, With a Preliminary Account of Excavations at Pecos,* Papers, Southwestern Expedition, Phillips Academy, No. 1, New Haven, Conn.
1931 *The Pottery of Pecos,* Vol. I, Papers, Southwestern Expedition, Phillips Academy, Yale University Press, New Haven, Conn.
1936 "Speculations on New World Prehistory," in *Essays in Anthropology Presented to A. L. Kroeber,* pp. 143–152, University of California Press, Berkeley, Calif.
1945 "George Clapp Vaillant: 1901–1945," *American Antiquity,* Vol. 47, pp. 589–602.
1958 *Pecos, New Mexico: Archaeological Notes,* Papers of the R. S. Peabody Foundation for Archaeology, No. 5, Andover, Mass.

BIBLIOGRAPHY

1960   "Reminiscences in Southwest Archaeology: I," *Kiva*, Vol. 25, No. 4, pp. 1–32, Arizona Archaeological and Historical Society, Tucson, Ariz.

1961a   "Archaeological Investigations at Kaminal juyu, Guatemala," *Proceedings of the American Philosophical Society*, Vol. 105, pp. 559–570, Philadelphia, Pa.

1961b   "A Possibly Unique Type of Figurine from Guatemala," in *Essays in Pre-Columbian Art and Archaeology*, S. K. Lothrop and others, eds., 176–181, Harvard University Press, Cambridge, Mass.

KIDDER, A. V. AND S. Y. GUERNSEY

1919   *Archaeological Exploration in Northeastern Arizona*, Bureau of American Ethnology, Bulletin 65, Smithsonian Institution, Washington, D.C.

KIDDER, A. V., J. D. JENNINGS, AND E. M. SHOOK

1946   *Excavations at Kaminaljuyu, Guatemala*, Carnegie Institution of Washington, Publication 561, Washington, D.C.

KIDDER, ALFRED II

1954   "Wendell Clark Bennett, 1905–1953," *American Anthropologist*, Vol. 56, No. 2, pp. 269–273.

KIRCHOFF, PAUL

1943   "Mesoamerica," *Acta Americana*, Vol. 1, pp. 92–107, Mexico City, D.F.

KLUCKHOHN, CLYDE

1940   "The Conceptual Structure in Middle American Studies," *The Maya and Their Neighbors*, C. L. Hay and others, eds., pp. 41–51, Appleton-Century, New York.

1956   "Alfred Marston Tozzer (1877–1954)," *Year Book of the American Philosophical Society*, 1956, pp. 128–131, Philadelphia, Pa.

KROEBER, A. L.

1901   "Decorative Symbolism of the Arapaho," *American Anthropologist*, Vol. 3, No. 2, pp. 308–336.

1904   "Dr. Uhle's Researches in Peru," *American Anthropologist*, Vol. 6, No. 4, pp,. 576–577.

1906   "Dr. Max Uhle," *American Anthropologist*, Vol. 8, No. 1, p. 202.

1909   "The Archaeology of California," *Putnam Anniversary Volume*, pp. 1–42, Philadelphia, Pa.

1916   *Zuni Potsherds*, Anthropological Papers of the American Museum of Natural History, Vol. 18, Pt. 1, pp. 7–37, New York.

BIBLIOGRAPHY

1917 "The Superorganic," *American Anthropologist*, Vol. 19, No. 2, pp. 163–213.

1919 "On the Principle of Order in Civilization as Exemplified by Changes of Fashion," *American Anthropologist*, Vol. 21, No. 3, pp. 235–263.

1923 *Anthropology*, Harcourt, Brace, New York.

1925a *The Uhle Pottery Collections from Supe*, University of California Publications in American Archaeology and Ethnology, Vol. 21, No. 6, Berkeley, Calif.

1925b *Handbook of the Indians of California*, Bulletin 78, Bureau of American Ethnology, Smithsonian Institution, Washington, D.C.

1925c *The Uhle Pottery Collections from Moche*, University of California Publications in American Archaeology and Ethnology, Vol. 21, No. 5, Berkeley, Calif.

1925d *Archaic Culture Horizons in the Valley of Mexico*, University of California Publications in American Archaeology and Ethnology, Vol. 17, No. 7, Berkeley, Calif.

1926a *The Uhle Pottery Collections from Chancay*, University of California Publications in American Archaeology and Ethnology, Vol. 21, No. 7, Berkeley, Calif.

1926b *Archaeological Explorations in Peru, Part I, Ancient Pottery from Trujillo*, Field Museum of Natural History, Anthropological Memoirs, Vol. 2, No. 1, Chicago, Ill.

1926c "Culture Stratifications in Peru," *American Anthropologist*, Vol. 28, No. 2, pp. 331–351.

1927 "Coast and Highland in Prehistoric Peru," *American Anthropologist*, Vol. 29, pp. 625–653.

1930 *Archaeological Explorations in Peru. Part II. The Northern Coast*, Field Museum of Natural History, Anthropology Memoirs, Vol. 2, No. 2, Chicago, Ill.

1937 *Archaeological Explorations in Peru. Part IV. Canete Valley*, Field Museum of Natural History, Anthropology Memoirs, Vol. 2, No. 4, Chicago, Ill.

1939 *Cultural and Natural Areas of Native North America*, University of California Publications in American Archaeology and Ethnology, Vol. 36, Berkeley, Calif.

1940 "Conclusions," *The Maya and Their Neighbors*, C. L. Hay and others, eds., pp. 406–490, Appleton-Century, New York.

1942a "On 'An Interpretation of the Prehistory of the Eastern United States'," *American Antiquity*, Vol. 7, No. 3, p. 326.

BIBLIOGRAPHY

1942b "Los Metodos de la Arqueologia Peruana," *Letras*, No. 22, pp. 205–226, Facultad de Letras y Pedagogia, Universidad Nacional Mayor de San Marcos, Lima, Peru.

1944a *Configurations of Culture Growth*, The University of California Press, Berkeley and Los Angeles, Calif.

1944b *Peruvian Archaeology in 1942*, Viking Fund Publications in Anthropology, No. 4, New York.

1946 *The Ancient Oikoumene as an Historic Culture Aggregate*, Huxley Memorial Lecture for 1945, The Royal Anthropological Institute of Great Britain and Ireland, London, U.K.

1948a *Anthropology*, revised edition, Harcourt, Brace, New York.

1948b "Summary and Interpretations," *A Reappraisal of Peruvian Archaeology*, W. C. Bennett, ed., pp. 113–121, Society for American Archaeology, Memoir 4.

1950 "Have Civilizations a Life History?" *A.A.A.S. Centennial, Collected Papers*, pp. 9–13, American Association for the Advancement of Science, Washington, D.C.

1953 *Paracas Cavernas and Chavin*, University of California Publications in American Archaeology and Ethnology, Vol. 40, No. 8, pp. 313–348, Berkeley, Calif.

1954 *Proto-Lima; A Middle Period Culture of Peru*, with Appendix on Cloths by D. T. Wallace, Fieldiana: Anthropology, Vol. 44, No. 1, Field Museum of Natural History, Chicago, Ill.

1956 *Toward Definition of the Nazca Style*, University of California Publications in American Archaeology and Ethnology, Vol. 43, No. 4, Berkely and Los Angeles, Calif.

1960 "Evolution, History, and Culture. Evolution After Darwin," Vol. II, *The Evolution of Man; Man, Culture, and Society*, S. Tax, ed., pp. 1–16, University of Chicago Press, Ill.

KROEBER, A. L. AND C. K. M. KLUCKHOHN

1952 *Culture: A Critical Review of Concepts and Definitions*, Papers of the Peabody Museum, Harvard University, Vol. 47, No. 1, Cambridge, Mass.

KROEBER, A. L. AND W. D. STRONG

1924a *The Uhle Collections from Chincha*, University of California Publications in American Archaeology and Ethnology, Vol. 21, No. 1, Berkeley, Calif.

1924b *The Uhle Pottery Collections from Ica*, University of

California Publications in American Archaeology and Ethnology, Vol. 21, No. 3, Berkeley, Calif.

KROEBER, A. L. AND OTHERS, EDS.

1953   *Anthropology Today,* Inventory Papers, International Symposium on Anthropology, Wenner-Gren Foundation for Anthropological Research, University of Chicago Press, Ill.

KROEBER, THEODORA

1961   *Ishi in Two Worlds,* University of California Press, Berkeley and Los Angeles, Calif.

1970   *Alfred Kroeber, A Personal Configuration,* University of California Press, Berkeley, Calif.

LACERDA, AUGUSTO

1882   "Documents pour servir a l'histoire de l'homme fossils du Bresil," *Memoires de la Societe d'Anthropologie de Paris,* 2nd Series, Vol. 2, No. 4.

LADD, JOHN

1957   "A Stratigraphic Trench at Sitio Conte, Panama," *American Antiquity,* Vol. 22, pp. 265–271.

1964   *Archaeological Investigations in the Parita and Santa Maria Zones of Panama,* Bureau of American Ethnology, Bulletin 193, Smithsonian Institution, Washington, D.C.

LARCO HOYLE, RAFAEL

1938–40 *Los Mochicas,* 2 vols., Casa Editora "La Cronica y Variedades", Lima, Peru.

1941   *Los Cupisniques,* Casa Editora "La Cronica y Variedades", Lima.

1946   "A Culture Sequence for the North Coast of Peru," *Handbook of South American Indians,* J. H. Steward, ed., Vol. 2, pp. 149–175, Bulletin 143, Bureau of American Ethnology, Smithsonian Institution, Washington, D.C.

1948   *Cronologia Arqueologica del Norte del Peru,* Hacienda Chiclin, Trujillo, Peru.

LATHRAP, D. W.

1970   *The Upper Amazon,* Ancient Peoples and Places Series, G. Daniel, ed., Praeger, New York.

1971   "The Tropical Forest and the Cultural Context of Chavin," *Dumbarton Oaks Conference on Chavin,* E. P. Benson, ed., pp. 73–100, Washington, D.C.

1973   "Gifts of the Cayman: Some Thoughts on the Subsistence Basis of Chavin," *Variation in Anthropology,* D. W. Lathrap and Jody Douglas, eds., pp. 91–107, Illinois Archaeological Survey, Urbana, Ill.

LATCHAM, R. E.
  1928 *La Prehistoria Chilena*, La Comision Oficial Organiza-
        dora de la Concurrencia a la Exposicion Ibero-Americana
        de Sevilla, Santiago, Chile.
  1936a "Indian Ruins in North Chile," *American Anthropolo-
        gist*, Vol. 38, No. 1, pp. 52–58.
  1936b "Atacameno Archaeology," *American Anthropologist*,
        Vol. 38, No. 4, pp. 609–619.
LINNE, SIGVALD
  1929 *Darien in the Past*, Goteborg Kungl. Vetenskaps-och, Vit-
        terhets-Samahalles Handlingar, Femte Foljden, Ser. A,
        Bid. 1, No. 3, Goteborg, Sweden.
LOTHROP, S. K.
  1919 "The Discovery of Gold in the Graves of Chiriqui, Pan-
        ama," *Indian Notes and Monographs*, Vol. 6, pp. 23–28,
        Museum of the American Indian, Heye Foundation, New
        York.
  1921 "The Stone Statues of Nicaragua," *American Anthropol-
        ogist*, Vol. 13, pp. 311–319.
  1924 *Tulum, an Archaeological Study of the East Coast of
        Yucatan*, Carnegie Institution of Washington, Pub. No.
        335, Washington, D.C.
  1926a *Pottery of Costa Rica and Nicaragua*, Contributions,
        Museum of the American Indian, Heye Foundation, Vol.
        8 (2 vols.), New York.
  1926b "Stone Sculptures from the Finca Arevalo, Guatemala,"
        Indian Notes, Vol. 3, No. 3, pp. 147–171, Museum of the
        American Indian, Heye Foundation, New York.
  1927 "Pottery Types and Their Sequence in El Salvador," *In-
        dian Notes and Monographs*, Vol. 1, No. 4, Museum of
        the American Indian, Heye Foundation, New York.
  1932a *Indians of the Parana Delta, Argentina*, Annals of the
        New York Academy of Sciences, Vol. 33, pp. 77–232.
  1932b "Aboriginal Navigation off the West Coast of South
        America," *Journal of the Royal Anthropological Institute
        of Great Britain and Ireland*, Vol. 62, pp. 229–256.
  1933 *Atitlan, An Archaeological Study of Ancient Remains on
        the Borders of Lake Atitlan, Guatemala*, Carnegie In-
        stitution of Washington, Publication No. 444, Washing-
        ton, D.C.
  1937–42 *Cocle, an Archaeological Study of Central Panama*,
        Memoirs, Vols. 6 and 7, Peabody Museum, Harvard Uni-
        versity, Cambridge, Mass.

1952   *Metals from the Cenote of Sacrifice, Chichen Itza, Yucatan*, Memoirs, Vol. 10, No. 2, Peabody Museum, Harvard University, Cambridge, Mass.

1955   "Alfred Marston Tozzer, 1977–1954," *American Anthropologist*, Vol. 57, No. 3, pp. 614–618.

1957a   George Gustav Heye—1874–1956, *American Antiquity*, Vol. 22, pp. 66–67.

1957b   *Pre-Columbian Art. Robert Woods Bliss Collection.* With W. F. Foshag and Joy Mahler, Phaidon Publishers, New York and London.

1959   "A Reappraisal of Isthmian Archaeology," *Mitteilungen aus dem Museum fur Volkerkunde und Vorgeschicte*, Vol. 25, pp. 87–91, Hamburg, W. Ger.

1961   "Early Migrations to Central and South America: An Anthropological Problem in the Light of Other Sciences," (Huxley Memorial Lecture, 1960), *Journal of the Royal Anthropological Institute of Great Britain and Ireland*, Vol. 91, Pt. 1, pp. 97–123.

1963   *Archaeology of the Diquis Delta, Costa Rica*, Papers, Vol. 51, Peabody Museum, Harvard University, Cambridge, Mass.

1964   *Treasures of Ancient America; the Arts of Pre-Columbian Civilizations from Mexico to Peru*, Skira Publishing, Geneva, Switzerland.

1966   "Archaeology of Lower Central America," in *Handbook of Middle American Indians*, Vol. 4, Robert Wauchope, ed., pp. 180–208, University of Texas Press. Austin, Tex.

LOTHROP, S. K. AND JOY MAHLER

1957   *A Chancay-style Grave at Zapallan, Peru*, Papers, Vol. 50, No. 1, Peabody Museum, Harvard University, Cambridge, Mass.

LOTHROP, S. K. AND OTHERS, EDS.

1961   *Essays in Pre-Columbian Art and Archaeology*, Harvard University Press, Cambridge, Mass.

LOWIE, R. H., ED.

1936   *Essays in Anthropology Presented to A. L. Kroeber in Celebration of His Sixtieth Birthday*, University of California Press, Berkeley, Calif.

MacCURDY, G. G.

1911   *A Study of Chiriquian Antiquities*, Memoir No. 3, Connecticut Academy of Arts and Sciences, New Haven, Conn.

MALER, TEOBERT
1901 *Researches in the Central Portion of the Usumatsintla Valley*, Memoirs, Vol. 2, No. 1, Peabody Museum, Harvard University, Cambridge, Mass.
1908 *Exploration of the Upper Usumacintla and Adjacent Regions*, Memoirs, Vol. 4, No. 1, Peabody Museum, Harvard University, Cambridge, Mass.

MANNERS, R. A.
1973 "Julian Haynes Steward, 1902–1972," *American Anthropologist*, Vol. 75, No. 3, pp. 886–903.
1964, ed. *Process and Pattern in Culture, Essays in Honor of Julian H. Steward*, Aldine Publishing Company, Chicago, Ill.

MASON, J. A.
1957 *The Ancient Civilizations of Peru*, Pelican Books, Baltimore, Md.

MATOS M., RAMIRO
1962 "William Duncan Strong, 1899–1963," *Revista Museo Nacional del Peru*, Vol. 31, pp. 335–340, Lima, Peru.

MAUDSLAY, A. P.
1889–1902 *Archaeology*, Biologia Central Americana, 4 Vols., London, U.K.

MEANS, P. A.
1931 *Ancient Civilizations of the Andes*, Scribner's, New York.

MELGAR, JOSE M.
1869 "Antiguedades Mexicanas, Notable Escultura Antigua," *Boletin de la Sociedad Mexicana de Geografia y Estadistica*, Vol. 1, pp. 292–297, Mexico, D.F.
1871 "Estudio Sobre la Antiguedad y el Origen de la Cabeza Colosal de Tipo Etiopico que Existe en Hueyapan del Canton de los Tuxtlas," *Boletin de la Sociedad Mexicana de Geografia y Estadistica*, Vol. 3, pp. 104–109, Mexico, D.F.

MERWIN, R. E. AND G. C. VAILLANT
1932 *The Ruins of Holmul, Guatemala*, Memoirs, Vol. 3, No. 2, Peabody Museum, Harvard University, Cambridge, Mass.

METRAUX, ALFRED
1946 "Ethnography of the Chaco," *Handbook of South American Indians*, J. H. Steward, ed., Vol. 1, pp. 197–370, Bul-

letin 143, Bureau of American Ethnology, Smithsonian Institution, Washington, D.C.

MILLS, L., ED.

1979   *The Puuc: New Perspectives*, Central College Press, Pella, Iowa.

MOOREHEAD, W. K.

1932   "Exploration of the Etowah Site in Georgia," *Etowah Papers*, Yale University Press, New Haven, for Phillips Academy, Andover.

MORLEY, S. G.

1920   *the Inscriptions at Copan*, Publication No. 219, Carnegie Institution of Washington, Washington, D.C.

1937–1938   *The Inscriptions of Peten*, 5 vols., Publication No. 437, Carnegie Institution of Washington, Washington, D.C.

MORRIS, E. H., JEAN CHARLOT, AND A. A. MORRIS

1931   *The Temple of the Warriors at Chichen Itza, Yucatan*, Publication No. 406, Carnegie Institution of Washington, Washington, D.C.

MURPHY, R. F.

1981   "Julian Steward," *Totems and Teachers*, Sydel Silverman, ed., pp. 171–208, Columbia University Press, New York.

NELSON, N. C.

1909   *Shellmounds of the San Francisco Bay Region*, University of California Publications in American Archaeology and Ethnology, Vol. 7, No. 4, Berkeley, Calif.

1910   *the Ellis Landing Shellmound*, University of California Publications in American Archaeology and Ethnology, Vol. 7, No. 5, Berkeley, Calif.

1914   "Pueblo Ruins of the Galisteo Basin," *Anthropological Papers of the American Museum of Natural History*, Vol. 15, Pt. 1, New York.

1916   "Chronology of the Tano Ruins, New Mexico," *American Anthropologist*, Vol. 18, No. 2, pp. 159–180.

NORDENSKIOLD, ERLAND VON

1913   "Urnengraber und Mounds im Bolivianischen Flachlande," *Baessler Archiv*, Vol. 3, pp. 205–255, Berlin, W. Ger.

NORDENSKIOLD, GUSTAV VON

1893   *The Cliff Dwellers of the Mesa Verde, Southwestern Colorado; Their Pottery and Implement*, Translated by D. L. Morgan, Norstedt, Stockholm.

NUNEZ, LAUTARO
  1978   "Northern Chile," in *Chronologies in New World Archaeology*, R. E. Taylor and C. W. Meighan, eds., pp. 483–512, Academic Press, New York.

NUTTALL, ZELIA
  1930   "The Round Temples of Mexico and Yucatan," *Art and Archaeology*, Vol. 30, No. 6, New York.

OUTES, F. F.
  1905   *La Edad de La Piedra en Patagonia*, Anales, Museo Nacional de Buenos Aires, Argentina, Vol. 12, pp. 203–575.

PARSONS, J. R.
  1968   "The Archaeological Significance of Mahamaes Cultivation on the Coast of Peru," *American Antiquity*, Vol. 33, pp. 80–83.

PATTERSON, T. C.
  1985   "The Huaca La Florida, Rimac Valley, Peru," *Early Ceremonial Architecture in the Andes*, C. B. Donnan, ed., pp. 59–70, Dumbarton Oaks, Washington, D.C.

PHILLIPS, PHILIP
  1940   "Middle American Influences on the Archaeology of the Southeastern United States," *The Maya and Their Neighbors*, C. L. Hay and others, eds., pp. 349–367, Appleton-Century, New York.

  1955   "Alfred Marsten Tozzer—1877–1954," *American Antiquity*, Vol. 21, No. 1, pp. 72–80.

PHILLIPS, PHILIP, J. A. FORD, AND J. B. GRIFFIN
  1951   *Archaeological Survey in the Lower Mississippi Alluvial Valley, 1940–1947*, Harvard University, Peabody Museum, Papers, Vol. 25, Cambridge, Mass.

PHILLIPS, PHILIP AND G. R. WILLEY
  1953   "Method and Theory in American Archaeology: An Operational Basis for Culture-Historical Integration," *American Anthropologist*, Vol. 55, pp. 615–633.

POHL, M. E.
  n.d.   *Excavations at Seibal, Department of Peten, Guatemala: Faunal Remains from Seibal and Other Peten Sites: An Ethnozoological Analysis*, Memoirs, No. 3, Vol. 17, Peabody Museum, Harvard University, Cambridge, Mass.

POLLOCK, H. E. D.
  1929a   "Report on the Casa Redonda," *Year Book, 28*, pp. 310–312, Carnegie Institution of Washington, Washington, D.C.

1929b "Report on the Coba Expedition," *Year Book, 28* pp. 328–329, Carnegie Institution of Washington, Washington, D.C.

1931 "Architectural Problems in the Maya Field," *Year Book 30,* pp. 117–119, Carnegie Institution of Washington, Washington, D.C.

1936a "The Architectural Survey," *Year Book 35,* pp. 122–125, Carnegie Institution of Washington, Washington, D.C.

1936b *Round Structures of Aboriginal Middle America,* Publication 471, Carnegie Institution of Washington, Washington, D.C.

1936c "The Casa Redonda at Chichen Itza," *Contributions,* Vol. 17, pp. 129–154, Carnegie Institution of Washington, Washington, D.C.

1937 "Architectural Details of Temples E-X and A-XVIII (Uaxactun)," in Ricketson and Ricketson, 1937, Publication 477, Carnegie Institution of Washington, Washington, D.C.

1940a "The Architectural Survey of Yucatan," *Year Book 39,* Carnegie Institution of Washington, Washington, D.C.

1940b "Sources and Methods in the Study of Maya Architecture," in *The Maya and Their Neighbors,* C. L. Hay and others, eds., pp. 179–201, Appleton-Century, New York.

1946 "Architectural Survey of Yucatan," *Year Book 45,* pp. 206–207, Carnegie Institution of Washington, Washington, D.C.

1948 "Architectural Survey of Yucatan," *Year Book 47,* pp. 218–219, Carnegie Institution of Washington, Washington, D.C.

1954a "Excavations in Mayapan," *Year Book 53,* pp. 277–279, Carnegie Institution of Washington, Washington, D.C.

1954b "The Northern Terminus of the Principal Sacbe at Mayapan," *Current Reports,* Vol. 2, No. 15, Carnegie Institution of Washington, Washington, D.C.

1955 "Excavations in Mayapan," *Year Book 54,* pp. 278–280, Carnegie Institution of Washington, Washington, D.C.

1956 "The Southern Terminus of the Principal Sacbe at Mayapan. Group Z.50," *Current Reports,* Vol. 2, No. 37, Carnegie Institution of Washington, Washington, D.C.

1958 "Annual Report of the Director of the Department of Archaeology, 1957–1958," *Yearbook 57,* pp. 435–448, Carnegie Institution of Washington, Washington, D.C.

1965 "Architecture of the Maya Lowlands," *Handbook of Middle American Indians*, R. Wauchope, ed., Vol. 2, pp. 378–440, University of Texas Press, Austin, Tex.

1970 "Architectural Notes on Some Chenes Ruins," *Monographs and Papers in Maya Archaeology*, W. R. Bullard, Jr., ed., Papers, Vol. 61, pp. 1–87, Peabody Museum, Harvard University, Cambridge, Mass.

1980 *The Puuc: An Architectural Survey of the Hill Country of Yucatan and North Campeche*, Memoirs, Vol. 19, Harvard University, Cambridge, Mass.

POLLOCK, H. E. D., R. L. ROYS, TATIANA PROSKOURIAKOFF, AND A. L. SMITH

1962 *Mayapan, Yucatan, Mexico*, Publication 619, Carnegie Institution of Washington, Washington, D.C.

PONCE SANGINES, CARLOS

1972 *Tiwanaku: Espacio, Tiempos, y Cultura*, Publicacion No. 30, Academia Nacional de Ciencias de Bolivia, La Paz, Bolivia

POPENOE, D. H.

1934 "Some Excavations at Playa de los Muertos, Ulua River, Honduras," *Maya Research*, Vol. 1, No. 2, pp. 61–86, New York.

PROSKOURIAKOFF, TATIANA

1954 "Mapping and Excavations at Mayapan," *Year Book, 53*, pp. 271–273, Carnegie Institution of Washington, Washington, D.C.

PUGH, MARION STIRLING

1981 "An Intimate View of Archaeological Exploration," *The Olmec and Their Neighbors, Essays in Memory of Matthew W. Stirling*, M. D. Coe, D. W. Grove, and E. P. Benson, eds., pp. 1–13, Dumbarton Oaks, Washington, D.C.

REED, E. K. AND D. S. KING, EDS.

1950 *For the Dean, Essays in Anthropology in Honor of Byron Cummings*, Hohokam Museums Association and the Southwestern Monuments Association, Tucson, Ariz. and Santa Fe, N. Mex.

REISS, WILHELM AND STUBEL, ALPHONS

1880–1887 *The Necropolis of Ancon in Peru*, 3 Vols., Berlin, W. Ger.

RICE, P. M.

1987 *Macanche Island, El Peten, Guatemala: Excavations,*

Pottery, and Artifacts, University of Florida Press, Gainesville, Fla.

RICKETSON, O. G., JR.

1929   *Excavations at Baking Pot, British Honduras,* Contributions to American Archaeology, Vol. 1, No. 1, Carnegie Institution of Washington, Publication No. 403, Washington, D.C.

RICKETSON, O. G., JR. AND E. B. RICKETSON

1937   *Uaxactun, Guatemala, Group E, 1926–1931. Part I: The Excavations; Part II: The Artifacts,* Carnegie Institution of Washington, Publication No. 477, Washington, D.C.

ROBERTS, F. H. H., JR.

1932   *The Village of the Great Kivas on the Zuni Reservation, New Mexico,* Bulletin 111, Bureau of American Ethnology, Smithsonian Institution, Washington, D.C.

1935a   "A Survey of Southwestern Archaeology," *American Anthropologist,* Vol. 37, No. 1, pp. 1–33.

1935b   *A Folsom Complex,* Smithsonian Miscellaneous Collections, Vol. 94, No. 4, Smithsonian Institution, Washington, D.C.

1937   "Archaeology in the Southwest," *American Antiquity,* Vol. 3, No. 1, pp. 3–33.

ROUSE, IRVING

1954a   "Wendell C. Bennett—1905–1953," *American Antiquity,* Vol. 19, No. 3, pp. 265–270.

1954b   "On the Use of the Concept of Area Co-Tradition," *American Antiquity,* Vol. 19, No. 3, pp. 221–225.

ROWE, A. P., E. P. BENSON, AND A. L. SCHAFFER, EDS.

1979   *The Junius B. Bird Pre-Columbian Textile Conference,* The Textile Museum and Dumbarton Oaks, Washington, D.C.

ROWE, J. H.

1960   "Cultural Unity and Diversification in Peruvian Archaeology," *Men and Cultures,* A. F. Wallace, ed., Selected Papers of the Fifth International Congress of Anthropological and Ethnological Sciences, pp. 627–631, University of Pennsylvania Press, Philadelphia, Pa.

1962   "Alfred Louis Kroeber, 1876–1960," *American Antiquity,* Vol. 27, No. 3, pp. 395–415.

ROYS, R. L.

1933   *The Book of Chilam Balam of Chumayel,* Publication No. 438, Carnegie Institution of Washington, Washington, D.C.

Ruppert, Karl
  1935 *The Caracol at Chichen Itza, Yucatan, Mexico,* Publica-
        tion No. 454, Carnegies Institution of Washington, Wash-
        ington, D.C.
Sabloff, J. A.
  1975 *Excavations at Seibal, Department of Peten, Guatemala:
        Ceramics,* Memoirs, Vol. 13, No. 2, Peabody Museum,
        Harvard University, Cambridge, Mass.
Sabloff, J. A. and E. W. Andrews V, eds.
  1985 *Late Lowland Maya Civilization, Classic to Postclassic,*
        University of New Mexico Press, Albuquerque, N. Mex.
Sanders, W. T.
  1981 "Ecological Adaptation in the Basin of Mexico, 23,000
        B.C. to the Present," *Supplement to the Handbook of
        Middle American Indians, Vol. 1, Archaeology,* J. A. Sab-
        loff, ed., pp. 147–197, University of Texas Press, Austin,
        Tex.
Saul, F. P.,
  1972 *The Human Skeletal Remains of Altar de Sacrificios: An
        Osteobiographic Analysis,* Papers, Vol. 63, No. 2, Pea-
        body Museum, Harvard University, Cambridge, Mass.
Saville, M. H.
  1929 "Votive Axes from Ancient Mexico," Parts 1 and 2, *Indian
        Notes,* Vol. 6, pp. 266–299, 335–342, Museum of the
        American, Indian, Heye Foundation, New York.
Schmidt, E. F.
  1928 *Time Relations of Prehistoric Pottery Types in Southern
        Arizona,* Anthropological Papers of the American Mu-
        seum of Natural History, Vol. 30, Pt. 5, New York.
Scholes, F. V. and R. L. Roys
  1938 *Fray Diego de Landa and the Problem of Idolatry in
        Yucatan,* Publication No. 501, Carnegie Institution of
        Washington, Washington, D.C.
Schufeldt, P. W.
  1950 "Reminiscences of a Chiclero," *Morleyana,* Boaz Long,
        ed., pp. 224–229, Museum of New Mexico and School of
        American Research, Santa Few, N. Mex.
Service, E. R.
  1962 *Primitive Social Organization,* Random House, New
        York.
Shetrone, H. C.
  1930 *The Mound-Builders,* Appleton-Century, New York.

BIBLIOGRAPHY

SHIMKIN, D. B.
1964 "Julian H. Steward: A Contributor to Fact and Theory in Cultural Anthropology," *Process and Pattern in Culture,* R. A. Manners, ed. pp. 1–17, Aldine Publishing Company, Chicago, Ill.

SHOOK, E. M.
1952 "The Great Wall and Other Features of Mayapan," *Year Book 51,* pp. 247–251, Carnegie Institution of Washington, Washington, D.C.

SHOOK, E. M. AND A. V. KIDDER
1952 *Mound E-111-3, Kaminaljuyu, Guatemala,* Carnegie Institution of Washington, Publication 596, Contribution 53, Washington, D.C.

SMITH, A. L.
1937 *Structure A-XVIII, Uaxactun,* Contribution 20, Publication 483, Carnegie Institution of Washington, Washington, D.C.

1950 *Uaxactun, Guatemala: Excavations of 1931–37,* Publication No. 588, Carnegie Institution of Washington, Washington, D.C.

1955 *Archaeological Reconnaissance in Central Guatemala,* Publication 608, Carnegie Institution of Washington, Washington, D.C.

1961 "Types of Ball Courts in the Highlands of Guatemala," *Essays in Precolumbian Art and Archaeology,* S. K. Lothrop and others, eds., pp. 100–125, Harvard University Press, Cambridge, Mass.

1968 "Reconstruction at the Maya Ruins of Seibal," *Monumentum,* Vol. 2, pp. 82–96, International Council of Monuments and Sites, Paris and Louvain.

1972 *Excavations at Altar de Sacrificios: Architecture, Settlement, Burials, and Caches,* Papers, Vol. 62, No. 2, Peabody Museum, Harvard University, Cambridge, Mass.

1973 *Uaxactun: A Pioneering Excavation in Guatemala,* Addison-Wesley Module in Anthropology, No. 10, Addison-Wesley Publishing Company, Reading, Mass.

1977 "Patolli, at the Ruins of Seibal, Peten, Guatemala," *Social Process in Maya Prehistory,* N. Hammond, ed., pp. 349–363, Academic Press, London.

1982 *Excavations at Seibal, Department of Peten, Guatemala: Major Architecture and Caches,* Memoirs, Vol. 15, No. 1, Peabody Museum, Harvard University, Cambridge, Mass.

SMITH, A. L. AND A. V. KIDDER
1943 *Explorations in the Motagua Valley, Guatemala*, Publication 546, Carnegie Institution of Washington, Washington, D.C.
1951 *Excavations at Nebaj*, Publication 594, Carnegie Institution of Washington, Washington, D.C.

SMITH, A. L. AND KARL RUPPERT
1952 "Mayapan, Yucatan," *Year Book 51*, pp. 243–244, Carnegie Institution of Washington, Washington, D.C.
1956 "Excavations in House Mounds at Mayapan: IV," *Current Reports*, No. 36, Carnegie Institution of Washington, Cambridge, Mass.

SMITH, A. L., LINTON SATTERTHWAITE, G. R. WILLEY, AND W. R. BULLARD, JR.
1961 "Leocadio E. Hopun, 1894–1960," *American Antiquity*, Vol. 27, No. 1, p. 101.

SMITH, A. L. AND G. R. WILLEY
1962 "Preliminary Report on Excavations at Altar de Sacrificios, Guatemala, 1959–60," *Proceedings, 34th International Congress of Americanists*, pp. 318–325, Vienna, Austria.
1966 "The Harvard University Explorations at Seibal, Department of Peten, Guatemala: The 1964 Season," *Actas y Memorias, 36th International Congress of Americanists*, Vol. 1, pp. 385–388, Sevilla, Spain.
1969 "Seibal, Guatemala in 1968: A Brief Summary of Archaeological Results," *38th International Congress of Americanists*, Vol. 1, pp. 151–158, Stuttgart-Munich, W. Ger.

SMITH, A. L., G. R. WILLEY, AND R. E. W. ADAMS
1962 "Altar de Sacrificios, Cuarto Informe Preliminar, 1962, *IDAEH, Antropologia e Historia de Guatemala*, Vol. 14, No. 2, pp. 5–38, Guatemala City, Guatemala.

SMITH, R. E.
1936a *Preliminary Shape Analysis of the Uaxactun Pottery*, Carnegie Institution of Washington, Guatemala.
1936b *Ceramics of Uaxactun: A Preliminary Analysis of Decorative Technics and Design*, Carnegie Institution of Washington, Guatemala.
1955 *Ceramic Sequence at Uaxactun, Guatemala*, Middle American Research Institute, Publication 20, Tulane University, New Orleans, La.

1971   *The Pottery of Mayapan*, Papers, Vol. 66, Peabody Museum, Harvard University, Cambridge, Mass.

SOLECKI, RALPH AND CHARLES WAGLEY
1963   "William Duncan Strong, 1899–1962," *American Anthropologist*, Vol. 65, pp. 1102–1111.

SPIER, LESLIE
1917   *An Outline for a Chronology of Zuni Ruins*, Anthropological Papers of the American Museum of Natural History, Vol. 18, Pt. 3, New York.

SPINDEN, H. J.
1917   "The Origin and Distribution of Agriculture in America," *Proceedings, 19th International Congress of Americanists*, pp. 269–276, Washington, D.C.
1928   *Ancient Civilizations of Mexico and Central America*, 3rd ed., Handbook Series, No. 3, American Museum of Natural History, New York.
1957   "Alfred Marston Tozzer, 1877–1954," *Biographical Memoirs*, Vol. 30, pp. 383–397, National Academy of Sciences, Washington, D.C.

STEWARD, J. H.
1933   "Archaeological Problems of the Northern Periphery of the Southwest," *Museum of Northern Arizona, Bulletin* 5, Flagstaff, Ariz.
1936   "The Economic and Social Basis of Primitive Bands," *Essays in Anthropology in Honor of Alfred Louis Kroeber*, R. H. Lowie, ed., pp. 311–350, University of California Press, Berkeley, Calif.
1937a   *Ancient Caves of the Great Salt Lake Region*, Bulletin 116, Bureau of American Ethnology, Smithsonian Institution, Washington, D.C.
1937b   "Ecological Aspects of Southwestern Society," *Anthropos*, Vol. 32, pp. 87–104, Vienna, Austria.
1938   *Basin-Plateau Aboriginal Sociopolitical Groups*, Bulletin 120, Bureau of American Ethnology, Smithsonian Institution, Washington, D.C.
1948a   "The Circum-Caribbean Tribes: An Introduction," *Handbook of South American Indians*, J. H. Steward, ed., Vol. 4, pp. 1–41, Bulletin 143, Bureau of American Ethnology, Smithsonian Institution, Washington, D.C.
1948b   "A Functional-Developmental Classification of American High" Cultures," *A Reappraisal of Peruvian Archae-*

ology, W. C. Bennett, ed., pp. 103–104, Memoir 4, Society for American Archaeology.

1949a ‴"Cultural Causality and Law: A Trial Formulation of the Development of Early Civilizations," *American Anthropologist,* Vol. 51, pp. 1–27.

1949b "South American Cultures: An Interpretative Summary," *Handbook of South American Indians,* J. H. Steward, ed., Vol. 5, pp. 669–772, Bulletin 143, Bureau of American Ethnology, Smithsonian Institution, Washington, D.C.

1953 "Evolution and Process," *Anthropology Today,* A. L. Kroeber, ed., pp. 313–325, University of Chicago Press, Chicago, Ill.

1955 *Theory of Culture Change: The Methodology of Multilinear Evolution,* University of Illinois Press, Urbana, Ill.

1960 "Evolutionary Principles and Social Types," *Evolution After Darwin,* Sol Tax, ed., Vol. 2, pp. 169–186, University of Chicago Press, Chicago, Ill.

1961 "Alfred Louis Kroeber, 1876–1960," *American Anthropologist,* Vol. 63, No. 5, Pt. 1, pp. 1038–1087.

1973 *Alfred Kroeber,* Columbia University Press, New York.

STEWARD, J. H., ED.

1946–59 *Handbook of South American Indians,* Vols. 1–7, Bulletin 143, Bureau of American Ethnology, Smithsonian Institution, Washington, D.C.

1967 *Contemporary Change in Traditional Societies,* University of Illinois Press, Urbana, Ill.

STEWARD, J. H. AND LOUIS FARON

1959 *Native Peoples of South America,* McGraw-Hill, New York.

STEWARD, J. H., R. A. MANNERS, E. R. WOLF, ELENA PASILLA, S. W. MINTZ, AND R. L. SCHEELE

1956 *The People of Puerto Rico,* University of Illinois Press, Urbana, Ill.

STIRLING, M. W.

1936 "Florida Cultural Affiliations in Relation to Adjacent Areas," *Essays in Anthropology Presented to Alfred L. Kroeber on His Sixtieth Birthday,* R. H. Lowie, ed., pp. 351–357, University of California Press, Berkeley, Calif.

1938 *Historical and Ethnographical Material on the Jivaro Indians,* Bulletin 117, Bureau of American Ethnology, Smithsonian Institution, Washington, D.C.

BIBLIOGRAPHY

1939 "Discovering the New World's Oldest Dated Work of Man," *The National Geographic Magazine*, Vol. 76, pp. 183–218, National Geographic Society, Washington, D.C.

1940a *An Initial Series from Tres Zapotes, Vera Cruz, Mexico*, Contributed Technical Paopers, Mexican Archaeology Series, Vol. 1, No. 1, National Geographic Society, Washington, D.C.

1940b "Great Stone Faces of the Mexican Jungle," *The National Geographic Magazine*, Vol. 78, pp. 309–334, National Geographic Society, Washington, D.C.

1943 *Stone Monuments of Southern Mexico*, Bulletin 138, Bureau of American Ethnology, Smithsonian Institution, Washington, D.C.

1950 "Exploring Ancient Panama by Helicopter," *National Geographic Magazine*, Vol. 97, pp. 227–246, National Geographic Society, Washington, D.C.

1953a "Exploring Panama's Unknown North Coast," *Royal Canadian Institute, Proceedings*, Ser. 3A, Vol. 18, pp. 29–30, Ottawa.

1953b "Hunting Prehistory in the Panama Jungles," *National Geographic Magazine*, Vol. 104, pp. 271–290, National Geographic Society, Washington, D.C.

1955a *Stone Monuments of the Rio Chiquito, Veracruz, Mexico*, Bulletin 157, Anthropological Papers, No. 43, Bureau of American Ethnology, Smithsonian Institution, Washington, D.C.

1955b "Hunting Prehistory in the Panama Jungles," *Indians of the Americas*, M. W. Stirling, ed., pp. 267–280, National Geographic Society, Washington, D.C.

1957 *An Archaeological Reconnaissance in Southeastern Mexico*, Bulletin 164, Anthropological Papers, No. 53, Smithsonian Institution, Washington, D.C.

1961 "The Olmecs, Artists in Jade," *Essays in Pre-Columbian Art and Archaeology*, S. K. Lothrop and others, eds., pp. 43–59, Harvard University Press, Cambridge, Mass.

1963 "A New Culture in Ecuador," *Archaeology*, Vol. 16, pp. 170–175.

1965 "Monumental Sculpture of Southern Veracruz and Tabasco," *Handbook of Middle American Indians*, Robert Wauchope, ed., Vol. 3, pp. 716–738, University of Texas Press, Austin, Tex.

1968 "Early History of the Olmec Problem," *Dumbarton Oaks Conference on the Olmec*, E. P. Benson, ed., pp. 1–8, Dumbarton Oaks, Washington, D.C.

1969 "Archaeological Investigations in Costa Rica," *National Geographic Society Research Reports, 1964 Projects*, pp. 239–247, Washington, D.C.

STIRLING, M. W. AND MARION I. STIRLING

1963 *Tarqui, An Early Site in Manabi Province, Ecuador*, Anthropological Paper 63, Bulletin 186, Bureau of American Ethnology, Smithsonian Institution, Washington, D.C.

STRONG, W. D.

1925 *the Uhle Pottery Collections from Ancon*, University of California Publications in American Archaeology and Ethnology, Vol. 21, No. 4, Berkeley, Calif.

1927 "An Analysis of Southwestern Society," *American Anthropologist*, Vol. 29, pp. 1–61.

1929 *Aboriginal Society in Southern California*, University of California Publications in American Archaeology and Ethnology, Vol. 26, Berkeley, Calif.

1933 "The Plains Culture Area in the Light of Archaeology," *American Anthropologist*, Vol. 35, pp. 271–287.

1935a *An Introduction to Nebraska Archaeology*, Smithsonian Miscellaneous Series, Vol. 93, No. 10, Smithsonian Institution, Washington, D.C.

1935b *Archaeological Investigations in the Bay Islands, Spanish Honduras*, Smithsonian Miscellaneous Collections, Vol. 92, No. 14, Washington, D.C.

1945 "George Clapp Vaillant, 1901–1945," *American Antiquity*, Vol. 11, No. 2, pp. 113–116.

1947 "Finding the Tomb of a Warrior-God," *National Geographic Magazine*, Vol. 91, No. 4, pp. 453–482, Washington, D.C.

1948 "Cultural Epochs and Refuse Stratigraphy in Peruvian Archaeology," *A Reappraisal of Peruvian Archaeology*, W. C. Bennett, ed., Memoirs of the Society for American Archaeology, No. 4.

1957 *Paracas, Nazca, and Tiahuanacoid Cultural Relationships in South Coastal Peru*, Memoirs of the Society for American Archaeology, No. 13.

STRONG, W. D. AND J. M. CORBETT

1943 "A Ceramic Sequence at Pachacamac," *Archaeological Studies in Peru, 1941–1942*, W. D. Strong, G. R. Willey, and J. M. Corbett, Columbia Studies in Archaeology and Ethnology, Vol. 1, Columbia University Press, New York.

STRONG, W. D. AND CLIFFORD EVANS, JR.

1952   *Cultural Stratigraphy in the Viru Valley, Northern Peru,* Columbia Studies in Archaeology and Ethnology, Vol. 4, Columbia University Press, New York.

STRONG, W. D., ALFRED KIDDER II, AND A. J. D. PAUL

1938   *Preliminary Report on the Smithsonian Institution-Harvard University Archaeological Expedition to Northwestern Honduras,* Smithsonian Miscellaneous Collections, Vol. 97, No. 1, Washington, D.C.

STRONG, W. D., J. H. STEWARD, AND W. E. SCHENCK

1930   *Archaeology of the Dalles-Deschutes Region,* University of California Publications in American Archaeology and Ethnology, Vol. 29, No. 1, Berkeley, Calif.

STRONG, W. D. AND G. R. WILLEY

1943   "Archaeological Notes on the Central Coast," in *Archaeological Studies in Peru, 1941–1942,* Columbia University Studies in Archaeology and Ethnology, Vol. 1, No. 1, pp. 1–26, Columbia University Press, New York.

TANNER, C. L.

1954   "Byron Cummings, 1860–1954," *The Kiva,* Vol. 20, No. 1, pp. 1–20, Arizona Archaeological and Historical Society, Tucson, Ariz.

TAYLOR, W. W., JR.

1948   *A Study of Archaeology,* Memoir No. 69, American Anthropological Association.

TELLO, J. C.

1923   "Vira-Kocha," *Inka,* Vol. 1, pp. 93–320, 583–606, Lima.

1929   *Antiguo Peru; Primera Epoca,* Editado por la Comision Organizadora del Segundo Congreso Sundamericano de Turismo, Lima, Peru.

THOMPSON, J. E. S.

1931   *Archaeological Investigations in the Southern Cayo District, British Honduras,* Anthropological Series, Vol. 17, No. 3, Field Museum of Natural History, Chicago, Ill.

1940   *Late Ceramic Horizons at Bengue Viejo, British Honduras,* Contributions to American Anthropology and History, No. 35, Carnegie Institution of Washington, Washington, D.C.

1941   "Dating of Certain Inscriptions of Non-Maya Origin," *Theoretical Approaches to Problems,* No. 1, Division of

Historical Research, Carnegie Institution of Washington, Cambridge, Mass.

1948 *An Archaeological Reconnaissance in the Cotzumalhuapa Region, Escuinta, Guatemala,* Contributions No. 44, Publication No. 574, Carnegie Institution of Washington, Washington, D.C.

THOMPSON, J. E. S., H. E. D. POLLOCK, AND JEAN CHARLOT

1932 *A Preliminary Study of the Ruins of Coba, Quintana Roo, Mexico,* Publication 424, Carnegie Institution of Washington, Washington, D.C.

TOURTELLOT, GAIR III

1988 *Excavations at Seibal, Department of Peten, Guatemala: Peripheral Survey and Excavation: Settlement and Community Patterns,* Memoirs, Vol. 16 (whole volume), Peabody Museum, Harvard University, Cambridge, Mass.

n.d. *Excavations at Seibal, Department of Peten, Guatemala: Burials: A Cultural Analysis,* Memoirs, Vol. 17, No. 2, Peabody Museum, Harvard University, Cambridge, Mass.

TOZZER, A. M.

1905 "A Navajo Sand Picture of the Rain Gods and Its Attendant Ceremony," *Proceedings, 13th International Congress of Americanists,* pp. 147–156, New York.

1907 *A Comparative Study of the Mayas and the Lacandones,* Archaeological Institute of America, New York.

1908 "A Note on Star-Lore Among the Navajos," *Journal of American Folk-Lore,* Vol. 21, pp. 28–32.

1909 "Notes on the Religious Ceremonies of the Navajo," *Putnam Anniversary Volume,* pp. 299–343.

1911a *Preliminary Study of the Prehistoric Ruins of Tikal, Guatemala,* Memoirs, Vol. 5, No. 2, Peabody Museum, Harvard University, Cambridge, Mass.

1911b "The Value of Ancient Mexican Manuscripts in the Study of the General Development of Writing," *Proceedings of the American Antiquarian Society,* Vol. 21, pp. 80–101, Worcester, Mass.

1912 "The Ruins of Northeastern Guatemala," *Proceedings, 17th International Congress of Americanists,* Mexico, pp. 400–405.

1913 *A Preliminary Study of the Prehistoric Ruins of Nakum, Guatemala,* Memoirs, Vol. 5, No. 2, Peabody Museum, Harvard University, Cambridge, Mass.

1916 "The Domain of the Aztecs and Their Relation to the Prehistoric Cultures of Mexico," *Holmes Anniversary Volume*, pp. 497–525, Washington, D.C.

1921a *A Maya Grammar with Bibliography and Appraisement of the Works Noted*, Papers, Vol. 9, Peabody Museum, Harvard University, Cambridge, Mass.

1921b *Excavations of a Site at Santiago Ahuitzotla, D.F., Mexico*, Bulletin 74, Bureau of American Ethnology, Smithsonian Institution, Washington, D.C.

1925 *Social Origins and Social Continuities*, The MacMillan Company, New York.

1927 "Time and American Archaeology," *Natural History*, Vol. 27, pp. 210–221, American Museum of Natural History, New York.

1930 "Maya and Toltec Figures at Chichen Itza," *Proceedings, 23rd International Congress of Americanists*, New York, pp. 155–164.

1944 *The Okinawas, a Japanese Minority Group*, Office of Strategic Services, Honolulu, Hawaii.

1957 *Chichen Itza and Its Cenote of Sacrifice: A Comparative Study of Contemporaneous Maya and Toltec*, Memoirs, Vols. 11–12, Peabody Museum, Harvard University, Cambridge, Mass.

TOZZER, A. M., ED.

1941 *Landa's Relacion de Las Cosas de Yucatan*, Papers, Vol. 18, Peabody Museum, Harvard University, Cambridge, Mass.

TOZZER, A. M. AND G. M. ALLEN

1910 *Animal Figures in the Maya Codices*, Papers, Vol. 3, No. 3, Peabody Museum, Harvard University, Cambridge, Mass.

UHLE, MAX

1903 *Pachacamac*, Department of Archaeology, University of Pennsylvania, Philadelphia, Pa.

1907 *The Emeryville Shellmound*, University of California Publications in American Archaeology and Ethnology, Vol. 7, No. 1, Berkeley, Calif.

1913 "Die Muschelhugel von Ancon, Peru," *18th International Congress of Americanists*, London, 1912, pp. 22–45, London.

1919 "La Arqueologia de Arica y Tacna," *Boletin de la Sociedad Ecuatoriana de Estudios Historicos Americanos*, Vol. 3, Nos. 7–8, Quito, Ecuador.

1922   *Fundamentos Etnicos y Arqueologia de Arica y Tacna,* Second edition, Quito, Ecuador.

VAILLANT, G. C.

1927   "The Chronological Significance of Maya Ceramics," Unpublished Doctoral Dissertation, Peabody Museum Library, Harvard University, Cambridge, Mass.

1930   *Excavations at Zacatenco,* Anthropological Papers, American Museum of Natural History, Vol. 32, Pt. 1, New York.

1931a   *Excavations at Ticoman,* Anthropological Papers, American Museum of Natural History, Vol. 32, Pt. 2, New York.

1931b   "A Bearded Mystery," *Natural History,* Vol. 31, No. 3, pp. 243–252, New York.

1932a   *Some Resemblances in the Ceramics of Central and North America,* Medallion Papers, No. 12, Gila Pueblo, Globe, Arizona.

1932b   "A Pre-Columbian Jade," *Natural History,* Vol. 32, No. 6, pp. 512–520, 557–558, New York.

1933   "Hidden History," *Natural History,* Vol. 33, No. 6, pp. 618–628, New York.

1934a   "The Archaeological Setting of the Playa de los Muertos Culture," *Maya Research,* Vol. 1, No. 2, pp. 87–100, New York.

1934b   "The Sculpute of Pre-Columbian Central America," *Natural History,* Vol. 34, No. 3, pp. 259–272, New York.

1935a   "Chronology and Stratigraphy in the Maya Area," *Maya Research,* Vol. 2, No. 2, pp. 119–143, New York.

1935b   *Excavations at El Arbolillo,* Anthropological Papers, American Museum of Natural History, Vol. 35, Pt. 2, New York.

1935c   *Early Cultures of the Valley of Mexico: Results of the Stratigraphical Project of the American Museum of Natural History in the Valley of Mexico,* Anthropological Papers, American Museum of Natural History, Vol. 35, Pt. 3, New York.

1938   "A Correlation of Archaeological and Historical Sequences in the Valley of Mexico," *American Anthropologist,* Vol. 40, No. 4, pp. 535–573.

1939a   *Indian Arts in North America,* Harper and Brothers, New York.

1939b   "By Their Arts You Shall Know Them," *Natural History,* Vol. 43, No. 5, pp. 268–277, New York.

1940 "Patterns in Middle American Archaeology," *The Maya and Their Neighbors*, C. L. Hay and others, eds., pp. 295–305, Appleton-Century, New York.

1941 *Aztecs of Mexico*, Doubleday Doran, New York.

1945 "Shadow and Substance in Cultural Relations," *The Scientific Monthly*, Vol. 60, No. 5, pp. 373–378.

VAILLANT, S. B. AND G. C. VAILLANT

1934 *Excavations at Gualupita*, Anthropological Papers, American Museum of Natural History, Vol. 35, Pt. 1, New York.

WAUCHOPE, ROBERT

1934 *House Mounds of Uaxactun, Guatemala*, Contribution 7, Publication 436, Carnegie Institution of Washington, Washington, D.c.

1938 *Modern Maya Houses: A Study of Their Archaeological Significance*, Publication 502, Carnegie Institution of Washington, Washington, D.C.

1965 "Alfred Vincent Kidder, 1885–1963," *American Antiquity*, Vol. 31, No. 2, Pt. 1, pp. 149–171.

WEBB, C. H.

1968 "James Alfred Ford, 1911–1968," *Bulletin of the Texas Archaeological Society*, Vol. 38, pp. 135–146.

WEIANT, C. W.

1943 *An Introduction to the Ceramics of Tres Zapotes, Veracruz, Mexico*, Bulletin 139, Bureau of American Ethnology, Smithsonian Institution, Washington, D.C.

WEYERSTALL, ALBERT

1932 "Some Observations on Indians Mounds, Idols and Pottery in the Lower Papaloapam Basin, State of Vera Cruz, Mexico," *Middle American Research Series, Publication No. 4*, pp. 23–69, Tulane University, New Orleans, La.

WILLEY, G. R.

1937 "Notes on Central Georgia Dendrochronology," *Tree Ring Bulletin*, Vol. 4, No. 2, University of Arizona, Tucson, Ariz.

1943 "Excavations in the Chancay Valley," *Archaeological Studies in Peru, 1941–1942*, Columbia Studies in Archaeology and Ethnology, Columbia University Press, New York.

1945a "The Weeden Island Culture: A Preliminary Definition," *American Antiquity*, Vol. 10, No. 3, pp. 225–254.

1945b "Horizon Styles and Pottery Traditions in Peruvian Archaeology," *American Antiquity*, Vol. 11, pp. 49–56.

1946a "The Chiclin Conference for Peruvian Archaeology, 1946," *American Antiquity*, Vol. 12, pp. 132–134.

1946b "The Archaeology of the Greater Pampa," *Handbook of South American Indians*, J. H. Steward, ed., Vol. 1, pp. 25–46, Bulletin 143, Bureau of American Ethnology, Smithsonian Institution, Washington, D.C.

1948 "A Functional Analysis of 'Horizon Styles' in Peruvian Archaeology," in *A Reappraisal of Peruvian Archaeology*, W. C. Bennett, ed., pp. 8–15, Memoir 4, Society for American Archaeology.

1949 *Archaeology of the Florida Gulf Coast*, Smithsonian Miscellaneous Collections, Vol. 113, Washington, D.C.

1950 "Growth Trends in New World Cultures," in *For the Dean, Essays in Honor of Byron Cummings*, E. K. Reed and D. S. King, eds., pp. 223–248, Hohokam Museums Association and Southwestern Monuments Association, Santa Fe, N. Mex.

1951a "A Preliminary Report on the Monagrillo Culture of Panama," *29th International Congress of Americanists, The Civilizations of Ancient America*, S. Tax, ed., Vol. 1, pp. 173–180, University of Chicago Press, Chicago, Ill.

1951b "The Chavin Problem: A Review and Critique," *Southwestern Journal of Anthropology*, Vol. 7, pp. 103–144, University of New Mexico, Albuquerque, N. Mex.

1953a *Prehistoric Settlement Patterns in the Viru Valley, Peru*, Bulletin 153, Bureau of American Ethnology, Smithsonian Institution, Washington, D.C.

1953b "Archaeological Theories and Interpretation: New World," *Anthropology Today, An Encyclopedic Inventory*, A. L. Kroeber and others, eds., pp. 361–385, University of Chicago Press, Chicago, Ill.

1953c Review of *Excavations at Nebaj* by A. L. Smith and A. V. Kidder, *American Anthropologist*, Vol. 55, pp. 258–260.

1956 "Problems Concerning Prehistoric Settlement Patterns in the Maya Lowlands," *Prehistoric Settlement Patterns in the New World*, G. R. Willey, ed., Viking Fund Publications in Anthropology, Wenner-Gren Foundation, New York.

1960 "Historical Patterns and Evolution in Native New World Cultures," *Evolution After Darwin*, S. Tax, ed., *Volume*

II. The Evolution of Man, pp. 111–141, University of Chicago Press, Chicago, Ill.

1962 "The Early Great Styles and the Rise of the Pre-Columbian Civilizations," *American Anthropologist*, Vol. 64, No. 1, pp. 1–14.

1966 *An Introduction to American Archaeology, Vol. 1. North And Middle America*, Prentice-Hall, Inc., Englewood Cliffs, N.J.

1967 "Alfred Vincent Kidder, 1885–1963," *Biographical Memoirs*, Vol. 39, pp. 293–322, National Academy of Sciences, Washington, D.C.

1969 "James Alfred Ford, 1911–1968," *American Antiquity*, Vol. 34, No. 1, pp. 62–68.

1971 *An Introduction to American Archaeology, Vol. II. South America*, Prentice-Hall, Inc., Englewood Cliffs, N.J.

1972 *The Artifacts of Altar de Sacrificios*, Papers, Peabody Museum, Vol. 64, No. 1, Harvard University, Cambridge, Mass.

1973a "William Rotch Bullard, Jr., 1926–1972," *American Antiquity*, Vol. 38, No. 1, pp. 80–83.

1973b *The Altar de Sacrificios Excavations: General Summary and Conclusions*, Papers, Peabody Museum, Vol. 64, No. 3, Harvard University, Cambridge, Mass.

1974 "The Viru Valley Settlement Pattern Study," *Archaeological Researches in Retrospect*, G. R. Willey, ed., pp. 149–178, Winthrop Publishers, Inc., Cambridge, Mass.

1976 "Samuel Kirkland Lothrop, 1892–1965", *Biographical Memoirs*, Vol. 48, pp. 253–272, National Academy of Sciences, Washington, D.C.

1978 *Excavations at Seibal, Department of Peten, Guatemala: Artifacts*, No. 1; Vol. 14, Memoirs, Peabody Museum, Harvard University, Cambridge, Mass.

1981a "Spinden's Archaic Hypothesis," *Antiquity and Man*, Evans, J. D., B. Cunliffe, and C. Renfrew, eds., pp. 35–42, Thames and Hudson, London, U.K.

1981b "Maya Lowland Settlement Patterns: A Summary Review," *Lowland Maya Settlement Patterns*, W. Ashmore, ed., pp. 385–415, University of New Mexico Press, Albuquerque, N. Mex.

1983 "Harry Evelyn Dorr Pollock, 1900–1982," *American Antiquity*, Vol. 48, No. 4, pp. 782–784.

BIBLIOGRAPHY

1985   "Junius Bouton Bird and American Archaeology," in *Early Ceremonial Architecture in the Andes*, C. B. Donnan, ed., pp. 7–28, Dumbarton Oaks, Washington, D.C.

n.d. 1   "Macon, Georgia: A Fifty Year Retrospect," prepared for the 50th Anniversary Celebration of Ocmulgee National Monument, Macon, Ga.

n.d. 2   "Augustus Ledyard Smith, 1901–1985," submitted to *American Antiquity* in 1986.

n.d. 3   *Excavations at Seibal, Department of Peten, Guatemala: General Summary and Conclusions*, No. 4, Vol. 17, Memoirs, Peabody Museum, Harvard University, Cambridge, Mass.

WILLEY, G. R. AND W. R. BULLARD, JR.

1956   "The Melhado Site, A House Mound Group in British Honduras," *American Antiquity*, Vol. 22, pp. 29–44.

1965   "Prehistoric Settlement Patterns in the Maya Lowlands," *Handbook of Middle American Indians*, R. Wauchope, ed., Vol. 2, pp. 360–377, University of Texas Press, Austin, Tex.

WILLEY, G. R., W. R. BULLARD, JR., J. B. GLASS, AND J. C. GIFFORD

1965   *Prehistoric Maya Settlements in the Belize Valley*, Papers, Vol. 54, Peabody Museum, Harvard University, Cambridge, Mass.

WILLEY, G. R. AND J. M. CORBETT

1954   *Early Ancon and Early Supe Culture: Chavin Horizon Sites of the Central Peruvian Coast*, Columbia University Studies in Archaeology and Ethnology, Vol. 3, Columbia University Press, New York.

WILLEY, G. R. AND C. R. McGIMSEY

1954   *The Monagrillo Culture of Panama*, Papers, Vol. 49, No. 2, Peabody Museum, Harvard University, Cambridge, Mass.

WILLEY, G. R. AND PHILIP PHILLIPS

1955   "Method and Theory in American Archaeology II: Historical-Developmental Interpretation," *American Anthropologist*, Vol. 57, pp. 723–819.

1958   *Method and Theory in American Archaeology*, University of Chicago Press, Chicago, Ill.

WILLEY, G. R. AND J. A. SABLOFF

1974   *A History of American Archaeology*, Thames and Hudson, London, U.K.

1980   *A History of American Archaeology,* 2nd edition, W. H. Freeman and Co., San Francisco, Calif.

WILLEY, G. R. AND A. L. SMITH

1963   "Recent Discoveries at Altar de Sacrificios, Guatemala," *Archaeology,* Vol. 16, No. 2, pp. 83–90, New York.

1967   "A Temple at Seibal, Guatemala," *Archaeology,* Vol. 20, No. 4, pp. 290–298, New York.

1969   *The Ruins of Altar de Sacrificios, Department of Peten, Guatemala: An Introduction,* Papers, Vol. 62, No. 1, Peabody Museum, Harvard University, Cambridge, Mass.

WILLEY, G. R., A. L. SMITH, W. R. BULLARD, JR., AND J. A. GRAHAM

1960   "Altar de Sacrificios, A Prehistoric Maya Crossroads," *Archaeology,* Vol. 13, pp. 110–117, New York.

WILLEY, G. R., A. L. SMITH, GAIR TOURTELLOT III, AND IAN GRAHAM

1975   *Excavations at Seibal, Department of Peten, Guatemala: Introduction: The Site and Its Setting,* Memoirs, Vol. 13, No. 1, Peabody Museum, Harvard University, Cambridge, Mass.

WILLEY, G. R. AND T. L. STODDARD

1954   "Cultural Stratigraphy in Panama: A Preliminary Report on the Giron Site," *American Antiquity,* Vol. 19, pp. 332–342.

WILLEY, G. R. AND R. B. WOODBURY

1942   "A Chronological Outline for the Northwest Florida Coast," *American Antiquity,* Vol. 7, No. 3, pp. 232–254.

WILLIAMS, J. M.

1975   *Stubbs Mound in Central Georgia Prehistory,* Florida State University, Tallahassee, Fla.

WILLIAMS, STEPHEN, ED.

1970   *Philip Phillips, Lower Mississippi Survey,* Peabody Museum, Harvard University, Cambridge, Mass.

WOLF, E. R.

1981   "Alfred L. Kroeber," *Totems and Teachers,* Sydel Silverman, ed., pp. 35–66, Columbia University Press, New York.

WOODBURY, R. B.

1973   *Alfred V. Kidder,* Columbia University Press, New York.

LUXURY

JOHN SEKORA

THE CONCEPT IN
WESTERN THOUGHT,
EDEN TO
SMOLLETT

THE JOHNS HOPKINS UNIVERSITY PRESS
BALTIMORE AND LONDON

This book has been brought to publication with the
generous assistance of the Andrew W. Mellon Foundation.

Manufactured in the United States of America

The Johns Hopkins University Press, Baltimore, Maryland 21218
The Johns Hopkins Press Ltd., London

Library of Congress Catalog Card Number 77-4545
ISBN 0-8018-1972-5

Library of Congress Cataloging in Publication data
will be found on the last printed page of this book.

FOR BILL,
AND FOREVER RUTH

CONTENTS

PART TWO: SMOLLETT AND LUXURY

PART THREE: THE ATTACK UPON LUXURY
AND THE FORMS OF *HUMPHRY CLINKER*

CONCLUSION

PREFACE

Running through eighteenth-century English writing—considered broadly enough to embrace Ned Ward as well as Edward Gibbon—is a typology of values and characters that, much simplified, would include the following: young – mature, urban – country, feminine – masculine, innovative – traditional, unnatural – natural, uncontrolled – serene, immoderate – temperate, irrational – wise, dull – witty, unruly – obedient, corrupt – virtuous, subjects – rulers, the mob – men of substance, "they" – "we." It was in the attempt to discover the roots of such polarities, usually described as simple conventions, that this book began. The search led as a matter of course to earlier literature and, because the typology is as much moral as literary, to philosophers, theologians, and eventually lawmakers. To give short circuit to a long journey, all paths led to the ancient concept of luxury. One of the most inclusive theories of human relationships employed in antiquity, the concept of luxury explained much about the polar relationships employed in the later period. But the initial task I had set myself proved not as restricted as I had assumed. For I could discover no adequate published scholarship to draw upon: neither on the influence and transmission of the concept from antiquity, its effect upon eighteenth-century controversy, its place in the thinking of any valued writer, nor its significance to any major literary work.

At that point the study lost its original focus upon literary convention and took on its present concentration upon luxury, with special reference to the eighteenth century. For it became clear that that century was a turning point in men's thinking about luxury; in 1700 the edifice of laws and attitudes surrounding the concept seems wholly intact; yet by 1800 it is rubble. Hence this period of English history and literature offered not one but several opportunities, principally for three concrete and interrelated kinds of illustration: an account of the polemics surrounding the classical conception of luxury during its twilight and sunset; an analysis of an important author who absorbed himself within the classical tradition; and a description of how the concept shaped one highly regarded literary work. The goal may be conceived as a series of concentric and concentrating circles.

The study is equally historical and literary. I present the complex of relationships subsumed under the concept of luxury in historical terms: the way it evolved, accumulating power and influence over time. That history is given point and precision when it is brought to bear upon a writer who was immersed in the intellectual currents of his own day and who is still respected in ours. Standing alone, the historical discussion of luxury would be incomplete and perhaps inconclusive. Standing alone, the literary study would be vacuous, perhaps incomprehensible. Standing together, they encompass one of the oldest and most potent traditions of Western literary and intellectual life. As examples of the literary influence of the idea of luxury during its final years of potency, as many as two dozen significant writers are available. The novelist Tobias Smollett proved especially appropriate, for he is probably the last major English writer to accept wholly the classical conception, and his career spans the last outburst of controversy and its later moderation. And as culmination *Humphry Clinker* is similarly apt: it is Smollett's last work as well as his best, the finest novel of the 1770s, and the last major English literary work to be informed by the older sense of luxury.

From the decision to treat Smollett at length, three possibilities ensued. One was to treat the whole range of his historical, journalistic, and miscellaneous writings as well as his better-known fiction. The second was to treat only one novel but to treat it fully, not as a cultural anthropologist collecting artifacts, but as a literary critic searching for value and meaning. To add *Ferdinand Count Fathom* or *Launcelot Greaves* (or *Tom Jones*) would mean either expanding the study greatly or reducing the value of individual works to the level of mere examples. This gave rise to a third possibility: to note as fully as might be pertinent previous evaluations of Smollett's work generally and his achievement in *Humphry Clinker* in particular. If my reading of the novel is to have merit, that is, it should be able to stand with the judgments of those critics from whom I have learned so much. I do not intend a specialist's study, chiefly for those already interested in Smollett; yet such a study is included. Like most readers I admire scholarly books that are lean and swiftly to the point; contemplating the pages that follow, I console myself with the hope that I have written such a book—indeed, several of them.

If the concept of luxury is as momentous as I believe it to be, it follows that my own contribution to its understanding can be no more than partial, tentative, and suggestive. Only an encyclopedic work by many scholars in many fields could do it full justice. Rather than the encyclopedia, I offer a series of related essays. The Introduction compares classical and modern conceptions of luxury, reviews scholarship on the idea (practically all of which is founded on the modern sense), and questions the place Smollett is usually assigned in literary history. Chapter 1 traces the attack upon luxury from the Hebrews to about 1700 and notes the sumptuary laws drawn to enforce the attack. Chapters 2 and 3 treat in more detail the fierce disputes that arose between 1700 and the mid-1760's, after which the concept was often given a 180-degree turn of meaning. Chapters 4, 5, and 6 concentrate upon the role of luxury in the novelist's many-sided works of the 1750s and 1760s. The first of these, on the historical writings, presents his account of the origin, rise, and consequences of luxury in English life. The concrete day-to-day progress of the vice as he viewed it during the most critical period of his career—indeed his maturity—is described in chapters 5 and 6; these seek also to identify as particularly as possible the contemporary persons and behavior he considered luxurious. Chapters 7 through 9 suggest some of the implications of the attack regarded as a literary mode, using as exempla the political nature, the characterization, and the narrative structure of *Humphry Clinker*. The Conclusion attempts a final synthesis and reinterpretation of the concept and of Smollett's achievement. Throughout I have resisted several strong temptations. Presenting an anthology of the chief discussions of luxury, with commentary, would establish more vividly than I can in these pages the strength and continuity of the concept; but the result would be barely readable and would detract from a larger purpose—to indicate the ways the concept was put to practical use. Another temptation was to give a full account of sumptuary and related legislation as it regulated conduct beyond spending; though one is certainly needed, I could not provide it here. And while I have not tried to respond to all the studies that see luxury as merely the obverse of primitivism, I do notice the most prominent. It is sufficient at the outset to say that an approach by way of primitivism cannot account for the social, political, or theological implications of luxury, or for the repeated attacks upon the alleged luxury of women, slaves, and paupers.

Much that is of interest in the history of luxury, moveover, lies before and after the three millennia treated here. The origin of the concept is obscure. There are indications that even before the Hebrews it was a deduction from religious dogma, a luxurious act being construed as human enjoyment of that intended as sacrifice to the gods: for example, gold, birds, animals, children, and virgins. There are other indications that the crime of luxury was associated with justifications for slavery. What is clear—as well as commonplace—is that the main Western philosophical systems posited perfect (i.e., absolute) forms of degradation as well as models of perfect virtue and freedom. To describe the decline into depravity of an individual or group, they created various theories of entropy, the concept of luxury being among the most prominent. Such theories sought to comprehend the origins of depravity, its nature, psychology, stages of development, and inevitable consequences. Their attractions remain visible in our language today as in our odd phrase "falling in love." To mark the decline and fall of a person or nation, we enjoy a vocabulary rich in nuance and technical distinction. But to describe the kinds and stages of success and fulfillment, we make do with a stock of bloodless yet incessantly used platitudes. In the ancient world the concept of luxury withstood all sorts of historical change: poverty as well as prosperity, republican as well as imperial governments, benighted as well as advancing civilizations. It was largely unaffected by Chrisitanity and came to the end of its classical phase in Europe only when certain economic and political circumstances undermined its original assumptions. But those assumptions did not themselves wither away, for many were transplanted to that new birth of freedom, America, where the ideas and often the exact language of the classical attack upon luxury were used to defend the most brutal form of slavery the world has known.

For the study that follows, 1776 is of cardinal significance as the year of Adam Smith's *Wealth of Nations* and the affirmation of American independence from European corruption. Yet it was also the year Congress struck from the Declaration of Independence Jefferson's charge that George III had carried on "cruel war against human nature" by capturing and enslaving many of his fellowmen. For the American slave no less than the Athenian slave, freedom was considered a luxury, something for which he had neither need nor right. The assumption held fast beyond the legal demise of slavery, to the extent that, in an address to the National Education Association in 1910, a southern superintendent of schools knew he would find sympathy for his region's policy of keeping black schools isolated and poor:

> Public peace and the safety of the state demand that the less developed race be subordinated to the more developed, under conditions as they exist in the South today. The Caste of Kin is the practice of the theory that blood is thicker than water. . . . If these widely different races cannot blend their blood—and instinct and science say nay—the only real foundation for democracy, equality actual or potential, does not exist and cannot be created. . . . Southerners understand the apparent cruelty imputed to the God of Israel who is represented as commanding the extermination of non-assimilable peoples. But the more refined killing of today in the South is not the taking of a negro's life but the impassive and relentless murder of a people's hopes. But better this than worse that might be.

To bring the record nearer to the present, one could cite three stories reported by the *New York Times* within one month during 1976. A white woman who heads a group in Boston opposed to school bussing explained that, "Black parents aren't really interested in desegregated schools. They care about more essential things like jobs." A male legislator from Florida said he was leading the opposition to the Equal Rights Amendment in his state because "Women already have more rights than they can handle." And a district court judge in Illinois ruled that, while uncovering graves of persons of European descent was "criminal desecration," the same act regarding native American graves was "legitimate archeology." All these attitudes and incidents represent atavisms of the ancient distinction between necessity and luxury and the ancient choice of who should draw the distinction.

Notwithstanding the good counsel I have received from many generous scholars, specialists in several fields may, at the minimum, question my decisions of emphasis and selection. I cannot yet resolve to my own satisfaction important issues raised by Smollett's work; it is far less likely that I can say anything conclusive about Sallust or Bolingbroke. For another instance, I have sorted out the phases of eighteenth-century discussion of luxury according to domestic controversy; a specialist in diplomatic affairs could well perceive international influences I have missed. And it is true that English writers on painting and gardening occasionally speak of luxury in a favorable sense I have not attempted to treat here. The few sentences I offer concerning the Romans or major English authors are simply illustrative and do not attempt to gauge their richness. While Smollett does receive the bulk of attention, that attention is again selective. I treat his social and political attitudes insofar as they are included within his conception of luxury, leaving largely untouched such otherwise important areas as his Scottish background.

It may be enough to say that, although I have not been able to resolve them, I am aware of the problems of dealing with a copious heterogeneity of material and with large, philosophically charged questions of historical change and description. Since any study that includes political controversy must cross lines closely guarded by the followers and doubters of Namier, the joining of certain controversies has been unavoidable. Without wishing to enter either list, I can plead that in general I follow Smollett's habitual uses of the terms *Whig* and *Tory*. I accept Namier's contention that well before midcentury England had for practical purposes (and in contemporary terms) a one-party government, and also Plumb's thesis that Walpole followed Cromwell in finding means to reconcile the interests of land and money. By 1756 Smollett apparently accepted as fact—not as enthusiastically, but as certainly, as a Pitt or a Beckford—that England was set on an unalterable commercial course. The battles he wished to lead were over hard political divisions and questions that yet remained: What kind of men would regulate national commerce and garner most of its profits? What products would be traded and with whom? Would commerce be made servant and guardian of the traditional English order of things? Or would it be permitted to undermine that order? Although he lagged behind many of his contemporaries in understanding political economy, he grasped more acutely than most the politics of status and privilege. He certainly knew what he meant when he dismissed an opponent as "a mere Whig" (and so did the opponent), and the divisions he posed were, indisputably, historical phenomena. They are not retrospective constructs or categories but are divisions embodied in living people at a discernible time over interests perceived as vital. This is one point among many made most recently by John Brewer in *Party Ideology and Popular Politics at the Accession of George III* (Cambridge, 1976).

A final stylistic point. Like most authors before him, Smollett uses the word *luxury* variously for the intellectual concept, the moral vice, and some concrete thing. In context such usage is seldom confusing, and to avoid distracting repetitions of "the concept of luxury" or "the vice of luxury" I have normally followed his practice. All citations from *Humphry Clinker* are drawn from the edition by Lewis M. Knapp in the Oxford English Novels series (London, 1966). In the last portion of the study, devoted to the novel, I revert to Smollett's way of dating the fictional letters—month first, then day—which Knapp and other editors have retained.

Any book like this depends upon the research and generous advice of many scholars. Although I would claim for it a moiety of originality, it would have been quite impossible but for the work of many eminent scholars, particularly M. I. Finley, David Brion Davis, P. A. Brunt, and Sarah Pomeroy on the ancient world; J. G. A. Pocock, Isaac Kramnick, Caroline Robbins, and George Rudé on eighteenth-century England; and Lewis M. Knapp, Paul-Gabriel Boucé, Byron Gassman, and Robert Donald Spector on Smollett. Having ventured into many fields, I am especially indebted and equally aware of the risks of having tried so much, and I will not excuse my errors by pressing them upon those who have helped me. Yet the errors I have made would have been far greater had not portions of the manuscript been read by Louis A. Landa, Lawrence Lipking, Henry Knight Miller, Ian R. Christie, Duncan Isles, Ronald Paulson, Jean H. Hagstrum, and J. G. A. Pocock. I mourn the circumstance that three gracious men who saw early drafts—Jack W. Jessee, Geoffrey Tillotson, and Lewis M. Knapp—will not see the final version. For their patience in enduring many hours of talk on the subject and their persistence in clarifying many of its problems, I am grateful to my friends Steven Bates, Anne Hargrove, June Frazer, Paul-Gabriel Boucé, William Park, and Anthony Wadden. I owe thanks to the National Endowment for the Humanities for a fellowship that allowed me to complete the manuscript. William P. Sisler of the Johns Hopkins University Press, an editor's editor and an author's friend, put it all together.

Whatever value this study may ultimately possess owes most to those teachers who offered a model as admirable as it was demanding. Toward Josephine A. Pearce, Warren F. Dwyer, G. E. Bentley, Louis A. Landa, and Henry Knight Miller, I feel a sense of obligation this volume cannot exhaust; yet I am happy for the chance to express it publicly. And only that teacher I know best, Ruth my wife, can realize how much this was written with and for her.

LUXURY

Introduction

WHY LUXURY? WHY SMOLLETT?

SOME PRELIMINARY

OBSERVATIONS

This is the study of a relationship—one compassing a major intellectual tradition, its twilight in England, a writer who during that twilight became its spokesman, and the masterpiece he created. For us, luxury is less a concept than a mere term, far less a single coherent social theory than the merest part of many theories.[1] Although the term has retained a mite of its ancient power, its conceptual significance has been absorbed by modern political philosophies, principally the varying "isms" that condition life in the contemporary world. The devaluation from transcendental principle to quibbling word was so slow as to be imperceptible to all but the most sensitive. Even in retrospect it is obscured by related but more palpable and dramatic changes: the Enlightenment, the French and American Revolutions, the founding of the British Empire, the Industrial Revolution, the growth of cities and of the bourgeoisie. As an intimate part of all of these, the changes in meaning of the concept of luxury represent nothing less than the movement from the classical world to the modern. For the concept of luxury

1

is one of the oldest, most important, and most pervasive negative principles for organizing society Western history has known. As an intellectual construct it is similar to the Great Chain of Being and other such figures for metaphysical relationships; on a "lower" level it is akin to such ideas as the divine right of kings, law and order, and manifest destiny in European and American history. In its more abstract senses, the concept was used to explain God's plan for mankind and thus the movement of human destiny. Rendered concrete through politics and the law, it evolved into a potent element of the whole range of secular institutions, expressing man's plan for man and thus the desired movement of everyday social affairs.

As over centuries the concept of luxury grew more influential, it also became increasingly complex and controversial. Tension, conflict, and controversy were inevitable as eminent men used the concept to identify those things within their societies they most distrusted. By the eighteenth century in England such controversy was climactically fierce, for the traditional concept was thought to be endangered, losing by degrees the religious and political sanction it had possessed since antiquity. To many prominent Englishmen it was most precious when most threatened. After centuries as a tacit, axiomatic supposition, it was now occasionally challenged, reinterpreted, and, stranger still, even ignored. The debate that ensued was pivotal in intellectual history, yielding a general sense of luxury radically different at the end of the century from what it had been at the beginning. A short list of the major figures who took part would include Mandeville, Addison, Steele, Defoe, Pope, Swift, Bolingbroke, Fielding, Chesterfield, Hume, Johnson, Pitt father and son, Walpole father and son, Goldsmith, Gibbon, Ferguson, Steuart, Wesley, and Adam Smith.

By midcentury a central position in the controversy had been assumed by Tobias Smollett (1721–71), whose distinction it is to have been one of the last, most adamant, and most forceful proponents of the classical view. In the early 1750s, while writing his first major history, Smollett became absorbed in social and political issues of national import and thereafter did as much as any single writer to keep the dangers of luxury ever before the public eye. To this task he brought distinct advantages. After 1754, when Fielding died and Richardson published his last work, Smollett was often praised as the most talented novelist in England. He was at the same time one of the nation's foremost political journalists, serving as defender of Leicester House, then Bute and George III, and directing two major reviews. He also came to be regarded as the most influential historian after Hume, and he was easily the most prolific, producing three dozen volumes within a decade. The specific vehicles of his involvement were the seventy volumes of nonfiction he wrote or edited between 1756 and 1771: The *Critical Review* (1756-), the *British Magazine* (1760-), the *Briton* (1762-63), *The Complete History of England* (1757-58), *The Continuation of the Complete History* (1760-65), *The Modern Part of the Universal History* (1759-65), the *Travels through France and Italy* (1766), *The History and Adventures of an Atom* (1769), and *The Present State of All Nations* (1768-69).[2] Several hundred times in these volumes he resorted to the concept of luxury to explain what he considered seriously wrong in England and the world.

In his last years, after more than a decade of intense activity, Smollett left England, ill and disillusioned with the state of national politics, to concentrate a large portion of his remaining energies upon the novel by which he is known best today, *The Expedition of Humphry Clinker*. Published just three months before his death in September 1771, this final book can be seen in retrospect as equally masterpiece and testament, his preeminent creation as well as his summing up of the lessons of history, experience, and natural law. He utilized the concept of luxury variously and repeatedly within the larger patterns of meaning, structure, and characterization. For him it was the hinge linking the two aspects of the novel, which is at once a harsh indictment of the newer England he repudiated and a nostalgic memoir of the Old England he honored. For us it demonstrates again that a work of art exists within a tradition, the artist perfecting and completing the work of his predecessors. For us too it may provide a further definition of *masterpiece*: a work that not only grows out of a tradition but actually contains it.

Whether this argument is valid and substantial is something that must emerge over subsequent chapters. Yet, put this baldly, it cuts across various assumptions current in social, literary, and intellectual history. It certainly raises a series of legitimate objections, which in summary form might run as follows. "We already know everything of consequence about the canard of luxury, during Smollett's lifetime as well as before. Moralists of the eighteenth century were naturally concerned with increasing signs of extravagance and self-indulgence within their society. And, in any case, what is valuable in Smollett has little to do with luxury or any other concept. In no genre is his work notable for its ideas, and *Humphry Clinker* owes its vitality not to any intellectual content but to its easy flow of comic characters and situations. Even if he sometimes did refer to luxury in the novel, there would be little point to a book-length gloss of a single idea in a single work by so unintellectual a writer."

Each of these judgments must be considered before we proceed, for each represents a serious objection to the entire process of revaluation attempted here. I have abbreviated the objections and limited them to the most pertinent; yet I have not tried by caricature to reduce their force. There is no satisfaction in besting straw men, and all can be pursued in the notes to their original sources. The basic question concerns the state of our knowledge of the concept of luxury. Even within the relatively new and always difficult study of the history of ideas, luxury presents an unusual problem in meaning, since it is not susceptible to ready definition. Context is important, and during three thousand years this has shifted many times and in many ways. Ideas concerning, say, death or marriage or monarchy are more easily sorted, for they possess a definite subject. Luxury, however, embraces a network of fluctuating social, philosophic, and theological presuppositions. For eighteenth-century Englishmen, certainly, it was not so much an idea to be analyzed as an idea to be lived by—or at least lived with. In Michel Foucault's valuable phrase, it is a system of discourse: both the mental discourse that guides thought and the social discourse that governs behavior.

Most perplexing for modern students is the additional complication that luxury represents a *lost* system of discourse, the loss disguised by a superficial resemblance between the classical and the modern usage of the term. On the lower level of modern usage, our ordinary language is of course something of a churchyard of ancient philosophies, and present-day references to luxury are to the original as a gravemarker is to an ebullient human life. On the higher level of doctrine, although the vocabulary and social vehemence are often the same, there is as little similarity between a classical opponent of luxury like Augustine and a modern one like Marx as between patristic theology and messianic socialism. We seem to recognize fully that Aquinas and Darwin mean quite different things by the phrase "natural law," but we have yet to draw such distinctions regarding luxury. Perhaps the most informative analogues lie in that specialized branch of the history of ideas, the history of architecture. A temple erected during the reign of Marcus Aurelius has recently been reconstructed to house concerts of popular music. The harmony of a Roman temple was as much cultural as physical; its mass, power, and plastic body were expressions of political philosophy as much as of aesthetic theory. To a modern Roman the rehabilitated shell might argue a renewal of history or a sign of its continuity; but its altered interior speaks volumes of profound change. For another example, a contemporary visitor to the Kremlin could well view Uspenski cathedral as an instance of permanent, unyielding grandeur, for its outward form has been carefully preserved since the fifteenth century. Yet its function and inner spirit have undergone vast upheavals between the czars who built it and the soviets who use it.

Ideas associated with a particular kind of social, religious, political, or economic organization can be finely analyzed long after the organization itself has lapsed or changed. The situation is quite different with ideas like luxury, which appear to absorb and comprehend many varieties of historical change. Like temple and cathedral, luxury has endured.

To indicate briefly that durability over time and fashion, one might examine the opinions of two Englishmen very different from Tobias Smollett. Roger Ascham devotes a large part of the opening Book of *The Scholemaster* (1570) to an exposure of Italian luxury and its imported effect upon educated English youth. When young men become luxurious or "Italianate," there begins a chain of events that ends in certain national degeneracy. First, individual youths dress absurdly and grow vain, lustful, and idolatrous. Contentious factions then develop within families and cities, and the public virtues of respect, honesty, and learning are forever lost. For Ascham luxury is "that sweet and perilous poison of all youth" that has directly caused the chaotic state of private and public life in sixteenth-century Italy. He concludes with the warning that vigilance against luxury must never waver, for the vice is not "open, fond and common," but always "subtle, cunning, new, and divers."[3] Writing two centuries later, Henry Fielding redirects Ascham's warning as he seems to repeat it. Fielding's *Enquiry into the Cause of the late Increase of Robbers* (1751) is a semiofficial report upon a specific situation at midcentury, and he feels obligated to review English history to account for that situation. He finds that the "vast Torrent of Luxury which of late Years hath poured itself into this Nation" has altered and disrupted all levels of society, but he is most alarmed that it has "almost totally changed the Manners, Customs, and Habits of the People, more especially of the lower Sort." A *political* evil, luxury has inspired in the poor a desire for things they may not and cannot have, hence what Fielding considers their wickedness, profligacy, idleness, and dishonesty. Like Ascham, he ends with a call for public vigilance, but of the kind made permanent by stringent laws.[4]

Brief, out of context, and randomly chosen from thousands of possible examples, these two instances cannot reveal much about the nature or history of luxury. Yet they can demonstrate something of its protean quality. The one concurs with the other that luxury is as potent an enemy as England faces. But Ascham's anxiety for the morals of wealthy, educated young Englishmen, while an important facet of the Renaissance conception of luxury, is not wholly congruent with the common eighteenth-century alarm over the luxury of the illiterate poor. Moreover, both Ascham and Fielding are concerned with states of interior wholesomeness, whether of persons or nations, and this

characteristic alone is sufficient to distinguish the classical or pre–
nineteenth-century concept of luxury from its modern version, with its
emphasis on externals like extravagant spending and the waste of natural
resources. The distinction between classical and modern conceptions
will be taken up later in this chapter.

Notwithstanding the tens of thousands of references to luxury in
Western literature, there is as yet, so far as I can discover, no thorough
investigation of the concept. Before the eighteenth century, European
readers had little need to question its meaning and significance, for they
were living in the midst of a vital tradition, one that asserted itself every
time a classical text or author was cited. Scholars and other readers
since the eighteenth century have in the main assumed that the meaning of luxury was self-evident and self-contained, that it referred to the
kind of ostentatious indulgence every right-minded person would oppose.[5] Studies of the eighteenth century generally, of other writers
concerned with luxury, and of Smollett have shared this assumption.[6]
I have tried to forego the particularity of previous definitions of luxury
—definitions that are often more rigorous than the material will allow
and that fall victim to misplaced concreteness—attempting instead to
discover the assumptions all have in common. Luxury has been always
despised and always loved, Voltaire ventured in the *Philosophical
Dictionary*. The issue is compounded, consequently, as much by
paradox and ambiguity as by controversy; the history of luxury is as
much one of various attempts to *enforce* a single meaning over all
others as of inevitably evolving meanings. It also encloses the full range
of human expression, from the "higher" peaks of philosophical speculation to the "lower" depths of disorganized sentiment and ineffable
passion. The power to unite men of differing goals and values—at least
tenuously and perhaps below the level of consciousness—remains one of
the most fascinating features of the idea.

If a revaluation of luxury is possible, then a redress of judgment
regarding Smollett will follow. For several reasons, his prominence and
importance in the intellectual life of the middle decades of the
eighteenth century have never been fully recognized. The very topicality
of much of his writing provides part of the explanation and at least
indicates why there is no brilliantly caustic portrait by Macauley to
rebut. But the main reason is seemingly temperamental, for Smollett
was a perpetual outsider, standing against or aloof from the influential
literary coteries of his day. He would find no welcome among the Whig
circle of patrons, writers, and booksellers; Horace Walpole saw to that.
He was too busy, too irascible, too pugnacious to compete for honors
within The Club, and therefore remained beyond the preservative power
of Boswell's pen. What time he did have for social diversion seems to

have been spent with his *own* circle of family and close associates. And this group, with the partial exceptions of John Moore and Alexander Carlyle, did not leave informative letters or memoirs. Smollett's own letters are relatively few, usually short, and generally utilitarian. They do not provide what we would most wish, "his own life in his own words." Indeed he appears to have been too much the proud Scotsman either (like Johnson) to feel altogether comfortable anywhere in London or (like Pope) to use personal letters to broadcast his fame.

The contention that Smollett's work is unintellectual is relatively recent, predicated on a superficial reading of his fiction and an almost total neglect of his nonfiction. In a brief essay in *Reason and Romanticism* (1926), Herbert Read argued that Smollett's mind "is innocent of ideas, and indeed of abstractions of any sort."[7] With the revival of interest in Smollett's fiction in succeeding decades, this presumption guided interpretations of the whole canon and of particular novels, Smollett becoming the pure storyteller among the great eighteenth-century novelists. Writing of *Peregrine Pickle,* James L. Clifford summarizes the most learned version of this view: "Although the writing is largely free from abstract ideas, this does not mean that Smollett's work lacks serious purpose. He merely refuses to philosophize, to brood, or to waste time in useless introspection. He is a story-teller, who is also an observer and satirist, with a world of folly to expose. But the demands of the narrative always have first claim."[8] Nor could critics like Alan D. McKillop discern any "philosophizing" in his final work. "The world of *Clinker* is still Smollett's world, a jungle in which amazing fauna are to be found, a region of endless absurdities, but there is no longer so much talk about fierce indignation [as in earlier novels]. There is a general parallel with Sterne here: while the great world may rage without, the obliquities of these originals are harmless, and manifest themselves in a well-grounded order of things.... Smollett's humorous characters never require long study."[9]

One kind of response to the misgivings of a magisterial man of letters like Read—and those who agree with him—is to bring to court the opinion of another. W. H. Auden has written:

> we cannot fully understand Pope and any other writers of his period without knowing something about the general climate of thought and opinion by which they were surrounded. It was one of the few historical periods in which one could with accuracy speak of an educated élite who, whether as writers or as readers, shared the same artistic tastes and general ideas about Nature, Man, and Society—a period, therefore, when "originality" and "alienation" were not regarded as the hallmarks of genius.[10]

Another response is to note that Read's notion of an idea was not Smollett's, nor that of numerous other eighteenth-century figures justly respected as thinkers. To a progressive critic like Read, *idea* connotes novelty, originality, innovation, bold speculation, a leap beyond the margins of conventional thought. But to Locke, Dryden, Swift, Pope, Johnson, Goldsmith, Reynolds, and Smollett, to cite but a few, intellectual apprehension was something quite different.[11] To call upon Johnson, it was a revelation of "the general truths of nature," "just and universal truths," "general and transcendental truths, which will always be the same." In the *Life of Cowley* appear the distinction of three levels of wit, the disparagement of novel insights as merely "metaphysical," and the famous summary, "Great thoughts are always general, and consist in positions not limited by exceptions, and in descriptions not descending to minuteness."[12] Whatever his other differences and disagreements with these contemporaries, Smollett shared their view of truth and the goals of meaningful thought. To him possession of an idea was a process of ever-growing, ever-deepening apprehension of a truth known from time immemorial. To hold an idea meant to make it one's own, to feel it, to use it, to renew its strength, to apprehend its manifestations, to become sensitive to its immediate implications; and to exercise the imagination meant to give an idea force, vitality, and immediacy. Like the old priest in Graham Greene who twice daily for fifty years polished the gilt crucifix he had received at ordination, Smollett furbished his conception of luxury with many volumes of what he considered closely argued prose.

A secondary objection, related to Read's, is that Smollett rarely appears self-consciously concerned with abstractions of any sort. It is perhaps this very habit of mind, common to active writers, that has obscured Smollett's stature as a thinker. To a contemplative philosopher like Hume, luxury could be an object of detached curiosity, a fascinating study in the clashes and combinations of various attitudes. But to Smollett it was of necessity something else—a tool for use, an automatic, reflexive instrument to simplify and clarify his work. Once accepted, the classical approach to luxury took on for him the strength of doctrine. It was to him what the Pauline epistles were to Wesley—not a pale relic of a remote culture, but a vivid, immediate presence of timeless certainty. It is hence not surprising that at no point in the seventy volumes he wrote after 1756, with their hundreds of references to luxury, did he define his use of the concept or reduce it to its essentials. He had no more use for such a definition than Wesley had for a definition of the Incarnation. Rather his habit is to associate it with other concepts and events or to illustrate it through its social consequences. It existed not to be defined, but to be displayed, vivified, personified, worked with, written from. It began with people, described people, described people, and returned to people. Finding the concept equally fertile and crucial, he turned time and again to luxury to guide his thinking and his writing, for the truth could easily bear incessant repetition. To John Locke the process of association would have been a familiar one, for "once set going" predominant ideas "continue in the same steps they have been used to, which by often treading, are worn into a smooth path, and the motion in it becomes easy, and as it were natural."

In such a "motion," moreover, the novelist was neither lax nor confused; he was reflecting the common habit of his time. The enveloping context and vocabulary of the controversy over luxury had been established perhaps as long as three millennia before he was born and were not to be revised substantially until after the publication of *The Wealth of Nations,* five years after his death. To this context and vocabulary the vast majority of Smollett's countrymen who wrote on the subject gave their assent, regarding the idea not as hackneyed or indeterminate, but as resonant with the implications of experience and the lessons of history. To most literate Englishmen of his lifetime, the continual reminders of the fall of Rome appear to have been like the annual feasts of the Jewish and Christian calendars, regular commemorations of the most important event in European history. Such reminders enabled eighteenth-century Englishmen to develop what was to them a sharp sense of history and thereafter to carry that sense with them day after day, generation after generation. As many Europeans would today say "Never again!" to the atrocities of Nazi Germany, just so did many Englishmen then respond to the luxuries of ancient Rome.

This legacy of dread had manifold consequences for eighteenth-century English thought. Since nearly all moralists assumed that luxury was one of the most dire forms of human vice, the only dispute possible was over its manifestations. In a century of accelerated change, these manifestations were to be found virtually everywhere. Politicians saw luxury rampant within the church, and clergymen found it infesting Westminster. While military men blamed the merchants, the merchants blamed the literati. Save for one conspicuous break, the controversy would have been flawlessly circular. Almost all writers on luxury blamed The People. As that amorphorous body found its spokesmen and then its own voice, the controversy over luxury reached probably its highest peak in European history. Although it may be impossible ultimately to assess the influence of an idea, particularly such a protean one, it is arguable that luxury was the single most significant social and political idea of eighteenth-century England. It became a popular cliché flowing easily from the pens of aspiring writers on religion, society, political economy, and politics. Yet it is also at the center of many works of the first order: from *Leviathan* to *The Wealth of Nations,* from *The Fable of the Bees* to *The Decline and Fall of the Roman Empire,* from *Tom Jones* to *The Man of Feeling,* from the *Spectator* to the *Annual Register,* and from Pope's *Epistles* to *The Deserted Village.* In his review of Jenyns's *Free Inquiry,* Johnson ventures the audacious, divining in the Platonic doctrine of plenitude a profound philosophical contradiction. With somewhat more temerity, critics occasionally called attention to the theoretical and practical inconsistencies present in the conventional concept of luxury.

Discussing the idea of the Great Chain during the eighteenth century, Lovejoy argued that questions of rank and power could be tacitly absorbed into the higher unity of theological metaphysics. Many Englishmen were simultaneously aware that questions of political and legal privilege, the concentration of wealth and property, the state of education and the arts, and many related issues could be absorbed openly into the allegedly higher unity of luxury. Although the position of literature in this process has been little noticed by literary historians, an economic historian, Jacob Viner, has essayed a general description. Regarding satirists from the Restoration to about 1760, Viner writes: "Satire was . . . an upper-class preserve in the main, with the satirists in the free or paid service of their social superiors. . . . I have not succeeded in finding a clear-cut *English* instance in which a satirist, on an economic issue, was attacking a social group clearly higher than the one he belonged to or had been hired to serve."[13] He argues further that during this period satire "had its darts pointed horizontally or downwards in the social scale, but not upwards." Smollett was not a satirist in the strict sense, and his last novel did not appear until 1771; yet his work otherwise falls within such a pattern. Later chapters indeed will seek to suggest his affinity with the earlier generation of Tory satirists. Viner recommends additional study of the interrelations of literature and society. Knowledge of the manner in which the concept of luxury influenced a major novelist goes far, I believe, to explain what he calls "institutional *status quo* conservatism." If language does in fact greatly influence perception, then the conservative perceptions of many eighteenth-century Englishmen were influenced by an intellectual tradition whose taproots lay deep in the soil of antiquity.[14]

Viner's researches help to anticipate the objections of literary scholars who, while granting the importance of luxury to the history of ideas, would question its pertinence to literary history. In the concluding portion of this study I argue that the attack upon luxury represents a literary mode as distinct and as ancient as the idea itself. If Smollett had never written a line, there would be value in a wholly literary investigation of luxury, on a scale I can only indicate here. For even beyond the question of narrative mode, condemnations of luxury possess a quality rare outside Gothic fiction and eschatological homilies—an eloquence of horror. Heuristic figures and flourishes abound, and the imagination is compelled to number the abominations of desolation. Frequently there is the further fascination of an author or fictional speaker extending himself to befoul that which he most ardently and most secretly covets, as in the rhetorical glory of lascivious clerics in Webster and Diderot.

The final pair of objections involve the nature of Smollett's achievement in *Humphry Clinker.* The one holds that his two decades of journalistic labor were an unfortunate distraction from his mature work as a novelist, rather than a contribution to it.[15] The other regards the novel as too much a comic tour de force to depend upon a "serious" or controversial context.[16] Both assume a series of disjunctions within his career and can be treated together. Regarding a major writer of voluminous output, literary historians usually are able to perceive that, when taken together, his different creations form a single, consistent oeuvre, one portion of which illuminates all others. But this overarching assessment has not been carried out for Smollett. Because of the obscurity of eighteenth-century controversy and his role in it, and because he did not publish an important novel between 1751 and 1771, it has generally been assumed that he had entered an arid period, writing much but accomplishing little. Contemporary readers, however, apparently had little difficulty recognizing the consistency and continuity his work possesses. They came to *Humphry Clinker* fully aware of his numerous nonfictional works of the 1750s and 1760s and of the positions he assumed during these last decades of his life. Of these decades, Herbert Read aptly notes that they were "years of the most unremitting literary labour, and to omit to reckon them in any estimate of Smollett is as though we were to ignore in Milton's case the twenty years that elapsed between *Lycidas* and *Paradise Lost.*"[17] But Smollett's contemporaries, of course, could not omit these years in their evaluation of the writer. While they may have known him as "the author of *Roderick Random,*" as the title pages of all the novels proclaimed him, they did not know him exclusively, or even primarily, as a novelist. For his fiction is but a small fraction of his total work, and at no time in his career was he a full-time novelist. Rather, they knew him as the contentious editor of the *Critical Review* and the *Briton,* the writer equally praised and damned for his histories of Europe and England, the jaundiced observer of the *Travels,* and the acidulous creator of the *Atom.* For them, as potentially for us, his authority derived from his immersion in the intellectual currents of his age: as a leading controversialist and defender of the king's causes, a man of medicine, a historian of his country, and the guiding spirit of some of the most considerable periodicals of the day. Indeed the Italian physician who visited him during his last days was informed that Smollett was a writer of "political and historical studies."

Whether hostile or favorable, contemporary estimates of Smollett's nonfiction remark upon two qualities: the ease of his narratives (i.e., his ability to shape large masses of material into a meaningful whole) and the force of his ideas. He was himself proud of the breadth of his reading and his interests and professed that he formed his opinions from "the best thoughts of our age and those of the past." It is part of his power that he genuinely believed he could absorb all of what was known to the English world of ideas. Since much of what was known was summarized by the traditional concept of luxury, Smollett could write rapidly and economically—expressing a constant theme with many variations. Like any comprehensive social concept, luxury gave him the habit and the ability to think in terms of *types* of people, *classes* of events, and *patterns* of behavior. In the histories he revealed the theme through people, events, and behavior of the past; in the periodicals, through those of the present. The habit and the ability combined to make him the eighteenth-century Aristarch of luxury. And in this respect he does far more than merely echo his time; to use Roy Fuller's phrase, he is its very ticking.

By revealing the way eighteenth-century Englishmen read *Humphry Clinker,* the contemporary reception of his last novel serves to affirm the respect Smollett's ideas received. First, the descriptive and expository portions of the novel were commonly distinguished and discussed apart from the narrative. I have located thirty-two notices published within three months of the appearance of the novel, and of these twenty-seven were devoted almost exclusively to the facts and opinions Smollett had included. Virtually all of the twenty extracts that were printed were of this kind of material and were given such titles as "The Present State of Bath," "The Present State of London," "Description of Harrigate," "A Description of Edinburgh," "Some Observations on Glasgow and Lachlomond," and "Considerations on the Union by . . . Dr. Smollett."[18] Second, these portions of the novel were seen, in the words of a reviewer for the *Universal Magazine,* as a "conduit-pipe, through which our author conveys his own real sentiments of men and things." "The work is by no means a novel or romance," the *Gentleman's Magazine* announced, "nor is it indeed principally a narration of events, but rather a miscellany containing dissertations on various subjects, exhibitions of characters, and descriptions of places." The *London Magazine* in its turn called it "a cyclopedia of opinion." The presence of two misanthropic characters notwithstanding, no reviewer doubted

that the serious opinions expressed were the author's own.[19] Third, although placed in an imaginative setting, the descriptive and expository
passages were granted as much authority as Smollett's earlier writings in
current affairs, history, and travel, seemingly because they were read as
extensions and continuations of those works. As the editors of contemporary periodicals realized and as Louis Martz has reminded us,
Humphry Clinker was frequently accepted as a fictional rendering of
The Present State of England and Scotland. John Moore, one of the
novelist's editors and closest friends, gave one kind of support to this
view when he wrote, in a memoir to the 1798 edition of the works, that
Smollett "hardly attempted any story" in his last novel, but used the
plot as "a mere vehicle for characters and remarks on life and manners." Horace Walpole provided another in his *Memoirs of the Reign of
King George the Third,* calling the book "a party novel, written by the
profligate hireling Smollett, to vindicate the Scots and cry down juries."
(*Profligate,* it should be noted, was one of Smollett's own favorite terms
of abuse.) Thackeray, one of the most sympathetic readers the novelist
has had, put the situation with admirable brevity: Smollett, he said,
"did not invent much."

Thus those readers most familiar with Smollett's previous work were
neither surprised nor disappointed to find in *Humphry Clinker* a miscellany of fiction and opinion, and no critic, friendly or harsh, had difficulty finding amid the several points of view represented in the novel
those most characteristic of the author. Such unanimity argues not
critical naivité, but the reverse. With the examples of Pope and Swift,
Fielding and Hogarth before them, eighteenth-century readers expected
a blend of general and particular satire and realized that profound moral
themes could be expressed as well through humor as through wrath. In
the *Treatise of Human Knowledge* (1739), Hume accepted the challenge
to define "what is commonly, and in a popular sense, called reason."
This he decided is "nothing but a general and a calm passion which takes
a comprehensive and distant view of its object." And what is commonly
termed "strength of mind" is actually but "the prevalence of calm passions over the violent." In a similar fashion the essential distinction
between, say, Smollett's essays in the *Critical Review* on the one hand
and *Humphry Clinker* on the other is not that the novelist had grown
less political, or had altered his social views, or had become a better
writer. Rather it is that he had gained sufficient time and favorable
circumstances to write another kind of book. We indeed know that
during the early 1760s, while he was writing for the *Critical,* he was
also gathering material that would later be incorporated into *Humphry
Clinker.* Moreover, we find in the *Critical,* the *Briton,* and the *Present
State of All Nations* anticipations of specific portions of the novel.

When Smollett gave over the exigencies of periodical journalism for travel and rest, he did not relinquish his combat with luxury. He selected new weapons.

To distinguish sharply between "the appealing humor" of *Humphry Clinker* and its "mere essay material," as many critics have done, is to create a false dichotomy, certainly one Smollett would not have permitted. For at heart the issue is one of elementary literary craftsmanship. Nearly all the humor as well as the "essay matter" is conveyed by two characters, Bramble and Jery. Smollett must convince us, as he did his original readers, that the uncle and nephew are worthy, responsible reporters of events; otherwise their humor would be as reflexive and their characters as absurd as those of Tabby and Dr. L——n (Linden). It is in fact a measure of his success that *Humphry Clinker* can be at once (as Thackeray wrote) "the most laughable story that has ever been written since the goodly art of novel-writing began" and one of the most despairing. Smollett had learned well the art of limits and balances, and the world he created in his final novel is rich and full because of the lesson.

It was as familiar a paradox to eighteenth-century critics as to those of the twentieth that fiction is often truer than philosophy. If Smollett's social and political ideas are accepted as essential elements in his creation of *Humphry Clinker,* they may still be interpreted in different ways. From a formalist point of view, they call attention not so much to themselves as to the characters and situations they animate. Fiction does not shackle its readers to a dogma from which we must later free ourselves. Rather it repeats, reorders, and reveals anew the values we already possess. A fine novel disengages us from ourselves by placing us in the midst of an assembly of fascinating characters. Ideas here must be not true, but ample, compelling, vivifying. A great novel gives not ideas to affirm, but a fullness of experience to appreciate. Against this view, a contemporary structuralist would say that most fiction, most of the time, offers an author's promise of deliberate commentary upon the phenomenal world; that Smollett—no less than Dickens, Balzac, Zola, and Richard Wright—is urging the truth of his ideas upon us. [20] To come to *Humphry Clinker* by way of his political and historical writing is, I think, to offer a way to resolve such theoretical questions. As Hardy late in his life turned in disappointment from fiction, so Smollett turned to it. Over the social reality he described in his nonfiction there was little dispute. It was there: simple, solid, and palpable. And many of his readers were repelled. But when he recreated that reality in *Humphry Clinker* they were delighted. In this last work he is among the *masters,* in Pound's sense of the term, authors who, "apart from their own inventions, are able to assimilate and co-ordinate a large number of preceding inventions . . . they either start with a core of their own and accumulate adjuncts, or they digest a vast mass of subject-matter, apply a number of known modes of expression, and succeed in pervading the whole with some special quality or some special character of their own, and bring the whole to a state of homogeneous fullness."[21]

It is no detraction, but plain fact, to observe that large portions of human existence were closed to Smollett. There was much in English life that he either missed or dismissed. Yet what he saw, he saw clearly. He was for many years preoccupied with the social, political, and literary relations of his time, and regarding these he was able to penetrate the immediate surface of mid–eighteenth-century events to a depth perhaps only a Swift could appreciate. Like Burke and Paine in their zeal a generation later, he believed he had been given special sight into the fundamental workings of human history. Gifted with such sight, he was able to create, in *Humphry Clinker* and elsewhere, a vital order of vision—what he would have called knowledge of the nature of things— that he could himself draw upon while also sharing with others. It is with questions about the nature of such an order that this study is ultimately concerned: what it sought from the Western intellectual tradition, how it accommodated change in human relationships, where it demanded continuity and where reversal and return.

Such questions encompass the whole of Smollett's later career but have special application to his last novel. In it he invested the routine, ordinary bustle of Bath, London, Edinburgh, and other places with a transcendental significance it surely did not of itself possess. Why, one may ask, did he weave into such rich and original cloth the features of a commonplace nemesis, luxury? Why is one of Smollett's voices, Bramble, so appalled by what another, Mr. S——, finds quite engaging? Why, on its surface, is *Humphry Clinker* savage, witty, silly, and tender by turns? If Walpole was just in calling it "a party novel," why has it been enjoyed by readers of all shades of political opinion across Europe and America (as editions and translations reveal it to have been)? If the early English novel as a genre offers a view of the world that is "subjective, individualistic, private," why does *Humphry Clinker* return to the objective, social, and public orientation of the classical world? If Sterne had converted English critics after 1760 to delicacy, sentiment, and amiability, why was Smollett's novel so popular a decade later? Why did so learned a man consciously reject the theories of Voltaire, Hume, Smith, Rousseau, Steuart, and others? Why in several places did he claim to perceive the collapse of British civilization in the pallor of London bread? And why does he often seem a vestige of an earlier generation of English satirists? It is on the broad middle ground of Smollett's conscious attitudes that the elements of this study converge.

Standing together, tradition, age, author, and work take on a significance each lacks when separated, and the light cast upon one illuminates all at once.[22]

Before concluding these preliminary remarks, it is necessary to return to the place of luxury in Western history. I have assumed that the concept must be approached historically, that though altered it remained strong into the nineteenth century, and that its meaning remains moot today. To examine these assumptions is to reply to one of the most profound objections ever raised against historical research, phrased thus by Samuel Johnson: "Life is surely given us for higher purposes than to gather what our ancestors have wisely thrown away, and to learn what is of no value but because it has been forgotten." In *Humphry Clinker* Smollett gives Bramble's attacks upon the luxury of Bath and London a discursive quality, a cogency growing out of immediate indignation and careful reflection—a quality familiar to readers of his earlier work. In such passages luxury is held responsible for two related kinds of disorder in contemporary England, in public life and in personal behavior. Of the first Bramble cites careless architecture and shoddy construction, narrow pavements, crowded houses, "noise, tumult, and hurry," "confusion, glare, and glitter," rampant commerce and high prices, oppressive assemblies and entertainments, vulgarization of Ranelagh and Vauxhall, great increases in the numbers of country houses, town houses, servants, black cattle, and horses, wine and tea drinking, "folly and extravagance," "fraud and sophistication," but great decreases in the total population. Of the second he notes the insolence of merchants and tradesmen and servants, debauchery of farm boys, large increases in the numbers of thieves, sharpers, and highwaymen, idleness of the poor, mixture of classes and sexes, drunkenness, "ignorance, presumption, malice, and brutality," "stupidity and corruption."

To show that Smollett's conception of luxury varies significantly from nineteenth-century usage, one need go no further than the turn of the century to find several authors for contrast. Yet for an effective contrast a later decade would be preferable, one that demonstrates that the issue of luxury had been settled and that the rough quarrels over meaning of the previous century had receded into a nostalgic past. Ideally the demonstration would involve a mid-century novelist, one with a shared sense of his society's values, and one who was nearly as fascinated by luxury as Smollett had been. Indeed either of the authors who leap to mind, Dickens and Thackeray, would serve. Thackeray is particularly apt. He was one of Smollett's greatest admirers, and his esteem for *Humphry Clinker* remains unsurpassed. A recent study of his major fiction by Barbara Hardy is entitled *The Exposure of Luxury: Radical Themes in Thackeray* (1972).[23] And his account of the age of

George III in *The Four Georges,* written in 1856, is valuable for our purposes, for it seeks to capture the flavor of Smollett's own time—re-creating it in what Thackeray assumed was its own terms. Although he was a careful reader of Smollett and acknowledged his indebtedness to him, the contrast in meaning between the two novelists is virtually complete.

The axis of the opening half of Thackeray's description is itself a studied contrast between the aristocratic culture of latter eighteenth-century England and the middle-class culture of the Victorian age. For illustrations of social life after 1760, he selects from the published letters to George Selwyn. "As one reads the Selwyn letters—as one looks at Reynolds's noble pictures illustrative of those magnificent times and voluptuous people—one almost hears the voice of the dead past. . . . How fine those ladies were, those ladies who heard and spoke such coarse jokes; how grand those gentlemen!"[24] He seeks, in his choice of adjectives, an initial sense of nostalgia that he will proceed to qualify, an atmosphere he wishes to capture in order to banish.

> I fancy that peculiar product of the past, the fine gentleman, has almost vanished off the face of the earth, and is disappearing like the beaver or the Red Indian. . . . In the days when there were fine gentlemen, Mr. Secretary Pitt's undersecretaries did not dare to sit down before him; but Mr. Pitt, in his turn, went down on his gouty knees to George II.: and when George III. spoke a few kind words to him, Lord Chatham burst into tears of reverential joy and grati-tude; so awful was the idea of the monarch, and so great the distinctions of rank. . . . At the accession of George III., the patricians were yet at the height of their good fortune. Society recognized their superiority, which they themselves pretty calmly took for granted. [Pp. 63–64][25]

Where Bramble saw only insubordination and plebeians bent upon in-sulting their betters, Thackeray perceives servility and flatterers. Reverence for the patrician world, Thackeray thinks was well-nigh uni-versal: "To Smollett, to Fielding, even, a lord was a lord: a gorgeous being with a blue ribbon, a coroneted chair, and an immense star on his bosom, to whom commoners paid reverence" (pp. 64–65). And in Selwyn he finds that world displayed in easy dishabille, "the real original men and women of fashion of the early time of George III." Inspecting a new club or abroad on the Grand Tour, at court or at home in the country, English high life compelled fascination and wonder.

Having conceded the attraction of the latter part of the eighteenth-century, Thackeray proceeds to bring it to judgment. Citing one of Selwyn's correspondents, the chaplain Dr. Varner, he finds its religion lukewarm, shallow, and politic. Citing Lord Carlisle, he finds the management of public affairs frivolous at best, corrupt at worst: "one of the English fine gentlemen who was well-nigh ruined by the awful debauchery and extravagance which prevailed in the great English society of those days. Its dissoluteness was awful" (p. 67). To Thackeray Carlisle is significant as a representative of an aristocracy rendered impotent and dissolute by luxury. "Besides the great London society of those days, there was another unacknowledged world, extravagant beyond measure, tearing about in the pursuit of pleasure; dancing, gambling, drinking, singing; meeting the real society in the public places (at Ranelaghs, Vauxhalls, and Ridottos, about which our old novelists talk so constantly), and outvying the real leaders of fashion in luxury, and splendour, and beauty" (pp. 67-68). But compared with many of his fellow patricians, Carlisle's sins of luxury were venial and temporary; he had caught the distemper of the times. "He found himself, in the midst of a dissolute society, at the head of a great fortune," was forced into luxury, suffered, and repented (pp. 68-69).

The point is clear. Although Smollett and Thackeray agree that luxury is idleness, extravagance, and dissolution in society, and both look for it at Ranelagh and Vauxhall, they disagree radically on its social locus. Thackeray leaves no doubt that luxury is a vice indigenous to the ruling classes: "If, in looking at the lives of princes, courtiers, men of rank and fashion, we must perforce depict them as idle, profligate, and criminal, we must make allowances for the rich men's failings, and recollect that, we, too, were very likely indolent and voluptuous, had we no motive for work, a mortal's natural taste for pleasure, and the daily temptation of a large income. What could a great peer, with a great castle and park, and a great fortune, do but be splendid and idle?"

> It is to the middle class we must look for the safety of England: the working educated men, away from Lord North's bribery in the senate; the good clergy not corrupted into parasites by hopes of preferment; the tradesmen rising into manly opulence; the painters pursuing their gentle calling; the men of letters in their quiet studies; these are the men whom we love and like to read of in the last age. . . . Their minds were not debauched by excess, or effeminate with luxury. [Pp. 70-71]

To Thackeray luxury is a vice of limited scope. Although a pervasive tendency among the predominant classes, it *could not* cause or account for all the many and various breaches Smollett sees. It could not, that is, cause shoddy architecture, impudence in workingmen, or an increase in robberies. Indeed on the issue of building and architecture their concepts are openly contradictory. For Thackeray, luxury would tend to produce buildings that were magnificent, grand, and fine: great wealth squandered where simplicity at less cost would have sufficed. For Smollett, in contrast, luxury produced buildings that were cheap in both senses, inexpensive as well as tawdry and inefficient, overly vulgar rather than overly refined. For the one man, luxury as a vice could not, by definition, reach down to the lower levels of English society; it was a vice of the rich. For the other, luxury had nothing to do with the idleness of a Carlisle or the sycophancy of a Varner. It could not, by definition, directly touch the behavior of royal, noble, or gentle society; it was a vice of the middling and poorer sort of Englishman. Between their respective uses of the same concept there is not only logical contradiction, but also social tension. Between 1771 and 1856 one of the basic principles for understanding the relationships within a society underwent fundamental transformation. That much is certain. Yet one is still left with the question so often asked during the eighteenth century— with irony by Mandeville, curiosity by Hume, and exasperation by Adam Smith. What does this chameleon of a concept *mean?*

Part One

A HISTORY OF MEANINGS

Luxury . . . turns men into greedy brutes. —Lycurgus,
according to Plutarch

Luxury is the source of this female insurrection.
—Cato, according to Livy

Luxury is the abandonment of nature. —Seneca

*Luxury is as the thirst of a man who has a fever . . . which is in
no degree like the thirst of a man who is in health.* —Epictetus

Luxury . . . the fount and origin of all evil. —Sallust

Luxury is slavery. —Ambrose

*   *   *   *

*. . . this ambiguous term, Luxury. There is no word more
incontantly used and capriciously applied to particular actions.*
—Warburton, The Divine Legation *(1737)*

*Luxury is a word of uncertain signification, and may be taken in a
good as well as a bad sense.* —Hume, Political Discourses *(1752)*

*Few writers, when they treat of luxury, ascertain the idea of it
in a proper manner.* —Critical Review *(1765)*

*There is scarce any subject that has been more frequently
treated by political writers than that of luxury, and yet few have
been treated in a more vague and superficial manner.*
—Monthly Review *(1772)*

NECESSITY AND HIERARCHY:
THE CLASSICAL ATTACK
UPON LUXURY

In the beginning was the Word, and for Western man the essential words of early history had the dual function of revealing God's Law and accounting for the human condition. While not the earliest source for the criticism of luxury, the story of Adam and Eve in Genesis 2–3 is a natural starting point for a survey, for it contains the simplest definition of luxury: *anything unneeded*. To understand the initial intertwining of luxury with human destiny, one must recall the elaborate Hebrew conception of history. What is distinctive to it is the conviction that it is God and not the world that is fearsome to man. Like the garden of Eden, the historical world of the Old Testament is the sacred and magnificent work of God's creation. It is Yahweh himself whom men must fear, for while he is the source of all good, he is also the source of terrible punishment. The world is but the ground upon which Yahweh works.

For the Hebrews the world is cultic and nonrational, governed only by the rules of Yahweh, the Law. The injunction to Adam is thus entirely consonant with the remainder of Mosaic Law: it is arbitrary, inviolable, and immutable. It seeks not moral perfection, but legal righteousness. It asks not choice, but obedience, for there can be no mitigating circumstance for disobedience. It is satisfied only by resignation, continually demonstrated, to the will of God. Out of this conception grew the conviction that luxury represented a changeless, eternal violation of God's Law.

The archetypal luxury of Adam and Eve involved five elements ever present thereafter. The first is the legislator, Yahweh, who defines the limits of necessity and thereby the threshold of luxury; it is an arbitrary distinction comprehensible only in terms of the will of the legislator. The second is the object of testing or temptation. In Genesis the fruit of the forbidden tree is by definition inessential to sustenence and comfort, for before it had been created "every tree that is pleasant to the sight, and good for food." It is present to fulfill not human happiness, but the conditions of the Law. Third, there is the tempter, an agent either external or internal which seeks to thwart the Law. The serpent appears as an external tempter, a force attempting to betray man's state of innocence, almost an anti-God, intent as its reason for being upon frustrating God's will.

The fourth element is imperfect human nature, incarnate as subject to the Law and victim of the tempter. Initially the sin of luxury is committed by "the woman." It is significant to all later interpretations of luxury that Adam's helpmeet is not named until after the Fall and just before the Expulsion, in Gen. 3:20. In the language describing the Fall itself (3:6) there is indication of a remarkable agreement of opinion. As much for early Jewish commentators as for the Jacobean translators of 1611 and political orators a century later, luxury is a single process: thought arousing desire impelling action. In the King James Version the process is expressed in a single sentence: "And when the woman saw that the tree was good for food, and that it was pleasant to the eyes, and a tree to be desired to make one wise, she took of the fruit thereof, and did eat, and gave also unto her husband with her; and he did eat." Punishment is the final element, a movement from enjoyment of all good things to enjoyment of few or none, a translation from arbitrary happiness to arbitrary grief.[1]

For Christian writers the lesson of Genesis was sufficient. But for the Hebrews it told merely the first half of the story of luxury. The Deuteronomic writers interpreted the Fall as an event of philosophic reconciliation, an explanation of Creation by an all-perfect God, on the one hand, and the predicament of the Israelites on the other. If no further, historical lapse into luxury had occurred, then the Israelites as a nation would have lived on earth with the same peace and security enjoyed by Adam and Eve before their violation. The Deuteronomic writers were speculating retrospectively, however, after the second great lapse and the consequent Diaspora. Recorded in the four successive books of Samuel and Kings, the latter half of the Hebrew account of the ravages of luxury is the most mordant chapter of Old Testament history and the type of subsequent devolutionary national histories, amplifying the social and political meaning of luxury: *anything to which one has no right or title.* Samuel and Kings recount the rise and fall of the nation of Israel, from the elevation of its first king to the period of infamy when a ruler of the southern kingdom would be slave to the king of Babylon. From 2 Samuel onward it is a tale of almost unrelieved calamity, six centuries of whoring after strange gods. On a deeper level, it is the story of human happiness forever squandered, a state of luxury becoming a state of accursedness. As in Genesis, only when the accursed thing has been expelled and isolated will God renew his blessing upon the Hebrews.[2]

The conflict of the whole arises at the outset, between the judgment of Samuel and the collective will of the people. Samuel has been a wise and just interpreter of the Law, but the people would throw off the rule of a moral judge in favor of a warrior king. He warns that a monarchy will subvert the Mosaic ideal of a theocratic nation in which God and God alone is the source of power, wealth, and authority. He warns, that is, that the object of testing is now the fundamental design of the Hebrew world. When the Israelites demand a king, they persist in the most serious of human errors: they yearn for something they do not need and may not claim, something that cannot profit or deliver. And when they place the power of God in the hands of an earthly ruler, it is to be expected that the ruler too will want, and take, what he does not need. With Saul begins the chain of misdeeds that decimate the ruling house, the domestic evils afflicting the monarch becoming the political evils afflicting the Israelite nation. Each of the leaders of Israel is perverted by luxury: to denial of the source of his authority, to neglect of the Lord, to unjust and unnatural wants. Saul's pride will not brook God's admonitions and impels him to apostasy, attempted assassination, and civil war. David's sense of justice is turned aside to lust and murder. Once satisfied, Amnon's desire for Tamar is transformed into disgust. Absalom's anger leads to fratricide, attempted regicide, and greater revolt. Solomon's wisdom is twisted to lechery and idolatry.

After Solomon, individuals are of less importance than the general pattern of punishment in national degeneration. From 1 Kings 12, the Deuteronomic writers present a rapid panorama of catastrophe: purges, massacres, usurpations, barbarities, and assassinations. The second fall and destruction of Jerusalem mark the physical dissolution of the nation of Israel, as the enslavement of Jehoiachin, its last king, marks the spiritual. For the royal house and the people of Israel alike, the wages of luxury are death and desolation.

Throughout these pages of moralized history the guilt of a leader of Israel comes to envelop his people: "his sin wherewith he made Israel to sin." (1) Luxury is shown to be an *active* sin. It cannot be merely avoided or ignored. Since it is rebellion against the Law, it must be confronted, conquered, eradicated. (2) Luxury is a *generic,* cardinal sin. From it follows general immorality and impiety. It is a violation of divine order, upsetting the relation not only of man to God but also of man to man. (3) Given the Jewish conception of history, luxury is necessarily a *political* crime as well as a violation of Law. By the time of Samuel and Kings it is something far more than an abstract theological vice; it is a palpable, irrational presence, a folk devil. (4) Luxury is a *national* sin, in which the folly of the people is transmitted to their leaders and then refracted in aggravated form to the nation as a body. When monarch and subject together pursue God's will, the nation is secure, satisfied, and prosperous. Yet, in an example of divine irony, when security, satisfaction, and prosperity are pursued as ends in themselves, then monarch and subject alike are devastated. Samuel's words are equally admonition and prophecy: "And turn ye not aside: for then should ye go after vain things, which cannot profit nor deliver. . . . Only fear the Lord. . . . But if ye shall still do wickedly, ye shall be consumed, both ye and your king."[3] (5) Luxury becomes associated with *original* sin. When the Hebrews move from monolatry to monotheism, the desire for luxury is transformed from a national failing to a universal one, the human malaise. Presence of this desire is taken as a sign of corruption of the whole species, and the prohibition of luxury henceforth extends to all of mankind. When the frailty transmitted from Adam reaches the kings of Israel, it destroys the nation but not itself. In obscure fashion, luxury has passed beyond the chosen people to infect the whole Gentile world as well. The Old Testament account of luxury has come full circle.[4]

Because the history of luxury is immense and complex and the purposes of this chapter are limited, it may be of use to review its elements at the outset. Already for the Hebrews the concept of luxury is what Lovejoy would call a complex idea, a fabric rather than a thread. It conveys the most decisive response possible to the human condition, a theory of entropy that explains as it describes how men, singly or collectively, lose vitality and fall from grace. For individuals it bears a theory of ethics, for nations a theory of history. Yahweh's Law is singular and establishes the moral unity of the Hebrew testament. All values are one, subsumed by obedience; the antithesis of luxury is not simplicity but obedience, the beginning and end of morality. Love is obedience. Virtue is obedience. Happiness is obedience. Freedom is obedience. Wisdom is obedience.[5] Within the Creation such unity is immutable and indivisible. But the Fall is a breaking of faith, a fracture perpetuated in the divisions that beset mankind. In retrospect the oneness of Creation can be analyzed, for with its loss came the manifold ruptures of human society. The entire raison d'être of human law, religion, and philosophy is to regain, as far as humanly possible, the harmony of Creation, to restore the principles of Necessity and Hierarchy that sustained it.

The Law of Genesis expresses the priority of natural law, antedating civil law in its founding of moral obligation within divine creation. As Aristotle, Cicero, Grotius, and Aquinas were to phrase it, natural law defines that which it is man's nature to observe. Thus it is also reason's law, plain to all rational creatures—nature's simple, universal plan. It ordains Necessity. As Necessity is made explicit by the Law, so too is Hierarchy. Eden is Yahweh's creation, not Adam's. Its perfection is that of divine plenitude, not human aspiration. Within the terms of the divine mandate Adam is free; he is free as Evangelus, steward to Pericles, is free, to enjoy the pleasures of his master's estate in the course of his duties, but not at their expense. Because he comprehends Eden, Yahweh is the legislator who determines all ramifications of the Law. Emphatically and repeatedly in Samuel and Kings, Yahweh demands submission to hierarchy; for the luxury of a secular ruler the Israelites pay with their sorrow and their children's sorrow. It was their duty to accept theocratic authority as they had accepted the bondage imposed by the Egyptians. Since all men are God's slaves, social and political relations among men are nugatory.

The Israelites fell as Adam and Eve did. They would have that for which they had no need and to which they had no claim. Luxury in the Old Testament begins in the neglect of necessity and the forgetting of one's place in the hierarchy. The Law teaches that one must be indifferent to personal and social condition. Only God's favor will ease pain, shatter physical bonds, and liberate the soul from mundane constraints. God permits the Israelites to enslave other nations and even each other; he does so to demonstrate that spiritual shackles alone are real. Hierarchy makes palpable for human understanding the unfolding of the Law. It declares who is the legislator, what is the object of testing, who is the tempter, who is subject to the Law, and how violators will be punished. Hierarchy determines, in ordinary terms, who gets what and who makes that decision. As it determines what one may covet, so it decides what one may love. The Israelites may not covet the form of government of their neighbors; a slave may not love freedom—or a free woman. Clear to all rational creatures is a natural relationship of legislator and subject, superior and inferior, master and servant.

The perfect subject of the Law is a person at one with the legislator, someone who fulfills his nature by becoming an instrument of the legislator's will. Since his nature is defined by the terms of the Law, he is the type from which particular models may be drawn: for example, the good child, wife, tradesman, soldier, servant, or slave. But the paradigm will hold merely in the abstract, in the perfection of the Law, for human nature is deficient. The attractions of luxury multiply, moreover, and the tempter grows in cunning. Because of his weakness the subject inevitably becomes the victim, first of the tempter and then of the sanctions prescribed by the Law. As luxury is the most heinous of sins, its punishment may be justly fierce, extending to enslavement and execution. In Genesis the dishonor of Ham brings perpetual bondage upon his descendants; in Kings Yahweh punishes the pride of the rulers of Israel with servitude to the Babylonians. Whether poor sinner or mighty nation, those who fall victim to the tempter will fall victim to the ineluctable Law.

Between the Hebrews and eighteenth-century England there is a demonstrable continuity in the conception of luxury—a continuity of form, the persistence of what I have called its five elements and their use in sustaining Necessity and Hierarchy. Since Englishmen inherited their sense of luxury not from the Old Testament but from classical Latin writers and the Christian church, such continuity is itself remarkable. (Historians of the language have traced the term to two Latin nouns: *luxus,* dative *luxu,* "sensuality, splendor, pomp"; and its derivative, *luxuria,* "riot, excess, extravagance."[6]) Yet it is not altogether surprising. Given the generalizing habit of moralists and jurists, often drawing upon the exact phrasing of their predecessors, the concept could remain relatively uniform over time and geography. To note this fact, however, is to distinguish between luxury as an intellectual entity and its concrete effects upon people and institutions. As slaves could not write about slavery as freely as their masters, so the subjects of the Law left far fewer records than the legislators. An important consequence is that we know much more about luxury in the abstract than we do about its influence upon people's lives. We do know enough to declare that it was never negligible. Philosophers, princes, and judges were able comfortably to shape their applications to their own ages and requirements. The power of legislators fluctuated over time, as did the type of punishment they would wield; objects of testing were construed one way by the Greeks, another by the church fathers. Spartans considered Athenians tempters, Cato suspected all Greeks, Augustine denounced Greek and Roman alike, Calvin blamed the pope. And while the injunctions of the Law might be virtually identical over three thousand years, its primary subjects could be quite diverse—from Athenian slaves and the widows of wealthy Romans to Tuscan apprentices and London merchants.

To simplify somewhat, one might say that both Smollett and Thackeray retain the Hebrew conception of luxury but apply it differently, particularly in deciding who is subject to its commands. For the significance of luxury is to be found not so much in a unique proper meaning as in the history and variety of its many meanings, a history in which inveterate elements are given a distinctive pattern in each succeeding age. Within a context of nominal identity and conservation of tradition, moralists made large changes and drew material distinctions in their application of the idea. Over centuries such changes came to express quite different and (usually) unrecognized alterations in experience and circumstance. While widely employed and universally accepted, it was kaleidoscopically fluid and demonstrably complicated, one aspect sometimes seeming to negate or contradict another. It could mean many things to many people because its content could be infinitely distended and adjusted. With such dynamic and generative possibilities, it was an idea to be used, not defined.

THE SEARCH FOR RATIONALITY IN GREECE AND ROME

The Greek view of luxury is a secular and rational complement to the Hebrew view. Luxury was as threatening to the Apollonian ideal of *sophrosyne* as to the Hebrew ideal of obedience. The Apollonian tradition exhorted men to recall that necessity and mortality set strict limits upon individuality and that pleasure and happiness were subject to the constraints of rationality. Luxury was therefore regarded as a retreat from order, a violation of harmony, and the introduction of chaos into the cosmos, preventing the individual and the community from realizing their natural ends. Theoretically, as in Hesiod's *Theogony* or Plato's *Timaeus,* luxury is an ever-present threat to the unity of the *cosmos;* concretely, as in Herodotus or the *Republic,* it is an immediate threat to the polis.

In Plato and Aristotle the temptation to luxury is described not as an anti-God seeking to frustrate the divine will, but as a constant drive of man's psychological nature. Later, in the church fathers, the two views will be joined even more closely, reconciled in the belief in both an external satanic tempter and a corrupted inner nature. For the Greeks the vice cannot be eradicated but must be suppressed. In that conviction originates the practice of defining putative instances of luxury with juridical precision, a process greatly accelerated by the Romans. Throughout the *Republic* Socrates speaks of the luxurious man as a man of mere appetite, in whom the lowest part of the soul predominates, a creature of impulse and passion unable to distinguish necessary from unnecessary desires. The luxurious man cannot be eliminated, for in the workaday world it is he who does the labor of the polis and produces the commodities essential to its existence. He can be controlled, however, by segregation, severe laws, and increased labor.[7] Punishment must be harsh, since the vice is like a disease whose contagion, particularly to those of some wealth, makes it the lethal enemy of the state.

The just and healthy state Socrates proposes—like Augustine's City of God and Hobbes's Christian Commonwealth—enforces two related principles. Man's needs are few, and incipient luxury is incipient anarchy. When Glaucon insists that the state ought provide for its citizens' wants as well as their needs, Socrates enunciates the classical Graeco-Roman indictment against luxury (2. 372c–373c). Quoted here in full (but without Glaucon's short statements of agreement), it makes plain that for Plato all men are subject to the Law and that all items of comfort and refinement are potentially dangerous; from personal adornment through warfare, the depredations of luxury are so well known that they may not only be seen but also foreseen.

> Yes, I said, now I understand: the question which you would have me consider is, not only how a State, but how a luxurious State is created; and possibly there is no harm in this, for in such a State we shall be more likely to see how justice and injustice originate. In my opinion the true and healthy constitution of the State is the one which I have described. But if you wish also to see a State at fever-heat, I have no objection. For I suspect that many will not be satisfied with the simpler way of life. They will be for adding sofas, and tables, and other furniture; also dainties, and perfumes, and incense, and courtesans, and cakes, all these not of one sort only, but in every variety; we must go beyond the necessaries of which I was at first speaking, such as houses, and clothes, and shoes: the arts of the painter and the embroiderer will have to be set in motion, and gold and ivory and all sorts of materials must be procured.
>
> Then we must enlarge our borders; for the original healthy State is no longer sufficient. Now will the city have to fill and swell with a multitude of callings which are not required by any natural want; such as the whole tribe of hunters and actors, of whom one large

class have to do with forms and colours; another will be the votaries of music—poets and their attendant train of rhapsodists, players, dancers, contractors; also makers of divers kinds of articles, including women's dresses. And we shall want more servants. Will not tutors be also in request, and nurses wet and dry, tirewomen and barbers, as well as confectioners and cooks; and swineherds, too, who were not needed and therefore had no place in the former edition of our State, but are needed now? They must not be forgotten: and there will be animals of many other kinds, if people eat them.

And living in this way we shall have much greater need of physicians than before?

And the country which was enough to support the original inhabitants will be too small now, and not enough?

Then a slice of our neighbors' lands will be wanted by us for pasture and tillage, and they will want a slice of ours, if, like ourselves, they exceed the limit of necessity, and give themselves up to the unlimited accumulation of wealth?

And so we shall go to war, Glaucon. Shall we not?

Then, without determining as yet whether war does good or harm, thus much we may affirm, that now we have discovered war to be derived from the causes which are also the causes of almost all the evils in States, private as well as public.

[Trans. Benjamin Jowett]

Here and in the memorable attack upon the luxurious quality of democracies (8. 555b ff.), Socrates poses the central question of Platonic order. Will the disordered and irrational multitude, driven by evanescent passions, be permitted to wield human destiny? Who will preserve necessity against "insolence and anarchy and prodigality and shamelessness"? Natural law furnishes the only satisfactory answer. As the body is subordinate to the mind, the appetitive part of the soul to the rational, and the servant to his master, so must subjects be ruled in all things by the guardians of the state.

The *Laws* makes yet clearer that for Plato only the intellectually superior partake of the rational and divine, possess the soul of gold, and thereby attain freedom. For the many, reckless and bewildered, the proper role is submission to the will of the virtuous guardians. It is luxury and a violation of order for a bondsman to seek freedom, a woman to rule a household, or a mechanic to govern an estate. It is luxury to seek that for which one has neither capacity nor understanding. Freedom belongs to the truly rational. All the rest is luxury.[8]

Plato's reshaping of the elements of luxury perforce affected the principles of necessity and hierarchy. To the former he added a theory of politics. If the syndrome of luxury is so plain in history, it will be as plain in the present and future. It will explain, that is, the contemporary rivalries of faction or party that erupt whenever groups seek to defend their present luxury against virtue and the law and to contend for more. To the latter he added a system of dualisms that divide humankind into those assumed to be virtuous and those whose capacity for virtue is doubtful. Thus the immediate division between the few legislators and the many subjects. Aristotle surpassed Plato not in presenting new arguments against luxury—found primarily in the *Ethics* and the *Politics,* they are elaborations of Plato—but in his specificity in defining necessity and hierarchy.

In the *Rhetoric* and the *Politics* Aristotle deduces the forms of authority from the primitive household. Nature, custom, and reason— whose union creates virtue—testify that as members of the house are subject to the father, so most persons must be subject to the dominion of the legislator. The child may wish to rule the father, but like the slave coveting freedom the desire is illusory and destructive, for he cannot govern even himself. Domestic hierarchy gives rise to social and then to political hierarchy—all from natural differences in moral-intellectual capacity. "From the hour of their birth," runs his memorable assertion in the *Politics,* "some are marked out for subjection, others for rule." To legislators he commends the arts of coercion and warfare, that they may with ease master "those who deserve to be enslaved." As contemporary legal entities, the estate and the nation are distinctive; yet they represent the kind of community where, because of economic dependence upon the master, all members are assumed to be united by common interest. And while involuntary servitude is mandatory for the wants of the community, such dependence marks a narrowness of soul and a deficiency of intellect.

For thinkers as late as Blackstone, Aristotle had established the inviolable distinctions between necessity and luxury, virtue and sin. No longer the arbitrary test of Yahweh, that distinction was seen as an a priori component of all nature. The frame of Law had been demonstrated: moral, paternal, and agrarian. The natural legislator had been identified in the man of the land whose birth, wealth, and intellect had elevated him to independence of other persons. All other human beings were subordinate to his will, which was codified in the laws of custom and the state. The ground of testing had been affirmed to be the complete spectrum of human activity. The virtue of dependent persons, necessarily of a lower and mechanical sort, was to be determined by the degree of their union with the rationality of the legislator, their ability to anticipate and satisfy his will; the most virtuous were those whose individual wills had been expunged. In the fulfillment of function lay the rationality of dependent mortals; in its neglect lay their luxury—strictly defined and rigorously punished. Aristotle's purpose was to harmonize nature and society. His accomplishment was to identify dependent persons as potentially luxurious and thus potentially subversive. His depreciation of women—that the rational part of woman's soul is impotent—is well known; among others without the deliberative faculty he placed servants, tradesmen, artisans, mechanics, freedmen, slaves; the immature, the illiterate, the weak; and such outsiders as non-citizens and foreigners. Within such groups legislators would discover the enemies of the state. At their best they might prove loyal; yet they were predisposed to be lazy, moronic, rebellious, irresponsible, and sexually dissolute.[9]

Without the explicit injunction of God that guided the Hebrews, Plato and Aristotle grounded their attack upon luxury in what they considered the universal norms of nature, which they associated with origin and birth as well as a presumptive primeval state. Paradoxically, the most thoroughgoing assault upon luxury came from men who repudiated the Platonic sense of hierarchy but extended much further the principle of necessity. Utter rejection of luxury is the foundation of Cynic, Sophist, and early Stoic philosophy, for it was regarded as the abiding impediment to self-sufficiency. Yet their adherents refuse to identify the legislator with secular power, placing it instead within the individual conscience. Unlike Plato and Aristotle, they did not assume that nature and society were—or could be—harmonized. Universal reason, they held, revealed that men of all ranks were consumed with blind craving for what they did not need—fame, wealth, possessions. It likewise revealed that extant social institutions were mere conventions or, worse, active restraints upon individual liberty. Philosophical dissidents, they sought truth and freedom in independent reason and independent conduct. Distinctions between old and young, male and female, rich and poor, citizen and alien were but accidental and superficial, irrelevant to the true principles of natural law. Every person might gain rational freedom from the passion and prejudice of luxury, at least from the omnivorous desire for things. Diogenes said that the true slaves of the world were everywhere to be seen walking free, men in rich robes enslaved by fleeting desires; things were their masters; things alone were self-sufficient. In the world they observed about them, Antisthenes, Crates, Zeno, Diogenes Laërtius, Chrysippus, and Panaetius saw the great majority of men enfeebled by luxury, a multitude that, lacking moral discipline, could not conceivably achieve virtue and rationality. Hence they regarded luxury as even more pervasive than did Plato and Aristotle. And while they rejected the philosophical validity of hierarchy, they accepted it as being as ubiquitous as ignorance. Putting the case more forcefully, Diogenes held that slavery was a tolerable convention so long as neither master nor slave was depraved by the relationship. He and the others taught individual, not social, reformation; toward society they taught indifference. They provided the perspective for uncovering luxury in *every* man, even the most exalted legislator; for the Roman historians' search for national decadence; for the joining of Hebrew and Christian social teachings; and for the intellectual theme we have come to call primitivism.[10]

From the middle Stoa of Panaetius through the late Stoa of Seneca, Greek philosophy was adapted to the practical ends of Roman statesmen and soldiers; so modified, it was the first postulate of countless Roman attacks upon luxury. Seneca himself, while elaborating the doctrine that the soul cannot be diminished by external circumstance, certainly seeks a practical civic virtue different from Zeno's social disdain. Luxury he terms the abandonment of nature, a perversion of both personality and politics that age by age has been growing stronger in Rome. Upon the nation it is like acid, dissolving the natural bonds that form men into a community and turning them from mutual fellowship to mutual plunder. In his own time he sees men slashing and bruising each other not over essentials but over luxuries. Intellect has been made slave of vice.[11] In the pseudo-Senecan pastiche *Octavia*, the Senecan indictment of the present is given mythic elaboration as the writer joins history, politics, and philosophy in his description of the birth of luxury. The character Seneca has described the Golden Age, the intermediage ages, and has now come to his own time.

> But another breed less gentle then appeared. A third race arose, cunning in new arts, yet holy. Soon came a restless race which dared pursue the wild beasts in the chase, to draw out fishes in nets or by the light rod from their hiding places in the waters, to catch birds, or with wicker stockades to fence in the fat cattle, to master fierce bulls by subjecting them to the yoke, to dig the earth, until then immune, with the wounding plough, earth who hid her fruits deep in her sacred womb. But this degenerate age dug into its mother's bowels; it dragged forth heavy iron and gold, and soon armed its savage hands. Boundaries marked out divided kingdoms, and new cities were built. Men defended their root-trees with their own weapons, or, threatening plunder, invaded the dwellings of other men. Astraea the Virgin, great glory of the stars, neglected, fled from the earth and the savage ways of men and hands polluted by gory slaughter. Desire for war grew and hunger for gold. Throughout the whole world the greatest evil arose, luxury, an

alluring plague, to which the long lapse of time and grievous error gave strength and power. All these many vices, heaped up through long ages, now overflow on us. We are crushed beneath the heavy burden of an age in which crime rules, mad impiety rages, violent lust dominates in shameful love, and triumphant luxury has long since seized the huge wealth of the world with greedy hands, only to lose it. But lo! with thundering step and savage countenance Nero comes. I shudder in my mind at what he may bring.

[Trans. Lovejoy and Boas]

Like Seneca and most Roman moralists, Cicero assumed that the origin and nature of luxury had been established beyond dispute. It was understood, yet for generations it had been allowed to spread unabated. What was wanted was not more analysis but more rhetoric, of the kind that compels effective law and public administration. Cicero is remarkable for the sheer volume of his calls for suppression of luxury and for his dexterity in applying diverse arguments to contemporary conditions in Rome. He is as willing as Seneca to censure the luxury of the mighty, at least among his political adversaries. And his debt to the Stoics is everywhere visible in his demands for thrift, self-denial, sobriety, and simplicity. He writes, for instance, in *Pro Roscio Amerino:* "The city creates luxury, from which avarice inevitably springs, while from avarice audacity breaks forth, the source of all crimes and misdeeds. On the other hand, this country life . . . teaches thrift, carefulness, and justice" (27, trans. John Henry Freese). But his sense of simplicity is less that of Diogenes of Sinope than Trimalchio of the *Satyricon*. In *De officiis* he attempts to define the qualities of the good life and feels the need to distinguish the various occupations available to the man seeking it (1.150–51).[12] He immediately dismisses money-lending and the collection of harbor taxes, then all labor for wages, since the wage is a warrant of slavery. All crafts and most trades are too mean. (He specifies fishmongers, butchers, cooks, poulterers, fishermen, dancers, and music-hall performers, but does not mention miners or servants; these are too mean even to dismiss.) He calls teaching, medicine, and architecture reputable occupations, for they call for some intellect and "are respectable for those whose status they befit." Domestic trade is mean, foreign is reputable. "But of all things from which one may acquire [wealth], none is better than agriculture, none more fruitful, none sweeter, none more fitting for a free man."[13]

What this passage suggests is that Cicero's denunciation of urban luxury and praise of rural austerity are in large part rhetorical conventions. *De officiis* belongs to a tradition running from Xenophon's *Oikonomikos* in the fourth century B.C.—and including Cato's *De agri cultura*, Varro's *Rerum rusticarum*, Columella's *De re rustica*—to Charlemagne's ninth-century *De villis* capitulary. No more than Cicero does any of these champions of agriculture concern himself with the specific tasks or techniques of farming. Like many other scourges of urban luxury—Seneca, Sallust, Apuleius, Atticus—they are very wealthy men, of the class Defoe in his *Tour* would have called Great: not farmers, but masters or managers or gentlemen farmers. For them agriculture means the ownership of land—the best possible occupation since it entails no occupation at all. For them and their followers in eighteenth-century England—like Pope, Swift, Bolingbroke, Fielding, and Smollett's Matthew Bramble—occupational categories are not (in the modern sense) economic, but moral. The rustic, virtuous simplicity Cicero commends is not a life of frugal fare and rigorous toil. It is a life of comfortable leisure, free from labor. It is the mean who must labor and labor meanly.[14]

Cicero represents one of the Roman contributions to the history of luxury, the impulse to purge the disorder—by draconian legislation if necessary—from every phase of Roman life, a practical approach that preoccupied most European nations until the middle of the eighteenth century. The wit and invective of the literary attacks by Horace and Juvenal represent another.[15] In the most important, historians of the late Republic treated luxury not as object but as subject, discovering in it an essential, causative factor in the narrative of national calamity they were obliged to impart. They were telling again the Deuteronomic story of national disaster without resort to divine intervention and recasting the plot of *Octavia* with specific dates, events, and persons; and they were searching in accounts of the confusion of the second century B.C. for the origins of first-century corruption. The result was an account that has fascinated readers to the present day and that indelibly linked luxury to the demise of republican greatness. Of all the moralists Sallust was the most systematic and highly reputed. To the younger Seneca, Martial, and Tacitus, Sallust was the foremost of the Roman historians, a classic and a model. Jerome and Augustine revered him as much as they did Cicero and Vergil. Erasmus recommended his work over that of Livy and Tacitus, Milton called him a sublime moralist, Johnson praised him as "the great master of nature," Arthur Murphy and others provided fresh eighteenth-century translations. In the wealthier parishes of London, historically minded clergymen made his name a commonplace.[16]

Roman history as Sallust viewed it took on an immediately visible pattern, and as identifiable as the pattern of the whole was the line of degeneration into *luxus* and *luxuria*. Described in the prologues to *Bellum Catilinae* and *Bellum Jugurthinum*, Sallust's thesis can be briefly stated. Rome prospered when it possessed *virtus* and sought *gloria.* This, the ancient way, kept the Republic secure as well as virtuous, but was undermined about the time of the destruction of Carthage.[17] The event marked the advent of *luxus,* which brought with it ambition, pride, avarice, and luxury, and these in turn overwhelmed justice, honesty, industry, and sobriety. In the *Catilinae* itself he outlines the major events. Rome was founded when a disparate and contentious mob was transformed into a group of citizens by the action of *concordia.* Kings ruled the city until they fell victim to the lust of domination. With their expulsion and the establishment of the Republic, Rome enjoyed a long era of *virtus* and *concordia maxima,* an era that ended with the sacking of Carthage. Avarice was then preeminent until the furthest stage of corruption, that of *luxuria,* was reached in the age of Sulla. Luxury was brought to Rome from Asia by Sulla's returning army, and in a short time it consumed the city, leaving little of the old values and bringing the Republic, in Sallust's own day, to the edge of moral, social, and political ruin. In the interim, Rome was filled with every species of vicious luxury, a city fit only for a Catiline. In the *Jugurthinum* he elaborates upon certain of these elements, particularly the role of party politics. Both parties, the *nobiles* and the *populus,* craved luxury, but the appetites of the aristocrats were insatiable and their superior resources gave them the instruments of oppression: the luxury of the few enforcing the poverty of the many and private opulence standing alongside public indigence.[18]

From the time of Sallust through the life of Macrobius in the fifth century after Christ, historians of Rome were to give luxury a causative role in the tale of republican decline. Although they do not agree on its dating, the historians are virtually unanimous that a moral crisis of profound significance occurred during the second century B.C.[19] For Sallust, *luxuria* appears comparatively late, but for most writers its appearance was the beginning of the process of devolution. In the annalistic tradition represented by Livy, luxury enters the bloodstream of Rome with the return of a victorious army from Asia in 187 B.C., as the material wealth and luxurious debauchery it brings with it form *luxuriae peregrinae origo* and *semina futurae luxuriae.* As Shakespeare's Romans see Antony corrupted by Egypt and eighteenth-century moralists were to see the decadence of France as the wellspring of luxury, so the Roman historians looked to the rankness of the East as the source of national ills. Livy marks the spread of luxury in the city itself with a long oration by Cato against the extravagance of women, many of whom were demanding the repeal of several sumptuary laws. To capitulate to the demands, Cato declaims, would be to allow the passions to rule over reason, to abandon masculinity, and to relinquish proper subordination in society—themes to be reiterated for the next eighteen centuries. For Plutarch too, Cato is a model of the upright Roman legislator, as Lycurgus is of the Spartan. Both had used eloquence and legal sanctions to combat a national disease; Lycurgus was successful; Cato, given the virulence within Rome, could not be.

Tacitus uses senatorial debates in the *Annals* to disclose how corruption reached the highest precincts of the Republic. He describes with contempt how the *nobiles* maneuver to write laws that will not apply to themselves and reports the argument of their spokesman, the infamous Gallus Asinius:

> In household establishments, and plate, and in whatever was provided for use, there was neither excess nor parsimony except in relation to the fortune of the possessor. A distinction had been made in the assessments of Senators and knights, not because they differed naturally, but that the superiority of the one class in places in the theatre, in rank and in honour, might be also maintained in everything else which insured mental repose and bodily recreation, unless indeed men in the highest position were to undergo more anxieties and more dangers, and to be at the same time deprived of all solace under those anxieties and dangers.
>
> [2, trans. Alfred John Church and William Jackson Brodribb]

This argument, turning upside down Socrates' reasoning in the *Republic,* so enrages one senator, Lucius Piso, that he will endure no more. The city is so replete with luxury, Piso declares, that it is no longer fit for the habitation of honest men (precisely the charge to be brought later against Bath and London). Luxury is daily corrupting the courts, bribing the judges, and hiring false witnesses. For him the only honorable option is to fly to a distant retreat.[20] When Tacitus summarizes the course of luxury from Tiberius through Vespasian, he introduces a note of generosity unusual among Roman moralists and anticipates Hume's comments in 1752 upon the progress of English commerce and the "new men" of the middle order. The passion for luxury was not exhausted, Tacitus notes, until large numbers of great families were themselves exhausted. "The new men who were often admitted into the Senate from the towns, colonies and even the provinces, introduced their household thrift, and though many of them by good luck or energy attained an old age of wealth, still their former tastes remained." Also anticipating Hume is his vague optimism (as rare among writers of the late Republic as among those of the earlier eighteenth century) and his unwillingness to concede all to the ancient position: "possibly there is in all things a kind of cycle, and there may be moral revolutions just as there are changes of seasons. Nor was everything better in the past, but our own age too has produced many specimens of excellence and culture for posterity to imitate."[21]

CHRISTIANITY: SYNTHESIS AND ACCOMMODATION

One of the first lessons Augustine seeks to teach in the *City of God* is that prosperity begets luxury and then avarice, and to that end he cites Sallust (at great length), Seneca, Cicero, Aristotle, and Plato. In the writings of the church fathers from the second century onward, the ravages of luxury recounted by the Roman historians are stated as indisputable fact and often cited seriatim. The Stoics held that all men possessed the inner resources to lift themselves from the mire of worldly things; yet in calling attention to the discrepancy between the capacity of the whole and the achievement of the very few, they raised more questions than they tried to answer. For Christians the answers were present throughout the Gospels, as when Jesus asserts that freedom lies in bondage to the Lord (John 8:31–35). The practical clarity of this position makes it more than a restatement of the Stoic paradox. All men are by nature enslaved, yet all men have the choice of master—God or mammon. Bondage is inescapable, but it may be the ennobling kind that brings redemption or the luxurious kind that brings corruption. Like Moses, Jesus places the legislator beyond individual consciousness; for him the Law is fixed and immutable and antedates human creation. Whereas the Stoics generally see the natural man as virtuous and free of social contamination, Jesus sees him as a slave to luxury, a sinner. For Hebrews and Christians alike, that is, the alternative to luxury is not Stoic primitivism, but obedience. As Paul wrote, the sinner seeks freedom from righteousness, while the saint seeks bondage to righteousness (Rom. 6:15–23). Or as a seventeenth-century Christian has Abdiel express it,

Unjustly thou deprav'st it with the name
Of *Servitude* to serve whom God ordains,
Or Nature; God and Nature bid the same,
When he who rules is worthiest, and excells
Them whom he governs. This is servitude,
To serve th' unwise, or him who hath rebell'd
Against his worthier, as thine now serve thee,
Thy self not free, but to thy self enthrall'd.

[*Paradise Lost*, 6.174–81]

A distinction there is, but it lies elsewhere. In the books of the Old

Testament and the Apocrypha—especially Samuel, Kings, Proverbs, Job, Ecclesiastes, Ecclesiasticus, and the Wisdom of Solomon—the motive for the renunciation of luxury is adherence to God's will, not denial of self. In the New Testament, however, this distinction is not maintained. When Jesus calls the disciples, "whosoever will come after me, let him deny himself, and take up his cross, and follow me" (Mark 8:34), he is yoking the negative message of self-abnegation to the positive one of obedience. The Evangelists often repeat the double injunction (e.g., Matt. 10:38, John 12:25) and on occasion advocate the abandonment of all material possessions (Matt. 19:21, Mark 10:28, Luke 9:57–62) and perpetual chastity (Matt. 19:12). To the Deuteronomic writers, earthly prosperity flows upon the Israelites as a direct consequence of their righteousness. To the Evangelists earthly reward is needless and even suspect.[22] The former treat luxury as a threat to the destiny of the Israelite nation as a whole, using it as a theory of history; the latter regard it as the curse of individual souls—a theory of ethics. Perfect virtue and freedom come only in absolute conformity to the will of the Lord. Neither king nor serf can slip God's shackles. What the Christian emphasis and synthesis does effectively, Lecky has observed, is to raise the moral stature of servitude. For the Greeks and Romans, servility was synonomous with vice; for Christians, fidelity, humility, obedience, and resignation are among the cardinal virtues.[23]

About necessity, therefore, early Christians were as stringent as Diogenes, about hierarchy as respectful as Aristotle. And to recognize that Christianity absorbed the classical attack upon luxury is, in effect, to understand why the concept seemed so vital for so long to European moralists. The Christian virtues were essential in service to God and valuable in service to temporal authority. The early Christians demanded revolution in spiritual aspiration, not in social hierarchy. Because all men were brothers in Christ, secular status was of no moment. In God's plan one man's temporal condition was no better—or worse—than another's, and a herdsman could be as devout a servant of the Lord as a king. Christian faith was one thing, material dependence another; no tension need exist between the two realms so long as the dependent believer served his master "as unto Christ."[24]

Given the teachings of the New Testament, then, luxury was *ex hypothesi* condemned by the leaders of the early church; given their preoccupation with individual morality, it was often associated with physical self-indulgence. Yet in noting this preoccupation, one must also recall that *luxuria* was never simply a minor taint but was the seed of all vices of the will and the flesh. Tertullian delivered a scathing denunciation of the luxury of his age in the *Apology,* and in *De cultu feminarum* analyzed "this vice of women," the source of corruption and effeminacy. Clement of Alexandria in the *Paedagogus* and Origen in the *Exhortation to Martyrdom* cite and use Stoic ideas in arguing that the denial of all forms of luxury is a needful preliminary step in the purification of the soul, an element of spiritual psychology much elaborated in the third century. In the *De officiis ministrorum*, Ambrose asserts with Epictetus that a luxurious man is not really a man, but a slave to vice and anxiety. And it was to become a central teaching of the Fathers of the Desert and the founders of monasticism in the fourth century. All the major figures argue that virtue is confined to no station. Clement and Augustine indeed maintain that the rich are more liable to luxury, for their wealth allows them to exercise their inherent vanity and sensuality. Since all of the secular realm is subject to the injunctions of the Law, the poverty and distress of the lowly may be viewed as valuable discipline of the spirit.[25]

In the *City of God* appear what came to be regarded as the definitive patristic condemnations of luxury, accepted without apparent reservation by Albert, Aquinas, and Bonaventure in the thirteenth century. Augustine was of two minds about luxury, and Christian Europe through the Renaissance generally preserved the different but related views he proposed. On the one hand, he did more than any other early Christian writer to keep alive and vivid the classical Platonic and Stoic condemnations.[26] In turn, Christian theologians, political theorists, and legislators would cite him as the source of their belief that the appearance of luxury signaled the onset of the death fever of civilization. The *City of God* is his treatise against the vice, inasmuch as it rules the enemy, the earthly city. While the heavenly city has put off the old man and put on the new, the earthly city continues its wicked and licentious course. The implication is that Christians must learn well "the calamities which befell Rome and its subject provinces" through luxury and impiety. In the opening five books he rehearses the decline of Rome and other ancient kingdoms. Book 1.30, entitled ''That those who complain of Christianity really desire to live without restraint in shameful luxury,'' is in essence a paraphrase of Sallust, arguing that contemporary pagans threatened the Christian world as sottish libertines did Neronian Rome.

First concord was weakened, and destroyed by fierce and bloody seditions; then followed, by a concatenation of baleful causes, civil wars, which brought in their train such massacres, such bloodshed, such lawless and cruel proscription and plunder, that those Romans who, in the days of their virtue, had expected injury only at the hands of their enemies, now that their virtue was lost suffered greater cruelties at the hand of their fellow-citizens. [Trans. Marcus Dods]

A "nation corrupted by avarice and luxury" is a nation mired in original sin, where tyranny and injustice are commonplace (1.30). Yet even where luxury reigns, the Christian can free himself; misery and submission expiate as well as manifest sin. Even where unjust, hierarchy can act as a check upon the crooked wills of the dissolute. No man may complain of utter injustice, he remarks, for no man is utterly innocent (19.15).

On the other hand, Augustine was absorbed with the proselytizing mission of the young church and came to stress luxury as the carnal lust of individual men—a lust that could be fought successfully only through the divine grace dispensed by the church. In consonance with earlier patristic emphasis upon the ideals of virginity and asceticism, he subsumes the meanings of *luxus* under those of *luxuria* and uses the latter to mean individual self-indulgence in general and lechery in particular. In the *Confessions,* the *Homilies,* and the later parts of the *City of God,* he concentrates not on the political effects of luxury but on the psychological. Especially in books 9 through 14 of the *City of God,* he recasts the Stoic psychology of luxury in Christian form. In the life of Jesus, he declares, Christians have found the perfect model of renunciation. A man must be judged by what he loves. The upright man loves God, but the luxurious man pledges all his love, his desire, and his energy to the world. Luxurious man is spurred by vain ambition and by concupiscence of the eyes and the flesh. He is fallen man, a worldly man; his punishment for disobedience to God is disobedience to himself. Since he has willed *not* to do what he could do, he now wills to do what he cannot. He has fallen, indeed, to the level of the beasts.[27]

The age of Augustine in all likelihood marks the time when the condemnation of luxury became practically universal in Western Europe. With a partial shift in emphasis to the personal, the classical attack had been embraced by the church and its secular instruments. Luxury was no longer a sin of abhorrent kind, as it had been for the Hebrews, but was remade into one of abhorrent degree, loathsome yet still pardonable through the offices of the church. Something vivid and concrete, it was no longer the concern, primarily, of the educated, but was brought into the daily lives of ordinary Christians. Although there were several others, the main popular vehicles were the soul drama and the deadly sins, depicted together or independently.[28] The pattern of the soul drama, as described by Samuel Chew, is relatively consistent. Man has forfeited immortality through Sin and must pass into the World of Time, ruled by Fortune. Here he will be faced with the Two Paths. If he chooses aright the strait and narrow, he will be beset by the Deadly Sins but will also gain the assistance of the Cardinal Virtues. At the end of his journey-struggle he will confront Death; yet with the courage of purity in his heart he will realize he is about to enter the City of God. According to Morton Bloomfield, the allegory arose from the homilies, late apocrypha, Latin poetry, and Prudentius; it passed over into the visual arts, and about the time of Aquinas into vernacular literature, dramatic and nondramatic. It is to be found, for instance, in most of the morality plays, Huon de Mari's *Le tournoiment de l'Antichrist,* Chaucer, Langland, Alanus's *Anticlaudianus,* and the *Cursor mundi.* Later versions appear in Spenser, Cervantes, Bunyan, and Goethe. A secularized variant is present in eighteenth-century fiction, certainly in the stories of Bramble, Jery, Humphry, and Lismahago in *Humphry Clinker,* in varying degrees in *Moll Flanders, Pamela, Clarissa, Joseph Andrews, Tom Jones, Amelia, Rasselas,* and the Gothics.

The soul drama motif suggests that early Christianity accepted the Hebrew view of Eve's Fall as a single process, then analyzed that unity into the infernal trinity and again into the seven (or more) deadly sins. From the Fall came, in Chaucer's rendering of 1 John 2:16, "the thre enemys of mankinde, that is to syn, the Flessche, the Feend, and the World," and thereafter the group usually composed of Luxuria, Superbia, Avarita, Gula, Ira, Accidia, and Invidia. That is, by the Middle Ages Christian writers had not only made luxury as familiar and repugnant as a folk devil, they had also rendered it virtually omnipresent. In its pilgrimage the soul must encounter luxury in three forms. In the beginning it is the cause of the primal Fall. Then it is the fundamental carnality that unites the world, the flesh, and the devil against God's Law. Augustine, Gregory the Great, and Aquinas all agree that luxury can be seen as: (1) the visible sign of the presence or activity of the devil, (2) the comprehensive sin of humanity and the worldly state, and (3) the devil's strongest type of temptation, which binds the flesh to the world and thereby to himself. And finally it is among the most formidable of the mortal sins. In iconographic terms the three forms of luxury came to be represented by three figures: Eve, Worldly Temptation (or Fleshly Pleasure), and, in her own garb, Dame Luxury. Furthermore, Dame Luxury threatens the pilgrim soul not once but at least twice, for it is vulnerable to her charm at two stages of life, in youth, when the delights of the flesh are most insistent; and later in maturity, when worldly power is most attractive. This presumed vulnerability of youth is of course very influential in the careers of most of the young men in English literature, but has particular application to such eighteenth-century figures as Lovelace, Joseph Andrews, Tom Jones, Rory Random, Pery Pickle, Rasselas, Humphry Clinker, and Jery Melford.

In the vast amount of literary and visual material dealing with the soul drama and the deadly sins, spanning 1,500 years, there is naturally little uniformity in many things. The ages of man depicted in the drama vary from three to twelve. The name, number, and position of the sins often change from writer to writer, illustrator to illustrator, century to century. About luxury, nevertheless, there is an arresting degree of agreement. In the early lists of cardinal sins influenced by John Cassian, luxury is usually placed first, regarded as primary in the sense of generative. Later ones, probably derived from Gregory the Great, place it last and refer to it as the ultimate sin, the culmination of all others. The lists also often switch the places of luxury and pride. When luxury is put first, pride is last and vice versa, suggesting a dread circularity of luxury evolving into pride and pride manifesting itself in luxury. And while it is usually identified with physical lust, it is often used by learned writers to stand for lust in figurative senses. Thus they often associate *luxuria* with lust for revenge, lust for worldly goods belonging to others, and lust to retain material possessions. In such instances the sin of luxury encompasses wrath, envy, avarice, and pride, as well as lechery. A popular parallel is revealed in didactic retellings of the Fall, with Eve guilty of pride, Adam of lechery, wrath, envy, and avarice all together.

There is moreover more consistency in the personification of luxury than with any other chief sin. With the major exception of the *Faerie Queene,* almost all personifications of luxury are feminine. Prudentius in the *Psychomachia* depicts Luxuria as a beautiful woman astride a splendid chariot. She has perfumed hair, graceful and languishing airs; her car is made of gold, silver, and precious stones. In her train come Amor, Jocus, and Petulantia. Unlike the other vices, she enters battle unarmed, violets and rose petals her only defense; and against her alone the virtues seem confused. At last Sobrietas steps in front of the chariot with the sign of the cross, the horses rear, the car upsets, and Luxuria falls groveling in the mire, to be killed by Sobrietas with a single blow.[29] Thereafter the portrayal of Luxuria as a lustful woman is continued in Jean de Meun, Langland, Dante, and Chaucer. In *Doctor Faustus*, Marlowe makes luxury the only female sin. The personification became a favorite device of Romanesque sculptors in the south of France and was carried over to the great Gothic cathedrals of France, Germany, and England, and later, in a figure by Cellini, into the ducal palace of Venice. In early illustrations of the *Roman de la rose,* as in the windows of Notre Dame, Chartres, and Amiens, she appears carrying the comb and mirror of cupidity and self-love; in some places she also holds a scepter to mark her omnipotence and sexual domination over men. Elsewhere she is less attractive. In the churches of Toulouse, Moissac, and Braisne, she is a nude figure being attacked at breasts and genitals by snakes or toads. In some illustrations she is a semidraped figure exuding sulfur to kindle the flames of delight. As though the point required underscoring, several medieval and early Renaissance depictions carry beneath the name a subtitle, "The Power of Woman." Some combination of these types was to remain in the visual arts through the Renaissance.[30]

Medieval theological speculation is brought to a climax with Aquinas. Taking Augustine's teaching as his ground, he provides an analysis of luxury that is narrow but deep, the most thorough examination of luxury as sin before the eighteenth century. Like the Roman jurists, Aquinas is a consolidator, and in retrospect the decisive point is that he does unify, rather than diminish, neglect, or deny. He was not in Augustine's position, impelled to accommodate the political structure of the Roman world. For now the church was itself powerful, and its teaching was always potentially subversive of the classical suppositions about necessity and hierarchy. Did it not preach the equality of all men under God, and the existence of a world of spirit in which all men were free? Slavery was gradually disappearing in western Europe, moreover, and some of the most brutal forms of subjugation were being ameliorated. The repeated eruption of egalitarian—and heretical—sects demonstrated that some Christians were accepting as literal the fraternal teaching of the church. Why then did not the egalitarian ideal of Christianity overmaster its previous practical compromises? David Brion Davis's study of slavery suggests some answers. The first is the potent legacy of two millennia that associated luxury with original sin and divinely conceived necessity and hierarchy. Second, to challenge the traditional conception of luxury would be to question fundamental Christian postulates about God's purpose and man's nature. For if luxury was to be accepted or redefined, then why had God enjoined it in Scripture and every nation enjoined it in law? If the attack upon luxury did not possess a divine function and instead violated a natural law of equality or a divine law of brotherhood, then whence the authority of state, legislator, landowner, and social arbiter? The tensions within Christianity are many and complex. It is enough here to note that for several centuries after Aquinas they were held in conservative equilibrium.[31]

Far from denying them, Aquinas emphatically reasserts the traditional principles of necessity and hierarchy. He argues that original sin is to be understood as luxury, the penchant for needless, temporal things. Once tainted, Adam and Eve and all subsequent parents transmit the sin to their children as a genetic predisposition for sensuality. (Aquinas thus retains Augustine's union of metaphysical and physical luxury while seeming to distinguish them; only with Adam and Eve is the distinction philosophically or historically meaningful.) Luxury is the enemy of chastity, for in contrast to the chaste man, the luxurious man is unable to contain his passion for self-aggrandizement, especially his sexual desires. He is precisely dissolute, for luxury leads to a general dissolution of personality. Having sinned against reason, he eventually loses his reason and intelligence, and reality is lost, hidden by blinding desire. And as the luxurious man has lost reason, so too he begins to lose will. He becomes rash, headstrong, and quarrelsome. Since he is closed to religious joy and the pursuits of the spirit, only the gross and the foolish have power to move him. In its most advanced form, luxury entails sin not only against reason, but also against nature. This stage, which might be termed the Neronian, culminates in bestiality, unnatural acts, and setting oneself in opposition to God who has ordained the nature of things.[32]

Perceiving the true nature of things, the godly man transcends worldly needs in order to find fulfillment in God, to recognize his place in the harmony of divine creation. And for Aquinas the plenitude of creation represents a monumental series of progressive hierarchies rising to several classes of angels in heaven. Before the Fall man was unfettered, but now he is obliged to preserve his proper place and function. The rationality of creation is manifest in plenitude and gradation, human rationality in recognizing an eternally fixed order of being. Luxury would undermine that order and disrupt the rational processes of nature (1.2.71–82, 96). To higher authority the Christian relinquishes both his will and his body. Regarding luxury, then, Aquinas is more Augustinian than Augustine and brings the patristic and scholastic traditions into essential accord. It was to be an important union, augmenting the church's concern for matters of individual morality and sexuality, while reaffirming her involvement in the governance of public affairs. It is reflected in the works of Boethius, Berchorius, Thomas à Kempis, Guido Faba, and Robert Holcot, and not altered in any significant way by either Luther or Calvin.

The major writers of the English Renaissance for the most part retain the medieval emphasis upon lust in their use of the term. Spenser writes of "lustfull luxurie and thriftless wast," Marlowe of "unchaste luxury." Webster has Ferdinand address the Duchess of Malfi: "Marry? they are most luxurious / Will wed twice."[33] A principal villain of Tourneur's *Revenger's Tragedy* is the young lecher—whose "heat is such were there as many concubines as ladies he would not be contained"—named Lussurioso. Almost all of Shakespeare's sixty or so uses of the term are in lascivious contexts, as in "he most burnt in heart-wish'd luxury," and "She knows the heat of a luxurious bed." In *Henry V* Pistol calls a French soldier a "damned and luxurious mountain goat"; in *Hamlet* the ghost terms Gertrude's bed a "couch for luxury and damned incest."[34] Probably the most memorable of Shakespearean uses is Lear's cry of despair:

> Let copulation thrive; for Gloucester's bastard son
> Was kinder to his father than my daughters
> Got 'tween the lawful sheets.
> To't, luxury, pell-mell, for I lack soldiers.   [4.6][35]

In other seventeenth-century poets, however, luxury is connected less exclusively with lust and more with all the deadly sins together. Donne in the second Satyre writes of the lawyer "spying heires melting with luxurie, / Satan will not joy at their sinnes, as hee." Milton, returning to Old Testament and Roman sources, returns also to their associations. Using the story from the book of Samuel, he has luxury appear in the wake of Belial,

>   who fill'd
> With lust and violence the house of God.
> In Courts and Palaces he also Reigns
> And in luxurious Cities, where the noise
> Of riot ascends above thir loftiest Tow'rs,
> And injury and outrage.   [PL, 1.495–500]

Book 4 of *Paradise Regained* contains Christ's denunciation of the Romans, a once virtuous people, "just, frugal, and mild, and temperate." Now they are guilty of

>   lust and rapine; first ambitious grown
> Of triumph, that insulting vanity;
> Then cruel, by thir sports to blood inur'd
> Of fighting beasts, and men to beasts expos'd
> Luxurious by thir wealth, and greedier still,
> And from the daily Scene effeminate.   [4.137–42][36]

SOME THEORETICAL AMBIGUITIES

The narrowly physical aspect of the concept—the "foule lust of luxurie" of Chaucer, Spenser, and Shakespeare—was not one that eighteenth-century writers chose to emphasize. For reasons to be adduced in the next chapter, their sense of luxury was more Roman than scholastic. As for Smollett, at no point in his writings from 1756 have I been able to discover an exclusive identification of luxury with lechery. Bramble acknowledges without remorse that he has left bastard children scattered about England and Wales. And while Smollett did see Britain menaced by the forces of luxury, lechery was not numbered in their lists. However, the survival of medieval attitudes into the sixteenth, seventeenth, and even eighteenth centuries does indicate something of the protean—not to say colossal—quality of the vice and does explain the readiness with which ordinary Englishmen came to associate it with base and ignoble human conduct. The 1707 edition of *Glossographia Anglicana Nova* indeed gave "carnal Pleasure" as the basic definition of the word. More learned or abstract associations might escape them, but from ballad or sermon they knew what they knew.

This brief survey serves to indicate part of what Englishmen in the early eighteenth century "knew" about luxury. Since all of the nuclear ideas included in that conception had been present long before the birth of Christ, its continuing and growing place in European thought might be accounted for in different ways. From the point of view of stern moralists, the charge of luxury was the most incisive criticism that could be directed against Western civilization. But on a more popular level, the idea was a *crambe repetita* for writers of varying and conflicting interests. In either case luxury had become a fluid and complex concept in which moral, religious, economic, and political attitudes were mixed into a vague and sometimes contradictory amalgam. From at least Cato onward, writers had devoted much attention to elaboration, little to definition. Assuming that their readers knew what luxury meant, they could begin their discussions with what was essentially a conclusion. Such a beginning, in turn, logically precluded any neutral or value-free discussion. Thus conventional usage demanded that when the issue of luxury arose it was for rhetorical or polemical purposes—to be denounced as sin and as a matter of course.

These assumptions and conventions can be reduced to three interrelated suppositions about the nature of luxury. In the first place, the pursuit of luxury, however considered, was viewed as a fundamental and generic vice from which other, subordinate vices would ensue. In the Old Testament, where it is equated with disobedience to God, it is *the* cardinal sin of the Israelites. In Plato and Aristotle, the Cynics and the Stoics, it is the first and most important violation of nature and reason. For the Roman historians, it is the primary factor in the dissolution of the Republic. For the Christian theologians, it is prima facie evidence of both disobedience to God and love of a degraded world. For all of these systems, from the Hebrews through the Protestants, luxury represents the starting point of historical or philosophical speculation. In ethical systems it is an index of human sinfulness and moral or intellectual deficiency, calling forth the requirement for inner regeneration and self-surrender. In the social realm it is an index of chaos and irrationality in the workings of public affairs, calling forth the demand for order, discipline, authority, and hierarchy (and, implicitly, self-surrender and self-sacrifice). All of these theories, moreover, make luxury a generic vice in another sense, using some metaphor like contagion to describe the movement of its corruption from the one to the many. When it strikes a man, it has the fatal power to dissolve his character and to destroy his estate—that is, his social position and financial well-being. When it has struck a sufficient number of individuals, luxury will sap a nation's economic and military strength and subsequently bring down the nation itself.

Second, while the vicious nature of luxury was regarded as immutable, its manifestations were viewed as virtually infinite. One way to explain this assumption is to assert with Diogenes that the objects of man's illicit desires are numberless. Each change in station or fashion or aspiration brings a concomitant set of new wants. Indeed on the level of simple desire all men are equally rich, bound only by the capacity of their imaginations. Another explanation is that few writers distinguished nicely between cause and effect, between a disposition toward luxury and the manifest consequences of that disposition. Socrates hypothesizes a luxurious man accumulating wealth and material goods, then banding together with others of his kind in order to preserve and extend his possessions. When completed, the process would encompass social division, economic competition, political corruption, war, rapine, and conquest. And at each stage of this series, Socrates seems to see luxury—not simply its operation. For Sallust, the rich spoils taken by Sulla's army are luxurious, as are the diverse uses to which that booty is put. Gilt swords, ivory daggers, and purple robes are luxuries, but so equally are drunkenness, prostitution, and pederasty. To Suetonius practically everything Nero touched turned to luxury, from costly rings to fair-haired boys. Augustine and Aquinas speak of physical lust as luxury at least as often as they do the more general trait of self-indulgence. Yet another explanation is that many writers included, on occasion, items of their own dislike or disapproval in their castigation of luxury. Diogenes had no use for baths, Seneca for cold drinks, Cato for the laughter of slaves. Less obvious but possible examples might be the frivolous dress Socrates sought to banish, the intellectual pertness of women that offended Cicero, the speech and manners of the patricians that repelled Sallust and Tacitus. What is certain, amid these possibilities, is that each of the major critics of luxury believed that in his own time its manifestations were increasing at an accelerated rate.

Third, to explain the relative absence of information about many native American tribes, some cultural anthropologists have proposed that happy people leave no history. If the obverse is also true, that unhappy people readily chronicle their woes, then the concept of luxury reveals a history of deep and bitter division. Throughout Western history men have called upon tradition to account for the terrors and surprises of the unknown and the irrational. For Hebrews and Christians the Fall became a cogent symbol of the corruption of mankind, and the major Greek philosophers agreed that not all men and not all of nature were subject to the order of reason. Roman writers frequently referred to their world as an *urbs deis hominibusque communis*—a household common to gods, men, beasts, all living things—yet they too felt required to explain why this household was often in open rebellion against itself. At virtually every point in the history surveyed here some figure could be found to warn that his society was in danger of degenerating into barbarism or hardening into tyranny. When a people or its leaders felt themselves the victims of misfortune they regularly saw in luxury the enemy that caused it. Ancient writers describe three main types of crisis: divine anger, political disturbance, and natural catastrophe. Luxury was interpreted as the direct source of the first two, and to the extent that a writer like Herodotus or Augustine would see in a plague, drought, or military defeat the sign of God's wrath, then it would account for all forms of disaster. Luxury was thus an absolute, a natural reflex of mind that could explain the new, the dissonant, the disturbing. The very durability of the concept suggests that it was psychologically satisfying, consolidating while it was dividing.

Luxury readily accommodated, even encouraged, belief in a historical division of mankind into a virtuous "we" standing against a luxurious "they." In a psychological sense, it *proved* the existence of lower, corrupted, imperfect humanity, whether called Gentile, pagan, plebeian, heterodox, or damned. In this vague sense of abhorrence and negation, luxury is akin to insanity as described by Michel Foucault in *Madness and Civilization,* to heresy in Frederick Heer's *Intellectual History of Europe* and *God's First Love,* to savagery as treated by the authors of *The Wild Man Within,* to racial inferiority as studied by Winthrop D. Jordan, Roy Harvey Pearce, Gary B. Nash, and others. Each of these concepts has a distinct history, and there are probably as many differences among them as similarities. Yet all represent conditions of almost universal reprobation among all strata of society. All stand for persons, thoughts, and behavior that have been branded as unacceptable. Individually and collectively, all represent "the Other"—that which is beyond the pale.[37]

Like insanity, heresy, and savagery, luxury was probably an idea born of psychological necessity. The men who defined it did so in order to describe the unspeakable, to classify the abhorrent, to name the vile. One might say it was named specifically to be abhorred. It provided its users with a powerful measure of self-worth, for it identified all they *were not*. It thus became a mode of self-justification and, by negation, of self-definition. There were of course other ancient theories of entropy, such as that of the Book of Esdras: "So you too must consider that you are smaller in stature than those who were before you, and those who come after you will be smaller than you, for the creation is already growing old . . . and past the strength of youth" (2 Esdras 5:54–56). But these comprehend a universal condition allowing no exceptions. Luxury, on the other hand, permitted Tobias Smollett, like thousands of moralists before him, to declare in effect, "A perfect man I am not, but assuredly I will not countenance luxury in any of its forms." Ordinary Europeans even might not be able to say precisely what made them good or normal or frugal or orthodox citizens, yet they could at least testify that they were not luxurious.

Foucault's *Madness* supplies an apt analogue, with one significant difference. Laws could not easily be drawn to prevent or punish insanity, but certainly were so drawn regarding luxury. The mere existence of such legislation indeed ensured that a great proportion of Europeans would consciously consider, if not fear it. It evolved into a concept difficult to ignore with impunity. In practical political terms perhaps the closer parallel would be heresy. Although there is no military campaign against luxury to compare to the wars of the Reformation, it is certain that men and women were ostracized, fined, beaten, imprisoned, and executed for instances of alleged luxury. Such punishments do not equal any single act of war, yet over centuries they were as deadly.

The concept of luxury can be seen as much as a cluster of symbols as it can as a cluster of ideas, sustaining one type of code while rejecting another. Augustine could admit the strength and attraction of the earthly city, yet be certain of its doom. God punishes the luxurious. The ruling groups of societies as distant as those of Israel in the eighth century B.C. and England in the eighteenth century A.D. alike tried to exercise their authority by convincing the majority that only they possessed the possible and legitimate means of satisfying human needs; all other methods were luxurious, anathema.

SUMPTUARY LAWS AND THE POLITICAL CONVERGENCE

In retrospect, the issue of luxury seems to have been almost perpetually surrounded by controversy. Part of that history of dispute can be traced, as we have seen, to logical or theoretical ambiguity. Yet perhaps a larger part derived from *practical* ambiguity. All the philosophical systems or theories noted thus far have taken as self-evident man's pursuit of pleasure and satisfaction; the most rigid Stoic admitted that, in the world he saw about him, every man was as luxurious as he was able to be. The condemnation of luxury was therefore an admonition that touched everyone. To recall Voltaire, although all men condemned luxury, all men practiced it. How could this contradiction be resolved in the everyday world of men?[38]

The practical answer to the inconsistency of precept and practice was government intervention. Because luxury had always been regarded as a primary threat to the state, the state was obliged to defend itself through sumptuary laws and similar measures. The institutes of Lycurgus, Solon, and Demosthenes are far from being the earliest, and such legislation absorbed the attention of the English Parliament as much as it did the Roman Senate. Two consequences flow from government regulation of luxury. It brought the concept from the empyrean of philosophy, theology, and abstract ideas down to the forum of institutions, politics, and power. In that forum, so ruled by compromise, there evolved a tacit double standard regarding what actually was luxury. Legislators in general drew a sharp distinction between the immoral and illegal lust for false wealth and station that corrupted men and nations, on the one hand, and the natural and admirable expression of position and self-interest that produced genuine value, on the other. In theory all men were subject to the prohibitions of luxury; in reality persons of authority were free to do as they pleased. To the philosophers as well as to the powerful, the contradiction was illusory. For man in his primal state was vicious, a slave to his passions, and thus of necessity subject to the laws of state and church. As Aristotle had put it, "No man can practice virtue who is living the life of a mechanic or laborer." The cultivated man, refined by wealth and education, could be assumed to be virtuous, hence subject to no authority other than his God or his conscience. While Epictetus, himself once a slave, argued that women and the young needed protection against luxury, the Senate actually drafted laws protecting the state against women and young people. Whereas Seneca wrote eloquently of the corruptions of wealth, many rich senators united to combat the luxury of the poor. The rabble was the greatest threat to the empire, these senators held, for, lacking everything, it coveted everything; not freedom or possessions but the lack of them signaled luxury. Had Seneca written the sumptuary laws, all men might have been in jeopardy; but, as Tacitus shows, the laws were actually made by the kind of men Seneca most distrusted. Seneca's own life was hardly the perfect expression of Stoic virtue. First tutor then advisor to Nero, he accumulated a vast fortune through political "gifts" and usury. A longtime opponent, Publius Suilius, attacked him publicly as a "hypocrite, an adulterer, and a wanton, a man who denounces courtiers and never leaves the palace; who denounces luxury, and displays 500 dining tables of cedar and ivory; who denounces wealth, and sucks the provinces dry by usury." Two monarchs renowned in their own times for extraordinary enforcement of laws against luxury were Nero and Louis XIV; they were vigorously opposed to the luxury *of others.* And Sallust, the arch-foe of extravagance, was known to his contemporaries as a man who had become immensely wealthy in politics and had then built himself a living monument, the *horti Sallustiani,* which would be coveted by Nero, Vespasian, Nerva, and Aurelian. Like many great contradictions, those enveloping the control of luxury could be absorbed into a higher unity: wise and virtuous authority ruling the irrational forces of the world. The aversion to luxury inherited by the eighteenth century had been incorporated into not only one or two, but the whole range of Western institutions.

Seldom can the historian of a seemingly lost world of ideas point to thousands of palpable monuments to its once incontestable vitality. Yet the plethora of European laws drawn to combat luxury represents just that, standing to the concept of luxury as, say, the Linear B tablets do to Mycenaean Greece. They are available, what is more, in abundance for almost every age and region of Europe from archaic Greece to industrial England. Despite their virtual ubiquity, they have been little studied and are often referred to as minor, paternalistic regulations of dress and spending.[39] A mere glance at the history of sumptuary legislation, however, discloses that they are certainly much more than that. All the moralists surveyed thus far attacked luxury in order to preserve their measure of necessity and hierarchy. Granting the negative quality of such attacks and the negative thou-shalt-not quality of Western law, the major philosophers were perforce de facto lawgivers.[40]

Fundamental to every attack has been the statement of the Law, and over three thousand years there was little disagreement over the general features of that Law. Xenophon's *Oikonomikos* is a useful gloss on the way Greek statutes incorporated those features. The sort of work standing between the richness of Socratic dialogues and the bleakness of legal codes, it is amateur philosophy, a collation of platitudes that would be unexceptionable to its audience—gentlemen landowners like its author— the type of what I have called the legislator, for whom ethics, politics, economics, and farm management are indissoluably one. Xenophon holds as a fact of nature that the good life is the free life and that, to obtain the freedom to which he is entitled, the legislator must cultivate the practical art of governing his inferiors, those who labor in his behalf. Right to the good life is certainly his; yet to reap its fruits he must carefully train and manage his slaves, servants, children, and wives. The *Oikonomikos* bore for centuries the reputation of a charming and reliable conduct book, telling clear truth clearly. It was cited admiringly by Plato and Aristotle, translated by Cicero and others, and quoted often by eighteenth-century philosophers like Francis Hutchinson (and sometimes by men who were truly interested in the techniques of farming, like Jethro Tull and Arthur Young). Smollett gives Xenophon's view of natural law clear voice in *Humphry Clinker* through one of his most sympathetic characters, one who will himself become a gentleman farmer, when Lismahago says he hopes he shall "never see the common people lifted out of that sphere for which they were intended by nature and the course of things."

With Xenophon, Greek writers equated citizenship and its attendant rights with the ownership of land, and the Romans certainly elaborated the equation. Most people in antiquity lived off the land; for the few who were owners this meant no labor; for the many, incessant labor. As the philosophers deduced the sources of moral and material good from the land, the legislators framed laws that would ensure full enjoyment of that good. Since such mundane burdens as taxes drastically limited the enjoyment of landowners, the law allowed them to pass the burden on to their dependents. The possession of wealth and status carried with it the right to preserve wealth and status.

By the very arbitrariness of his injunction, Yahweh sought to create order out of Law. Seeking rationality, the Greeks and Romans reversed the process, attempting to create Law out of the social order. The model of civil polity became agrarian, paternal, and hierarchical. Politically the nation was associated with the hierarchy of the household, economically with that of the estate. At its apex were the all-powerful masters, those who possessed the land, *potestas, manus,* and *dominium,* who according to Aristotle were economically independent and hence truly free; all other persons were inferior and dependent. Masters were ordained for political rule, for only they were free to pursue other than basic, physical needs. Their birth granted independence, their education confirmed it. From independence flowed leisure, which led to responsibility for government, a central function of which was to ensure that the great majority of persons remained dependent and continued to perform the essential and involuntary labor that sustained the legislators' independence.

Founded upon slavery and other forms of involuntary servitude, the economy of the ancient world gave rise to a society of orders and status. P. A. Brunt has observed that in Rome this hierarchical structure was even more aggravated by continued warfare, with its concomitants of conscription, confiscation, and ever more harsh and demanding laws.[41]

Indeed several of the most comprehensive Greek and Roman sumptuary codes were enacted after the outbreak of war and retained when the fighting ceased—thus accumulating crisis upon crisis. They could be enacted quickly and retained permanently because they were directed against those traditionally regarded as dissolute, unpatriotic, and un-reliable—specifically those groups, that is, who were excluded from government. In the context of universal history, M. I. Finley calls compulsory labor the norm, not the exception. To understand a society founded upon legally defined status, Finley recommends the metaphor of a spectrum, but one that removes the polar extremes of total free-dom and total lack of freedom. Between the two extremes falls the range represented by ancient Greece and Rome, where status and rights were defined simultaneously.

> A person possesses or lacks rights, privileges, claims and duties in many respects: he may be free to retain the surplus of his labour after payment of dues, rents and taxes, but not free to choose the nature and place of his work or his domicile; he may be free to select his occupation but not his place of work; he may have certain civil rights but no political rights; he may have political rights but no property rights so long as he is . . . *in potestate;* he may or may not have the right (or obligation) of military service, at his own or public expense; and so on. The combination of these rights, or lack of them, determines a man's place in the spectrum, which is, of course, not to be understood as a mathematical continuum, but as a more metaphorical, discontinuous spectrum, with gaps here, heavier concentrations there.[42]

Although intended to clarify the societies of Greece and Rome, Finley's metaphor does much to bring clarity to all the European sumptuary laws accumulated over three thousand years. They may be national, as in England and France; municipal, as in the cities of Germany and Switzerland; written into published ordinances; discretionary, upon the judgment of monarch or ruling council; enforced by secular govern-ment or by the church or by both together.[43] Yet all are designed to effect the legislators' sense of necessity and hierarchy, to place all subjects within the spectrum. More concretely, all are designed to ob-tain by coercion a person's labor (or service or property) and proper conduct; and further, to establish by law some form of social and psychological discrimination among groups of people.

To ancient legislators the model of a properly ordered society was what it was for Xenophon: a great estate, where it was assumed that only persons of the same goals and values were admitted and where status was patent and fixed by type of labor. Here tempters, strangers, interlopers, and foreigners could be easily excluded. Here value for all could be dictated from above, by the master. The worst kind of place by this standard would be one where tempters were many and diverse, where the population was heterogeneous and (in the sociologist's sense) unintegrated, and where goals, values, and masters were various. In short, a city. Keeping workers on the land was the first function of the laws; the second was controlling social behavior in places without the hierarchy of farm labor—the market towns and the cities. At the latter the obvious badges of farm labor would be missing or cunningly disguised, and subversive persons—artisans, mechanics, servants, women, and young people—might congregate in numbers. Hence the gravity of laws defining status and costume in Athens and Rome and later in Genoa, Venice, Paris—and London.

Jurists assumed that the lower orders were tempted with ease and with ease turned tempters themselves. With Aristotle they held that the lower forms of humankind corrupt the higher and must therefore be classified and separated. From this assumption followed the immense profusion of legal terms required to define status. To cite but a tiny fraction: there would be substantial differences in the quality of life among the *ptochos,* the *penēs,* and the *plousios* in Greece; the *sclavii, adscripticii, vasii, coliberti, coceti, servi,* and *coloni* in Rome; and the slaves, villeins, serfs, clients, agents, tenants, debt-bondsmen, and vassals in medieval Europe. In death there was segregation; a Roman law of the second century B.C. ordered the maintenance of separate common ditches for burial of the lowly. For the living multitude many outward signs of status were available: identification tablets, shorn heads, uniforms, brands, tattoos, and bonds (for foot, ankle, wrist, or neck). Although dress and outward marks were the most common devices for designating status, less visible means were as numerous and important, including the ability to enter apprenticeship and a guild, to travel or reside in a parish, to use weapons, to marry across status lines or to marry at all, to rear one's children, to enter into a contract, to appear before a magistrate, and so on.[44] To select an example from the Christian era, Gratian in the fourth century declared that any servant or slave charging his master with a crime (other than high treason) would be burned alive regardless of the validity of the accusation.[45]

Such legislation was viewed as a simple means to a very difficult end. Trying to persuade the lower orders to restrain their desires was as futile as trying logical argument upon imbeciles. A single law properly drawn, however, could impose discipline upon people who would otherwise have been ruled by impulse to fleeting gratification. It could assign a man to a specific kind of labor, regulate his general conduct, and visibly fix his status. To the legislator it conserved necessity and hierarchy and was humane as well as useful. It permitted his subjects to exercise their own peculiar form of virtue, the fulfillment of an assigned function. Subjects had no independent sensibility, philosophers and jurists concurred, for the whole of their beings was predicated upon the use the legislator had for them. Everything not mandatory, it could be assumed, was forbidden.

Subjects to the law could be regarded as things—the slave is merely the extreme example—who possessed no rights, no family, no name even unless granted one by the legislator.[46] In their elaborate codes the Romans were consolidating systematically the practice of many earlier societies when they defined the position of laborers. They merely made explicit what the Greeks and Hebrews took for granted: a dependent laborer is not free *not* to enter the work force, and once in it is not free to withdraw. When the empire was dissolved, its legal influence was maintained through the concrete institutions of servitude—in England, for example, through the continuance of large-scale slavery until the thirteenth century. It was reasserted in written form once French jurists recovered the Justinian Code and became the basis for Bracton's work, the poor laws, for villenage, and for feudal law generally.[47] Sumptuary legislation drawn specifically to meet English conditions dates from the fourteenth century, and significant extensions occurred during each succeeding century. Major codification of existing laws came in 1463, further legislation was passed in 1533, and the Act of Precedence —which sealed the social order in law as if in amber—followed in 1539.[48] The culmination of these efforts was the act known commonly as the Statute of Artificers of 1563. With it Parliament sought to preserve England, socially and economically, as a permanently agrarian nation, enjoining persons who sold their labor from shifting from one trade to another (the seven years' apprenticeship already enforced in some trades was made mandatory for all), one district to another, one social order to another, and one kind of apparel to another.[49]

The Statute of Artificers, to look no earlier, suggests that the legal means devised to maintain necessity and hierarchy were becoming as complicated as their ends. It was not especially hard for legislators to translate the agrarian ideal of Xenophon, Aristotle, and Cicero into the juridical matrix of feudal Europe. But it was another thing altogether to hold an altered economy within those legal bounds. English law attempted to keep laborers on the land even when feudal service was economically obsolete. By the sixteenth century villenage had largely given way to rents, contracts, and monetary payments, yet the law continued to add circumstances—that is, crimes—for which a man could be placed in bondage for the rest of his life. The tensions that resulted were present well into the eighteenth century. Landowners who entered into contracts with laborers were among the legislators who prohibited such agreements; legislators became divided amongst themselves, and individual legislators were divided between their practice and their principles. Subjects too were thus divided between the growing number with indulgences and those without. Bolingbroke attempted to reduce the chance for division with the Landed Qualification Act of 1711, proposing that no man represent a shire in the House of Commons unless he held land in annual value of £600, or, for a borough, £300. Then the laws themselves seemed to require closer guarding and greater severity. Beyond church and Parliament, surveillance and enforcement were in the hands of mayors, baliffs, sheriffs, aldermen, justices of the peace, and committees of selected citizens. The number of offenses against property classed as capital quadrupled during the eighteenth century, from about fifty to more than two hundred. The Waltham Black Act of 1723 not only provided capital punishment for vandals, poachers, and the like, but also encouraged landowners to supply their own punishment in the form of mantraps and spring guns. According to Leon Radzinowicz, the measure standing alone constituted a complete criminal code: "There is hardly a criminal act which did not come within the provisions of the Black Act; offences against public order, against the administration of criminal justice, against property, against the person, malicious injuries to property of varying degree—all came under this statute and all were punishable by death."[50] By one count Radzinowicz finds 50 distinct offenses punishable by death under the act; by another, stricter interpretation (which takes in accessories, second and third principals, etc.), he discovers between 200 and 250. Men like Pope, Swift, Fielding, Goldsmith, Smollett, Boswell, and many others reviled the movement of laborers away from the land and called for more laws to keep them put. What we can see in retrospect is that legislators were not lax, that laws did what they could to preserve the sanctity of the country estate.

Subjects to the sumptuary laws included all persons whose labor was required or whose dependence was undenied. While all were burdened, women were triply so. Because natural law was interpreted as barring them from office as legislators, they were necessarily reduced to subject-victims. When by chance a woman like Elizabeth was elevated to the role of legislator, the anomaly was explicable in terms of a male legislator's requirements of inheritance. The law first stipulated their dependence, irrespective of birth, fortune, or education, then regulated their conduct according to sex and again according to status. Aristotle's contempt for feminine reasoning had already been codified in classical Greece. Early Athenian law prohibited the erection of memorial steles to women, and Solon in the sixth century B.C. promulgated laws controlling their walks, dress, food, drink, and holidays; he established the conditions under which women were allowed to marry and approved the sale into slavery of a ward or daughter not a virgin. Demetrius in the fourth century B.C. followed Aristotle's advice directly and founded boards of "regulators of women," men who would censor all aspects of feminine conduct. The Oppian law (215 B.C.) confiscated for the state virtually all the wealth held by Roman women. It restricted to one-half ounce the amount of gold a married woman could hold and expropriated all the wealth of wards, widows, and single women. Roman law determined what woman was fit to ride in a chariot, on a horse, a pack animal, an ass, or not to ride at all. (English law followed suit, distinguishing among the honorable, gentle, worthy, and several orders below common; for each respective order was mandated length and material of coat and dress, number of flounces, width of lace, length of shoe points, height of bonnet, and so on.)[51] In Greek and Roman law women were regarded as a national resource, to be specially cultivated like the land during periods of war and natural calamity. Reasons of state dictated if and when women might marry or remarry and bear children; only during times of war were citizens legally required to rear their daughters, an obligation never relaxed regarding sons. Graeco-Roman sumptuary codes also enforced the principles of woman as "in-house slave," *partus sequitur ventrem,* and feminine incapacity for public affairs.[52] From early Christianity came an ambivalent conception of woman: holy–threatening, passive–active, AVE–EVA. Mary was to be honored, but the ordinary daughter of Eve was another case, Chrysostom in the fourth century calling her a "necessary evil, a natural temptation, a desirable calamity, a domestic peril, a deadly fascination and a painted ill." Aquinas said that woman could legitimately be considered "defective and misbegotten," for she produces the mere matter of humanity while man produces the essential form, and that, moreover, she was not part of the original creation, having been generated not from divine material but at one remove, from Adam. And in a sermon preached before Elizabeth, Bishop John Aylmer described woman as "in every way doltified with the dregs of the devil's dunghill."[53]

The preservation of sumptuary legislation into the Christian era was but the outward sign of Christian acceptance of the attack upon luxury. No less than the Deuteronomic writers, Aristotle, or Seneca, the church fathers wished to impose virtue upon the recalcitrant masses. In the Old Testament the concept of luxury formed an implicit link between spiritual discipline and social control. The decision in favor of a warrior-king is unwise both religiously and politically. It alters not only the moral atmosphere of Israel but also its mode of government. In the classical Greek and Roman authors the connection between religious and secular realms is made explicit, and after the novel synthesis of the New Testament that connection would remain fast for nearly 1,800 years. Plato, Critias, Isocrates, Polybius, Scaevola, Varro, Cicero, Livy, and Vergil were among the many thinkers who, although themselves skeptics, argued that religious dogma must be maintained in order to control the masses. In the *Republic* Socrates defends the habit of rulers' "lying for the public good." In the *Histories* Polybius argues that the fickle and violent multitude can be held in check only by the piety and terror of religion devised by the rulers of the state, a religion that, while without a claim to truth, would be politically useful. Luxury allied patriotism with religious devotion and cloaked the management of the multitude in the worship of Mars, Jupiter, and Minerva.[54]

As a social issue, luxury is no less blatant within the Christian era, and no less effective. With its emphasis upon the universal but individual nature of sin, early church theology could decry all men as sinners yet honor extant social distinctions.[55] Even without such accommodation, there need be no philosophical contradiction between moral absolutism and legal-political relativism. For Greek and Roman philosophers as well as Christian theologians found means to come to terms with the imperfections of the world. For many of the Cynics and Stoics, the state of the present world had degenerated irretrievably from some earlier condition, usually identified with the Golden Age. For Tertullian, Augustine, and Aquinas, the nature of fallen man rendered his works inevitably degraded. From the perspective of either the Golden Age or the City of God, that is, human history and human society were of course fatally flawed. Luxury could no more be eliminated than could mortality. On the level of doctrine, therefore, pagan and Christian alike taught a kind of indifference to history and society that amounted to silent toleration of luxury. True freedom involved self-transcendence and disengagement from one's immediate environment. The world meanwhile could be expected to continue its guilty course, and the men in charge of secular affairs could not be expected to be any better than they had ever been.[56]

On the level of concrete, day-to-day existence, moreover, still more direct compromises with the world became prudent. As the Christian church survived the presumptive millennium and saw the need to accommodate itself to a sturdy world, it came to accept the institutions of the state as valuable instruments for doing God's work and extending its own influence into secular affairs.[57] Several studies have revealed that on many issues church and state of the Middle Ages moved to a relationship not of mere accommodation but of mutual support and encouragement. Luxury was the hub of such agreement, for the concept could be made to comprehend any sort of behavior—social, political, economic, or moral—that seemed to undermine the authority of the present order. The church, on its side, devoted increasing attention to canon laws that served to reinforce extant civil legislation, as in the protection of property (including slaves) and the stipulation of status. Civil government gradually but increasingly assumed some of the moral functions and proscriptions of the church, as in the prosecution of "victimless crimes" such as profuse spending, drunkenness, swearing, and gambling. Together they evolved the doctrine of "consumption by estates" under which standards of conduct and comfort were fixed according to social rank; liberty and magnificence were reserved for the highest rank but prohibited to all others, and so on down the great chain of social being. Until the nineteenth century it was customary for sumptuary laws to be read from the pulpit in every church at least once a year—a daunting task, since ordinances regarding dress alone often ran more than one hundred duodecimo pages. Until the Reformation the legislation against luxury enacted by secular European governments was administered by ecclesiastical courts (on the Continent called consistories); thereafter the clergy retained several places on the court. In seventeenth-century Germany and Switzerland the courts were called *Reformations-Kammer* or *Reformations-Rath*.[58] The reformation intended by such bodies was not of theology but of morals and conduct, and when influential men in London, many clergymen included, decided that the sumptuary laws were being neglected, they formed in 1692 a Society for the Reformation of Manners that became the model for similar societies begun in other cities throughout the eighteenth century. A parallel organization explicitly uniting the church with the call for stronger sumptuary codes was established in 1698 (and flourishes today) as the Society for Promoting Christian Knowledge. The Society for the Reformation of Manners did not attempt to police the whole spectrum of luxuries or even the whole of southeast England. Nevertheless, it claimed responsibility for 91,899 arrests by 1725.[59]

A final example: in the 1590s, while Shakespeare was using luxury as a synonym for lechery, civil and ecclesiastical leaders were maintaining its widest application. In June of 1592 the bishop of London and various other church officials joined the lord mayor and council of London to condemn the riotous and luxurious behavior of apprentices at the playhouses. Boys and young men were temporarily forbidden the right of free assembly, and the Rose was closed for three months. A similar reaction occurred in the summer of 1595, when the London price of certain staples, including eggs and butter, doubled and often more than doubled. When the young and the poor protested violently, church and state again cried out in one voice against luxury and insolence. Prices remained high, martial law was invoked, and those agitators who could be found were hanged, then drawn and quartered on Tower Hill.[60] Englishmen of the eighteenth century owed their understanding of luxury more to the bishop and lord mayor of London than to Chaucer or Shakespeare. Like religious and secular authorities 160 years earlier, Smollett and his contemporaries came to fear the discontented mass of the London poor. Particularly when spurred by allegedly unscrupulous politicians, the poor seemed always on the brink of collective insurrection. They seemed to represent a potent threat to property and status and that nexus of political power implicit in the ownership of property. Such was the protean inner logic of an idea used to decry the barbarities of a Nero that it could be brought to bear, at the height of England's quest for empire, upon the poorest of the poor.

Two

LEGISLATORS DIVIDED:
THE ATTACK UPON LUXURY
IN THE EIGHTEENTH CENTURY

*Every society has a right to preserve public peace and order, and
therefore has a good right to prohibit the propagation of opinions
which have a dangerous tendency . . . no member of a society
has a right to teach any doctrine contrary to what society
holds to be true.—Samuel Johnson*

When Smollett's type of the natural legislator, Matthew Bramble, revisits several English cities after long absence in Monmouthshire, he is shocked to discover how deeply luxury has eroded the habits, manners, and institutions of Old England. In London he finds the management of public affairs in the hands of base and incompetent men, the result, he says, of "luxury and corruption"; he thereupon advances the proposition that all institutions arranged in a "democratical form" will soon "degenerate into cabal and corruption." In Bath and again in the metropolis he is jostled and insulted, cheated and confounded by tradesmen and their wives and by common people who are surly, insolent, and restless in their station; all of which he terms the working of "luxury and insubordination." At the end of his travels, Bramble observes that these related forms of luxury have turned the natural order in England upside down.

The subversion of necessity and hierarchy in government and every-day life—corruption and insubordination, in contemporary shorthand—which so exercises Bramble in a novel of 1771 had outraged writers throughout the earlier part of the century and became, for readers with appetite enough, the weekly fare of those common rooms of public philosophy, the political papers and pamphlets. Corruption of the civil polity was the incandescent charge brought in almost every number of the *Craftsman*. In one example, the pseudonymous editor Caleb d'Anvers rehearses the parlous state of English affairs, then draws an ominous parallel: "This was the Case of the *Roman Common-wealth* of old, and of others of much later Date. Luxury and Profuseness led the Way to Indigence and Effeminacy; which prepared the Minds of the People for Corruption; and Corruption for Subjection; as they have con-stantly succeeded one another, and will do so again, in the same Circumstances, in all Countries, and in all Ages" (no. 56 [29 July 1727], 2:73). Later d'Anvers turns from history to fable to draw his moral, describing a dream-visit to an island Edenic in its native liberty and prosperity. As long as its inhabitants can remember, d'Anvers learns, the island has been happy and fruitful. Then suddenly, a dark tree shoots forth, grows with amazing velocity, and envelopes the entire land in the shadow of its branches. "I saw it put forth a vast Quantity of beautiful Fruit, which glitter'd like burnish'd Gold, and hung in large Clusters on every Bough. I now perceived it to be the Tree of Corrup-tion, which bears a very near Resemblance to the *Tree of Knowledge,* in the Garden of *Eden,* for whoever tasted the Fruit of it, lost his Integrity and fell, like *Adam,* from the *State of Innocence*" (no. 297 [25 March 1732], 9:53). The fruit of corruption bears inscriptions that identify it with the national debt, stockjobbing, and the moneyed companies. An obese little man perched in the tree tosses the poisoned fruit into the crowd, which is beguiled, then sickened with the new diet. Soon the island is fouled and blighted, and no healthful food remains. From the once-happy island now arises a general lamentation, relieved only by the sinister chortle of the fat man and his minions.

Attacks upon the intransigence of the common people became com-mon about mid-century and found their way even into the pages of relatively nonpolitical periodicals like the *Gentleman's Magazine.* During the autumn and winter of 1757–58, for example, the *Gentleman's* carried a heated and lengthy series of letters from members of the provincial gentry. With more vigor than was usual in the regular letters column, they wrote of their indignation at the crimes committed in their shires and towns by the forces of luxury. Various as their complaints were, they agreed that the laboring poor had become so licentious as to be no longer manageable. When, for the major example, the price of common grain had been increased, large numbers of laborers had refused to pay the new price or to buy an inferior grade. After demanding a return to the previous level of prices and being refused, many laborers rioted. Food riots, sporadic but common in the summer of 1757, provided landowners with what seemed to them cogent instances of the depravity of the times. Their letters summarize popular notions of luxury in the 1750s and indicate how easily disparate events could be explained by a single concept. One of the most revealing of the letters assumes that the evil forces have been condemned sufficiently, but that practical action has been lacking. Printed under the heading "The Mob Must be Conquered," it argues that, unless the luxury of "the lower sorts of people" is suppressed, Britons will lose the property, "laws, religion, and natural blessings of our country."[1]

Reflecting a sense of anxiety rising to alarm, such correspondence echoed current debates in the House of Commons and was carried in many English periodicals during the 1750s and well into the 1760s.[2] For more than a decade the *London Magazine* was a regular outlet for anguished protest against the enveloping tide. In the issue for September 1754, "Civis" writes that, "Amongst the many reigning vices of the present age none have risen to a greater height than that fashionable one of luxury, and few require a more immediate suppression, as it not only enervates the people, and debauches their morals, but also destroys their substance" (23:409). He denounces in particular the rise of the fashion among the lower orders and calls for speedy enforcement of sumptuary laws against urban laborers. In January 1756 another correspondent notes that, while he usually disapproves of "those common place declamations against the degeneracy of the present times," he now believes that luxury has increased so prodigiously as to "threaten the undermining of our constitution and the downfall of our state. . . . Our riches may perhaps be greater than formerly, but I am sure that our virtue is less" (25:15-16). Two years later, in May 1758, "Britannicus" seeks to describe in detail "to what degree this pestilence hath spread itself through the nation" and to forewarn readers of the certain ruin facing England if it is not eliminated (27:223). Although the storm of denunciation had moderated by 1764, occasional outbursts persisted, and in December "Aurelius" writes: "A little rational consideration will enable us to discover the kindred links between luxury, rapine, meanness, extravagance, misery, idleness, vice and guilt; for they are of one family, as scandalous as pernicious, and alike fatally destructive in their effects" (33:620).[3]

These letters represent a mere droplet in the last great wave of public condemnation to sweep England during the eighteenth century. For the period of Smollett's lifetime, 1721–71—roughly the time between the enlarged edition of the *Fable of the Bees* and the *Wealth of Nations*— the British Museum and London School of Economics possess more than 460 books and pamphlets in English that discuss luxury; for the whole century the number would nearly double. This estimate includes works, like Hume's *Political Discourses,* of which only part is devoted to luxury. But it does not include the vast number of comments in periodicals. If comments of all types during the century were counted, the number would be several thousand. Although not a matter to be ascertained with statistical certainty, the controversy over luxury prob- ably reached its highest pitch in British history in the years 1756–63. These are also the terminal years of the Seven Years' War and of Smol- lett's active involvement in polemical journalism. When the novelist and three other "gentlemen of approved abilities" issued the first number of the *Critical Review* on 1 March 1756, armed conflict with the French had already been under way for months. His tenure as editor and probably sole writer of the pro-government sheet the *Briton* ended 12 February 1763, two days after the war had been officially concluded. The coincidence of these circumstances is not fortuitous.

As the previous chapter has indicated, cries against luxury have been loudest when a people is under unusual stress. From at least the time of the Philistine attacks upon the Israelites through the War of the Spanish Succession, public dispute over the issue was the visible sign of a sense of crisis. When war or domestic discord appeared to threaten important interests and values, then old theories were respun to clothe new situa- tions. Luxury arose time and again, for it could account for any un- wanted or unforeseen shift in the scales of military, economic, social, political, moral, and even literary forces. The specific occasion might be sudden outbreaks of crime, violence, and immorality, or fierce partisan quarrels in politics (often over the goals and tactics of war), a lost battle, bad harvests, interruptions in foreign commerce, high taxes, or unex- pected financial reversals (as in the South Sea Bubble). Most often, all these events occurred together. In all cases, men of civic spirit demanded explanation and resolution: the sources of discontent had to be dis- covered, the traitors identified. So it was in eighteenth-century England, and Smollett's anxiety over luxury was a normal one for his contempo- raries.

To understand the particular nature of the controversy over luxury during the century, it is useful to turn first to the best summary of contemporary ideas, provided by Mandeville:

> It is a receiv'd Notion, that Luxury is as destructive to the wealth of the whole Body Politic, as it is to that of every individ-

ual Person who is guilty of it, and that a National Frugality enriches a County in the same manner as that which is less general
increases the Estates of private Families. . . . What is laid to the
Charge of Luxury besides, is, that it increases Avarice and Rapine:
And where they are reigning Vices, offices of the greatest Trust
are bought and sold; the Ministers that should serve the Public,
both great and small, corrupted, and the Countries every Moment
in danger of being betray'd to the highest Bidders: And lastly, that
it effeminates and enervates the People, by which the Nations
become an easy Prey to the first Invaders.[4]

Thus the received notion of luxury near the beginning of the eighteenth
century was essentially what it was in Old Testament times and in Rome
of the first century B.C. The first portion of Mandeville's definition
reveals that luxury continued to express a theory of value, an ethic for
both individuals and nations; the second, that it remained a theory of
history, an explanation of both personal and collective decline in the
past. One needs to go beyond Mandeville, however, for an explanation
of the complex mutations the concept had undergone by Smollett's age.
Several related questions require at least tentative answers: Why the
attack upon luxury remained as important to the English as it was to
the Romans, why it was not met by countervailing or competitive
theories of national history, why it was applied so massively after 1688,
why it fit partisan polemics so well, why in common parlance "corruption" and "insubordination" acquired such special significance, and
what kinds of challenges were at work. In fine, what was old in the
eighteenth-century situation, and what new. Although full justice to
the situation is not possible within the limits of a chapter, present
purposes can be served by an overview, drawing upon major studies of
English society by J. G. A. Pocock, Peter G. M. Dickson, and Isaac
Kramnick, followed by an account of the main phases or periods of
debate over luxury.

The primary answer is that what is new is a congeries of economic,
political, and social circumstances, while what is old is the way those
circumstances are perceived. The seventeenth century gave rise to a new
series of relationships among Englishmen as well as to new relationships
between them and their principal institutions. It carried English
thought, according to Pocock, from its post-medieval to its early modern stage. What was involved in this transition was a willingness to look
more closely, to analyze more exactly the flux of history. Change could
be seen as something more particular than the sheer disorder Herodotus
or Augustine observed; now it could be seen "in terms of intelligible
social and material processes." But while a century of revolution could
induce attention, it could not compel approval. The conceptual universe

of early eighteenth-century England remained essentially what it was for the ancients—a universe bound by a "rigorously limited epistemology of the secular," in which particular events and their causes were ill understood. This universe of ideas obliged men to interpret change negatively, as a subversion of the divinely and naturally ordained principles of necessity and hierarchy and as a degeneration from grace, virtue, stability, and rationality.[5] Since the Hebrews, the concept of luxury had possessed the capacity to communicate those values and to describe the consequences of their violation. Hence it was one of the very few traditional concepts in which aspects of change were inherent. Embodied in holy Scripture, in the works of the great philosophers and theologians, and in the corpora of Hebrew, Greek, Roman, and Christian law, it provided a reflexive doctrine upon which opponents of any instance of change might base their misgivings or resentment. At once, luxury accommodated change, absorbed it, explained it, and judged it. Regarding the concept of luxury, the classical world extended from the rule of Moses to that of George III.

Second, with ample documentation Dickson calls the years 1688–1756 the period of "financial revolution in England," the Bloodless Revolution standing as watershed between the older agrarian England and the newer commercial nation. The new financial order encouraged a trend toward a more urban and bourgeois society, more centralized economic and political institutions, and became the requisite ground for the industrial revolution to follow.[6] Over this congeries of changes, the eighteenth-century battles of luxury were fought. For to adherents of the classical conception, a vocal if not overwhelming majority for much of the century, the Revolution of 1688 was a Pandora's box setting loose a spirit of luxury the natural order could not contain. To them the world was spinning not only beyond control, but almost beyond comprehension. Luxury was fast begetting new, false, and artificial wealth, a new and noxious economic order, and a new and sinister breed of men whose sole office was to multiply by some nefarious means the new man-made values. Taxes, credit, public funds, stock-jobbing, a standing army—all of these misbegot, from nothing, the innovators, the moneyed men who set out to break the nation to their own ways. They bought influence with cash and political power with corruption; they used them solely for subversion—of the constitution, the machinery of government, the spirit of the country, the morals and manners of its people. With loud anguish Bolingbroke phrased the situation in his *Dissertation upon Parties* (1733–35): "THE POWER OF MONEY AS THE WORLD IS NOW CONSTITUTED IS REAL POWER."

Third, as it accounted for devolutionary change and the genesis of corruption, so the concept of luxury described the character of the agents, the actual human beings engaged in the destructive process. To the Hebrew sense of degradation, it conjoined the Greek sense of natural duality. Luxury was not the sole theory of entropy available to the ancient world, but it was the most attractive, I believe because it allowed (or required) the exclusion of exceptional men from the devolutionary course. As we have seen, the legislators—the men who in Greece, Rome, and feudal Europe wrote the laws, sermons, histories, and philosophical treatises—felt themselves proof against the dread temptations of luxury. Lesser beings would succumb, but the natural legislator was held aloft—by his land, his wealth, his birth, his education, his status—in eighteenth-century terms, by his estate. From Plato onward it was assumed that humankind was divided between the legislators and the subjects, the select few and the ignorant multitude, the men of honor and everybody else (including, with significant emphasis, the men of profit). It was further assumed that legislators would be united and act as one, for they tended to be males of similar background, training and philosophy; indeed they were to use the Law to atomize their subjects, to guarantee industry, and to prevent insubordination. If Birth was their throne, Law was their sword.

But in eighteenth-century England, throne and sword had been thrust apart. Power was no longer the exclusive prerogative of the natural legislators and sometimes fell into the hands of what was to them a bastard simulacrum. In the illegitimate world ushered in by the financial revolution, men of mere profit were in the ascendancy. Now place and power were divided between natural and unnatural claimants. The situation was sufficiently grave for the men of honor to sound alarum, to rouse themselves to wrest control from the venal. They, Aristotle's independent men, possessed the right to rule, not the moneyed men who were natural subjects, who had no virtue themselves and who led a herd of blind mercenaries. They, noble of birth and noble of character, alone had the right to determine necessity and hierarchy for England. Hence the decades-long cry of corruption: luxury as it threatened the constitution. Men like Pope, Swift, and Bolingbroke had been forced to discard belief in the monarch as sole or even chief upholder of the constitution. Now they were being goaded to explain how that role had devolved upon mere subjects—those of the middle orders against whom Greek and Roman law had been written. The Deuteronomic writers would tolerate no usurers, bakers, confectioners, or the like. Socrates, Cato, Cicero, and Augustine agreed. Sumptuary codes had for centuries suppressed or limited their numbers and activities. Now they were claiming influence in government, a certain sign of corruption of the civil polity. They were guilty of what in civil law was termed jactitation, a claim falsely made, and as yet stood unpunished. Again Bolingbroke puts the case succinctly, in his *Letter on the Spirit of Patriotism* and again in the *Idea of a Patriot King* (both 1749): "THE LANDED MEN ARE THE TRUE OWNERS OF OUR POLITICAL VESSEL; THE MONEYED MEN, AS SUCH, ARE NO MORE THAN PASSENGERS IN IT."

Despite Bolingbroke's capitals, the usurpers continued to thrive, not only diluting the power of the natural legislators, but succeeding even in sundering them from it. Perhaps the most galling aspect of Opposition strategy during the 1720s and 1730s was that it had to be extra-parliamentary, forged mostly outside the arena of power. For a generation before Walpole's rise and nearly a generation after his fall, many leaders of the great families echoed Bolingbroke's anguish. Here, they cried, was an infernal paradox born of the corruptions of luxury: they were intended by the nature of things to guard the constitution, that part of natural law deduced specifically for the governance of England; yet they could not get into the ministry. Isaac Kramnick has argued persuasively that to the Opposition Walpole's cardinal sin was moral, in the sense that the sumptuary codes were moral, delimiting moral capacity as well as legal culpability. By reducing government to administration and mediation, Walpole appeared to have reduced politics to an acquired skill. But to most of the Opposition, statecraft was a thing of the spirit, requiring proper birth and classical education, social grace and rhetorical eloquence. A skill might be learned by anybody, when to be anybody was to be nobody. The concept of luxury and the workings of natural law, on the other hand, dictated that only the men of land and family could observe necessity and hierarchy. Kramnick writes:

> To Bolingbroke, Walpole's political corruption was the symbol of a much larger corrupt society. . . . The financial revolution of 1690–1740 was, then, the most meaningful social experience in the lives of Bolingbroke and the others in his circle . . . it informs all their writing on politics and society, and it feeds their gloom, their satire, and their indignation. They saw an aristocratic social and political order being undermined by money and new financial institutions and they didn't like it.[7]

Fourth, division among eighteenth-century legislators and the concomitant vituperation of attacks upon luxury appear in retrospect to have been unavoidable. The pattern of argument after 1688 suggests that all of the conflicts inherent in the classical concept were aggravated in the growth of a more fluid and complex society. What is revolution to men on one side of the wheel is devolution to those on the other.

Where European society had been relatively static, as in rural areas of medieval England, the authority of the natural legislator went largely unchallenged. However, in the market towns and the capital, where expansion was the desideratum for legislator and merchant alike, challenges were frequent, and the law was called into play to enforce order. Where the law was neglected or rescinded, the apparent cause was the new power won by the middle orders. "Stadluft," the Germans claimed, "macht frei." A process visible in imperial Rome, Renaissance Venice, and seventeenth-century Paris was asserting itself once again in London, as several forces marched together: prosperity and aspiration on one side, resentment and attacks upon luxury on the other. By the middle of the eighteenth century, London was the largest city in Europe and contained the greatest proportion of national population—one in ten. She was also the greatest port, the largest center of international trade, and the largest center of ship-owning and shipbuilding in the world. Through these enterprises she eventually became the world center of banking, finance, and insurance.[8] One consequence of this concentration was that the city exercised an enormous influence over the British economy. Defoe called her the great octopus that sucked to itself the vitals of the nation's trade, and Hume noted that "[Our] national debts cause a mighty confluence of the people and riches to the capital, by the great sums levied in the provinces to pay the interest." Another was that she evoked an enormous amount of envy and suspicion, suggested by Defoe and Hume and voiced loudly by the societies bent upon reforming city manners and by those who identified with the provinces. The lines of division are indicated by the host-narrator in the opening chapter of *Tom Jones:* "we shall represent Human Nature at first to the keen appetite of our reader in that more plain and simple manner in which it is found in the country, and shall hereafter hash and ragout it with all the high French and Italian seasoning of affectation and vice which courts and cities afford."

The sumptuary codes of the ancient world testify that societies ordered by juridical status were usually fragile and insecure, alert subjects continuously seeking new privileges, alert legislators continuously seeking new restrictions. In Rome, M. I. Finley has noted, as the empire prospered, the number of slaveholders grew, as did the number of slaves. A worried Senate responded with additional controls over slaves and slave owners. A similar dilemma faced the natural legislators of England. They could try either to halt the new prosperity or to find means to control it. The former course was futile, for even before 1688 commercial expansion was virtually irrevocable. The latter was at best difficult, for with their influence diluted in court and Parliament they could not hope to institute the drastic measures required to renew the old model of necessity and hierarchy. Throughout English history the disturbance of any kind of national equilibrium was likely to be followed by fresh condemnations of luxury. This reflexive offering of a placebo recurred because verbal tirade was, it seems, virtually the only method accepted for solving inveterate problems. Especially after 1688, when numerous types of equilibrium were being violated, the very tenacity of such problems insured that luxury grew not less important, but more. For when effective means to resolve difficulties were unknown or unacceptable, then ineffective ones were pressed with greater insistence—if only to allay popular anxiety. Changes in English society had been growing apace for decades, most of them set off by deliberate decisions of the traditional natural legislators. By the eighteenth century such changes had created serious human problems, principally for women, the poor, and the urban middle orders. When enclosure or poor harvests or other pressures pushed a farming family toward the city, for example, the family became enmeshed in an obvious double bind. If it remained in the country seeking a new site for old labor, it was accused of truculence and insubordination. If it sought new work in the city, it was decried for indigence and restlessness. As with the occupational roles of the poor, so with the social roles of educated women and the financial roles of merchants and tradesmen. In each instance English traditions generated serious difficulties, and English traditions condemned whatever solutions were sought. And in each instance the leaders of Old England could issue their denunciations of luxury with genuine satisfaction. A campaign of moral rearmament, they could assume, had been opened. The enemy had been identified and located; victory would follow shortly. Thus the concept of luxury again served its consolidating function, and the discovery of luxury among the laboring poor became the social equivalent of detecting French agents concealed in St. John's Woods.

Victory did not usually follow, however. By the late seventeenth century Englishmen were certainly aware of land, labor, capital, and raw material as the ingredients of a commercial economy. This much at least is revealed by the adventures of the Mississippi Company in Paris in 1718 and the South Sea Company in London two years later. But economic theory hobbled behind economic reality. Johnson wrote justly that "There is nothing which requires more to be illustrated by philosophy than trade does." Not until the last quarter of the century did a prolegomenon to such a philosophy appear in Smith's *Wealth of Nations*. Until the 1760s there seemed little hope of reconciling the buoyant, optimistic proponents of material progress who were translating economic power into political power with the dubious, pessimistic observer of material decay. No longer could a man of the land rise with the confidence of a Roman born to wield power, assert the harmony of nature and society, and deduce the unity of all values. Arguments questioning traditional authority were surfacing in treatises and even appearing weekly in the papers. If it was toppled, the whole edifice surrounding the conception of luxury might follow.

Fifth, that edifice seemed to be under siege on several fronts at once. To the natural legislators the most insidious threats were also the most predictable. Centuries of experience had prepared them for the guile of foreign enemies and the unbridled middle and lower orders. Such tempters were expected to act with cunning, for they represented inveterate resistance to natural virtue, resistance that it was the design of law and government to contain. Although it was quite clear by the time of Walpole's Robinocracy that those controls were no longer working, a change of administration might bring about their renewal. What was not so predictable was the apparent treason of some philosophers and writers, men who were the normal allies or servants of the traditional order. Hobbes was a fervent ally, but a dangerous one; for his reduction of necessity and hierarchy to issues of fear, power, and self-interest had stripped natural law of its divine sanction.[9] Locke was an equally dangerous foe, for his redefinitions of legitimate authority seemed to cast natural law away from its ancient agrarian center. Some mercantile writers, it is true, continued the attack upon luxury in a classical way. Others however were not so careful and suggested that the economic order was best governed by its own laws. These held that economic behavior was of itself morally neutral; luxury could be justified if it provided a market for the nation's goods and increased the circulation of money.[10]

Besides Locke and the economic writers, the important figures symbolic of national division were Defoe and Mandeville. The one challenged the classical notion of hierarchy in his defenses of women, laborers, pauper children, and the commercial interests. In scores of exuberant, commonsensical works he ventured to say that the new freedoms won by the middle orders could never reasonably be called luxury. The other, an audacious conservative who because of his conservatism sought to jettison the old taboos against luxury, flatly denied the classical notion of necessity. Neither Defoe nor Mandeville had any real power, yet each possessed enough notability to be branded infamous. Neither was at all radical—as, say, Milton and the Levellers had been. Both were intent upon strengthening extant English society by clearing it of the detritus of patent contradiction.[11] But to the natural legislators such mediation was pointless and uncalled for—indeed, exacerbating. They would brook no talk of contradiction, because their most abiding anxiety lay, it seems, in the fear that their supremacy was being undermined by a dark and demonic force that they could sense but not comprehend. To face the moneyed men on their own terms in the political arena was one thing, and a familiar one. But to be told that they were facing the impassive workings of a relentless social and economic process—that was another, and a damnable one.

The hostility that greeted Defoe's and Mandeville's social writings suggests that rancor and tension were as much a part of eighteenth-century controversy as division. They were bridge figures attempting to reconcile the past to the present and calling attention to the fact that English society—in our terms, the field of testing—had been thoroughly secularized. Their reception showed how desperate and controversial the issue of luxury remained and indicated that such contradictions as they found would persist. As much as Defoe and Mandeville, the defenders of necessity and hierarchy were obliged by momentous events to emphasize the secular workings of luxury—in philosophical basis as well as everyday articulation. Moral arguments, whether Platonic, Augustinian, or Calvinist, were certainly used, but mainly in passing. Even churchmen came to concentrate upon the putative economic and political consequences of luxury; even they were more alarmed over its predicted effects upon the nation than upon the individual soul. In practice, that is, they grasped for the same sword wielded by Hobbes and their adversaries, making economic and political theory the fount of moral norms. And they found it double-edged. They were not trying to say something novel about the vice; indeed nothing new or significant was added to the classical attack during the century, not even by Rousseau. Instead, the traditional arguments were culled for their collective and economic implications. A domestic hurricane was raging, and any text in a storm. What original thinking about luxury did occur during the century was carried out by men who rejected some part of the classical attack. Men like Defoe, Mandeville, Hume, Johnson, Kames, Ferguson, and Smith were not attempting to betray the values of European civilization. Rather they were arguing that the ancient dogma of luxury was not essential to those values.

Sixth, the protean quality of the classical attack upon luxury—informing every traditional institution and judging the conduct of every subject—insured that its spirit would persist in many forms. At any particular moment, the number of Englishmen bold enough to challenge it was relatively small. In the popular mind at least, it would be generations before the traditional horror would be moderated or redirected. Beyond all questions of philosophy and historical movement, therefore, there remain complicating habits in usage. Mandeville demonstrates that luxury entered two distinct levels of usage. On one it is, for men like Bolingbroke, Hume, Harris, Ferguson, and Smollett, a nuclear and organizing concept in an elaborate social and political system. Swift, for example, supplements his philosophical quarrel with luxury by claiming, in the *Proposal for Correcting . . . the English Tongue* (1712), that the vice is responsible for debasement of the language. On the other level, a vulgarization of the first, it has passed into general currency as a commonplace element in various kinds of dispute. Many anonymous pamphlets could be cited to illustrate this popular level of usage, tracts that hold luxury responsible for a multiplicity of circumstances: for both high prices and low, prosperity and hardship, crime and discourtesy, brutality and effeminacy, martial weakness and unsuccessful diplomacy. As a springboard for vulgar controversy, the idea was of enormous utility, for it was inherently polemical and customarily vague. Popular discussions of economic topics reveal this tendency in the extreme, often totally neglecting such elemental distinctions as those among necessities, conveniences, and comforts— all of which were changing during the century. Numerous writers of the first rank, moreover, who generally possessed a learned view of luxury, on occasion also utilized popular senses of the term—for example, as a synonym for physical indulgence or sexual immorality. Similarly, writers felt free to excoriate the presumed dissipation of every class and sector of society but their own. Men of the middle orders rejected out of hand the argument that their claims upon government were luxurious. But many were willing to entertain the same argument directed against the working poor. William Temple of Trowbridge, friend of John Wilkes and defender of City causes, was at once a voluble supporter of the commercial interests against charges of luxury and a fierce enemy of the luxury of laborers. Nathaniel Forster criticizes oligarchs like the Walpoles and the Pelhams for insensitivity toward the privations of the poor. Horace Walpole derides the extravagances of Clive and other nabobs. Clive is shocked by the luxurious apparel of servants in London.[12] In the *Travels,* Smollett finds occasion to ridicule many instances of French and Italian luxury, but he is incensed by the absence of comfort in his own lodgings; these are not luxurious enough. For Bramble, the comforts of Lord Queensberry savor of refinement and hospitality; those of Squire Burdock reek of dissipation and bad taste.

Variations in usage were natural and common throughout the century, for luxury probably *was* the greatest single social issue and the greatest single commonplace. The situation apparently posed no extraordinary difficulties to contemporaries, but it is bedeviling to modern students. Elizabeth Gilboy's comments upon luxury are not altogether compatible with those of Norman Sykes; each is regarding only part of the concept, and that from a specialized perspective. Smollett's contemporaries, particularly among major intellectual figures, were no more confused in their discussions of luxury than modern writers are in their analyses of, say, liberalism or communism or democracy.[13] As men brought the concept to bear upon the whole spectrum of human activity, luxury became an increasingly centrifugal constellation of ideas. To note this evolution is merely to recast the distinction between luxury as form and luxury as content. Thus, while Greek, Roman, and Christian arguments of a general sort persisted through much of the century, specific examples or manifestations continued to accumulate—at an increasing rate. On the one hand, a writer would tend to repeat the maledictions of his predecessors while adding a few uniquely his own. On the other, each new social disturbance—from the South Sea Bubble and the '45 rebellion to increased prices of porter and the decline of education at Oxford—could provide further instances of the reign of luxury. Critics of the *Estimate of the Manners and Principles of the Times* chided John Brown not for his relatively narrow view of the nature of luxury, but for his restricted perspective of its consequences. They accordingly extended Brown's list of grievances with contributions of their own. Bramble's "catalogue of London dainties" and his list of English affectations are closely related in motive and form to earlier strictures against luxury.

A final complication should be noted as a caveat. The issue of luxury was volatile and political, the period one of rapid and drastic change. The coincidence of these circumstances made for controversy that is overblown and division that is too schematic. When a flaming political issue is raised and a simple answer required, many men will respond who would ordinarily remain silent or venture a cautious "maybe." Such probably was the case during the eighteenth century, else the flames of dispute would have continued burning as high after 1763. Ordinary Englishmen probably were not as certain of their own minds as the philosophers and lawmakers of previous centuries. Our understanding must take into at least tacit account the tepid, the dubious, and the confused. The division, moreover, could not have been throughout the period a simple one of gentlemen versus merchants, since well before 1750 there were several fine gentlemen who were merchants and as many merchants who considered themselves fine gentlemen. And political combatants, as is their wont, routinely shifted sides. Defoe, the famous example, could write for one side, then the other, and later for both at once. He could—and in fact did—write a fiery pamphlet in October refuting a fiery pamphlet he had published in July. With John Trenchard, Thomas Gordon produced the scathing *Cato's Letters;* yet about 1724 he accepted a place from Walpole and thereafter became foremost government writer. Journeying in the other direction was the

Earl of Bath, William Pulteney. After breaking with Walpole over a position in the ministry, he joined the Opposition and produced some of its more effective pieces of polemic. Such examples are too extreme to represent the ordinary Englishman, but they do reveal the danger of interpreting character entirely through politics. The issues of a great debate can remain consistent, but most human participants cannot.

STAGES IN THE ATTACK

Despite such complications, the bases of the attack upon luxury through 1763 are relatively clear. The upholders of traditional privilege sought first to remind England of the Law known from antiquity that set limits upon what most men *may* do by defining the limits of what they *can* do, and which condemned categorically all forms of luxury. From that law they deduced their own status as guardians and legislators, the embodiment of the law and its interpreters. They argued that the very essence of English nationhood was endangered and represented the immediate field of moral testing—challenging legislators and subjects alike to unite in the effort to reestablish the natural order of virtue. The new moneyed men and their many imitators, they held, were at best rebels acting out of pride and greed and falsely claiming privileges to which they had no right; at worst these men were tempters, witting or unwitting agents of infernal destruction. The series of crises and disruptions the nation had undergone since the previous century they viewed as decisive instances of the punishment that follows violation of the law. Conflict was implicit in each of these positions, for few of their opponents—their reluctance to defend luxury notwithstanding—were willing to grant their title to dominion, far less all of their premises. The ensuing controversy appears to have followed the political temperature in England. During relatively normal times, there issued a seemingly constant flow of attacks upon luxury, usually along familiar moral and religious lines; in 1794 two pamphlets were published each of which asserted it would deliver the final answer to Mandeville. This constant base was increased and aggravated whenever political emotions grew fevered, and at least five phases or periods of aggravation can be distinguished. The earliest occurred about 1698–1702 during the Court and Country debates over a standing army. The next is represented by the last four years of the reign of Queen Anne, when Whig fought Tory over the direction of government policy. Responses to Mandeville and the South Sea Bubble of 1720 dominated the third; a few were elicited by "The Grumbling Hive" of 1705, most to editions of the *Fable of the Bees* of 1714, 1723, and 1728. During the latter 1720s and 1730s the terms of the debate were widened with the superaddition of Tory theories of history and politics to older criticism of luxury. Luxury here became a weapon in the serious paper battles against Walpole and his supporters, and a banner of attack for the Opposition. In the final phase, from about 1750 to 1763, the controversy widened once more to include a concerted attack upon the habits of the laboring poor. During this last stage, in which Smollett was a prominent figure, previous arguments against luxury flowed together and raised the tide of condemnation to its highest crest in English history.

The first period centered on the writings of a group of men—John Toland, John Trenchard, Walter Moyle, Andrew Fletcher, and Charles Davenant—often referred to as the Commonwealthmen.[14] Their resistance to a permanent army was the manifestation of a larger reaction against the drift of English politics. Luxury, not patriotism, was guiding public affairs, they feared, and the result was a loss of moral and political stability. In his *Discourse of Government with Relation to Militias* (1698), Fletcher asserted that nothing of the old order remained except "the ancient Terms and outward Forms," and that "the generality of all Ranks of Men are cheated by Words and Names" (p. 5). He perceived luxury besetting Europe in strength about the time of the Renaissance, in the wake of the new learning, new inventions, new wealth, and new trade. As Pocock has shown, he opposed a standing army and the new version of patriotism it represented because he saw a substitution of money values for feudal duty. The men of this latter kind of army were not faithful vassals rallying to their lord's call, but mercenaries whose services had been purchased. Where once service was owed, now it was bought, and all essential elements of life were measured by monetary value.

> By this means the Luxury of Asia and America was added to that of the Antients; and all Ages, and all Countries concurred to sink Europe into an Abyss of Pleasures; which were rendered the more expensive by a perpetual Change of the Fashions in Clothes, Equipage and Furniture of Houses.
>
> These things brought a total Alteration to the way of living, upon which all Government depends. 'Tis true, Knowledg being mightily increased, and a great Curiosity and Nicety in every thing introduced, Men imagined themselves to be gainers in all points, by changing from their frugal and military way of living, which I must confess had some mixture of Rudeness and Ignorance in it, tho not inseparable from it. But at the same time they did not consider the unspeakable Evils that are altogether inseparable from an expensive way of living. [Pp. 12–13]

By expensive way of living, Fletcher means one absorbed with money and its concomitant values. By unspeakable evils, he means the loss of station and function, of the social harmony implicit in the ancient order. By frugality, he means the absence of choice, the coincidence of duty and station. Now luxury has enabled many men to choose what they would do; if they would not fight, they can hire others to take their places. The innovations of luxury have weakened the warrior quality of subjects and legislators equally.

Fletcher was alarmed over the physical and psychological corruption the financing of war produced. Davenant was appalled by the new breed of men who did the financing, men "whom peace would have left in their original obscurity, in troublesome times shine forth; but they are like portentous meteors, threatening ruin to the country that is under their malevolent aspect."[15] In his *Discourse on the Public Revenue and on the Trade of England* (1698), Davenant held that as it had corrupted Rome, so luxury was corrupting England. Everyone was money-grubbing, and the worst were merely those grubbing the most. Not only did the bankers, stockjobbers, and moneyed companies control the destiny of the nation during war, they also sucked it dry during peace. *The True Picture of a Modern Whig* (1702) is his portrait in dialogue of the projectors and financiers who care only about cash. Tom Double, spokesman for the modern Whigs, boasts that in 1688 he was shoeless, but after fourteen years as a stockjobber is worth £50,000. To anyone attracted to his party, he is ready with counsel: "In general, detract from and asperse all the men of quality of whom there is any appearance that either their high birth, or their great fortunes, or their abilities in matters of government should recommend them to the future administration of affairs. . . . It is our interest to humble the ancient gentry because they know our originals and call us upstarts and leeches that are swollen big by sucking up the nation's blood" (4:179). Davenant gives plain statement of the source of England's ills in the *Essay upon the Probable Methods of Making a People Gainers in the Balance of Trade* (1699):

> Trade, without doubt, is in its nature a pernicious thing; it brings in that wealth which introduces luxury; it gives rise to fraud and avarice, and extinguishes virtue and simplicity of manners; it depraves a people, and makes way for that corruption which never fails to end in slavery, foreign or domestic. Lycurgus, in the most perfect model of government that was ever framed, did banish it from his commonwealth. But, the posture and condition of other countries considered, it is become with us a necessary evil. We shall be continually exposed to insults and invasions, without

such a naval force as is not to be had naturally but where there is an extended traffic. However, if trade cannot be made subservient to the nation's safety, it ought to be no more encouraged here than it was in Sparta. [2:275]

The next period serves in part to demonstrate the vitality of classical attitudes toward luxury. From 1711 to 1714, the *Spectator* commented upon luxury a half-dozen times or so, suggesting that the vice did not loom so large to writers of Whiggish bent. Taken together, they provide useful contrasts in tone to the acrid polemics of Tory and Country journalists, for all are written with a temperate reasonableness spiced with wit. Addison's no. 55 is the earliest, longest, and most important, offering a fable of modern times in which Luxury and Avarice, once enemies, now unite to despoil the world. Quoting Persius and Sallust, he asserts that luxury was responsible for the demise of Rome and could devastate Britain. In nos. 260 and 294, Steele calls luxury a harking after fashion, the chief way the wealthy waste their money. Budgell, in no. 331, asks sardonically if the growing of beards will not become another fashion to advance the luxury of the times. Steele returns to satire in no. 478, arguing that tradesmen favor luxury because it and all other forms of folly increase their business. Finally, in no. 574, Addison declares that, contrary to ordinary thinking, luxury cannot bring happiness. Persons who succumb to its temptations are victims of artificial wants and, unable to satisfy themselves, are in a continuing state of artificial poverty.

Direct responses to Mandeville were mainly of two kinds. More learned writers like John Dennis and William Law reiterated Platonic and Stoic ideas. Law's riposte, founded on the necessity for reason and order, is contained in *Remarks upon a Late Book, Entituled the Fable of the Bees* (1724). In *Vice and Luxury Publick Mischiefs* (1724), Dennis finds luxury threatening on grounds of both fact and reason. He finds the evidence incontrovertible that the vice was responsible for the falls of Sparta and Rome and for the present exorbitant size of the English national debt. Passion and vanity are the sources of luxury, and these must be quelled or all civil order will be lost: "Reason will approve of just so much of them [dress, furnishings, housing] as is requisite for the Distinction of Rank, and the keeping up of that Subordination, which is absolutely necessary to Government" (p. 54). Again, "Where Luxury once prevails and becomes habitual, the Passions have entirely got the upper Hand of Reason, have banished all consideration, and ruin'd all Oeconomy" (p. 73). Unlike Law and Dennis, however, most of Mandeville's adversaries did not sense the existence of a genuine intellectual issue. Pope's reply appears, in effect, in the "Epistle to Bathurst":

What Nature wants (a phrase I much mistrust)
Extends to Luxury, extends to Lust:
And if we count among the Needs of life
Another's Toil, why not another's Wife?   [11.25–28]

Instead they saw an outrageous threat to the normal order of things. Representative of many such replies is George Blewitt's *An Enquiry whether a General Practice of Virtue tends to the Wealth or Poverty, Benefit, or Disadvantage of a People?* (1725):

> The Dearness of Labour of all sorts, the Largeness of Wages and other Perquisites of Servants, their Idleness and insolence are all the effects of Luxury; of which . . . though the Example arise among idle Persons, yet the Imitation is run into all Degrees, even of those Men by whose Industry the Nation subsists. To this we owe the Scarcity of Servants where they are *really* wanted; and from hence arises the prodigious loss to the Publick, that Draught of lusty and able-bodied men from Husbandry or Country Business, to add to the magnificence of Equipages: *A sort of idle and rioting Vermin, by which* (we are told) *the Kingdom is almost devoured, and which are everywhere become a public nuisance.* [P. 208]

From Mandeville's point of view, the received notion of luxury amounted to an intellectual cliché, the bogeyman of the educated. It had retained the pattern and weight of great menace, but not the substance; it was an anomaly, like an old toad that lives on though buried under a stone. Thoughtful men at least should not regard it seriously, he argued. Mandeville and his critics did share one piece of common ground: luxury definitely was useful as a generalized theory of history. The distinctive use of the concept during the 1730s, however, is as a *specialized* theory of contemporary English history. Reviewing events of the past half-century, various writers of Tory inclination reported finding in luxury the source of a nefarious process that had robbed them and their patrons of their accustomed rank, power, and privilege. In sermon and treatise, broadside and history, they elaborated a series of indictments against the men who had profited from the events of 1688, especially those who were without birth, breeding, formal education, or history of family involvement in government. In the Glorious Revolution, they attempted to demonstrate a sharp break in the continuity of English history, a devolution from the high standards of Old England, a subversion of the English constitution, and a deterioration in the quality of English life and art. In the new Whigs and the moneyed interest, they sought to expose a group guilty of the rankest usurpation and insubordination.

For more than a generation, writers articulating either the gentry position or the somewhat narrower one of the Opposition held that the course of contemporary English history was precisely that foretold by countless ancient philosophers. They wished, as Pocock has said, to subsume particular modern events under the vocabulary of the ancients. The workings of luxury they saw as congruent with the movement of history. The sense of decline explicit in such identification accurately reflected the disconsolate temper of the times. A progressive theory of history was available through continental—particularly French—writers, yet it could have little appeal for men who felt acute grievance. To such men only two conceptions of history could possibly accommodate their experiences: one of cumulative deterioration, the other of cyclic rise and fall. Luxury fitted both. When considering the past, furthermore, Whig and Tory alike were searching for practical lessons in ethics and politics, and once again luxury provided specific examples. One of Bolingbroke's central theories concerned the pragmatic uses to which historical writing and thinking should be put, as a guide to political and ethical truth. In the eight letters of the *Study and Use of History* (1735–36), he disdains the erudition of the annalistic tradition, proposing instead the drawing of "political maps." As an example of the kind of writing he favors, he includes a sketch of European history from about 1500, which incidentally vindicates by reference to "general laws" Tory principles and his own career.[16]

On the professional level, this view is represented by Smollett's histories, written largely amid the slough of despond stimulated by the unsuccessful early stages of the Seven Years' War and by Gibbon's preoccupation with the dismemberment of Rome. Popularly, it can be seen in numerous pamphlets even before the 1730s, especially those condemning the War of the Spanish Succession and the South Sea Bubble. An anonymous work published the year after the Bubble, *An Essay Towards Preventing the Ruin of Great Britain* (1721), blames the spread of luxury for the debacle and possesses the tone of angry despair Smollett was to recreate in his histories. The author calls the Bubble a visitation from God, a lesson intended to show the fatal effects of the nation's luxury, corruption, and folly. National reformation is necessary; religion, industry, subordination, public spirit, and patriotism must be reinstated in men's hearts. England could regain genuine wealth and prosperity only through the natural and traditional means of agriculture and trade. It could never be regained through the public gaming table where "money is shifted from hand to hand in such a blind fortuitous manner, that some men shall from nothing in an instant acquire vast estates with the least desert; while others are as suddenly stript of plentiful fortunes" (p. 5). While luxury is the natural cause of national decay and ruin, national and personal virtue is the strength and sustenance of the body politic. The lessons of Rome are going unattended, and the English are rapidly becoming corrupt and impotent, drowning in luxury. All persons in the kingdom have been tainted with the corruption; so all persons must renounce their obsession with private interest.

> The south sea affair is not the original evil or the greatest source of our misfortune; it is but the natural effect of these principles which for many years have been propagated with great industry. And as a sharp distemper by reclaiming a man from intemperance may prolong his life, so it is not improbable but this public calamity that lieth so heavy on the nation may prevent its ruin . . . if it should turn our thought from cousenage and stock-jobbing to industry and frugal methods of life; in fine if it should revive and inflame that native spark of British worth and honor which hath too long lain smothered and oppressed. [P. 25]

The fourth great wave of protest against luxury took place between approximately 1726 and 1742, terminal dates that coincide with Bolingbroke's return to active engagement in politics (and the founding of the *Craftsman*) and Walpole's resignation. In the emphasis upon luxury as a divisive political issue, Bolingbroke is apparently the foremost figure—as theorist, financier, and spokesman for the opposition to Walpole.[17] And although it was not used massively until the later 1720s—compare a tract by Fletcher or Davenant with a number of the *Craftsman*—this highly polemical interpretation of the concept probably had its source in the violently partisan strife between Whig and Tory earlier in the century, between 1710 and 1714. These bitter years were the seedtime not only of Bolingbroke's theories but also of Tory attitudes toward expansionist wars—attitudes voiced most persistently later by Tobias Smollett.

The Tory government led by Harley and Bolingbroke, which ruled between the Sacheverell incident and the death of Anne, had two principal goals: destruction of its opposition and conclusion of the war with France. For Harley and Bolingbroke, the objectives of the war had been already achieved in the containment of Louis's power in the Netherlands and Italy. But for the Whigs, the Dutch, and the Duke of Marlborough, the war would have to be continued until the French were driven totally out of Spain. In order to discredit the Whigs and "their war," the government launched a vast paper war which sought to make three points: that the war enriched only the moneyed interest and proportionately drained the landed interest; that England had already contributed enough to a continental campaign that benefited only the

Dutch and the Austrian emperor; and that Marlborough and other leaders of the Whigs had made fortunes by corrupt management of war moneys. These were the themes Swift sounded in the *Examiner* and in his highly successful *Conduct of the Allies* (1711). In the latter he wrote: "We have been fighting to raise the Wealth and Grandeur of a private Family [Marlborough's]; to enrich Usurers and Stock-jobbers; and to cultivate the pernicious Designs of a faction by destroying the Landed-Interest." Names changed, these are the staple arguments and phrases Smollett used against the City in the years 1756–63.

Enveloping the specific goal obtained in the Treaty of Utrecht, however, was a deeper complex of Tory grievances. The Glorious Revolution had been only the visible beginning of change. The Revolution Settlement, to the extent that it reconciled Anglican and Purtian, Tory and Whig, to that same extent compromised the material and political interests of traditional high Tories. The Act of Settlement of 1701 then settled the reversion of the English crown upon the Protestant Electress of Hanover and her children, jettisoning Tory claims of divine right and hereditary succession. Opposition to the war with France was therefore merely one sign of that mixture of fear and anger with which Tories regarded "the Modern Whigs." There was the Whig lust for commerce: expansion, inventions, new manufacturers, new trading centers, the movement of economic and political power from the land to the cities. Then there was the new financial order erected to support commerce: land taxes, national debt, stockjobbing, moneyed corporations, foreign alliances, the Bank of England, and the East India Company. All of this and more convinced the Tories that the traditional structure of Old England—the structure that had upheld them for so long—was being undermined. In his open Letter to Sir William Windham, written in 1717, Bolingbroke reflected upon the political campaign begun in 1710:

> We looked on the political principles which had generally prevailed in our government from the Revolution in 1688 to be destructive of our true interest, to have mingled us too much in the affairs of the continent, to tend to the impoverishing of our people, and to the loosening of the bonds of our constitution in church and state. We supposed the Tory party to be the bulk of the landed interest, and to have no contrary influence blended into its composition. We supposed the Whigs ... to lean for support on the presbyterians and other sectarians, on the bank and the other corporations, on the Dutch and the other alllies.[18]

The most vexing characteristic of the new moneyed middle class was its social inferiority. As Swift wrote in the *Examiner* for 2 November 1710: "Let any man observe the equipages in this town, he shall find the greatest number of those who make a figure, to be a species of men quite different from any that were even known before the Revolution."[19] The most dangerous was its growing influence in Parliament, and both Country and Court deplored its concomitant financial and political prosperity. While the landed gentry carried the full weight of national expense, Bolingbroke wrote, the moneyed men reaped huge profits but "contributed not one bit to its charge." (This is another accusation reiterated by Smollett in his polemical writings and by Bramble in his first letter from Bath.)

The complex of conservative attitudes evoked by the events of 1710–14 and provoked afresh by the Hanoverian Succession lay behind what has been termed the gloom of the Tory satirists. It also informs much of the power of the *Dunciad,* the *Beggar's Opera,* and *Gulliver's Travels.* Part 3 of Swift's masterpiece, published in 1726, is a valuable guide and bridge to both periods of Tory polemics, reflecting the atmosphere of 1710–14 and anticipating the issues of the 1730s. Chapter 8 of the voyage to Laputa and other places makes three charges that would be developed at length in the pages of the *Craftsman.* First, Gulliver remarks upon the *recent* introduction of luxury into England, a comment cast in the form of an observation upon Roman history: "I was surprized to find Corruption grown so high and so quick in that Empire, by the Force of Luxury so lately introduced."[20] Second, Gulliver voices his rejection of events of the recent past and of the writing of history, concluding with a thinly veiled reference to the revolution of 1688:

> I was chiefly disgusted with modern History. For having strictly examined all the Persons of greatest Name in the Courts of Princes for an Hundred Years past, I found how the World had been misled by prostitute Writers, to ascribe the greatest Exploits in War to Cowards, the wisest Counsel to Fools, Sincerity to Flatterers, Roman Virtue to Betrayers of their Country, Piety to Atheists, Chastity to Sodomites, Truth to Informers. How many innocent and excellent Persons had been condemned to Death or Banishment, by the practising of great Ministers upon the Corruption of Judges, and the Malice of Factions. How many Villains had been exalted to the highest Places of Trust, Power, Dignity, and Profit: How great a Share in the Motions and Events of Courts, Councils, and Senates might be challenged by Bawds, Whores, Pimps, Parasites, and Buffoons: How low an Opinion I had of Human Wisdom and Integrity, when I was truly informed of the Springs and Motives of great Enterprizes and Revolutions in the World, and of the contemptible Accidents to which they owed their Success.

Third, Gulliver expresses acceptance of the degenerative theory of history, finding occasion for "melancholy Reflections" upon "how much the Race of human Kind was degenerate among us, within these Hundred Years past." Luxury and corruption had altered the English countenance, shortened physiques, "unbraced the Nerves, relaxed the Sinews and Muscles, introduced a sallow Complexion, and rendered the Flesh loose and rancid." Surrounded by degeneration, Gulliver yearns for a return to simple, virtuous Old England:

> I descended so low as to desire that some *English* Yeomen of the Old Stamp, might be summoned to appear; once so famous for the Simplicity of their Manners, Dyet and Dress; for Justice in their Dealings; for their true Spirit of Liberty; for their Valour and Love of their Country. Neither could I be wholly unmoved after comparing the Living with the Dead, when I considered how all these pure native Virtues were prostituted for a Piece of Money by their Grand-children; who in selling their Votes, and managing at elections have acquired every Vice and Corruption that can possibly be learned in a Court.

In chapter 10 the point is underscored, Gulliver noting "the several Gradations by which Corruption steals into the World" and the "continual Degeneracy of human Nature so justly complained of in all Ages."[21]

For the Opposition, the special utility of the concept of luxury was to explain not so much how they fell as how the unworthy Whigs rose. In this respect Bolingbroke and his group offer an elaboration of the arguments of 1698–1702 and lay the immediate ground for those of the 1750s. From the earliest essays of the *Craftsman,* the coalition of "Patriots" made prosecution of luxury the paper's predominant philosophical theme, uncovering the vice nearly everywhere and insisting upon the foreboding parallel with Rome. The ideal polity for the Opposition was largely what it was for Aristotle and Cicero: a derivation of the natural, traditional social order, where the masters of the land are the masters of the nation. In a "genuine" polity—as opposed to the "bastard" polity of contemporary England—Bolingbroke finds the emblem of "a free people" in the patriarchal family, where all values are set by the father. Birth, rank, and independence are the marks of the natural legislator—"Men of the *highest Dignity, the most acknowledg'd Wisdom,* and *try'd Integrity,*" in Pulteney's words—without which the civil polity is inevitably debased and unnatural.[22] Bolingbroke distinguishes between "subjects" and "tutors and guardians"; between "the multitude designed to obey, and . . . the few designed to govern." Since the design in question is both divine and natural, the *Craftsman* is a clarion call to all genuine leaders. In its number for 10 January 1730 appears a representative exhortation:

> As for you, *Gentlemen,* who are possessed of *large Estates* and a *natural Interest* in the Counties, where you live, I think there can be no Occasion for many Arguments to excite you to a Conduct, which is now happily become both your *Duty* and your *Interest.* Whatever Attachments you may have to *this* or *that Party;* whatever Engagments you may be under to *particular Men;* or by whatever *Names* you may distinguish your selves; you will certainly unite, as one Man, in this common Cause, and support each other against the Incroachments of *Stock-jobbers,* or *beggarly Tools of Power,* who are sent amongst you, without any Recommendation of Merit or Virtue, to supplant you in the Esteem of your Tenants, Neighbours and Dependants; and to get themselves chosen, by indirect Means, as well as for vile Purposes, to be your *Representatives.* [No. 184, 6:10-11][23]

Under its natural leaders, England would regain its inherent unity and rid itself of factious diversity. Calling luxury the *fons et origo mali,* Bolingbroke identified it as the root source of individual corruption and the original sin of nations; money, he wrote, had become "a more lasting tie than honour, friendship, consanguinity, or unity of affections."[24] Division into parties was a visible sign that personal gain had replaced national interest and that individual independence was no longer valued. To him, as earlier to Shaftesbury and later to Smollett, the model politician was an independent country gentleman drawing his virtue and freedom from the land, wise enough to join other natural legislators in ruling the nation, brave enough to resist tyrannical crown or executive. To Walpole, on the other hand, the ideal politician was a sycophant. Quoting *Cato's Letters* the *Craftsman* frequently advised, "Forget . . . the foolish and knavish Distinction of *High-Church* and *Low-Church,* of *Whig* and *Tory;* Sounds, which continue in your Mouths, when the *Meaning* of them is gone, and are now only used to set you together by the Ears, that Rogues may pick your Pockets." Wedded to such counsels were arguments over place bills and demands for new sumptuary laws.[25]

With ancient history as his text, Bolingbroke could foresee only disaster for Britain. When Sparta, Athens, and Rome fell under the spell of mean men, they lost all capacity for virtue and public valor. As they fell, so "will the people of Britain fall, and deserve to fall." The present situation was indeed more serious, for superimposed upon ancient luxury were the monsters introduced with the financial revolution—the national debt, stockjobbing, and moneyed companies—simultaneously instances of luxury and constant temptations to new forms of corruption. For the Opposition the model of economic polity was the great estate; it followed that such an unholy trinity would ruin the nation. No estate could withstand a huge debt, a division of management, and a piecemeal parceling out of ownership.[26] As the alleged panderer of impending catastrophe, Walpole was the Lucifer of Bolingbroke's demonology. He was seen as guilty of two types of political crime. On the one hand, he was supposed cynically and resolutely to have subverted English morals in order to achieve his personal aggrandizement. To this end he, like Mandeville, called luxury useful and perhaps necessary. On the other hand, he was seen as the progenitor of faction, selfishness, and insubordination, forces that were now remolding English society. To the Opposition the most bitter proof of Walpole's venality was that he had given a voice in public affairs to men "whose talents would scarce have recommended them to the meanest offices in the virtuous and prosperous ages of the commonwealth," men "who had not, either from their obscure birth, or their low talents, or their still lower habits, the least occasion ever to dream of such elevation."[27]

Like Fletcher and Davenant a generation earlier, Bolingbroke was convinced that England was depraved beyond redemption. With luxury the reigning standard, the arts and the professions could only lapse into dullness and stupidity; wit, learning, good sense, and public spirit declined together. The *Idea of a Patriot King* was to be his political testament, providing his catalog of the forms of luxury obtaining in the nation and his final prescription for unity and reform: rule by a single great man who stood above all divisions and differences. This, his ultimate statement that legislators were now hopelessly divided, cited Cato, Sallust and the Roman historians, and Machiavelli to demonstrate that when luxury cannot be abated by normal means, only the great man can uphold the general welfare.

Bolingbroke's political despair was to be echoed frequently during the 1750s, and the similarities between Opposition and later attacks upon luxury are many. Both identify the issue as economic and political. Both locate a historical watershed in the recent past. Both contrast the older virtuous order of birth with the newer degenerate values of an order dominated by money. Both assert the death of patriotism and public spirit and the omnivorous vitality of riot, faction, self-interest, and insubordination. Both declare the corruption of most politicians and call for some form of moral rearmament. Both are deeply pessimistic about the future of Britain. The main distinction lies in the broad scope of later attacks. In the 1750s and 1760s writers included both the middle and lower orders in their campaigns against the vice. Bolingbroke earlier concentrated his hostility upon his immediate political opponents, the wealthy Whigs and their mercantile supporters. Toward the lower orders he seems a benevolent patron, writing in the "Fragments, or Minutes of Essays" that for the masses luxury could prove a benefit. If defined as added comforts of life, he writes, luxury would be valuable to the majority of men, as an increase in the amount of "physical good" possessed by mankind. When he wrote of the corruption of luxury, he was referring to the comparatively limited condition: the influence upon public affairs of new men and new money.

> That luxury, which began to spread after the restoration of king Charles the second, hath increased ever since; hath descended from the highest to the lowest ranks of our people, and is become national. Now nothing can be more certain than this, that national luxury and national poverty may, in time, establish national prostitution. Beside this, it is to be considered, that the immense wealth of particular men is a circumstance which always attends national poverty, and is in a great measure the cause of it. . . . Now, as publick want, or general poverty, for in that sense I take it here, will lay numbers of men open to the attacks of corruption; so private wealth will have the same effect, especially where luxury prevails, on some of those who do not feel the public want; for there is imaginary as well as real poverty. He who thought himself rich before, may begin to think himself poor, when he compares his wealth . . . with those men he hath been used to esteem . . . far inferiour to himself. . . . Thus may contraries unite in their effect, and poverty and wealth combine to facilitate the means and the progress of corruption.[28]

Although the partisan controversy over luxury appears to have abated immediately upon Walpole's fall, the campaign waged by the Opposition had made an indelible impression upon the minds of many Englishmen. Attacks upon luxury would continue to grow for at least another generation, and the Opposition version of that attack would be absorbed into the body of older criticism. Hence, by the middle of the century the condemnation of luxury was practically unanimous among the traditionally privileged groups of England. While such opposition did little to define one's position, it did signify one's quarrel with the present age. It therefore appealed to very disparate persons: Jacobites, Tories, political "outs" of many varieties; Catholics and Puritans; monarchists, primitivists, and classicists; philosophers, moralists, and ecclesiastics; pessimists and malcontents; those who had lost rank and fortune and those who had rank and fortune to lose. Even so generous a man as Henry Fielding found cause in 1749, in *A Charge delivered to the Grand Jury . . . of Westminster,* to exclaim: "The fury after licentious and luxurious pleasures is grown to so great a height, that it may be called the characteristic of the present age." What is distinctive in the polemics of the period is, as Samuel Johnson saw, the new animus directed against the English poor. Surveying this last and most relevant period in the controversy over luxury, the immediate context of Smollett's own writings, one notices not so much the voice of argument as the cacophony of curse and threat. Whatever their political stripe, eighteenth-century legislators were largely united in a policy of firm control over labor—an element of national well-being thought to be as essential as control of the prices and quantities of goods. Domestic social and economic policy could thus be subsumed under the attack upon luxury, combating idleness, mobility, insolence, and prosperity among the common people. Population could be considered the source of national wealth only if it was productively and profitably employed, with the definitions of *profit* and *productivity* left to employers. Many writers earlier in the century had identified the luxury of the poor with idleness. Some cited the notion of the utility of poverty to demonstrate that any wage above bare subsistence, even in times of abundance, was a contribution to luxury. Some, like Defoe in *The Great Law of Sub-ordination Consider'd* (1724), complained that the habits of the rich had corrupted the poor by making them discontent. Some, like William Wood, used all three ideas: "where riot and luxuries are not dis-countenanc'd, the inferior rank of men, become presently infected, and grow lazy, effeminate, impatient of labour, and expensive, and conse-quently cannot thrive by trade, tillage, and planting."[29] There was a liberal contribution to this argument, but a weak one. When certain writers held that luxury invariably reduced population, increased unem-ployment, raised the price of food, and ruined poor families, they presumed to be speaking for the national interest and not for special privilege. Yet they could summon no conclusive empirical corrobora-tion for their position, and later evidence, like the census of 1801, found it untenable or misleading. Studies of sumptuary and related laws, it should be recalled, record thousands of warnings, arrests, and convictions during the seventeenth and eighteenth centuries in England. But not one, so far as I can discover, was directed against a person of noble or gentle birth. As Adam Smith noted, many writers could grant freedom and prosperity to England only by denying them to English-men.

What is clear is that during the 1750s and early 1760s fear and anxiety brought forth by national and international conflicts nourished the conventional criticism of luxury. Rising crime, grain riots, and general increases in the price of staples were among the social and economic factors that gave fresh impetus to the pamphlet-writers. Upon the outbreak of war at mid-decade, writers found additional grounds for alarm, lest luxury should drain national resources and hasten national defeat. Fielding's *Enquiry into the Cause of the late Increase of Robbers* (1751) is significant in this context, for it reveals the extent to which the Opposition's method of social analysis had become normal. As journalist and as magistrate, Fielding had seen closely the miseries and dislocations of the city; the experience led him to make luxury the major premise in his attack upon the effects of social change.

His starting point is economic:

> nothing hath wrought such an Alteration in this [the lower] Order of People, as the Introduction of Trade. This hath indeed given a new Face to the whole Nation, hath in great measure subverted the former State of Affairs, and hath almost totally changed the Manners, Customs, and Habits of the People, more especially of the lower Sort. The Narrowness of their Fortune is changed into Wealth; the Simplicity of their Manners changed into Craft, their Frugality into Luxury, their Humility into Pride, and their Subjugation into Equality. [P. xi]

His principal argument is that luxury, not poverty, is the immediate cause of crime among the poor:

> I think that the vast Torrent of Luxury which the late Years hath poured itself into this Nation, hath greatly contributed to produce among many others, the Mischief I here complain of. I aim not here to satirize the Great, among whom Luxury is probably rather a moral than a political Evil. But Vices, no more than Diseases will stop with them . . . in free Countries, at least, it is a Brand of Liberty claimed by the People to be as wicked and as profligate as their Supperiors. . . . It reaches the very Dregs of the People, who aspiring still to a Degree beyond that which belongs to them, and not being able by the Fruits of honest Labour to support the State which they affect, they disdain the Wages to which their Industry would entitle them; and abandoning themselves to Idleness, the more simple and poor spirited betake themselves to a State of Starving and Beggary, while those of more Art and Courage become Thieves, Sharpers and Robbers. [P. 3]

Like Smollett, Fielding senses a dangerous insubordination among the "Dregs of the People" and urges, as a short-run measure, their exclusion from all places of amusement—a proposal Smollett repeated. For the longer range he seeks to establish "How far it is the Business of the Politicians to interfere in the Case of Luxury." He recommends two types of action, both involving sumptuary laws. The first and more important is legislative, "effectively to put a Stop to the Luxury of the lower People, to force the Poor to Industry, and to provide for them when industrious" (p. 126). The second is judicial, the rigorous and universal application of comprehensive laws.[30] His half-brother, John, seconded his call for strong laws to combat dissipation:

> Time is the Labourer's Stock in Trade; and he that makes the Most of it by Industry and Application is a valuable subject. A Journeyman can no more afford to give or throw away his Time than a Tradesman can his Commodity; and the best Way of preventing this useful Body of Men from this species of Extravagance is to remove from their Sight all Temptation to idleness: and however Diversions may be necessary to fill up the dismal Chasms of burdensome Time among People of Fortune, too frequent Relaxations of this Kind among the Populace enervate Industry.[31]

The interrelationship of luxury, population, and labor was among the common topics of political and economic works. Josiah Tucker, in *Reflections on the Expediency of a Law for the Naturalization of Foreign Protestants* (Bristol, 1751), asks rhetorically: "Was a Country *thinly* populated ever rich?—Was a populous Country ever *poor*?" (p. 19). His negative answer is supported by William Horsley in *The Universal Merchant* (1753), which argues that the ideal laborer for the British economy is a poor man with a very large family: "Herein consists the Marrow of that Maxim, *that Numbers of People are the Wealth of a Nation:* as where they are plenty, they must work cheap, and so Manufacturers are encouraged for a foreign Market, and their Returns is a Wealth of a Nation, which numbers thus procure."[32] Since it threatened to eliminate large families, luxury was attacked as a menace to the whole nation. The presumed decline in national spirit appeared all the more dangerous with the outbreak of war. Among the many alarmist pamphlets published within a few months was the anonymous *The Parallel; or, The Conduct and Fate of Great Britain in regard our present Contest with France; exemplified from the Histories of Macedon and Athens* (1756). Reviewers drew the same point from Thomas Leland's translation of *All the Orations of Demosthenes* (1756). They held luxury the primary cause of Athenian defeat and selected from Leland extracts that seemed to support their charge.[33] The urgent need for discipline and a rejection of luxury were central to Francis Fauquier's *Essay on Ways and Means for Raising money for the Support of the Present War without increasing the Publick Debt* (1756) and the anonymous *The True National Evil* (1756). The latter, a sermon, used as its text a paraphrase of a line from the seventh chapter of Joshua: "There is an accursed thing in the midst of thee, O Britons." In the anonymous *Trial of the lady Allured Luxury* (1757), the *lady* is a notorious foreign spy, convicted of every charge brought against her, who is rescued by the fools and knaves of England.

Insofar as the ferment over domestic and foreign problems could be epitomized in a single work, the work would be John Brown's *Estimate of the Manners and Principles of the Times,* the first volume of which appeared in 1757. The *Estimate* is basically a bill of indictment against the English people, particularly the commercial classes, and supplies a catalogue raisonné of the evils of luxury. In this respect it follows a pattern familiar after Bolingbroke, but it is more concise and more concrete than anything done by him. It was also one of the most popular works of the decade, the first volume running through seven authorized and pirated editions in the first year, far surpassing any comparable work and calling forth an extraordinary response from correspondents and reviewers in the periodicals.

What immediately distinguished the content of the *Estimate* from dozens of other works of the fifties was the breadth and particularity of Brown's indictment. Where other writers had railed in abstruse or historical terms, Brown offers pungent details and contemporary names. He laments that the inconsequential essays of Hume are preferred to the substantial achievements of Bolingbroke and Warburton. Opera and pantomime have driven Shakespeare off the boards. Military officers, politicians, and clergymen all neglect their high callings in favor of self-gain. Cowardice, hypochondria, and suicide are but various symptoms of the same national disease of luxury. In the current period of crisis only a total reformation will preserve the nation. Honor, religion, public spirit, and renunciation of self-interest must be returned to their traditional places in English life. Otherwise the disciplined French will overrun the plains of Salisbury as they have overrun the plains of America.[34]

For the evils of his age, Brown blames the *new* commercial interests, as ominously novel to Brown in 1757 as they had been to Bolingbroke in 1710 and Davenant in 1698. He writes, "The spirit of Commerce, now predominant, begets a kind of regulated Selfishness, which tends at once to the Increase and Preservation of Property" (1:22). And, "the Spirit of Trade in its Excess, by introducing Avarice, destroys the Desire of *Rational Esteem*" (1:173). Since the interplay of economic forces must not be left to determine British affairs, firm moral and political regulation is required. Increased wealth at this stage brings not order, but "superfluity, avarice, effeminate refinement, and loss of principle" (1:157–58, 195–96).

It was from a vantage very similar to this that Smollett judged the effects of economic change. He certainly concurred with Brown's estimate of the weakness of human nature: "Humanity neither improved nor controlled, is always defective and partial; and may be very dangerous in its effects" (2:38). For both men the source of a "National Spirit of Union" lay in a strong monarchy, Brown claiming that strength and unity are to be gained most easily in absolute monarchies. In "free Countries," unity is continually threatened by selfishness, faction, and "Freedom of *Opinion* itself" (1:105). Like Smollett, he saw the liberty of the press outrageously abused. For its critical short-range exigencies, Britain needed government by an elite, "whose Superiority is approved and acknowledged . . . who have been so unfashionable as to despise the ruling System of Effeminacy: and [who have] *laboured* and *shone* in a College" (1:77).[35]

Again like Smollett, Brown has no high regard for the common people:

> the Manners and Principles of the common People will scarce find a Place in the Account. For though the Sum total of a Nations immediate Happiness must arise, and be estimate, from the Manners and Principles of the Whole; yet the Manners and Principles of those who *lead,* not of those who *are led;* of those who *govern,* not of those who are governed; of those, in short, who *make* Laws or execute them, will ever determine the Strength or Weakness, and therefore the Continuance or Dissolution, of a State.
>
> For the blind Force or Weight of an ungoverned Multitude can have no steady nor rational Effect, unless some *leading Mind* rouse it into Action, and point it to it's proper *End:* without this, it is either a *brute* and random Bolt, or a *lifeless Ball* sleeping in the *Cannon:* It depends on some superior *Intelligence,* to give it both *Impulse* and *Direction.* [1:24-25]

The masses of people, moreover, do not gain materially from increased national wealth and may be left comparatively poorer. Luxury thus begets more "Murmurs, Sedition, and Tumults." His distress is almost apocalyptic: "Or what can come forth from such Scenes of unprincipled Licentiousness, but Pick-pockets, Prostitutes, Thieves, Highwaymen, and Murderers! These are your Triumphs, O BOLINGBROKE, TINDAL, MANDEVILLE, MORGAN, HUME" (2:86).[36]

Within a year and a half of the publication of volume 1, the *Estimate* had prompted a vast amount of commentary. Almost all the periodicals of the day reviewed it, many correspondents offered their opinions, and answering pamphlets appeared. Perhaps because Brown had criticized so many of his contemporaries and had severely rebuked the weekly and monthly journals, its reception was mixed and sometimes ambiguous. Yet there could be little doubt that Brown had written what many others had been thinking. Reviewers found his arguments against the periodicals unfounded, and clergymen thought his remarks on their profession too harsh, but few challenged or contradicted his censure of luxury. Rather he was chastised for misjudging its nature, not identifying all its manifestations, or not citing all its consequences. The upshot was a new round of popular debate and self-castigation. The *World* deplored the liberalism of the British constitution; the *Grand* rejected as vain all hope for honest government. The *Universal* lamented the depravity of human nature, and the *New Royal* called for ruthless measures by the government. The *Universal Visitor* said that reliance upon trade destroyed the customs and stability of English society. All seemed to agree, however, on the need for immediate action. In the words of a correspondent to the *London Magazine:*

> The time of war, when people are obliged to contribute largely for its support, and consequently cannot spare so much for superfluities, seems the fittest to suppress luxury; for experience shows, that peace always promotes it: And indeed, if men will be luxurious, when in distress and under pressures of war, there can be little hopes of their leaving it off in times of peace, and when their circumstances are more affluent.[37]

The year the *Estimate* appeared also saw the widespread anxiety over the provision and price of grain indicated earlier. By 1760 some forty pamphlets had been published condemning either the adulteration of bread or the general high prices of grain. The discussion of high prices, in fact, lasted more than a decade. Many of the writers related their arguments to the current excitement over luxury; among these were James Manning, *Poison Detected; or, Frightful Truths* (1757); *The Causes of the Present High Price of Corn and Grain* (1758); *A Modest Apology in Defense of Bakers* (1758); and *A Dissertation on Adulterated Bread* (1758). Bramble's letter of June 8 from London, it will be recalled, included adulterated bread in the "catalogue of London dainties" produced by luxury. "The bread I eat in London," Bramble wrote, "is a deleterious paste, mixed up with chalk, alum, and bone-ashes; insipid to the taste, and destructive to the constitution." The same charge had been made in 1758, in *An Essay on Monopolies; or, Reflections upon the Frauds and Abuses Practiced by Wholesale Dealers in Corn and Flour*. The author holds "the vain and luxurious" responsible for the existence of such monopolies.

> After all that has been urged on this subject, we are obliged to acknowledge one melancholy truth, that *mistaken luxury* and

general folly have laid the foundation, and afforded incitements to all these frauds. We know that a few years ago a fancy prevailed amongst persons of elegance, to paint all their wainscots with a dead white; but why that should be the colour of their bread, too, is not easy to be accounted for, as it certainly is a very unnatural one. . . . There is known to be a yellowish cast in the best and purest flour, especially when mixed with yest; but it is a matter of astonishment, that people who boast of taste, should merely for the sake of a colour, exchange the sweetness, elasticity and consistence, of a pure home-made loaf, for a harsh, dry, and crumbling composition of, *they really know not what.*[38]

Anxiety of a less material sort preoccupied many writers for several years after 1757. In a comparative flood of sermons, pamphlets, and books, they warned of a national malaise of disturbing proportions, a sickness of which luxury was both cause and symptom. The whole of Goldsmith's *Enquiry into the Present State of Polite Learning* (1759) reflects this view. Wherever he looks, Goldsmith sees avarice controlling behavior and policy. Learning and culture have been debased by "luxurious affluence" to the point that vulgarity alone finds applause. The course of his inquiry leads him "to deduce a universal degeneracy of manners, from . . . the depravation of taste; . . . as a nation grows dull, it sinks into debauchery . . . vice and stupidity are always mutually productive of each other" (pp. 195–96).

Historical precedents for the current crisis were presented in a tone of urgency. One of the lessons of Thomas Leland's *History of the Life and Reign of Philip King of Macedon* (2 vols., 1758) was that luxury had corrupted Persia in the time of Xerxes: "When Princes, either through inattention, defect of judgment, or want of virtue, suffer their subjects to sink into all the excesses of effeminate luxury; from such subjects they are not to expect generous sentiments, or great and gallant actions. Ruin and slavery [are] the necessary and natural consequences of such corruptions" (2:104). Edward W. Montagu interrupted his *Reflections on the Rise and Fall of Ancient Republics* (1759) to attack Mandeville and the corruption of English life he had ostensibly endorsed (p. 159). The anonymous *Additional Dialogue of the Dead* (1760) seems written for the specific object of comparing the Athens of Pericles and the Britain of Pitt. Aristides at one point asks:

Arist. . . . suppose that, by the excess of commerce, and overflow of wealth, or by any other cause, a pernicious *luxury* should creep in, and steal unperceived on the highest ranks . . . and suppose this political *venality* should, in fact, creep in along with luxury; what consequence should you expect?

Pericles.   You terrify me by the representation. I behold the state
on the brink of *ruin.*[39]

Similar omens were further identified in M. P. Macquer, *A Chronological
Abridgment of the Roman History* (1760); *The History of the Roman
Emperors from Augustus to Constantine* (1760); *The Private Life of the
Romans* (1761); volume 3 of N. Hooke's *Roman History* (1763); and
John Mill's third volume of *Memoirs of the Court of Augustus* (1763).

Many economic tracts meanwhile broadcast the demoralizing effects
luxury had upon the laboring classes. Two anonymous pamphlets,
Populousness with Oeconomy the Wealth and Strength of a Kingdom
(1759) and *A Letter to the Right Hon. Sir Thomas Chitty* (1760),
dwell upon the dangers of depopulation and demands for higher wages.
A View of the Internal Policy of Great Britain (1763) maintains that
only the resettlement of poor families in uninhabited areas could insure
a steady flow of "hardy industrious people." Other works contended
that those of the laboring population who had settled in the city—the
resort of sickness, laziness, and libertinism—were already lost, for they
had succumed to a fashion that ruined the constitution and prevented
healthful reproduction. The coordinate issue—the relationship of luxury,
idleness, and insubordination—is explored in James Ridley's *The
Schemer* (1763); *Remarks on the Present State of the National Debt*
(1764); and *North Briton Extraordinary* (1765). Containing an otherwise commonplace argument, the *Remarks* reveal one sign of a decided
shift in popular notions concerning luxury: its author regards only idleness among the poor as *dangerous* luxury; all other forms are mere
refinement or innocuous luxury. Later in the century William Cobbett
was to insist that in his own lifetime the attitudes of the rich had become much harsher, a deterioration reflected in common language. By
the time of the *Rural Rides* the old term "the commons of England"
had given way to "the populace," "the pesantry," and "the lower
orders."

Religious objections to luxury continued to be offered in a traditional
vein, but increasing emphasis was given to its political effects. In *Sermons on Public Occasions* (1761), Charles Bulkey declares that Christianity and patriotism stand together against the vice.[40] Thomas Cole's
Discourses on Luxury, Infidelity, and Enthusiasm (1761), which was
highly praised in at least three periodicals, makes the same point at
greater length. Cole devotes much of the first half of his work to a
repudiation of Mandeville; the latter half is an attempt to prove that
luxury has been and will always be "the utter ruin of every nation
where it prevails." Within a period of five years, another clergyman,
Edward Watkinson, published seven sermons and tracts attacking
luxury. One, *An Essay upon Oeconomy* (1762), which saw three

editions its first year and eight within five years, held that "the *Glory* of a Nation was never founded on the *Luxury* of the People. . . . *Luxury* always relaxes the Sinews of Government" (p. 34). Another, *An Essay upon Gratitude* (1764), calls discontent a blameworthy kind of envy and states that it is a *religious* duty for Englishmen to feel affection and gratitude toward their government. Samuel Cooper's *Definitions and Axioms relative to Charity* (1764) finds vicious only the luxury of the poor; the pleasures of life are permissible when confined to the "middling and higher orders of people." Cooper's chief practical proposal is the prohibition of "plays and shews of every kind" before an audience of laborers.

Such jeremiads continued beyond the Treaty of Paris, although with declining frequency and with less absorption in immediate crises. Samuel Fawconer's *Essay on Modern Luxury* (1765) is a summing up of the concerns of the 1760s, as Brown's *Estimate* had been of the previous decade. Assured of England's military survival, Fawconer wishes to uproot the social manifestations of luxury that persist despite the imprecations of wartime. His language and point of view have the added interest of anticipating Bramble's attacks upon Bath and London in *Humphry Clinker.* His main target is the aspiring middle orders, particularly their fashions in dress, amusement, equipage and retinue, and their "new and unprecedented" claims for inclusion in public affairs. Such concerns, he says, are properly the exclusive domain of rank and wealth. Encroachments upon that domain can lead only to chaos and insubordination. The crises weathered by government and constitution followed directly from faction, sedition, and riot spawned by luxury. For the aspirations of the middling sort of people, he has only ridicule; though they are ridiculous, they do pose a threat to national order, especially in London. He is horrified by the state of life in the capital, likening it to an overgrown head, whence luxury moves to the rest of Britain like a "distemper," a "frenzy," and a "madness."

Fawconer reveals that for some Englishmen the Aristotelian principles of necessity and hierarchy still held fast. For natural legislators splendor and elegance is fitting, for,

> it may be right for people of family and fashion to live up to their quality and fortune: as it gives mankind an opinion of their dignity and opulence, and promotes the circulation of the materials of happiness. But here lies the danger: luxury is of that assimilating insinuating nature, that its infection, like a pestilence, runs thro' every order of the community, from the throne to the cottage. And, whether tempted by inborn pride or seduced by the power of all-prevailing fashion, every impertinent inferiour treads

on the heel of his betters. This emulation of pomp and parade is not confined to equals in point of rank or fortune, but extends itself to the most distant degrees in both. [Pp. 4-5]

(Six years later, the letters of Bramble would twice return to the image of ignorant and impertinent plebeians treading on the heels of their betters.) Suitable laws would have prevented such abuses of liberty, but they were not enacted: "Hence it is that so many make a figure in the eye of the world, and keep up a farce of grandeur without anything to support it. Like an *ignis fatuus,* they shine and glitter for a while, and in a moment disappear" (p. 6). For the same reasons as Bramble, Fawconer finds London oppressive:

> it is observable, that luxury generally abounds, in proportion to the populousness of the capital city. It is become a fashion for every body to crowd to the metropolis, to spend part of the year in town, for the sake of its pleasures and diversions. . . . And, where the exteriors form our judgment of the man, and appearance in the vulgar eye passes for the only criterion of true worth: every one is ready to assume the marks of a superior condition, in order to be esteemed more than what he really is. [Pp. 6-7]

> Nor is this the only inconvenience that is suffered in a city, whose inhabitants are continually on the increase. For these temporary inmates must be accommodated with lodging . . . there is reason to apprehend, that this overgrown metropolis must in a few years be crushed with its own weight. Already the head is too large for the body. The prodigious increase of inhabitants raises the price of provisions to an exorbitant height. The additional consumption is so large, that the produce of the neighborhood is unequal to the supply. And when the necessaries of life are procured from a distance, they must fall into the hands of dealers and factors: who are too often led, by this temptation, to monopolies and combinations, to make their own advantage of the necessities of others. [Pp. 8-9]

Spreading outward from the capital, the distemper had infected all parts of Britain. Spas are now "public marts of folly and misery"; what was once a center of recreation has become the seat of "public riot and dissipation, the place of general resort for the sick, and idle, and people of fashion and fortune; and persons of figure without any pretensions to either" (p. 10).

For the fashionable entertainments of the present age are the most empty and trifling that can possibly be imagined; arguing not the want of good taste only, but even of common sense. And this must always be the consequence, whenever sensual pleasure is suffered to assume the empire over our rational faculties. [Pp. 10–11]

In his discussion of luxury in dress and furnishings (pp. 13–21), Fawconer urges an alliance of religion and government to suppress the vice, for it is dishonest and reprehensible for a person to dress or live above his station and thereby undermine hierarchy. Persons of rank and fortune are degraded, Fawconer argues, when their inferiors are permitted to dress, speak, or behave like them.

The custom of all civilized countries, hath regulated some general standard of dress, as most convenient to discriminate one from another in point of sex, age, and quality. The propriety and necessity of such a regulation, is evident from the mischiefs that could ensue from the want or neglect of it. For on whatever levelling principle the reasonable distinction of merit and degree is confounded, the order of government is broken in upon and destroyed. [Pp. 16–17]

Having ruined the health, property, fortune, and family of individuals, luxury then subverts the foundations of national economy and government: "O luxury! Alas! patriotism!" (p. 24 n).

LATER DEVELOPMENTS

Within a decade of the unprecedented attention given Brown's *Estimate,* the concept of luxury had lost much of its power instantly to arouse indignation and partisan fervor. After several generations of expanding the concept to fit new social and financial situations, Englishmen began to reconsider its uses. Luxury had become so cumbersome, it appears in retrospect, that in order to become manageable once again it had to be redefined and hence renewed. Pocock has argued well that the history of political ideas is also a history of political language. Both concept and language became ambiguous when English legislators concentrated upon the use and consumption of *things*—when they were constrained to give luxury a primarily economic construction. An emphasis upon hierarchy subverted their position on necessity, and vice versa. If imported foods or textiles were dangerous in and of themselves, why were they not as dangerous to legislators as to subjects? Tiberius found a way to square that circle; George III did not try. Pocock writes:

Because men in speaking commit themselves to a load or fabric greater than they can control, it is possible for others in reply to employ the same words to convey the loads of meaning they desire to select. Communication is possible only because it is imperfect. Because we affect one another's most intimate behavior by the spins we impart to words as they pass to and fro between us, it is possible for the linguistic polity to synthesize conflict with the recognition of interdependency. Politics is a game of biases in the asymmetrical universe of society. What we have called paradigms are linguistic constructs recognized as carrying increasingly complex loads in excess of what can be predicted or controlled at a given moment.[41]

The political games played over the idea of luxury would never again be quite the same.

The history of luxury from about 1763 to the end of the century proceeds along three lines: strict continuity, moderate redefinition, and radical change. The *Essay on Modern Luxury* is interesting as a prelude to Smollett, and it would be notable among dozens of attacks published at the outbreak of the Seven Years' War. Appearing as it does nearly a decade later, however, Fawconer's pamphlet is noteworthy as an example of a declining genre, reflecting a diminution in both the number and the intensity of attacks upon luxury.

Such changes were neither sharp nor consistent. The *Fable of the Bees* continued to evoke outraged replies through the 1790s. Edward Watkinson's *Frugality and Diligence* (York, 1766) reproduces without significant modification the religious argument common to the seventeenth century. And like Richard Price, in *Observations on . . . the Population* (1779) and *An Essay on the Population of England and Wales* (1780), writers continued to worry over the relation between luxury and the supply of labor. Persistent disquiet among the laboring population, moreover, continued to prompt warning against luxury. As Arthur Young wrote of his *Eastern Tour* (1771), "every one but an idiot knows, that the lower classes must be kept poor or they will never be industrious" (4.361).[42] To men like these, a large majority in 1750 but a minority fifty years later, luxury remained an absolute vice, to be suppressed or eradicated.

Yet another and growing trend attempted to moderate between old attitudes and new situations, arguing that luxury represented an inevitable condition of English life, to be understood and if necessary controlled. It is to this latter development of thought that Goldsmith refers, in hyperbolic terms, in his dedication to the *Deserted Village* (1770):

In regretting the depopulation of the country, I inveigh against the encrease of our luxuries; and here also I expect the shout of modern politicians against me. For twenty or thirty years past, it has been the fashion to consider luxury as one of the greatest national advantages; and all the wisdom of antiquity in that particular, as erroneous. Still however, I must remain a professed ancient on that head, and continue to think those luxuries prejudicial to states, by which so many vices are introduced, and so many kingdoms have been undone. Indeed so much has been poured out of late on the other side of the question, that merely for the sake of novelty and variety, one would sometimes wish to be in the right.[43]

Goldsmith's judgment is doubly revealing. Elsewhere, in the *Citizen of the World*, he had voiced approval of certain forms of luxury. He also attributes its defense to "modern politicians." The implication, supported by other evidence, is that with the successful conclusion of the war luxury ceased to be an incendiary social and political issue. British imperial conquests, with the increased commerce they implied, together became translated into a new popular acceptance of "the commercial vice." Even writers for the *Critical Review*, formerly arch-foes of luxury in any form, expressed themselves in reasoned, judicious tones. Two years after Smollett left the journal, the reviewer of a French work declares:

Few writers, when they treat of luxury, ascertain the idea of it in a proper manner. Some of them . . . comprehend profusion and intemperance, and therefore declaim against it as inconsistent with the maxims of Christianity and the welfare of society. Others . . . mean costly furniture, magnificent buildings, splendid equipages, elegant entertainments, and other things of the nature, and agreeably to this notion, maintain, in opposition to the first, that it promotes the circulation of money and the advantage of the community. On both sides there is truth; and each party would allow, were they mutually to explain the meaning of the expression, that they differ more in appearance than in reality.

Luxury, (this author) observes, is contrary or favorable to the enrichment of nations, according as it consumes more or less of the produce of their soil and of their industry, or as it consumes more or less of the soil of foreign countries; and it ought to have a greater or a less number of objects, according as these nations have more or less wealth. With such an extensive commerce as now prevails, with so universal a spirit of industry, with such a multitude of arts brought to perfection, it would be a vain scheme to think of bringing Europe back to her ancient simplicity, which would be only bringing her back to weakness and barbarism. The only point should be to give luxury a proper direction, and then it would contribute to the grandeur of nations and the happiness of man kind.[44]

More concisely, a later writer for the *Monthly Review* repeats the point: "There is scarce any subject that has been more frequently treated by political writers than that of luxury, and yet few have been treated in a more vague and superficial manner. The generally received opinion is, that luxury has proved the ruin of the greatest empires, and that, in whatever state it prevails, it must in the end be fatal to it; and on this topic orators, moralists, philosophers, and divines are eternally declaiming."[45]

Boswell provides an illustration of the new judiciousness in a conversation between Johnson and Goldsmith dated 13 April 1773. Goldsmith seeks to draw Johnson "on the common topick, that the race of our people was degenerated, and that this was owing to luxury." Johnson doubts the fact of degeneration and also denies that luxury could ever cause it. He asks consideration of a contrary, indisputable fact: "how very small a proportion of our people luxury can reach. Our soldiery, surely, are not luxurious, who live on sixpence a day; and the same remark will apply to almost all the other classes. Luxury, so far as it reaches the poor, will do good to the race of people; it will strengthen and multiply them. Sir, no nation was ever hurt by luxury; for, as I said before, it can reach but to a few." In the *Decline and Fall of the Roman Empire* Gibbon also distinguishes between harmless and harmful luxury, along the same lines as Johnson and Adam Smith. Discussing the age of the Antonines in chapter 2 (published in 1776), he remarks that "in the present imperfect condition of society, luxury, though it may proceed from vice or folly, seems to be the only means that can correct the unequal distribution of property." While the rich strive to enjoy every possible type of pleasure and refinement, the mass of the people must labor incessantly to provide them. In this process, which Gibbon sees as occurring in all ages, luxury acts as "a voluntary tax" paid to the poor by the possessors of land. However, when luxury has so pervaded a society that no other pursuit is possible, as occurred in Rome under Theodosius, then the situation has altered entirely. Luxury is no longer a distributive tax, but "that indolent despair which enjoys the present hour and declines the thoughts of futurity." When it reaches the army it is "a secret and destructive poison," under whose influence the infantry lays aside its heavy armor, later to be overwhelmed "naked and trembling" by the cavalry of the enemy (chap. 27, 1781).

In Scotland, where Enlightenment views on luxury were more warmly received than in England, several major writers were also challenging the received opinions of men like Arthur Young. Beginning in the 1750s a group of writers on social theory began to portray social development as directly related to means of subsistence. This group—including Dalrymple, Ferguson, Kames, Smith, and Smith's student John Millar—proposed that all societies pass through successive stages of hunting, pasturage, agriculture, and commerce, each stage possessing its own distinctive complex of values and institutions. Flowing from this four-stage theory were a more favorable view of commerce, an assertion of modest progress in human affairs, and a criticism of primitivist theories.[46] In his chapter on luxury in the *Essay on the History of Civil Society* (1767), Ferguson attempts to remove the concept altogether from the arena of polemics. Following an argument put forward by Hume in 1752, Ferguson suggests that luxury possesses a positive and important meaning directly related to the material progress of a society: the capacity to use the accommodations and conveniences the age has developed. He largely reduces the question of visible luxury to one of mere changing tastes; Smollett four years later was reducing visible changes in taste to a question of dangerous luxury. In a direct challenge to attacks upon the luxury of the poor, Smith argues in the *Wealth of Nations* (1776) that if the effects of British trade are economically beneficial, they should also be socially welcome. The economy *required* the free exercise of self-interest. Indeed the economic, then social, benefits that filtered through to the mass of laboring people returned to the nation as multiplied economic security:

> The common complaint that luxury extends itself even to the lowest ranks of the people, and that the labouring poor will not now be contented with the same food, cloathing, and lodging, which satisfied them in former times, may convince us that it is not the money price for labour alone, but its real recompence, which has augmented.
>
> Is this improvement in the circumstances of the lower ranks of the people to be regarded as an advantage or as an incoveniency to the society? The answer seems at first sight abundantly plain. Servants, labourers and workmen of different kinds, make up the far greater part of every great political society. But what improves the circumstances of the greater part can never be regarded as an inconveniency to the whole. No society can surely be flourishing and happy, of which the far greater part of the members are poor and miserable. It is but equity, besides, that they who feed, cloath and lodge the whole body of the people, should have such a

share of the produce of their own labour as to be themselves tolerably well fed, cloathed and lodged.[47]

It was the redefinition of the concept, which had been attempted long before 1763 and will be discussed in the following chapter, that eventually led to a complete reversal in its conventional usage and thence to Thackeray's and the modern sense of luxury. Perhaps most influential in the process of redefinition was Hume's *Political Discourses* of 1752. Hume had at least three incisive criticisms against contemporary, all-embracing uses of the term. Philosophically, such uses were frequently untenable, based as they were upon vague or unspecified assumptions. Historically, they were inaccurate, founded upon a reading of ancient and modern history for which there was no evidence. And socially, they were very biased, defending the few against the many. In calling attention to the political and social animus contained in the theory of luxury, Hume distinguished between luxury as criterion of value and luxury as vehicle of prejudice. His views had little effect upon the young Scottish writer who had just published his second novel or upon the Scottish nobleman about to begin the education of the future monarch. But they were influential upon the work of two other Scots, Ferguson and Smith, who together delivered the intellectual coup de grace to the more blatant political purposes to which the idea of luxury had been put. Yet because luxury was far more than an intellectual construct, the arguments of brilliant minds alone would not alter it greatly.

It is important that Hume was not the only reputable Tory to help dissolve its social animus. Another staunch conservative, undeservedly regarded as extreme in his political views, began a number of the *Literary Magazine* in 1756 with the assertion, "The time is now come, in which *every* Englishman expects to be informed of the national affairs, and in which he has a right to have that expectation gratified." Thus Johnson at the opening of the Seven Years' War, at the conclusion of which Smollett was yet arguing the contrary position. It was also Johnson who understood better than most "the maxims of a commercial nation": "To entail irreversible poverty upon generation after generation only because the ancestor happened to be poor, is in itself cruel, if not unjust, and is wholly contrary to the maxims of a commercial nation, which always suppose and promote a rotation of property, and offer every individual a chance of mending his condition by his diligence." And perhaps his most pertinent comment in the review of Soame Jenyns: "The shame is to impose words for ideas upon ourselves or others." A third notable Tory, although somewhat equivocal about luxury, included in his novel *The Vicar of Wakefield,* published five years before *Humphry Clinker* and written earlier, a chapter extolling the virtues of the English middle class and especially its contributions to domestic trade and domestic liberty. Echoing Hume, Goldsmith calls that class of which he and Johnson were members:

> that order of men which subsists between the very rich and the very rabble; those men who are possest of too large fortunes to submit to the neighbouring man in power, and yet are too poor to set up for tyranny themselves. In this middle order of mankind are generally to be found all the arts, wisdom, and virtues of society. This order alone is known to be the true preserver of freedom, and may be called the People.[48]

English success in the war accelerated acceptance of this view, for political change was needed before a political concept would be altered. In the mid-1750s Horace Walpole had often evoked a genuinely desolate mood: "Between the French and the earthquakes, you have no notion how good we are grown; nobody makes a suit of clothes now but of sackcloth turned up with ashes." The tone of his metaphors in 1757 had not lightened: "It is time for England to slip her own cables, and float away into some unknown ocean." Yet with the Treaty of Paris his sense of English greatness had more than returned: "Throw away your Greek and Roman books, histories of little peoples." Walpole's allusion seemed apt, for with the peace had emerged the second and greater British Empire. His elation, too, reflected a common sentiment. "French superiority . . . received a death-blow on the heights of Abram," wrote Leslie Stephen, "and Englishmen, finding that they had not become cowards, forgot the alarm or remembered it only as a good jest." Modern historians have perceived the same response. "The British . . . were overtaken by hubris after 1763," Ian R. Christie has written; "Everywhere the theme was expansion."[49]

Expansion presumed cooperation between government and commercial interests; put in the terms of those interests, expansion presumed that industry and commerce would operate on a grand scale, as part of a concerted national policy. English victory seemed to indicate that at least one kind of human progress, the commercial, was attainable. (In the paper war of the early 1760s, the *Critical Review* continued for a time to warn against luxury in situations where the *Monitor* saw only "commercial progress.") French defeat provided a complementary lesson upon the vulnerability of an empire held by force of arms alone. What befell the French colonial armies could easily recoil upon the English (and in the American colonies soon did). Far better to found a trading empire bound to England by shipping routes and self-interest, not by chains and fear. While Burke came to regret that an age of "sophists, economists, and calculators" had succeeded the age of chivalry and that "the glory of Europe is extinguished for ever," he nevertheless saw Adam Smith as a new Moses, declaring: "The laws of commerce are the laws of nature, and therefore the laws of God." Once Smith's views had found a solicitor, they would soon find a singer; and in the fourth book of *The Progress of Civil Society: A Didactic Poem in Six Books* (1796), Richard Payne Knight provides a redaction into verse of the lessons of the *Wealth of Nations*:

> Each found the produce of his toil exceed
> His own demands, of luxury or need;
> Whence each the superfluity resign'd,
> More useful objects in return to find:
> Each freely gave what each too much possess'd,
> In equal plenty to enjoy the rest.
>
> Hence the soft intercourse of commerce ran,
> From state to state, and spread from clan to clan;
> Each link of social union tighter drew,
> And rose in vigour as it wider grew.   [Pp. 77–78]

By 1780 two events of symbolic importance had occurred. James Watt, who once wrote bitterly that the gentry treated him as a mechanic no better than a slave, had joined Matthew Boulton in the production of steam engines for industry—science and invention entering into partnership with manufacturing. And for the first time in English history Parliament found it worthwhile to levy a tax upon retailers' shops. Within the decade every statistical measure of production turned sharply upward; the revolution in commerce and industry was visibly upon England. The popular counterpart of these changes is the history of John Bull: a figure of ridicule in Arbuthnot's pamphlets of 1712, a commonplace of political caricature until the late 1750s, and the typical, *good* Englishman from the 1770s onward.[50]

The dispute over high prices to be described below will demonstrate that in learned works of the early 1760s luxury could be turned 180 degrees, loosed from its aristocratic moorings, and set against the bastions of the rich. In Addison, Steele, and Defoe we have already witnessed the penchant of Whiggish writers to turn an argument against luxury into an indictment of the upper orders, a tendency continued in Gray's association of luxury with pride and wealth in the *Elegy* (1751), in Churchill's location of luxury exclusively at court in book 1 of *Gotham* (1765), and in Burns's attack in *The Cotter's Saturday Night* (1786). It finds a transatlantic parallel in the movement of American Quakers for the abolition of slavery, a movement that inspired the English Quaker Thomas Day to compose the highly influential *The*

Dying Negro (1773).[51] By 1771 the reversal of target in condemnations of luxury was sufficiently acceptable to appear in a popular novel. In *The Man of Feeling,* published in the same year as Smollett's last novel, Mackenzie has a passing stranger explain to Harley how the luxury of the rich harms the poor and corrupts civil government, his comments on education sounding like a gloss on the careers of Jery and Lydia Melford.

"Indeed, the education of your youth is every way preposterous: you waste at school years in improving talents, without having ever spent an hour in discovering them; one promiscuous line of instruction is followed, without regard to genius, capacity, or probable situations in the commonwealth. From this bear-garden of the pedagogue, a raw unprincipled boy is turned loose upon the world to travel; without any ideas but those of improving his dress at Paris, or starting into taste by gazing on some paintings at Rome. Ask him of the manners of the people, and he will tell you, That the skirt is worn much shorter in France, and that every body eats macaroni in Italy. When he returns home, he buys a seat in parliament, and studies the constitution at Arthur's.

"Nor are your females trained to any more useful purpose: they are taught, by the very rewards which their nurses propose for good behaviour, by the first thing like a jest which they hear from every male visitor of the family, that a young woman is a creature to be married; and when they are grown somewhat older, are instructed, that it is the purpose of marriage to have the enjoyment of pin-money, and the expectation of a jointure.

"These indeed are the effects of luxury, which is perhaps inseparable from a certain degree of power and grandeur in a nation. But it is not simply of the progress of luxury that we have to complain: did its votaries keep in their own sphere of thoughtless dissipation, we might despise them without emotion; but the frivolous pursuits of pleasure are mingled with the most important concerns of the state; and public enterprise shall sleep till he who should guide its operation has decided his bets at Newmarket, or fulfilled his engagement with a favourite-mistress in the country."[52]

Similar charges were to be repeated in a series of important works in the middle of the decade. The year 1776 saw not only the publication of the *Wealth of Nations,* but also Paine's *Common Sense,* Bentham's *Fragment on Legislation,* and Richard Price's *On Civil Liberty;* it also brought the first comprehensive proposal for parliamentary reform.

The wide social gulf between the nobility and gentry, on one hand,

and the merchants on the other certainly persisted alongside such signs of change. Writing of London around 1780, Archenholtz records the suspicion and jealousy existing between the groups, and though Smollett would have quickly recognized the sources of the hostility the foreign visitor describes, he might have been surprised by its terms of expression.

> This difference which holds even in the hours of eating and drinking, in the kind of amusements, the dress and manner of speaking etc. has given rise to a degree of mutual contempt by the inhabitants of each of these quarters for the other. Those of the city reproach them of the other end for their idleness, luxury, manner of living, and desire to imitate everything that is French: these in their turn never mention an inhabitant of the city but as an animal gross and barbarous, whose only merit is his strong box . . . this mutual dislike is sung in the streets, it is introduced upon the stage, and even in parliament it is not forgotten.[53]

Smollett's total and uncompromising classical denunciation of luxury in 1771, then, is anachronistic. It is wholly consistent with his earlier pronouncements on the subject, but it is less consistent with the development of British attitudes after the Treaty of Paris. Rather than the confidence of the end of the 1760s, *Humphry Clinker* reflects the doubt of the beginning of the decade, supporting the contention that in the novel Smollett is returning with gusto to some of his earlier political quarrels. In his many attacks upon luxury, the novelist is returning also to an ancient rhetorical mode, and *Humphry Clinker* must be read in the light of its traditions. He seeks no novelty or conscious originality for his arguments. On the contrary, his strength sustains itself upon ancient convention, invoking the familiar and the commonplace in order to reflect the patterns of truth and experience. The burden of controversy taxed that strength, demanding that he deny economic arguments in favor of luxury in order to express his social and political antipathies. In this respect he could be called the last Patriot.

~Three~

SUBJECTS RAMPANT:
DEFENSES AND REDEFINITIONS OF
LUXURY IN THE
EIGHTEENTH CENTURY

Hume's essay "Of Luxury," among the *Political Discourses* of 1752, is a devastating commentary upon the type of thinking outlined in the previous chapter. Yet only eight years later, while gathering his essays for a new collection, Hume altered the title, substituting the word *refinement* for luxury. Confident that his own view of the matter would soon hold the day, he was willing to forego at least part of the taunting edge of his earlier position. His aplomb is, for us, both revealing and deceptive. It certainly was prescient, for his general estimate of luxury stands as the usual one today, when leisure and convenience are meant. But for the English world of ideas it was also quite premature. A generation later, in 1776, Johnson was still correcting Boswell: "Many things which are false are transmitted from book to book, and gain credit in the world. One of these is the cry against the evil of luxury. Now the truth is, that luxury produces much good." Hume's recasting of the concept, like Johnson's defense of its effects, is an example of a rare genre. It is a liability of progressive treatments of intellectual history that to the twentieth century the best-known discussions of luxury are those of the few heretics rather than the many true believers.[1]

For the first three-quarters of the century there are probably fewer arguments in support of luxury than there are defenses of deism or greater democracy. Traditional condemnations were so widely accepted during most of the century that few writers were bold enough to meet them frontally. For writers in every field—with the partial exception of political economy—the classical attack upon luxury amounted to precious orthodoxy. There is a real paradox in this. For if one accepts the view of the commonwealthmen, then the reign of luxury began with William and Mary and should have received concerted support thereafter. If one takes another view, making Walpole the serpent of the British Eden, then defenses should have flowed massively from hired pens after 1720. Yet little of this did follow. In fact, Walpole's party journalists usually responded to Bolingbroke's charges not with approval of luxury but with counterattacks upon the motives and integrity of the Opposition. Whether defending George II, Newcastle, Pitt, or Beckford, later writers sought as a matter of course to shift the terms of dispute from luxury to a more immediate, concrete political issue. Even those men audacious enough to voice approval of some aspect of luxury—a group that includes some of the foremost intellectual figures of the period—generally did so obliquely: Mandeville with irony and epigrammatic sallies, Johnson in conversation, Steuart, Ferguson, Smith, and others as part of comprehensive revaluations of social and economic theory or policy. The essential issue was of course not moral courage, for no defense of luxury however straightforward would have entered a favorable climate of opinion much before 1763. The situation is clearest with those writers of the 1750s and 1760s who tried to defend the poor against charges of debauchery. They wished to initiate debate over the material evidence of luxury in English society, especially in the lives of the homeless and miserable. In a few instances they received replies ostensibly couched in terms of manifestations of luxury: empirical testimony and the corollary comparison of life past and present. For the most part, however, they were answered only with repetitions of the original charges. Their opponents were not much concerned with logic and evidence, and the basic difference between the two groups was not merely descriptive or empirical but was of a more profound sort. Rather than a learned disagreement over the course of social and political change, the controversy reflected a collision over the ancient principles of necessity and hierarchy—whether they represented the sole expressions of ultimate virtue.

So long as the leaders of England, of all sorts, adhered to the traditional conception of luxury, it possessed the power of religious dogma: self-sustaining, self-confirming, and invulnerable to internal contradiction or even argument. Precisely how and why it lost that support cannot be answered with certainty. The development of British Protestantism, frequently remarked by students of the century, no doubt acted as a cultural catalyst. A fully secular social philosophy, an ethic of benevolence spurring liberalism, sentiment, and tolerance; a socially powerful evangelical movement: these and other forces prompted some Englishmen to ask anew the ancient questions of what people needed, and where, socially, they belonged. What is clear is that the reaction, when it arrived, came from outside the normal context of English beliefs—in new social, economic, and political relationships, international as well as domestic, signaled by division among the legislators. Internal arguments against traditional attitudes did not simply prevail by virtue of intellectual force. Rather they were left holding the field as older positions were abandoned. To account fully for the transition, one would need the kind of grand cultural analysis provided by Kuhn in *The Structure of Scientific Revolutions* or Foucault in *The Order of Things*. (One could contend, for example, that in its setting it represented as complex a change, with sources as diverse, as the Reformation.) More modestly, one can note that by the end of the century the traditional concept no longer satisfied many of England's intellectual and political leaders. Political economy had come to emphasize the latter half of the phrase as much as the former, and here writers discovered not only demonstrably new knowledge about the economic mechanism, but also what was perceived as a new economic structure itself. Under such circumstances luxury as it had been viewed for centuries underwent a lasting devaluation: from a myth to a fiction, from an ethic to a prejudice, and from an essential, general element of moral theory to a minor, technical element of economic theory.

In what might be called the "macroeconomic" sense, the modernizing of luxury of course passed beyond Smollett's comprehension. But on the "microeconomic" level of palpable month-to-month changes in political and economic relationships, he was more aware of what was happening in England than most of his educated fellow countrymen. And most of what he saw he did not like. The present section is intended as a clarifying interchapter, indicating some of the sources of eighteenth-century controversy as well as present-day thinking about luxury and relating the general criticism of luxury sketched above to Smollett's own, traced in following chapters. There is no need here fully to recount the flux of argument that sustained the controversy outlined in the previous chapter. At each stage of the attack, there were a few writers able in some manner to respond. Of these the most inter-esting—including Mandeville, Defoe, Walpole's party writers, and Hume—were also the most influential, at least in the sense that they could not be wholly ignored. Those of the novelist's contemporaries who in some fashion defended luxury were surely important to him and were perhaps also influential in shaping *Humphry Clinker.* More obviously, they provide two gauges of his antipathy toward luxury: indirectly as exponents of the theories of society that were available to him but that he either tacitly rejected or publicly repudiated; directly as targets of severe criticism in the pages of the *Critical Review,* particularly during debates over the high price of food.[2] Less obviously, they probably altered the classical form of the condemnation of luxury. From ancient times this condemnation had expressed codes of religion and morality. Eighteenth-century defenders of luxury, on the other hand, chose to deemphasize morality in favor of economics, arguing in the main that luxury could increase and redistribute wealth and was there-fore a laudable trait in a society. Whatever its moral blemishes, they said, luxury served a needful economic function. To meet this new challenge at least partway, traditionalists needed to reshape their tirades, at a minimum to glance briefly at the actual economic condi-tion of the nation as a whole.

Historically the men who in some measure commended luxury were harbingers of "classical" economic theory, were instrumental in dis-mantling the older mercantile system, and represented a thoroughgoing challenge to the classical principle of necessity. In comparison with the critics of luxury, they are far fewer in number, more recondite in treat-ment, more cautious in language, and more empirical in approach. Unlike the critics, they analyzed both the causes and the effects of luxury in order to isolate its various elements. Some, like Mandeville, went further, arguing in anticipation of Adam Smith that causes and effects could not in practice be separated at all. If trade was accepted as a beneficial activity for the nation, then a rise in the consumption of luxuries would necessarily be a part of those benefits. Recognizing with Johnson that "every state of society is as luxurious as it can be," most of these writers couched their defenses or redefinitions of luxury in terms of the expansion of industry, employment, and population. Two corollary arguments were also advanced. The first held that a state of at least partial luxury had always been a precondition of liberty, educa-tion, and refinement. The other—treated here with the controversy over prices—held that the improvement of men's lot through the extension of physical luxury was a laudable end in itself.

The influence of the *Fable of the Bees* upon this tradition would be difficult to overestimate. Mandeville's argument, or a distorted version of it, was still under attack by pamphlet writers as late as 1794, and at least fourteen appeared during the 1760s with the stated intention of answering his position once and for all.[3] We have far more evidence than Johnson's that Mandeville was at the heart of part of the controversy during the century. In the face of orthodox classical and Christian denunciations of luxury, he assumed that men were proud, egoistic and governed by their passions, and therefore he posited three theses that in this context were relatively novel. (1) National frugality—the contemporary term for necessity—is a vice, not a virtue, since prodigality, among other things, redistributes wealth and provides for the whole of the population. (2) Luxury is a concomitance of, perhaps even a prerequisite to, national greatness: it is inevitable. (3) The pursuit of individual self-interest normally redounds to the prosperity of the state. It was indeed the increased prosperity of the state that he sought ultimately to release. He had no moral objections to the extant economic structure of England—indeed he was more conservative than most of his apparent adversaries—but he wished to point out that by traditional standards the whole of that structure would be called immoral. The notoriety of the *Fable* derived from Mandeville's unmistakable statement that Englishmen said one thing but, fortunately, did another.[4]

Mandeville was very much a part of the fevered quarrels outlined in the previous chapter, the "Grumbling Hive" being a response to several political poems of the turn of the century, and the 1714 edition of the *Fable* answering several Tory attacks of Anne's reign.[5] He was aware that his critics objected not so much to the wealth generated by trade as to the men who acquired that wealth. Such critics routinely associated luxury with pride, proof to him that they saw vice and hypocrisy only in those they considered their social inferiors. If they wished to brand as luxury all the changes English society was undergoing, Mandeville said, so be it: let them rest content with *verbal* victory and *moral* satisfaction:

> Thus every Part was full of Vice,
> Yet the whole Mass a Paradise . . .
> Such were the Blessings of that State;
> Their crimes conspir'd to make them great.

In addition to challenging conventional assumptions about society, Mandeville sought to clarify both the issues and the language informing the concept of luxury. To the current attitude that said luxury must be a vice because frugality, its supposed opposite, was a virtue, he answered that frugality had never been a *national* virtue. Historically it had rather been a mere necessity, avoided whenever possible. To the other dominant attitude, which held that luxury, by corrupting a nation and wasting its resources, was economically dangerous, he responded that the charge had no historical foundation. In fact luxury was necessary for economic prosperity and had always been found together with it. He therefore ridiculed the careless way most men used the concept.

> If everything is to be Luxury (as in strictness it ought) that is not immediately necessary to make Man subsist as he is a living Creature, there is nothing else to be found in the World, no not even among the naked Savages; of which it is not probable that there are any but what by this time have made some Improvements upon their former manner of living.
> . . . if once we depart from calling everything Luxury that is not absolutely necessary to keep a Man alive . . . then there is no Luxury at all; for if the wants of Man are innumerable, then what ought to supply them has no bounds. [1:107–8][6]

Similarly, he spurred five generations of sermon-writers, usually to indignation, with his perception of moral paradox: "It is the sensual Courtier that sets no limit to his Luxury; the Fickle Strumpet that invents new fashions every Week . . . the profuse Rake and lavish Heir . . . : It is these that are the Prey and proper Food of a full grown Leviathan. . . . He that gives most Trouble to thousands of his Neighbours, and invents the most operose Manufactures is, right or wrong, the greatest Friend to the Society" (1:355–56).

The next major philosophical defender of luxury was Smollett's contemporary and fellow historian, Hume. But in the years between the *Fable* and Hume's *Political Discourses* (1752), Mandeville's argument, though usually not Mandeville himself, earned a certain modicum of intellectual respectability. Without granting it anything approaching universal applicability, writers could allow its usefulness in understanding the undisciplined members of mankind. The dissolute, the weak, the unorthodox—all indeed who did not behave according to strict principles—all these could be seen as driven by the desire for luxuries to harder and more efficient work. Thus surrounded by a host of proper qualifications, luxury might be viewed as an independent force in the scales of national production, one capable of increasing labor by energizing laborers.

Yet the men most responsible for capturing the new energies abroad in Britain were of a more humble cast than the great Hume. Represented by Defoe and Walpole's party writers, they wrote largely for the moment. But the abundance of that moment earned them an enduring stature; in Pocock's words, they were among "the first intellectuals on record to express an entirely secular awareness of social and economic changes going on in their society, and to say specifically that these changes affected both their values and their modes of perceiving social realities."[7] By intent, Defoe was neither defender nor redefiner of luxury. He was not, like Locke or Mandeville, a philosopher of the new commercial age. Rather he was, as G. D. H. Cole has said, its poet laureate. And Walpole's stable, although it included several able minds bestirred at times to philosophy, was designed to protect a ministry, not a stoa.

Defoe wrote nearly as much and as often about luxury as did Smollett. The resemblance, however, ends there. While Smollett stayed fast within the classical tradition, Defoe, two generations earlier, was closer to the moderns Dickens and Thackeray. Violations of necessity and hierarchy he certainly sees everywhere about him, but the usual notions of these principles he curtly dismisses. In a series of consecutive issues of the *Review,* beginning with no. 9 for 18 January 1706, he describes the corruption that disturbs him: "the Luxury and Vanity of a Court, and the Extravagances of the Gentry." In no. 10 he reports that his readers object to such a construction of luxury; he will therefore elaborate his position and show that the "Luxury and Extravagancies of the *English* Nobility, have been the Advantage of the Common People." The "Ancient Nobility and Gentry" have brought "Havock and Destruction" upon themselves and are fast losing their ancestral estates. Where have the estates gone? They have "been swallow'd up, by the Commonalty and Tradesmen, who are now Richer all over the Nation." He thus turns on its head the argument used by Fletcher and Davenant earlier, Bolingbroke and Pulteney later. They held that the luxury of the common people threatened the great families and thereby the constitution. He holds that the luxury of the great families harms only themselves, encourages trade, redistributes wealth, and thereby strengthens the nation as a whole.

Over thirty years of polemical writing, Defoe's consistency on the matter of luxury cannot be of the letter-for-letter variety. He is acutely aware of the complex of customs and attitudes branded luxury, especially their use in political thinking. Hence he tries to accomplish two quite different ends: to use luxury himself as a political weapon against the landed interests; and, alternatively, to insist that luxury must be considered dispassionately without recourse to immediate political point-scoring. In no. 34 of the *Review* he notes that the freedoms, "Pleasures and Conveniences of Life" that all men should have are commonly stigmatized "in that ill-natur'd Term Luxury." At least thirty numbers of the paper say luxury is beneficial to trade; at least five, that it is harmful. For twelve consecutive numbers starting 7 February 1706, he argues that what is "a Vice in Morals, may at the same time be a Virtue in Trade"—but only so long as tradesmen and laborers are not caught up in it. His ambivalence is plainest regarding the working poor, toward whom he seems to feel both sympathy and suspicion. Numerous times in the *Review* and several times in the *Tour,* he rejects the charge that a decent wage is a luxury. Laborers, he says, have the right to as much leisure and as high wages as they can get, for these amount to "the vast Hinge on which the Wealth of the Nation turns." But far more frequent, in the *Review* as well as in his work of the 1720s, is his own charge that the poor are sexually loose, shirk their work, waste their wages, spend their time on backs and bellies, and generally live a "Riot of Luxury."[8]

Luxury for Defoe is associated with idleness, and he is often uncertain who is more morally luxurious, the garishly rich or the dismally poor; neither meets his measure of necessity. About the middle orders, however, he admits no serious doubts, and his major nonfictional works of the 1720s are strenuous defenses of the commercial interests against the prevailing attack upon luxury. What he will continue to defend to the end of his life, that is, is not luxury, but those men interminably accused of it. *The Complete English Tradesman* (enlarged ed., 1727) is the manifesto of a new and ascendant social order, the *trading* gentry. To landed men, tradesmen are mostly vile and mean wretches; to Defoe they are sturdy, vigorous men of sense and dignity. Most important, they are productive and industrious, not idle like the men of land. If they will avoid the luxuries that have sapped the old legislators, they will gain power and recognition proportionate to their merit. They have done more than transform England into a trading country, for it is now the greatest trading nation in the world. The transformation they have worked upon commerce they can work upon society and government (pp. 304-19). Written about 1728-29 but not published until 1890, *The Compleat English Gentleman* is a companion volume, a plan for reform of English education. Most in need of genuine education, Defoe feels, are the youth of the great landed families, since they are at present vain, weak, idle, and ignorant. Indeed for long they have not possessed the virtue, learning, and ability that the title of gentleman originally implied; elsewhere he calls them the victims of luxurious fathers, "bred boors, empty and swinish sots and fops." Now that title more properly belongs to the tradesman, the man who is great because of personal achievement, the *novus homo.*

Some of the earliest numbers of the *Review* allege that Tories will remain enemies of unfettered trade, for such trade carries with it the new liberties that so revolt the landed interests. This argument remains, twenty years later, at the heart of his strategy for a robust international power, *A Plan of the English Commerce* (1728). The classical sense of luxury and concomitant notion of fixed hierarchy he dismisses out of hand, as "Family Jargon, for it is no more."[9] History read aright, he says, teaches that tradesmen were nearly as important in antiquity as they are today. The ancient division of peoples into "Gentry and Commonalty" he calls nonsense born of false pride (p. 4). His own division is between a landed gentry who are truly luxurious, since they live off rents and the labor of others and have mere pride of purse, and the manufacturers who are truly virtuous, since they live off their own industry and possess pride of achievement (pp. 37–38). This, he says, is the crux of all quarrels surrounding luxury and trade: "Employment is Life, Sloth and Indolence is Death." When commerce expands, the purse-proud lose relatively, the industrious gain. Hence present attacks upon luxury, which any man of sense could expect and dismiss:

> Trade is the Wealth of the World; Trade makes the Difference as to Rich or Poor, between one Nation and another; Trade nourishes Industry, and Industry begets Trade; Trade disperses the national Wealth of the World, and Trade raises new Species of Wealth, which Nature knew nothing of. [P. 51]

For fifteen years Defoe had been Walpole's man, but far from his only man. Throughout Walpole's administration, government writers met Opposition charges of luxury with arguments of their own (though drawn in large part from Locke), some of which had the effect of moderating the classical attack. First, natural law was not what the Opposition supposed. All men are equal in the state of nature. To their persons and the property they might honestly acquire, no other man may lay claim a priori. Government derives from a voluntary relationship intended for security, not subordination; it was not designed to shackle dependents to masters, but to provide life, liberty, and property for all.[10] Second, where the Opposition saw 1688 as the engine of England's climactic devolution, Walpole's press saw it as the inauguration of her glory. The *London Journal* called the Glorious Revolution the nativity of national freedom, the end of tyranny, and the beginning of true progress in, for example, representative government, a responsive economic system, and a distribution of power suited to the range of English talents.[11] Third, the Opposition called parties a pernicious division within what was by nature a family united by paternal authority and mutual interest. The Whig papers responded with the proposition that, since all men could not concur over the national interest or even their own self-interest, political divisions were inevitable and wholesome. Better to express disagreement through parties than to suppress them through tyranny; it was the intent of the Glorious Revolution to permit such differences. Parties were like the two sides of "an express contradiction"; they could be stated but, short of blood-shed, not reconciled.[12]

Finally, to the charge that Walpole ruled by luxury and corruption, they made several responses. It was not the duty of a magistrate to dictate how people may dispose of their persons and property so long as they injured no one else, they argued in a version of Locke's call for tolerance and a limited government. Similarly but rarely, they held that few of the habits and freedoms the Opposition called luxurious deserved such stigma. What Bolingbroke and his coterie sought was to limit the opportunities of persons other than themselves, "under a pretense of preventing luxury."[13] They admitted that Walpole used Treasury funds, but denied that such use was corruption. Rather it was patronage, the reward of service in government as much as in the arts; if placemen were examples of luxury at work, then the vice was innocuous enough.[14]

In approach Hume is more distant than the ministerial press could afford to be. In three of the essays (and parts of three others) of *Political Discourses* (Edinburgh, 1752), he attempts to refute all the long-standing objections to luxury. "Of Commerce" replies to the charge that trade subverts political liberty. "Of Luxury" argues against previous definitions of the concept. And "Of the Populousness of Ancient Nations" challenges current thinking on depopulation. Taken together, his discourses amount to an all-encompassing reappraisal of mercantile society. On major points he assumes a position antithetical to the tradition embraced by Smollett. Whereas the novelist deplored the rapid growth of the cities, Hume approved it, arguing that people gathered in urban areas to receive and communicate knowledge, thereby increasing their humanity. Smollett writes often from the common assumption that luxury leads to venality and corruption in government and the demise of political liberty. Hume, by contrast, sees a parallel growth in luxury and commerce, on the one hand, and humanity and sympathy on the other. Where Smollett stresses the authority of traditional morality, Hume emphasizes its flaws. The existence of such a contrast is in itself instructive, for Smollett in 1771 was repeating most of the objections to luxury that Hume in 1752 saw himself as answering. Hume moreover regarded his position as a moderating one, one about which men of unprejudiced common sense might gather. The fact that Smollett found this position too moderate indicates much about his own social and political attitudes, particularly with regard to the role of merchants and their representatives in English affairs.

Hume's study of English and European history yielded his fundamental premise: the rise of materialism, individualism, and economic power outside the court had stimulated political freedom and parliamentary government. Indeed the increase of European power and grandeur during the previous two hundred years was directly attributable to the fruits of luxury. In contemporary England, the interests of the class of tradesmen and merchants, "the middling rank of men," had had a liberating influence upon the policies of the House of Commons. As a group they were "the best and firmest basis of public liberty." "These submit not to slavery and meanness of spirit; and having no hopes of tyrannizing over others, like the barons, they are not tempted, for the sake of that gratification, to submit to the tyranny of their sovereign. They covet equal laws, which may secure their property, and preserve them from monarchical, as well as aristocratical tyranny." This phenomenon is furthermore a universal feature, to be found in every society whose economy is evolving from primitive agriculture to sophisticated manufactures.

> A state is never greater than when all its superfluous hands are employ'd in the service of the public. The ease and convenience of private persons require, that these hands should be employ'd in their service. The one can never be satisfied, but at the expense of the other. As the ambition of the sovereign must entrench on the luxury of individuals; so the luxury of individuals must diminish the force, and check the ambition of the sovereign. [P. 6]

> If we consult history, we shall find, that in most nations foreign trade has preceded any refinement in home manufactures, and given birth to domestic luxury. [P. 16]

Hume ascribes the controversies surrounding luxury to the absolutist sense in which the term is used. Few writers consider the all-important relative factors of nation, time, and condition of individuals.

> Since luxury may be consider'd, either as innocent or blameable, one may be surpriz'd at those preposterous opinions, which have been entertain'd concerning it; while men of libertine principles bestow praises even on vitious luxury, and represent it as highly advantageous to society; and on the other hand, men of severe morals blame even the most innocent luxury, and represent it as the source of all the corruptions, disorders, and factions incident to civil government. [P. 24]

The remainder of the discourse "Of Luxury" is an attempt to correct and mediate between the men of libertine principles like Mandeville and those of severe morals like Dennis and Law. Hume's argument is threefold. (1) Far from being reprehensible, the ages of innocent luxury and refinement have in fact been the happiest and most virtuous in world history. (2) When luxury is excessive, it must be recognized as "the source of many ills," but it becomes a vice only when "pursu'd at the expence of some virtue, as liberality or charity." (3) Even a society tolerating vicious luxury is preferable to one entirely without luxury.

Hume's method is no less distinctive than his conclusion, for he is one of the few writers to speak with both authority and sympathy of ordinary laborers. Luxury was a continual spur to working men, Hume held, because initially it led them to work, then gave a sense of liveliness to its performance, and finally provided pleasure at its completion. From such private or individual happiness flowed the more public happiness of industry, knowledge, and humanity. As the laborer gains satisfaction in the mechanical arts, so the larger society acquires the liberal arts. While industry is increasing order and discipline, understanding is diminishing ignorance and superstition. Although moralists persist in advocating "the monkish virtues," it is luxury that renders "the government as great and flourishing as [it renders] individuals happy and prosperous" (p. 28).

> What has chiefly induc'd severe moralists to declaim against luxury and refinement in pleasure is the example of antient *Rome,* which joining, to its poverty and rusticity, virtue and public spirit, rose to such a surprising height of grandeur and liberty; but having learn'd from its conquer'd provinces the *Grecian* and *Asiatic* luxury, fell into every kind of corruption; whence arose sedition and civil wars, attended at last with the total loss of liberty. All the *Latin* classics, whom we peruse in our infancy, are full of these sentiments, and universally ascribe the ruin of their state to the arts and riches imported from the East: insomuch that Sallust represents a taste for painting as a vice no less than lewdness and drinking, and so popular were these sentiments during the latter stages of the republic, that this author abounds in praises of the old rigid *Roman* virtue, tho' himself the most egregious instance of modern luxury and corruption. . . . But it would be easy to prove, that these writers mistook the cause of the disorders in the *Roman* state, and ascrib'd to luxury and the arts what really proceeded from an ill model'd government, and the unlimited extent of conquests. Luxury or refinement on pleasure has no natural tendency to beget venality and corruption. [Pp. 32–33]

To the charge that British government since 1688 had been corrupt and venal, Hume replied that nothing could "restrain or regulate the love of money but a sense of honour and virtue; which, if it be not nearly equal at all times will naturally abound most in ages of luxury and knowledge" (pp. 33–34).

The house of commons is the support of our popular government;

and all the world acknowledge, that it ow'd its chief influence and consideration to the encrease of commerce, which threw such a balance of property into the hands of commons. How inconsistent, then, is it to blame so violently luxury, or a refinement in the arts, and to represent it as the bane of liberty and public spirit. [P. 36]

Compared with his rebuke of stern moralists and disappointed politicians, however, his answer to advocates of libertinism is rather weak. Referring directly to Mandeville, he comments that, "it seems, upon any system of morality, little less than a contradiction in terms, to talk of a vice, that is in general beneficial to society" (p. 39).

Hume nevertheless concludes his discourse on luxury strongly, affirming that there is no just alternative to the function of luxury. Whereas Smollett and others said that fear of punishment and starvation was sufficient motive for labor, Hume favored a more positive stimulus, the anticipation of reward and pleasure.

Luxury, when excessive, is the source of many ills; but is in general preferable to sloth, and idleness, which wou'd commonly succeed in its place, and are more pernicious both to private persons and to the public. When sloth reigns, a mean uncultivated way of life prevails amongst individuals, without society, without enjoyment, and if the sovereign, in such a situation, demands the service of his subjects, the labour of the state suffices only to furnish the necessaries of life to the labourers, and can afford nothing to those, who are employ'd in the public service. [P. 40]

The discourse "Of the Populousness of Antient Nations" assumes a related agnostic position. Just as the critics of luxury have no evidence for the corruption of English life, so there is no valid evidence concerning luxury and depopulation. In the first place, Hume writes, there exists no reliable information about size of population in any nation of classical or medieval times. In the second, if such evidence existed and if it did show a trend toward depopulation, then luxury still could not be held responsible for the situation. The same trend could easily have been caused by some other factor or group of factors. Hume thus dismissed the common luxury-degeneracy-depopulation argument as specious, founded as it was on unsupportable assertions.

The *Discourses* have a threefold significance for the study of luxury and Smollett. They answer directly many of the charges the novelist raised against the temper of his times. By 1771, Hume and Smollett had been friends for perhaps longer than a decade. Smollett had an obvious respect for his abilities and called him "one of the best men, and undoubtedly the best writer of the age."[15] Hume's essay on population, moreover, elicited an anonymous pamphlet that anticipates the major distinctions between England and Scotland that Smollett makes in *Humphry Clinker*. The author of *A Dissertation on the Numbers of Mankind in Antient and Modern Times: In which the Superior Populousness of Antiquity is maintained . . . and some Remarks on Mr. Hume's Political Discourse of the Populousness of Antient Nations* (1753) is content to repeat the assertions Hume attempted to discredit.[16] He contends that Egypt, Palestine, Greece, Italy, Sicily, and Gaul were better populated, particularly after being converted to Christianity, than contemporary Europe. In earlier times the simple, frugal, Christian life prevailed; at present an irreligious life of luxury dominates. Beginning with Alexander the Great and continuing during the Roman Empire, luxury destroyed simplicity and fertility.

> The magnificence and splendor, shows and diversions, excesses and debaucheries of the courts of princes, would allure vast numbers [of rural folk]. By all these methods, the world daily declined in temperance, frugality and virtue, and of course the people were continually diminished. . . . Nor indeed has the world ever recovered the antient taste of frugality and simplicity, but is either barbarous . . . or corrupted by luxury and false refinements. [P. 197]

As the most relevant example of this idyllic, primitive state, simple, frugal, and happy Scotland is contrasted with vain, luxurious, debauched, and unhappy England. In Scotland the author finds that "the most humble virtues are found to be not only consistent with, but greatly conducive to the populousness and grandeur of society" (p. 198).

Later, Joseph Harris and Oliver Goldsmith followed Hume in arguing that luxury increased happiness by allowing men to produce and consume freely. Harris, in *An Essay upon Money and Coins* (1757), is careful to exclude the objects of vanity from his defense of luxury. "The word *luxury* hath usually annexed to it a kind of opprobrious idea; but so far as it encourages the arts, whets the inventions of men, and finds employment for more of our own people, its influence is benign, and beneficial to the whole society" (p. 30). Luxury achieves these benefits by increasing trade, industry, and efficiency. As these rise, the mechanical arts are perfected and production grows. At each stage of the process wealth increases faster than population: owners receive higher profits, more workers are employed, and taxes can be reduced. In letter 11 of *The Citizen of the World* (collected ed., 2 vols., 1762), Goldsmith gave voice to a point of view quite different from that of the earlier *Enquiry into the Present State of Polite Learning*. His letter-writer finds luxury leading to refinement and meditation.

Certainly those philosophers, who declaim against luxury have little understood its benefits; they seem insensible, that to luxury we owe not only the greatest part of our knowledge, but even of our virtues. . . . The more various our artificial necessities, the wider is our circle of pleasure; for all pleasure consists in obviating necessities as they rise; luxury, therefore, as it encreases our wants, encreases our capacity for happiness. [P. 35]

Examine the history of any country remarkable for opulence and wisdom, you will find they would never have been wise had they not been first luxurious; you will find poets, philosophers, and even patriots, marching in luxury's train. The reason is obvious; we then only are curious after knowledge when we find it connected with sensual happiness. The senses ever point out the way, and reflection comments upon the discovery. [P. 35]

Politically, luxury is no threat, for "the greater the luxuries of every country, the more closely, politically speaking, is that country united" (p. 36). Hence Goldsmith's conclusion is favorable.

In whatsoever light, therefore, we consider luxury whether as employing a number of hands naturally too feeble for more laborious employment, as finding a variety of occupation for others who might be totally idle, or as furnishing out new inlets to happiness, without encroaching on mutual property, in whatsoever light we regard it, we shall have reason to stand up in its defense, and the sentiment of Confucius still remains unshaken: *that we should enjoy as many of the luxuries of life as are consistent with our own safety, and the prosperity of others, and that he who finds out a new pleasure is one of the most useful members of society.* [P. 37]

During the two decades before *Humphry Clinker* appeared, a few further works were published that gave qualified support to certain aspects of luxury. William Temple of Trowbridge, in *A Vindication of Commerce and the Arts* (1758), for instance, says luxury is benign so long as it is an incentive to risk-taking and free spending. Adam Anderson, in *An Historic and Chronological Deduction of the Origin of Commerce* (2 vols., 1764), concludes that in the major European cities luxury is the inevitable concomitant of commerce. To weaken one is to weaken the other. Yet these works are overshadowed in significance by another group that, even though they did not treat the question of luxury directly, are perhaps more central to an understanding of England and Smollett.

This latter group of writers was concerned over the recurring crises brought about by fluctuations in the price of staples. More particularly, they sought some way to alleviate the sufferings of the laboring class that invariably followed a rise in prices. In comparison with the majority of writers cited previously, they entered the controversy over luxury almost inadvertently, since they were generally addressing themselves to the economic position of laborers. In varying degrees they dissented from the normal economic attitude and practice of the century: that the wages a worker received should provide for only slightly more than mere subsistence. They argued rather that higher wages and an improved standard of living should be ends in themselves. Beyond this heretical tenet, most of them made one or more of the following observations: (1) Few laborers were actually idle or dissolute. (2) Idleness, when it did prevail, was largely beyond the laborers' control. (3) The standard policy of wage depression was deplorable, destroying incentive and reducing workers to despair. (4) Higher wages would reward labor and spur the demand of laborers for goods. (5) Increased spending by laborers could create a more stable and equable society. Such attitudes led the writers to a position extraordinary, if not paradoxical, for the time. To different extents, they condemned the luxury of the rich, while redefining or defending the luxury of the poor. Although this body of material is too large to treat adequately here, a brief outline of it is needed further to define Smollett's attitudes. It is a position with which Smollett was certainly acquainted, for the *Critical* reviewed several works containing it while he was editor and afterward. These reviews, furthermore, were consistently hostile toward plans for assisting the laboring poor. The pattern of such hostility becomes even clearer when one compares reviews of the same works in the *Critical* and in the *Monthly*.[17]

Besides Hume and Harris, writers who were sympathetic to the plight of the poor during the period 1750–70 included W. Hazeland, Malachy Postlethwayt, William Mildmay, Nathaniel Forster, James Steuart, and, surprisingly, Soame Jenyns.[18] Three of the most famous of these, Forster, Steuart, and Jenyns, merit specific notice. Forster's *Enquiry* attacks luxury almost exclusively from the point of view of the poor majority of Englishmen. Forster condemns as "as false, as it is inhuman" the doctrine that "the poor will be industrious only in the degree that they are necessitous" (p. 55). Oppression leads not to increased production, but to "desperation and madness." "I cannot but think it is as good a general maxim as ever was advanced, that the sure way of engaging a man to go through a work with vigour and spirit is, to ensure him a taste of the sweets of it" (p. 60). At the same time that he carefully redefined the "necessaries" required by the poor, saying they too needed luxuries, Forster called the luxury of the rich both the immediate and long-term cause of high prices.

> Articles of luxury are of no consideration in comparison to the necessaries of life. Nothing but a plenty of these [last] can make the people tolerably happy, or at all increase their numbers. A nation, therefore, cannot more fatally mistake its own interest, than in giving the least encouragement to luxurious productions, when they are in any degree inconsistent with such as are necessary to general subsistence.

After granting Hume's point that luxury should be a stimulus to industry, Forster says it cannot possess such motivating force in contemporary England. For it is not permitted the poor and certainly has no effect upon the rich; they are not stimulated even to work, much less to work harder (pp. 37–39). At present, luxury serves only "more and more to widen the fatal gap between the very rich, and the very poor" (p. 42). "They that work the hardest live too the hardest. And it seems to be looked upon by some as an act of generosity, that they, who have naturally the best right to live, are suffered to live at all" (p. 191).

Most of the *Enquiry* is devoted to minute and learned examination of the effects luxurious fashions have upon the poor. One chapter is given to bread, another to cattle, a third to horses. Regarding horses, Forster says that the fashion for personal horses and equipages has hurt poor farmers by taking away tillage land from cattle, replacing useful animals with useless ones, driving many farmers off the land, and sending up the prices of hay, straw, and oats. Since Forster's attack upon luxury is presumably from the opposite end of the political spectrum from Smollett's, it is perhaps surprising to find Bramble in his letter of May 29 from London complaining that, "The incredible increase of horses and black cattle, to answer the purposes of luxury" has driven men from the farms. It is, in any case, one of Forster's purposes to show the process by which food and animals which are necessities for the rural poor are, through increases in prices, transformed into luxuries for the urban rich.[19]

Steuart's *Inquiry* is far broader and much more theoretical than Forster's book. Like Hume, Steuart identifies luxury with commerce and calls for control rather than suppression. So long as trade and luxury support the national economy, they are to be encouraged. And while his defense of luxury is more neutral than Forster's, he advocates the extension of prosperity to English laborers. In the section on trade, he seeks to distinguish between moral and economic issues.[20] The narrow moralist sees luxury as self-indulgence and excess. The descriptive economist, however, views it as the inevitable consequence of the introduction of money. Once money dominates economic organization, then a desire for luxury is the main motive for industry and one of the main regulators of production and consumption. It is precisely because luxury is so central to economic activity, Steuart says, that it must be controlled. An exporting nation must control its domestic luxury lest foreign competitors undersell the same products. Discussing the position of laborers, Steuart says an improved standard of consumption for the poor majority is a precondition for economic progress, and he warns of an economic as well as a social danger in a very unequal distribution of wealth. If prices continually outstrip wages, production will fail; but deserved increases in wages will yield greater production.

Jenyns's short pamphlet *Thoughts on the Causes and Consequences of the Present High Price of Provisions* is in at least one respect the most unusual of all the works arguing for more humane treatment of laborers. Half of it appears to be a conventional diatribe against all forms of luxury, in whatever class it is found. Jenyns wants everyone to be frugal, especially the government. Yet in the second half, when he seeks to particularize his grievances, he finds that luxury, like taxes and the national debt, enriches only a few already wealthy individuals. As the few grow richer, the many grow poorer. The present exorbitant price of all staples is but one sign of the wretched position of the laboring classes. While rejecting such a solution as unlawful, he admits that the only permanent answer would be a more equable division of the country's wealth (p. 23).

Forster, Steuart, and Jenyns are but a small sample of the heterogeneous group of writers who defended laborers against charges of idleness and luxury. In addition to preparing the ground for the *Wealth of Nations*, they served partially to untangle the knot of issues labeled luxury, rebutting such charges as Fielding's of the criminal luxury of the poor. In effect, they argued that insofar as luxury was good, the poor must be extended its virtues; insofar as it was bad, the poor were incapable of its vices. Addressing the immediate situation of high prices, they made three observations. (1) Wages should be proportionate to prices. (2) Wages should be sufficient to provide for marriage, self-improvement, occasional leisure, and unpredictable need. (3) Unless unemployment or underemployment were general in the country and encouraged by the government, higher wages would prompt faster and more careful work and would discourage idleness. This perspective upon luxury was available to Smollett, but in his signed work he either rejected or ignored it. Yet the *Critical,* because of its reviewing policy, could not ignore it altogether.

Writing in 1767, a reviewer for the *Critical* said that at least five hundred pamphlets had been published during the past ten years on the high price of provisions. However accurate this estimate, the review was highly selective in its notices, extracts, and comments. In the period from the spring of 1765 to the winter of 1767—during which the works of Forster, Steuart, and Jenyns were appearing—the *Monthly Review,* its rival, noticed sixty books or pamphlets on the subject. The *Critical,* meanwhile, was giving notice to twenty-one. And of this small fraction of a voluminous controversy, the only ones to which it gave space and praise, so far as I can discover, were those that condemned the working poor for their luxury and insubordination. The issue of April 1765 carried an extract and comment upon the anonymous *Considerations on taxes . . . also some Reflections on the General Behavior and Disposition of the Manufacturing Populace of this Kingdom* (1765). Its author is quoted as believing that taxes on necessaries are not, as others think, too high. Rather they are much too low and must be higher if Britain is to retain its advantages in foreign trade. The manufacturing populace is also so idle and debauched that they will not work when the price of provisions is low; only fear of starvation will force them to work: "*"taxes on the necessaries of life* tend to enforce general industry, to restrain idleness and debauchery, to improve our manufacturers, and to make labour cheap a *variety of ways*"" (19:308). The reviewer then remarks that the author's argument is strong because of "the habitual indolence of the English common people, who will not work half the week if they can possibly subsist without it" (19:310). He is assured that there is no validity behind the current clamor over the high price of wheat: "We are of the opinion that the facts [the author] has brought to support this are true, and that the principle is therefore irrefragable. The publication is the more useful on account of the public discontents that are so artfully propagated on its subject" (19:310).

In November 1766 the periodical highly recommended the anonymous *Some Observations upon setting the Assize of Bread* (1766) as a work containing "several matters of the highest importance to the poorer of our fellow-subjects" (22:386). In the long extract the *Critical* printed, the author of the pamphlet calls the dispute over prices of bread exaggerated and malicious. From political and disreputable motives, evil persons voiced the cry; it was heard because of "'the universal clamour and tumult raised throughout the kingdom, chiefly among the poor (the vagrant, the idle, the dissolute, not the industrious poor) and either through ignorance, ostentation, false popularity, or some worse motive, so fatally countenanced . . . by persons of every rank'" (22:387). (This latter charge of false motive Smollett leveled against Pitt in the *Briton* and against all those who solicited votes in the *Briton* and in *Humphry Clinker.*) In the following issue the *Critical* noticed two more anonymous pamphlets on the topic. Of the first, *Political Speculations; or, An Attempt to discover the Causes of the Dearness of Provisions, and high Price of Labour, in England* (1766), it printed a short extract that blamed the idleness of laborers and the lack of severity of the poor laws (22:461). The second, *Reflections on the present high Price of Provisions* (1766), took up the raging argument over monopolies. Hazeland, Forster, and many others had called upon the government to act against the grain monopolies that had forced prices even beyond the critical level. The grain cartels were charged with allowing distillers first and complete choice over the harvest, setting exorbitant prices, regardless of supply, and sending English grain abroad while Englishmen starved for want of it. About the new work, the reviewer for the *Critical* wrote: "The author's professed design in this pamphlet, which is sensible, and written upon generous public-spirited principles, is to show, that the free currency of buying and selling both among ourselves and with other nations, will always prove the most effectual expedient for removing a public scarcity, and that the laws against forestallers, regulators, etc., are as unjust and ridiculous as those formerly in force against witches and wizards" (22:462).

Equally revealing is the treatment the *Critical* accorded Forster, Steuart, and Jenyns. On Forster's *Enquiry*—which such modern economic historians as Furniss, Gilboy, and Coats have called one of the most important tracts of the time—the reviewer in the April 1767 issue begins with an attack upon Forster's presumption, in writing on a topic about which everything has been said, and criticizes the work for lack of learning, taste, and observation. He continues:

> We cannot think ourselves greatly edified . . . because it contains no more than what has appeared in different shapes, within these 10 years, in at least 500 other pamphlets. The author's observations on luxury are equally unimportant, and principally drawn from Montesquieu and certain flimsy French writers, who, whatever they may pretend, are ignorant of the British constitution; and whose maxims never can be applicable to the English manners and interests. [23:305-6]

With the *Inquiry* of Sir James Steuart the periodical was not so curt. It devoted twenty-three pages to the work, all but a few paragraphs being extract or paraphrase. Yet it was highly selective; from the lengthy work it extracted the least controversial and most conventional of Steuart's analyses. His definition of luxury is summarized in one sentence, his defense of it in another. After the latter, the reviewer says he respectfully disagrees (23:323). About Steuart's recommendation that the government step in to ensure equilibrium between prices and wages and to promote a more equal division of wealth, the reviewer comments:

> The author, we hope, will pardon us in saying, that we can have no idea of any statesman interfering in the commercial concerns of a free country. They are too delicate to be touched even by an assembly of statesmen. . . . Nothing ought to appear more uncontrouled, or can be more permanent, than the principles of commerce; and nothing ought to be so independent of a statesman, because they are self-evident; and, as they spring from mutual necessities, they never can be mistaken. [23:411]

Jenyns's *Thoughts* received similar treatment in the December 1767 issue. One paragraph of the work—on the need to lower taxes if prices are to be reduced—is quoted, with the comment that the author's argument is rational. Jenyns's remarks on the poor are ignored.[21]

For the *Critical*, then, as for Bramble and Lismahago, luxury remained a negative concept, in social reality an unalloyed evil to be identified and eradicated. Against this backdrop of evolving attitudes toward luxury, Smollett's position can be seen, in one aspect, as entirely static. *Humphry Clinker* is at least as vehement in opposition as were the *Complete History* and the early volumes of the *Critical* fifteen years earlier. The arguments of Hume, Goldsmith, Harris, Forster, Steuart, Jenyns, and others had no perceptible influence in modifying Smollett's attitude. But seen from a second aspect, Smollett's position had indeed developed. In the *Complete History* he traces the turmoil in the nation during his century to the luxuriousness of the middle classes, especially the merchants and tradesmen of London. But in his later writings he sees unrest among the poor as another, equally dangerous manifestation of luxury. If a wigmaker from Stepney challenged the structure of English society when he shoved his way into the Pump Room at Bath, then a tenant farmer from Derby did so even more forcefully when he demanded higher returns or lower prices, or both at the same time. Thus those writers who favored or redefined luxury may have influenced Smollett indirectly by demonstrating that national economic and political issues—and not religious or moral ones—lay behind the discontent of the laboring poor. As Hume, Harris, and Forster argued for more concern and compassion for laborers as a group, Smollett may have seen the need for increased severity and vigilance, especially so during the early 1760s when wigmakers occasionally supported the demands of tenant farmers. And as he had always worked from a panoramic form, he may have seen the desirability of extending it as far socially as he had geographically, to include not only the customary lords, squires, and merchants, but also an occasional and representative farmer or laborer as well. Such indeed is the difference between the earlier volumes of the *Complete History* and the later *Travels, Present State, Atom,* and *Humphry Clinker.*

Part Two

SMOLLETT AND LUXURY

THE POLITICAL HISTORY OF
LUXURY: THE *COMPLETE HISTORY*
AND OTHER WRITINGS

*We must consider how very little history there is; I mean real
authentick history. That certain Kings reigned, and certain battles
were fought, we can depend upon as true; but all the colouring,
all the philosophy, of history is conjecture.—Samuel Johnson*

Chancing upon a classical attack upon luxury, a twentieth-century
reader would, I think, find the text mute. He would meet hard nouns
and fevered adjectives but be left in doubt over the intense human
experience they strain to express. Where, exactly, was the plague
Socrates tried to stem? What, exactly, were the crimes Cicero called
loathsome? Who, exactly, were the jaded sinners Tertullian sought to
reform? Some parts of the long history of classical attacks are doubtless
beyond recovery; yet to follow Smollett through the copious work of
his last decades is to answer comparable questions for much of the
eighteenth century. It is in fact to grangerize the final, climactic chapter
of the history. Of his time he was representative in both senses, leader
and example. He is as explicit as anybody as to the substance of the

135

Law, the identity of legislators, subjects, and tempters, and the nature of tests and punishments. He is always ready to inform his contemporaries about what they need and where they belong. And through the potency of his art he has preserved the classical tradition, creating in *Humphry Clinker* a book that is very much alive today.

For Smollett luxury is a hanging matter. From 1756 through 1771 he treated it as a capital crime against British civilization and as the unresolved issue upon which the future of that civilization depended. Given their diversity of form, purpose, and occasion, the nonfictional works of his last sixteen years possess a remarkable singleness of vision. The *Complete History of England* (1757-58), its *Continuation* (1760-65), the *Critical Review* (1756-), the *Briton* (1762-63), the *Modern Part of the Universal History* (1759-65), the *Travels through France and Italy* (1766), the *Present State of All Nations* (1768-69), and the *History and Adventures of an Atom* (1769) reveal the novelist organizing and controlling his material according to a small number of principles. Although the exposure of luxury is but one of these, it is the most prominent and pervasive. In the *Travels* he inquires to what extent France and Italy are more luxurious and decadent than England, and in what ways. In the *Present State,* less concerned with details, he asks how far each nation has been able to defy luxury and retain its necessity and hierarchy. The political arguments of the histories, the journalism, and the *Atom* are complex, for here he also stresses related concepts, using them normally as subordinate to luxury, sometimes as coordinate. On certain issues Smollett was a man of adamantine constancy, and his nonfictional works contain several hundred references to luxury. This chapter will trace his theory of the introduction of the vice to England, given in the *Complete History,* and demonstrate the persistence of the theory in two quite different works, the *Travels* and *Present State.* Chapters 6 and 7 will deal with the *Critical, Briton,* and *Atom,* works that represent his attempts not only to describe the manifestations of contemporary luxury but also to eradicate them.

The seventy volumes Smollett wrote or edited during his later career represent the most sustained attack upon luxury of the period and bespeak the continuity of previous attitudes into the 1750s and 1760s. His opposition to luxury is stated in language that is strongly traditional. He either dismissed or ignored new concepts introduced into discussions of economics in general and of finance and technology in particular. He apparently believed, for example, that all economic problems could be solved by monetary policy, that a mathematically exact balance of trade was necessary from month to month, and that a nation increased its wealth by no other means than did a private individual. His standards for judging his world were semifeudal, paternal, agrarian, mercantilist, and Augustinian. He regarded land and its resources as the ultimate economic units of a society. And his view of human nature was decidedly dark, developing into the belief that the conduct of the great majority of his fellow Britons must be strictly controlled. He supported the landed interest politically as well as socially, and like Bolingbroke called for a return to the conditions obtaining before the Glorious Revolution. Finally, his arguments are virtually all rationalistic, calling for support upon custom, authority, and tradition rather than upon empirical evidence.

Smollett's political writings of this period are of interest on several grounds. They have the attraction of all of his prose: he knows how to charge his words with effective meaning. And they articulate the social and philosophic suppositions of a large portion of educated England. To Smollett politics meant something far wider than mere electioneering, extending to everything that shapes the national character. As the previous chapter sought to show, in ideas he was nothing if not representative. His originality lay in his fictions and his combination of forms; in politics novelty was something he abhorred. In these writings he was to conservative Englishmen what Paine was to rebellious Americans—a passionate logician, a speaker of vigorous common sense. His basic texts were very different from Paine's, as his lessons were antithetic. He courted the authority of the ages while Paine appealed to the instincts and experiences of his readers. He would have fled scandalized from the men and the experiences Paine sought to touch, and Paine would have thought wasted the energy Smollett spent trying to goad the gentry into action. Yet each sought assurance from what he thought to be the fundamental force of political life.

From the beginning to the end of this period Smollett insisted that the spread of luxury carried with it profound political implications. It is therefore not surprising that in his last novel he should include about forty overtly political references, characters, and situations and should frequently link them to the effects of luxury. Most of his writing, it should be remembered, is political and historical, and luxury was a basic criterion by which he judged the movement and tendency of British society from the great historical watershed of 1688 until his own day. When brought to bear upon the events of his day, this habit of approach, I contend, provided him with specific targets for his attacks upon luxury in the novel. If in the English portion of *Humphry Clinker* Smollett is describing the political world of England during the later 1750s and early 1760s, then he is recalling and repeating parts of his earlier campaign against the City Whigs. When placed in this immediate mid–eighteenth-century context, even the most olympian judgments of a Bramble or a Jery or a Lismahago assume a different coloring.

Exactly when and how Smollett became fervent and partisan in his political thinking we do not know. However, we do have one of his own comments on a related matter: when and how he came to repudiate the Whigs. After the publication of the last volume of the *Complete History,* on 2 January 1758, he wrote to Dr. Moore:

> The last Volume will, I doubt not, be severely censured by the west country whigs of Scotland; but for you and other persons of sense and probity, I desire you will divest yourself of Prejudice, at least so much as you can, before you begin to peruse it, and consider well the Facts before you give Judgement. Whatever may be its defects, I protest before God I have, as far as in me lay, adhered to Truth without espousing any faction, though I own I sat down to write with a warm side to those principles in which I was educated. But in the Course of my Inquiries, the whig ministers and their abettors turned out such a Set of sordid Knaves that I could not help stigmatizing some of them for their want of Integrity and Sentiment. [*Letters,* p. 65]

Yet signs of Tory inclination are present from at least as early as 1756, and they increased to the determined partisanship of the *Briton* and the acidity of the *Adventures of an Atom.* In his nonfictional works, such committed advocacy gives Smollett's language a distinction certain to endure. Boldly and vividly he brought into focus the ruthless, disruptive effects of unbridled commercialism nearly a century before Carlyle. There can be no doubt of Smollett's foresight into the ravages of an industrial England. No one who knows Dickens or Mayhew, Engels or the Hammonds can believe Smollett exaggerated the social effects of unreformed capitalism. To this task he brought not only the mind of a Tory believer, but also the heart of a satirist and the eye of a novelist. It was probably to this achievement that Moore referred when he said Smollett was at his best depicting "the inferior societies of life." When trying to describe the larger forces at work in the present and immediate past of his country, however, he relied upon a conventional idea already worn smooth by writers of sermons. Used as a neutral metaphor for the effects of increasing affluence in portions of a society, the idea of luxury could be brilliantly suggestive—as it was in Mandeville, Hume, and Forster. But as a social touchstone it was burdened with theoretical and practical difficulties. For Smollett, nevertheless, luxury was apparently never a neutral or a complex issue, and he accordingly became one of those described by Hume as "men of severe morals [who] blame even the most innocent luxury, and represent it as the source of all the corruptions, disorders, and factions incident to civil government." For this pertinacity five reasons may be suggested.

First and most obvious, luxury was one of the very few social and political ideas current in Smollett's time that was generic or encompassing enough to include all the things the novelist opposed. He saw England menaced by chaos, faction, corruption, insubordination, and lack of patriotism—and only luxury could account for all of them. Second, he had a basically imperious approach to social complexities, an imagination drawn to severe diagnoses and drastic solutions, impatient of compromise. Third, his polemical métier was negative and critical. He was most vigorous and engaged in social criticism, in the politics of status and privilege, and in the defense of tradition against the onslaughts of the vulgar. About matters of actual day-to-day political policy and their repercussions he was less interested and less confident. And when called upon to be positive in his assessment of government maneuvers, as for many months in the *Briton,* his usual force declined notably.

Fourth, as a thinker Smollett was, by his own admission, not deep or systematic. His acceptance of the traditional arguments against luxury therefore gave to his thinking and writing an intellectual cohesion and confidence they might not otherwise have had. It made his writing more vivid, more complete, more immediate, more intelligent. With it he could point a moral as well as adorn a tale. Indeed it provided the intellectual frame essential for anything beyond mere hackwork: a historical perspective, the rudiments of social and political philosophy, and even something of a view of social psychology. For his work in the *Complete History,* the *Continuation,* and the *Modern Part of the Universal History,* it furnished a means both to measure and to evaluate historical change. For his articles in the *Critical Review,* the *Briton,* and the *Present State,* it supplied similar standards with which to judge contemporary affairs in society and government. It gave him grounds to criticize and to predict the behavior of the middle and lower classes, armed as he was with a panoply of historical portents and analogies. It provided a key to the base designs of the City Whigs and to the purposeless depravity of the mob. It suggested that political opposition could often be regarded in terms of status—the attempt by vain, greedy, and overweening men to overtop their betters. It revealed in imitation the source of working-class insubordination and in inspiration by treacherous men the source of popular discontents. It provided, in short, much that was of practical necessity to a hard-pressed writer who was, on the one hand, a proud, thin-skinned Scotsman of conservative and aristocratic bent impelled to make his way in Whiggish, ever-changing London; and, on the other, one of the most active and prolific writers of the 1750s and 1760s, always working but often ill, seldom having enough money, and never, at least from 1756 until 1763, with leisure for random study.[1]

The fifth and overarching reason was Smollett's deep sense of loss in

English social cohesion. He saw himself within a period of devolutionary social change and in effect echoed Aristophanes: Zeus was gone and Whirl was king. He strongly distrusted the effects of such change upon the social fabric and especially upon political institutions. The desire for luxury was for him the root of change, threat, and destiny, goading men of low birth and no breeding to covet the power, the station, the social perquisites of their superiors. Such covetousness had been raging unabated since 1688. The Glorious Revolution, Walpole, the buying of Parliaments, and the South Sea Bubble were among its early symbols. Moreover, its contemporary manifestations—unrest, rioting, demagoguery, Mr. Monitor, the City Radicals, Wilkes—all proved that rather than flagging, covetousness had grown epidemic. In "a vile world of fraud and sophistication," as Bramble calls London society, Smollett must have felt increasingly isolated, by his awareness of its moral squalor and by his adherence to an older and purer aristocratic ideal.

Among his historical works, Smollett introduces the ideas of luxury and national decline in, significantly, the same place—at the opening of the fourth and final volume of the *Complete History*, in his discussion of the reign of William III. Whereas in previous volumes he had not treated any portion of the sixteenth and seventeenth centuries as a golden age of English life, he seemingly regarded the social relations of those centuries, civil war apart, as embodying a vital, organic society lost to his own time. However indefinite and ahistorical this pre-1688 condition may have been to Smollett, it was of decided value to his thought and is present at least by implication in virtually all his works— even *Humphry Clinker,* where it is represented by Brambleton Hall, which Bramble describes (MB, June 8) as the seat of all that is virtuous and harmonious in British country life and a vestige of the older ideal. This last volume, covering the years 1688–1748, contains, by way of Smollett's regular commentary, his one extended treatment of national luxury and its influence on English politics. Although written near the beginning of his career in polemical journalism—it was completed by June 1757 and published in January 1758—the volume, Smollett felt, reflected a mature and independent view of English history, representing as it did the culmination of fourteen months of arduous work on the *Complete History*. It certainly shows him essaying more than the recounting of sixty years of military and parliamentary affairs. Rather, he was tracing the continuity of present and past, discovering the source of contemporary ills in the parliamentary victory he disdained to call glorious.

The notion that history should be useful, an admonition to its readers, is one of the apparent assumptions of Smollett's historical works. It follows from the belief that history is cyclical or otherwise repetitive:

that every government or nation is constantly declining toward corruption and must be rescued periodically by a revitalizing of its constitution and first principles. The historian can assist in this critical process by bringing his knowledge and judgment to bear upon important events and situations. Like Plato and Hobbes, Smollett desires a nation at one with itself, unified inwardly as much as outwardly. He would encourage unanimity of beliefs and sentiments through the identification of subjects with their government. Although his histories stand apart from the major achievements of European historiography of the seventeenth and eighteenth centuries, his concern with the consequences of luxury led him to broaden the usual narrative of political events to include social phenomena. Signs of discontent and mediocrity could be neither isolated nor ignored, for they exemplified a challenge to the unity and authority a nation must possess.

It could be argued that the *Complete History* and *Continuation* are fundamentally unhistorical. Like Smollett's other historical writings, they appeal to a tacit version of natural law, that in essential matters men are always and everywhere the same, and that contrasts between ages are apparent and superficial. He would probably have agreed with Hume's remark that "History's chief use is only to discover the constant and universal principles of human nature." Since genuine, cumulative progress would therefore be impossible, Smollett could account for the vicissitudes of English history only in terms of the quality of the country's leaders. Hence political strife, though deplorable, is made inevitable in times of incompetent leadership. Natural law is qualified further in his account of the very recent past. Deliberately or not, he indicated that, while progress was illusory, deterioration was an accomplished fact. During his own lifetime, he felt, England had been brought low by paltry leaders and greedy factions, so low in fact that her survival was in doubt. This sense of the significance—uniqueness even—of the present contradicts an underlying assumption of the histories at the same time that it gives his writing a sense of involvement and urgency. An immersion in the present, if it can be said to detract from the histories, gives Smollett's fiction its characteristic flavor. A generation earlier than Burke, the novelist was seeking to forestall the moment when the age of chivalry would pass and the glory of Europe be extinguished forever.

Specifically how the evil influence of luxury penetrated English institutions that were basically sound is not a question Smollett addresses. Instead he treats luxury as a spirit that enters the nation from the Continent about the time William and Mary assume the throne. Thereafter it is always associated with money, and the implication is strong that it was imported by merchants bent upon financial gain, an abnormal excrescence attached to England by brutal and avaricious men. In any case the revolution of 1688 becomes an irreparable fracture in the cincture of Old England, and luxury descends upon the nation not with the infinite (or historical) slowness of a stalactite, but with the overwhelming onrush of a torrent. Discussing the Whig merchants, faction, corruption, the South Sea Bubble, the Walpole era, and the position of the common people, Smollett views luxury as "an irresistible tide," "an impetuous current," "a delerious flood," "a deluge," "a torrent" overwhelming morality and tradition—precisely those metaphors to which he returned in *Humphry Clinker.* The prime movers of the revolution and those who most profit by it are the arrogant Whig merchants, the "Moneyed-Interest," and Smollett reflects thus on the state of England in 1692:

> Intoxicated by this flow of wealth, they [the Moneyed-Interest] affected to rival the luxury and magnificence of their superiors; but being destitute of sentiment and taste, to conduct them in their new career, they ran into the most absurd and illiberal extravagancies. They layed aside all decorum; became lewd, insolent, intemperate, and riotous. Their example was caught by the vulgar. All principles, and even decency was gradually banished; talent lay uncultivated, the land was deluged with a tide of ignorance and profligacy. [4:93]

No evidence accompanies this identification of luxury with the merchants and the common people, but in substance the charge is repeated about thirty times in later works. Throughout the reign of William III, Smollett writes, luxury continues to flourish: the interests of the kingdom are sacrificed to "the interests of money," the constitution and public weal are weakened, and public spirit is sacrificed to faction. An unmistakàble sign of national decline is given when positions of leadership pass from men of learning and virtue to men born "to serve and obey." Men of low birth, no abilities, and gross habits could so rise not by merit, but only by fraud and corruption. Meanwhile men of true substance—"men of landed substance," *not* "mere moneyed men"—go into exile or retirement.

Hope for reform is strong at the accession of the Electoral House, for the country by this time is in a perilous, vulnerable position. National degeneracy has proceeded so far, however, that George I is unable even to slow its pace. A steady decline in public spirit and governmental integrity has made England prey to an unscrupulous faction. Smollett writes of George I as "extremely well disposed to govern his new subjects according to the maxims of the British constitution," but the monarch unfortunately fell victim to the machinations of the Whigs and the moneyed interest. It was during the reign of George I that there occurred the single most important event that the novelist associated with the new economic order. In his description of the South Sea Bubble of 1720, he displays an intense disgust, seeing in the economic collapse a damning symbol of the social chaos ensuing whenever established ranks and distinctions are weakened. The bubble is for him an apt symbol of the abettors of luxury—with their sinister innovations, their companies, projects, funds, debts, and stockjobbing:

> The South-sea scheme promised no commercial advantage of any consequence. It was buoyed up by nothing but the folly and rapacity of individuals, which became so blind and extravagant, that [Sir John] Blunt, with moderate talents, was able to impose upon the whole nation. . . .
>
> Without entering into the details of the proceedings, or explaining the scandalous arts that were practiced to inhance the value of the stock, and decoy the unwary, we shall only observe, that by the promise of prodigious dividends, and other infamous arts, the stock was raised to one thousand; and the whole nation infected with the spirit of stock-jobbing to an astonishing degree. All distinctions of party, religion, sex, character, and circumstance, were swallowed up in this universal concern, or in some such pecuniary project. Exchange-alley was filled with a strange concourse of statesmen and clergymen, churchmen and dissenters, Whigs and Tories, physicians, lawyers, tradesmen, and even multitudes of females. All other professions and employments were utterly neglected; and the people's attention wholly engrossed by this and other chimerical schemes, which were known by the denomination of Bubbles. . . . The nation was so intoxicated with the spirit of adventure, that people became a prey to the grossest delusion. [4:484–85] [2]

The Bubble of 1720 was a portent. Smollett felt that, since national catastrophe was always imminent in a time of luxury, the seeds of economic collapse or political revolution were germinating in his own time.

Since political venality is the twin of economic folly, so by the advance to the throne of George II in 1727 the Whigs had rationalized their policies "by establishing a system of corruption, which at all times would secure a majority in Parliament." Luxury had thus,

> prepared the minds of men for slavery and corruption. The means were in the hands of the ministry: the public treasure was at their devotion: they multiplied places and pensions to increase the

number of their dependents: they squandered away the money of the nation without taste, discernment, decency, or remorse: they enlisted an army of the most abandoned emissaries, whom they employed to vindicate the worst measures, in the face of truth, common sense, and common honesty; and they did not fail to stigmatize as Jacobites and enemies to the government all those who presumed to question the merit of their administration. [4:518–19]

In the *Continuation,* Smollett often remarks that the concomitant growths of luxury and commerce endanger the spirit of the nation. On the state of affairs after the treaty of Aix-la-Chapelle in 1748, he writes:

Commerce and manufacture flourished again, to such a degree of encrease as had never been known in the island: but this advantage was attended with an irresistible tide of luxury and excess, which flowed through all degrees of the people, breaking down all the mounds of civil polity, and opening a way for licence and immorality. The highways were infested with rapine and assassination; the cities teemed with the brutal votaries of lewdness, intemperance, and profligacy. [1:56]

On events of the year 1752, his reflections are similar.

The tide of luxury still flowed with an impetuous current, bearing down all the mounds of temperance and decorum; while fraud and profligacy struck out new channels, through which they eluded the restrictions of the law, and all the vigilance of civil polity. New arts of deception were invented, in order to ensnare and ruin the unwary; and some infamous practices, in the way of commerce, were countenanced by persons of rank and importance in the commonwealth. [1:128]

Indignation against Whig methods of controlling Parliament, especially Walpole's, Smollett raised to the level of doctrine, to be reiterated in at least three other works, including his final novel.[3] In the *Continuation* he laments:

The extensive influence of the c——, the general corruptibility of individuals, and the obstacles so industriously thrown in the way of every scheme contrived to vindicate the independency of p——ts must have produced very mortifying reflections in the breast of every Briton warmed with the genuine love of his country. He must have perceived that all the bulwarks of the constitution were little better than buttresses of ice, which would infallibly thaw before the heat of m——l influence, when artfully concentrated . . .

and that, after all, the liberties of the nation could never be so firmly established, as by the power, generosity, and virtue of a patriot king.

A few years later, in the *Present State,* his language is not so neutral.

The constitution of England, though said to be as perfect as human wisdom could suggest, and human frailty permit, yet, nevertheless, contains in itself the seeds of its own dissolution. While individuals are corruptible, and the means of corruption so copiously abound, it will always be in the power of an artful and ambitious prince to sap the foundations of English liberty. . . . The crown being vested with the executive power, the command of the forces by sea and land, the prerogative of making treaties and alliances, of creating peers and bishops, to secure a majority in the upper house, and being reinforced by a venal house of commons, may easily acquire and establish an absolute dominion. [2:165–66]

In his historical works Smollett's normal technique is to associate luxury with the most shocking crises and excesses of the post-1688 period.[4] Yet within this pattern he weaves a further design. He represents luxury as the source of venality, ambition, fraud, corruption, faction, envy, insolence, insubordination, riot, and other similar evils, then identifies each with the practices of the Whigs. On the one hand, luxury leads to venality which leads to fraud which leads to corruption . . . which leads to the tyranny of the Whig oligarchs. On the other, luxury also leads to envy to ambition to insolence to demagoguery to insubordination to riot and finally to the sedition of the metropolitan Whigs. The careful reader is thus able to trace the major portion of Whig policy and practice during the eighteenth century to the hateful influence of luxury. The reviewer of Brown's *Estimate* for the *Critical Review,* if not Smollett himself, could have had Smollett's history mentally before him when he wrote of "the lowest and vilest of mankind" as those who profited from that "inelegent luxury . . . which attended the revolution."[5]

As luxury had created certain political evils, so it had exacerbated others. Writing of the condition of the common people of England, Smollett uses luxury in a sense approaching the modern, of excess. Luxury here is the relaxation of strict control, of the breach of traditional barriers (the same sense, that is, in which he uses the term when condemning commerce). In describing the effects of luxury upon the multitude, he appears almost swept away by his own language. He writes that the example of the Whig merchants "was caught by the vulgar," that "the whole nation was infected" by the South Sea scheme and "All distinctions of . . . sex, character, and circumstance, were swallowed up in this universal concern," and that a generation later commercial affluence was a direct cause of murder on the highways. While Smollett used his metaphors of inundation with conviction and wished his readers to understand that they clothed an irrefutable truth, modern historians have nevertheless demonstrated that few eighteenth-century Englishmen could have engaged in social competition or would have been aware of, far less affected by, stock operations in 1720. His habits of overgeneralization do however reveal his adamant belief that luxury had broken the traditional and necessary barriers between classes. The merit of social distinctions is one of the recurring themes of his writing: *Roderick Random* and *Peregrine Pickle,* like the later *Travels* and *Humphry Clinker,* record worlds of minute social discriminations, where a man can—or should—be *known* by his dress and manner.

The comingling of classes for mere business or amusement would appear moderately harmless did it not signal another, deeper disorder. Smollett is particularly scandalized by the mingling of both classes and sexes. Exchange Alley during the bubble drew "a strange concourse of statesmen and clergymen, churchmen and dissenters, Whigs and Tories, physicians, lawyers, tradesmen, and even multitudes of females." The Paris of the *Travels* reveals itself as the hub of continental luxury and dissipation in its confusion of the places of men and women.

As individuals the submerged majority of Englishmen lie outside the pale of the *Complete History.* As in *Humphry Clinker* and especially the *Atom,* they are nameless and faceless. Yet they are very much within the scope of Smollett's thinking, for in his way he was as much concerned with humiliation, crime, and evil as Dickens. His characteristic habit is to assign the poor and the déclassé to the distant confines of a category. Later English novelists were to be as hostile to the working-class "mob" as he—Dickens in *Barnaby Rudge* and Conrad in *Under Western Eyes,* for example—but they were to see the mob as a union of individualized men caught up in mass action. There is no one in Smollett to approach a Sim Tappertit or a Joe Gargery, however, for he appears to have been what modern sociologists term an essentialist, someone who believes that social status is fixed and immutable and that any attempt to breach the barriers between classes is both unnatural and wicked. He certainly relaxes his powers of narration and description into a mere flow of adjectives whenever his subject is the activity of the lower orders. Moreover, he is led to occasional lapses of consistency. He regards individual benevolence as the locus of morality, especially in dealing with one's inferiors. The deserving poor are to be encouraged by individual, infrequent, and arbitrary acts of generosity.

But their undeserving brethren are to be discouraged by organized, collective, and systematic acts of punishment and control.

The multitude, the common people in the aggregate, of Smollett's historical and fictional writing have few if any redeeming features. No warm and humane face looks out of the crowd toward Bramble the traveler or Smollett the historian. Indeed one might say that the crowd possesses no human, individual characteristics at all. In places of social resort it may be derisory and ridiculous. But luxury has made it dangerous as well as foolish. When aroused by seditious persons to meddling in matters of economy and politics, it becomes, in Bramble's words, "The mob . . . a monster I never could abide."[6] The mob does not attract Smollett's serious attention until the five volumes of the *Continuation,* where in examining the years 1748 to 1765 he makes its conduct one of the main forces in English political events and one of the great threats to the constitution. Yet, as described occasionally in the final volume of the *Complete History,* the mob is already monstrous. Or, rather, it is asserted to be so, for Smollett does not usually describe or specify the conduct he indicts. The following comments on his treatment of the common people, although based upon volume 4 of the *Complete History,* find their fullest substantiation in the *Continuation.* First, Smollett's language is normally one of deprecation or revulsion. When he notes the physical presence of a crowd in a lane or a square, his common metaphors are "drunken," "intoxicated," and "inebriated," continuing the liquid imagery of his passages on luxury. The following is a partial list of the adjectives used to portray the behavior of the common people: absurd, low, indelicate, vicious, depraved, insensible, lewd, corrupt, mean, intemperate, venal, gullible, insolent, mercenary, clamorous, riotous, lunatic, intractable, indecent, wretched, licentious, ignorant, loose, savage, profligate, dissolute, slavish, abandoned, tasteless, idle, brutal, drunken, fierce, debauched. Such a list does more than indicate the vigor of Smollett's language, for no comparable list of even a few neutral or favorable terms can be gathered.

Second, his portrayal of the life of the common people during the eighteenth century is strangely incomplete. He devotes a full six volumes (of nine in the original editions) to events since 1688, and in the *Continuation,* where he is narrating events into 1765, he is increasingly concerned with the activity of the masses. Yet nowhere, so far as I can discover, is there an attempt to anlayze the abiding condition of the great majority of Englishmen. He laments the depopulation of Midland farms but is silent on the plight of the dispossessed farmers. He speaks of the desperate men besieging the roads but says nothing of the sources of their despair. He does not distinguish between the position of the laboring poor and that of the unemployed. The seasonal agricultural laborer is not distinguished from the London apprentice. He passes over times of acute shortage as periods of discontent and faction: gin riots and grain riots are equally pernicious. In short, he does not display that understanding of the miseries of the multitude one finds in Fielding, Hume, Johnson, Goldsmith, or Adam Smith. The most sympathetic passage in all of his historical works regarding the poor presents at the same time the belief that they are ineluctably degraded. Writing in the *Continuation* of a measure proposed in 1759 to amend a law regarding debtors, he says:

A man, who, through unavoidable misfortunes, hath sunk from affluence to misery and indigence, is generally a greater object of compassion than he who never knew the delicacies of life, nor ever enjoyed credit sufficient to contract debts to any considerable amount: yet the latter is by this law intitled to his discharge, or at least to a maintenance in prison: while the former is left to starve in gaol, or undergo perpetual imprisonment amidst all the horrors of misery, if he owes above one hundred pounds to a revengeful and unrelenting creditor. . . . Wherefore the legislature should extend its humanity to those only who are the least sensible of the benefit, because the most able to struggle under misfortune? And wherefore many valuable individuals should, for no guilt of their own, be not only ruined to themselves, but lost to the community? are questions which we cannot resolve to the satisfaction of the reader. Of all imprisoned debtors, those who are confined for large sums may be deemed to be most wretched and forlorn, because they have generally fallen from a sphere of life where they had little acquaintance with necessity, and where altogether ignorant of the arts by which the severity of indigence are alleviated. On the other hand, those of the lower class of mankind, whose debts are small in proportion to the narrowness of their former credit, have not the same delicate feelings of calamity. They are inured to hardship, and accustomed to the labour of their hands, by which, even in a prison, they can earn a subsistence. Their reverse of fortune is not so great, nor the transition so affecting. Their sensations are not delicate; nor are they, like their betters in misfortune, cut off from hope, which is the wretch's last comfort. It is the man of sentiment and sensibility who, in this situation, is overwhelmed with a complication of his pride, his ambition blasted, his family undone, himself deprived of liberty, reduced from opulence to extreme want, from the elegancies of life to the most squalid and frightful scenes of poverty and affliction; divested of comfort, destitute of hope, and doomed to linger out a wretched being in the midst of insult, violence, riot, and uproar. . . . He scorns to execute the lowest offices of menial services, particularly in attending those who are the objects of contempt or abhorrence. [3:34–36][7]

Third, Smollett was clearly appalled by the general violence of common life in England. He feared what he considered ever-increasing riots and ever-increasing crime and was disgusted by the sources of recreation favored by the vulgar: hangings, gin-drinking, boxing women, bear-baiting, cockfighting. At their height the gin shops of London numbered about 17,000 and crimes classed as capital 250; "Scarce can our fields, such crowds at Tyburn die, / With hemp the gallows and the fleet supply," was Johnson's view. But Smollett's essential, conscious anxiety was political. Luxury, he came to believe, had changed the traditional submission of the common people into envy, discontent, insolence, and insubordination. His historical study, he felt, demonstrated that in their ignorance the common people were attracted by only *false* examples and *destructive* leaders.[8] Easily aroused by faction and popular incendiaries, they seemed to him a senseless mass covetous of active political power. It was at this point that his parallel suspicions of the Whig middle classes and the poor converged. Under the sway of a vulgarizing, emotional demagogue, a gullible crowd could easily be turned into a mob bent upon destroying hallowed English institutions: insubordination spurred to violent sedition. Smollett thus tends to see the machinations of political opportunists—never identifiably of the Opposition—behind quite diverse examples of potential or actual rioting: for gin and against "crimping," for popular heroes and against wage-cutting, for public executions and against high prices. He tends furthermore to see riots in the context of false issues or grievances. That is, he tends to reject the possibility that rioting arises from either legitimate grievance or random aggression. His linking of the leaders of faction to the mob gives the impression of an English third estate, ranging from Alderman Beckford to Welsh smugglers. At the least, his attitudes toward rioting possessed considerable acumen. He evidently realized what many of his contemporaries, like the Fieldings, did not—that the lower orders were not the only groups to riot. Among the rioters were often many merchants, craftsmen, and tradesmen who not only expressed their own grievances on such occasions, but also articulated the grievances of their less eloquent fellows.[9]

A comparison of the *Complete History* and *Humphry Clinker* suggests that Smollett's regard for the quality of English political life did not change greatly between 1757 and 1771. He seems to have retained with some tenacity the attitude toward luxury and its effects he had developed more than a decade earlier. Although we do not have enough direct information about Smollett's social and political ideas before the 1750s to call his later position a conversion, in one respect at least he is like T. S. Eliot after 1932. In their later careers both concentrated with increasing rigor upon the implications of their acceptance of an older ideal, an ideal honored if at all in its transgression. Martz has accounted for the concreteness of observation in *Humphry Clinker* by calling attention to Smollett's labors with encyclopedic compilations. One may cite the further and probably prior and greater influence of his political engagement. In the first three volumes of the *Complete History,* for example, Smollett assembled from various sources the "factors" of English history. In its last volume and in the *Continuation* he was writing *felt* history—specific heroes and villains, virtues and vices replacing the more abstract and impersonal forces of the preceding volumes. Bramble's later catalogs of intolerable conditions at Bath and London can also be seen as the result of Smollett's controlled observation, his inquiry into the effects of luxury and degradation in his own time.

The *Travels* and the *Present State* are useful comparison pieces for both the *Complete History* and *Humphry Clinker*. In the form of international tours, they reveal Smollett a decade after the *Complete History* continuing to use social status as his divining rod in the search for luxury. In the *Travels* part of his intention is chauvinistic—to display for English readers the follies and degeneracy of the French and Italians and, by contrast, the wholesomeness of their own country. He organizes his comments according to social order, describing "the noblesse or gentry, the burghers, and the canaille" of each town he visits (letter 4). He can find only the middle and lower ranks guilty of luxury. Letters 6 and 7 are devoted to a general description of the extremity and absurdity of French luxury: "France is the general reservoir from which all the absurdities of false taste, luxury, and extravagance have overflowed the different kingdoms and states of Europe. The springs that fill this reservoir, are no other than vanity and ignorance" (letter 7). The luxury of French women carries "human affectation to the very farthest verge of folly and extravagance" and serves as "plain proof that there is a general want of taste, and a general depravity of nature" (7). In one of many examples of overgeneralization, Smollett declares that *every* poor woman is likewise infected by luxury: "That vanity which characterizes the French extends even to the canaille. The lowest creature among them is sure to have her ear-rings and golden cross hanging about her neck" (5).

The luxury of the bourgeois is normally ludicrous, and Smollett describes the parvenus of Nice as he does those of Bath, by means of a satiric listing: "One is descended from an advocate; another from an apothecary; a third from a retailer of wine; a fourth from a dealer in anchovies; and I am told, there is actually a count in this country, whose father sold macaroni in the streets" (17). But at other times they are disgusting. At Boulogne tradesmen have napkins on every cover, silver forks, and stamped linen; but their homes are filthy, "Indeed they are utter strangers to what we call common decency" (5). The artisans and shopkeepers of Nice are lazy, awkward, and greedy, for the city, "being a free-port, affords an asylum to foreign cheats and sharpers of every denomination" (20).

In city after city, village after village, Smollett finds the commonality idle and dishonest. Of the French he declares, "I have a hearty contempt for the ignorance, folly, and presumption which characterize the generality" (7). One sign of their presumption is that they wish to travel as comfortably as their betters (9). Another is their impertinent attitude toward strangers: "The natives themselves are in general such dirty knaves, that no foreigners will trust them in the way of trade" (20, cf. 28). More than once he finds them turning into a mob and behaving like barbarians (34), and at St. Remo he reacts with horror upon being invited to sit in a "common room among watermen and muleteers" (25). He is most sympathetic when he finds them exercising proper subordination, as in Nice:

> All the common people are thieves and beggars; and I believe this is always the case with people who are extremely indigent and miserable. In other respects, they are seldom guilty of excesses. They are remarkably respectful and submissive to their superiors. The populace of Nice are very quiet and orderly. They are little addicted to drunkenness. [20]

Throughout the *Travels* Smollett strikes the attitude of a meritocratic *noblesse de robe* jealous of his accomplishments and ready to unite with the *noblesse d'épée* against the comic but dangerous Third Estate. The *Present State of All Nations,* published in the same year the *Encyclopedia Britannica* began to appear, is for the most part a more factually descriptive work. In seven of the eight lengthy volumes in the series, Smollett and his writers resort only four times to the concept of luxury in their analyses, finding the vice to be the major cause of meanness and poverty in Denmark, Asia, Paraguay, and Peru (1:156; 7:4; 8:394, 417). In the remaining volume, for which the novelist was personally responsible, however, luxury is an important part of the discussion.[10] Indeed he opens the introductory plan of the series with an attack, recalling those of Brown and Goldsmith, on the intellectual consequences of luxury: "In this frivolous age, when the powers of the understanding are all unbraced by idleness, and the mind (as it were) overborne by tides of vanity and dissipation, it requires some address to reclaim the attention to subjects of real utility, and to render the voice of instruction agreeable to the votaries of pleasure" (1:iii). Smollett's main task thereafter is the description of England and Scotland. As Martz has pointed out, the *Present State* was apparently designed for English readers, and Smollett withheld virtually all criticism of their country, reserving it for use in *Humphry Clinker*. The manners and morals of the nation receive almost fulsome praise; the places of amusement in London, Bath, and Bristol are held up as models of urban recreation. Smollett in fact permits himself only one rather mild reproof of English life. In the section on diseases, he notes that illnesses due to luxury and gross intemperance "are rife in England, especially in the great towns" (2:222). A smaller deviation might also be noted, censuring not the mainlanders, but the natives of the Isle of Jersey: "Those of the inhabitants, who are temperate, live to a great age; but luxury being more prevalent here than formerly, has brought in distempers unknown to their ancestors" (3:328).

The section on Scotland, which immediately precedes that on England, is in two respects a striking contrast. Smollett does not reprove the English for their luxury, but for obvious reasons neither does he applaud their frugality. Yet in at least eight instances—and in the manner anticipating the Scottish half of *Humphry Clinker*—Smollett explicitly praises the Scots for being *strangers to luxury*.[11] The following, for example, are his comments on the inhabitants of the Hebrides and St. Kilda:

> [The people of the Hebrides] are, in general, strong, vigorous, and healthy, their constitutions being steeled with labour, and preserved by temperance. Happy in their ignorance of luxury and ambition, they live without pride, avarice, and almost without contention, enjoying the hard-earned necessities of life. . . . Perhaps these people might be justly deemed the happiest of mortals, were not their felicity invaded by the horrors of superstition. [1:431–32]

> With respect to their manners [the people of St. Kilda] are a model of innocence and simplicity; and perhaps the happiness of the golden age was never so much realized as in St. Kilda. Unknown to envy and ambition, ignorant of luxury and vice . . . they obtain the necessaries of nature without money, of which they are wholly destitute. [1:451]

Furthermore, whereas Smollett is generous toward English institutions but not toward Englishmen, here his tactic is the reverse. His descriptions of Scottish institutions are generally unfavorable, but he applauds ordinary Scotsmen for their simplicity, industry, and subordination. The majority of his fellow countrymen (in contrast to those of France and Italy) are good laborers because, "a man of the lower class, who has been taught from his infancy to bridle his passion, to behave submissively to his superiors, and live within the bounds of the most rigid economy, will, through the whole course of his life, retain the color of his education" (2:10). Such a laborer will never defy his betters, the law, or any aspect of social decorum: "On the contrary, he will save his money and his constitution: he will pay due deference to those whom fortune hath placed in superior sphere: even when he thinks himself injured, he will rather devour his resentment, than gratify it at the hazard of losing a friend or employer" (2:11).[12]

In a general sense, we need not pass beyond the *Complete History* in order to discover an ultimate source of the opinions voiced in *Humphry Clinker*. In the attack upon luxury Smollett found a form, as well as a theme, that would do him full service for the remainder of his writing career. His discussion of the effects of luxury upon a weakened society in the history can be said to anticipate and account for his portrait of a decadent England in the fiction; his description of the unscrupulous tactics of leading Whig figures is sufficiently angry and inclusive to explain his continued condemnation in the 1760s. Yet to identify the attitudes of the last volume of the *Complete History* with those of the novel would distort the experience that produced *Humphry Clinker*. According to internal evidence, the most probable dates for the composition of the first three-quarters of the novel are 1765–68. That is, the last volume of the history was composed near the beginning of the chaotic and transitional years of the Seven Years' War and the novel some years after its close, with the *Continuation*, the *Present State*, the polemical journalism of the *Critical* and the *Briton*, and the *Atom* intervening. It is likely that the political tone and substance of *Humphry Clinker* were the result of specific political issues and trends of the late 1750s and early 1760s, and, further, of Smollett's disillusionment over his involvement with them.

These issues amount to a calendar of the controversies in which the nation—and consequently Smollett—was engaged between 1756 and 1763. They revolved centripetally about two of his inveterate concerns —the degeneracy and prostitution of an age of omnivorous luxury and the dangerous conduct of the City Whigs and their myrmidons in the metropolis, both in the immediate context of the tactics and purposes

of the war with France. The long years of war seemed to many contemporary Englishmen a time of ever-shifting domestic crises: the death of
one monarch and the accession of another, the transfer of power from
one political group to another, the fall of four ministries, increased
agitation by the middle orders for a voice in policy-making, and controversies over the royal prerogative, colonial trade, food prices, standing
armies, German alliances, and the costs of war. For the politically
inclined, the times compelled increased activity, reassessment, and
realignment. For Smollett they brought forth the occasion and the
audience for his two journals of political commentary—the *Critical
Review* and the *Briton*.

THE POLITICS OF WAR:
THE *CRITICAL REVIEW*

For my part, I cannot bear the tumult of a populous commercial city. —*Smollett,* Travels

I saw a Parcel of People caballing together to ruin Property,
corrupt the Laws, invade the Government, debauch the People, and
in short, enslave and embroil the Nation; and I cry'd Fire.
—*Defoe on the function of the* Review

Smollett's histories amply demonstrate that his objection to luxury was not pure like a theorem, but concrete and personal like an indictment. In this respect he came prepared to the bruising world of metropolitan journalism. By the time he began the *Critical Review,* some forty eighteenth-century periodicals had already carried out prolonged crusades against luxury. Many editors had already explained their motives in terms of the highest patriotism. Thus Fielding in the *True Patriot* (no. 7): It was the duty of every Briton to combat luxury, for its presence aborted all virtue as it spawned all vice. With precedent and principle established, a political paper could settle into its real business, to identify and denounce that "Parcel of People" bent upon corrupting the nation. Smollett broadcast his indictment of luxury in nearly everything he wrote, but he delivered its bill of particulars in the *Critical* and

the *Briton*. Many Englishmen in each decade—certainly the more influential ones who financed and wrote the papers—regarded luxury as
not only the curse of the age, but also the threat of the very hour. Like
many writers before him, Smollett used the opportunities of his monthly and weekly journals to mark the movement of that hour. Here the
roles of social critic and political commentator were one, and here
luxury could be exposed at its source—in the antics of unprincipled
politicians, fatuous tradesmen, and a swinish mob.[1]

It is significant to an understanding of Smollett's temper that the
world of journalism he entered in the 1750s was altogether different
from that of later centuries. He began his career, not like Dickens, in
the scrupulous verification of factual detail, but in commentary upon
men, books, and events. Almost his entire experience in journalism was
as editor and polemicist, his realm that of opinion and controversy. The
pattern of his journalistic writing becomes the pattern of the later
Travels, Atom, and *Humphry Clinker:* he takes notice of the large,
incontestable fact—the book *was* published, the Louvre and the British
Museum *are* there, the war is *still* on—and proceeds quickly to what
interests him more, his own judgment of the fact and its circumstances. The political tumult of the 1750s encouraged this pattern, for
it reflected two levels of crisis—one caused by major changes in domestic and international affairs, the other brought about by the failure of
older theories adequately to explain these changes. The visible result
was a period of inflamed debate, burning with such intensity that many
Englishmen were convinced that the ultimate destiny of their country
hung in day-to-day balance. Public commentary, especially on the conduct of the war, subsisted on a pinch of fact, a pound of opinion. The
Critical Review could not observe the flow of national affairs without
also altering it. It became, itself, a new weight in the balance of contending forces. And the attack upon luxury of the *Complete History* was
applied, as it had been from Plato to Bolingbroke, to events of the present and predictable future and thus became a politics.

In the early stages of the war the *Critical* attempted to bring down
the Newcastle administration, condemned the Whigs as inveterate
rabble-rousers almost as often as they attacked the French, and repudiated mercantile arguments in favor of the German alliance. As the war
was entering its third and fourth years without a sign of eventual victory, Smollett and his writers raised a chorus of deprecation against the
presumed evils of the age and most particularly against the evils of their
political opponents. They resumed the offensive later when victory did
appear assured, with attacks upon those who opposed an early peace.
In the *Briton* Smollett was himself called upon to praise the terms of
the peace treaty as well as the characters of George III and the Earl of

Bute and to disparage their adversaries among the City Whigs. What remains constant through the entire length of these many-sided campaigns is not so much the language or the logic or the argument or even the immediate political position of Smollett's periodicals. Rather, it is the object of attack—the independent Whigs of the London middle class. Indeed, of the twenty-five or so journals that flourished during the period, Smollett's are the most adamant and complete foes of the City Whigs.[2]

Although we do not know the full extent of Smollett's contributions to the *Critical*, we do have sufficient evidence to say that he dominated the review from its inauguration in March 1756 to his departure from England in June 1763.[3] In the first place, his public and especially his enemies—it is significant that he attracted more decided enemies than mere opponents—identified him as its presiding genius, to the extent that a preface was attached to the sixth collected volume (1759) asserting that Dr. Smollett did not write all of the articles in the review.[4] Furthermore, in a list he composed of his published works he added "Great Part of the Critical Review," and he had earlier indicated that he approved virtually everything that went into the journal. In addition, he described himself in a letter written in 1762 as "proprietor" of the *Critical*, although in such a context as to suggest he may not have been sole proprietor.[5] Finally, a copy of the first volume marked with the names of reviewers suggests Smollett as its main author, Knapp surmising that both his editorial control and the number of his reviews increased in succeeding years. After surveying Smollett's work for the *Critical*, Knapp speculates that he was "the leading reviewer in London for the period from 1756 to 1763."[6] During this period the political point of view of the journal remained relatively constant: a consistency reflected in the fact that the first, and rather feeble, defense of luxury ever to appear in the *Critical* was not published until two years after Smollett relinquished active involvement in it.

France and England were already in armed conflict in North America when the first issue of the review appeared. The coincidence was not altogether happy, for Smollett and his writers were deeply suspicious of combat over trade rivalries in the colonies. Of all the major issues the *Critical* confronted during Smollett's editorship, it was on only this initial one that it seemed confused and ambivalent. Always hostile toward the French, it was nevertheless nearly as hostile toward the men who supported the war and its aims: the merchants and tradesmen, the newly affluent, the optimistic and hearty. Some of the journal's early critics accused it of a belligerent antimetropolitanism and an antagonism toward commercial expansion. Others meanwhile perceived in its attitude a primitive, agrarian, and peculiarly Scottish defiance of English policy, whatever its direction.[7] Yet the review was in something of a dilemma. It had announced in a preface to the first volume its patriotic intention to combat sedition and to join controversy. As rapidly as it became a brutal fact, however, war with France faded as an issue of dispute. By mid-1756 Smollett and his writers were faced with a problem that, with historical hindsight, can be summarized thus: How could a new review very much devoted to public affairs survive during a period of war if it were simultaneously isolationist on international issues and aggressive on domestic matters? The practical answer the *Critical* evolved was a three-sided attack not upon the war itself, but upon the Whigs and their handling of the conflict, the effete temper of the times, and "popular" demands upon government. Such a compromise was equally imaginative and successful: while the *Critical* not only survived but prospered, this compromise remained a fundamental feature of its position during Smollett's active editorship.[8]

In one of the earliest examples of the policy, articles attributed to Smollett led an assault upon Newcastle's administration after Admiral Byng's retreat from Minorca.[9] When the incident first became known, the *Critical* joined in the public consternation expressed against the admiral himself, but eight later reviews attempted to deflect indignation onto the duke and his ministers, charging them with deficiencies in experience, leadership, and preparation. These reviews, appearing as judgments of the many pamphlets by ministerial and antiministerial writers, also contained a second theme, that both ministerial and opposition Whigs were rousing the mob with scurrilous and irresponsible rhetoric—a charge Smollett would repeat many times and in many circumstances during the next eight years.[10] The review's vituperative tone in challenging Newcastle and Smollett's later defense of Byng in the *Continuation* reveal that the actual target of the dispute was the old minister himself and not his unfortunate admiral.[11] The flavor of this campaign against Newcastle can be justly gauged in the *Briton,* which although written later represents Smollett's writing alone. In no. 32 of the *Briton* Newcastle is depicted as a "superannuated original" scurrying about madly, "as usual in a sea of absurdity." Yet more harsh is the portrait in no. 38 of him as a senile fool in "the vineyard of sedition": "an old pilot conveyed through the public streets upon an ass, his face turned to the tail, with a cap and bells upon his head, a slavering bib under his chin, and a rattle in his hand."

To the *Critical,* Newcastle was merely the leader of a political faction and the temporary favorite of the fickle multitude—a gloss upon Smollett's use of the term. During the Byng affair the *Critical* was part of the faction opposing Newcastle, but to this group the review gave the title "patriots." As defense of the royal prerogative became much more significant to Smollett and his writers under George III, so they allowed the "popular voice in public affairs" its due when it removed Newcastle but vigorously deplored it when it sought to bring down Bute.

Perhaps because he saw an end to the power of the Whig junta, perhaps because he foresaw a rapid end to the war, Smollett welcomed the elevation of Pitt, Newcastle's successor as principal minister. While opposing many of his plans for conducting the war, the *Critical* termed Pitt "the most venerable character of our age" and called abuse of him in the press "invidious and unjust."[12] Smollett had paid personal tribute to Pitt in a handsome dedicatory statement prefaced to the *Complete History*. Yet the *Critical*'s support of the minister was relatively brief and did not extend, even in moderated form, beyond 1759, after which he was regularly denounced by Smollett and his writers. They deplored the continental campaigns and argued with equal vehemence against naval ventures. They likewise opposed all German alliances and the increased influence being assumed by the City interests, who urged an expansion of the aims of the conflict. So long as the nation appeared united behind Pitt and no Tory alternative seemed practicable, the *Critical* attacked his policies but not his leadership.[13] When the terms of that unity were altered in 1760 by signs of eventual victory and by the death of George II, however, the review again became partisan in opposition. It recalled earlier grievances and soon came to call Pitt's ministry "the most despotic that ever reigned in England . . . he resigned because he could not retain his despotism."[14]

Thus it was that in his writings of the 1760s—especially the *Briton* and the *Continuation,* but also *Humphry Clinker*—Smollett was to repudiate his earlier praise of Pitt. His themes were two: Pitt had enkindled faction, and he had sought support among the dregs of the people. In the *Continuation* he wrote that Pitt's resignation "savoured of disgust and resentment, and implying a disapprobation of the k——g's measures, acted as a ferment upon the ill humour of the people. Such a commotion could not fail to clog the wheels of government, obstruct the public service, and perhaps have some effect in alienating the affections of the subjects" (4:333-34). He charges Pitt with responsibility for the "heats and dissentions which inflamed and agitated the nation." In a similar vein, he discloses his attitude toward Pitt's followers when he comments upon a tribute made him in October 1761 by the London common council:

> Whether this resolution was not in fact an arrogation of right to decide upon the merits of a minister, the particulars of whose conduct they could not sufficiently distinguish; and implied a

disapprobation of their S——n and his council, because they had not implicitly surrendered their own faculties of perception and reflection, to the ideas of one man; nay more, because they had not complied with the violent measures he proposed, in diametrical opposition to their own sentiments and judgment; posterity will be candid enough to determine, when those clouds of prejudice which now darken the understanding, are dissipated, and all the rancour of personal animosity is allayed and forgotten. [4:335]

The *Briton* contains many of Smollett's most vitriolic comments on Pitt, as upon other topics and figures. He is disparaged in no. 3 for alleged ingratitude toward George III; in no. 5 as a man "who raised himself into a colossal idol of popularity"; in no. 7 as greedy but undeserving of a royal pension; in no. 15 as a man without principles, a man "who changed his party as often as he changed his cloaths." Two other attacks are notable for their similarity to Bramble's remarks in *Humphry Clinker* and for their double condemnation of the minister and the groups he supposedly led. In no. 37 Smollett rejects a comparison between Pitt and Scipio Africanus because the latter did not "climb upon the shoulders of the mob to the first offices of the state . . . nor use the lowest arts of popularity to play upon the passions of the vulgar, and raise the most dangerous spirit of discontent among his fellow-citizens." This is precisely Bramble's position when he decries gentlemen who stoop to the level of the mob. In a longer statement of this theme, the *Briton* no. 11 presents a portrait of Pitt that, although no doubt unjust and malicious, anticipates the technique Smollett used with so much skill in *Humphry Clinker*. In the guise of a letter-writer, the novelist identifies Pitt with one Luca Pitti, a Florentine demagogue of the fifteenth century. This letter, significant enough to be quoted in full, fully utilizes the devices of fiction and grasps the novelistic opportunity to create memorable and convincing details of Pitt's tyranny. It thereby presents a substantial case, with concrete evidence, something Smollett could not or would not do in his other non-fictional writing against the elder Pitt. It also contains the simile of the minister as a political comet, to be used again in the novel.

Smollett opens the letter with a straightforward statement of one of his fundamental political assumptions: "A wise man will scorn alike the censure and applause of the multitude; the first as an impotent attack which virtue cannot avoid, and innocence has no cause to fear; the last as a contemptible bubble, without solidity or duration." In *Humphry Clinker* Barton restates this position in order to explain Newcastle's periods of popular support. The letter in the *Briton* then proceeds with the evidence of history.

There are some examples on record, of good men and great patriots sacrificed by popular frenzy; but I could fill a whole volume with instances, both from ancient and modern history, of men without real merit, whom the mob, without reason, has raised into idols, worshipped for a season; and then their adoration changing into disgust, abandoned to contempt and oblivion. Reverses of this nature might be found in the annals of this country, even within my own remembrance: but as such a review might be displeasing to some persons still living, whom I have no intention to offend, I shall select one remarkable instance from a foreign republic, the case of a famous demagogue in Florence, called *Luca Pitti*, who flourished, and fell in the fifteenth century. He was a plebeian of a bold and turbulent spirit, who sought to gratify the most aspiring ambition, by courting the favour of the populace. This, he found no difficulty in acquiring, possessed as he was of a natural flow of eloquence, perfectly adapted to the taste and understanding of the vulgar. By dint of exerting this talent in the council of the state, and espousing the cause of the multitude on all occasions, he raised himself into such consideration among the lower class of citizens, that nothing was heard but the praise of Pitti. When he appeared in public, the mob rent the air with acclamations; and every mechanic of any substance, presented him with some valuable token of his esteem. Cosmo de Medicis the first, the wealthiest and the best subject of the republic, who knew his disposition, and was well acquainted with his aim, employed his influence in such a manner, that Pitti was chosen gonfalonier of justice; and then his real temper appeared without restraint. He no longer kept any measures with his fellow-citizens. He treated his superiors with insolence, and his equals with contempt: he fleeced the people without mercy: he granted protection and encouragement to the most abandoned profligates, who were endued with any art or talent which could be turned to his private advantage; and the multitude, which he had formerly courted and caressed, he now held in the most mortifying subjection. Afterwards, when the family of Medici was supposed to aspire to sovereign power; when the people were alarmed for their liberty; when opposited factions were on the point of drawing the sword, and his country was threatened with the horrors of a civil war: in this emergency, when certain patriots entreated him to interpose his influence towards an accommodation, or declare himself in favour of those who wished well to the constitution; he shrunk from the service of his country in the day of danger and distress, he lent a deaf ear to all their solicitations; and wrapt himself in the shades of inglorious retirement, at a critical juncture, when public freedom was at stake, and his country in an especial manner demanded the full exercise of his faculties and interest. His behaviour on this delicate occasion, though palliated by a few hireling emmissaries, provoked his former adherents to such a degree, that their attachment was changed into hatred; their applause into reproach. The gifts they had formerly bestowed with rapture, they now recalled with disdain: not one gold box or trinket was left as a testimony of his former credit! Their indignation, however, gradually subsided into contempt. *Luca Pitti,* who had appeared like a comet in politics, now set, never to rise again. He passed the evening of his life in disgraceful solitude, and died in utter oblivion. It must be owned, however, in behalf of this man, that when he quitted the helm, he was quiet. He did not attempt to disturb the operation of that machine which he would no longer manage; and if he did not exert himself to the utmost of his power, for the service and advantage of the public; so neither did he employ or countenance a set of desperate incendiaries, to kindle the flames of civil dissention in the bowels of his country. If any turbulent *Pitti* is living at this day, he will do well to take warning from the fate of this Florentine; or should such infamous partisans be at work, I hope every good man will think it a duty incumbent upon him to detect and expose them to the detestation of their fellow-subjects.

During Smollett's years of intense political involvement, Pitt was not only a formidable opponent, but also the foremost representative of a succession of related forces the novelist found threatening. As a purposive cause standing beyond immediate appearances, luxury was ever in the background of Smollett's political purview. In the midst of an arduous and unpredictable war which he felt might well end in calamity, in the years 1756–60 Smollett apparently came to see luxury as having depleted a once-proud nation he honored under the rubric of "Old England." It had weakened both its men and its institutions; it had squandered land, food, animals, raw materials, and other national resources. The enervation begun in 1688 seemed to be nearing its fateful climax. Especially during the *Critical's* period of support for Pitt, but also as early as its first issue, it was denouncing "the age of shop-keepers" in terms at least as harsh and as comprehensive as John Brown's in the *Estimate* and Goldsmith's in the *Enquiry into the Present State of Polite Learning in Europe.* Many of its pages indeed provide the corroborative tone to Bramble's cheerless nostalgia for better times past. In *Humphry Clinker* Smollett is certainly reviewing this mood when he has Bramble ask rhetorically:

whether the world was always as contemptible, as it appears to me at present?—If the morals of mankind have not contracted an extraordinary degree of depravity, within these thirty years, then I must be infected with the common vice of old men, *difficilis, querulus, laudator temporis acti;* or, which is more probable, the impetuous pursuits and avocations of youth have formerly hindered me from observing those rotten parts of human nature, which now appear so offensively to my observation. [MB, June 2]

The answer, in fact, comes immediately: "We have been at court, and 'change, and every where; and every where we find food for spleen, and subject for ridicule." As evidence that Bramble is not being merely peevish, we have Smollett's own even more savagely pessimistic observation in the *Continuation:*

From the frivolous pursuits of the people, the rage for novelty, their admiration for show and pageantry, their ridiculous extravagance, their licentious conduct, their savage appetite for war and carnage which they had for some time avowed, and the spirit of superstition with which they began to be possessed, one would be apt to believe that the human mind had begun to degenerate, and that mankind was relapsing into their original ignorance and barbarity. [4:19]

The *Critical's* crusade against luxury was as fierce as that of the *Craftsman* had been twenty years earlier. It conceded only once through 1766, in a review already cited, that its effects would not be devastating to the nation, retaining Smollett's policy of condemnation for at least four years after his resignation from the review.[15] Seven aspects of its comments on luxury merit particular attention. First, the *Critical* gave considerably more notice to works decrying luxury than did the other leading review, the *Monthly Review.* Second, it was highly selective in the notice it gave works that discussed social conditions, a tendency already noted with regard to rising prices. Reviewing a book that called for both higher productivity and higher wages, for example, it would report or extract only the former position, ignoring the latter. Third, more than once its writers held that the most dangerous form of luxury was the idleness or insubordination of the poor. Fourth, it gave the most curious of all reviews of John Brown's *Estimate of the Manners and Principles of the Times,* deploring its alleged appeal to mass emotions. The same review reiterates the charge that luxury came to England in the wake of William III and the Whig moneyed interest. Fifth, it chose to extract from the many volumes of the *Modern Part of the Universal History,* which was edited by Smollett, those portions that describe the vicious effects of luxury in other nations. Sixth, it antici-pated one of the major themes of *Humphry Clinker* by twice attempt-ing to establish that the poverty of Scotland was directly caused by the luxury of England. Finally, it renewed the Opposition's contention that the liberal arts and graces of England had been dissipated by the forces of luxury.

In the preface to the first volume of the *Critical Review,* Smollett wrote that the periodical was determined to combat the seditious ten-dencies then obtaining in England. He and his fellow writers apparently viewed luxury as among the foremost of such seditious trends, since they used virtually every issue to attack it. With so many books and pamphlets being published on the topic, occasions for comment were manifold. Thus by either direct statement or approbation of the opinion of others, writers for the periodical summoned up practically all the arguments against luxury cited in chapters 1 and 2. On the abstract level, luxury was held responsible for political faction, social chaos, economic decline, popular discontent, and national degeneracy. More specifically, it was regarded as the root of depopulation, crime, high prices, grain riots, losses at war, and an unfavorable balance of trade.[16] Instances of luxury were condemned as vain, silly, sinful, vicious, and unpatriotic. Arguments against luxury, one reviewer said, must be repeated as often as possible, however old or unoriginal they may be.[17] Perhaps it was this belief that led Smollett and later editors to give so much attention to sermons denouncing luxury. The *Critical* occasionally chided clergymen for straying into matters of commerce and science, but it was generous with its space and its praise when the clergy damned luxury.[18]

As an indication of editorial policy, luxury was continually made a political issue. In the issue of August 1756, one writer warns that individual resistence to luxury will be inadequate, for "the best endeavours of virtue will be vainly exerted to save us from ruin, should indolence, luxury, and corruption become the sole ends of the adminis-tration" (2:84). Another, writing in the same issue, concludes a discus-sion of the luxury and effeminacy of Athens with the comment: "Few of our Readers, we imagine, will be able to pass over this character of the degenerate *Athenians* without an application, but too obvious, and some melancholy reflections on the striking resemblance between *them,* and a nation *now subsisting,* sunk into universal corruption and depravity, and perhaps on the very brink of ruin" (2:2). Foreseeing English defeat in the war with France, a third, in December 1756, saw luxury as the source of national weakness: "We are become a most venal and mercenary people,—that there is little or no public virtue left amongst us—that selfish regards have swallowed up all true social affection—" (2:460). Even in less fearsome times, the periodical continued to see luxury as a political evil. Writing in March 1761, a reviewer called luxury the central issue of the forthcoming parliamentary elections. He therefore recommended a particular sermon against luxury "to the electors of Great Britain at the present important juncture, when the love of our country is so immediately necessary towards the making of a proper choice of their representatives in the ensuing parliament" (11:201).

This conservative bias, regarding virtually all change as a sign of luxury and degeneracy, is revealed further in the *Critical's* reviews of economic works. As in the controversy over high prices, the periodical ridiculed or ignored those books and pamphlets (or parts thereof) that called for a more equable treatment for the mass of English people. Nominally reviewing a pamphlet that called for an end to the adulteration of bread, a writer in the May 1758 issue used the opportunity to damn as sedition current popular discontent: "The pipe of self-interest played upon by these wretches [the bakers], has become a trumpet of sedition, arousing the turbulence of popular uproar to revenge their oppressors" (5:443).[19] Similarly, in its reviews of two of Malachy Postlethwayt's books on commerce, the periodical neither mentions nor extracts the author's suggestions for relief of the poor and the better distribution of national wealth. Of Postlethwayt's *Great Britain's True System* (1756) it published sixteen pages of extracts and comments, but those concerned only monetary policy (2:432–48). Phillip Cantillon's *Analysis of Trade, Commerce* (1759) contains several passages calling for changes in attitude toward labor and the structure of society, but the periodical's long notice of the work in March 1759 refers only to the history of money (7:241–49). Indeed this reduction of economic problems to questions of monetary value characterizes the *Critical's* attitude during the controversy over high prices. Writers who addressed themselves to problems of misery, starvation, monopolies, insufficient wages, restrictive distribution, and unfair division of wealth were perilously close to treason, the journal argued, for the situation "cannot be remedied [by means other] than by preserving an exact and true proportion between gold and silver" (9:469; June 1760).

With other writers, those of the *Critical* increasingly came to identify the idleness and insubordination of the laboring poor as the form of luxury most threatening to the national interest. They rejected, that is, Defoe's contention that luxury was the immediate cause of idleness in all classes. They had identified effect with cause and applied this line of reasoning with special vehemence to one group only: the laboring poor. They also brought mercantilist thinking to bear on the alleged excesses of the poor. Returning to the older proposals for a tax on such luxuries as French lace, they recommended that laborers be taxed when they were unemployed. They criticized the charity schools, as they had been attacked in the 1720s, for placing too much emphasis on reading and writing and not enough on "labour and industry." The idea that the economy depended upon very low wages was likewise put to peculiar use. Demands for higher wages were possible only when laborers felt secure in their jobs. They could feel so only when the number of jobs equaled the number of workers. That, in turn, was possible only when the country had been depopulated. Thus a controversy over wages was a certain sign of depopulation, and both were signs of national luxury. A writer in the July 1760 issue rhetorically asks why it is

> that there is not that order, regularity, and subordination main-
> tained among the manufacturing poor of this as of other countries;
> that our poor are in their morals more loose, dissolute, and
> abandoned; that we daily hear of combinations among journey-
> men in manufacturing towns to extort exorbitant wages, without
> ever growing richer; nay, on the contrary, growing more idle,
> drunken, and debauched, in proportion to increased wages?
> [10:43][20]

The causes he cites are of course luxury and depopulation.

Yet the most curious demonstration of the *Critical*'s antipathy to the common people of England came in its long review of Brown's *Estimate* in the issue for April 1758. One would have expected the periodical's editors to hail Brown as a welcome ally, for they had attacked the same agents of luxury and shared his uncompromising aversion toward luxury itself. As has been shown, moreover, Smollett's language of condemna-tion often echoes that of the *Estimate*. But rather than praise, the periodical gave Brown stern rebuke. His book was to be deplored and repudiated, the review stated, not so much because of its argument, but because of its appeal to anarchical, mass emotions. Precisely because of its popularity, the work threatened to arouse the public to a degree of irresponsible zeal. At the same time that the *Gentleman's Magazine* and the *London Magazine* were commending Brown as an erudite and patriotic writer, the *Critical* was reacting extremely in the opposite direction. It compared him with Smollett's notorious antagonist, Dr. John Shebbeare, whose *Letters to the People of England* were consid-ered treasonable incitements to riot. And while threatening domestic order, Brown was also giving comfort to England's enemies.

The review first questions Brown's knowledge of the origins of contemporary luxury in precisely the terms Smollett had used in the *Complete History of England* to describe the aftermath of the Glorious Revolution.

The inelegant luxury, the degeneracy of taste, the universal profligacy of manners, which attended the revolution, were owing to causes very different from those which this estimator has assigned. They were the natural consequences of money-corporations, funding, stock-jobbing, and the practice of corrupting p——ts, which began to be reduced into a system in the reign of King William. Deluges of wealth flowed in upon contractors, stock-jobbers and brokers, the lowest and vilest of mankind, utterly destitute of taste, knowledge, or liberality. They were seized with the ambition of rivalling their betters: they substituted expense in the room of elegance, and gave into all the absurdity of extravagance. Their example influenced the common people, who knew their origin and envied their affluence. These began to thirst after the same enjoyments, and scrupled at nothing to attain them. . . . Such was the origin and progress of that degeneracy which we now lament. [5:285]

The effect of the *Estimate* can be only unfortunate.

Our author speaks . . . with a becoming severity of the writers of such books as tend to overturn religion . . . but many will be apt to put a hard question to our author, by asking him, Who is to be looked upon as the greatest pest of society—the writer, who, tho' he attacks the principles of religion, writes only to a few metaphysical readers, or the writer who published a treatise level to all capacities, in which the most hideous picture is drawn of his fellow subjects: the community to which he belongs is libelled without any regard to truth and decency, and held up to the view of the neighboring nations, as lost to every generous, manly, and virtuous principle; a nation of poltroons, and on the very brink of destruction, by our degenerate manners? . . . a character which every true Englishman will read with indignation, and every Frenchman with joy and triumph. [5:313]

And such adverse effects, furthermore, are likely to continue. "The more popular a writer is, the more dangerous, because his efforts are adopted, his falsehoods believed, and the world apt, like *Mirabel* in the comedy, to fall in love even with his faults" (5:319). The periodical expresses approval of only one of Brown's positions, his charge that servants "are now generally left to the workings of unbridled passions, heightened by idleness, high living, and dissolute example." About this passage, the reviewer writes: "What this writer has said concerning the manners of servants in the present age, it is but justice to him to acknowledge, is very fit and proper, and expressed with that warmth and indignation which their shameful licentiousness so highly deserves" (5:312).

For some reason not readily discoverable, the *Critical* interpreted the thesis of the *Estimate* to be democratic and leveling. Yet as we have seen (and as Leslie Stephen has shown) Brown's position was highly traditional and conservative, depending in part upon Tory ideas on luxury from the 1720s and arguing for a more nearly omnipotent monarch and a more elitist Parliament. Although this position was more flexible than the *Critical*'s normal preference for absolute monarchy, it was certainly not leveling, and Smollett's periodical was alone in seeing it thus. That the periodical persisted in this interpretation for at least three years is revealed by its review in June 1760 of the anonymous *Additional Dialogue of the Dead, between Pericles and Aristides* (1760). From the beginning the reviewer presumes Brown to be the author and calls Brown's praise of the Greek ideal of democracy "equally pernicious and deceptive" (9:466). He continues by arguing, in language almost identical to Smollett's description of the reign of George II in the *Complete History* and to Lismahago's tirade in *Humphry Clinker* (MB, July 15), that even the present English form of limited representative democracy is evil.

> What shall our author say to great, powerful, and civilized people, who delegate their rights to a certain number of representatives, chosen by themselves! To a people who, void of every idea regarding public virtue, barter their rights for the mean gratuity given by a candidate for a seat in the senate! Who have absolutely reduced to system this species of corruption, whereby the price of every corporation is exactly ascertained! Who entrust the liberties of the nation to representatives, who have wasted their influence in soothing, cajoling, corrupting and destroying the morals of their constituents? Who are sensible that the broken fortunes of these representatives must be repaired by methods inconsistent with freedom; that they are assembled in one house under the immediate eye of a court, rich in lucrative posts and preferments, and liberal in pensions, out of the public money? What, shall influence, and power of bribes, avail nothing here? [9:466]

The review concludes with a mordant statement of conservative disillusion: "Consult history, consult your own mind . . . there can [never] be a dependence on the integrity of the people, where luxury and interest contribute in rendering corrupt, those on whom they have devolved their rights, and constituted their representatives" (9:467). As in its review of the *Estimate,* the *Critical*'s reaction is peculiar. It alone of all the reviews saw in the *Additional Dialogue* any signs of liberalizing or reforming tendencies. The *Monthly Review* for July 1760 termed it a tract on the gullibility and dependence of the masses (13:30); my own reading of it is similar.

While the *Critical* was pursuing its immediate opponents, it also sought to ensure that the presumed historical consequences of luxury were kept before its readers. One of its methods was to extract pertinent sections from historical works that blamed luxury for national degeneration. Between 1759 and 1765, the multivolume *Modern Part of the Universal History,* prepared by Smollett and others, was used in this way,[21] the periodical extracting about four hundred pages of the work in all, usually in its lead article. Since the *Modern Part* was a vast survey, extending to sixteen volumes, the editors of the *Critical* had an abundance of material suited to its purposes. Among the extracts they published were discussions of the laudable tax on luxury instituted by the Venetian Republic, the general effects of luxury on European trade, the ways luxury had led to the corruption of various legislative bodies, and the effrontery instilled by luxury in the merchant class throughout Europe.[22]

The *Critical's* judgments on the economic relations between England and Scotland run parallel to those voiced by Bramble and especially Lismahago in *Humphry Clinker.* In Bramble's letter of December 20, Lismahago denies that the Union has brought a significant amount of benefit to Scotland; rather, the Scots themselves have labored hard for what they have achieved. In a review of Robert Wallace's *Characteristics of the Present Political State of Great Britain* (1758), a writer for the *Critical* in April 1758 says:

> With respect to the riches of North Britain, which seem to be our author's native country, we shall not pretend to dispute. This, only it may be proper to observe, that he, in imitation of all the Whig writers, ascribes the late improvements which have been made in the agriculture, manufacture, and commerce of Scotland, to the union of that kingdom with England: whereas, in fact, it seems owing to the natural progress of trade, which has been increasing in the same proportion, during that period, in other improveable countries. [5:290]

Lismahago holds that Scotland has improved in spite of English policies, not because of them. The reviewer of the Wallace book writes:

> We cannot allow the truth of his assertion that the present trade and wealth of this nation are owing to the security and liberty which the nation gained at the revolution above what they had enjoyed in the preceding period. It is well known, that trade

flourished during that period to a very great extent; that navigation was as free, and commerce much less clogged with duties and restrictions, than it has been since the revolution; that the subsequent increase of trade was a natural consequence of improvement and extended industry, assisted by the wretched policy of France, which by persecuting its protestant subjects, drove them into England, where they were hospitably received in the reign of James II, and where they established the manufactures of silk, hats, toys, etc. to the inconceivable emolument of the kingdom. [5:290-91]

The echo is yet stronger in the October 1766 issue, in a review of M. V. D. M. [Mons. Vivand De Mezague], *A General View of England . . . translated from the French* (1766), which focuses upon the relative luxury of the two countries. The reviewer disdains the book as a "wild production" but quotes part of it at length, as Lismahago listens patiently for a while to Bramble, in their *débat*.

How well informed this very superficial but assuming Frenchman is, may be gathered from his observations upon Scotland, when speaking of the benefit which England receives from that country. "As to the money that the Scotch proprietors may perhaps spend in England, you are to observe, that Scotland is but a very poor country: that those landed gentlemen of theirs who come into England, generally carry back with them more than they brought, and that the other people of that country, who go into England, carry little or nothing ever with them, and always carry back something, and often pretty considerable too. It is not the Limousine that enrich Paris . . . they go thither only, because they are wanted, in order to carry back with them all that they can save, out of the wages paid them for their labour. It may be safely affirmed, that this article, far from contributing to England, swallows up more than the three millions of livres raised by the taxes levied in Scotland, which, moreover, may be presumed, to have been already exhausted by the pensions, salaries, and appointments of those, who are employed in the different branches civil and military, of the government of that country. Thus then, the territorial income of Scotland, considered abstractly, from all kinds of commerce, contributes nothing to England, whereas England may be said to contribute largely to Scotland."

A Scotchman who understands the present state of his own country, could inform this writer, that though manufactures and commerce are of late years incredibly encreased in Scotland, yet they carry on their trade chiefly, if not wholly, by paper-money;

and that one of the principle reasons for this is, because their great landholders rake together all the specie they can get among their tenants that they may spend it in England from whence they bring nothing down to their own country, but a knowledge of the vices and fashions of the places where they resided.

"It is impossible," continues our author, "that Scotland should contribute the least tittle to the art of trade with England. It is even certain, the balance is greatly in its favour; for, having nothing to sell, to enable it to buy, all its conveniences must arise from its national industry and oeconomy. Its sales therefore are few, and its purchases still less, insomuch, that it dares not venture to purchase the very wheat that it wants; were it to purchase such wheat, it would be forced to go without many other necessary articles, and would soon become more depopulated than it is at present. A great number of its inhabitants content themselves with eating oatcakes, and very often a kind of oatmeal soaked in water. Scotland sends into England nothing but some black cattle, linen, salt herrings, salmon, and a particular kind of coal that is burned in the houses of people of fashion only. It is true, indeed, that Scotland furnishes swarms of lawyers, physicians, surgeons, military officers and soldiers, shopkeepers, artizans, and pedlars, but very few seamen. Now any country that has nothing, or what is next to nothing, can't but be great gainers by trading with a country that has a great deal. It is not France that gets by Savoy; but Savoy certainly gets by France. The only benefit therefore that England reaps by its trade with Scotland, is, first, by drawing from thence a number of men, whose labour and industry comes cheaper to them than that of their own people, which therefore is a great saving to them. Secondly, by drawing men from thence, who serve to replace those that she is continually losing by her luxury, by her trade, by navigation, and by her wars, which necessarily therefore, makes her less subject to depopulation."

Never, perhaps, was such a string of absurdities and mistakes crowded in so few lines as in the preceding paragraph. The Scotch mention it as a melancholy truth, that their luxuries are so much encreased by their trade, and the improvement of their estates, that they purchase the chief articles of their expences (in household furniture especially) from England; that their houses are as elegantly furnished, their attendants as numerous, and even their tavern expences as dear as in any part of England; that the housekeeping of their nobility and gentry is as extravagant; and that all their trade can scarcely supply the demands the English have upon them for the several articles they import. If anything was wanting to show the ridiculous mistake of this author with regard to the poverty of Scotland, we might appeal to that infallible criterion, the price of land in Scotland, which is said to be as high, at this very time, as in England. [22:300-301][23]

Finally, in the arts and sciences, as well as in government, commerce, and trade, the fruits of civilization seemed rotten to the *Critical*.[24] Reason had become corrupted, liberty abused, and "the public" depraved. Nearly every issue contained at least one discussion of "the degeneracy, want of taste, trifling pursuits, and dissipation of the present age," as the issue for April 1759 (7:375) termed the English condition. The review seemed to be preparing its readers for an impending national catastrophe:

> There is not a stronger mark of the corruption and depravity of any state or kingdom, nor perhaps a more certain symptom of its approaching dissolution, than a visible contempt of the arts and sciences, with an universal coldness and neglect in regard to every branch of literature. We have too much reason to think from the love of indolence and pleasure, which distinguishes the age we live in, that this species of degeneracy is every day gaining ground upon us. [4:46; July 1757]

Most of the periodicals of the time, as before noted, at some time and to some degree participated in such national recrimination. Yet the *Critical's* contributions are distinguishable on a number of grounds. Its repeated calls for English reformation were most insistent and confident and had more obvious social and political biases. It emphasized, in effect, not what *we* can do, but what can be done to *them;* not general responsibility, but particular blame. The review often lamented the lack of *amor patriae* in persons "too cold, indifferent, and mercenary," yet sought to identify itself and its individual writers, Smollett especially, as the "true patriots."[25] Besides denouncing luxury, Smollett and his writers chose to attack what they thought were its particular manifestations. The review of Brown's *Estimate* already cited is a cardinal example of the periodical's habit of turning a general indictment into an occasion for pursuing specific enemies.[26] Unintentionally but rather accurately, Smollett is describing the practice of his own periodical when he has Bramble lament to Dr. Lewis: "I should renounce politics the more willingly, if I could find other topics of conversation discussed with more modesty and candour; but the daemon of party seems to have usurped every department of life. Even the world of literature and taste is divided into the most virulent factions, which revile, decry, and traduce the works of one another" (MB, June 2). The

Critical's demands for reform are in consequence essentially different from the calls for moral and ethical regeneration being made by dozens of other periodicals and pamphlets. It was arguing for a stronger monarchy, a reassertion of traditional controls over most Englishmen, a resumption of power "by men born to wield it."

Such goals went well beyond even those of John Brown and certainly were the antithesis of what the City merchants meant by political reform. When the *Monitor* called for reform, it was asking for a wider franchise and some redistribution of parliamentary seats.[27] To Smollett such calls were in themselves evidence of the degeneracy of the times, and from 1756 through 1763 the *Critical* poured its ample fund of scorn upon them. Reviewing Joseph Warton's essay on Pope, Smollett in 1756 anticipates one of his principal theses in the *Briton* and reveals the characteristic tone of the earlier *Critical:*

> We think the author of the essay mistaken, when he asserts . . .
> that the sciences cannot exist but in a republic. The assertion
> savours too much of a wild spirit of Democratic enthusiasm,
> which some people have imbibed from the writings of the *Greeks.*
> —. . . it betrays its owner into all the absurdities of an overheated
> imagination.—The sciences will always flourish where merit is en-
> couraged; and this is more generally the case under an absolute
> monarchy, than in a republic, for reasons so obvious, that they
> need not be repeated. [1:233; April 1756]

Two months later, a review of *A Vindication of Natural Society* misses the work's irony and proposes a choice between the status quo and "total anarchy and confusion."

> In regard to our author's arguments (if any argument there be)
> we cannot but esteem them weak and inconclusive: for although
> it will very readily be granted, that every species of society and
> every form of civil government is attended with many evils, and
> subject to inconveniences and abuses, it will yet, by no means fol-
> low, that total anarchy and confusion, which would be the inevi-
> table consequence of (what he terms) *natural* society, are therefore
> *eligible.* The grievances and imperfections of which he so heavily
> complains, must always continue whilst men are men, unless he
> could persuade his friend [Bolingbroke] in the shades to send us
> one of his *Utopian* patriot kings to govern us, and a better rule
> than his *first philosophy* to regulate our moral conduct. [1:426;
> June 1756]

Subsequent issues called the desire for political change "the seed of civil dissension," a disruption of "public order and national tranquility," and a sign of "resistance and opposition."[28] A review in 1760 already cited pronounces an author's admiration for the Greek ideal of democracy "equally pernicious and deceptive" and cautions that merely representative government leads inevitably to "storms of popular faction" and "narrow jealousies of rival merit."[29]

The proximate cause of English degeneracy, the City mercantile interests, Smollett kept constantly in the foreground of his political scrutiny. Of association with them, Pitt was guilty in both person and policy—sufficient grounds alone to disturb the *Critical*. To adapt two of Smollett's metaphors, if luxury was the tide inundating English society, then the City Whigs were the sharp rocks upon which the society would be broken.[30] His hostility toward the City, extending in his nonfictional work from the beginning of the *Critical* in 1756 through the publication of the final volume of the *Continuation* in 1765, was widely publicized on Grub Street. It was the subject of dozens of pamphlets and articles in periodicals. Yet for the twentieth-century reader it is obscured by the apparent vagueness of both Smollett's language and the nature of the City and its goals. Respecting the customs of controversy and the libel laws of his time, Smollett did not normally name names in his attacks, Admiral Knowles notwithstanding. Like most controversialists he instead used obvious and convenient titles like Mr. Monitor, Mr. Addressor, Mr. Alderman, Mr. Freeman, The Old Woman of the Monthly, Liverymen of London, and later, Mr. North Briton and Mr. Patriot. A variant is the type of name he used so often in his fiction, such as Alderman Grog, Freeman Vain, and Yelper. Other references are geographical, to the wards or streets where merchants and tradesmen lived or had their presses, as in "the Shadwell mob," "the mob at Temple-Bar and Guild-Hall," "the worthies of St. George-in-the-East," and "the Monmouth St. reformers." Thus in *Humphry Clinker,* Bramble refers with malice to the "delicate creatures from Bedfordbury, Butcher-row, Crutched-Friers, and Botolph-lane" (MB, April 23). A further category would include such terms of evident disparagement as "cits," "zealots," "rabble-rousers," "republicans," "incendiaries," and that trinity of scorn he used so often—it appears in the *Complete History, Continuation, Critical, Briton,* and *Humphry Clinker*—"contractors, stock-jobbers, and brokers."

Although they would not have answered to such names, City merchants apparently recognized Smollett's contempt and returned it. For decades at the center of the English economy, they had also become, since the early 1750s, a significant factor in national politics. By 1760 the City had a population of about 150,000 and was the undisputed focus of banking, insurance, overseas trade, and the older crafts. At the top of its financial pyramid were "the moneyed-interest," the Whig oligarchy: the governors and directors of the Bank of England, the principal insurance companies, and the great merchant companies like the East India Company. Whig by tradition and self-interest, these men were largely unreformed and a law unto themselves. They were attached by business and taste to the court and the current ministry; they were themselves fashionable and lived in fashionable districts. The actual heart of the City's community and political life, however, was not with the few oligarchs but with the larger, more middling sort—the 8,000 liverymen and 12,000 to 15,000 freemen who belonged to the City's sixty or so companies. From this group, attached to the City by both occupation and residence, came the 236 members of the London Common Council, representing twenty-six wards and one hundred vestries. Such a large concentration of interest and activity made the Common Council a potent political force in its own right and, equally important, a political forum second only to Parliament.[31]

The large measure of unity and experience displayed by the Common Council during Smollett's day came as the result of a traditional division of forces within the City. While the council amounted to the lower house of metropolitan government, the Court of Aldermen, composed of one representative from each of the wards, was the upper. The councilmen normally initiated political action but were often opposed by the aldermen, who tended to be wealthier, more aristocratic, and "better connected." The aldermen, in addition, acted as though they composed a gentlemen's club, were fewer in number, met more frequently, had the decisive vote in such decisions as selections of a lord mayor, and were either more receptive or more vulnerable to manipulation from court. The division between aldermen and councilmen led on the one hand to unrest and suspicion, but on the other to a creative friction that bound the City together as it seemed to rend it. The liverymen and freemen found common interests and kept a continual pressure upon the aldermen, who, in response, were less inflexible than they would otherwise have been. The City was thus a source of political ferment, or at least motion, which to opponents like Smollett appeared subversive, leveling, and radical.[32]

Far from seeking the favor of court or ministry, the City as a whole and the Common Council in particular took great pride in a tradition of independence and usual opposition to Whitehall and St. James. For twenty years a center of steady opposition to Walpole, it became, according to Lucy Sutherland, a major political force during the Seven Years' War. At some point during the latter 1750s its leaders determined that the City should no longer accept the roles the oligarchs had previously set it, as stalking-horse and scapegoat. Among the signs that City interests were restive in their secondary positions was the establishment of their own periodicals of opinion and controversy, like the *Monitor* (founded 1755), the *Con-Test* (1756), the *Patriot* (1762), and the *North Briton* (1762). In their pages, and in a plethora of pamphlets, writers claiming to represent a unified City point of view vociferously supported Pitt and the war, opposed concessions, and reviled the surrender of conquests. Overall, they argued for a greater and more visible share of political power. Yet by far the greatest amount of dispute arose over more specific, month-to-month political and economic issues that fell outside the conduct of the war, especially those raised at election time and as questions or legislation in the Common Council and Parliament. These were items of metropolitan, sometimes even national, interest and captured notice in the newspapers and reviews (Smollett's opportunity for criticism). Representatives of the City, both within and without Parliament, argued that England could not be a great and just nation when fixed and often exorbitant prices subsidized the landed aristocracy at the expense of the needy, when a wealthy junta dominated overseas trade through state monopolies, when national monopoly franchises were granted for manufactures, when the gentry's laissez-faire attitude toward wage rates kept laborers at mere subsistence, and when landed interests virtually controlled commercial policy and set harmful customs and excise taxes. In place of these policies they proposed parliamentary regulation of grain prices, to fluctuate with the size and quality of harvests; independence of trade from the crown and freedom for competition; expansion and competition in manufactures; higher labor rates, to be set by Parliament if necessary; and governance of commerce in the hands of men engaged in commerce. Beyond such largely financial matters, City spokesmen advocated seemingly radical changes in political and social custom, ranging from the publication of parliamentary debates and ministerial decisions to the opening of certain streets and sections of London heretofore closed to tradesmen.

Because they were essentially gradualist and reformist—"true sons of the Glorious Revolution"—members of the Common Council and its sympathizers in Westminster and the Court of Aldermen strove for parliamentary recognition of their contributions to the nation. Hence the movement for parliamentary reform, a repeated issue in the 1750s and yet more so in the 1760s, subsumed many of the other social, political, and economic goals of the City. The movement had its origins in the period of Walpole's dominance and of course found not even partial satisfaction until 1832, but to traditionalists during Smollett's time it often seemed as large a threat as the armies of Louis XV. As elaborated over a number of years, the fundamental demands of the City Whigs were four: (1) shorter (three-year) and more frequent parliaments; (2) stronger and more effective, though nonetheless traditional, means of restraining the power of the crown; (3) elimination of those centers of aristocratic—as well as royal—power, the rotten boroughs; and (4) binding of parliamentary representatives to the wishes of their constituents by means of contractual pledges made at election time. All these points were in the political air while Smollett was writing and receiving his lasting opprobrium—in great measure because both Smollett and the leaders of the City had profound hopes for change at the accession of George III. While the novelist trusted that the young monarch would, with Bute's guidance, repudiate Whiggish principles, the City hoped (with considerably less confidence, however) that he would be persuaded by Pitt to elaborate, extend, and purify them.

Sutherland finds a new phase of City politics opening with the resignation of Pitt in 1761. Disabused of hope for court support or even neutrality, the City appeared to possess much greater self-confidence and political competence, to the extent that it became the dominant partner in its alliance in opposition with the Rockingham group. It was united against Bute and his terms for peace and was determined to press its petitions and its demands for reform. William Beckford, City alderman and lord mayor during the period of the *Briton,* concentrated his parliamentary election campaign in 1761 on the issue of electoral reform, declaring in a speech in March that, "our Constitution is defective only in one point, and that is, that little pitiful boroughs send members to parliament equal to great cities."[33] Pitt's principal lieutenant in the City and the chief backer of the *Monitor,* Beckford resumed his argument in the House of Commons after the election. During a Commons debate in November 1761, he said that the government was not always in harmony with "the sense of the people" and went on to clarify the phrase.

> The sense of the people, Sir, is a great matter. I don't mean the mob; neither the top nor the bottom, the scum is perhaps as mean as the dregs, and as to your nobility, about 1200 men of quality, what are they to the body of the nation? Why, Sir, they are subalterns, I say, Sir . . . they receive more from the public than they pay to it. If you were to cast up all their accounts and fairly state the ballance, they would turn out debtors to the public for more than a third of their income. When I talk of the sense of the people I mean the middling people of England, the manufacturer, the yeoman, the merchant, the country gentleman, they who bear all the heat of the day. . . . They have a right, Sir, to interfere in the condition and conduct of the nation which makes them easy or uneasy who feel most of it, and, Sir, the people of England, taken in this limitation are a good-natured, well-intentioned and

very sensible people who know better perhaps than any other nation under the sun whether they are well governed or not.[34]

For this and earlier campaigns the more active aldermen, councilmen, and their supporters, especially in the press, gained the name, City Radicals, which many of them cherished. Yet during the 1760s they were also known as "the Bill-of-Rights people" because of a famous chain of events in which Smollett played an important part. For more than two years before Bute became chief minister, his allies in court and in the press had been attacking the *Monitor* as seditious and had at least four times threatened government suppression. Then on 25 May 1762, Bute was made first lord of the treasury (and the next day a knight of the garter), and Whig rule was at an end. Within four days Smollett produced the first number of the *Briton*, whose function, that initial number stated, was "to oppose and expose and depose *The Monitor*." Two weeks later Arthur Murphy was engaged to assist Smollett with a second ministerial weekly, the *Auditor*. Soon thereafter the ministry began intercepting mail to and from important journalists and politicians of the opposition. In November a warrant was issued for the arrest of one of the principal writers of the *Monitor* on grounds of sedition. The City had henceforth another unifying issue of resistance—the suppression of freedom of speech, a freedom, it held, guaranteed by the revolution of 1688. That cause had of course been trumpeted five months earlier in the first number of the *North Briton*, in whose opening lines Wilkes had written:

> The *liberty of the press* is the birth-right of a BRITON, and is justly esteemed the firmest bulwark of this country. It has been the terror of all bad ministers; for their dark and dangerous designs, or their weakness, inability, and duplicity, have thus been detected and shown to the public, generally in too strong and just colours for them long to bear up against the odium of mankind. Can we then be surpriz'd that so various and infinite arts have been employed, at one time entirely to set aside, at another to take off the force, and blunt the edge, of this most sacred weapon, given for the defence of truth and liberty? A wicked and corrupt administration must naturally dread this appeal to the world; and will be for keeping all the means of information equally from the prince, parliament, and people.

Although many in the City itself doubted Wilkes's motives, they were yet more anxious over the government's response to the periodical: further warnings of suppression, a duel, a dozen or so threatened legal actions, a general warrant, and final suppression. Their own eventual reaction, summarizing years of political agitation, was the cry for "Wilkes and Liberty."[35]

Smollett's treatment of the City Whigs in the *Critical,* the *Briton,* the *Continuation,* and *Humphry Clinker* turns inside out the City's conception of itself. Smollett was apparently convinced that, because they had neither judgment nor learning, the men of the City could have no awareness of how foolish and ignorant (and therefore alarming) they appeared to cultivated Britons. A group of men bent upon insulting their betters could expect no quarter from the *Critical* and received none. Within this general policy of disparagement, the review's criticism of the City Whigs had five specific characteristics. First, an immeasurable but probably small part of it derived from a continuing rivalry between Smollett's review and Griffiths's *Monthly Review* (and to a lesser degree between the *Critical* and Scott's *Monitor*). The *Critical* and the *Monthly* were to some extent contending for the same audience, and they frequently assumed adversary positions for the sake of simple opposition as much as for political partisanship.[36] Second, from its inception the *Critical* found little favor and much hostility in the City, and the review typically returned abuse in kind. When in *Humphry Clinker* Newcastle calls his opponents a "pack of rascals . . . Tories, Jacobites, rebels," Smollett is recalling the epithets most often hurled by City writers at the *Critical.*[37] Third, the review's identification of the City Whigs with luxury is almost certainly a function of nationality, politics, and class. That is to say, nowhere in the pages of the *Critical* through 1763 have I been able to uncover any of the following types of (British) persons or causes associated with luxury: Scottish, Welsh, Irish, Tory, noble, aristocratic, gentle. All of Smollett's writings, the *Present State* especially, proclaim that within the British Isles only the English have been infected with the virulence of luxury. Of the English, only persons of inferior birth—the mercantile or middle and lower classes—display its symptoms. And of these, the contagion is most visible in those men who claim to be heirs of the Whig revolution, who are striving, ambitious, mobile, and disdainful of social and political traditions. The Whig oligarchs are pernicious because of what they do; but the metropolitan Whigs are despicable because of what they *are.*

The most obtrusive and positive example of this identification of the City with luxury appears in the *Adventures of an Atom.* This political apologue, Smollett's *Gulliver's Travels,* published twelve years after the *Complete History,* reflects the effects of the journalistic conflicts of 1758-63, with Smollett distinguishing between the two main groups of Whigs and attacking each in turn. It also anticipates his method of invective in *Humphry Clinker,* ridiculing specific Whig aristocrats like Newcastle in extended individual portraits, while condemning the popular Whigs of the City almost exclusively as a group. Early in the work Smollett describes this political division during the reign of George II.

> The two factions that divided the council of Japan [i.e., England], though inveterate enemies to each other, heartily and cordially concurred in one particular, which was the worship established in the temple of Fakku-basi [Whiggism], or the White Horse. This was the orthodox faith in Japan, and was certainly founded, as St. Paul saith of the Christian religion, upon evidence of things not seen.[38]

After depicting the leading members of the junta, Smollett proceeds "to describe many other stars of an inferior order."

> At this board there was as great a variety of characters, as we find in the celebrated table of Cebes. Nay, indeed, what was objected to the philosopher, might have been more justly said of the Japanese councils. There was neither invention, unity, nor design among them.—They consisted of mobs of sauntering, strolling, vagrant, and ridiculous politicians. Their schemes were absurd, and their deliberations like the sketches of anarchy. All was bellowing, bleating, braying, grinning, grumbling, confusion, and uproar. It was more like a dream of chaos than a picture of human life. . . . Here, however, one might have seen many other figures of the painter's allegory; such as Deception tendering the cup of ignorance and error, opinions and appetites; Disappointment and Anguish; Debauchery, Profligacy, Gluttony, and Adulation; Luxury, Fraud, Rapine, Perjury, and Sacrilege; but not the least traces of the virtues which are described in the groups of true education, and in the grove of happiness. [P. 415]

In the *Atom,* as in *Humphry Clinker,* Newcastle and his ilk are marked by extremes of foolishness, guile, and sham. Yet by the nature of things they are immeasurably greater in stature than the mobs of an inferior order who induce anarchy, confusion, uproar, chaos, "Disappointment and Anguish; Debauchery, Profligacy, Gluttony, and Adulation; Luxury, Fraud, Rapine, Perjury, and Sacrilege." The plebeians at Bath expose themselves at the general tea-drinking: "There was nothing but justling, scrambling, pulling, snatching, struggling, scolding, and screaming" (JM, April 30). The political plebeians expose themselves at Whig councils: "All was bellowing, bleating, braying, grinning, grumbling, confusion, and uproar." The nobility can control and improve this mass of anarchy, as Quin says, "as a plate of marmalade would improve a pan of sirreverence."

Smollett's reluctance to identify luxury with the aristocratic Whigs and *all* of the City merchants may seem to argue a confusion or inconsistency of point of view. But, as earlier sections have indicated, very little rigor could be expected in application of a concept that by the 1750s was a polemical convention and at worst a hasty slogan. Given such patterns of usage and the additional exigencies of almost daily political controversy, Smollett was indeed consistent. He observed nice distinctions of class and was yet more certain of the identity of his political adversaries. As discussion of the *Briton*, for example, will show, the attacks upon the licentiousness of the press in *Humphry Clinker* that Smollett places in the context of a universal weakening of moral integrity have their historical basis in his journalistic disputes with the City Whigs. For the only periodicals that carried out a sustained attack upon government policies and personalities in the period 1761–63—and the only ones he denounced by name—were those either sympathetic to, or actual organs of, the City. It is revealing of the social-political divisions of the time that the same writer, Arthur Murphy, was hired to defend the Whig Newcastle against the City in 1756 (in the *Test*) and the Tory Bute against the City in 1762 (in the *Auditor*.)[39]

The fourth major feature of the *Critical*'s treatment was the alternately hot and cold language it employed against the City, both styles bearing the same refrain. On the one hand, when the City commented upon matters of great moment, like the conduct of the war, the *Critical* rejoined in tones of righteous alarm. In the early dispute over the German alliance no less than during the later one over the terms for peace, the review argued against a strategy of mercantile expansion, holding that such measures were the desire of only a clique of greedy, selfish, and insubordinate men leading a mindless mob. Of the sixteen review articles condemning the alliance that were printed between 1756 and 1758, a minimum of eight are attributable to Smollett. In one of the earliest he held that: "It is well known . . . how great a clamour was raised, and still subsists, artfully propagated by the enemies of government. . . . But these are clamours which could never have existed, or gained ground, but amongst persons totally ignorant of the views and motives aimed at by the bringing over of Germans" (2:121; September 1756).[40] By statement as well as innuendo, the review insisted upon the existence of sordid and often seditious motives behind the various positions the City Whigs took through the signing of the peace treaty.[41] In effect, the *Critical* said that the arguments of the City should be quickly dismissed, for they merely cloaked the intentions of base and mercenary men.

On the other hand, the City Whigs were base in yet another sense, and

Smollett's periodical used the language of ridicule to expose their vulgarity. When concerned with matters of lesser importance, the *Critical* derided their lack of education and manners, their trades and crafts, and sneered at their competence to hold, much less express publicly, views on art, government, and international affairs. Much of this derision was directed toward the *Monitor,* whose writers, the *Critical* alleged in some of its earliest issues, were narrow, stupid plebeians.[42] But the *Critical's* attitude to the opposition journal depended in most instances upon the current political situation. In January 1759, with George II seemingly well and Pitt seemingly impregnable, it could make the necessary identification of the *Monitor* with faction while also indulging in a measure of relatively tolerant irony: "We should imagine that there is very little occasion for a Monitor, while a *Mentor* stands at the helm of government; while faction and opposition are, in a manner, annihilated; and every individual joyfully acquiesces in the wisdom and uprightness of the administration. What occasion, therefore, is there for this champion, to fight for the Rex or the Grex [?]" (7:22-23). Yet two years later, in May 1761, with a new monarch adamantly hostile to the Commoner, its tolerance had vanished. Speaking of the opposition press, particularly the *Monitor,* a reviewer predicts that "the present times will be distinguished in future ages for political rancour. Every subject of a political nature is debated with as much indecent warmth and animosity as if persons were sworn enemies, though possibly the writers may be entire strangers to each others faces, names, and characters" (11:363). More representative of the *Critical's* raillery is a notice in February 1757 of an anonymous open letter to Pitt on the topic of trade in the colonies.

> The author of this perplexed and absurd letter ["a merchant of the city of London"], begins with this modest assertion; "That as he has been conversant with commercial affairs for upwards of twenty years, in the course of that time he cannot fail to have made such observations and remarks upon our trade and navigation, as may tend, at this juncture, to the advancement of both!" Notwithstanding this claim to infallibility, his whole performance demonstrates the great possibility of failing, and that a bourgeois may be all his life employed in commercial affairs, without being qualified to direct a minister of state even in matters relating to trade and navigation. As the letter is addressed to the r——t h——ble W—— P——, Esq; the public is not immediately concerned in it, therefore we hope the bookseller, upon perusal of the ms, has had the precaution to print a very few copies, which the author may present to his friends at the club, to show that the new ministry

must certainly prosper, as they are assisted by such an able counsellor. [3:186]

This notice might be taken as typical of the majority of the *Critical*'s reviews of works it interprets as Whiggish in intent: it neglects most of the letter's contents, distorts the rest ("claim to infallibility"), and ridicules its author. As men of the City do not know even their own business, so they are by nature incapable of higher refinement. Hence a caricature in the April 1760 issue:

> Should it enter into the brain of a phlegmatic alderman to open Pindar, it is probable he would regard the flights of that poet as the extravagancies of a disturbed imagination, and his admirers as the dupes of prejudice and superstitious veneration for antiquity. From the very first line he would conclude him a milk-sop, and prefer the pertness of a *Marriot,* or the solid dullness of a *Richmond Groves,* to the impetuous fire and luxuriant fancy of the Greek. Dead to all sensibility, and the warm emotions of the heart, vainly should we strive to give his tastless soul a relish of the beauties, or convince him that genius ever existed out of the countinghouse, or taste out of Billingsgate and Leadenhall-market. [9:289]

In the period 1761 to 1763, while Smollett was at work on the *Briton,* the *Critical* gave its full support to Bute and his policies. In practice this support meant not only continuing, but substantially increasing its denunciations of the City, Bute's primary opposition, and within its own review format the *Critical* pursued a course parallel to Smollett's own defense of the ministry, a course owing as much to political consistency as to loyalty to its former editor.[43] From the beginning of the war the review had assumed positions nearly identical to those favored by Leicester House and the opposition in Parliament. From the death of George II it had argued with a tone of great urgency for a cleansing of English politics, a new reformation designed to recapture old glories. The issue of March 1761 contains what amounts to a manifesto of the new order. The writer calls for a return to a unified nation under the direction of a strong monarch who would bring an early peace and dispel those clouds of jealousy and faction that too long had oppressed the country. A reassertion of the royal prerogative would necessarily put an end to those claims of influence made by men with no inherent right to opinions in governmental affairs (11:233–37). More than two years later—after Bute's fall and Smollett's departure for France—the review was repeating its call for a powerful monarchy. One example appears in the issue of October 1763, in a review of the collected numbers of the *North Briton*. Number 39 of the *North Briton* had drawn a fairly elaborate comparison between the Treaty of Paris of 1763 and the allegedly infamous Treaty of Utrecht of 1713. Of it the reviewer for the *Critical* wrote: "The 39th number is very arch, and a great part of it very true. But, after all, what is the substance of all our author advances, when digested in the alembic of national interest, or weighed in the ballance against public peace and unanimity?" (16:283).

A final characteristic of the *Critical's* attitude toward the City was its repeated charge that the Popular Whigs were engaged in criminal agitation among the common people. On its surface this charge appeared difficult for Smollett's opponents to credit, for it comprehended mobs and discontent in Shropshire, Warwickshire, and Cumberland, where the City Whigs were not directly or physically present, as well as in London, where their influence was undisputed. Yet, as we have seen, the charge certainly does follow from two of Smollett's assumptions about the nature of luxury. If, as he believed, the mob was a mindless, insensate mass, then its public activity was occasioned by either imitation or instigation. If, as he also believed, opposition to authority was permitted in one place, then it would surely spread to another, the insolence of London plebeians quickly infecting the vulgar of the provinces. In this sense, then, the general unrest of the lower orders followed inevitably from the political opposition of the City. Indeed, Smollett's normal attitudes precluded belief in any other possible source of unrest.

The charge of agitation was most pronounced in the controversy over electoral reform, but was also used by the *Critical* in a variety of other contexts. In the dispute over reform, the review chose to widen the issue considerably. As Beckford and the *Monitor* were at pains to make clear, the City was definitely not urging the inclusion of the masses in the electoral process. Yet the review used the idea of reform to raise a specter of riot, chaos, and drunkenness as "the mob" and "the people" were permitted free expression of their political views. Smollett and his writers foresaw hordes of soldiers, sailors, thieves, smugglers, and whores arriving gaily at polling places.[44] It is notable that not once over eight years, so far as I can discover, did they use the phrase "the people of England" in the favorable (and limited) sense in which it was constantly used by the *Monthly,* the *Monitor,* and the *North Briton.* Indeed in the *Briton* Smollett attacked as illegitimate and outrageous the concept of equality the phrase implied. When laborers in London banded together to resist impressment into the navy and when provincial journeymen united to demand higher wages, the *Critical* saw nefarious schemes to disrupt civil government and the end of all "order, regularity, and subordination."[45] In such pages we can also trace Smollett's attitude toward servants and their "shameful licentiousness," an attitude that led in *Humphry Clinker* to Bramble's instant dismissal of the footman John Thomas, "who is naturally surly," at the servant's first sign of impudence (JM, May 24).[46] As Smollett did in the *Continuation,* the review applauded proposals for closing all places of working-class resort and amusement.

The *Critical's* attitude toward the Methodists can be seen as parallel to, or a part of, its opposition to the middle-class Whigs. From one contemporary point of view, Methodism represented the challenge of emotion, enthusiasm, and innovation to the bulwarks of reason, tradition, and orthodoxy in religion. Seen in this way the Methodists were religious anarchists but not otherwise dangerous. But from another perspective, which the review seems to have held, the Methodists were but one of many groups of ignorant upstarts assaulting the institutions of English society. For Smollett and his writers, orthodoxy in religion was apparently inseparable from orthodoxy in politics. Such views were clearest in reviews of Voltaire and Rousseau but also appeared in discussions of Methodism.[47] The *Critical's* demands for orthodoxy indeed placed the City in a position of double jeopardy, since many of the freemen and liverymen were religious dissenters as well as Popular Whigs. In the *Present State* Smollett had noted a parallel instance, writing that members of the middle class in Edinburgh were, "like the burghers of every opulent city, a better kind of vulgar, consisting of merchants and tradesmen, the majority of whom are religionists of the presbyterian leaven, sour and censorious" (2:123). English merchants and tradesmen often seemed to more respectable persons to be engaged in the same activity of stirring up the rabble that characterized the Methodist leaders. Whitefield opened his tabernacle in London about the same time that the *Critical* began publication, and the review maintained a steady denunciation, terming him the grimy "apostle of Tottenham-Court" and lumping him with Wesley as "the false apostles" of the age.[48] Reviewing the collected sermons of a clergyman of the Church of England, a writer in the issue of March 1761 noted: "This is talking like a cool, dispassionate, sensible preacher, who appeals not to the passions, like our ranting hypocritical roarers at the tabernacle, but to the understanding of his audience" (11:200). In October 1763, the review carried an attack upon the characters of Whitefield and Wesley couched in largely the same terms as its invectives against the Whigs.

> The rapid and dangerous progress of *methodism* amongst us, is, to the last degree, astonishing and unaccountable, in a nation so justly and universally esteemed as our own for its good sense, penetration, and sagacity, especially when we consider what poor and contemptible characters figure at the head of it. The fanatics

of the last age, though equally absurd in their doctrines, had men amongst them who were professed of some parts, learning, and capacity; but the leaders of the methodists are a set of the most stupid and illiterate creatures that ever pretended to mislead a multitude. [16:293-94]

In this review Wesley is called a "vehement roarer at the Foundry," and "a true Pharisee" guided by "pride and insolence" who should be "the object of universal contempt and aversion in the eyes of every unprejudiced and impartial man." Two issues later the whole Methodist movement is called "infidelity" against religion.[49]

Smollett maintained this unmodified and unsparing condemnation in the *Continuation,* where, surveying the events of the year 1760, he writes:

> The progress of reason, and free cultivation of the human mind, had not, however, entirely banished those ridiculous sects and schisms of which the kingdom had been formerly so productive. Imposture and fanaticism still hung upon the skirts of religion. Weak minds were seduced by the delusion of a superstition styled Methodism, raised upon the affectation of superior sanctity, and maintained by pretensions to divine illumination. Many thousands in the lower ranks of life were infected with this species of enthusiasm, by the unwearied endeavours of a few obscure preachers, such as Whitfield, and the two Wesleys, who propagated their doctrine to the most remote corners of the British dominions, and found means to lay the whole kingdom under contribution. [4:121-22]

Although himself very much of an enthusiast in political affairs, Smollett stated his abhorrence of enthusiasm in religion, and in the *Travels* found occasion to analyze the fanatic as type.

> The character of a *devotee,* which is hardly known in England, is very common [in France]. . . . For my part, I never knew a fanatic that was not a hypocrite at bottom. Their pretensions to superior sanctity, and an absolute conquest over all the passions, which human reason was never yet able to subdue, introduce a habit of dissimulation, which, like all other habits, is confirmed by use, till at length they become adepts in the art and science of hypocrisy. Enthusiasm and hypocrisy are by no means incompatible. The wildest fanatics I ever knew, were real sensualists in their way of living, and cunning cheats in their dealings with mankind. [Letter 5][50]

In the activities of the Methodists, Smollett certainly saw insubordination: the pretensions of the lower orders to some measure of religious authority and religious illumination, and the leveling of class distinctions in ecclesiastical practices. In the activities of the City, he saw a great but comparable example of insubordination. An indication that the two types remained linked in his thinking is the character of Humphry Clinker himself, who in the novel is brought to represent the antithesis of both luxury and fanaticism. In all the novelist's work from 1756 there is no direct reference to the positive, spiritual side of Christianity, certainly nothing approaching the Christian devotion of a Johnson, a Smart, a Cowper, or even a Boswell. It would seem that for him the valuable service of religion is to supply not a metaphysic, but an ethic. In the relationship between church and government, government is necessarily the dominant partner. And as ethics could be brought into the service of politics, so the eradication of luxury could be made as much a religious duty as a civic one.

Six

THE POLITICS OF PEACE:
THE *BRITON* AND THE *ATOM*

Smollett's ventures into periodical journalism were probably undertaken as necessary jobs of work. He had a sizable stable of writers and
translators as well as a family to support. Yet however pressed for time
and money he was, his journalistic writing is not mere hackwork. Like
Swift, he had both the habit and the ability to turn an occasion into an
opportunity, a job into a crusade. Whenever he put pen to paper he
resumed his lifelong debate with his own time, for he seemingly wished
to do more than acknowledge the movement of history: he wished to
alter it. His earlier periodical ventures permitted engagement in controversy. What was to be his last demanded it. By the spring of 1762 the
conditions of 1710–14 appeared to have returned. Old lines of contention were being redrawn, old arguments rehearsed. And Smollett had
taken Swift's place in the center of the storm.

It was to promote public peace and unanimity, as these were conceived by Bute, that Smollett undertook the *Briton*. Largely by chance,
the founding of the *Critical Review* coincided with the initial stages of
the Seven Years' War. By conscious design, the complete span of the

Briton coincided with the war's concluding stages. Capitulation of the French at Montreal in September 1760 was taken as a sign that eventual victory belonged to the English. Canada had been secured, and further military action, it was thought, would serve both to extend and to consolidate English conquests. With victory evidently assured, fierce controversy erupted over its terms. To the commercial interests and apparently to much of literate London, on one side, a favorable peace meant the end of the French trading empire—in Europe as well as in the western hemisphere. To this end City spokesmen were arguing at the accession of George III for a continuation of the continental campaign and the retention of all the rich conquests in the Americas (to include, by the end of 1762, Puerto Rico, Florida, Havana, Guadaloupe, Martinique, and the many smaller islands of the West Indies). Economic considerations were equally important to the other side, as George III suggested when he wrote to Bute that the waste of the war must end before "the reign of virtue" could commence. To the young monarch, his chief advisor, most of the court, and the country gentry, a favorable peace meant a rapid close to a very costly war. This position was founded on a willingness to end the German alliance, and hence the European war, and to barter away the newly acquired territory in favor of an early treaty. Thus from what may be called the Tory point of view the goal of the peace was a return to the European balance of power of the late 1740s. From that of the City Whigs, the only satisfactory goal was English hegemony over European and American trade.[1]

From 29 May 1762, four days after Bute assumed control of the Treasury, to 12 February 1763, two days after the signing of the Treaty of Paris, Smollett engaged in the defense of Bute's terms for peace and of Bute himself. His brief from the ministry had no doubt been more positive, yet the force of circumstance in mid-1762 placed him in a constrained position. If members of Parliament, upon whom acceptance of the terms of peace actually depended, would not be moved by the resources of a Treasury well-prepared to reward its friends, then they would not be persuaded by the lucubrations of a new political sheet of transparent origins. Nor could massive popular support be expected, given the general metropolitan view of the peace, its designer, and its defender. In the event, the mere existence of the *Briton* seemed indeed to spur new animosity toward the ministry and to raise political issues, like that of a government-controlled press, previously dormant—emotions and issues that persisted well beyond February 1763. Bute's lieutenants, moreover, did not give Smollett the practical support he needed to wage an even moderately successful campaign. For an important example, the novelist was evidently unaware of the details and even the timing of the preliminary articles of the peace before they were signed and made public in November 1762.[2]

But if in one sense Smollett was severely constrained, in another he was correspondingly free. He had four to six pages to fill every Saturday for eight months, a situation allowing for both the scope of the elaborate serial essay and the concentration of the single short essay. Such opportunity came seldom in the review framework of the *Critical* or in the time- and space-bound pages of the *Complete History* and *Continuation.* The nature of his task, furthermore, was such that he probably accepted it with alacrity and gusto. In order to represent Bute and the peace in the best possible light, he had two direct and plausible methods at hand: identification of Bute's position with the wisdom of the royal prerogative and ultimately with the king himself, and exposure of all those who challenged the chief minister and the negotiations. Since the novelist applauded what he took to be the young monarch's principles of government, and since the main detractors in the opposition were old enemies, Smollett was being asked simply to continue his political efforts of the past seven years, this time under governmental aegis. The outsider found himself inside at last. Thus, as the *Atom* is his version of *Gulliver's Travels,* the early numbers of the *Briton* have the flavor of nos. 14 and 15 of the *Examiner* of October 1710. In the first issues of the new periodical, Smollett displays a confidence and assertiveness approaching ebullience rare in his political and historical writings. Although this tone did not last beyond June 1762, the more fundamental moral earnestness it overlaid was never diminished. To put the situation another way, the assignment he accepted called for the talents of a nimble party writer of the more proficient class, of whom there were many readily available, as Arthur Murphy easily proved. Although he took on a job of hackwork, Smollett brought to it neither the methods nor the motives of a hack. His opponents in 1762 and 1763 charged that the *Briton* contained merely the standard partisan diatribe of the time. While granting the partial truth of that charge, one can point to the more important fact that the attitudes Smollett expressed in such language were definitely his own, however much they may have also been the ministry's, and had been expressed at least seven years earlier and were to be reaffirmed in publications at intervals over the succeeding eight years. In the *Critical* and the histories, Smollett played a large part in framing what by 1762 had become the language of political controversy. And indeed the *Briton* probably lost much of its propaganda value to the ministry precisely because Smollett was not taking dictation from the palace of St. James.

The *Briton* therefore represents Smollett's single most concentrated attack upon the manifestations of luxury: its agents and abettors and their specious self-justifications. It is to the *Critical* as the second layer of a palimpsest is to the first. Smollett's attacks upon the integrity of writers and politicians in the 1750s and 1760s are not only connected with, but similar in tone to, his condemnation of luxury. All were refrains in the *Critical,* major themes in the *Briton,* and figures of contempt in the *Continuation* and the *Atom.* Yet, just as he makes no attempt to define precisely what he means by luxury, neither does he disclose anywhere his criteria for a responsible politics or a responsible press. To take the latter issue, nowhere in his voluminous signed writings or in the periodicals he edited can one discover anything approaching a philosophical discussion of the nature of public commentary. Nowhere do he and his writers suggest rules to govern the publication of news and opinion; nowhere does he attempt to delimit the duties and responsibilities of the press. What one does discover are pejorative statements about the integrity of his opponents; on political questions the charges are specific, practical, and partisan. When the *Critical* or the *Briton* deplored an item in another periodical or, more severely, called for legal action to be taken against it, they were customarily referring to a particular journal whose point of view clashed with Smollett's. And in his journalistic work, this point of view was controlled by more immediate and practical concerns than the integrity of the press. His reviews were of course themselves known for their pugnacious and tendentious methods and language, and the novelist spent eleven weeks in King's Bench Prison convicted of public libel. Given then the sufficiency of the evidence, the conclusion is inescapable that in decrying the press in *Humphry Clinker* Smollett was recalling his own personal rivalries, particularly the months of inflamed dispute with the *Monitor* and the *North Briton* in 1762 and 1763.

Scholars as late as 1974 have tended to take the novelist's language at face value. Unlike Smollett's contemporaries, they tend to assume that his use of such terms as *reason, good order,* and *corruption* was absolute, objective, and self-evident.[3] Some hold that Smollett's opposition to the continental war was based on humanitarian grounds and therefore interpret Bramble's attacks upon the press as a condemnation of some of the obvious excesses of the time. In each case, scholarly eludidation has merely repeated Smollett's positions without analyzing them. Yet proponents of the continental campaign also stated their arguments in humanitarian language, saying that without England's assistance her European allies would be left to the ravages of Louis's armies. Again, the *North Briton* may well represent one aspect of the journalistic excesses of the 1760s, but so do the *Briton* and the *Auditor.*

In many places Smollett calls attention to the excesses of the City; nowhere does he undertake the same task against the Tories, the court, or the landed interest. In the *Briton* he seeks to expose putative inconsistencies in the arguments of the City papers; so many and so gross

are they, he asserts, that they prove the worthlessness of their proponents. Yet he is himself capable of several lapses in argument. For one
instance, he portrays Pitt as solely a creature of the main chance, then
has no explanation for the minister's forsaking the largest opportunity
of his later career. Pitt's retirement, by Smollett's own testimony, brings
rebuke from both friends and enemies. Again, Smollett calls the mob as
foolish in its rejection of Pitt as it had been in its earlier adulation. Yet
he claims that Pitt had come to treat "mere citizens" with patent contempt—a circumstance that if true would certainly justify rejection,
however belated. He charges that when in power Pitt did nothing but
fleece the people. What talents and what influence would Pitt then have
"to rescue a beleaguered constitution"? When Bramble and Lismahago
term canvassing for votes an "avowed system of venality," they are not
so much expressing a philosophical judgment as repeating a partisan
political slogan used against the popular methods of certain Whig politicians. In actuality, the only practical alternative to the solicitation of
votes—and one frequently used—was the purchase and distribution of
parliamentary seats by the Treasury. When Bramble likewise despises a
politician of birth who will "put himself on the level with the dregs of
the people," he is, first, almost certainly denouncing Pitt and, second,
giving a characteristically Smollettian meaning to the phrase, *the dregs
of the people.* The bottom 40 to 60 percent of the people, on an economic scale, were regarded as untouchable by all political groups, as
Smollett, Pitt, and Beckford alike knew well. To an unsympathetic
observer, it may have seemed that Pitt put himself on the level of the
middling sort of tradesmen, but these last could hardly be described in
any objective sense as "the dregs of the people." Similarly, it was not an
impartial observer who saw canvassing for votes as inherently more
selfish and illiberal than Bute's purchase of the loyalty of provincial
placemen.[4] Here as elsewhere Smollett is utilizing the partisan slogans
of the court and ministry. Indeed, he uses the terms *dregs* and *vulgar* in
precisely those contexts where Beckford uses *people.* In no. 31 of the
Briton, for instance, Smollett sought to refute the anonymous but decidedly Whiggish author of the pamphlet *An Address to the Cocoa-Tree*
(1762). He writes:

> I know our addresser and his friends, in all their speeches and
> writings, take it for granted, that the *people* of England, in their
> collective capacity, are disaffected towards the present minister.
> I deny the supposition; I am under no difficulty of admitting, that
> the *vulgar* of London are; but, I am certain, so far as any fact of
> that kind can be ascertained, that the majority of the *people* of
> England, at this very instant, is greatly in his favour. [Italics added]

It would, in short, be difficult to find, after Swift, a major eighteenth-century author who uses with more regularity not only the issues but also the actual language of contemporary politics.

The *Briton* is at once the most ample illustration of Smollett's habits in the use of political language and the best single gloss on that language. In individual numbers he is concerned not with definition but with persuasion; his normal mode is emotive assertion. Yet when taken together, the whole collection of the essays of the *Briton* serves to clarify each part. For eight months Smollett had one principal message: The Whig opposition is base. Stated in the first, it was reiterated in virtually every one of the thirty-eight numbers. In the course of those months he stated and restated his thesis in so many ways—extension, simplification, elaboration, deduction, and others—that his essential meaning is unmistakable.

Certain issues were intended to be unmistakable from the beginning. And to the City Whigs the most arresting aspect of the first number (29 May 1762) of Smollett's new journal must have been its masthead. Under the coat of arms of the king of England and in tones of a manifesto, Smollett declared that the function of the *Briton* was "to oppose and expose and depose *The Monitor*," an infamous sheet that had "undertaken the vilest work of the worst incendiary" and had had "recourse . . . to insinuation against the throne and abuse of the ministry."[5] Thus one half of his rhetorical formula: the opposition was unspeakably bad. The other followed directly: the government was ineffably good. The ministry was unquestionably able and had the complete confidence of the monarch. His emphatic identification of George III with Bute's policies was an open invitation to the City to challenge the king's judgment and was to appear often in his pages. In this opening number he wrote:

> Our Sovereign's character is in all respects so amiable as to engage the affection of every one not blasted with envy . . . his heart benevolently sympathizes with all the children of distress . . . his hand is liberally opened to every appearence of merit . . . his sole aim is to augment and secure the happiness of his people with the independence of his crown.

In no. 4 he said, "The Sovereign can have no interest independent of the happiness of his people." Later, in no. 17, he calls George III a "Patriot-king, whose chief aim is the happiness of his people." The direct identification is repeated in no. 18:

> Let us depend upon the paternal affection of a virtuous Sovereign, who can have no views distinct from the interest and happiness of

his people. Let us depend upon the care and fidelity of an honest minister, who is engaged by every tie of loyalty, of honour, and of interest, to promote the patriot designs of his Master, to consult the glory and welfare of the nation.

Friend and foe alike, contemporary observers found the *Briton* least persuasive when Smollett undertook such positive defense of Bute's policies. Henry Fox secured Murphy's services for a second ministerial weekly within days of the appearence of Smollett's, and Temple affirmed "that *The Briton* left to himself is left to his worst enemy."[6] It was soon pointed out, for example, that Smollett was representing the monarch as both extremely cordial to the ministry and also judiciously independent of it. The novelist responded with the assertion that the role of the ministry, like that of the whole Tory party, was to protect the king's independence and his royal prerogative. He compounded the paradox by noting further that, in any event, Bute's ministry could not be termed either Whig or Tory.[7] A comparable dispute arose over no. 3, in which he replied to a challenge from the *North Briton* to state the achievements of the current ministry by citing the conquest of Martinique and the neutral islands of the West Indies. The *Monitor* and the *North Briton* retorted quickly that he had previously extolled Bute's war policy precisely because it condemned further conquest, and that the capture of the islands merely fulfilled the plans and preparations made by Pitt.

Smollett's evident slowness in the ebb and flow of week-to-week practical politics has caused the *Briton* to be largely ignored, even by scholars. Yet it could be argued that his role of apologist was uncharacteristic and therefore of lesser significance for an understanding of the work. In his historical and journalistic writings, his most effective defenses—and there are many—are of himself and his personal associates, and even these are for the most part attacks upon their detractors. What he most enjoyed was jamming common sense down the throats of men he considered fools. He was the man of wit turned man of the nation's business. The *Complete History* is vivid in representing the events of 1688 as a devolution from some earlier, more wholesome condition of English society, but that earlier state is not defined or described. In the *Briton*, likewise, Smollett's writing is most vigorous in those essays from which the personalities and the policies of the ministry are absent. Vindication of Bute, I contend, was but a necessary distraction from what he took to be his major task: to destroy the political influence of the City and its allies. To this end he needed to make no efforts to link the City with Pitt in opposition to the peace, for Pitt had already done so publicly. On 9 October 1761, Pitt and Temple resigned from the cabinet. Shortly thereafter, in order to explain his reasons for resigning and accepting a pension, Pitt addressed an open letter to Beckford which was published by City periodicals. And as early as the *Briton* no. 2, Smollett opened the assault upon Pitt's integrity that was to continue to the end of the journal.[8]

From the beginning of June 1763, Smollett was compelled to include the new political review, the *North Briton,* in his indictment of the City press. In this early stage of rivalry with Wilkes and Churchill, he argued that the government and the laws were too lenient against the treasons of the opposition press, and, alternatively, that legal action against an opposition author was an almost certain means of creating popular sympathy for him. In no. 4 Smollett compares the author of the first *North Briton* with Orator Henley, who "was in hopes of attaining the pillory, or of being brought to the cart's-tail; events which would have given him consequence among the multitude on whom he depended." The novelist retained this divided view on the value of legal suppression to the writing of *Humphry Clinker.* In the final volume of the *Continuation,* probably written sometime in 1764, he voiced both opinions. Describing the origins of the *North Briton,* he said: "One Mr. Wilkes, member of parliament for Aylesbury, was at very little pains to conceal that he was the author of the paper, which, in point of wit, language, or argument, could never have attracted the attention of the public, had not the minds of the people, by the arts of faction, been inflamed to a degree of madness" (5:220).[9] Writing earlier about the rumors of an amorous connection between Bute and the Queen Mother, he had said that swift suppression would have resolved the affair.

> Had the promulgators of the first defamatory libels that appeared against the k——g and his family, been apprehended and punished according to the law, the faction would have found it a very difficult task, in the sequel, to engage either printer or publisher in their service . . . but they were emboldened by impunity to proceed in their career, to confirm their calumnies by unrefuted falshoods, and to give a loose to the most audacious scurrility; until the minds of the people were so deeply and so universally tainted, that it became hazardous to call the libellers to account. [5:120]

In its campaign against the City press, the *Briton* naturally received the support of the *Critical Review* and the *Auditor.* In September 1762 a reviewer for the *Critical* gave praise to a pamphlet that called for the suppression of "the torrent of abuse issued daily from that fountain of impurity against the most respectable characters." A later review stated: "We have often known it foreseen and lamented, that licentiousness may prove fatal to liberty; but of all licentiousness, that of the press is grown the rankest." At least one-third of Murphy's essays in the *Auditor* contained vilification of the opposition press, the remainder being taken up with glorification of the ministry. In a typical comment, Murphy called the authors of the *Monitor* and the *North Briton* "banditti of incendiary writers" and lamented "the unexampled lenity of the administration" in not punishing them.[10]

In no. 4 of the *Briton,* Smollett combines his attack upon the City press with one directed against the concept of popular government. This number expresses the conviction that the City is more irresponsible when it seeks popular support or, in his phrase, "appeals to the mob." Smollett asserts that the popular appeals of the *Monitor* can lead only to extravagance, disorder, and decline: "It is not to people who exercise their reason, that such appeals [those of the *Monitor*] are made. . . . No, they apply to the million; to the base illiberal herd, who have neither sense to attain conviction, nor sentiment to own the force of truth, who fatten upon the spoils of reputation and greedily snuff up the fumes of scandal, even to intoxication." Two issues later, in no. 6, he explains that, in contrast to City writers, when he addresses "the English people," he is *not* referring to "the base, unthinking rabble . . . without principle, sentiment or understanding." In no. 8 he equates those who want a quick end to the war with the "sensible and honest part" of the nation and calls the trading interests the "refuse of the vulgar." No. 11 contains the memorable fictional letter of Winifred Bullcalf, godmother and prototype of Win Jenkins, who protests in mangled English against the deceit of City politicians. Her husband had been promised huge reward for exhorting the mob around the Guildhall and Temple Bar, she writes, but for all his exertions got merely five shillings and a jug of rum. Most Londoners, Smollett would have his readers believe, knew Bullcalf under the name John Wilkes.

By August 1762, Smollett's accusations against the City had become harsh and blunt. Without circumlocution, he began calling the writers of the *Monitor* and *North Briton* scandalmongers and traitors, desperate men who would be appeased by the disgrace of their country and their natural superiors. "It would be doing too much honour to the talents of these revilers, to suspect they are employed by the French king as incendiaries, to raise a cumbustion in the bowels of their country," he wrote in no. 14, "but it cannot be unfair to charge them with having engaged as volunteers in this honourable service." The next number contained a yet greater amount of emotive abuse, as when Smollett asks,

whence flow these tides of scurrility and treason, these deluges of filth and sedition that drown our daily papers, and stink in the nostrils of mankind?—From a fourth estate distinguished by the name of *Rabble,* which I divide into three corporations, *viz.* Hedge coffee-house politicians, bankrupt mechanics soured by their losses, and splenetic sots, who change their no-opinions oftener than their linens.

No. 14 continues this level of invective in a direct attack upon Wilkes. Smollett had been ridiculing the authors of the *North Briton* individually by giving them ridiculous names; Churchill appearing in the *Briton* as Bruin, Robert Lloyd as Paedagogus Latro, and Wilkes as Captain Iago Aniseen or Jacky-Dandy.[11] For the fourteenth number he concocted an Arabian Nights fable in which Wilkes is cast a Jahia Ben Israil Ginn, a goggle-eyed moral and physical monster. The great and liberal caliph of the time had established a paradise of freedom and prosperity for his people, but Jahia, an insignificant malcontent, wishes only to overturn the prosperity and to vilify his generous and forgiving ruler: "In this season of general felicity, there was a remnant of miserable wretches, who, from disappointed ambition, or inveterate envy, repined at the success of merit, and like so many demons, damned without all prospect of redemption, derived fresh torments from the happiness which their fellow-creatures seemed to enjoy."[12]

No. 16 of the *Briton,* published 11 September 1762, is at once a high point in Smollett's battle against the City, in which he gives vent to the quotidian resentments of many years, and, more significantly, one of the best summaries of the political views he had been expressing since 1756. Specifically, he seeks to make two points. First, the City and its allies are like the savage Goths who sacked Rome: "Uninspired by sentiment, unenlightened by science, and unrestrained by laws; instigated by sedition, and inflamed by intoxication." Second, the City advocates the leveling principle "that every individual has an equal right to intermeddle in the administration of public affairs"; at best this is "a principle subversive of all government, magistracy and subordination; a principle destructive of all industry and national quiet, as well as repugnant to every fundamental maxim of society." As a whole the number is the longest plain statement in all of Smollett's writings of his adherence to classical hierarchy and necessity and of his aversion to theories of social and political equality. Here is the wraith of the Country party under William and Mary and of Bolingbroke's Opposition under Walpole, still keening the world's ill fortunes, three-quarters of a century after the Glorious Revolution.

As so often in the *Critical Review,* he opens his attack upon luxury with an appeal to the lessons of ancient history. He proceeds by means of his customary method in controversy: having rendered a comprehensive assertion, he then argues within that assertion.

Every kingdom, and every age, for a series of centuries, has produced a set of speculative philosophers, who have endeavored to refine upon the constitution of their country; and almost all of these projectors have either affected, or actually felt, an enthusiastic attachment to the democracies of ancient Greece. Some have commenced advocates for the liberty of the people, merely from the pride of classical knowledge, and have extolled the laws of Solon, for no other reason but because they were written in Greek. Others have conceived republican principles from envy of their superiors in wealth and affluence. A third sort of reformers have espoused the plebeian interests, from an innate aversion to all order and restraint. And it is to be hoped, for the honour of human nature, that some few of those theoretical legislators have been actuated by motives of humanity and benevolence. This, however, I take to be a mistaken philanthropy, which, conceiving every individual to be equally free by nature, draws this erroneous inference, that every individual has an equal right to intermeddle in the administration of public affairs; a principle subversive of all government, magistracy and subordination; a principle destructive to all industry and national quiet, as well as repugnant to every fundamental maxim of society.

To give us a just idea of a mob-ruled commonwealth, we need only peruse the histories of Athens and of Rome, during those periods at which their government was purely republican. There we shall meet with nothing but faction, animosity, persecution, ingratitude and disquiet. We shall find the people of Athens led about by every turbulent orator in their turns, like an ill-tamed monster, from vanity to vice, from folly to caprice, from the lowest depth of despondence, to the most giddy height of elation. All was violence, tumult, injustice, and presumption.

Yet if the sensible, patriotic Greeks and Romans were susceptible to such extravagances, what, Smollett asks, is to be expected from the unrestrained and savage populace of a Gothic nation? Very simply, brutality, sedition, and intoxication: "Such were the mob-reformers which have appeared at different times, in almost every kingdom of Christendom." Lest his readers fail to apply this lesson to contemporary England, he moves rapidly to the present. He notes that, "the malcontents of our days have not yet proceeded to open insurrection . . . but . . . they have exactly followed the footsteps of their ancestors in those circumstances we have already mentioned, as well as in divers other particulars." They have boldly criticized the government and attempted to usurp the king's prerogative, keeping in constant view the example of Wat Tyler's rebels: "they have had the courage to scatter the seeds of sedition in public; to practice every species of defamation; to insult the government, and belie the ministry; to laugh at Bridewell and flagellation; and despise and brave the pillory, and even set the gallows at defiance." For his conclusion, Smollett drops all vestige of temperate language in favor of open diatribe, an attack upon the motives, character, and personalities of the opposition that seemed severe even to the strong tastes of the time.

As these Reformers have, upon all occasions, assumed the title of Free-born Englishmen, and denominated themselves *the good people of England;* it will not be amiss to enquire who the individuals are that compose this respectable community. Are they persons of wealth, property, or credit?—No.—Have they distinguished themselves as valuable members of the commonwealth?—No such matter.—Do they contribute to the necessities of the public, or of the poor, by paying scot or lot, King's tax, or parish-tax?—Not a farthing. They reverence no King: they submit to no law: they belong to no parish. Have they a right to give their voice in any sort of election, or their advice in any assembly of the people? They have no such right established by law; and therefore they deduce a right from nature, inconsistent with all law, incompatible with every form of government. They consist of that class which our neighbors distinguish by the name of *Canaille,* forlorn Grubs and Garetteers, desperate gamblers, tradesmen thrice bankrupt, prentices to journey-men, understrappers to porters, hungry pettifoggers, bailiff-followers, discarded draymen, hostlers out of place, and felons returned from transportation. These are the people who proclaim themselves free-born Englishmen, and transported by a laudable spirit of patriotism, insist upon having a spoke in the wheel of government.[13]

After its earliest numbers, the *Briton* received hardly any notice in the *North Briton.* Wilkes had been content to point out that Smollett was working for a Stuart—John, Earl of Bute—whose apparent goal was the restoration of the days of an earlier Stuart. When this point was driven home by repetition, Wilkes sought out larger targets than the author of the *Briton.* But no. 16 was extraordinary and called for rebuttal, and hence in no. 19 of the *North Briton* Wilkes printed a letter in response to Smollett from William Temple, the merchant from Trowbridge, which merits attention for several reasons. It reveals the heat surrounding Bute and his policies and represents the type of argument often used against Smollett. Besides replying in Lockean terms to no. 16 of the *Briton,* it paints a flattering picture of the City Whigs that shows beyond doubt that contemporaries were aware of Smollett's meaning and the actual objects of his opprobrium.

As the BRITON, of Saturday the 11th instant, is an impudent libel on all the good people of *England* in general, as well as on the city of LONDON in particular, representing all the *nobility, gentry, merchants, tradesmen, yeomen,* and all the commonalty, as a seditious rabble, which despises all government, because they express a dislike to some measures relative to a *peace;* and as our constitution is reproached with being an *ochlocracy,* or mob-common-wealth, because it permits our people to murmur with impunity at the conduct they cannot approve, which by-the-bye is inculcating the vilest tyranny ever practised by the worst monsters of all the *Roman* emperors, pray indulge me in communicating to the public a few remarks upon so extraordinary a performance. . . . He informs us *"that there are a set of speculative philosophical reformers.".* . . This extraordinary species of philosophers was reserved for the discovery of the *extraordinary genius,* the author of the BRITON. Well; . . . Could any poor creature write such stuff unless one lately eloped from *Bedlam?* But now for the root of this political evil, this philosophical aversion to order, arising from a regard to the interests of the people. This, our author tells us, proceeds from (remark him!) *the opinion that every individual is equally free by nature.* . . .

Government is a just execution of the laws, which were instituted by the people for their preservation: but if the people's implements, to whom they have trusted the execution of those laws, or any power for their preservation, should convert such execution to their destruction, have they not a right to intermeddle? nay, have they not a right to resume the power they have delegated, and to punish their servants who have abused it? If *our king can do no wrong,* his ministers may, and are accountable to the people for their conduct. This is the voice of *Locke,* the voice of our laws, the voice of reason; but we own not the voice of tyrants and their abetters, not the voice of the Briton. On the contrary, this wretch preaches up the doctrine, that some part of mankind, nay, the mass, are born slaves, who ought implicitly to be submissive to the caprices of a few, who by accident, knavery, or cunning, shall wriggle themselves into power. . . . Observe, *Britons,* what this despicable wretch, and tool of some in power, would reduce you to. Are these the sentiments of his paymasters? Is this the cue given him in his instructions, to boldly assert, that *Englishmen* are all born to be slaves. . . .

[The *Briton* holds that] the present citizens, merchants, traders, commonalty of LONDON, are just such another rabble as the mob under *Wat Tyler* and Jack *Straw* was formerly. He has given all manner of latitude and scope to his imagination, and indulged falsehood in all her wanton levities. . . . You neither want for capacity to discern his insults, nor for spirit to resent the abuse: no; for to do you justice, I must say, whatever the pride of presumption and the swell of vanity may induce some persons to think, the *merchants* of *London,* in their collective capacity, possess more honest, useful, political knowledge, and understand more of the true interest of their country, than all the ministers of state ever discovered, or were masters of.

Smollett meanwhile, sensing that the opposition was for the moment on the defensive, had no intention of meeting these arguments from Walpole's age, but attempted to pursue his advantage in no. 17 of the *Briton* by castigating the City and its press as "the vile retainers to a desperate faction" actuated by base and mercenary motives. He asks rhetorically which persons "so industriously blow the coals of discord" by opposing the peace treaty:

we must search for it [the answer] among the idle and profligate, who have neither diligence nor virtue to earn a subsistence in any calm, pacific course of life; among a set of selfish people who find their account in the war; an iniquitious band of money-brokers, usurers, contractors, and stock-jobbers, who prey upon the necessity of their country, and fatten on her spoils. These are joined by certain individuals in the public service, who sacrifice every patriotic sentiment to the desire of preferment: but those who raise their voices the highest in this discordant cry, are the vile hackneyed retainers to a desperate faction, actuated by implacable malice, rancorous envy, and guilty ambition.

Smollett's use of the pejorative term *faction* here and elsewhere in the *Briton* is to some extent uncharacteristic, inconsistent with the way he used it from 1756 until 1761. In defense of Bute, Smollett used the word to designate any political group or party in opposition to the existing administration. Previously he had usually used it—in the *Complete History* and the *Critical Review*—in a broader and looser sense to include all his political opponents, whether in government or without, as when he termed the Whig oligarchs under Walpole "an ambitious and greedy faction" unrepresentative of the English people. Once again the *North Briton* found occasion to gloss the novelist's habits in the use of political language and to turn the situation to its own advantage. In no.

30 the author says that most readers understand *faction* to be a careless term of abuse without meaning.

> But if by a *faction* we mean, according to a general acceptation, a set of men formed into a party on seditious and selfish principles, and determined, at all events, to oppose the friends and sacrifice the interests of the public to their own base and private views; in this sense of the word, it becomes us to be extremely cautious how we apply it.

> One sure and infallible *criterion,* by which every man may find out a *faction* with the most absolute certainty, is, the wicked art of sowing discord, and infusing the groundless jealousies among the people; whether directed against their old and firm friends, or their great and spirited allies. The first weekly political paper, which has appeared since the change of the ministry, and has been countenanced and paid by the government, was the BRITON, who has abused in the most indecent terms, his Majesty's royal grandfather, our protestant ally, the king of Prussia, the city of London, its first magistrate, and the *people of England.* This was the first wretch hired to ring the alarum bell of discord and sedition.

> Let facts speak. Are we not now become an uneasy, distrustful, and divided people? and, were we not a happy, confiding, and united nation, respected abroad, and blessed at home? Does not the present ministry occasion the greatest disunion and animosity ever remembered in this country? Are they not in the highest degree culpable of engendering the alienation of the best-intentioned subjects from the most gracious of sovereigns? Did not the late ministry preserve union and harmony in the nation; and had they not the confidence of the public in an unlimited manner? Whence has the change arisen? . . . a faction . . . seized the helm of government.

Having brought the *Briton* to a new and higher level of controversy, Smollett largely kept it there during the autumn of 1762. No. 20 reiterates some of his regular charges against the writers of the *Monitor* and the *North Briton,* calling them a "vile crew of incendiaries, the professed enemies of their Prince and his government, the prostitutes of a desperate faction, and, as far as in them lies, the parricides of their country." To these political charges he added, in no. 21, the explicit connection with luxury. Return of acquired territories is necessary, he declares, because conquest would merely aggravate further the syndrome of luxury: "The acquisition of Mexico and Peru would serve only to hasten the ruin of Old England. It would enervate our minds, debauch our morals, destroy our industry, and depopulate our country."[14] The following number, like the *Atom* and *Humphry Clinker,* declares indeed that such enervation is already apparent. The City could have supporters and its periodicals readers only if Londoners had gone insane.

> When we hear the present ministry reproached in every coffee-house, in every ale-house, and almost in every private house within the city of London: when we hear the plebeian politicians accuse them of want of capacity, of want of spirit and activity; and ex-claim with an air of contempt . . . what can we think, but that heaven hath actually deprived the people of their senses; or that they are blinded by the most absurd prejudices, and transported by the most ungenerous and unjustifiable resentment.
>
> Is it possible, that rational beings should be so weak, so humble, as to resign all their own ideas and reflections, and listen with implicit faith, to the idle declamation of a few worthless incendi-aries, who do not even take the trouble to amuse them with the faintest shadows of reason; but seem to overbear their intellects with a foul torrent of general abuse, totally devoid of truth, argu-ment, and probability?
>
> To these abandoned wretches, who have devoted their talents, such as they are, to the propagation of slander and sedition, and perpetually ring the change upon *venal pens, ministerial hirelings, and mercenary writers, attempting to defend an infamous peace;* what should I oppose but an ineffable contempt, and silent dis-dain?

Smollett's disdain could not remain silent for more than a week, how-ever. Opposition to Bute remained extraparliamentary and had no discernible effect upon the minister's plans for peace. On 1 November 1762 the king's emissaries signed the preliminary articles of the peace.[15] The opposition had failed in its primary objective, and circumstances called for a new ministerial offensive to complete the rout. The last three and one-half months of Smollett's writing for Bute accordingly reverted to his original positions of May and June, even though he altered their presentation and added a few novel thrusts. The first num-ber after the signing of the preliminary treaty, no. 24, declared that: "The present, is the first aera in the annals of Great Britain, distin-guished by a torrent of the foulest slander and abuse, poured upon the character of a Prince, who deserves to be the darling of his people; upon the reputation of a minister, whose conduct has defied the severest scrutiny of mallice." The next contains a strong attack, one of many to appear in the *Briton,* upon Beckford, now lord mayor of London. He is ridiculed for his want of character, his plantation holdings in Jamaica, and his sheeplike minions, "the common mob of that great metropolis."[16]

In no. 26, Smollett returned to the form of the fictional letter and produced one of the most effective issues of his paper and an anticipation of many of the letters of *Humphry Clinker,* especially those concerning the trials of Baynard and his luxurious wife. He recounts a political parable of one Mr. Fitz-George and his insolent servants, led by Will Pitot and Tom Give-place, or Buy-vote. While successfully ridiculing his opponents, he also provides a short history of the political events of the early 1760s. He seeks further to counter the City's main argumentative metaphor by using it himself: if the *Monitor* and the *North Briton* said the sovereign was the principal servant of the people, the *Briton* would reply that the people are nothing more than servants of the king. This unsigned letter served not only to stigmatize all Whig opposition as illegitimate, but also allowed Smollett to castigate specific personalities who had incurred his wrath: Pitt, Newcastle, Temple, Dashwood, Wilkes, Beckford, and Charles Say, most of whom were to reappear in *Humphry Clinker.* It is reproduced in full in an appendix to this book.

He was to resume his general castigation of the Whigs in January 1763 with a history of that party during the century, this time without the framework of fable. No. 35 repeats in exaggerated and summary form the attitudes he expressed in the final volume of the *Complete History* and looks toward the invective of the *Atom.* The premise of his argumentative essay is the singular nature of the royal prerogative: "British monarchy, however independent, must be limited by the constitution; if it is not, it is no longer British monarchy, but despotism. As to independency, unless it is independent within itself, if it is subject to the controul either of foreign power or domestic insolence, it equally ceases to be British monarchy." Throughout the century, he continues, the Whigs have been the constant source of domestic insolence, in part because they sought to reduce the strength of the monarchy: "The Whig ministers have always been known to plume themselves in the feathers they plucked from the prerogative; and have added to their own persons, that importance which they have filched from the crown." But this will never be tolerated again. The first two Georges were weak sovereigns overwhelmed by the machinations of the Whigs; their successor is of nobler fiber. Moreover, the Whigs were guilty of yet another type of treason against the crown, one now difficult to suppress. Some privileges that they usurped from the sovereign they distributed to the people at large, against their will. In some weak-minded persons the notion of popular government resulted, and it was these persons who created present-day scandals. But Whig attempts "to widen the bottom of government" had been defeated once and for all, and every reasonable man now agreed that "the popular principle of Whiggism" was naturally abhorrent to the great majority of Englishmen, who preferred a strong monarchy. Smollett concludes the essay with a repudiation of the Whigs as complete as that of no. 16.

The final issues of the *Briton* are dominated by recriminations against the City press. No. 31 distinguishes between "the People of England" for whom Smollett wrote, on the one hand, and "the vulgar of London" to whom the *Monitor, North Briton,* and *Patriot* appealed, on the other. No. 32 is replete with warnings that the government will not continue to endure the foul rantings of those "dregs of the populace," the writers for the opposition. In fierce tones, which find their reverberation in the words of Bramble (especially the letter of June 2) and Lismahago, Smollett asks what can stop this defamation: "What punishment does the malicious wretch deserve, who . . . lifts the murderous quill to stab the reputation of innocence, to sully the fair fame of the most shining merit, and unite the most treacherous disloyalty, with the most rancorous defamation." (Lismahago, in Bramble's letter of July 15, says liberty of the press "enabled the vilest reptile to soil the lustre of the most shining merit.")

> The shameless scribbler, like the village-idiot, when the clock was silent, still continues to strike sedition, from the force of habit, even though the springs that first moved him have ceased to operate. The weekly libel still appears, replete with nonsense, falshood and scurrility, and tho' banished with disgrace from every creditable society, finds readers among the vulgar herd of alehouse politicians. The most shocking exhibitions of infamous scandal and stupid obscenity, are publicly vended in the shops of this metropolis, to the reproach of government, and the disgrace of the nation, as if our people delighted in malice and indecency, and there was no law in the kingdom to punish the most brutal licentiousness.

He leaves no doubt that he demands the most severe punishment possible.

> We know it hath been adjudged, that an attempt, *forcibly to prescribe laws to the K——g, and to restrain him of his power, implies a design to deprive him of his crown and life; that words spoken to draw away the affection of the people from the K——g, and to stir them up against him, tend to his death and destruction, and are T——n;* and we know that *Scribere Est Agere.* [Original italics]

No. 33 calls the *North Briton* and the *Monitor* enemies of the nation whose address is "to the lower class of mortals," the rabble, to whom the City would give over the reins of government.

Smollett concludes the *Briton* on those themes with which he opened it. In the penultimate issue, no. 37, he avows that he was forced to come to the defense of the ministry. "The reader will remember, that I did not lift the pen in this dispute, until I saw my S——n, whom I am bound to honour, and his M——r whose virtue I had cause to respect, aspersed with such falshood, and reviled with such rancour, as must have roused the indignation of every honest man." The final number, no. 38, published on 12 February 1763, is another broadside against the Whigs generally and the City in particular.

The signing of the Treaty of Paris ended Bute's patronage and the life of the *Briton*. Smollett's letters and the *Travels* suggest that these eight months were among the most intense in his eventful life. In retrospect, they also seemed to him the most frustrating, even harrowing. A year after he had begun the journal he was broken in both body and spirit, and in June of 1763 he took his family away to France. Earlier he had written of his failing health to Moore: "My constitution will no longer allow me to toil as formerly. I am now so thin you would hardly know me. My face is shrivelled up by the asthma like an ill-dried pippin, and my legs are as thick at the ankle as at the calf."[17] In the opening letter of the *Travels,* written later, he spoke of the bitterness induced by his work on the *Briton;* he had been "traduced by malice, persecuted by faction" and "abandoned by false patrons" in a "scene of illiberal dispute, and incredible infatuation."

This period of his life was embittering not so much because the task he accepted was unfamiliar or difficult as because its results were so unsatisfactory. Personally Smollett went unrewarded; whatever he had been promised, he received no sizable remuneration. Politically the results were at best ambiguous. The ground swell of conservative, royalist support the *Critical* had been predicting since mid-1760 never materialized to embrace the *Briton* or its sponsors. The peace treaty had been drafted and ratified as Bute wanted, yet the minister remained in power only a few months beyond its ratification. Intended as a first step toward "the reign of virtue," the peace had exhausted its designer as well as its defender. The means had become an end and, for Bute, a dead end. Though Bute had won his campaign for the peace, moreover, the City had not altogether lost. In the course of his months of writing for the minister, Smollett had been compelled to reverse several of his positions on important political issues, such as the integrity of Pitt, the reliability of the French government, and the value of territorial conquests. Although he was regularly denounced for inconsistency, his consistency actually never faltered and was of the most basic sort: he sought by all arguments available to him to destroy the influence of the City Whigs. Yet he and Murphy had not succeeded in their smaller, preliminary task, that of destroying the credibility of the City press; if anything, ministerial attacks assisted in raising such credibility. The *Monitor, North Briton,* and *Patriot* had no hope of swaying members of parliament, and they did not. But with their selected audience, the middling group of the capital, their credit had grown prodigiously. The ministry in 1763 was weak in victory. The City, beginning twenty years of accelerated political agitation, was strengthened in defeat.[18]

In 1763 as in 1714, the Tories could gain the peace they desired, but not the stability and authority: they could manage a negotiating conference but not a country. Smollett's responses were much like Swift's. He soon abandoned England and later composed a political apologue, a summing up of his attitudes beyond the threshold of hope. *The History and Adventures of an Atom* retraced the historical ground Smollett had traveled before without presenting any new "facts." But it provided him with two opportunities he did not have in his periodical work: to express his disappointment over the chances lost by Bute and his administration, and to restate with the license of fiction his utter detestation of Whig politicians, especially Newcastle and Pitt, and their myrmidons, the Legion. The resulting work grows expressly from his earlier concerns. It outlines again the political history of luxury in the corruption of Whig power and describes the source of that power in what the novelist saw as its full obscenity. And it contains what amounts to his final statement of independence from partisan, practical politics—a partial explanation, at least, of the political detachment of *Humphry Clinker.*

Although the *Atom* is relatively short, it presents more of what Smollett took the actual stuff of politics to be than do the *Complete History* and *Continuation.* It represents a secret history of private maneuvers, behind closed doors and among milling crowds. The chronicle is narrated by an omniscient and indestructible atom, now lodged in the pineal gland of one Nathaniel Peacock, which is able once every millennium to impart the enormous knowledge it possesses: "For the benefit of you miserable mortals, I am determined to promulge the history of one period, during which I underwent some strange revolutions in the empire of Japan, and was conscious of some political anecdotes now to be divulged for the instruction of British ministers."[19] The one period the atom wishes to describe minutely lies between the death of Henry Pelham and the rise of Newcastle in 1754 to Bute's failure in 1763. The opening portion of the atom's story concerns the general condition of England from the revolution to 1754.

The major elements of this condition are by now familiar in Smollett. The English are a fickle, stupid, and docile people: "such inconsistent, capricious animals, that one would imagine they were created for the purpose of ridicule. Their minds are in constant agitation. . . . They seem to have no fixed principle of action, no certain plan of conduct. . . . One hour [an Englishman] doubts the best established truths; the next, he swallows the most improbable fiction. His praise and his censure are what a wise man would choose to avoid, as evils equally pernicious" (pp. 392-93). Moreover the English,

> value themselves much upon their constitution, and are very clamorous about the words liberty and property; yet, in fact, the only liberty they enjoy is to get drunk whenever they please, to revile the government, and quarrel with one another. With respect to their property, they are tamest animals in the world; and, if properly managed, undergo, without wincing, such impositions, as no other nation in the world would bear. In this particular, they may be compared to an ass, that will crouch under the most unconscionable burden, provided you scratch his long ears, and allow him to bray his bellyfull. They are so practicable, that they have suffered their pockets to be drained, their veins to be emptied, and their credit to be cracked, by the most bungling administrations, to gratify the avarice, pride, and ambition, of the most sordid and contemptible sovereigns, that ever sat upon the throne. [Pp. 393-94]

Monarchs who are contemptibly weak and foolish are perhaps apt but nonetheless incompetent rulers for such a people. George I is an ignoramus, but his successor is worse—expelled, not born, "*a posteriori* from a goose." "He was rapacious, shallow, hot-headed, and perverse; in point of understanding, just sufficient to appear in public without a slavering bib; imbued with no knowledge, illumed by no sentiment, and warmed with no affection. . . . His heart was meanly selfish, and his disposition altogether unprincely" (p. 397). His favorite amusement is "kicking the breech" of his ministers, an office assumed naturally by the Whigs, for they are the only group totally without honor or decency.

The Whigs are natural heirs of early Hanoverian policy because they are at once stupid and unscrupulous. For a time Newcastle is the most powerful political figure in the nation because he enjoys having his arse kicked: "He presented his posteriors to be kicked as regularly as the day revolved; and presented them not barely with submission, but with all the appearance of fond desire; and truly this diurnal exposure was attended with such delectation as he never enjoyed in any other attitude"

(p. 401). This admirable appetite is supported by a politic vacuity of mind, an actual "hollowness in the Brain"; "He had no understanding, no economy, no courage, no industry, no steadiness, no discernment, no vigour, no retention. He was . . . profuse, chicken-hearted, negligent, fickle, blundering, weak, and leaky" (p. 398). He is in fact the perfect specimen of the Whig oligarch: "A statesman without . . . the smallest tincture of human learning: a secretary who could not write; a financier who did not understand the multiplication table; and the treasurer of a vast empire who never could balance accounts with his own butler" (p. 400).[20] The inferior, metropolitan wing of the Whig party, led by fat aldermen who dine on turtle and venison, are more anarchic, disreputable, and unpredictable than the old duke and his friends. Yet they too are imbeciles willing to unite under the Hanoverian creed: "that two and two make seven; that the sun rules the night, the stars the day; and the moon is made of green cheese" (p. 416).

When Smollett reaches the period of the Seven Years' War, there is a sharp change in tone, one he himself notes: "I shall now proceed to a plain narration of historical incidents, without pretending to philosophize like H——e, or dogmatize like S——tt" (p. 416). The first two Georges, Newcastle, and their ilk Smollett can ridicule, for they are absurd and their activities make for farce. But from the mid-1750s the plain narration must also include Pitt and the mob, whom he can only loathe, for they are horrible. According to him, the old Whigs helped create the new sordid turn of affairs by initiating a policy of pandering to the mob: "'The multitude . . . is a many headed monster—it is a Cerberus that must have a sop:—it is a wild-beast, so ravenous that nothing but blood will appease its appetite: it is a whale that must have a barrel for its amusement:—it is a demon to which we must offer up human sacrifice. Now, the question is, who is to be this sop, this barrel, this scape-goat?'" (p. 426). The victim chosen is of course Admiral Byng.

Pitt wanders into this opening as leader of the "self-constituted college of the mob." He possesses a loud braying voice, a fluency of abuse ("a species of music to the mob") which earns him the title, "first demogogue of the empire." His chief gift in diplomacy is to feign service to others while pleasing only himself. Performing the osculation a posteriori required of all public officials, he secretly disables his rivals. Filling his pockets with the treasure of the empire, he contrives a new food to beguile the starving, "a mess that should fill their bellies, and, at the same time, protract the intoxication of their brains, which it was so much his interest to maintain." Turning national policy to disgrace and apostasy, he holds the mob spellbound with his tricks, twists, and tumbles. Smollett sees Pitt as a virtuoso in the new English politics, mobocracy, having him declare, "I will ride the mighty beast whose name is Legion." He is the first power in the kingdom because he is a professional "mob-driver," a modern politician self-trained "to bridle and manage the blatant beast whose name was Legion." His natural constituency comprises the new order of public philosophers: "grocers, scavengers, halter-makers, carpenters, draymen, distillers, chimney-sweepers, oyster-women, ass-drivers, aldermen, and dealers in waste paper." Recognizing the stench of its own filth, the beast follows its master everywhere, and Pitt "milked the dugs of the monster till the blood came." Pitt's rivals are equally fascinated and horrified, convinced that the orator had sold his soul to the devil in exchange for power to move the mob. This is an interpretation the atom can credit: "I not only know there is a devil, but I likewise know that he has marked out nineteen-twentieths of the people of this metropolis for his prey" (pp. 461–62).

To the narrator-atom, Pitt and the Legion are practically inseparable and indistinguishable, and a full third of his tale is taken up with such passages as, "This furious beast not only suffered itself to be bridled and saddled, but frisked and fawned, and purred and yelped, and crouched before the orator, licking his feet, and presenting its back to the burdens which he was pleased to impose." And, "No fritter on Shrove Tuesday was ever more dextrously turned, than were the hydra's brains by this mountebank in patriotism, this juggler in politics" (both p. 437). Thus, as its Victorian critics charged, the *Atom* is indeed a scurrilous and virulent broadside against English politics during Smollett's lifetime. It does use such physical acts as eating, kissing, licking, vomiting, defecating, and many more to express a sense of disgust past despair. Most of the novelist's enemies pass in opprobrious review: Beckford as "an half-witted politician, self-conceited, headstrong, turbulent, and ambitious"; Churchill as a lewd priest able to rouse the blatant beast "by dint of quaint rhymes"; Wilkes as an artist in "making balls of filth which were famous for sticking and stinking." However, it was considerably more to Smollett's contemporaries, and should be so to anyone interested in the ideas of the age.

It expresses the novelist's final estimate of Bute, as a man of capacity and public spirit who is also checkered with "childish vanity, rash ambition, littleness of mind, and lack of understanding." The minister erred greatly when he prevailed upon the monarch to vest him with all the trappings of honor available in the kingdom; his fate was then sealed. It contains Smollett's disarmingly candid assessment of his own work on the *Briton*. He calls himself a dirt-thrower who played his part tolerably well. Although his missiles "were inferior in point of composition" to those of the City, they did at least bring a smarting to the eyes of Pitt and his minions (pp. 526–27). Finally, it shows Smollett near the end of his career reclaiming the role of objective statesman he had set for himself in 1756. Actual reference to the two political parties that divide England does not appear until near the close of the work (though the Whigs had been condemned all along), and then the purpose is to call for a plague upon both. One is composed mostly of fools, the other of knaves; both operate by "every art of corruption, calumny, insinuation, and priestcraft. . . . In short, both parties were equally abusive, rancorous, uncandid, and illiberal" (pp. 498–99). Very abrupt and appropriately bleak, his ending discloses Bute "hurried by evil counsellers into a train of false politics," facing with horror the prospect of yet another war, this time with the American colonists. The *Atom* reveals its author in an attitude of grave concern for, but personal detachment from, Britain's future. It is this uncommon sense of simultaneous involvement and disengagement that Smollett in his final work lent to Bramble and Lismahago.

Part Three

THE ATTACK UPON LUXURY AND
THE FORMS OF *HUMPHRY CLINKER*

. . . if research requires a division of forces, a humane
education requires a synthesis, however provisional, of the results
of their labours, and to encourage us, by seeing these results,
not as isolated fragments, but as connected parts of a body of
living tissue, to acquire a more synoptic and realistic view of the
activities composing the life of society. The subject . . .
is concerned not merely or mainly with the iridescent surface
of manners, fashions, social conventions and intercourse,
but with the unseen foundations, which, till they shift or crumble,
most men in most generations are wont to take for
granted.—R. H. Tawney, "Social History and Literature"

Seven

THE POLITICS OF
HUMPHRY CLINKER

We are not what we were; patriotism is not the growth
of these days; luxury has taken root too deeply for sudden
eradication.—Critical Review, *1756*

. . . the wise patriots of London have taken it into their heads, that all
regulation is inconsistent with liberty; and that every man ought to live in
his own way, without restraint—Nay, as there is not sense enough left
among them, to be discomposed . . . they may, for aught I care, wallow
in the mire of their own pollution.—Matthew Bramble, *June 8*

Thus far it has been necessary to consider luxury in its material aspect
—its presence and influence in European history, in eighteenth-century
controversy, and in Smollett. It is now possible to make the inevitable
transition to its formal features. For three millennia the attack upon
luxury conveyed the dominant values and attitudes of Western society,
and moralists pursued their condemnations with certain impunity, for
no one would seriously defend immorality. Well before the birth of
Christ the attack had acquired a distinctive form. It had become so
common as to be conventional, so familiar as to take on a definite
shape. Individual writers would retain this general shape—as preachers
would keep the overarching form of the homily—while contributing
their own specific details. Theirs would be variations upon a traditional
theme, contemporary manifestations of a universal malaise.

The attack upon luxury may be regarded as a relatively distinct literary mode, with its own characteristic devices and methods of persuasion. It can more usefully be considered a mode rather than a genre, for it has been expressed in many genres. Because it seeks to reveal the (often hidden) dimension of causes, relations, and devolutions, it is primarily a heuristic, narrative mode, usually found in those forms which express developing awareness or expanding experience: quest, journey, psychomachia, imaginary voyage, retrospective elegy, nostalgic pastoral, panoramic survey, or moral history. It is the mode of Cato and Seneca, the *Republic* and the *City of God, Paradise Lost* and *Aureng-Zebe, Joseph Andrews* and the *Deserted Village;* of Swift and Bolingbroke, Davenant and John Brown. When that awareness is directed toward the historical past—as in Samuel and Kings, Sallust, Plutarch, and Gibbon—it nonetheless culminates in lessons drawn to redeem the present. And even in those rare instances where the attack has been shown to be successful—as in Prudentius and the Christian theologians—that victory over luxury must be guarded by constant vigilance and discipline.

From the Deuteronomic writers through Brown, Fawconer, and Goldsmith, the attack upon luxury normally represented an explanation and a warning, a portrait of a nation in rapid decline, perhaps in final devolution. The lesson is stated, then demonstrated in a series of marked contrasts: obedience – rebellion; old glory – new misery; political unity – competition and insubordination; social harmony – crime and ambition and confusion; the proud men of the ancient order – the debased representatives of the present; places of past greatness – sites of new debauchery; rural felicity – urban corruption; disciplined youth – depraved youth; a society guided by divinity and masculinity – one ruled by effeminate passion. So terrible and so persistent was the idea of luxury that it made an indelible imprint upon the European sensibility, and the list could be extended almost indefinitely. What had been a theological lesson became a theological pattern, forecasting God's punishment onto the present and future. It then yielded a logical pattern, a historical one, and a literary one. One sign of the vitality of the literary pattern is its early refinement. By the time of Herodotus the story is told by someone who is (or claims to be) relatively objective—a sage, historian, or foreign visitor. And within a generation, by the time of Aristophanes, the technique is developed further, with the superaddition for contrast of the views of various kinds of victims—the young, the naive, the gullible, and the unscrupulous.

Preceding chapters have sought to demonstrate that Smollett used this familiar mode in his major nonfiction after 1756. Is there reason to believe it is present also in his final work, the novel that is considered his masterpiece? On the prima facie level of direct textual evidence, the answer is clear. Twice in the first quarter of *Humphry Clinker,* Bramble delivers long and memorable tirades against the social customs of his time, first in Bath, then in London. He concludes his diatribe against Bath with the generalization: "All these absurdities arise from the general tide of luxury, which hath overspread the nation, and swept away all, even the very dregs of the people" (MB, April 23). In London he again sees a "tide of luxury" inundating the capital in social evils he has taken pains to specify: "they may be all resolved into the grand source of luxury and corruption" (MB, May 29). As Bramble turns his mind, briefly, to more pleasant matters during the journey northward, the theme—and the metaphor—is taken up by Lismahago: "Mean while the sudden affluence occasioned by trade, forced open all the sluices of luxury and overflowed the land with every species of profligacy and corruption; a total pravity of manners would ensue, and this must be attended with bankruptcy and ruin" (MB, July 15). Such open, direct denunciation is voiced by five different characters—Bramble, Jery, Lismahago, Dennison, and Baynard—and elaborated in eighteen different letters, letters that as a rule are the longest in the novel.

Such evidence establishes that the attack upon luxury is materially present, but it does not establish its necessity to a work of fiction. For this latter task only close analysis of forms will suffice. I shall argue in this and the following two chapters that *Humphry Clinker* does indeed deserve to be read in the light of the Western tradition, eighteenth-century controversy, and Smollett's own two decades of attack—in their light and as their epitome. While this contention is in no way iconoclastic, so far as I can discover no major work of English or Continental literature has been the subject of such a reading. The argument follows from the earlier portion of this study and from two truistic assumptions. First, the novel is inexhaustible and merits reading in as many ways as possible. The attack upon luxury is not the single golden key that will unlock its treasures. There is no such unique key, for Smollett is patently engaged in tasks (like the celebration of Scotland) other than the exposure of luxury. Yet it is the only approach not yet pursued by modern criticism, and it does provide access to much that can be gotten at in no other way: Smollett's method of combining general and particular satire, his cultivation of a mixed response for a bittersweet portrait of contemporary Britain, and the tradition in which it was written and read. The value of further access is clear if one accepts the argument of E. D. Hirsch that readers usually approach a new work through mode or type.[1] Retrospectively, we today tend to view eighteenth-century fiction under the all-absorbing rubric of *novel.* Contemporary readers, however, could not and did not. For what we know as the early novel was a fluid and hybrid form, the major writers incorporating much that was old into the "new species of writing." One has but to recall the influence of spiritual autobiography upon Defoe, model letters upon Richardson, the epic upon Fielding, and Rabelaisian satire upon Sterne to realize how comfortable Smollett would have been expressing his loathing of luxury in the new form.

Second, an idea like luxury can easily enter into the formal constituent part of a literary work. To admit that the attack upon luxury can be a literary mode is to acknowledge that ideas can be embedded in the narrative structure itself. An accomplished novelist like Smollett requires us to absorb the experience of his fictional characters, to assume it, to comprehend it, to regard it as natural. To present a luxurious world in action is by definition to make a series of metaphysical statements, for luxury is precisely that concept which for Smollett and others encloses all vital issues of human value. Novel-writing could be akin to cultural criticism. Moreover, the attack upon luxury may be metaphysical in still another sense. In an early essay Lionel Trilling writes of "the real basis of the novel" in England and on the Continent as "the tension between a middle class and an aristocracy which brings manners into observable relief as the living representation of ideals and the living comment on ideas."[2] Trilling's observation is not self-evidently valid for all great novels, but to the extent that it holds for many it elevates the importance of luxury. A traditionalist like Smollett would explain the tension Trilling finds in terms of the cultured few upholding a standard, a national way of life, a sanctified truth, "an England," against the subversive luxury of the barbarian horde. Extending Trilling, one could say that the attack upon luxury is "the real basis" of "the real basis of the novel."

To read *Humphry Clinker* as formally an attack upon luxury is to alter several modern critical emphases, including those that see Smollett as essentially simple (or if that is too harsh, then *transparent*), separate the man from his work, dismiss the social and political commentary, regard all main characters as coequal, reduce Bramble and Lismahago to decorative eccentrics, and see the organization of the novel as random and purposeless. To cite but one example, in a work cited earlier McKillop considers the milieu of the novel a region of endless absurdity but little indignation: "While the great world may rage without, the obliquities of these originals are harmless, and manifest themselves in a well-grounded order of things."[3] This is a plausible modern reading. But contemporary readers were aware that the great world indeed roars within the pages of the novel as the genesis of the endless absurdities McKillop notes; and if the obliquities of Bramble and Lismahago now strike us as harmless the reason is far different from the one he finds.

The well-grounded order of things Smollett cherished has in fact been much eroded, and the imprecations of his characters are delivered against a changing order they regard as disturbing and inferior. A Bramble and a Lismahago possess the confidence of buoyant assertation and do indeed embody values which are clear and self-confident, but they stand together as adversaries, not representatives, of the development of English society. So deeply and so carefully is the attack upon luxury embedded in the novel that the task of criticism is almost one of excavation. This and the following two chapters will seek to uncover the primary elements of Smollett's attack, in the political configurations, development of characters, and narrative structure of the novel. The remainder of this chapter attempts to demonstrate, in plain but ample fashion, that *Humphry Clinker* is a highly political novel, one of the most politically charged of the century.

To call *Humphry Clinker* a political novel might strike a modern reader (to put it charitably) as mildly paradoxical. Although many political figures are introduced, few are worthy, most contemptible; at best we meet men like the monarch who keep aloof from the routine duplicity of factions and parties. Political action, insofar as it is shown, is enveloped by chaos—sometimes hilarious, sometimes mortifying; political policy, we learn, is deceit practiced upon ignorance. Yet there is a familiar resonance to the scene. It had been predicted by Plato, Seneca, Bolingbroke, and Smollett—the time when the public graces have been swallowed up by the voracious maw of luxury. It is moreover the scene explained and described by Bramble in his first letter from London, May 29. Luxury has been as acid upon the nation he once revered, dissolving all into corruption, rebellion, and political frenzy. Moving from the general to the particular, Bramble personalizes the dissolution in several ways, most poignantly by reference to past friendships: "I have seen some old friends . . . but they are so changed in manners and disposition, that we hardly know or care for one another." The sentiment returns, he finds, throughout his tour of England, for merit and reward no longer travel together. Most of his old friends have changed for the worse: those who have retained their integrity have lost income and standing; those who have kept social position have squandered their morality. The traveler's sense of loss is indicative of the political tone of the novel, a withdrawal approaching despair. The madness luxury has released has driven out all hope for major, public reform; English politics is exhausted in vain self-interest. Only private hope, personal dreams remain. This fact marks a certain diminution in Smollett's ambitions, literary as well as political, and may explain part of the vitality and attraction of the novel. In contrast to his other projects, *Humphry Clinker* is a work of limits, restraint, proportion.

Relatively, it is a work of modest ambition, the kind appropriate to an age of rancor and excess. Certainly not mellow, it is simply measured— a political novel for a time when legitimate politics is dead.

On the one hand, Smollett sought to give the novel an appearance of political involvement but impartiality. This was the role he has assumed for himself as early as the *Complete History,* writing in it, the *Continuation,* the *Critical Review,* and the *Briton* that he was of no party. (In the last he also wrote that neither Bute nor any member of his ministry was politically partisan. Like contemporary opponents, however, later historians have tried in vain to discover a genuine Whig within the administration.) In the novel his chief male characters are close observers of contemporary politics, Bramble as a former Member of Parliament, Jery as an aspirant to its chambers, and Lismahago as a student of the law. Yet they are explicitly noted to be nonpartisan. Introducing Barton, a friend and fellow Oxonian, Jery remarks:

> He has not gall enough in his constitution to be enflamed with the rancour of party, so as to deal in scurrilous invectives; but, since he obtained a place, he is become a warm partizan of the ministry, and sees every thing through such an exaggerating medium, as *to me, who am happily of no party,* is altogether incomprehensible—Without all doubt, the fumes of faction not only disturb the faculty of reason, but also pervert the organs of sense; and I would lay a hundred guineas to ten, that if Barton on one side, and the most conscientious patriot in the opposition on the other, were to draw, upon honour, the picture of the k— or m—, *you and I, who are still uninfected, and unbiassed,* would find both painters equally distant from the truth. [JM, June 2, italics added]

In the same letter Bramble mentions his own political independence: "Whilst I sat in parliament, I never voted with the ministry but three times, when my conscience told me they were in the right." In Namier's terms, Bramble was therefore of the independent country party during the ministries, presumably, of Newcastle and Pitt, and hence a proper commentator upon those two politicians. As a freeholder and country gentleman, he is placed in a relatively disinterested political position, untainted by the selfish motives of professional politicians, courtiers, merchants, and financiers.[4] The third major character, Lismahago, is represented as equally free from partisan spirit. Himself a victim of much political chicanery, he calls for a plague upon both parties. The specific political commentary, wide-ranging though it is, is largely confined to five of the more than eighty letters of the novel: JM, June 2; MB, June 2; JM, June 5; MB, July 15; and MB, September 20. Even in these, Smollett feels compelled to defend its inclusion. In Bramble's letter of September 20, for instance, Lismahago's political opinions—identical to Bramble's—are reported in detail, and the novelist has Bramble conclude: "So much for the dogmata of my friend Lismahago, whom I describe the more circumstantially, as I firmly believe he will set up his rest in Monmouth'shire." Bramble seeks to limit the influence of that "daemon of party" not only in his own life, but also in the life of literature and the arts; hence his alarm that "the daemon of party seems to have usurped every department of life. Even the world of literature and taste is divided into the most virulent factions, which revile, decry, and traduce the works of one another" (MB, June 2). For Smollett, who wrote or edited nearly seventy volumes of historical and political commentary between *Count Fathom* and *Humphry Clinker* and was increasingly associated with partisan causes, such isolation and restraint are quite striking. They may be interpreted as either the self-restraint demanded by the novel or the reduction to proper size of the role of partisan issues in everyday life; I would argue that they are both, the transcendence of false politics by the true. What is certain is that Smollett endured a series of bitter disappointments after 1763; vicious personal attack, the failure of the *Briton,* Bute's ingratitude and later fall from power, repeated acute illness joined to chronic ill-health, failure to receive a government post abroad, continued worry over money, and most important, the death of his only child, the fifteen-year-old Elizabeth. Political and paternal grief are intermingled in his summary of recent years for the opening letter of the *Travels* (1766):

> You knew, and pitied my situation, traduced by malice, perse-cuted by faction, abandoned by false patrons, and overwhelmed by the sense of a domestic calamity, which it was not in the power of fortune to repair.
>
> You knew with what eagerness I fled from my country as a scene of illiberal dispute, and incredible infatuation, where a few worth-less incendiaries had, by dint of perfidious calumnies and atrocious abuse, kindled up a flame which threatened all the horrors of civil dissention.

On the other hand, he fashioned in *Humphry Clinker* a highly political design: the counterpointing of England and Scotland, city and country, change and tradition; the major characters' Welsh background; Bramble's flight from moral squalor to moral virtue, the equation in his person of physical sensitivity and moral sensibility; the journey of education of Jery and Lydia; the presence of a distressed veteran of the colonial wars; the alternation in the letters of frivolous and mature points of view. Each of these circumstances underlines Smollett's intention to provide serious comment upon familiar, public topics. Moreover, the novel is at its most vigorous as a tract against the times. Giving colorful illustration of what it condemns, *Humphry Clinker* proceeds with the logic of discourse. The irritations of Hot Well are succeeded by the provocations of Bath and the enormities of the capital. At Bath we are introduced to the nature and manifestations of luxury, at London to its agents and brutal consequences. Similarly, in discussing London Smollett first gives us the venal politicians who pander to false tastes (June 2, June 5), and then their handiwork in the near ruin of everyday living (June 8). Famous personages appear together in the three London letters, where they are introduced as if on permanent exhibit in a great hall of statuary. Thus Bramble asks, in the midst of the tour, "'Well, Mr. Barton, what figure do you call next?' The next person he pointed out, was the favorite *yearl;* who stood solitary by one of the windows" (JM, June 2). Barton makes his judgment, Bramble sustains or denies, and Jery finds for his uncle. Commenting upon issues, the London letters reinforce one another closely, with an opinion broached in the first letter repeated in the second and again in the third. To a lesser extent Smollett uses the same method with personalities, such as Newcastle, who is *said* to be an ass in the first and *shown* to be one in the third. The two later letters from Scotland, representing Lismahago's political disquisitions, serve to recall and further reinforce those of the English half. Smollett insured that his considered thoughts on luxury and politics would appear in each of the original three volumes of *Humphry Clinker.*

Certain opinions, such as that of the licentiousness of the press, are sustained throughout the five letters. Jery asserts the evil of the press in the first. In the second Bramble affirms the charge and Barton reaffirms, then illustrates it. In the third Bramble repeats himself; in the fourth and fifth Lismahago echoes and reechoes Bramble. On many occasions in the Scottish half of the novel, it will be remembered, Bramble is allowed to forget his earlier positions in order to stand as temporary adversary to Lismahago, thereby softening a little the lieutenant's didactic voice. Yet Lismahago does have his own particular function as political spokesman for Smollett, as he describes the methods of English exploitation of Scotland. And it is he, proud Scotsman and veteran soldier, who is called upon to defend the Treaty of Paris. Two-thirds of the way through the novel—hundreds of miles away, that is, from the king, Bute, Pitt, and the City—Smollett inserts a brief reference to the cause linked so intimately with his name: "One of the company chancing to mention lord B——'s inglorious peace, the lieutenant immediately took up the cudgels in his lordship's favour, and argued very strenuously to prove that it was the most honourable and advantageous peace that England had ever made since the foundation of the monarchy" (MB,

July 15). Bramble, acting here in the uncommon role of disinterested narrator, immediately closes the episode for Dr. Lewis by noting: "Nay, between friends, he offered such reasons on this subject, that I was really confounded, if not convinced."

Smollett's powers of dramatic presentation are at full stretch not with the glories of Edinburgh, but with the horrors of London. Even within the Scottish half, the pattern recurs. Whereas we are told of the hospitality of Commissary Smollett, we are shown the household of Lord Oxmington, and Jery's comments come not as summary but as introduction: "His lordship is much more remarkable for his pride and caprice, than for his hospitality and understanding; and indeed, it appeared, that he considered his guests merely as objects to shine upon, so as to reflect the lustre of his own magnificence.—There was much state, but no courtesy; and a great deal of compliment without any conversation" (JM, September 28). In addition, Smollett seems to be offering solutions to quasi-political problems. More often than not, the resolution of temporary grievance is not through persuasion and agreement, but through the direct use of force. To obtain quiet in his lodgings at Bath, Bramble must cudgel the offending musicians. He and Lismahago both recommended the severe beating of libelous printers. The travelers can gain Oxmington's respect only by a massive show of arms and strength, and Lismahago's kick is shown to be the proper response to the nobleman's lackey. Baynard cannot salvage his estate merely by following wise counsel: he and his affairs must be placed totally in the hands of Bramble and Dennison.

Seldom varied, the pattern of Smollett's political tour of England is renewed each time the party travels to a new place. Upon arrival, one of the males—usually Bramble and usually in the manner of the *Present State*—provides a synoptic view of the ills pervading the town. Against later letters from the same place, this introduction is taut and concise, vivid and impassioned: it is so relentless a portrait of human folly that we at first assume it must be eccentric to a novel of comic intentions, so extreme that it must be qualified, if not erased. As the party moves about the town, however, subsequent letters reveal the incarnation of those very ills in the men and women who dominate social affairs. The later letters, penned mostly by Jery, are more numerous, tentative, disinterested, and tolerant; yet their ultimate effect is to affirm the keenness and truth of the opening survey.[5]

Humphry Clinker includes many of Smollett's old crotchets, and the overarching issues are the most familiar, what we have come to know through his own work as the syndrome of luxury. In the wake of the vice flows an unholy emphasis upon trade and commerce. Hence Bramble follows his attack upon the luxury of Bath with a tirade against merchants and their morality of profit (MB, April 23), Lismahago asserts that "a glut of wealth . . . destroys all the distinctions of civil society; so that universal anarchy and uproar must ensue" (MB, September 20), and the Scotsman exposes, in the long passage already cited, the effects of English luxury in the depletion of the Scottish economy. Explaining why commerce must be tightly supervised, Lismahago also voices in a metaphor the novelist's rather feudal view of fluctuations in trade: "the nature of commerce was such, that it could not be fixed or perpetuated, but, having flowed to a certain height, would immediately begin to ebb, and so continue till the channels should be left almost dry; but there was no instance of the tide's rising a second time to any considerable influx in the same nation" (MB, July 15). He observes further:

> That commerce would, sooner or later, prove the ruin of every nation, where it flourishes to any extent. . . . He observed, that traffick was an enemy to all the liberal passions of the soul, founded on the thirst of lucre, a sordid disposition to take advantage of the necessities of our fellow-creatures. . . . Mean while the sudden affluence occasioned by trade, forced open all the sluices of luxury and overflowed the land with every species of profligacy and corruption; a total pravity of manners would ensue, and this must be attended with bankruptcy and ruin. [MB, July 15]

As Smollett had done in his histories, Lismahago in a later letter conjoins the effects of commerce and the behavior of the multitude.

> "Woe be to that nation, where the multitude is at liberty to follow their own inclinations! Commerce is undoubtedly a blessing, while restrained within its proper channels; but a glut of wealth brings along with it a glut of evils: it brings false taste, false appetite, false wants, profusion, venality, contempt of order, engendering a spirit of licentiousness, insolence, and faction, that keeps the community in continual ferment, and in time destroys all the distinctions of civil society; so that universal anarchy and uproar must ensue." [MB, September 20][6]

Bramble and Lismahago likewise express by implication what Smollett elsewhere states directly: commerce is the efficient cause of English degeneracy. It is associated in the novel with virtually all the horrors of London life and most of the ills of the rest of Britain—inflation, highway crime, depopulation of the country, ruin of the small landowner, eradication of frugality and simplicity, the decline of education and the arts.

Corruption of government is the most despicable of the many horrors of the capital, and among its many contemporary manifestations

Bramble continually remarks a nearly universal currying of favor. Instead of doing the work of the kingdom, English politicians are absorbed in endless rounds of otiose flattery and bribery, the ugliest of which is cultivation of the mob. In an oblique reference to Pitt, Bramble exclaims:

> Notwithstanding my contempt for those who flatter a minister, I think there is something still more despicable in flattering a mob. When I see a man of birth, education, and fortune, put himself on a level with the dregs of the people, mingle with low mechanics, feed with them at the same board, and drink with them in the same cup, flatter their prejudices, harangue in praise of their virtues, expose themselves to the belchings of their beer, the fumes of their tobacco, the grossness of their familiarity, and the impertinence of their conversation, I cannot help despising him, as a man guilty of the vilest prostitution, in order to effect a purpose equally selfish and illiberal. [MB, June 2]

A sure sign that Smollett's polemical flame was still lambent, this passage covers three-quarters of the population under the slurs "mob" and "dregs of the people." It recalls the criticism of Antony by a cold Octavius that Antony would "keep the turn of tippling with a slave" and then "stand the buffet / with knaves that smell of sweat." A figure like Pitt would certainly come into physical closeness with the middle-class voters of the City. But "dregs," "low mechanics," "prejudices," "belchings," "beer," "grossness," and "impertinence"—these terms identify the mass of workers and unemployed who, whatever their fearsome habits, had no voting rights and no direct political influence. Smollett would have his readers dismiss such distinctions.

With Lismahago the indictment becomes broader, as the old soldier argues that elections are themselves a species of bribery and that even the English form of limited representative democracy is evil. Calling Parliament "the rotten part of the British constitution," Lismahago traces present corruption to Walpole's putative habit of buying a legislature to suit him. Elections, at least those under George II, therefore amount to no more than "an avowed system of venality, already established on the ruins of principle, integrity, faith, and good order, in consequence of which the elected and the elector, and, in short, the whole body of the people, were equally and universally contaminated and corrupted." As if to anticipate all ripostes, Lismahago pursues his logic to a fatal stop:

> He affirmed, that of a parliament thus constituted, the crown would always have influence enough to secure a great majority in

its dependence, from the great number of posts, places, and pensions it had to bestow; that such a parliament would (as it had already done) lengthen the term of its sitting and authority, whenever the prince should think it for his interest to continue the representatives. . . . With a parliament, therefore, dependent upon the crown, devoted to the prince, and supported by a standing army, garbled and modelled for the purpose, any king of England may, and probably some ambitious sovereign will, totally overthrow all the bulwarks of the constitution; for it is not to be supposed that a prince of a high spirit will tamely submit to be thwarted in all his measures, abused and insulted by a populace of unbridled ferocity, when he has it in his power to crush all opposition under his feet with the concurrence of the legislature. [MB, July 15][7]

This passage reflects two aspects of Smollett's polemical writing. He strives to produce a bold and vivid assertion and then argues aggressively within the terms of the original assertion. More a habit than a conscious technique, this aspect of the novelist's style gives his argument an air of confidence while also avoiding the disquieting problems of definition, qualification, and evaluation. It also leads on occasion to a clash of conflicting assertions. If, as Lismahago holds, the crown has the power to create a Parliament of its own design and thereafter to retain it, then that Parliament is the impotent, not the rotten, part of the British constitution. The passage further shows the novelist's penchant for repeating with small changes of phrase his cherished statements from earlier works. To his familiar warnings of a manipulated Parliament, he here adds a reference to the political controversies of the earlier 1760s— "a prince of high spirit . . . abused and insulted by a populace of unbridled ferocity"—which would recall the alleged libels of the *North Briton*.

If Lismahago is anxious over the possibility of a tyranny imposed from above, Bramble is yet more exercised over signs of a revolution from below. Like thousands of moralists before him, the Welshman is convinced that insubordination represents the death fever, the final madness of a nation infected by luxury. In almost every English city he visits, he perceives its symptoms, particularly in social leveling, factions, freedom of the press, and the operation of the jury system. Since he believes that the various ranks of a society are immiscible, he finds frequent occasion to deplore such places as Vauxhall where classes and sexes mix more readily than elsewhere. On the one hand, the respectable persons found there are guilty of degrading themselves: "When I see a number of well-dressed people, of both sexes, sitting on the covered

benches, exposed to the eyes of the mob . . . I can't help compassionat-
ing their temerity; while I despise their want of taste and decorum"
(MB, May 29). On the other, the common people are guilty of criminal
failure to conform to class distinctions in dress: "Every clerk, apprentice, and even waiter of tavern or coffee-house . . . assumes the air and
apparel of a petit maitre—The gayest places of public entertainment are
filled with fashionable figures; which, upon inquiry, will be found to be
journeymen taylors, serving-men, and abigails, disguised like their betters." Even small examples of social mixing, like Win's comically ill-
fated visit to the theater, can be interpreted as political rebellion if one
assumes that every inch of new freedom granted to an apprentice removes that amount from the prerogatives of a lord. Hence Bramble's
conclusion follows from his premise: "In short, there is no distinction
or subordination left—The different departments of life are jumbled
together—The hod-carrier, the low mechanic, the tapster, the publican,
the shop-keeper, the pettifogger, the citizen, and the courtier, all tread
upon the kibes of one another: actuated by the demons of profligacy
and licentiousness . . . and crashing in one vile ferment of stupidity and
corruption" (MB, May 29). Repeating Smollett's earlier contentions
from the *Complete History,* moreover, he finds that the insubordination
of the poor inevitably leads not only to sedition but also to crime.

> The tide of luxury has swept all the inhabitants from the open
> country—The poorest 'squire, as well as the richest peer, must have
> his house in town, and make a figure with an extraordinary num-
> ber of domestics. The plough-boys, cow-herds, and lower hinds, are
> debauched and seduced by the appearance and discourse of those
> coxcombs in livery, when they make their summer excursions.
> They desert their dirt and drudgery, and swarm up to London, in
> hopes of getting into service, where they can live luxuriously and
> wear fine clothes, without being obliged to work; for idleness is
> natural to man—Great numbers of these, being disappointed in
> their expectation, become thieves and sharpers; and London being
> an immense wilderness, in which there is neither watch nor ward
> of any signification, nor any order or police, affords them lurking-
> places as well as prey. [MB, May 29]

In a nation beset by luxury, spurious political divisions are encouraged, while genuine authority and legitimate order go ignored.
Various groups are permitted to compete for the leadership that can
never rightfully be theirs. They rival one another with false claims, false
reports, false promises. As Bramble's above letter has raised the central
issues, Jery's next, of June 2, begins the process of illustrating the stinks
given off by the vice, noting, "Without all doubt, the fumes of faction

not only disturb the faculty of reason, but also pervert the organs of sense." In the same letter Bramble is quoted as saying that while in power Newcastle was rightly ridiculed, but when he lost power and "unfurled the banners of faction" he was hailed as "a wise, experienced statesman, chief pillar of the Protestant succession." Barton explains this contradiction by identifying faction with mob mentality: "I don't pretend to justify the extravagations of the multitude; who, I suppose, were as wild in their former censure, as in their present praise." In his letter of the same date, Bramble repeats and extends these themes. Explaining to Dr. Lewis why needed improvements of the British Museum "will never be reduced to practice," he says, "Considering the temper of the times, it is a wonder to see any institution whatsoever established, for the benefit of the public. The spirit of party is risen to a kind of phrenzy, unknown to former ages, or rather degenerated to a total extinction of honesty and candour" (MB, June 2). He then promptly moves to the most egregious public example of faction. "You know I have observed, for some time, that the public papers are become the infamous vehicles of the most cruel and perfidious defamation: every rancorous knave—every desperate incendiary, that can afford to spend half a crown or three shillings, may skulk behind the press of a news-monger, and have a stab at the first character in the kingdom, without running the least hazard of detection or punishment" (MB, June 2).

Barton is then introduced in order to confirm Bramble's opinion. Referring to his penchant for eulogizing the current ministry, Bramble notes that he had seen one of Barton's favorites so stigmatized in the press, "that if one half of what was said of him was true, he must be not only unfit to rule, but even unfit to live." He tells Barton that at first he could not credit the charges, but when the favorite failed to vindicate himself he began to entertain suspicions. Smollett's manipulation of his main character is obvious: in the space of two sentences Bramble is transformed from a cynic to an innocent. Barton's considered response is thus elicited, and echoing the conversation in *Macbeth* between Malcolm and Macduff, it turns upon the depraved tastes and perverted loyalties of the mob:

"And pray, sir, (said Mr. Barton) what steps would you have him take?—Suppose he should prosecute the publisher, who screens the anonymous accuser, and bring him to the pillory for a libel; this is so far from being counted a punishment, *in terrorem,* that it will probably make his fortune. The multitude immediately take him into their protection, as a martyr to the cause of defamation, which they have always espoused—They pay his fine, they contribute to the increase of his stock, his shop is crowded with customers, and the sale of his paper rises in proportion to the scandal it contains. All this time the prosecutor is inveighed against as a tyrant and oppressor, for having chosen to proceed by the way of information, which is deemed a grievance; but if he lays an action for damages, he must prove the damage, and I leave you to judge, whether a gentleman's character may not be brought into contempt, and all his views in life blasted by calumny, without his being able to specify the particulars of the damage he has sustained." [MB, June 2]

This belief in the delicacy of a gentleman's honor, something not to be entrusted to the judgment of such gross plebeians as usually make up a jury, is part of Smollett's contention that the freedom of the press and the composition of juries are parallel instances of rank insubordination, which if permitted to continue will produce not only scandal but sedition: "This spirit of defamation is a kind of heresy, that thrives under persecution. *The liberty of the press* is a term of great efficacy; and, like that of *the Protestant religion,* has often served the purposes of sedition." When Bramble interrupts Barton's harangue to comment further upon juries, neither the tone nor the substance of the passage is altered in the least: "Certain it is, a gentleman's honour is a very delicate subject to be handled by a jury, composed of men, who cannot be supposed remarkable either for sentiment or impartiality—In such a case, indeed, the defendant is tried, not only by his peers, but also by his party; and I really think, that of all patriots, he is the most resolute who exposes himself to such detraction, for the sake of his country" (MB, June 2). Lismahago's later attack upon the "illiterate plebeians" who generally make up a jury seeks to expose the injustice of the jury system.

> Juries are generally composed of illiterate plebeians, apt to be mistaken, easily misled, and open to sinister influence; for if either of the parties to be tried, can gain over one of the twelve jurors, he has secured the verdict in his favour; the juryman thus brought over will, in despite of all evidence and conviction, generally hold out till his fellows are fatigued, and harrassed, and starved into concurrence; in which case the verdict is unjust, and the jurors are all perjured. [MB, July 15]

Bramble, however, is aware of a likelier means of redress than "the ignorance and partiality of juries." To a gentleman traduced in the press, he recommends recourse to "the publishers bones" and "the ribs of an author." Should the gentleman himself be reluctant to try such measures he may employ "certain useful instruments, such as may be found in all countries, to give [an offender] the bastinado." Thus Smollett does find some occasional value in the violence of the mob. Although he has found an effective solution, Bramble is not able to relinquish the problem.

As for the liberty of the press, like every other privilege, it must be restrained within certain bounds; for if it is carried to a breach of law, religion, and charity, it becomes one of the greatest evils that every annoyed the community. If the lowest ruffian may stab your good-name with impunity in England, will you be so un-candid as to exclaim against Italy for the practice of common assassination? To what purpose is our property secured, if our moral character is left defenceless? People thus baited, grow desperate; and the despair of being able to preserve one's character, untainted by such vermin, produces a total neglect of fame; so that one of the chief incitements to the practice of virtue is effectually destroyed. [MB, June 2]

And in the second half of the novel Lismahago is once more called upon to return attention to the seriousness of the problem: "He said, he should always consider the liberty of the press as a national evil, while it enabled the vilest reptile to soil the lustre of the most shining merit, and furnished the most infamous incendiary with the means of disturb-ing the peace and destroying the good order of the community. He owned, however, that, under due restrictions, it would be a valuable privilege; but affirmed, that at present there was no law in England suf-ficient to restrain it within proper bounds" (MB, July 15).

The viciousness of the press was thus to Smollett another conse-quence of a climate of luxury and insubordination. It seemed to him that the masses wished to erase the distinctions that by nature existed between themselves and men of rank, to drag men of character down to their own level. (Bramble's letter of June 2, it should be noted, applies the epithet of *mob* to men able to pay the fines of popular pub-lishers as well as to read their papers, and castigates as the *lowest* ruffian not only a man able to read and write but one who also can afford to buy the full apparatus of publishing.) The press became a vehicle of such infamous craving when it pandered to the tastes of the mob, a monster Bramble never could abide. The contemporary political condi-tion of England was doubly perilous, moreover, because certain politi-cians as well as the press appeared to be pandering to the masses. Hence in his letter of June 2 Bramble moves quickly and effortlessly from a denunciation of the press to an attack on the complementary evil, the gentleman who flatters the mob. This theme is of course repeated by Bramble and Lismahago throughout the novel. In an earlier letter

Bramble had said: "Indeed, I know nothing so abject as the behavior of a man canvassing for a seat in parliament—This mean prostration, (to borough-electors, especially) has, I imagine, contributed in great measure to raise that spirit of insolence among the vulgar; which, like the devil, will be found very difficult to lay" (MB, May 19). The fundamental assumption is that the traditional exclusion of the great majority of Englishmen from the political process must be maintained; the primary condition of good order is stated plainly by Lismahago: "He said, he hoped he should never see the common people lifted out of that sphere for which they were intended by nature and the course of things" (MB, September 20).

Being the folly of the mindless and tasteless, insubordination is represented in *Humphry Clinker* by men and women who are largely faceless. Some are named, but most are merely neutered members of one or another organ of the mob—the City, the Methodists, the Legion. One could say that for Smollett they are not human personalities to be described, but problems to be solved, at best groups to be controlled. This is certainly not to say that the novelist could exclude his adversaries among the Old Whig Gang; about certain heads he could be as driven as any Mr. Dick. The founder of the gang, Walpole, is ushered in briefly by Bramble as "a first-mover, who was justly stiled and stigmatized as the father of corruption" (JM, June 2). Pitt, the present leader, appears as "the great political bully" and "that overbearing Hector" (JM, June 5), and directly in Jery's letter of June 2: "Ha, there's the other great phaenomenon, the grand pensionary, that weathercock of patriotism that veers about in every point of the political compass, and still feels the wind of popularity in his tail. He too, like a portentous comet, has risen again above the court-horizon; but how long he will continue to ascend, it is not easy to foretel, considering his great eccentricity." Newcastle is presented as the clown prince of the gang in two of the most comically acid scenes of the novel. In the one Bramble calls him "an ape in politics" for thirty years, and Jery describes him as hopelessly senile (JM, June 2). In the other he moves from one absurdity to another at his own levee, scandalizing visitors like the ambassador from Algiers: "he scarce ever opened his mouth without making some blunder, in relation to the person or business of the party with whom he conversed; so that he really looked like a comedian, hired to burlesque the character of a minister" (JM, June 5). The gang is rounded off with Townshend, who is in constant fear of Pitt (JM, June 5), and the pseudonymous factota, Pitt's "two satellites." The first is probably Wilkes: "without a drop of red blood in his veins . . . a cold intoxicating vapour in his head; and rancour enough in his heart to inoculate and affect a whole nation." The second, Temple:

"Without principle, talent, or intelligence, he is ungracious as a hog, greedy as a vulture, and thievish as a jackdaw" (JM, June 2).[8]

Relatively, these individualized sketches are few, enveloped by the collective presence of the mob. Seemingly omnipotent and omnipresent in England, the mob befouls everything it touches, from the spas to the churches, the courts to the papers, Ranelagh to Parliament. Put politically, the Whig oligarchs require no strength of numbers, for they possess such willing tools in the City, the Methodist chapels, and the gin shops. Smollett felt obliged to expose the folly and ignorance of the men of the City. That lesson is certainly part of the intention of *Humphry Clinker*. The original title page carried lines from the *Sermones* of Horace: *Quorsum haec tam putida tendunt, / Furcifer? ad te, inquam.* (To what object are these disagreeable facts directed, you rogue? To you, I said.) The most disagreeable collective portrait in the novel is of the men of the middle orders who come down from London and in their barbarity despoil the graces of Bath.

Clerks and factors from the East Indies, loaded with the spoil of plundered provinces; planters, negro-drivers, and hucksters, from our American plantations, enriched they know not how; agents, commissaries, and contractors, who have fattened, in two successive wars, on the blood of the nation; usurers, brokers, and jobbers of every kind; men of low birth, and no breeding, have found themselves suddenly translated into a state of affluence, unknown to former ages; and no wonder that their brains should be intoxicated with pride, vanity, and presumption. Knowing no other criterion of greatness, but the ostentation of wealth, they discharge their affluence without taste or conduct, through every channel of the most absurd extravagance; and all of them hurry to Bath, because here, without any further qualification, they can mingle with the princes and nobles of the land. Even the wives and daughters of low tradesmen, who, like shovel-nosed sharks, prey upon the blubber of those uncouth whales of fortune, are infected with the same rage of displaying their importance; and the slightest indisposition serves them for a pretext to insist upon being conveyed to Bath, where they may hobble country-dances and cotillons among lordlings, 'squires, counsellors, and clergy. These delicate creatures from Bedfordbury, Butcher-row, Crutched-Friers, and Botolph-lane, cannot breathe in the gross air of the Lower Town, or conform to the vulgar rules of a common lodging-house; the husband, therefore, must provide an entire house, or elegant apartments in the new buildings. Such is the composition of what is called the fashionable company at Bath; where a very inconsiderable proportion of genteel people are lost in *a mob of impudent plebeians, who have neither understanding nor judgment, nor the least idea of propriety and decorum; and seem to enjoy nothing so much as an opportunity of insulting their betters.* [MB, April 23; italics added]

Once again the City Whigs represent the confluence of Smollett's national, political, and social antipathies, the intersection of large issues and small personalities. Bramble finds luxury and insubordination indigenous to London, whence they are carried outward, most notably to Bath, but also at times to the northern countryside (by persons like Mrs. Baynard and her aunt). The evils of the time encounter little resistance in England but much in Scotland, where they are fated to languish and die. Lismahago's two tirades (MB, July 15; and MB, September 20), though delivered on the road north, are directed against English influences. In Scotland neither commerce nor the men engaged in it are in any way subversive of the social and political order. On at least three occasions (MB, August 28; JM, September 12; and MB, September 20), Smollett gives praise to the effects of Scottish commerce and to the men who have brought it to such a productive state. In Scotland the pursuit of wealth is restrained by reason and virtue, as Lismahago asserts when he refutes the typical English notion of his country's deprivation:

> "Those who reproach a nation for its poverty, when it is not owing to the profligacy or vice of the people, deserve no answer. . . . The most respectable heroes of ancient Rome, such as Fabricius, Cincinnatus, and Regulus, were poorer than the poorest freeholder in Scotland; and there are at this day individuals in North-Britain, one of whom can produce more gold and silver than the whole republic of Rome could raise at those times when her public virtue shone with unrivalled lustre; and poverty was so far from being a reproach, that it added fresh laurels to her fame, because it indicated a noble contempt of wealth, which was proof against all the arts of corruption—If poverty be a subject for reproach, it follows that wealth is the object of esteem and veneration. . . . An absurdity which no man in his senses will offer to maintain.—Riches are certainly no proof of merit: nay they are often (if not most commonly) acquired by persons of sordid minds and mean talents: nor do they give any intrinsic worth to the possessor; but, on the contrary, tend to pervert his understanding, and render his morals more depraved." [MB, September 20]

Scots merchants, it can be assumed, are thus to their English counterparts as Captain Brown is to Paunceford. (Just as Smollett nowhere attacks an individual or group of Scottish merchants, nowhere does he rebuke any contemporary Scottish political figure.) Furthermore, because of his inherent abilities, a Scotsman's true merit cannot be known from his outward appearance. Lismahago seems an impoverished veteran, but in fact he is a cultivated man of the world, trained in the law. In the same fashion, Bramble calls his apothecary "a proud Scotchman, very thin skinned, and, for aught I know, may have his degree in his pocket—A right Scotchman has always two strings to his bow, and is *in utrumque paratus*" (MB, June 8).

This dispensation applies with especial force to young Humphry Clinker. As Bramble's long-lost son, he shares in his father's strength of character and hence cannot be the "poor Wiltshire lad" he at first appears. On that initial appearance (JM, May 24), Tabby calls him "a beggarly rascal" and "a filthy tatterdemalion," and Jery finds his condition "equally queer and pathetic."

> He seemed to be about twenty years of age, of a middling size, with bandy legs, stooping shoulders, high forehead, sandy locks, pinking eyes, flat nose, and long chin—but his complexion was of a sickly yellow: his looks denoted famine; and the rags that he wore, could hardly conceal what decency requires to be covered—[JM, May 24]

Like native-born Scots, however, the sons of Welsh gentlemen cannot be known by their first appearance, as Jery reports.

> In the afternoon, as our aunt stept into the coach, she observed, with some marks of satisfaction, that the postilion, who rode next to her, was not a shabby wretch like the ragamuffin who had drove them into Marlborough. Indeed, the difference was very conspicious: this was a smart fellow, with a narrow-brimmed hat, with gold cording, a cut bob, a decent blue jacket, leather breeches, and a clean linen shirt, puffed above the waist-band. When we arrived at the castle on Spin-hill, where we lay, this new postilion was remarkably assiduous, in bringing in the loose parcels; and, at length, displayed the individual countenance of Humphry Clinker, who had metamorphosed himself in this manner, by receiving from pawn part of his own clothes, with the money he had received from Mr. Bramble. [JM, May 24]

The revelation is made complete when, under Bramble's questioning, Humphry discloses that he too is *in utrumque paratus.*

> "Suppose I was inclined to take you into my service, (said he) what are your qualifications? what are you good for?" "An please

your honour, (answered this original) I can read and write, and
do the business of the stable indifferent well—I can dress a horse,
and shoe him, and bleed and rowel him; and, as for the practice of
sow-gelding, I won't turn my back on e'er a he in the county of
Wilts—Then I can make hog's-puddings and hob-nails, mend kettles,
and tin saucepans—" Here uncle burst out a-laughing; and enquired, what other accomplishments he was master of—"I know
something of single-stick, and psalmody, (proceeded Clinker) I can
play upon the Jew's-harp, sing Black-ey'd Susan, Arthur-o'Bradley,
and divers other songs; I can dance a Welsh jig, and Nancy Dawson;
wrestle a fall with any lad of my inches, when I'm in heart; and,
under correction, I can find a hare when your honour wants a bit
of game." "Foregad! thou art a complete fellow, (cried my uncle,
still laughing) I have a good mind to take thee into my family—"
[JM, May 24]

If the Scots and Welsh are invulnerable to luxury by reason of national
virtue, the English upper orders are similarly protected by reason of
superior birth. In his periodicals as in *Humphry Clinker,* Smollett attacks opponents among the higher classes not for their luxury, but for
their politics, or more specifically, for their political characters. Unlike
Bolingbroke thirty years before, he could not merely dismiss them as
upstarts. Newcastle is a dolt, Pitt a despot, Townshend a knave. Lord
Oxmington, likewise, is mean of spirit, but not luxurious (JM, September 28). Even Walpole is portrayed in the *Complete History* as not himself luxurious, but as the manipulator for his own corrupt ends of the
luxury of others. Yet even this class-bound view of luxury is open to
modification by politics. One English merchant, "G. H——," George
Heathcote (1700–68), does receive Smollett's praise in *Humphry Clinker*
as "really an enthusiast in patriotism." Although a lord mayor of London in 1742, Heathcote is not to be regarded as a Popular Whig. A
nephew of one of the founders of the East India Company, he was
usually allied with the oligarchic wing of Newcastle's coalition and
considered the leader of the Jacobite party in London in the 1740s. In
the 1750s he was denounced as "a great Jacobite" by members of the
Common Council, and later Horace Walpole wrote of him as "a paltry,
worthless Jacobite." A pamphlet Heathcote published in 1749 deplores
the depravity of the times in tones reminiscent of Bolingbroke. While
sharing many of Smollett's political attitudes, he is also an insider, and
thus an effective critic of the "citizens of London," telling Bramble,
"with the tears in his eyes, that he had lived above thirty years in the
city of London, and dealt in the way of commerce with all the citizens
of note in their turns; but that, as he should answer to God, he had

never, in the whole course of his life, found above three or four whom he could call thoroughly honest" (MB, May 19).[9]

The narrator-atom of the *Adventures of an Atom* claimed that nineteen-twentieths of the inhabitants of London were followers of the devil, and Smollett had not reduced that proportion by *Humphry Clinker*. While the City Whigs increase their sedition against authority, the Methodists openly promote sedition against reason. Walking through the city, Jery and his uncle discover Humphry haranguing a crowd in a lane behind Longacre. When Bramble berates him for presumption, Humphry pleads that he was moved by the new light of God's grace. To which his employer responds: "What you imagine to be the new light of grace . . . I take to be a deceitful vapour, glimmering through a crack in your upper story—In a word, Mr. Clinker, I will have no light in my family but what pays the king's taxes, unless it be the light of reason, which you don't pretend to follow" (JM, June 10). Bramble then continues:

> "Heark-ye, Clinker, you are either an hypocritical knave, or a wrong-headed enthusiast; and, in either case, unfit for my service— If you are a quack in sanctity and devotion, you will find it an easy matter to impose upon silly women, and others of crazed understanding, who will contribute lavishly to your support—if you are really seduced by the reveries of a disturbed imagination, the sooner you lose your sense entirely, the better for yourself and the community." [JM, June 10]

Bramble's suspicions are soon proved correct. What Humphry had felt as "such strong impulsions, as made him believe he was certainly moved by the spirit," Bramble discovers to have been the machinations of Lady Griskin, who sought out the Methodist meeting as part of a scheme to marry Tabby off to Barton and to that end prompted Clinker to mount the rostrum, "to the true secret of which he was an utter stranger" (JM, June 10). Humphry is shown to be free of fanaticism (MB, June 14), and after London his Methodism is hardly perceptible.

Meanwhile, however, Tabby has attached herself with zeal to the sect; she is of course both a silly woman and a person of crazed understanding, thus always vulnerable to the deceit and enthusiasm of the Methodists. Bramble is unable to admonish his sister as he did Clinker, but does guess that her religious devotion is no more than a convenient cloak for a less spiritual quest. We are thus permitted a knowledgeable smile upon learning that Tabby "has had the good fortune to come acquainted with a pious Christian, called Mr. Moffat, who is very powerful in prayer, and often assists her in private exercises of devotion" (JM, August 8). Later we appreciate the irony involved when Jery reports

that, "Mrs. Tabitha displayed her attractions as usual, and actually believed she had entangled one Mr. Maclellan, a rich inkle-manufacturer,
in her snares; but when matters came to an explanation, it appeared
that his attachment was altogether spiritual, founded upon an intercourse of devotion, at the meeting of Mr. John Wesley" (JM, September
3). Resolution of Tabby's search, in the shape of Lismahago, serves to
confirm Bramble's early observation, when the passion of love does
indeed abate the fervor of her devotion (MB, July 15). This view is
tinged with brotherly tolerance, and we have reason to surmise that in
this instance Smollett has transposed the usual roles of Bramble and
Lydia. Usually mild and romantic, Liddy is frank and harsh in her
appraisal of her aunt's behavior:

> My poor aunt, without any regard to her years and imperfections,
> has gone to market with her charms in every place where she
> thought she had the least chance to dispose of her person, which,
> however, hangs still heavy on her hands—I am afraid she has used
> even religion as a decoy, though it has not answered her expecta-
> tion—She has been praying, preaching, and catechising among the
> methodists, with whom this country abounds; and pretends to
> have such manifestations and revelations, as even Clinker himself
> can hardly believe, though the poor fellow is half crazy with
> enthusiasm. . . . God forgive me if I think uncharitably, but all this
> seems to me to be downright hypocrisy and deceit—[LM, Septem-
> ber 7]

In the activities of the Methodists, Smollett certainly saw insubordination: the pretensions of the lower orders to some measure of religious
authority and illumination, and the leveling of class distinctions in
ecclesiastical practices. In the activities of the City, he saw a complementary kind of political rebellion. He has Humphry Clinker assume
the repudiation of both. Humphry easily proves himself a stranger to
luxury, but remains suspect in Bramble's eyes until he can answer
charges of fanaticism. After catechizing him over his preaching to the
mob, Bramble affirms, "If there was anything like affectation or
hypocrisy in this excess of religion, I would not keep him in my service;
but, so far as I can observe, the fellow's character is downright simplicity, warmed with a kind of enthusiasm, which renders him very
susceptible of gratitude and attachment to his benefactors" (MB, June
14). In keeping with his habits of association, Smollett here suggests
that as simplicity with obedience is proof against luxury, so simplicity
with humility is proof against fanaticism.[10]

Discovery of Humphry brings Bramble much personal comfort during
the expedition, but it does nothing to allay his anxieties over the state

of England. He finds a companion and later a son, but his search for honest politics and decent politicians is futile; there are no worthy men of influence to be found in England. Against the venality of the times stands only one public figure, George III, whom Bramble calls "A very honest kind-hearted gentleman . . . he's too good for the times" (JM, June 2).[11] Yet the monarch cannot administer the kingdom alone and must make do with the caliber of politician elected to Parliament. The contrast is stark between honest, kindhearted king and dishonest, heartless ministers and sycophants. No *public* response to the ills introduced by luxury appears possible. The process of degeneration has gone too far. The people, their representatives, and their institutions have all been corrupted. What is left is a humbler, smaller opportunity. Private men of good will can maintain their privacy against the infiltration of the times; they can renounce public haunts and public squalor. When national values have been twisted, personal choices alone remain, and these cannot represent the ideal but merely the inevitable. Hence *Humphry Clinker* ends, for Bramble and Lismahago, with retreat and self-exile in Monmouthshire.

Eight

THE CHARACTERS OF
HUMPHRY CLINKER

For many twentieth-century readers the politics of Tobias Smollett is outrageous, repulsive, dead. But the politics of *Humphry Clinker* is cogent and alive. If this is paradox, it is the kind out of which literary history itself comes alive. The novel captures the essence of an attitude toward life, indeed toward an era, as only a work of nostalgia can do. Over two centuries it has enjoyed a large and diverse audience, and few have doubted the authenticity of that nostalgia. Like *The Way of All Flesh,* another work of nostalgia, Smollett's novel is a memoir and an indictment. While the one is a classic study of father-son enmity, the other examines the enmity dividing the social orders of a society. As Butler's use of the theory of acquired characteristics enhances rather than diminishes the accomplishments of his novel, so Smollett's use of the concept of luxury transcends the fading ideology of his time. Lamarckian theory provided a cogent frame for Butler's cautious optimism and his search for evolutionary purpose. Luxury provided an intellectual form for Smollett's cultural pessimism and sense of devolution: his preference for reason over enthusiasm, for logic over evidence, authority over empiricism, custom over innovation, and tradition over experiment. Ernest Pontifex enters a world freer and better than that known by his father; but Jery Melford will find the world far less hospitable than his uncle, in his youth, once did. As Butler repudiated Darwin's idea of purposelessness, so Smollett repudiated Hume's idea of limited progress.

Yet like irony, nostalgia does have its ambiguities. Source studies are often accused of diminishing the richness of a literary work, of reducing and flattening complexity into formula. The charge has its modicum of truth, for every compelling work of art encloses more activity than can be marked by a critic. But the accusation is ultimately unfair. Most twentieth-century critics have enjoyed *Humphry Clinker* as a work of ironic characterization, the partial and subjective views of its many comic figures qualifying one another; with contemporary reviewers of the novel I have argued that the acceptable views expressed in the novel radiate from Bramble. This latter interpretation does not, I think, deplete its fullness, but does the reverse. It grants Smollett yet more subtlety than do Jamesian critics: the achievement of a more effective unity under the surface of effective variety. If the novelist can perform his illusions upon the most adept of modern readers, then his reputation is indeed secure. Nor should awareness of his methods detract from their effects. The keenest followers of professional magicians, it is said, are the stagehands, from whom no sleight of hand can be concealed.[1]

By literary standards *Humphry Clinker* is, among many other things, the most successful conservative attack upon luxury written in any genre during the 1750s and 1760s, a pearl in a generation of sand. In it Smollett tapped one of the fountains of eighteenth-century emotion, taking the galvanic but nonetheless drab, gray stuff of old controversy and transforming it by the force of his powerful imagination. Like a Renaissance master, he captured the adventive moment and made all its colors fast. Among the reasons for this success, two are noteworthy. First, he could control the milieu of his novel, closing it to unanswered questions, unresolved ambiguities, and ambivalent conditions as he could not in his histories and journalism. Here there is no necessary division between the thing to be expressed and the medium of expression. Luxury need no longer be treated as an abstract entity to be denounced as a matter of course. It could be exposed where it actually existed—in the world of men. An acknowledged master of narrative design, Smollett could determine the terms and elements of both action and debate, thus fashioning a fictive world sufficient unto itself—and its readers. Vice, folly, and error appear of necessity in such a world, to arouse that response he declared he sought in *Roderick Random,* "that generous indignation which ought to animate the reader against the sordid and vicious disposition of the world." The Bramble party can be in that world but not of it. They are detached from their local roots and under no compulsion to defend their own estate against luxury. They are not beleaguered as Burdock and Baynard are, for they have each other and are welcome visitors in all remaining bastions. They are detached in precisely those ways Smollett himself was during the last eight years of his life.

Second, the attack upon luxury could in a natural way infuse the organization and characterization of *Humphry Clinker.* Smollett had not published a novel since the serialization of *Sir Lancelot Greaves* in 1760–61, and his last major novel, *Peregrine Pickle,* had appeared ten years before that, in 1751. As it had done in the *Travels* and the *Present State,* the attack upon luxury gave focus and coherence to his final work, whose travel form was not innately disciplinary. It was perhaps yet more useful to the novel than to the works of 1766 and 1768–69, for in *Humphry Clinker* it could be joined with ease to Smollett's inveterate habits of association and invention. In the final volume of the *Complete History,* to cite a long and early contrast, his use of luxury is not so clear and seems extrinsic—an appendage or superimposition. But in his last novel it is intrinsic, fully fleshed, and fully illustrated. It might indeed be argued that nineteenth- and twentieth-century students have been little concerned with Smollett's ideas precisely because of his successful integration of story with idea. *Humphry Clinker is* what Smollett thought about luxury in contemporary England, present, a Saintsbury might exclaim, in such a plenitude of substance that its essence need hardly be defined further.

Several of the foremost critics of luxury in the ancient world had fought the vice with deeds as well as words. Like Thucydides, Xenophon, Polybius, Josephus, Sallust, and Tacitus, they were active political partisans who, upon defeat of their practical hopes, turned to literary descriptions of the forums they had forsaken. Having done their best to reform their worlds directly and having failed, they withdrew a proper intellectual distance from practical affairs in order to transform fervent partisanship into reasoned analysis. Political loss would yield literary gain: history would be told by the men who made it, and it would acquire a distinctive blend of engagement and detachment.

Bramble's strategic retreat to Monmouthshire is a characteristic part of Smollett's attack upon luxury. He is an apt diagnostician of the distemper that is England, for he has been thoroughly inoculated, has known it intimately—as Augustine knew the city of men and Imlac the world beyond the Happy Valley. Having served long in Parliament and followed the antics of a generation of mercenary politicians, he has renounced direct involvement himself. He nevertheless declares practical experience in politics a necessity, seeking it for Jery and calling it superior to any amount of library reading. Engaged yet detached, he is intellectually involved yet physically distant. He has no hope that the disease of the age will be cured, but he does foster the humble aspiration that good men will do what they can to slow and isolate it. His valedictory journey has been shaped to that modest end, as a testimonial good-bye to all that, a form of contemporary history written by a patriot for the edification of other patriots.

In 1771 *Humphry Clinker* was a frankly topical book, but it also entered what George Steiner calls a field of prepared echo—resounding still to Seneca, Cicero, and Sallust, Augustine and Aquinas, Dennis and Law, John Brown and Samuel Fawconer, and to Smollett's own seventy much-read, much-discussed earlier volumes. Drawing upon a literary mode older than Europe itself, the novel could proceed by means of unfolding reiteration, allusion, and variation upon an established repertoire of motifs and characters. The gullibility of women and the mob had been preached—to cite but a few diverse examples—by Aristophanes, Cato, and Tertullian. The ruin visited upon men who were ruled by women was a refrain for Stoic and Christian alike. Commandments to cleanse the marketplace, to discipline the new rich, to distrust the claims of city-dwellers, to instruct carefully the young men who would guard the nation's future, to venerate the learning of age and experience—these are lessons carried from Plato's Athens to Smollett's London by way of all of the centers of learning in Europe. The repertoire would be eternally fresh and timely, for it was eternally fixed and timeless. Human nature was flawed: men are merely what they are, women more so.

In an attack upon luxury expressed through fiction, the central figure, as important as all others combined, is the moral guide. Although flawed himself, he must be acute and reliable. Although mortal, he must by his mere presence raise all the immortal issues—order, merit, justice, individual and social health. Although sharply individualized, his experience must embrace the range of social reality, from the minutiae of personal manners to the workings of national institutions. He is merely a man and that of a degraded age; yet he is a man of justice.

At first glance *Humphry Clinker* seems to possess two main narrators, for uncle and nephew share by far the greatest number of letters (and even greater number of pages) that make up the novel. Yet the division of focus is merely apparent, not substantial. By repetition the novel forces us to concentrate upon the scenes, characters, and issues it places before us. Jery provides the basic reportage, the journal of who traveled when, where, and by what route; Bramble examines the significance of the journey. While the nephew relates the event, the uncle gives us the feeling—often the taste and smell—of the event. Jery's letters after Bath seldom contain opinion; when they do, the opinion is normally Bramble's. Bramble's letters (certainly those in England) are virtually all opinion—first his own, later his and Lismahago's. It is through Bramble's offices that Smollett works his magic. Characterization becomes revelation and plot, confirming demonstration.[2]

The revelation of true character and motive first occurs with Bramble himself, for neither is clear at the start. In his opening two letters Bramble complains of his vexations—gout, constipation, melancholy—and soon thereafter refers to his bootless twenty-year search for happiness.[3] Jery's opening letter echoes the complaint: "My uncle is an odd kind of humorist, always on the fret, and so unpleasant in his manner, that rather than be obliged to keep him company, I'd resign all claim to the inheritance of his estate" (JM, April 2). Indeed Bramble seems as vulnerable to the luxury of the times as the other members of his household. Physically he has been indolent and splenetic, even his bowels, he laments, proving ungovernable. Psychologically he has been prey to discontent, a gnawing restlessness he feels is unsuited to his age and station. In his mid-fifties, with considerable wealth and influence, he is pestered by politicians who would find use for both possessions. His philosophical pursuit of true felicity has encompassed the life spans of Jery, Liddy, and Humphry (and perhaps has coincided with his period of direct involvement in politics), and he is determined to resolve it. The disquiet of Bramble's inner life converges at the opening with the outer disarray within his family. His sister has grown unmanageable, fantastically at odds with everyone in Monmouthshire, even the good Dr. Lewis. His nephew has seemingly gained nothing from Oxford save pertness and has embroiled himself in a low quarrel. The niece, his other ward, has formed a demeaning attachment with an indigent actor, the antagonist in Jery's quarrel. Even his servant grows more insolent by the day. The apparent situation is of an irascible, egoistic valetudinarian traveling for double relief, from the gout and from the demands of his dependents.

It is, however, no more than an opening gambit, a device to initiate interest and movement. Bramble is asking Lewis to prepare him something for the gout in his last letter (November 20) as well as in his first (April 2). The most perfect and salubrious place in all of Britain, Bramble makes clear, is Brambleton Hall, the place of departure, to which he would immediately return—he says eight times in the original opening volume of the novel—if he were not bound by other obligations. About his abrasiveness he comments more often and more forcefully than does any other character. Jery's one sentence of early criticism is mild in comparison, and even this is very soon dispelled by growing admiration:

> Mr. Bramble's character . . . opens and improves upon me every day.—His singularities afford a rich mine of entertainment: his understanding, so far as I can judge, is well cultivated: his observations on life are equally just, pertinent, and uncommon. He affects misanthropy, in order to conceal the sensibility of a heart, which is tender, even to a degree of weakness. This delicacy of feeling, or soreness of the mind, makes him timorous and fearful; but then he is afraid of nothing so much as of dishonour; and although he is exceedingly cautious of giving offence, he will fire at the least hint of insolence or ill-breeding. [JM, April 24]

Thus Smollett quickly opens and improves *our* first impression of Bramble: he is certainly a man of knowledge and responsibility. He quotes the Roman poets and historians, Shakespeare, and a variety of contemporary authors. Besides literature he has read law, art, politics, history, geography, and philosophy. He seems to know as much medicine as his physician-friend Lewis: "I forgot to tell you, that my right ancle pits, a symptom, as I take it, of its being *oedematous,* not *leucophlegmatic*" (MB, April 20). Although Jery has just come down from university, he cannot compete with his uncle in breadth of reading—or in depth of understanding. Jery's account of Bramble's misanthropy (April 2) is far more superficial than Bramble's own (April 17, 20, 23). The latter are both more harsh and more explanatory; Bramble knows and tells more about himself than any other character can or will. He explains his physical irritability by revealing his moral sensibility (something Jery later confirms). Where Jery in this instance merely recounts superficial effects, Bramble reveals profound causes. The contrast is of course yet greater with the remaining letter-writers, Lydia, Tabby, and Win. By the time the party reaches Bath, we realize that Bramble is not merely in selfish pursuit of comfort. For his family more than for himself, he is in search of the conditions of health— peace, honor, and contentment. In Bath he longs for "my solitude and mountains" as Ishmael in clotted Manhattan cries out for the sea. In London he acknowledges that the tour would be cut short were he the only traveler: "With respect to the characters of mankind, my curiosity is quite satisfied. . . . Every thing I see, and hear, and feel, in this great reservoir of folly, knavery, and sophistication, contributes to inhance the value of a country life" (MB, June 2). Personally appalled by this great reservoir, he endures its stench for the sake of his family, who as yet cannot tell incense from offal; he informs Lewis he will soon move northward: "But I must, in the mean time, for the benefit and amuse-ment of my pupils, explore the depths of this chaos; this mishapen and monstrous capital, without head or tail, members or proportion" (MB, May 29).

By the close of the novel Bramble's pupils have included, primarily, Jery, Liddy, and Humphry; secondarily, Lismahago, Tabby, Win, and such temporary attendants as Linden and Barton; by extension, nearly one hundred named characters; and by further extension all of Smol-lett's readers. To note his anxieties at the beginning is to esteem his achievement at the end. His powers of instruction have been taxed fully but happily; order and harmony have been restored and renewed at Brambleton Hall. Through good sense and good fortune, he has been able to redeem each member of his party, by the by performing the same office for meritorious acquaintances, like the mother of the con-sumptive child at Bristol, Martin the highwayman, Burdock, and Baynard. He has, moreover, learned as warmly as he has taught, the vigorous exercise of his faculties proving the precise regimen he has so long required. His venture—to "take a plunge amidst the waves of ex-cess, in order to case-harden the constitution" (MB, October 26)—has proved efficacious. His quest—like his nerves, estate, and future—has been settled. Never again, he remarks, will he allow his life to lose its balance (November 20).

Administrator and quixote, philosopher and modest citizen, Bramble possesses the varied nature needed to hold together a work seeking a mixed response. He is sometimes rash in his impressions, as about Jery's audacity, Humphry's fanaticism, and Lismahago's extravagance. Yet he is the first to speak against hasty judgments and does not remain per-manently deficient in any of his assessments. Though hardly flawless, within the bounds of the novel he is almost ideally just—to chance acquaintances as well as lifelong tenants, to women as well as men, to the base as well as the mighty. Though he appears initially a creature of blatant prejudice, he is shown to be extraordinarily free of blindness. He can with ease bring himself to applaud even urban and mercantile life—in Scotland, in Glasgow and Edinburgh—where luxury has not effec-tively penetrated. He has that quality which in shorthand form Smollett called intuition, a unique and active combination of learning, experi-ence, intelligence, and respect for natural law.

Because Bramble is a touchstone for justice, he suffers deeply and often. He is not a military hero like his friends Cockril, Balderick, and Lismahago, yet his code of honor is as demanding as theirs. He requires valor, dignity, and magnanimity of others, not merely because he requires them of himself, but because in a threatened civilization they are virtues of universal necessity. About the frailties of ordinary, individual human nature his tolerance is Roman. But about collective enterprises—war, politics, architecture, urban "improvement," public recreation, mercantile policy—he is adamant in his demands and scathing in his denunciations. In these he sees human folly magnified and deified. He will not allow the view that bleached bread and diluted beer represent minor abuses of taste, for under luxury no abuse is innocuous and all are connected. Perhaps in an earlier, more innocent age, an assembly at Bath provided trivial dissipation. But no longer. Now it provides *"a compound of villainous smells,* in which the most violent stinks, and the most powerful perfumes, contended for the mastery" (MB, May 8). With a phrase adapted from Falstaff and his own emphasis, Bramble discloses the assembly to be criminal as well as foul. His intuitive response given, he feels no need to describe further the shambles before him; it is more than enough that his senses cry out against a condition that would make a moral man sick: "arising from putrid gums, imposthumated lungs, sour flatulencies, rank arm-pits, sweating feet, running sores and issues, plasters, ointments, and embrocations, hungary-water, spirit of lavender, assafoetida drops, musk, hartshorn, and sal volatile; besides a thousand frowzy steams, which I could not analyze."

Bramble's exquisite senses also afford protection. In such a time of national disease, he says, every man must be his own physician. For this task most Englishmen are disabled, "their very organs of sense are perverted, and they become habitually lost to every relish of what is genuine and excellent in its own nature" (MB, June 8). For himself and his pupils, contemporary recipes for health and happiness are mostly degrading illusions. Hence he will distrust popular political and religious figures, refuse to believe the papers, avoid celebrated drinking waters, and take cold baths when conventional wisdom calls for warm (and the opposite). He realizes the journey may prove nuptial for some of his party, but he refuses to credit newer conceptions of marriage, for example, that sexual love can transform a man's character for the better. With Burdock, Baynard, Milksan, Sowerby, and others, he sees many men turned by women, and in each instance the man is worse for the transformation. For him sexual love must be judged by its social and political benefits, not seen as good in itself; he has himself been willing to pay for nine bastards, but no wife: "Thank heaven, Dick, that among all the follies and weaknesses of human nature, I have not yet fallen into that of matrimony" (MB, September 30). Physical attraction and marriage are merely fillips that should lead to masculine dominance in the family and social harmony in the nation. In luxurious England, however, goals have been eliminated and society has been turned topsy-turvy. Successful marriages for love are possible, he acknowledges in describing the Dennisons, but only when both partners are inoculated against the age; like Lewis and apparently Mr. S——, he prefers not to assume the risk.

In an age of tasteless insubordination, Bramble is a rare type, thorough individual *and* good citizen, a man who would abide by natural law even when the task calls for inordinate strength. "What temptation can a man of my turn and temperament have, to live in a place where every corner teems with fresh objects of detestation and disgust?" he asks in London (June 8). His answer is quick, for his duty to himself and his charges is self-imposed, although its fulfillment requires resistance to everything his age calls "fashion" and "society." He searches at large for honor, is disappointed, and therefore cherishes all the more those few friends in whom it remains alive. To the strong who can equal his demands, he gives his admiration. To the weak or unfortunate who cannot, he gives pity; if they are sensible enough to seek help, he supplies it readily. For the vain and frivolous who will not, he reserves his contempt. His quest for the good society must be ultimately disillusioning, since he seeks the conditions of national honor and finds only the possibility of personal ethics. Like Plato he believes that good politics best fashions good men. Like Cicero his conservatism is moral and aesthetic as well as political: he would have public life exemplary, glorious, and honorable. His is the dilemma of a search for the public good undertaken when legitimate politics is dead, the paradox of the man who while rejecting individual ethics as the primary touchstone discovers that only personal choices remain. And like Socrates he knows that the philosopher's dedication to his search appears ridiculous to the multitude.

The nature of that quest (as of Smollett's gifts) insures that Bramble will be a figure in comedy, if not a comic figure. Smollett follows Aristotle and Fielding in finding the ridiculous the spring of pure comedy. The most hilarious scenes are those that cause no lasting harm to anyone—such as ones precipitated by Win, Humphry, Lismahago, Bullford, Mackilligut, and Micklewhimmen. Like Parson Adams, Bramble is sometimes the object of laughter, as when Humphry "saves" him by the ear from still waters, or when he subjects himself to pills, purges, and pungent odors. More often he provokes laughter by seeking quixotically after decorum in situations inherently vile. In places like the Pump Room and Vauxhall, where all of polite society endures noise and stink, he demands peace and fragrance. In places ruled by sophisticators, he dares ask for pure food and drink. He is so at odds with English attitudes that he is continually caught up in contradictions, which to the fashionable world prove his boorishness. For Captain O'Donaghan, Lady Griskin, Lord Oxmington, and often Tabby, he is no more than a meddlesome oaf; yet we have reason to suspect that the derision he faces from "superior" personages in England is reflexive, without power to goad or alter him. Liddy nicely captures his reactions to the world of fashion assembled at Bath: "My uncle sometimes shrugs up his shoulders, and sometimes bursts out a-laughing" (LM, May 6).

If hearty laughter is one antidote to the distemper of the times, then simple avoidance is the other. After the refreshment of Scotland, Bramble is forced by the sorrows of Baynard back to an original question. "At what time of life may a man think himself exempted from the necessity of sacrificing his repose to the punctilios of a contemptible world?" (MB, September 30). The answer is found in his earliest letters, reiterated and demonstrated throughout the journey. In a contemptible world a man can create his own harmony, in retirement and vigilant cultivation of his own estate. "It must be something very extraordinary that will induce me to revisit either Bath or London," he tells Lewis in his last letter (November 20). Instead, the future will hold good exercise and good companionship: "I have got an excellent fowling-piece from Mr. Lismahago, who is a keen sportsman, and we shall take the heath in all weathers." Personal and political resolutions thereby coincide. When he determines that civic life in England has degenerated beyond recall, Bramble is prepared to accept the option of honor and retire. Like Cato and Lucius Piso, Cicero and Seneca, and like Smollett after mid-1763, he is self-exiled. He has fulfilled his moral obligation, that of passing on his knowledge of the fruits and frailties of the world to the young people of his family, as Cicero had done for his son in *De officiis*. Active, concerted resistance is now futile, and he will retreat to his small but comfortable lot in Monmouthshire, there to find remission from a wretched world for which he had become unfit. His just sense of history and his own worth dispels gloom. Other societies and other men have been under attack from luxury. He will not be intimidated; he will not despair.

Bramble is one of the outstanding creations in a great age of English fiction. Besides being a vital and interesting figure in his own right (independent in one's memory of the novel), he must bring about the communion of values that animates the novel. That is, he must win the assent and sympathy of his pupils and of Smollett's readers alike. He must convince them and us—fully and simultaneously. The task is not a simple one. Before the eighteenth century, literary attacks upon luxury could proceed under two presumptions: the clarity of the tradition and a direct, unmediated relationship between writer and reader. Yet by the time Smollett's last novel appeared, neither held with such tenacity. Although most readers might still regard luxury, traditionally conceived, as the great enemy, their relationship to authors had been radically altered by satire and the novel. Without the implicit authority of a Sallust or an Augustine directly addressing his readers, novelists resort to rhetorical devices of various kinds. Defoe and Richardson choose a first-person narrator of evident candor, Fielding an omnipresent narrator whose selection of language guides readers into his own unique angle of vision, Goldsmith a naive narrator whose strengths and limitations are for the most part transparent. Having used the direct approach in his histories and several devices of satire in his journalism and previous fiction, in *Humphry Clinker* Smollett tries something fresh.

As a literary mode, the attack upon luxury had for centuries depended upon an easy recognition of a series of contrasts elaborated into a typology: masculine – feminine, old – young, country philosopher – city sharper, and so on.[4] What distinguishes *Humphry Clinker* is not the mere inclusion of familiar patterns, but the lively variations Smollett plays upon them. With Bramble established as hub and touchstone, the novelist is free to roam like his travelers over character, circumstance, and geography, confident that his center will hold. (The reader's coming to terms with Bramble could be considered the earliest subplot of the book.) His contrasts are many and integral, but never simple and seldom static. As critic of the times Bramble stands opposed to Tabitha; as brother he stands watch over her. Seemingly, Quin is entrepreneur to the corruptions of Bath; actually, Bramble's claret-cousin, he is the city's secret scourge. Win Jenkins is always a jink; yet she is winsome, and by the end she is also a winner. Lismahago is one of the most poignant victims of the nation's moral squalor; he is likewise one of its keenest analysts. Paunceford is set against Serle, then Bramble and Jery, and finally Captain Brown. As Bramble's old companion, Baynard is a worthy man; as tool of a luxurious woman he is a pitiable wretch. As with other families in the novel, the Baynards provide an example and its opposite. Sons are to be compared with fathers, with mothers, and with other sons; wives with their husbands and with each other.

For the first third of the novel Smollett encourages the semblance of five discrete narrative versions of events: after Bramble come Jery the arch, Lydia the naive, Tabby the gullible, and Win the simple. Thereafter variations quicken. In her earliest letters, for instance, Lydia is an ingenue, less an observer than a girl acting out a fond role from remembered romances. These come hard upon her uncle's normative commentary and her own later letters, which represent the shrewd judgments of a penetrating young woman. As with Liddy and her uncle, much of the characterization and plotting moves by reversals: from official version to unbiased description, impression to certainty, appearance to reality, rind to heart. Wilson the nefarious actor turns effortlessly into George Dennison, paragon of young manhood. A cycle turns back upon itself when Matthew Bramble reveals a Matthew Loyd in his past in time to secure a Matthew Loyd for his future. Theatergoers and readers of fiction would be prepared for such revolutions of name and station; yet they might not expect the evolution of Jery the pup into Jery the prudent, or of Tabitha the terrible into Tabby the (relatively) tame. Thus while the characters of the novel must be considered in the light of the attack upon luxury, they are usually too full and too various to be stillborn types. And the groupings in which they appear pass unobtrusively through several levels of contrast into pairs, unions, reversals, balances, divisions, negations, equations, and juxtapositions.

Insofar as it is an attack upon luxury, *Humphry Clinker* is a novel about relationships: a social-political order that has been undermined, the many personal relationships that were destroyed in the collapse, and the few that have withstood the shock. Like the legislator in Genesis defining the threshold of luxury, Bramble defines for us the failures of merchants and politicians, citizens and families. From him radiate those relationships that impart movement and dimension, and through him we learn how well other figures cope with luxury and each other. For the most part the worth of a character in the English sections varies with the closeness of his relation to Bramble. Closest are his male friends and the young people of his blood, furthest the older men and women of inveterate luxury.[5]

The group that resembles Bramble most are the older, mature men who have been educated as he has and whose lives have been witness to the ravages of the age. It includes men who have small roles, like Serle, Balderick, Cockril, Bentley, Heathcote, and Mr. S—, as well as those with large roles like Lewis, Dennison, and Lismahago. It extends to the men who, although antagonists to luxury, are wedded to it by circumstance. Quin is bound by temperament to the stink of the Pump Room; Burdock, Baynard, Milksan, and Sowerby are bound by marriage. It is Bramble's respect that obtains our sympathy for such men, even as it is his own motive for assisting them. Half of his first letter, the first of the novel, it should be recalled, is devoted to specific, practical, and presumably effective advice on how to relieve various persons from temporary distress. His last is preoccupied with settling the affairs of his family and his household. As he has done for himself, he shall demonstrate to others that inner aspiration need not be crushed by external circumstance.

Humorous stranger to Bramble, then in stages gentle antagonist, friend, boon companion, and brother-in-law, Lismahago is of course the pivotal figure among the seasoned men carrying their experiences and misfortunes into the Bramble family. Our first view of him, like the first view of Bramble, is a ludicrous one. In two consecutive letters (July 10, 13) Jery details every comic feature of countenance, physique, dress, mount, accent, pride, and pugnacity. As he admits to Phillips, Jery at once grasps the amusement value in Lismahago's appearance: "In my last I treated you with a high flavoured dish, in the character of the Scotch lieutenant, and I must present him once more for your entertainment." In his initial report, however, Bramble plunges immediately into the Scotsman's opinions, with a few words of preface about the man's spirit of contradiction, indefatigable study, and desire "to refute established maxims" (MB, July 15). Though brief, this preface is adequate to Smollett's purpose. Lismahago has been legitimized, established as exactly the kind of man Bramble is himself, exactly the kind of character needed to introduce the Scottish portion of the book. Approaching Scotland, Bramble is required by Smollett's theme to relax, to enjoy fully a land free of England's disease. So that he may, Lismahago expounds the ramifications for his country of the luxury of the South, reiterating almost verbatim Bramble's earlier accusations against mob, press, juries, factions, inflation, commerce, merchants, effeminacy, and leveling politicians. The two men discover in Scotland that genuine friendship remains possible. That link forged, they discover in England that they can act in concert, in the affairs with Oxmington, Bullford, Baynard, and Tabby. By the close Bramble has succeeded in bringing good cheer to the lieutenant's austerity: Lismahago's joke in riposte to Bullford is so apt that it surprises and impresses all concerned (JM, October 3); and "His temper, which had been soured and shrivelled . . . is now swelled out, and smoothed like a raisin in plum-porridge" (JM, November 8).[6]

Thematically it is Bramble's relationship with older males, allowing for a rotating criticism of luxury, that anchors the novel. Formatively it is his relationship with Jery and the rest of his family that allows it gradually to unfold. Jery, and to a lesser degree Humphry and Liddy, are being tried, tested for intellectual ripeness. From Homer through Fielding Western literature has recast the story of a young man in quest of knowledge and a family: in *Joseph Andrews* and *Tom Jones* the title character is a youth seeking wisdom and a lost father. In *Humphry Clinker* this single figure has been divided into two, doubling thereby the kind and amount of instruction that can be rendered. As it divides the attention directed to the pupils, this device concentrates our focus upon the teacher. Similarly, *Joseph Andrews* offers two older male figures for Joseph's emulation: Adams as moral guide for the journey, and Wilson as discovered father and future model. In Smollett the roles of tutor and father are united in Bramble. Jery requires an education whose progress and consequences will become the substance of his letters; these in turn represent a form of notebook the reader is permitted to inspect. Humphry needs a family and a place; his education is subordinated to his needs and his service. Already possessed of his father's moral fitness—Fielding's "Good Nature"—he is not solely a pupil; at times he can and does teach.

Like the other young men in eighteenth-century fiction, Jery Melford requires a structured expedition before he will be fit to assume the responsibilities of manhood. As Rasselas must put aside bootless yearning before he is fit to rule, so Jery must discard the jejune arrogance he has put on at Oxford. Bramble notices Jery's immaturity, referring to him as "a pert jackanapes, full of college-petulance and self-conceit" (MB, April 17) and calling him down as an inexperienced pup, "a young fellow . . . when he first thrusts his snout into the world" (MB, May 6). But by the time the party reaches Bath uncle and nephew are commencing to respect each other. For Jery the process begins with greater contact.

> The truth is, his disposition and mine, which, like oil and vinegar, repelled one another at first, have now begun to mix by dint of being beat up together. I was once apt to believe him a complete Cynic; and that nothing but the necessity of his occasions could compel him to get within the pale of society—I am now of another opinion. I think his peevishness arises partly from bodily pain, and partly from a natural excess of mental sensibility; for, I suppose, the mind as well as the body, is in some cases endued with a morbid excess of sensation. [JM, April 18]

Bramble discerns that Jery's brittle edges cover a young man of character, and Jery remarks approvingly of the older man's fineness of feeling, against which his own seems quite coarse: "Mr. Bramble is extravagantly delicate in all his sensations, both of soul and body. . . . His blood rises at every instance of insolence and cruelty, even where he himself is no way concerned; and ingratitude makes his teeth chatter. On the other hand, the recital of a generous, humane, or grateful action, never fails to draw from him tears of approbation, which he is often greatly distressed to conceal" (JM, May 10).

Such perception discloses that hereafter Jery is prepared actually to join his uncle in uncovering instances of insolence and cruelty, especially among the nouveaux riches. In neglect of Serle, his former benefactor, Paunceford receives the censure of uncle and nephew alike. While both agree that Paunceford has violated all rules of decency and friendship, it is Jery who delivers their verdict:

> This man, after having been long buffetted by adversity, went

abroad; and Fortune, resolved to make him amends for her former coyness, set him all at once up to the very ears in affluence. He has now emerged from obscurity, and blazes out in all the tinsel of the times. I don't find that he is charged with any practices that the law deems dishonest. . . . But they say, he is remarkable for shrinking from his former friendships, which are generally too plain and home-spun to appear amidst his present brilliant connexions; and that he seems uneasy at sight of some old benefactors, whom a man of honour would take pleasure to acknowledge—[JM, May 10]

The phrases "tinsel of the times" and "practices that the law deems dishonest" demonstrate that Bramble's lessons have taken hold. Jery has begun to penetrate current fashions in morality in just those ways that characterize Bramble. He is indeed so apt a pupil that in his next letter, May 17, he is able to observe for himself the vagaries of a luxurious society, noting that the Bath season has ended "and all our gay birds of passage have taken their flight." With Bramble's eye for physical detail, he perceives signs of enervation all about him: "There is always a great shew of the clergy at Bath: none of your thin, puny, yellow, hectic figures, exhausted with abstinence and hard study, labouring under the *morbi eruditorum;* but great overgrown dignitaries and rectors, with rubicund noses and gouty ancles, or broad bloated faces, dragging along great swag bellies; the emblems of sloth and indigestion." Earlier Bramble had found all of Bath swollen and congested by insolence; here Jery discovers concrete examples. Earlier Bramble had denounced the fools who flocked to Bath to be sucked dry by parasites; here Jery closes his letter with the tale of a would-be politician, George Prankley, betrayed by cowardice and vainglory into giving preferment to a mercenary parson, Tom Eastgate.

The effect of Jery's learning is such that at Bath Smollett is able to add a major voice, subordinate only to those of Bramble and Lismahago, to the indictment of luxury. Without sacrificing any of his rich resources of language, the novelist has bestowed distinctive voices upon uncle and nephew. Bramble's style is usually that of intuitive judgment forcefully rendered, Jery's a more neutrally descriptive tone effectively verifying and elaborating the older man's generalizations. To his Oxford chum Phillips, Jery announces his intention to describe everything of interest; that is, only he among the writers formally commits himself to observation of detail. While Bramble may transcribe his or Lismahago's lengthy monologues, only Jery has the habit of recording dialect and dialogue. When Bramble finds novelty in England, it is normally of the repulsive kind he has no patience to remark minutely. Jery, however, must walk three times around an object before forming an opinion. Hence it is to Jery that the great set-pieces of the novel are given: Bramble's deeds of valor and honor, as with the distressed widow (JM, April 20); Sunday dinner with Mr. S——, which opens with Bramble's casual remark that brilliant writers are usually quiet in company and proceeds to show us S—— reigning by dint of physical presence alone (JM, June 10); and those scenes of high comedy whose effect arises from simple placement of incongruity against incongruity (Tabby against Mackilligut, Lismahago against Bullford, Bramble against Linden, Lismahago and his horse, Humphry and the coach). The dialectical relation between Bramble and Jery goes so far that on occasion Smollett forgets his illusions. Bramble at the close of his letter of July 15, for example, tells Lewis of an open contest for Win's affections between Clinker and Dutton. As if forgetting that he alone corresponds with Lewis, he adds: "Jery has been obliged to interpose his authority to keep the peace; *and to him I have left the discussion of that important affair*" (italics added).

As Lismahago is a bridge between the English and Scottish parts of the novel, so Humphry Clinker is a bridge between the elder, intuitive men and the younger men in want of instruction. Somewhat less obtrusively, he also calls attention to the rural-urban poles of English luxury. He joins the expedition on the road between Bath and London –appropriately outside the centers of city temptation and dissipation, where like Joseph Andrews and Tom Jones he might have been drawn into the general whirlpool of degradation. In the rural virtues he abounds: he is simple, talented, obedient. But he is not yet proof against urban deceptions and cannot fully protect himself, being taken in turn by Justice Buzzard, the Methodists, and Lady Griskin. From Bramble Jery requires education by demonstration, Humphry education by admonition. To Bramble the ward-nephew can return respect and admiration, the servant-son loyalty and devotion. The young men become complementary pupils, each learning and being taught according to his presumptive station, and suggesting, by the by, that readers of all levels can benefit from Smollett's novel. Until the final revelations, their differing stations are underscored; when referred to by name the nephew is virtually always called by his Christian name; the servant "Clinker" and "Humphry Clinker" more often than "Humphry."

Humphry enters at the point when Bramble is beginning to doubt the sanity of his mission-quest. With his irritability rising and the stench of Bath in his nostrils, he chances upon "honest Humphry"–as Jery and Bramble each three times call him–an undoubted example of honest virtue unblemished by the fraud and sophistication around him.[7] Uncle immediately perceives and nephew at length confirms him as a model of positive simplicity. Bramble writes, "the fellow's character is downright simplicity" (MB, June 2), and he is "pleased with the gratitude of Clinker, as well as with the simplicity of his character" (MB, June 12). For Jery, "Humphry Clinker . . . is a surprising compound of genius and simplicity" (JM, June 10). He is sufficiently aware of "the poor fellow's simplicity" to see correctly Humphry's sole flaw, the "danger of falling sacrifice to his own simplicity" (JM, June 11). When Clinker does indeed fall victim, taken as a highwayman, Bramble is certain of his innocence, for he is "the very picture of simplicity" (MB, June 12). Although Bramble does occasionally become vexed with his new servant, the emotion is quickly assuaged by Humphry's "great simplicity of heart" (MB, July 4). Jery terms his own new valet, Dutton, "the very contrast of Humphry Clinker" and distinguishes between the genuine and the luxurious: "Humphry may be compared to an English pudding, composed of good wholesome flour and suet, and Dutton to a syllabub or iced froth, which, though agreeable to the taste, has nothing solid or substantial" (JM, July 18).

Bramble is willing to devote his care and energy to the tuition of Jery and Humphry because they will be future models themselves; Jery, in fact, represents Bramble at an earlier stage of his life. For the same reason, we learn, young George Dennison has been thoroughly tutored by his father. The virtue of such young men in turn stands in stark relief to the youths whose instruction has been neglected or left to their mothers, like young Burdock and Baynard. The story of Martin, the man of parts turned highwayman, parallels then converges with that of Humphry, indicating that unprotected young men are easy prey to the metropolis. Bramble has little time to assist him—initiates wager "he swings before Christmas"—but with men of merit short is sufficient. Although Martin's accomplishments are many, he has fallen victim to the snares indigenous to a luxurious city. His past misfortunes he owes to attaching himself to the merchant class: "he lived some time as a clerk to a timber-merchant, whose daughter Martin privately married, was discarded, and his wife turned out of doors" (JM, June 11). His present situation derives from the male folly especially common to the tribe of Macheath: "namely, an indiscreet devotion to the fair sex, and, in all probability, he will be attacked on this defenceless quarter." As Martin has intervened to save Humphry, so Bramble intervenes to save him. The letter recommending Martin to the East India Company (founded perhaps on Heathcote's former connection with the company) is the sole use Bramble finds in the novel for the world of English commerce.

A luxurious society offers too few opportunities to the goodly young men of the novel; their capacities are too circumscribed by frivolous pursuit of fashion and lucre. On the other hand, a debauched society offers too many freedoms to young women; their capacities are taxed beyond their limits. Smollett introduces relatively few young women into his tale—the ratio of older to younger characters generally must be about twenty to one—and places only Liddy and Win in the foreground. Their role is to be guided by the models of mature womanhood Bramble discovers, all except one of whom are proper wives to sensible men: Moore, Campbell, Colquhoun, Melville, Queensberry, Dennison. (Mrs. Pimpernel, who is virtuous despite her tyrannical husband, gets but one sentence.) Yet these ideal figures remain faint. They have no independent existence, are introduced only after their husbands, and are extensions into another personality of the qualities of their husbands. The best of them, the uncommon Mrs. Dennison, is praised by Bramble as an apposite consort to Dennison: her "disposition is suited to his own in all respects," and she is therefore "admirably qualified to be his companion, confidant, counsellor, and coadjutrix" (MB, October 8). It may also be that they are extensions in a different sense of Bramble and Jery, since each time the men reach a new place, they need someone to care for the women; for example, at Drumlanrig, "The dutchess was equally gracious, and took our ladies under her immediate protection" (MB, September 15). In any case Bramble exerts himself more in denouncing, say, Mrs. Burdock, than he does in praising all the virtuous wives combined.

It is protection, Bramble makes clear at the start, that Liddy needs more than any other service, for while intelligent she is "soft as butter, and as easily melted" and "as inflammable as touch-wood" (MB, April 17). What instruction she does receive on her journey seems to be by example, positive from her uncle and negative from her aunt. Her two letters from Bath and two from London reveal a heart of naive wholesomeness. Because she is immature and sentimental, she is occasionally unable to distinguish the luxurious and false from the simple and genuine and must be rescued continually (seventeen times by rough count) from the predators with which England abounds. At Bath she is gulled into believing that "a great many gentlemen and ladies of Ireland" frequent the Spring Garden (LM, April 26). The situation recurs in London when she mistakes notorious women of pleasure for famous ladies of fashion (LM, May 31). In contrast to her uncle, she finds that "Bath is . . . a new world—All is gayety, good humour, and diversion," where "The eye is continually entertained with the splendour of dress and equipage, and the ear with the sound of coaches, chaises, chairs, and other carriages" (LM, April 26). In London she says that her "imagination is quite confounded with splendour and variety," and compares the city to the world of romance, "all that you read of wealth and grandeur, in the Arabian Nights Entertainment, and the Persian Tales" (LM, May 31). Like her experiences with the reality of England, her romantic effusions are few and short and are set between the caustic letters of Bramble and the realistic ones of Jery. The moral—stated by uncle and brother alike—is that Liddy must be closely watched lest her innocence betray her. She will not be entirely safe until she is delivered into the arms of a man as well inoculated against the degeneracy of the times as Jery and Bramble. Such a man, we know, is not likely to be found in Bath, and certainly not in London.

Smollett does not allow Liddy to mature as deeply or as quickly as her brother. Yet her appreciation of Scotland signals a quickened perception. The first letter she has devoted to the members of the party, from Glasgow, September 7, is a précis of the revelations we have been witnessing. Jery is an affectionate, constant brother, having only her interest at heart. Win is "really a good body in the main," but "is weak in her nerves, as well as in her understanding." Clinker "is really a deserving young man," but Dutton is "a debauched fellow." She is as acute in self-assessment, aware that Scotland "being exceedingly romantic, suits my turn and inclinations." Her most arresting insights turn upon the deplorable women she has encountered and on Tabby's hunt for a husband among the Methodists. These are as bluntly caustic as anything written by Bramble, charging her aunt with ranting hypocrisy and women generally with cunning and deceit: "My dear Willis, I am truly ashamed of my own sex." For those who might have missed Liddy's transformation and permanent conversion to her uncle's views, Smollett has her exclaim to Bramble, "My dear uncle!—My best friend! My father!" and provides her with the following reflection:

> Nature never intended me for the busy world—I long for repose and solitude, where I can enjoy that disinterested friendship which is not to be found among crouds, and indulge those pleasing reveries that shun the hurry and tumult of fashionable society—Unexperienced as I am in the commerce of life, I have seen enough to give me a disgust to the generality of those who carry it on—There is such malice, treachery, and dissimulation, even among professed friends and intimate companions, as cannot fail to strike a virtuous mind with horror. [LM, October 4]

A prologue to Liddy's own future, this is of course a conscious echo of Bramble's hymns to Brambleton Hall, delivered in Bath and London.

When Liddy reports that Win is in the main "really a good body," we realize her mind is another thing entirely and that she is in need of extraordinary protection. From Tabby her mistress she receives tyrannical control, from Jery amused surveillance, and from Humphry tender devotion. There is a nice symmetry in the affection shared by the two servants: Humphry genuinely simple, Win a genuine simpleton, each falling in love at sight of the other's bare backside. In England she is naturally drawn to luxurious fashions, but her errors are ludicrous, domestic, and harmless. Win errs by imitation: "Nature intended Jenkins for something very different from the character of her mistress; yet custom and habit have effected a wonderful resemblance betwixt them in many particulars" (JM, July 18). She is overly fond of propriety and shares Tabby's concern with her prize possessions, "Three-quarters of blond lace, and a remnant of muslin, and my silver thimble" (WJ, May 15). And like all the ladies of the family, she is overawed by the attractions of London: "O Molly! what shall I say of London? All the towns that ever I beheld in my born-days are no more than Welsh barrows and crumlecks to this wonderful sitty! Even Bath itself is but a fillitch, in the naam of God—One would think there's no end of the streets, but the land's end" (WJ, June 3). She of course possesses the weaknesses of her class and delights in dressing above her station: "Last night, coming huom from the meeting, I was taken by a lamp-light for an iminent poulterer's daughter, a great beauty—" (WJ, June 3). In the end the true goodness everyone has testified to brings Win her reward: she has the novel's last word.

Tabby, however, is another story. Whereas Bramble, Jery, and Liddy suffer the waves of excess in order "to case-harden the constitution," Tabby simply likes to get wet. In her Smollett unites the extremes of two satiric types: the weak and empty vessel of the woman, open to the whole spectrum of vanities; and the person possessed of the normally opposed vices of luxury and avarice.[8] If with Liddy his powers of characterization are not pronounced, with Tabby his gifts of travesty are at their fullest. Bramble's solicitude tells us early that she is silly, not wicked—in Fielding's terms a representation of the Ridiculous. He tells Jery that she is "insensibly a part of my constitution—Damn her! She's a *noli me tangere* in my flesh, which I cannot bear to be touched or tampered with" (JM, May 6). She redeems his tolerance by caring for him when he is ill, and at the end—when her "vinegar . . . is remarkably dulcified" (JM, October 14)—by a proper choice of husband, the same he wished for her. Yet along the way she affords a sacrifying enough picture of luxury to scotch the need for a Mrs. Burdock.

Tabby's first letter of April 2 actually introduces the attack upon luxury, since it like all the rest is concerned solely with her possessions. In none of her letters does she remark journey, place, or emotion. Nothing beyond self touches her; she exists below the attractions of art, nature, reason, and experience. She is oblivious, Slipslop tutored by Mrs. Western. Rather than attend to the journey, she concentrates her formidable energies upon maintaining her store of goods in Brambleton Hall, while adding to it in the item of one husband. Throughout the expedition her perversity of judgment has two sides. On the one, she is never merely mistaken, but is always *completely* wrong, wrong 180 degrees. When she applauds the mirth of Bath or the honesty of the Methodists or the beauties of London, we have confirmed the antithetical views of brother and nephew. When she sees Humphry as a worthless beggar, Mr. Moffat as a fine gentleman, and Brambleton Hall as an early Cold Comfort Farm, we obtain important information, delivered in code. What is more, the other characters themselves delight in breaking the code. Bramble reports that Tabby is "inclined to give the whole Scotch nation to the devil, as a pack of insensible brutes," then adds the crucial phrase, "upon whom her accomplishments had been displayed in vain." Jery records her peevishness in Edinburgh and her desire to leave—until she chances upon a susceptible male. Even Win joins the game; as Tabby is railing against all things Scottish, Win tells us, "As for mistress, blessed be God, she ails nothing.—Her stomick is good, and she improves in grease and godliness" (WJ, September 7). Left to herself, she and her topsy-turvy world harm no one.

But when her vice turns social, embroiling others, she moves in the direction of Lady Griskin and Mrs. Baynard. Initially Jery sees her as "exceedingly starched, vain, and ridiculous" (April 2). But after traveling with her for a month, his view is sharper—and darker: "In her temper, she is proud, stiff, vain, imperious, prying, malicious, greedy, and uncharitable. . . . Her avarice seems to grow every day more and more rapacious" (May 6). During that month she has begun to issue the insatiable demands that characterize her luxury and that will not be quelled until she is ruled by Lismahago. Lydia remarks that the atmosphere of Bath is too feverish, but "Aunt says it is the effect of a vulgar constitution, reared among woods and mountains; and, that as I become accustomed to genteel company, it will wear off" (LM, April 26). She not only doubts, but revolts against her brother's generosity to the widow and her consumptive daughter at Bristol, even after Jery explains the situation: "Child, child, talk not to me of charity.—Who gives twenty pounds in charity?—But you are a stripling—You know nothing of the world—Besides, charity begins at home—Twenty pounds would buy me a complete suit of flowered silk, trimmings and all" (JM, April 20). Her letter of diatribe, May 19, charts the distance between her selfish attitude toward the servants and her brother's compassion.[9] She flirts with dozens of false gentlemen, foolishly sees Barton's favors directed toward herself, tries to entice a bereaved Baynard, and would have everyone (Squikinacoosta included) dressed in the latest Parisian fashions.

When Bramble exclaims, "I an't married to Tabby, thank Heaven!" he is drawing a pertinent distinction. Tabby is guarded round by a family of inordinate strength bent upon protecting her from herself—brother and nephew comment regularly on her "manageability"—and her *folies des luxes* are normally witless. She is probably related, by misadventure, to another fictional sister, Bridget Allworthy, both modeled upon the focal female figure in Hogarth's "Morning" (see Jery's description, May 6). What would the consequence be if she were brighter or uncontrolled or married to a man weaker than she? Put another way: what would the result be for England if most *men* were as frivolous as she? It is the very pettiness of Tabby's vices that serves to stress the danger of a climate of luxury, for frivolity can be translated swiftly into disaster. Tabby has power merely to irritate her brother, but the social rabble can overturn Bath, the political mob destroy London, and Mrs. Burdock and Mrs. Baynard bring heartbreak to their husbands.

Avatars of luxury dominate England. Indeed Tabby is a direct link, since she attracts mercenary "gentlemen"—about two dozen named and unnamed—as a rich coach draws highwaymen. (In Scotland it is *she* who does the pursuing.) She also establishes that luxury can threaten even the most virtuous of families, a lesson repeated with the entry of Bramble's cousins, Lady Griskin and Squire Burdock. That the Bramble party itself does not succumb is proof not of the enemy's weakness, but of its own strength. The forces of luxury are led by the political hacks and "uncouth whales" of commercial fortune noticed in the previous chapter. Their followers are mostly parasitic men and women whom Bramble with ample cause disdains to name: "If you pick up a diverting original by accident, it may be dangerous to amuse yourself with his oddities. He is generally a tartar at bottom; a sharper, a spy, or a lunatic" (MB, June 8). The remainder range from agents like Sir Ulic, Jack Holder, Squire Prankley, Colonel Tinsel, and Paunceford to their working-class imitators like John Thomas and Dutton.[10] In order to maintain an emotional equilibrium against such fashionable vermin, Bramble finds some means to keep them at a distance. He flees them, refuses to acknowledge them, or drives them from his vicinity. Like Oxmington and Tabby's ersatz suitors, most are cowards easily dissuaded. Yet occasionally words are not forceful enough. When two slaves owned by Colonel Rigworm, "a Creole gentleman" with neither taste nor breeding, play their French horns on the common staircase, Bramble's indignation is fierce. He promptly batters both horns and heads, promises the same to their master, and is disturbed no more.

Certain instances of luxury Bramble is obliged to confront without flinching. As a visitor to England cannot easily avoid Bath or London, so Bramble cannot in conscience skirt the home of a relative like

Burdock or a friend like Baynard. In such households he must acknowledge the power of effeminacy blindly to destroy the ways of Old England. They reveal the consequences of female rule and disclose how wives prey upon the weaknesses of worthy men, obtaining control even when their husbands know the better course: "I believe it will be found upon enquiry, that nineteen out of twenty, who are ruined by extravagance, fall a sacrifice to the ridiculous pride and vanity of silly women, whose parts are held in contempt by the very men whom they pillage and enslave" (MB, September 30). Burdock and Baynard should be as steeled against luxury as the other seasoned men of the novel, but, schooled by their wives, they merely demonstrate that dissipation has reached well into the North of England.

A flagrant example of the new rich, Mrs. Burdock is insensitive, illiberal, arrogant, brutal, and cold. The house she has turned into "a great inn," "neither elegant nor comfortable," a house without warmth. For the older virtue of generosity she has substituted mere splendor; her husband admits, "Country gentlemen now-a-days live after another fashion.—My table alone stands me in a cool thousand a quarter, though I raise my own stock, import my own liquors, and have every thing at the first hand" (MB, June 26). All normal bonds of duty and affection she has broken. Hence the son is a young fool just returned from Italy who "slips no opportunity of manifesting the most perfect contempt for his own father." The servants, without loyalty or subordination, are insolent, inattentive, and rapacious, "so greedy," Bramble reports, "that . . . I can dine better, and for less expence, at the Star and Garter in Pall mall, than at our cousin's castle in Yorkshire." Her signal achievement is to be equally abusive to everyone, husband or chance visitor. At the moment Bramble arrives she and her son are expressing their love for Burdock by having him needlessly trepanned. The squire takes his near-death in stride, for he "hates her mortally; but . . . truckles to her dominion, and dreads, like a schoolboy, the lash of her tongue." Although he is a tough old dog, his dread is such that he cannot invite Bramble to stay the wet night.

When he visits the Baynards, Bramble meets with not an instance, but a whole colony of luxury, three men "driven by their wives at full speed, in the high road to bankruptcy and ruin" (MB, September 30). The women vie with each other and with wealthier women of the region for more and costlier clothes, plate, china, furniture, servants, horses, and carriages. Because their husbands are of differing temperaments, they must exercise "three different forms of female tyranny."

Mr. Baynard was subjugated by practising upon the tenderness of his nature. Mr. Milksan, being of a timorous disposition, truckled to the insolence of a termagant. Mr. Sowerby, who was of a temper neither to be moved by fits, nor driven by menaces, had the fortune to be fitted with a helpmate, who assailed him with the weapons of irony and satire.

Of all the fictional characters in *Humphry Clinker,* Mrs. Baynard most fully represents the vain triumphs of luxury; every detail Bramble provides in this, the longest inset story in the novel, reeks of social perversity. Her birth—"daughter of a citizen, who had failed in trade"— places her among those "shovel-nosed sharks," the English women of the middle orders, whom Bramble has deplored everywhere along the journey. As a tradesman, her father was certainly a rascal: "Your trades-men are without conscience" (MB, June 8). But what is worse, he was also a failure: if "cits" are not good for trade, they are good for noth-ing. In her own education "for the usual purposes of the married state," she has repeated his failure.

> She excelled in nothing. Her conversation was flat, her stile mean, and her expression embarrassed—In a word, her character was totally insipid. Her person was not disagreeable; but there was nothing graceful in her address, nor engaging in her manners; and she was so ill qualified to do the honours of the house, that when she sat at the head of the table, one was always looking for the mistress of the family in some other place.

Only after marriage does she disclose her guiding passion, "vanity . . . of a bastard and idiot nature, excited by shew and ostentation." Only then does she pronounce her intention to rule all (and spend all) they have. Only then does she reveal her answer to all expostulation—prolonged faints and violent fits.

Her trickery, elaborately described in one of Bramble's rare transcrip-tions of dialogue, summarizes all the major acts of deceit recounted in the novel. Through it she gains an extravagant house in the city, an extravagant estate in the country, and an extravagant tour of the Conti-nent. She tours Europe as Tabby does Britain, learning nothing, but gathering expensive parasites and bric-a-brac, disgusted with a country when her presence goes unnoticed. "Her travels," Bramble reports, "had no effect upon her, but that of making her more expensive and fantastic than ever." This is to be contrasted with the effect travel has had upon the Bramble family.

Upon returning to England, Mrs. Baynard assumes the rank of arbiter "in every article of taste and connoisseurship." She proves her genius by destroying the facade of the house and the perfection of the gardens and by duplicating the fashionable meals of London.

The pottage was little better than bread soaked in dishwashings, lukewarm. The ragouts looked as if they had been once eaten and half digested: the fricassees were involved in a nasty yellow poultice; and the rotis were scorched and stinking, for the honour of the fumet. The desert consisted of faded fruit and iced froth, a good emblem of our landlady's character.

The same as Jery proposed for Dutton, the lady's emblem is a syllabub, the emblem Bramble would choose for all of fashionable England. In her moments away from aesthetic projects, she superintends the tuition of her son, "a puny boy of twelve or thirteen," who according to Bramble "will be ruined in his education by the indulgence of his mother." She watches complacently as he steals a kiss from Liddy and thrusts his hand inside the bosom of her dress. With such guidance young Baynard will doubtless prove a fit companion in the Pump Room for young Burdock.

With exquisite care and expense, Mrs. Baynard has turned the estate into a gallery of contemporary English vices. Travelers with little time need not make the Bristol-Bath-London-Harrigate circuit, for here they may sample the same depraved food, morals, manners, architecture, and family relationships. Here they may meet individually those types that give the crowds of the spa and the capital their special stink: overbearing women, broken men, false friends, disloyal relations, insolent children, and thievish servants. A museum at once of English history and English destiny, it contains for Bramble "every thing . . . cold, comfortless, and disgusting." Chef d'oeuvre of the place is the lady herself, who, when not removed for fit or faint, may be viewed at length: form for the women who tread upon the kibes of their betters and the backs of their husbands; foil and warning to Liddy, Jery, Humphry, Baynard, Bramble, and the Dennisons.

Smollett's insistence upon this synecdochic epitome is so sharp that we hardly need, but cannot avoid, glosses by Dennison, Bramble, and Baynard. Dennison, Bramble tells us, is a beacon, a standard of reason in a disordered world—precisely the man into whose family Liddy should be entrusted. At every point where the Baynards fell victim to luxury, Dennison remained vigilant and carried his wife with him. He draws the contrast himself when he says he was resolute in avoiding "'pride, envy, and ambition. . . . Those, in times of luxury and dissipation, are the rocks upon which all small estates in the country are wrecked'" (MB, October 11). Bramble's commentary is more complex. At the Burdocks' he had been unsettled by a situation he could despise but not remedy. Baynard is a closer, worthier friend, willing to be advised, and moreover suffering the physical symptoms of mental distress that Bramble himself endured earlier. As he had cured himself, Bramble is determined to release his friend. Yet the exchange between the two men at first appears quite odd, with Bramble demanding, the other supplying, conversations of twenty years ago and humiliating confessions of weakness. Finally the gravamen become clear. When Bramble presses Baynard to resist his wife, the latter answers, "But there are certain lengths which my nature—The truth is, there are tender connexions, of which a bachelor has no idea—Shall I own my weakness? I cannot bear the thoughts of making that woman uneasy—" (MB, September 30). Bramble's response—"I was shocked at his infatuation, and changed the subject"—is thematic (he never willing changes the subject), since his companion's apology is of a piece with Adam's "the woman beguiled me and I did eat." Old Adam's plight remains pretty much the same into the eighteenth century. Whether the novelist seeks to recall the Fall is less important than his creation of a modern Eve. Whereas the archetype of feminine passion disobeyed the law and plucked the fruit, her descendant refuses to recognize any law beyond self and chops down the whole orchard.

If Bramble and Mrs. Baynard are polar opposites in the moral world of *Humphry Clinker,* they stand together in marking Smollett's gifts in the creation of character. The one stands above even the most famous tutor figures of the century: more vital, complex, and interesting than Grandison, Adams, Wilson, Allworthy, Imlac, or Primrose. The other is certainly more evocative of evil than the empty, dimensionless type of contemporary polemics. We glimpse her movements somewhat indirectly, through the magnifying projections of her curt dialogue, Bramble's bitter adjectives, and Baynard's lugubrious recollections. By careful preparation, the novelist can maintain the social definition of her type yet transcend its aesthetic limitations, allowing him to place her at the thematic climax of his narrative. To outline the form from the start, he offers us Tabby and Win, followed by dozens of anonymous female Yahoos in action at the Pump Room, Ranelagh, Vauxhall, and elsewhere. Thereafter he is ready to pause briefly over a figure like Lady Griskin, then to linger with a termagant like Mrs. Burdock. Coming immediately on the heels of such women on the trip north, Mrs. Baynard would not have been so surprising or effective. But Smollett withholds her until the visit to idyllic Scotland has passed, until Jery and Bramble have sung tributes to Scottish women, and until we have lapsed into the fond hope that the party has outdistanced the ravages of luxury. Then and perhaps only then will Baynard's wife provide a sufficient shock. Placed unexpectedly at the close of the book, she can be vapid in and of herself yet potent enough to evoke memories and resonances from everywhere in England. Her parts are entirely negative, yet she becomes greater than the sum of those parts.

The fact that Mrs. Baynard does draw together so many strands of the novel gives us a further instance of Smollett's achievement. He has dared to set his attack upon luxury in a land where luxury is the rule, the norm. On the most elementary level, five-sixths of the action (measured by the number of pages in the original edition) takes place in degenerate England, where the Bramble party and friends are outnumbered by villains in a ratio of hundreds to one. In power and influence good is easily overwhelmed by evil. Yet while England is dominated by villains, the novel is not. The party moves through pitch but is undefiled. It has many narrow escapes, but always extricates itself. The epistolary technique is essential in this regard. For we cannot look to the intervention of either Defoe's divine providence or Fielding's benevolent, omnipotent narrator. Instead, we watch while credible human beings help one another and at leisure write about their success. Smollett has projected a world in which the personal and the particular virtue of Bramble and his pupils is sufficient to withstand the general wickedness that envelops England.

At the opening of the novel Smollett pits a luxurious England at the peak of its material strength against a Bramble family at its psychological nadir. Faced with such omnivorous vice, Bramble is vexed, Jery callously amused, Liddy bewildered, Tabby and Win beguiled. In rapid succession at Bristol, Bath, and London we learn of other decent families who against their wills are pulled into the vortex or pushed into the hinterlands. Uniting around Bramble, this family will not be drawn or divided. At the close it is bound together as never before. It is moreover trebled in size and worth, having attracted Humphry, Lismahago, the three Dennisons, the Wilsons, Baynard, Miss Willis, and Archy M'Alpin. The family that had been Bramble's bane becomes his blessing, the source of his distress transformed into the spring of his joy—the first he has known in many years.

The political despair with which the novel concludes is thus balanced by the glow of personal renewal. Each positive character has completed a significant rite of passage, has achieved what he most needs, and has vanquished his own peculiar deadly sin. Perhaps to perpetuate his uncle's model pilgrimage, Jery himself appears ready to assume the role of moral guide; at the close of his last letter he offers to lead Phillips in a "scheme of peregrination." For his own part, Bramble covets the heath and hearth of Brambleton Hall, content to leave the fashionable English to "wallow in the mire of their own pollution."

THE STRUCTURE OF
HUMPHRY CLINKER

We have been at court, and 'change, and every where;
and every where we find food for spleen,
and subject for ridicule—Matthew Bramble, June 2

Of the eighty-two letters that make up *Humphry Clinker* Jery writes twenty-eight, Bramble twenty-seven, Liddy eleven, Win ten, and Tabby six. With two-thirds the total number of letters, the men also have seven-eighths the total number of pages; the only substantial letters by the women are three by Liddy. These surface facts suggest in a general way something about the nature of relationships in the novel. If pursued further they disclose part of the reading structure of the book. Jery has no "topics" that are uniquely his own, and his letters are in effect elaborations of Bramble's; Liddy's long letters provide either examples or extensions of her uncle's observations. The Bramble-Jery relationship of judgment and verification can then be traced with other male characters. Upon stopping in England, Bramble the traveler and outsider will characterize the new place, then converse at length with older men who are knowledgeable insiders—like Quin, Heathcote, Bentley, Balderick, Lismahago, Burdock, Baynard, and Dennison—and who confirm with incontestable detail his gravest suspicions. Smollett thus develops the incidents of *Humphry Clinker* in such a way that they constitute both the narrative itself and an attitude toward it, the structure he provides telling us not only what occurs but also how to interpret those occurrences.[1]

As it entered eighteenth-century England, the attack upon luxury possessed a closed, rationalist structure, expressing first principles from which no appeal—no new evidence or alternative interpretation—was possible. Yet over the century, as it grew more political and more closely allied to the genre and techniques of the novel, it also became increasingly empirical. Although some philosophers and theologians continued to pursue the attack by way of assertion and deduction, other writers proceeded by (or at least included a measure of) demonstration. In *Humphry Clinker* rationalist and empirical elements are in nice equilibrium. Political commentary is Smollett's way of describing the civic corruption of England as well as of accounting for its origins. Various characters are likewise led to gloss their own behavior and the workings of the plot. Jery is summarizing for us the effect of the journey upon all the young people of the party when he says, "Without all doubt, the greatest advantage acquired in travelling and perusing mankind in the original, is that of dispelling those shameful clouds that darken the faculties of the mind, preventing it from judging with candour and precision" (JM, October 14). Yet these rationalist devices are not sufficient for Smollett: they yield clarity but not force.

To say that *Humphry Clinker* is the story of an expedition told in letters is to call attention to its balanced elements. On the one hand, Bramble as head of the household sets the pace of the journey, its direction, route, and stopping points. It is at his insistence that the tour is panoramic, international, and comparative. Like Cato, Sallust, and Plutarch, and like Smollett in the *Travels, Present State,* and *Atom,* he demands that nation be judged against nation, people against people, city against country, vice against virtue, and present against past. His control is of itself sufficient to prevent stasis and to insure constant movement from place to place, time to time, and conversation to conversation. His control tells us, moreover, that threats to the family will be short-lived, that respite is always somewhere ahead. On the other hand, Smollett does not content himself with these traditional kinds of movement. By having five writers compose eighty-two letters over a period of about eight months, he multiplies many times the transitions of the novel. Each movement from day to day, style to style, or letter to letter carries the party forward but brings readers to a brief halt; we must pause to reorient ourselves, to recall who is writing, to fit together everything that has gone before. It is as though we were presented with a drama of eighty-two acts in which important action frequently takes place between the acts.

The two previous chapters have indicated some of the rationalist patterns of the novel, the *what* and *to whom* of what happens. The present chapter will concentrate primarily upon the empirical, the *how, when,* and *where.* Every attack upon luxury seeks to reveal a plenary truth: the horror of its nature and the virtual ubiquity of its influence. *Humphry Clinker* accomplishes this end through all the means available to a mature novelist with a consuming interest in the mechanics of human activity. A documentary, encyclopedic quality is present in most of Smollett's writing—as he seeks out how institutions are ordered, how various activities are organized, how people live and move about, how cities get planned and built, how machines are made and operate, what particular jobs actually entail, how influence is generated and diffused, how politicians are selected and corrupted. Converging with his symbolic sense, this inveterate interest in process generates much of the vitality of the novel. As he is fascinated by specific details of how things work, so his symbols are usually of the external or literal variety; that is, he chooses for figurative use people and places that actually exist and that take on a concentration of meaning by means of repetition and accumulation. The one habit will convey how luxury manifests itself, the other how it strikes and spreads its contagion: together they will make the darkness visible. Structurally they also explain why the novel seems obsessed with decadent England. Bramble is in search of peace for himself and protection for his charges, he tells us. Yet for much of the journey he leads them to and through the very heart of chaos and danger. Of course he explains the contradiction in several ways: his family must be case-hardened; no tour would be complete without the great cities; he wishes to visit old friends; and so on. Yet the suspicion persists that while Bramble is fleeing luxury, Smollett is actually pursuing it, searching out its tentacles, its spawn, and its foulings. Like the historians tracing luxury to Eve or Cain or Nero, he seems bent upon exposing the mainspring of evil, the universal villain, the omnipotent conspiracy, the invisible network embracing insolent children, diluted wines, and international commerce. Although there is no single criminal genius presiding over this morass, Bramble is given the task of investigating it thoroughly. His is the hard duty to reveal that the type of generic evil is no longer a fallen woman or a depraved tyrant, but a nondescript mob.[2]

A structure of unfolding demonstration serves to emphasize that luxury is a vice that destroys relationships among men as it destroys less palpable social institutions. It is a matter of integrity with Smollett's positive older males that fashion and misfortune do not change them. They are most themselves when under duress, their steadfastness becoming self-sufficiency, the signal value in the chaos of England. Their struggle—the struggle that brings them alive in the novel—is to keep themselves as they are. Their character is revealed not by inner process but by social and external conflict.

At the beginning of the novel all the letter-writers are testing themselves, each other, their correspondents, and the atmosphere of the spas. At Bristol, their first stopping place, Bramble perceives an air of neglect summarized in the widow and her sickly daughter. When he offers, privately, to relieve their distress, Tabby impugns his motive and deprecates his generosity. The clash between sister and brother reveals the nature of each and confirms Bramble's sense of the place. Jery, who recounts the episode, will not allow Bramble's judgment to be challenged so outrageously and responds on his behalf. By itself a diverting but minor scene, this is actually a small trial drawing together all that has gone before. Inadvertently losing his guise of amused observer, Jery is impelled to enter and judge the altercation, then to revise his estimates of uncle and aunt. The scene has accomplished much in a small compass and will be joined to subsequent scenes by another trial at the next spa.

Its temptations far greater, Bath receives far more attention than Bristol. As English luxury reveals itself more fully, the momentum of the novel gathers, larger challenge calling forth greater response. Here men of worth are sometimes merely ignored, but sometimes actively oppressed. Such distinguished friends of Bramble as Admiral Balderick and Colonel Cockril, "who have acted honourable and distinguished parts on the great theatre," are left to a life of indigence and frustration. They receive none of the distinction and reward their service to the nation merits, for Bath gives her attention only to the frippery and ostentation of new retainers of fortune. To Bramble's disgust and chagrin, men of true worth like Balderick and Cockril—who prepare us for the injustice that has befallen Lismahago—find the city not a haven, but "a stewpan of idleness and insignificance." "They have long left off using the waters, after having experienced their inefficacy. The diversions of the place they are not in a condition to enjoy. How do they make shift to pass their time? In the forenoon, they crawl out to the Rooms or the coffee-house, where they take a hand at whist, or descant upon the General Advertiser; and their evenings they murder in private parties, among peevish invalids, and insipid old women—This is the case with a good number of individuals, whom nature seems to have intended for better purposes" (MB, May 5).

Such scenes provoke Bramble but serve initially as a fillip to his nephew's entertainment. Jery's view of social intercourse at Bath will soon lead to another clash of personalities and judgments, and his pose of mediator will be thrust aside entirely.

> I was extremely diverted, last ball-night, to see the Master of the Ceremonies leading, with great solemnity, to the upper end of the room, an antiquated Abigail, dressed in her lady's cast-clothes; whom he (I suppose) mistook for some countess just arrived at the Bath. The ball was opened by a Scotch lord, with a mulatto heiress from St. Christopher's. . . . I cannot account for my being pleased with these incidents, any other way than by saying, they are truly ridiculous in their own nature, and serve to heighten the humour in the farce of life, which I am determined to enjoy as long as I can. [JM, April 30]

Similarly, he notes, "Another entertainment, peculiar to Bath, arises from the general mixture of all degrees assembled in our public rooms, without distinction of rank or fortune. This is what my uncle reprobates, as a monstrous jumble of heterogeneous principles; a vile mob of noise and impertinence, without decency or subordination. But this chaos is to me a source of infinite amusement." And again, "Those follies, that move my uncle's spleen, excite my laughter." From this divergence a demonstration will issue, as it does every time Bramble and Jery are coequal participants in a scene. It arises from a difference of opinion obvious from the opening of the novel and establishes the ground for all ensuing action. Smollett had begun contriving the situation in Jery's first letter and developed it carefully up to Bath. He gives the young man an air of jejune callousness modified by a sense of fairness: he has his opinion but is willing to have it tested. Already he calls the crowd a chaos and reports his uncle's views at greater length than his own.

> I took the liberty to differ in opinion from Mr. Bramble, when he observed, that the mixture of people in the entertainments of this place was destructive of all order and urbanity; that it rendered the plebeians insufferably arrogant and troublesome, and vulgarized the deportment and sentiments of those who moved in the upper spheres of life. He said, such a preposterous coalition would bring us into contempt with all our neighbors; and was worse, in fact, than debasing the gold coin of the nation. I argued, on the contrary, that those plebeians who discovered such eagerness to imitate the dress and equipage of their superiors, would likewise, in time, adopt their maxims and their manners, be polished by their conversation, and refined by their example. [JM, April 30]

Jery again gives himself the lesser argument, admitting he is "not much conversant in high-life," but insists that the argument be resolved by a "recourse to experience"—exactly the criterion Bramble has been suggesting all along. He recommends the general tea-drinking as an experiment, "no bad way of trying the company's breeding." Bramble and Quin agree to "abide by that experiment" provided they may watch from the safe distance of the gallery.

> The tea-drinking passed as usual; and the company having risen from the tables, were sauntring in groupes, in expectation of the signal for attack, when the bell beginning to ring, they flew with eagerness to the desert, and the whole place was instantly in commotion. There was nothing but justling, scrambling, pulling, snatching, struggling, scolding, and screaming. The nosegays were torn from one another's hands and bosoms; the glasses and china went to wreck; the tables and floor were strewed with comfits. Some cried; some swore; and the tropes and figures of Billingsgate were used without reserve in all their native zest and flavor; nor were those flowers of rhetoric unattended with significant gesticulation. Some snapped their fingers; some forked them out; some clapped their hands, and some their back-sides; at length, they fairly proceeded to pulling caps, and everything seemed to presage a general battle. [JM, April 30]

Smollett underscores the lesson by keeping Bramble's comments to a bare minimum; it will be Jery who will relate the "disgraceful situation" of the assembly, their "absurd deportment" and eventual "mortification." Quin is able to laugh at the result, for he had predicted that the different ranks of society would mix happily no more than "a plate of marmalade would improve a pan of sirreverence." But Bramble is hurt. "He hung his head in manifest chagrin, and seemed to repine at the triumph of his judgment . . . his victory was more complete than he imagined." Although Jery repudiates all of the combatants at the tea-drinking, the only persons he singles out for attention are women, "two amazons who singularized themselves most in the action." He reports: "One was a baroness, and the other, a wealthy knight's dowager." Bramble enforces the point by adding, "'I bless God . . . that Mrs. Tabitha Bramble did not take the field today.'" Jery concedes to avuncular wisdom and agrees that his proposed mixture leads to the disgrace and debasement of all. Never again in the novel will he challenge Bramble.[3]

The conversion of Jery at Bath recalls the events of Bristol and anticipates the lessons of the remainder of the expedition. The tea-drinking approximates the moment of recognition in drama, the point in dialectic when revolutionary change takes place, Jery abandoning his false conception of luxury with the realization that it had always been false. The process of discovery has involved change over time; yet the truth it discovers is changeless and timeless. Both characters are elevated: Jery is shown to have an authentic respect for truth, Bramble a genuine comprehension. The teacher-pupil distinction need no longer be so emphatic. One or more of such trial scenes will occur at every stage, testing the moral atmosphere of the new place, the integrity of new characters, and the triumphs of Bramble's judgment. In London, where virtue is openly attacked, Humphry will be the defendant at several—over his poverty, simplicity, religion, and innocence of robbery. All of these are actual tests except the last, when Clinker appears before an official magistrate, Justice Buzzard. Bramble will try a person only for just cause; English authorities prefer to seek out the patently innocent. Bramble's authority derives from his ability to discover reality. The influence of a Pitt, Newcastle, Wesley, or Buzzard, however, is due to his capacity for compounding error and misunderstanding. True justice survives in England only because private men recognize and dispense it for themselves; the representatives of law and religion are merely agents of luxury and deception. Humphry's experience in London will be repeated by Liddy, as she withdraws her trust from Tabby and Lady Griskin and places it more firmly with Bramble. No one in the novel bests Bramble; Lismahago is able to match him by reiterating his own arguments.

While they teach the young and reveal the honest, scenes of testing also expose the luxurious. From Bristol onward Bramble's senses are an outward monitor to the degeneracy of the age, to be flayed repeatedly until he crosses the Tweed. Compared with other English cities, Hot Well seems mild enough; still, Bramble finds it a place for fools: "the man deserves to be fitted with a cap and bells, who for such a paltry advantage as this spring affords, sacrifices his precious ⁄time, which might be employed in taking more effectual remedies, and exposes himself to the dirt, the stench, the chilling blasts, and perpetual rains, that render this place to me intolerable" (MB, April 20). And where fools reside, knaves will find them out. Here the reigning quack, playing hard upon the gullible, is the notorious Dr. Linden. For Smollett's purposes he is here to be exposed and purged. Bramble has little difficulty accomplishing the former task, telling Linden "with a view to punish this original . . . there was a wart upon his nose, that looked a little suspicious" (JM, April 18—Jery and Bramble again collaborating). Establishing that Linden cannot diagnose, Bramble allows him to show himself that he cannot prescribe. After a night of his own treatment Linden returns with "a considerable inflammation, attended with an enormous swelling; so that when he next appeared his whole face was overshadowed by this tremendous nozzle . . . ludicrous beyond all description." Bramble has thereby demonstrated to all present that the man is not to be trusted with anyone's health. That, however, is but part of Linden's function. He is present also to demonstrate in his own absurd person that charlatans are physically revolting. Hearing complaints of stench from the river, he enters "into a learned investigation of the nature of stink."

> He observed, that stink, or stench, meant no more than a strong impression on the olfactory nerves; and might be applied to substances of the most opposite qualities . . . that individuals differed *toto caelo* in their opinion of smells, which, indeed, was altogether as arbitrary as the opinion of beauty . . . that the Negroes on the coast of Senegal would not touch fish till it was rotten; strong presumptions in favour of what is generally called *stink* . . . that he had reason to believe the stercoraceous flavour, condemned by prejudice as a stink, was, in fact, most agreeable to the organs of smelling; for, that every person who pretended to nauseate the smell of another's excretions, snuffed up his own with particular complacency; for the truth of which he appealed to all the ladies and gentlemen then present: he said, the inhabitants of Madrid and Edinburgh found particular satisfaction in breathing their own atmosphere, which was always impregnated with stercoraceous effluvia . . . he affirmed, the last Grand Duke of Tuscany, of the *Medicis* family, who refined upon sensuality with the spirit of a philosopher, was so delighted with that odour, that he caused the essence of ordure to be extracted, and used it as the most delicious perfume: that he himself, (the doctor) when he happened to be low-spirited, or fatigued with business, found immediate relief and uncommon satisfaction from hanging over the stale contents of a close-stool, while his servant stirred it about under his nose.

With Linden's grotesquerie Smollett demonstrates that luxury is an affront to the senses as well as to the intellect; even the dullest should be repelled. At Bath the demonstration quickens and broadens, as Bramble is attacked through all his senses, and the atmosphere of luxury becomes evident, then oppressive, then horrid. The clamorous mob that crowds into the Pump Room will not be composed of the decent gentry Bramble had expected to find, but of broken-winded landladies, lame brandy-merchants, and paralytic attorneys who give off that "compound of villainous smells" that nauseates all but the degenerate; that is, no one but the Bramble family. The welter of sensory details Smollett provides is seldom gratuitous, for he gives them symbolic weight. Throughout England the simplest acts of everyday living are increasingly hard. Noise prevents conversation and rest, food is insipid or vile, foul odors beset one at every corner. Wines, ales, ciders, and perries are undrinkable. In life as in art England has entered "a degen-erate age, fast sinking into barbarism" (MB, April 28). At each major stopping point on the journey Smollett will insert a catalog of the effects of luxury, since for Jery and Bramble, history, nature, and sense all cry out against it: as Bramble says at Bath, "All these absurdities arise from the general tide of luxury, which hath overspread the nation, and swept away all, even the very dregs of the people."

Bramble describes Bath as he will London: clotted, congested, sickly, and sluggish. The streets are overcrowded with houses, set at odds, "want beauty and proportion." They extend without planning or order, as "growing excrescences" to create new confusion. He sees the city as Rowlandson would later, as a place of permanent disorder, precisely the spa to attract the very dregs of the people: "A national hospital it may be; but one would imagine that none but lunatics are admitted."

> Thus the number of people, and the number of houses continue to increase; and this will ever be the case, till the streams that swell this irresistible torrent of folly and extravagance, shall either be exhausted, or turned into other channels. . . . This, I own, is a subject on which I cannot write with any degree of patience; for the mob is a monster I never could abide, either in its head, tail, midriff, or members: I detest the whole of it, as a mass of igno-rance, presumption, malice, and brutality; and, in this term of reprobation, I include, without respect of rank, station, or quality, all those of both sexes, who affect its manners, and court its so-ciety. [MB, April 23]

The upshot is that Bath too is sinking into barbarism, "the very center of racket and dissipation" and a symbol of "a vile world of fraud and sophistication." All substantial families are forced to flee, "the madness of the times has made the place too hot for them, and they are now obliged to think of other migrations—Some have already fled to the mountains of Wales, and others have retired to Exeter. Thither, no doubt, they will be followed by the flood of luxury and extravagance, which will drive them from place to place to the very Land's End" (MB, May 5). Like a charming actress turned tu'penny whore, the once pleasant resort has been sophisticated by new and fast money. As Bramble has said, England has turned topsy-turvy: the very places people seek out for their health are sinks (and stinks) of disease, founts of infection rather than cure. This combination of luxury and the mob make the city intolerable for decent visitors. What is more, occasional insubordination has now become general usurpation.

Even the wives and daughters of low tradesmen, who, like shovel-nosed sharks, prey upon the blubber of those uncouth whales of fortune, are infected with the same rage of displaying their impor-tance; and the slightest indisposition serves them for a pretext to insist upon being conveyed to Bath, where they may hobble country-dances and cotillons among lordlings, 'squires, counsellors, and clergy. These delicate creatures from Bedfordbury, Butcher-row, Crutched-Friers, and Botolph-lane, cannot breathe in the gross air of the Lower Town, or conform to the vulgar rules of a common lodging-house; the husband, therefore, must provide an entire house, or elegant apartments in the new buildings. [MB, April 23]

Bath is become a mere sink of profligacy and extortion. Every article of house-keeping is raised to an enormous price; a circum-stance no longer to be wondered at, when we know that every petty retainer of fortune piques himself upon keeping a table, and thinks 'tis for the honour of his character to wink at the knavery of his servants, who are in a confederacy with the market-people; and, of consequence, pay whatever they demand. . . . This por-tentous frenzy is become so contagious, that the very rabble and refuse of mankind are infected. [MB, May 5]

The point for Bramble is that there is nowhere to hide from the con-tagion. The momentum of portentous frenzy peaks in the capital with repeated scenes in which revulsion and discovery are inextricably mixed. He prepares for Lewis what he calls a "catalogue of London dainties," which he says could easily "swell into a treatise" were he to partic-ularize every grievance he feels. With a full list of the most abominable foods in the civilized world, he includes the obstacles to a simple night of sleep:

I am pent up in frowzy lodgings, where there is not room enough to swing a cat; and I breathe the steams of endless putrefaction; and these would, undoubtedly, produce a pestilence, if they were not qualified by the gross acid of sea-coal, which is itself a perni-cious nuisance to lungs of any delicacy of texture: but even this boasted corrector cannot prevent those languid, sallow looks, that distinguish the inhabitants of London from those ruddy swains that lead a country-life—I go to bed after mid-night, jaded and restless from the dissipations of the day—I start every hour from my sleep, at the horrid noise of the watchmen bawling the hour through every street, and thundering at every door; a set of useless fellows, who serve no other purpose but that of disturbing the repose of the inhabitants; and by five o'clock I start out of bed, in

> consequence of the still more dreadful alarm made by the country
> carts, the noisy rustics bellowing green pease under my window.
> [MB, June 8]

Actually the situation is far more grave, for in London he cannot summon up adequate personal analogues for the despair to which he is subjected. Here alone on the expedition he finds life utterly contemptible.
Here his bodily pain is greatest and his family circle most vulnerable. At
every hand—in the arts, law, religion, politics, commerce, journalism—he
finds false schemes of "interest and ambition." Once the seat of wisdom and royalty, the jewel of Europe, London is now the *anus mundi.*

In two of the longest letters of the work, Bramble's of May 29 and
June 8, Smollett gives us three aspects of London: as an observed,
historical city; as symbol of a world in decline; and as theme, geographic
locus, source, and agent of that decline. As Rome was to the empire, so
London has become to Britain. In his writings of two decades, Smollett,
with these letters, comes closest to what his student Dickens achieved
in the Court of Chancery in *Bleak House* and Marshalsea prison in *Little
Dorrit:* the realization of a central, unifying emblem for what he
despised in society. On its surface, Bramble's attack is certainly conventional. Luxury had been regarded as the curse of cities from before the
time of Plato, and the association of the two was usual among Roman
writers. Among eighteenth-century English writers, moreover, satires
upon the capital were common, from Swift's two "Descriptions" to
Johnson's "London."[4] Yet, as previous chapters have shown, mid-
century London actually did contain all that the novelist stood against,
and his controversial writings are increasingly preoccupied with uncovering lines of influence within the city. The result in *Humphry Clinker* is
his use of two complementary images, invasion and degradation. London is certainly under attack from without by barbarian hordes, the
indigent poor of the provinces:

> the capital is become an overgrown monster; which, like a dropsical
> head, will in time leave the body and extremities without nourish-
> ment and support. The absurdity will appear in its full force, when
> we consider, that one sixth part of the natives of this whole ex-
> tensive kingdom is crowded within the bills of mortality. What
> wonder that our villages are depopulated, and our farms in want of
> day-labourers? . . . The tide of luxury has swept all the inhabitants
> from the open country—The poorest 'squire, as well as the richest
> peer, must have his house in town, and make a figure with an
> extraordinary number of domestics. The plough-boys, cow-herds,
> and lower hinds, are debauched and seduced by the appearance
> and discourse of those coxcombs in livery, when they make their
> summer excursions. [MB, May 29]

At the same time, it is being subverted by traitors from within, by base men intent upon fouling their own nest.

In these letters Bramble attempts to particularize for Dr. Lewis his charge that the metropolis is the fountainhead of luxury, the spring and channel of contemporary social vice. To a man of sense, it is uninhabitable. It is overcrowded and uncomfortable; all is hurry, noise, and confusion; prices are exorbitant, valuable goods scarce, and food adulterated; merchants are corrupt; the common people are depraved and intolerable; taste and friendship are impossible; necessary social divisions are eroded; women lose all decorum; fashions generally are silly, dress astonishing; crime and sickness spread unabated; servants are bold, greedy, and dishonest; the political situation is vicious and the government in constant danger; and much more. But the virulence of the contagion is such that it will not stop at the city's margins. London's demands for luxury are so voracious that it also despoils the remainder of the nation. The country is bereft of workers; population is falling; the land is stripped of resources; needed horses and cattle are plundered from the farms; small estates are wiped out and worthy men ruined; Scotland is exploited and Wales threatened; the primary virtues, especially subordination, economy, and simplicity, are banished. "There are many causes that contribute to the daily increase of this enormous mass," Bramble writes, "but they may be all resolved into the grand source of luxury and corruption" (MB, May 29). If Bath is a ruined actress, London is a queen grown blind, demented, and incontinent.

Smollett devotes more space to London than to the whole of Scotland. His party has looked into the abyss and his readers have been appalled. After this demonstration of England's decline he is able to resume the theme with allusion and variation. Jery reminds us that the rage of fashion respects no bounds, for "Harrigate treads upon the heels of Bath, in the articles of gaiety and dissipation" (JM, June 23); Bramble with his portrait of Mrs. Burdock testifies that shovel-nosed sharks also travel to northern waters. And Lismahago joins the group eager to discourse on the truth that "'a glut of wealth brings along with it a glut of evils; it brings false taste, false appetite, false wants, profusion, venality, contempt of order, engendering a spirit of licentiousness, insolence, and faction, that keeps the community in continual ferment, and in time destroys all the distinctions of civil society; so that universal anarchy and uproar must ensue'" (MB, September 20). Indeed the example of Mrs. Burdock and the warnings of Lismahago qualify the party's sojourn in idyllic Scotland. Enclosed on one side by Mrs. Burdock and on the other by Lord Oxmington and Mrs. Baynard, the visit to Smollett's homeland is like a holiday in a nostalgic past. Giving the Bramble party a much-needed respite, Smollett uses the Scots lieutenant to recall present economic and political realities. Lismahago holds that as London is plundering the rest of England, so England is plundering Scotland. Since the Union his country has relinquished vital portions of its trade, population, wealth, national resources, self-government, national spirit, and way of life. In return it has received merely a promise of military protection, dubious if not worthless.

Whatever the implications of this relationship, Bramble and his family are permitted to set them aside. To them Scotland is England turned right side up, a haven where relationships are radically altered. Gone are Bramble's pain, asperity, and craving for fellowship. Soon after arriving in Scotland, he finds, "I have met with more kindness, hospitality, and rational entertainment, in a few weeks, than ever I received in any other country during the whole course of my life" (MB, August 8). Where luxury has been withstood, felicity is still possible. North Britain is "the Scotch Arcadia," Edinburgh is "a hot-bed of genius," and the people greet one "not barely with hospitality, but with such marks of cordial affection, as one would wish to find among near relations, after an absence of many years." In answer to the proud Paunceford stands the good Scotsman Captain Brown, an "honest favorite of fortune" who also became wealthy in India. But unlike Paunceford, the captain gratefully returns to his devoted family, showering them with his generosity and moving Bramble (as Jery early said such acts would) to tears of joy (JM, September 12).

The nature of Smollett's demonstration has transformed the historical Scotland into a *paysage moralisé*. Most of the details seem chosen specifically to contrast with English habits. Scottish noblemen, politicians, merchants, professors, lawyers, doctors, farmers, and common people are all the subject of flights of eulogy. Every sign of English decay is here replaced with wholesome growth. Politicians are concerned only with national honor, merchants are restrained and honest, common people submissive, and juries properly constituted. And of course, "Scotch ladies . . . are the best and kindest creatures upon earth" (JM, August 8). Instead of the duplicity of a Justice Buzzard, Scotland offers a "college of justice" of unquestioned integrity. Instead of the churlish literati of London, Bramble finds Scots authors agreeable, instructive, and entertaining. Instead of the clerical drones and hypocrites of Bath and London, the Scottish kirk "abounds at present with ministers celebrated for their learning, and respectable for their moderation" (MB, August 8). A sense of the disparity—in Smollett's efforts as well as in national characteristics—is offered by two of Bramble's descriptions of food and drink, in London and in Cameron. In London, he says,

> If I would drink water, I must quaff the maukish contents of an
> open aqueduct, exposed to all manner of defilement; or swallow

that which comes from the river Thames, impregnated with all the filth of London and Westminster—Human excrement is the least offensive part of the concrete, which is composed of all the drugs, minerals, and poisons, used in mechanics and manufacture, enriched with the putrefying carcases of beasts and men; and mixed with the scourings of all the wash-tubs, kennels, and common sewers, within the bills of mortality.

This is the agreeable potation, extolled by the Londoners, as the finest water in the universe—As to the intoxicating potion, sold for wine, it is a vile, unpalatable, and pernicious sophistication, balderdashed with cyder, corn-spirit, and the juice of sloes. . . . The bread I eat in London, is a deleterious paste, mixed up with chalk, alum, and bone-ashes; insipid to the taste, and destructive to the constitution. The good people are not ignorant of this adulteration; but they prefer it to wholesome bread, because it is whiter than the meal of corn: thus they sacrifice their taste and their health, and the lives of their tender infants, to a most absurd gratification of a mis-judging eye; and the miller, or the baker, is obliged to poison them and their families, in order to live by his profession. The same monstrous depravity appears in their veal, which is bleached by repeated bleedings, and other villainous arts, till there is not a drop of juice left in the body, and the poor animal is paralytic before it dies; so void of all taste, nourishment, and savour, that a man might dine as comfortably on a white fricassee of kid-skin gloves, or chip hats from Leghorn. . . .

Of the fish, I need say nothing in this hot weather, but that it comes sixty, seventy, fourscore, and a hundred miles by landcarriage; a circumstance sufficient, without any comment, to turn a Dutchman's stomach, even if his nose was not saluted in every alley with the sweet flavour of *fresh* mackarel, selling by retail— This is not the season for oysters; nevertheless, it may not be amiss to mention, that the right Colchester are kept in slime-pits, occasionally overflowed by the sea; and that the green colour, so much admired by the voluptuaries of this metropolis, is occasioned by the vitriolic scum, which rises on the surface of the stagnant and stinking water—Our rabbits are bred and fed in the poulterer's cellar, where they have neither air nor exercise, consequently they must be firm in flesh, and delicious in flavour; and there is no game to be had for love or money. [MB, June 8]

To complete his catalog Bramble requires about ten pages of horrors; in Scotland he needs but one succinct paragraph to draw the contrast.

Do you know how we fare in this Scottish paradise? We make

free with our landlord's mutton, which is excellent, his poultry-yard, his garden, his dairy, and his cellar, which are all well stored. We have delicious salmon, pike, trout, perch, par, &c. at the door for the taking. The Frith of Clyde, on the other side of the hill, supplies us with mullet, red and grey, cod, mackarel, whiting, and a variety of sea-fish, including the finest fresh herrings I ever tasted. We have sweet, juicy beef, and tolerable veal, with delicate bread from the little town of Dunbritton; and plenty of partridge, growse, heath-cock, and other game in presents. [MB, September 6]

Bramble and Jery themselves draw one conclusion from such juxtapositions: Scotland represents a better because *older* way of living. Refusing to bend to the blasts of fashion from the south, the people and their institutions have kept fast the best of ancient traditions, remaining hardy and virile. Jery applauds the refusal of the Scots to accept the vices of the English, particularly their retention of "regulations of public and private oeconomy, of business and diversion" (JM, August 8). Bramble admires the Highlands because the "country is amazingly wild. . . . All is sublimity, silence, and solitude," and its men are admirably rugged.

When disciplined, they cannot fail of being excellent soldiers. They do not walk like the generality of mankind, but trot and bounce like deer, as if they moved upon springs . . . they are incredibly abstemious, and patient of hunger and fatigue; so steeled against the weather, that in travelling, even when the ground is covered with snow, they never look for a house, or any other shelter but their plaid, in which they wrap themselves up, and go to sleep under the cope of heaven. Such people, in quality of soldiers, must be invincible. [MB, September 6]

While the unity of the clans is weakened, the strength of the country endures, "founded on hereditary regard and affection, cherished through a long succession of ages." In another scene of sensory demonstration, Jery and Bramble visit the venerable Dougal Campbell in Argyleshire and are delighted by a household that is "equally rough and hospitable, and savours much of the simplicity of ancient times." They are gratified with the best of food, fellowship, music, and other entertainments. With no meddling Mrs. Burdock about to say nay, they are graciously invited to stay the night. They are shown to guest quarters while most of the household retire to beds made of heath. Jery continues, "My uncle and I were indulged with separate chambers and down beds, which we begged to exchange for a layer of heath; and indeed I never slept so much to my satisfaction. It was not only soft and elastic, but the plant, being in flower, diffused an agreeable fragrance, which is wonderfully refreshing and restorative" (JM, September 3).

With Scotland Smollett offers us the simple grandeur of Britain's past, embodied and embraced. (There is of course no room amid such greatness to note the poverty of ordinary Scotsmen.) That past has been in the background throughout, in Bramble's continual reflections upon Brambleton Hall. We need not be shown the estate in Monmouthshire, for we have seen its plenteous image. Scotland is a land of peace and refreshment; Brambleton Hall a retreat beyond retreat, a place of recreation beyond refreshment. Had the novelist sought to emphasize the practicability of an easy return to the past, he might have allowed the party to remain in Scotland or to pass immediately to Wales. Instead he makes Scotland a pivot, not a terminus. His art of contrasts has temporarily balanced Hades with Paradise, but the return journey through hell reminds us that Bramble and his family have not had an escape, merely a holiday. As Pope had it, he who would debase the sons, exalts the sires, and Smollett will balance Dougal Campbell with Oxmington and Mrs. Baynard.[5]

The epitome of Smollett's technical achievement in the novel is his ability successfully to transform matters of mere accidental taste into urgent moral issues. He is able to convince his readers that the bastard tastes of the English middle orders indeed signify falsehood and ignorance in morality, and further that the decline in morality portends the imminent dissolution of British civilization. When Bramble rails against the bleaching of bread, the scandalmongering of the papers, and the promiscuous mixture of classes at Vauxhall, he is particularizing a grievance greater than the sum of its manifestations, a national condition worse than anything he can say about it. And having once demonstrated his lesson, Smollett is able to give it resonance thereafter. After the spas and the capital we assume we have witnessed all possible variants of excess, have numbered all the abominations of desolation. Nevertheless, we are shaken and alarmed as Smollett unfolds the last long episode of the novel.

On September 30, Bramble writes to Lewis that his old friend Baynard is in the country and says, "I would not pass so near his habitation without paying him a visit, though our correspondence had been interrupted for a long course of years." The opportunity to renew his friendship gives Bramble a sense of delightful anticipation: "I felt myself very sensibly affected by the ideas of our past intimacy, as we approached the place where we had spent so many happy days together." Yet before he can set eyes upon his friend, his mood changes from eagerness to apprehension: "but when we arrived at the house, I could not recognize any one of those objects, which had been so deeply impressed upon my remembrance."

> The tall oaks that shaded the avenue, had been cut down, and the iron gates at the end of it removed, together with the high wall that surrounded the court yard. The house itself, which was formerly a convent of Cistercian monks, had a venerable appearance; and along the front that looked into the garden, was a stone gallery, which afforded me many an agreeable walk, when I was disposed to be contemplative—Now the old front is covered with a screen of modern architecture; so that all without is Grecian, and all within Gothic—As for the garden, which was well stocked with the best fruit which England could produce, there is not now the least vestige remaining of trees, walls, or hedges—Nothing appears but a naked circus of loose sand, with a dry bason and a leaden triton in the middle. [MB, September 30]

In six sentences Smollett has unobtrusively recalled the lessons of four hundred pages: the ubiquitous threat of luxury, the huge gulf between Old England and the present age, the internal significance of external signs. (He has also freely translated Horace's famous ode, "Of Luxury.") Although we are alarmed that contemporary degeneracy has encroached even within Bramble's circle, we are not surprised to find that Baynard, though desperate, remains the good, gentle man Bramble knew him to be. The intrusive agent of the changes in his estate—land, health, finances—as well as of his present despondency, is his wife. She *has* ruined her husband, but not in a spirit of gratuitous malice. Rather she had simply indulged herself with the tastes of the times. In place of the best fruit England could produce, middle-class taste has yielded loose sand, a dry bason, and a leaden triton. As the reader's sympathies are engaged in behalf of the unfortunate Baynard, his memory is recalled to Bramble's continuing verdict: "All these absurdities arise from the general tide of luxury, which hath overspread the nation, and swept away all, even the very dregs of the people."

Conclusion

LUXURY AND THE ACHIEVEMENT
OF *HUMPHRY CLINKER*

Examining what he calls the Norman yoke, Christopher Hill provides an apt analogue to the history of luxury. He recalls that the rulers of England had for centuries used the great myths of Western civilization to justify their superiority to an often resentful population. Vigilance was required, however, for the great myths had an unfortunate double-edged quality. They enabled medieval peasant rebels to ask,

> When Adam delved and Eve span
> Who was then the gentleman?

They nonetheless also obliged fourteenth-century bishops to recall the Fall of Man: Paradise could be gained only in heaven, and meanwhile sinfulness justified social inequality and subordination here on earth. When the Levellers asked for the creation of a New Jerusalem, Royalist and Puritan leaders alike spoke of the Tower of Babel—usually with the fall of Athens and Rome added for full measure. In the sixteenth and seventeenth centuries, when reformers insisted upon reclaiming the rights they had lost since the Golden Age, English rulers responded with the myth of primitive Arcadia.[1] For longer than the great myths, the attack upon luxury had served the interests of power and intellect, becoming the vital expression of their impulse to order. Any challenge to the social, political, or economic status quo could be dismissed as by definition a sign of wantonness. If a man wanted something he did not have, or if by chance he got something, he was perforce guilty of luxury. Certainly by the opening of the Christian era, the many different realms of human activity had been comprehended, laws laid down for the basic relationships—between man and woman and within the family, between man and God, and regarding wealth and authority—what the anthropologists term the primal trinity of sex, salvation, and sustenance.

This study has culminated in the attempt to reach and interpret the best-known of Smollett's works by way of some of the least-known. It has sought to understand the novelist's ideas as well as to explain them, to show the relationship that exists among the books of his last two decades, to reveal the personality that informed them, and to analyze that singular blend of genius, talent, and temperament that gives his writing its characteristic value and flavor. At the same time it has tried to be suggestive of an aspect of eighteenth-century thought older, larger, and more portentous than the social and political ideas of a single novelist. Once recognized and understood, Smollett's ideas can be seen to represent the tensions and ambiguities of an important portion of English society. With greater persistence and articulation, the novelist's work reveals the same concentration of attitudes to be found in generations of country gentlemen, politicians, clergymen, courtiers, and writers. What *Humphry Clinker* discloses is not merely a set of ideas, but also a mode or style of thought, a cluster of unspoken philosophic, social values.[2] Intellectually this mode of thought had been at bay from the early 1700s. But because its primary strength was not intellectual, the intellectual challenge was in the short run merely a minor irritation. When the formidable challenges did come—symbolically in 1745, economically in the 1750s, politically from 1763 onward—then the mode of thought clustered about the classical idea of luxury took on the aspect of a besieged garrison. English reformers, with the examples of the American, then French, radicals at hand, discovered that the old myths could be turned against the defenders of traditional privilege, and in 1783 Thomas Spence could claim with confidence that,

> The Golden Age, so fam'd by Men of Yore,
> Shall soon be counted fabulous no more.

Against this New Jerusalem Smollett and many others posed Old England.[3] To give the novelist his place in the currents of English life and thought, however, is in no way to deny the fullness of his achievement in either the nonfictional works or *Humphry Clinker*. Indeed his writings of the 1750s and 1760s in all likelihood represent the single most important body of conservative polemics of his generation. For nearly two decades he had used the classical concept of luxury to express a revulsion against certain aspects of historical change. This sense of the concept, infused into *Humphry Clinker*, was becoming increasingly ineffectual by the time the novel appeared in 1771. It was increasingly difficult, that is, for a ruling elite to demand effort and expansion while simultaneously urging restraint and retrenchment. Even as Smollett was writing in the mid-1760s the contradiction was apparent to many, and the attack upon luxury as a polemic weapon was being turned round by the insurgent middle orders, point blank against its previous aristocratic owners. He and Adam Smith were born but two years and sixty miles apart; yet on this issue they were separated by intellectual continents. In the age of Adam Smith, more nineteenth than eighteenth century, the Aristotelian view of luxury will not hold. When the classical conception was allowed to lapse into obsolescence, so too was the vast intellectual engine that supported it. Spence was premature, and it is too much to say with Burke that Smith had rediscovered God's law. But it is not too much to note that Richard Payne Knight had superseded Xenophon as interpreter of civilized values for Britain. Those values carried with them a tolerance for change and a sense of progress unacceptable to the age of Smollett. They allowed the growth of a different notion of human psychology, in which subjects need no longer be defined entirely by status and function but might be viewed as independent personalities. What had been regarded as devolution might now, under proper circumstances, be seen as evolution: in the lives of human beings, fictional characters, civilizations, and even nature itself. As Ronald Paulson has pointed out, narration now seemed to gain a new sense of purpose, in the pictorial as well as the literary arts.[4] Knight is far better known as the theoretician of the picturesque than as poet of the *Progress of Civil Society;* yet it may be that the two roles are not altogether different.

The attack upon luxury as Smollett used it was well fitted to his social and political pessimism, implicitly containing as it did the notion of a chronologically prior, ideal state. To private men like Bramble, Lismahago, Baynard, and Dennison—without, as the world turns, wealth or power—the struggle to preserve one's character and integrity inevitably led to a poignant sense of loss. To recall the past is not to renew it. Even the happiness of Smollett's ending—in which, to use Paulson's formulation, a missing father is found, lost lovers are united, a paternal estate is reclaimed, and everybody is rewarded—is essentially private and nonsocial. The triple wedding ceremony does not here have the over-tone of universal reconciliation that it has in Shakespeare. Rather, three specific women have subordinated their lives to three particular men; order and reconciliation have been sealed within one family alone. Integrity has not been vindicated in the arena of the great world; it has merely been protected unto another generation. The primary bene-ficiaries and youthful figures of hope—Jery, Liddy and George, Humphry and Win—are nevertheless much more pale and passive in their virtue than their tutors, the aging representatives of an older generation. Though their journey has been long, the young people have rarely earned a positive claim upon our attention. Fielding and Goldsmith use precisely this kind of resolution to express a world of new beginnings and new levels of vitality. Joseph and Fanny, Tom and Sophia, Sir William Thornhill and his Sophia, we must assume, will not permit the vigor of their lives to lapse into rural desuetude. To them the promises of a future England are at least as attractive as the achievements of Old England.

For Smollett the height of these achievements is implied in Bramble-Hall, the hub of the Bramble family's life and the terminus of the party's expedition. Yet in contrast to Paradise Hall or even Grandison Hall, Brambleton Hall is evanescent and abstract. Its characteristics are primarily negative, the negation of those of London. Its air is not pol-luted, its waters not stinking, its paths not clamorous, its veal not blanched, its bread not adulterated, its beer not sophisticated. Smol-lett's vision of genuine worth did not project an *alternative* society—as one in which charity should conquer selfishness. Rather he posited the values of an *earlier* society—one where life was simpler and where order, station, and identity were more firmly established and respected. (It is also, like Brambleton Hall, a world over which Matthew Bramble has undisputed sway.) In this retrospective search for a unified world, a better world we have squandered, *Humphry Clinker* anticipates such works as Carlyle's *Past and Present,* James's *The American Scene,* and Henry Adams's *Mont-Saint-Michel.*

The better world Smollett appealed to is at heart the world of in-herited rights: where the highest ranks of a society have exclusive responsibility for determining the nature of the good, where the laws of nature and the laws of tradition are regarded as synonymous, and where social position fixes one's activities and aspirations. In practice, the ethos of inherited rights was associated with that of inherited wealth, when land was the most important and lucrative real property. But as we have seen, land and the system of thought that supported it had lost their absolute supremacy by the time Smollett had reached his majority. The realities of wealth had changed substantially, and land was in many ways already less profitable than commerce. Mercantile economic theory exhausted itself when its categories of value became incapable of transformation, and the traditional condemnation of luxury degenerated into the scholastic, in the pejorative sense. That at least some educated laymen were aware of these changes in the 1750s is indicated by the essays of Hume and Johnson. Although politically conservative, each was aware that the past could not be preserved intact, that effective conservatism was also selective. Johnson's review of Soame Jenyns is a classic statement of the newer sensibility: the famous passage rejecting the utility of pain and misery indeed represents an almost revolutionary change in English sensibility.

The traditional concept of luxury accepted pain and misery as a permanent feature of the lives of the great majority of humankind. Smollett's attitude toward the English common people likewise carried an acceptance of their suffering and dispossession. His letters, especially those to Alexander Hume Campbell and Caleb Whitefoord, reveal an ardent claim to the rank of gentleman. In this respect he was like Dickens. But whereas Dickens upon attaining fame came increasingly to identify himself with the class below him, Smollett continued to aspire upward, identifying his interests with those of the men he considered the natural leaders of Britain. For most of his life Dickens was financially secure, but to his death Smollett was never so. To the gentlemen Smollett created, luxury is a many-sided threat. With its vulgarity and prostitution luxury undermines grace, hospitality, and fine manners. On a deeper level it directly threatens the material possessions upon which refinement is built. Deeper yet, it attacks the very ground upon which refinement and wealth are based: the ancient principles of necessity and hierarchy, summarized in the supposition that certain people have exclusive claim to the better things of life. It is perhaps one of the larger ironies of English and Scottish literary history that the Whig principles Smollett opposed so long and so vigorously should within the space of two generations stand as the foundation of the Tory Reaction. Smollett might not have noted the essential kinship between Bramble and the hero of the Waverley novels. The insolent Whigs of the City could never gain the breeding Smollett demanded, but they could very soon acquire the property.[5]

The terms of opposition in the novel are thus more varied and comprehensive than the city–country, Whig–Tory, England–Scotland contrasts in which they are usually conceived. Like his creations Bramble, Baynard, and Dennison, Smollett was educated by the city, and his journalistic career of a decade is testimony to the conviction that the future of Britain was to be determined, for good or ill, in the metropolis on the Thames. His tributes to Welsh country life are largely negative, to that of England stock, and to that of Scotland only slightly less perfunctory. What is more, he *does* praise urban life and urban commerce in Scotland, where social controls have not been relaxed. From one point of view the spirit of *Humphry Clinker* could be called Tory. Such a label would be adequate as far as it goes, but it would not go very far at all. For Smollett was interested in partisan politics only as a means, and the *Atom* makes clear that by the end of the 1760s no party or group approached his ideal of virtue. After 1763, it seems, he sought nothing so pedestrian as a new election, but a new and political reformation that would rid Britain root and branch of modernist influences. The spirit he wished to invoke through Bramble was of longer standing even than England. Among the Roman elements of the novel could be counted a reverence for Terminus, the god of bounds whom Ovid praised as the most admirable of Roman deities. It is a work into which he would pour everything of importance, but with every thing in proper place and proportion.

For the purposes of this study, the most significant contrast in *Humphry Clinker* is not between city and country, England and Scotland, or Mrs. Baynard and Mrs. Dennison. Instead it is the contrast between Smollett's own voices in the novel: Bramble and Mr. S——. On June 8 Bramble tells Lewis at great length why he will be pleased to quit London, asking "what is the society of London, that I should be tempted, for its sake, to mortify my senses, and compound with such uncleanness as my soul abhors?" And later, "Thank Heaven! I am not so far sucked into the vortex, but that I can disengage without any great effort of philosophy." Juxtaposed with Bramble's diatribe is Jery's long letter of June 10, in which he describes the obvious satisfaction Mr. S—— derives from life, especially literary life, in the capital. Encircled by entertaining and secretly admiring dependents (but no Mrs. S——), S—— rules benevolently and creates in his home in Chelsea one of the few places of positive value in England. For S—— London is the only possible cantonment, both a universe unto itself and a window from which to view the rest of creation. Smollett is the most urban of the five major novelists of the century—even more so than Defoe or Fielding in *Amelia*—and his final work is more engaged with the characteristics of urban life than any other major novel. If in his last years he should have been of two minds about the city and found means to project both onto the pages of *Humphry Clinker,* we have already seen some of the possible causes for ambivalence. Men of letters like Smollett and Mr. S—— could regard London as their proper habitat, the locus of wit, judgment, culture. Adamant traditionalists like Smollett and Bramble could regard it as barren ground, a once-proud haven ravaged by inferior men who befouled it and opened it to others more wretched than themselves. Charged with the social and intellectual history of its time, Smollett's *summa mundi, Humphry Clinker* summons up inventories of both aspects of the metropolis, perhaps more important to him at the end of his life, when he had abandoned it.

In Smollett the secondary world of imagination is always interpenetrated by the primary world of observation, and at many places in *Humphry Clinker* the two are almost indistinguishable. The commonplace about referential language in the novel takes on a further dimension in his last work. Whereas Fielding seeks to present fictions more complete and satisfying than disorderly reality could ever be, Smollett wishes to compel attention, which can be gained no other way, to the wretched condition of the phenomenal world. It is the difference, in our time, between Ralph Ellison and Richard Wright. Attempting ever to say complicated things straightforwardly, Smollett renders intensity of consciousness differently but no less fully than Sterne. The mediation of his many "originals" like Lismahago and Win works to heighten, not undermine, the seriousness of his moral—anticipating in practice an aesthetic theory that would absorb Dickens's generation. While a virulent attack upon luxury, the novel is framed by the letters of Dustwich and Davis, Tabby and Win. While providing all the refinements of moral judgment called for by Johnson in the *Rambler* no. 4, it also satisfies the demands of travel narrative, burlesque, domestic comedy, social satire, and comic romance. While written by a weakened, disappointed, dying man, it exudes vigor, vitality, and unquenchable spirit. While a portrait of social tragedy, it has for generations seemed one of the brightest of English comedies. While centered on the sensibility of a single character, it possesses the largest cast of memorable figures between Fielding and Dickens.

Smollett, it seems, was like his seasoned men, most himself when under duress, his gifts of fancy most engaged when most required. A mixture of the Rabelaisian and the rabbinical, he was prepared equally to laugh or to shame people free of what he considered absurd infatuations. In the course of the novel his gifts serve complementary functions: to expose injustice and to raise laughter. The scenes of England he gives us are disturbing and demoralizing; yet the retributive comedy he supplies is stabilizing, rejuvenating. It carries respite from the outrage of very real grievance. At Bath, for example, Bramble is mortified to find three of his old friends—Rear-Admiral Balderick, Colonel Cockril, and Sir Reginald Bentley—reduced to shells of men, overtopped by mere upstarts, and left to a cold day's dying. Yet our indignation at these injustices is controlled by a scene in immediate counterpoint. In the general tea-drinking at Bath, we are shown that upstarts and pretenders to fortune are shabby and disgraceful, sufficiently punished by their own absurdity. Instances of personal injustice abound in Smollett's narrative. Dr. Linden imposes his pretentious nonsense upon the gullible at Hot Well. Tabby mistrusts her brother's goodness to the mother at Bath and to the foundling, Humphry Clinker. Mrs. Burdock and her son attempt to have the squire needlessly trepanned. Micklewhimmen, the Scots lawyer, delights in gross and dangerous practical jokes. Dutton seeks to entice Win from Humphry. Lord Oxmington and his lackeys seek gratuitously to humiliate Bramble and Lismahago. Although each of these incidents reflects the overarching callousness and deceit obtaining in Britain, each is resolved in a fresh gust of retributive laughter.

As the earlier *Briton* and *Travels* attest, Smollett's years of writing against the progress of national luxury provided him with abundant insight into the luxurious person as comic type. In *Humphry Clinker* observation and facility yielded a deftness of touch able to mark age, rank, and disposition in a few strokes of concentrated detail. He is able in one short scene to convince us that Newcastle is indeed a senile old fool and a political liability for any age—everything, that is, that Bramble has said he is. The reader is left more in wonder than resentment that the old duke should ever have held great power. Smollett's humor has therefore fulfilled its social function. The degeneration of his contemporaries has been rendered more visible by his skill and fancy. The fruits of luxury are shown to be absurd, and the absurd ought to be laughed at. Smollett's laughter is cathartic: it furnishes a release from the strains of living in a decadent society. Its audience is taught to distinguish the plate of marmalade from the pan of sirreverence, to honor the one and disdain the other. As tragedy and comedy are not actual opposites, so the deep disgust of the *Atom* is not antithetical to the hearty humor of *Humphry Clinker:* they are two sides of one coin.

Appendix

THE *BRITON* NO. 26

20 November 1762

The sauciness of servants is now become an epidemical evil. Go where you will, you hear nothing but complaints of them: but methinks, the case of one Mr. Fitz-George deserves particular notice and commiseration. This young gentleman, it seems, came to the possession of a plentiful estate, about two years ago, by the death of his grandfather. Being a humane, generous, good-natured man, he suffered most of the servants who were in the house in his grandfather's time to continue; and as for the few whom he found it prudent to part with, he gave them pensions for life. Mr. Fitz-George enjoyed his house and family with great peace and comfort for about a twelve-month, when one Will Pitot (for so I think they called him by way of nickname) gave his master warning in a great passion. People were very much surprised at this as they knew Will had had a very good place of it. But Will himself soon unfolded the mystery, by publishing a letter, in which he told us, that he had given his master warning, because he was not allowed to rule his master and the whole house. Many of the tenants of the manor were not sorry for

Will's leaving his place; for they say, that though he had been very zealous in maintaining the rights of the manor, yet he had such a number of over-seas acquaintances, to whom he sent presents out of the manor, that he some years laid out the whole rents upon them, which were about six millions. This the tenants murmured at very much; for in consequence of this, their Lord was obliged to raise their rents every year to maintain his house, and supply the exigencies of the manor, even to the amount, they say, of twelve millions a year sometimes. This they reckoned very hard, as they had nothing to do with, nor received any advantage by, these acquaintances of Will's. And this they looked upon as the more unaccountable still, because Will, when he was an out-door servant, had exclaimed most bitterly against the servants before him, who had followed these practices, though they had never spent the half of the money upon their foreign acquaintances, that Will did upon his. But what provoked them most of all was, that they had helped Will to the place, merely with a view that he might break the neck of these things; and then they found, that instead of this, he increased them. But Will was a strange sort of fellow, and had got some peculiar notions of oeconomicks; for what was wrong when done by another, he thought right when done by himself. Nay, when he heard some whispers through the manor with respect to these things, after he left his place, he told the tenants in the letter already mentioned, that indeed he should give himself no trouble to sollicit the return of their favour. This they considered as worse than all the rest, first to deceive them, and then to bid them defiance; but Will knew what he was saying, for, he had somehow or other, got an annuity for three lives.

Things continued in this posture about half a year, when another servant, who had lived long in the house, and been kindly used, I think his name was Tom Give-place, or Buy-vote, I don't know which, took it into his head to give his master warning also, unless he would double his wages. This was thought to be a very odd proposal, as Tom was now far advanced in years, and almost past his labour. The case, it seems, was this; money was wanted in the office to which Tom belonged; application was made to Mr. Fitz-George for it. He asked how much would do for such a time. Tom answered two millions. Mr. Fitz-George (as the money was to be raised upon his tenants) was willing to be as gentle to them as possible; he therefore asked some of his other servants, whether a less sum would not suffice; they replied, that, considering the burden the tenants had lain under for a great while, they thought one million was as much as they could in conscience demand of them, and that, with good management, would do very well; or if it would not hold out till the time proposed, their Lord might make a second demand when it was found necessary. Tom, taking this much amiss, left his place. Upon this, a great many of the out-door servants, raised a clamour, as they had done in Will's case before. The reason was, that Will had often cajoled some of them by saying, he liked their livery, *viz.* an alderman's-gown, better than his own, tho' he only played on them; so Tom had often employed others of them in jobbs about the house, for which he had every now and then given them a bit of a sop. This they were afraid they would now lose, and therefore mouth'd very undeservedly both against the master and the new servant he put in Tom's place. They objected that he was a stranger, though both he and his progenitors had belonged to the manor for several centuries; and long before some of themselves were so much as heard of in it. When this could not be denied, they then urged that he was however born on the northern part of the manor, and themselves in the southern or western; to this it was rationally enough answered, that the northern part belonged to the manor as well as the southern; and to prevent all objections of that kind for the future, proposed that the manor-house should be built exactly in the middle of the estate, and then the tenants would be all equally near it, according to their respective divisions. When they found therefore that these objections were treated only with ridicule by the opposite party, and people who had taken no side, they then trumped up a story, that he was not qualified for the place, because he did not know the way of the house. To this it was replied, If they meant the former way of it, they were undoubtedly right; for it was allowed, that formerly there had been a great deal of waste and profusion in it; but if they meant a way which would be most advantageous, both to the master and the tenants, they were mistaken, for he understood that as well as any man; and as a proof of it, they urged, that it was now plain from fact, that he had done the same service for one million, for which Tom (as mentioned above) had demanded two. This new servant's name, I find, was Jack Scot, and related, they say, to Mr. Fitz-George's family. This fellow, it seems, had been much addicted to reading, which gave him something of the college, together with the court air. However, it made him master of a good deal of polite and useful literature, which afforded a handle to some to upbraid him with learned disquisitions upon cockle-shells, plants and flowers: and others, whose genius could not soar so high as this happy flight, came nevertheless very near it, by the curious invention of the name Jack-a-boot, which, it seems, they struck out by an uncommon effort of wit, from a titular name his family had long borne.

All these objections operated wonderfully upon many sensible people, both without and within the house; for one Harry Chamberman soon after gave his master warning likewise. Harry, we hear, had absented himself from his service for some time past; his master advertised him twice, but to no effect. However, whether of his own accord, or in consequence of a third advertisement, is not material, Harry did return; but it appears it was not to ask his master's pardon, or to apologize for what he had done, but to let him know he would serve him no longer. So Harry gave up his livery, and after dining with an old acquaintance, viz. Tom Give-place, went down to his friends in the country. In consequence of this, one Charley Check, whose business in the house was to see that the cooks, and other servants, put nothing to waste, gave Mr. Fitz-George warning also; the reason, they say, was not want of victuals, ill-paid wages, or being over-wrought, but that, being a relation of Harry Chamberman's, he would not stay in the house after he was gone. The same, we hear, was the case of one Peter Post-boy. His office was to carry his master's letters to and fro; but tho' his master paid him very liberally for it, kept him always in good livery, and never made him go in dark nights, yet he has given him warning too. Such is the way this young gentleman has been used by his servants; so that people of lower rank need not wonder if they are ill-used by theirs. Which of them have taken the example of the other, I cannot tell; but as to the designs of Mr. Fitz-George's servants in acting so, people seem to be universally agreed, that they want to force every body else out of the house, and to have the whole of it to themselves, and such as they shall put it. Whether Mr. Fitz-George will thus give up his house to them or no, no body as yet pretends to say. Many of the tenants heartily wish he would not; for they think it is a shame they should be so presumptuous: but however these things may be, there are two or three foolish curs, commonly called Monitor, North-Briton, Patriot, &c. but I understand their true name is Yelper, and all of one litter, who post themselves in dark corners, and snarl in an angry manner, both at Mr. Fitz-George, and his new servants, whenever they pass by; but when any of the old ones happen to come in their way they fawn, and lick their feet most wishfully, particularly Will Pitot's, tho' he has been longest out of the house. Whether Will had been kind to them while he was in it, by throwing them a little bone now and then, or whether they wanted to bespeak his favour beforehand, in case he should chance to come into it again, or whether they had something of an inbred antipathy against Scot, can't be certainly determined. Some are of opinion that there is a mixture of all three: be that as it will, Mr. Fitz-George and his servants, have hitherto gone out and in about their business, without taking any notice of them, because, I suppose, they don't think them worth their while.

This is the best and fullest account I can give you of this matter at present; but if you want further information about it, perhaps one

Charles Say, a news-man, or his eldest brother, may be able to satisfy you. These gentlemen have generally very early intelligence, with respect to what passes in Mr. Fitz-George's family, and one of them let us know the other day, that there is talk of seventeen more of that gentleman's servants going to give him warning. Whether this is true or false, time only can discover. But it is thought, if they should do so, Mr. Fitz-George will be in no difficulty to supply their places, as there are many in all parts of the manor who would be glad to serve him.

NOTES

INTRODUCTION

1. See, for example, the articles on luxury in the *Encyclopedia of Religion and Ethics,* ed. James Hastings (New York, 1916); *Encyclopedia of Social Sciences,* ed. E. R. A. Seligman (New York, 1954–59); *International Encyclopedia of the Social Sciences,* ed. David L. Sills (New York, 1968); *Dictionary of the History of Ideas,* ed. Philip P. Wiener (New York, 1973); and *Encyclopedia Britannica,* 15th ed. (Chicago, 1974).

2. In addition, he produced a seven-volume edition, *Compendium of Authentic and Entertaining Voyages,* in 1756, and a thirty-five-volume English edition of the works of Voltaire in 1765.

3. Roger Ascham, *The Whole Works of Roger Ascham,* ed. J. A. Giles (London, 1864), 3:153, 159. The discussion of luxury appears in 3:148–67.

4. Henry Fielding, *Enquiry into the Cause of the late Increase of Robbers* (London, 1751), p. 3.

5. Since 1800 approximately four hundred books and articles have appeared that discuss luxury in one connection or another. The usual context is of course the history of Rome. Three examples will suffice. Morris Bishop recounts the traditional causes assigned for the fall of Rome, among them "the moral answer: license, luxury, a decline in character and in discipline" (*The Middle Ages* [New York, 1970], p. 3). Crane Brinton provides a list of the ordinary daily luxuries of wealthy Romans: boasting, gambling, gluttony, drunkenness, sexual license, ostentatious display, and conspicuous consumption (*A History of Western Morals* [New York, 1959], pp. 114–17). W. E. H. Lecky, on the other hand, emphasizes the more extraordinary luxuries: the mutilation and crucifixation of house slaves to gratify the sadism of guests (*History of European Morals from Augustus to Charlemagne,* 3d ed. [1889; reprinted New York, 1955], 1:302–3). Even so profound a classical scholar—and one to whom I am in so great debt—as M. I. Finley conceives of luxury in modern terms. See his *Ancient Economy* (Berkeley and Los Angeles, 1973), e.g., p. 60. And to note that this conception is not limited to the world of

English-speaking scholars, see Paul Louis, *Ancient Rome at Work: An Economic History of Rome from the Origins to the Empire,* trans. E. B. F. Wareing (1929; reprinted London, 1965), pp. 126–30, 234–36. Some of the major works of scholarship on Rome argue with ample documentation that early views of Roman luxury are absurdly exaggerated. That is, they contest the conventional estimate but not the conventional definition of luxury. Among these are Ludwig Friedlander, *Roman Life and Manners under the Early Empire,* trans. J. H. Freese (1909; reprinted New York, 1968), 2:131–230; J. E. Sandys, *A History of Classical Scholarship,* 3rd ed. (Cambridge, 1920), esp. vols. 1 and 2; M. Rostovtzeff, *The Social and Economic History of the Hellenistic World,* 3 vols. (Oxford, 1941), passim; and Theodor Mommsen, *The History of Rome,* trans. William Purdie Dickson, 5 vols. (New York, 1900), passim.

Economic studies that use luxury to mean exorbitant spending are represented by E. J. Urwick, *Luxury and the Waste of Life* (London, 1908); R. I. MacBride, *Luxury as a Social Standard* (New York, 1915); Werner Sombart, *Luxury and Capitalism* (German ed., 1913), trans. W. R. Dittmar (Ann Arbor, 1967); and Emile De Laveleye, *Luxury* (London, 1891). Only two studies have attempted to view the concept historically—one directly, the other obliquely—and both assume the modern definition. H. Baudrillart, in his four-volume *Histoire du luxe privé et public, depuis l'antiquité jusqu'à nos jours,* 2d ed. (Paris, 1880–81), provides an informal but wide-ranging survey of ostentation in food, dress, building, and domestic arrangements. He finds the sources of luxury in the universal traits of vanity and sensuality. The controversy over it he discovers in the tension between two schools of ethical theory. One, typified by Rousseau, would prohibit all ostentation on moral grounds; the other, represented by Voltaire, would encourage it on economic grounds. By the final volume his historical goal is clear: he seeks to account for the French Revolution by contrasting the private opulence of eighteenth-century France with its public squalor. In *Primitivism and Related Ideas in Antiquity* (Baltimore, 1935), Arthur O. Lovejoy and George Boas note luxury several times as one of the ideas related to their central concern. Regarding primitivism they do proceed sensitively and historically. But they are committed to the search for but *one* unknown and therefore are impelled to treat luxury logically, as at all times and in all places the obverse of primitivism. They are unable with such an approach even to hint at the religious and political dimensions of luxury.

6. Even within the limited context of a single century, estimates of its significance vary widely. Leslie Stephen writes, "The cant of the day used the phrase 'luxury,' and luxury was admitted on all hands, to consist in a departure from the simplicity of nature" (*History of English Thought in the Eighteenth Century,* 3d ed., 2 vols. [London, 1902], chap. 10, 69). Duncan Forbes calls luxury one of the most familiar clichés of the time (introduction to Adam Ferguson, *An Essay on the History of Civil Society* [Edinburgh, 1966], p. xxxi). Hume's biographer, Ernest C. Mossner, takes it to mean simple consumption (*Life of David Hume* [Austin, Tex., 1954], p. 270). Maynard Mack, in *The Poet and the City* (Toronto, 1969), p. 199 n, uses it as nearly synonymous with greed. James William Johnson terms it "economic prosperity and cultural affluence" in *The Formation of English Neo-Classical Thought* (Princeton, 1967), p. 48. See also F. B. Kaye's introduction to *The Fable of the Bees* (Oxford, 1924), 1:xciv–xcvii; and Susie I. Tucker, *Protean Shape* (London, 1967), esp. pp. 82–83, 137–69.

Those studies that mention or discuss the concept with most respect tend to do so within narrow and specialized limits: as in studies of population, crime, European trade, mercantile theory, the decline of religion, the development of law, and the position of the laborer. Among the more prominent examples are: J. H. Plumb, *The Growth of Political Stability in England, 1675–1725* (London, 1967); Elizabeth Gilboy, *Wages in Eighteenth Century England* (Cambridge, Mass., 1934); André Morizé, *L'apologie du luxe au XVIIIe siècle* (Paris, 1909); Edgar Furniss, *The Position of the Laborer in a System of Nationalism* (New York, 1920); Jacob Viner, *Studies in the Theory of International Trade* (London, 1937); Eli Heckscher, *Mercantilism,* trans. Mendel Shapiro, 2d ed. 2 vols. (London, 1955); E. A. J. Johnson, *Predecessors of Adam Smith* (New York, 1937); Philip Buck, *The Politics of Mercantilism* (New York, 1942); and A. W. Coats, "Changing Attitudes to Labour in the Mid-Eighteenth Century," *Economic History Review,* 2d ser., 11 (1958–59): 35–51. The one paragraph M. Dorothy George devotes to the idea in *London Life in the Eighteenth Century* (London, 1925), p. 14, is representative of the approach of such studies and also to the broadest generalization available:

Then, there was in the latter part of the eighteenth century, as in most times of social change, a general cry of national deterioration. This is based largely on two ideas, one, the terrible effects of increasing luxury, as seen for instance, in the nabob, or the lamplighter with silk stockings or the labourer's family consuming tea and sugar. The other is the decline of what Defoe called the Great Law of Subordination, a theory of course much stimulated by the fears of Jacobinism roused by the French Revolution. Though connected with opposite schools of thought, the two ideas merged; the well-dressed lamplighter for instance might be regarded as a symbol of either of the two great causes of degeneration.

A few studies of Smollett have noted his use of the concept, but usually in passing. Like most recent scholars, M. A. Goldberg follows Lovejoy and Boas in regarding luxury as the antithesis of primitivism. In *Smollett and the Scottish School* (Albuquerque, 1959), pp. 146–53, Goldberg associates the novelist with the moderate reformers Kames, Robertson, Ferguson, and others. Taking a different tack, David Bruce (*Radical Dr. Smollett* [New York, 1964], pp. 111–14) sees Smollett's opinions as those of a Radical Whig but offers no evidence. The most perceptive commentary appears in Byron Gassman, "The Background of Tobias Smollett's *The Expedition of Humphry Clinker*," diss., University of Chicago, 1960, p. 68. Gassman argues that Smollett's use of luxury is part of a pastoral tradition of opposition between city and country, a tradition that includes Pope, Fielding, and Goldsmith as well as Smollett. This approach reveals some notable similarities among literary figures but leaves the novel unrelated to Smollett's previous writings and to the social and political history of which they are a significant part. Finally, Lewis Knapp and André Parreaux follow Gassman in their respective introductions to the novel. Parreaux contrasts Bramble's "town grievances" with his "country comforts" (introduction to *The Expedition of Humphry Clinker* [Boston, 1968], pp. xxv–xxvi). And Knapp writes, "Another seemingly personal motif in *Humphry Clinker* is a strong love of the virtues of country life as opposed to the socially corrupting luxury and affluence of urban existence" (introduction to *The Expedition of Humphry Clinker* [New York, 1966], p. xiv).

7. Herbert Read, "Tobias Smollett," in his *Reason and Romanticism* (London, 1926), p. 192.

8. James L. Clifford, introduction to *The Adventures of Peregrine Pickle* (London, 1964), pp. xxviii–xxix.

9. Alan D. McKillop, *The Early Masters of English Fiction* (Lawrence, Kans., 1956), pp. 174–75.

10. W. H. Auden, *Forewords and Afterwords* (New York, 1973), p. 111.

11. This distinction has been made many times—to cite only works from this century—from Leslie Stephen's *English Literature and Society in the Eighteenth Century* (London, 1904) to Walter Jackson Bate's *From Classic to Romantic* (Cambridge, Mass., 1946) and Peter Gay's *The Enlightenment: An Interpretation*, 2 vols. (New York, 1966, 1969).

12. Also according to Johnson, the artist was "the interpreter of Nature and the legislator of mankind" who would preside "over the thoughts and manners of future generations" and "superintend the taste and Morals of Mankind." Johnson's emphasis upon the moral and the general is familiar to students of the century and is treated at length in René Wellek, *A History of Modern Criticism* (New Haven, 1955), 1:79–104; Bate, *The Achievement of Samuel Johnson* (New York, 1955); Jean H. Hagstrum, *Samuel Johnson's Literary Criticism* (Chicago, 1952); and Paul Fussell, *Samuel Johnson and the Life of Writing* (New York, 1971).

13. Jacob Viner, "Satire and Economics in the Augustan Age of Satire," in *The Augustan Milieu: Essays Presented to Louis A. Landa*, ed. Henry Knight Miller, Eric Rothstein, and G. S. Rousseau (Oxford, 1970), p. 86; see also pp. 87, 90–101.

14. Reviewing Viner's essay, Bernhard Fabian notes that at present eighteenth-century scholarship cannot explain the phenomena Viner discloses. He says further, "What is alarming about Viner's statements is that in the face of so much scholarship on satire he should find the satiric territory inadequately mapped by the literary historian and, moreover, many modern studies so esoteric as to be of limited value" (*ECS* 7 [1973–74]: 114).

15. Most literary studies of Smollett are silent on this period. The exacting ones are Gassman, "*The Briton* and *Humphry Clinker*," *SEL* 3 (1963): 397–414; and Robert Donald Spector, *English Literary Periodicals* (The Hague, 1966), pp. 95–99. For the remainder, Knapp, Fred W. Boege, and McKillop are representative. In his biography *Tobias Smollett, Doctor of Men and*

Manners (Princeton, 1949), p. 245, Knapp passes over the *Briton* as so much "vexation and drudgery" for which Smollett "was temperamentally unfitted." Boege writes: "Of Smollett's next literary undertakings, the editing of the *British Magazine* and the *Briton*, little needs to be said. The first seems to have gained him a firm friend in Goldsmith . . . the second cost him a good friend, John Wilkes, and his affiliation with Bute's administration was surely not designed to make him more popular. But his unhappy venture into political journalism had no direct effect on the fortunes of his novels" (*Smollett's Reputation as a Novelist* [Princeton, 1947], p. 23). McKillop states the conventional opinion in one sentence: "He was unfortunately involved in politics, and published the *Briton* (1762-63) in support of Bute's administration" (*Early Masters*, pp. 174-75).

It is true that at least twice in the late 1760s Smollett did complain of his earlier polemical efforts; yet his regret was, I believe, directed not toward the labor itself but toward its hostile reception. In any case, my argument is that, fortunate or not, he had been involved in politics long before 1762, and that social and political themes preoccupied his writings for most of the last two decades of his life. See his letter to William Hunter, 24 February 1767, in *Letters*, ed. Knapp (Oxford, 1970), pp. 132-33.

16. This is the view expressed in almost all histories of the novel; it can be traced from Thackeray through Saintsbury, Wilbur L. Cross, and Ernest A. Baker to Walter Allen, Lionel Stevenson, and others. It also informs the more specialized studies of Knapp, Parreaux, and McKillop. The most important demurrer is Paul-Gabriel Boucé, *Les romans de Smollett* (Paris, 1971), pp. 248-98.

17. Read, *Reason and Romanticism*, p. 192.

18. *Whitehall Evening-Post*, 15-18 June, 18-20 June, 22-25 June 1771; *Town and Country Magazine* 3 (1771): 317, 319, 327; the *Weekly Magazine; or, Edinburgh Amusement* 13 (1771): 76, 105, 272; *Edinburgh Advertiser*, 9-12 July, 16-19 July, 22-25 October 1771; *Hibernian Magazine* 1 (1771): 324.

19. *Universal Magazine of Knowledge and Pleasure* 49 (1771): 256; *Gentleman's Magazine* 40 (1771): 317.

20. Jonathan D. Culler, *Structuralist Poetics: Structuralism, Linguistics and the Study of Literature* (Ithaca, 1975), pp. 189-238, esp. pp. 192-93. The antiformalist position is stated more emphatically by David Caute throughout his *The Illusion: An Essay on Politics, Theatre and the Novel* (London, 1971), esp. pp. 23-25, 241-67. Caute holds that "the novel remains to this day an extremely fluid, open-ended literary form, sharing a lot and borrowing a lot from history, biography, philosophy, journalism, as well as other art forms like the drama and the cinema. This whore-like, open-legged personality is both a charm and a virtue of the novel; but the illusionists, the refiners and polishers, the magicians and conjurors, the mimetic realists and the salesmen of empathy, the hidden Gods—they would all have us believe that our coarse and rugged courtesan is in fact a porcelain princess without debts or duties" (pp. 264-65).

21. Ezra Pound, *How to Read* (1931; reprinted New York, 1971), p. 22.

22. This middle ground is coincident with Smollett's attitudes toward government and the desired organization of English society. Hence in chapters 4-6 I attempt a tentative outline of his political view during the final portion of his career. Such an outline, however incomplete, is needed because of a persistent confusion over his political ideas and because of the integral relationship between them and his concept of luxury.

As a sampling of comments on Smollett's political position, the following are notable and representative: (1) Smollett himself, writing of his labors on the *Complete History*, said, "I have kept myself independent of all Connexions which might have affected the Candour of my Intention . . . I have cultivated no Party." The statement appeared in a letter to William Huggins and is quoted in L. F. Powell, "William Huggins and Tobias Smollett," *MP* 34 (1936): 185. (2) The *Critical Review*, 6 (September 1758): 226-39, repeatedly asserts that the novelist is attached to neither party and is independent of both. (3) Scott, in his *Lives of Eminent Novelists and Dramatists* (London, n.d.), pp. 451-52, calls Smollett a moderate Tory and a monarchist. (4) Saintsbury, in his introduction to *Sir Launcelot Greaves* (London, 1895), calls him a Whig; but in the introduction to *Peregrine Pickle* in the same edition he says he has a Tory bent. (5) In his *Autobiography* (Edinburgh, 1860), p. 191, Alexander Carlyle says Smollett was unmistakably a Tory. (6) Thomas Seccombe, in his edition of the *Works* (Westminster,

1899–1901), 12:xiv, writes, "Smollett is clearly a political Ishmael, who has severed his ties with all parties." (7) Louis L. Martz, *Later Career of Tobias Smollett* (New Haven, 1942), p. 131, implies that he was politically ambivalent if not uncommitted. (8) In his biography, *Tobias Smollett,* pp. 303–4, Knapp holds that Smollett began the *Complete History* as a Whig but converted to the Tory point of view as he began to uncover the corruption of earlier Whig ministries. This contention is repeated in Laurence Brander, *Tobias Smollett* (London, 1951), p. 9; and Robert Gorham Davis's introduction to *Humphry Clinker* (New York, 1952), p. xv. (9) Goldberg opens his book, p. 3, with the assertion, "Smollett's political position is equally ambiguous and contradictory." (10) Bruce, throughout his book, finds the novelist's position to be that of a radical Whig. (11) Robert Donald Spector, in *Tobias Smollett* (New York, 1968), pp. 29, 33, finds him a conservative Tory. (12) Boucé (p. 50) notes the reception of his histories: "Ses critiques lui reprochaient une certaine partialité pour les "Tories," sa haine des "Whigs" et ses tendances jacobites."

23. Barbara Hardy, *The Exposure of Luxury: Radical Themes in Thackeray* (London, 1972). Significantly for my argument, Hardy does not attempt to define luxury but cites its usual associations in Thackeray: "rank, class, trade, commerce, money, insincerity and artifice, the corruptions of hospitality, fellowship and love . . . corrupt relations and values shown in object-worship and conspicuous consumption" (pp. 13–14). That is, while assuming a meaning quite different from Smollett's, Thackeray in the nineteenth century and Hardy in the twentieth use the same method of discussion—association—as Smollett used in the eighteenth.

24. William Makepeace Thackeray, *The Four Georges* (London, 1901), p. 63. Future references to this work will be to the same edition and will be given in the text.

25. Thackeray here tends to support one of Smollett's main contentions but contests another. While the latter may have agreed that the eighteenth century as a whole was probably the last period of patrician dominance, he would have said that his own lifetime—four-fifths of which coincided with the reign of George II—marked the time of visible vulgarization of English life.

CHAPTER ONE

1. Robert Graves and Raphael Patai, *Hebrew Myths: The Book of Genesis* (1963; reprinted New York, 1966), pp. 70–81; Louis Ginzberg, *The Legends of the Jews,* trans. Henrietta Szold (Philadelphia, 1909), 1:64–83; John Skinner, *A Critical and Exigetical Commentary on Genesis* (New York, 1900); Gerhard von Rad, *Genesis, A Commentary,* trans. John H. Marks (Philadelphia, 1961). A general treatment of women as tempter-victim is contained in H. R. Hays, *The Dangerous Sex: The Myth of Feminine Evil* (New York, 1964). More specialized are two works by Joseph Epstein: *Marriage Laws in the Bible and Talmud* (Cambridge, Mass., 1942), and *Sex Laws and Customs in Judaism* (New York, 1948); and J. J. Bachofen, *Myth, Religion and Mother Right,* trans. Ralph Manheim (Princeton, 1967). The belief in "Eve's curse" can be observed in a chronological and intellectual spectrum ranging from ancient Jewish law to the code of contemporary pimps. According to the latter, Adam was not the first man, but the first *trick* or fool; and women must continually be regulated by physical force. See Christina and Richard Milner, *Black Players: The Secret Life of Black Pimps* (Boston, 1972), chap. 6.

2. To understand the Hebrew conception of history I have drawn upon George W. Anderson, *The History and Religion of Israel* (London, 1966); C. F. North, *The Old Testament Interpretation of History* (London, 1946); and especially Johannes Pedersen, *Israel: Its Life and Culture,* 2 vols. (London, 1954). For Calvin and other later commentators, another basic text for the condemnation of luxury was Isaiah 2; see *Calvin: Commentaries,* trans. Joseph Haroutunian (Philadelphia, 1958), pp. 350–51.

The Deuteronomic sense of accursedness was often transposed to seventeenth- and eighteenth-century England and was caught well in Dryden's *Absalom and Achitophel* (1681):

The sober part of Israel, free from stain,
Well knew the value of a peaceful reign;
And, looking backward with a wise affright,
Saw seams of wounds, dishonest to the sight:

In Contemplation of whose ugly scars
They curs'd the memory of civil wars. [11.154–59]

3. 1 Sam. 12:21–25. This and all further quotations from the Bible are drawn from the King James Version; future citations will be given in the text. A comparable message is contained in Deut. 17:14–20.

4. The eighteenth-century English conception of luxury of course derives from later Roman and Christian commentary. There are nevertheless dozens of echoes of the Hebrew association of luxury, pride, and decadence. In a letter published in 1702, the traveler John Marshal describes the natives of the East Indies as "ignorant of all Parts of the World but their own; they wonder much at us, that will take so much Care and Pains, and run thro so many Dangers both by Sea and Land, only, as they say, to uphold and nourish Pride and Luxury. For, say they, every Country in the whole World is sufficiently endow'd by Nature with every thing that is necessary for the Life of Man, and that therefore it is Madness to seek for, or desire, that which is needless and unnecessary." John Marshal, "A letter from the East Indies . . ." (1702), quoted in Ray W. Frantz, *The English Traveller and the Movement of Ideas 1660–1732* (1934; reprinted Lincoln, Neb., 1967), p. 115.

It can be argued that the positive events of Jewish history also need to be associated with luxury. For it was only after Israel had been exhausted by luxury and crushed by the Babylonians that there arose the idea of a tragic fate and national identity for God's chosen people. In the midst of suffering and persecution, says the latter part of Isaiah, the task of the Jews is to bring about a reconciliation between God and all other peoples of the world.

5. Cf. Stanley Eugene Fish, *Surprised by Sin: The Reader in Paradise Lost* (New York, 1967), p. 332.

6. Walter W. Skeat, *An Etymological Dictionary of the English Language*, 4th ed. (1910; reprinted New York, 1956); A. Ernout and A. Meillet, *Dictionnaire etymologique de la langue latine*, 3d ed. (Paris, 1951); Eric Partridge, *Origins*, 2d ed. (New York, 1959); *Oxford English Dictionary*. The editors of the *OED* and Ernout and Meillet raise the possibility that the noun *luxus* derives from the adjective *luxus*, "dislocated, sprained"—a sense quite apt to the purposes of Greek and Roman historians.

7. Plato, *Republic* 2.372e–373e, 9.590b; *Timaeus* 4, 8; *Laws* 6.781a–b, 7.805d ff., 8.841a, 11.919b.

8. Cf. the fable of the unruly, luxurious steed in the palinode of the *Phaedrus* 253–54.

9. In Aristotle this position can be traced in the *Topics*, throughout the *Politics*, in the *Ethics* and *Athenian Constitution;* in the historians, Herodotus *History* 6–7; and Thucydides *Peloponnesian War* 3–6, 8.

10. Eduard Zeller, *The Stoics, Epicureans and Sceptics*, trans. Oswald J. Reichel (London, 1880), pp. 268–81, 301–4; E. Vernon Arnold, *Roman Stoicism* (Cambridge, 1911), pp. 332, 353–56; Ludwig Edelstein, *The Meaning of Stoicism* (Cambridge, Mass., 1966), pp. 22–44; A. A. Long, *Hellenistic Philosophy: Stoics, Epicureans, Sceptics* (London, 1974), pp. 205–9.

11. See *De benef.* 3.17–18; *Phaedra* 11.483–558; and the *Dialogi* 1.4, 4.21, 5.36. The elder Pliny's *Naturalis historia* and the *Discourses* of Epictetus elaborate further on the necessity for man to see rightly his place in nature. In the proemium to book 7, Pliny asserts the superiority of animals to men, for man alone of all living things courts grief in his endless pursuit of luxury, in every mode, for every member. Epictetus in book 4 of the *Discourses* used vividly for individuals the figures Socrates had applied to the state. He holds that most men can never attain virtue because they cannot comprehend it; their aspirations are entirely bound by luxury, which is to the soul what disease is to the body.

12. I follow the interpretation of Finley, *Ancient Economy*, pp. 40–44.

13. Diogenes had insisted that masters were more in bondage than their slaves; they *needed* slaves, but slaves did not need them. Cicero often illustrates this paradox when he shows that free men depend upon their dependents, those who are not free. Finley cites two further instances. About 400 B.C. an Athenian publicly pleaded poverty because he had no slaves to maintain him. Eight hundred years later Libanius the rhetorician argued before the council of Antioch the case of impoverished lecturers, so destitute they could afford no more than two or three slaves each (*Ancient Economy*, p. 79).

14. W. E. Heitland in *Agricola* (Cambridge, 1921) argues that such proponents of rural toil as

Cicero do indeed wish to keep most people on the land, but "the ever-repeated praises of country life are unreal. Even when sincere, they are the voice of town-bred men, weary of the fuss and follies of urban life, to which nevertheless they would presently come back refreshed but bored with their rural holiday" (pp. 200–201). For consideration of the influence of *De officiis* on the eighteenth century, see Henry Knight Miller's introduction to Henry Fielding, *Miscellanies* (Oxford, 1972), 1:xvii–xxvii. Other statements of Cicero's position may be found in *De finibus, Orationes Philippicae, Oration in Pisonem, Pro M. Caelio, Pro L. Murena,* and *De lege agraria.*

In *De oratore* (2.23) Cicero gives the concept of luxury aesthetic as well as moral value, declaring that an overripe style befits only a luxurious audience. Horace makes a similar point in the second of the *Epistolae,* and in *De sublimitate* (6.44, 95) Longinus warns that luxury destroys the spirit of a people and hence of their poets and writers.

15. Horace notes in the first of his epistles that though he belongs to no school he is indebted to the Stoics. Elsewhere he declares that wisdom teaches moderation and the rejection of luxury to poets as well as other men; the simple man is likely to be a *better* man than the spendthrift. See *Epistolae* 2.2. 122, 146–204; and *Ars Poetica* 71–72. In eighteenth-century thinking about luxury, Horace was probably best remembered for the fifteenth in his second book of odes. Usually given an English title like "Of Luxury" or "The Invasion of Luxury," this ode was doubtless well known to most literary men:

> Soon few for tilth the acres will remain,
> Such princely piles we raise. On every side
> > Fishponds, than Lucrine lake more wide,
> > > We'll see. The Bachelor-plane
>
> Will oust vine-wedded elms; and violets blue,
> And myrtle's fragrance, and flower-scents untold,
> > Will scatter sweetness, where of old
> > > The owner olives grew.
>
> Soon sultry sunshine by thick-planted bays
> Will be shut off. Not so taught Romulus' rule,
> > Or the unshaven Cato's school
> > > And old folks' simpler ways.
>
> With them men's private wealth was scant indeed,
> But great the common good. No colonnade
> > With northern outlook yielded shade,
> > > To please a private greed.
>
> None dared for house-building chance turf eschew;
> Cities and public temples, these at most
> > The laws bade deck at public cost
> > > With pomp of stonework new. [Trans. John Marshall]

See also the *Satires* 1.1, 2.2; and Ovid *Remedia Amoris.* At least three—the first, sixth, and eleventh—of Juvenal's satires contain attacks upon luxury. The first calls the gross and luxurious fit targets for satire, citing men who "gorge whole patrimonies in a single course." The sixth calls luxury an evil of peace, more ruthless than war, which broods over Rome.

16. M. L. W. Laistner, *The Greater Roman Historians* (Berkeley and Los Angeles, 1947), p. 171; D. C. Earl, *The Political Thought of Sallust* (Cambridge, 1961), pp. 41–43. In these paragraphs I follow Earl's analysis of Sallust's thought.

17. *Catilinae* 10; *Jugurthinum* 41. Gibbon challenges this view in vol. 1, chap. 2, of the *Decline and Fall.* Cautionary tales of the subversive effects of luxury upon a victorious army can be traced at least to Alexander the Great. After defeating the armies of Darius about 330 B.C., Alexander and his generals reputedly adapted overwell to the indulgent life of the Persians. First rumors passed among the troops that Alexander had given himself utterly to the vice. Then, according to Plutarch, Alexander himself became alarmed at the ostentation and extravagance of his generals and cautioned them to "avoid the vices and follies of those we have conquered."

18. See esp. 41-42.

19. Cato, fragments 58-66, 154-75, in *Oratorum Romanorum fragmenta*, ed. H. Malcovati, 2d ed. (Turin, 1955); Livy *History of Rome* 1-2, 23, 35-43; *Periochae* 43, 47-48; Valerius Maximus *Factorum ac dictorum* 2, 6; Plutarch *Marcus Cato;* Polybius *Histories* 18, 35, Velleius Paterculus *Historiae Romanae* 1; Diodorus Siculus *Bibliotheca historica* 31; Aulus Gellius *Noctes Atticae* 2; Pliny *Naturalis historia* 10. Cf. Macrobius *Saturnalia* 3, 7.

Hellenistic writers may have been as influential as earlier Stoics upon the thinking of the historians. Philo Judaeus and Dio Chrysostom were among the philosophers attempting to discover the nature of luxury through the language used to describe it. They particularized the vices and passions of luxury in ways comparable to the jurists and do make clear where luxury was thought to be nurtured: in cities and the haunts of women, tradesmen, and the lowly. An environment of virtue is a place of men steeled by a simple rural existence devoid of possession.

20. In book 3 of the *Annals* Tacitus notes several speeches that blame women for the luxury to be seen in Rome. He also recounts that rare episode of political candor, Tiberius's famous letter to the Senate on luxury. When the Senate was pressed for stronger sumptuary codes, it equivocated and redirected petitions to the emperor. After some delay Tiberius responded with an open letter on the political exigencies surrounding the issue. He asks which of the manifold things called luxuries he is expected to limit. Each of his critics asks that a different item or freedom be banned, and those crying loudest for prohibitions are also those most busy seeking to exempt themselves. "The cure for other evils must be sought in our own hearts. Let us be led to amendment, the poor by constraint, the rich by satiety. Or if any of our officials give promise of such energy and strictness as can stem the corruption, I praise the man, and I confess that I am relieved of a portion of my burdens" (trans. Church and Brodribb).

21. Nero is described in books 13-16; Tacitus gives him and Agrippina the habits of both cruel rapacity and sadistic luxury. In his biography of Nero, Suetonius makes him the epitome of luxury: vain, wanton, greedy, lecherous, brutal, degraded. According to Suetonius he had two favorite sayings. Good for all occasions was, "True gentlemen always throw their money about." Reserved for the appointment of a magistrate was, "You know my needs, eh? You and I must see that nobody is left with anything" (trans. Robert Graves). He also particularizes what many others refer to, Nero's rage at the luxury of senators and knights and his enforcement and enactment of statutes to limit private expenditure. See also Annaeus Florus *Epitomae* 1-2.

22. The doctrine of self-denial and its sources are treated in K. E. Kirk, *The Vision of God* (London, 1931). In the story of Christ and the gift of the precious ointment (Luke 7:36-50, John 12:3-8) there is a striking parallel of the ancient injunction against human use of something intended for the divine. In John the scene is sharply dramatized: Mary's gift and her offer of her hair for drying Jesus' feet, the taunting of Judas and Jesus' response, "For the poor always ye have with you; but me ye have not always." Jesus' words were often used to justify the elaborate decoration of churches and cathedrals during periods of deprivation.

23. Lecky, *History of European Morals,* 2:66-68.

24. The best extended discussions are R. W. Carlyle and A. J. Carlyle, *A History of Medieval Political Theory in the West,* 6 vols. (Edinburgh and London, 1915), 2:56-75, 102-13, 3:92-114, 4:4-85; and David Brion Davis, *The Problem of Slavery in Western Culture* (Ithaca, 1966), pp. 87-121.

25. See e.g., *City of God* 4.3; and *Confessions* 6.15.

26. For Augustine's influence in the preservation of the Platonic tradition, see R. Klibansky, *The Continuity of the Platonic Tradition during the Middle Ages* (London, 1939).

27. See esp. *Confessions* 9, 12-13; *Tenth Homily* 4; *De vera religione* 38.69; *City of God* 9.17, 13.13; 14.15; and for useful background information, Herbert A. Deane, *The Political and Social Ideas of St. Augustine* (New York, 1963).

28. In the following paragraphs I draw upon Samuel C. Chew, *The Pilgrimage of Life* (1962; reprinted Port Washington, N.Y., 1973), pp. 1-34, 61-78, 144-73; and Morton W. Bloomfield, *The Seven Deadly Sins* (1952; reprinted East Lansing, Mich., 1967), pp. 59-66, 353.

29. In one of the few anticipations of my thesis, C. S. Lewis notes that Luxuria here also possesses the characteristics of Gula and Superbia: *The Allegory of Love* (New York, 1936), pp. 70-71. Sixteenth-century personifications of luxury are treated by Rosemond Tuve in *Allegorical Imagery* (Princeton, 1966), pp. 119, 182-83, 207-11, 442.

The alternative tradition of representation, in which luxury turns human beings into wild animals—usually asses, goats, hogs, and apes—is well illustrated by the engravings of Andrea Alciati in Geoffrey Whitney, *Choice of Emblems* (1586).

30. Some sense of the pervasive, familiar quality of Renaissance depictions of luxury is contained in Frances A. Yates, *The Art of Memory* (Chicago, 1966). It is also striking that images of luxury were allowed to stand during the sixteenth-century Reformation in England; it was not one of the cluster of images destroyed by reformers and discussed by John Phillips in his *Reformation of Images: Destruction of Art in England, 1535-1660* (Berkeley and Los Angeles, 1974).

Typical representations are to be found in Chew, *Pilgrimage of Life*, figs. 75, 77, 79, 82, 89, 90, 103, 104, 141; Tuve, *Allegorical Imagery*, figs. 50, 51, 82-84; D. W. Robertson, Jr., *A Preface to Chaucer* (Princeton, 1962), figs. 2, 15, 16, 34, 68; Emile Mâle, *The Gothic Image*, trans. Dora Nussey (1913; reprinted New York, 1958), figs. 49, 50, 57, 59; and Erwin Panofsky, *The Life and Art of Albrecht Dürer*, 4th ed. (Princeton, 1955), fig. 216.

Jean Seznec discusses the transformation of Venus into Luxuria in *The Survival of the Pagan Gods*, trans. Barbara F. Sessions (New York, 1953), part 1, chap. 3. And in *Pandora's Box*, 2d ed. (New York, 1962), Dora and Erwin Panofsky describe the variety in Renaissance versions: Rosso Fiorentino's *Pandora Opening the Box*, René Boyvin's *L'ignorance chassée*, Bronzino's *Exposure of Luxury*, Andrea Mantegna's *Virtus combusta et virtus deserta*, and Jacques Callot's *Luxuria*.

31. Davis, *Problem of Slavery*, pp. 91-92.

32. Primary discussions of luxury and the passage where Augustine's influence is clearest is *Summa theologica*, first part of the second part, questions 6 through 89 (on Human Acts: Habits, Virtues and Vices), noted here as 1.2.6–89. Further discussion appears in 2.2.153-54. All are glossed by Etienne Gilson, *The Christian Philosophy of St. Thomas Acquinas*, trans. L. K. Shook (New York, 1956), part 3.

33. For Marlowe see verses signed "Ignoto"; for Webster, *The Duchess of Malfi*, 1.1.325-26. For Spenser see the following in the *Faerie Queene*, 1.4.1.5; 1.4.21.3; 1.12.14.9; 2.11.12.6; 4.10.23.1.

34. *Lover's Complaint*, 314; *Much Ado*, 4.1.41; *Henry V*, 4.4.19; *Hamlet*, 1.5.83. See also *Troilus*, 5.4.8; *Titus*, 5.1.88; *Richard III*, 3.5.80; *Macbeth*, 4.3.58; *Antony*, 3.13.120; *Merry Wives*, 5.5.94; and *Measure for Measure*, 5.1.501.

35. As usual Shakespeare looks as far forward as backward. *Lear* contains several speeches that use luxury in the sense of lust; it is also, throughout, very much about luxury in the modern sense. The famous "O, reason not the need!" speech of Lear (2.4) is but one of many places where Shakespeare's characters question the separation of necessities from superfluities in modern, psychological terms. Others are Lear to Edgar (3.2) and Gloucester to Edgar (4.1). Then, in the "What, art mad?" speech of 4.6, Lear in his mad lucidity penetrates to the core of the moral-social issue. When all distinction hangs upon office, "The usurer hangs the cozener. / Through tatter'd clothes small vices do appear; / Robes and furr'd gowns hide all. Plate sin with gold, / And the strong lance of justice hurtless breaks; / Arm it in rags, a pigmy's straw does pierce it."

36. See also *PL*, 11.711-13; *PR*, 3.297; 4.110-14.

37. In *The Savages of America: A Study of the Indian and the Idea of Civilization* (Baltimore, 1952), p. 5, Pearce notes that the Indian "became important for the English mind not for what he was in and of himself, but rather what he showed civilized men they were not and must not become." Jordan, in *White over Black: American Attitudes toward the Negro, 1550-1812* (Chapel Hill, N.C., 1968), comes to the same conclusion about the English perception of Africans. In this discussion I am indebted to Hayden White's illuminating essay, "The Forms of Wildness: Archeology of an Idea," in *The Wild Man Within*, ed. Edward Dudley and Maximillian Novak (Pittsburgh, 1972), pp. 3-38.

38. An obvious feature of the history of luxury has been its integral relationship with ideas concerning wealth. From the Attic kingdoms through the French Revolution, there was a parallel increase in the denunciation of wealth and its accumulation. The best-known statements of this point are to be found in Johan Huizinga, *The Waning of the Middle Ages*, trans. F. Hopman (London, 1924); Max Weber, *The Protestant Ethic and the Spirit of Capitalism*, trans. Talcott

Parsons (London, 1930); Ernst Troeltsch, *The Social Teaching of the Christian Churches,* trans. B. Wyon (London, 1931); Richard Schlatter, *Private Property: The History of an Idea* (London, 1951); and Crane Brinton, *A History of Western Morals* (New York, 1959). Since the censure of wealth was usually contained in an attack upon luxury, the intellectual situation of the eighteenth century becomes intelligible when it is understood that, historically, opposition to luxury was not an attempt to *prevent* the accumulation, but rather to *regulate* it. The year 1757 probably marked the peak of public condemnation of luxury in England, as represented by the reception of John Brown's *Estimate.* Yet in the same year Samuel Johnson could write with ample justification, "There was never from the earliest ages, a time in which trade so much engaged the attention of mankind, or commercial gain was sought with so general emulation."

39. A few comments on sources are required here:

1) There are several detailed studies of sumptuary laws in the ancient world and at least one for each modern European nation. For the most part these works acknowledge that the laws were intended to control behavior and spending; then they proceed to discuss only the latter kind of regulation. For example, a standard work on England is F. Elizabeth Baldwin, *Sumptuary Legislation and Personal Regulation in England* (Baltimore, 1926; also published with other works in vol. 44 of *Johns Hopkins University Studies in Historical and Political Science*). At the outset Baldwin describes such legislation as an effort to limit individual spending; next she establishes motives: "the desire to preserve class distinctions, so that any stranger could tell by merely looking at a man's dress to what rank in society he belonged; the desire to check practices which were regarded as deleterious in their effects, due to the feeling that luxury and extravagance were in themselves wicked and harmful to the morals of the people; economic motives; the endeavor to encourage home industries and to discourage the buying of foreign goods, and the attempt on the part of the sovereign to induce his people to save their money, so that they might be able to help him out financially in time of need. Sheer conservatism and dislike of new fashions or customs might be mentioned as a fourth factor which led to the passage of English sumptuary laws" (pp. 9-10). This is a fair statement as far as it goes, and it leads one to ask about those aspects of the legislation that went beyond spending to other forms of control upon class distinction and deleterious practices. And it leaves unasked the questions why some ranks were considered exempt from the laws and how the definition of luxurious practices was arrived at. The upshot is that, almost universally, modern studies of sumptuary codes use the modern sense of luxury as something known and deplorable and treat the laws as minor, moral, and paternalistic. They are to be distinguished from valuable contemporary works, such as Nicolas Baudeau, *Principes de la science morale et politique sur le luxe et les loix sumptuaires* (1798).

2) The most useful modern studies tend to be those that approach the law indirectly, by way of some larger concern: e.g., Peter Garnsey, P. A. Brunt, and M. I. Finley on social conflicts in Greece and Rome; W. W. Buckland and David Brion Davis on slavery; Sarah Pomeroy and Verena Zinserling on the position of women in antiquity; Doris M. Stenton on women in England; E. P. Thompson on the working class.

40. *Sumptuary* is the traditional adjective for a type of legislation that had several titles in antiquity and more in the Christian era; using a narrower range of laws from the seventeenth and eighteenth centuries, Maurice J. Quinlan in his fine study, *Victorian Prelude: A History of English Manners, 1700-1830* (New York, 1941), terms them vice laws. Often called "luxury statutes," or "laws against luxury," they have in common the philosophical purpose I have outlined and the announced purpose to combat the luxury rampant at the moment, usually opening with a preamble that declares that the present age is far more luxurious than any of the past and has evoked the following measure of restraint. (Annually, on the average, for three thousand years, with few long interludes, legislators pronounced their own age the most depraved the world had seen. This was entropy indeed.) Contemporary indexers for the *British Parliamentary Journals* tended to use the categories of "luxury," "poor law," and "civil disorder." Survivals in modern Britain and the United States would include the American Constitution (in its original distinctions of rank, race, and sex), the slave codes and later Jim Crow laws, and the temperance and "blue" laws of both nations. Parliamentary debates that led to the current English pub-closing statutes reveal that some legislators maintain a strong sense of the function of such

laws; they argued that regulating the hours pubs could be open would both restrict the profit a tradesman-owner could make and discourage laborers from avoiding work.

41. P. A. Brunt, *Italian Manpower, 225 B.C.–A.D. 14* (London, 1971), p. vii. See also Brunt's *Social Conflicts in the Roman Republic* (London, 1971).

42. Finley, *Ancient Economy*, pp. 67-68.

43. An obvious example, in force in most European countries from the establishment of the monarchy to the present day, is that royal marriages were exempt from the restrictions imposed upon the rest of the nation by nuptial laws. Louis XIV was involved in one of the most widely discussed examples of royal discretion exercised in the seventeenth century. In August 1661 the French minister of finance, Nicholas Fouquet, invited the young monarch (and six thousand others) to view his newly built estate, Vaux-le-Vicomte. Louis's response to the sumptuous establishment was a combination of jealousy and rage. He charged Fouquet with *luxe insolent et audacieux*, had him immediately imprisoned, and confiscated the treasures of Vaux for himself.

44. We have little direct information about how ordinary people were affected by a system of orders and status, but we do have such creative reconstructions as Eileen Power's *Medieval People* (London, 1924). The most important single mark of status was that of citizenship. Aristotle had held that politics was the business only of citizens, and in Greek and Roman law this threshold of favored status was legislatively defined and jealously guarded. In Athens citizens alone were entitled to hold land and to enter freely into marriage; their number, Finley estimates, was between one in six and one in three of all males. In 91 B.C. Augustus estimated about four million citizens of Rome in an empire of fifty to sixty million persons. See Finley, *Ancient Economy*, pp. 45-48; for the number and classification of Roman citizens, within Italy and without, see Brunt, *Italian Manpower*, pp. 61-83, 204-65; and, generally, see Peter Garnsey, *Social Status and Legal Privilege in the Roman Empire* (Oxford, 1970).

45. For this and other examples, see William L. Westermann, *The Slave Systems of Greek and Roman Antiquity* (Philadelphia, 1955), pp. 75-76, 91-93, 115.

46. The longevity of this view with all its contradictions is indelible in the Dred Scott case (1857), in deciding which the chief justice of the United States Supreme Court declared that black people "had no rights which the white man was bound to respect; and that the negro might justly and lawfully be reduced to slavery for his benefit." This judgment he noted was "an axiom in morals as well as in politics." The justice was of course historically quite correct, for the sumptuary laws defined not only legal culpability, but also moral-intellectual capacity. Four years later a judge in Alabama put the contradiction concisely: "Because they are rational *human beings*, they are capable of committing crimes; and, in reference to acts which are crimes, are regarded as *persons*. Because they are *slaves*, they are incapable . . . of performing civil acts; and in reference to all such they are *things;* not persons."

47. See [Andrew Horn], *The Mirror of Justices*, ed. William Joseph Whittaker (London, 1895), originally written or edited in the late thirteenth century; Brian Tierney, *Medieval Poor Law: A Sketch of Canonical Theory and Its Application in England* (Berkeley and Los Angeles, 1959); Paul Vinogradoff, *Villainage in England: Essays in English Medieval History* (Oxford, 1892); and Pierre Kramer, *Le luxe et les lois somptuaires au moyen âge* (Paris, 1920).

48. Baldwin, *Sumptuary Legislation*, pp. 12, 101, 164-78; Lawrence Stone, *The Crisis of the Aristocracy, 1558-1641* (Oxford, 1965), pp. 27-30.

49. To observe the continuity of laws drawn to protect the land, one might compare, say, the Lex Agraria of 111 B.C. with the Statute of Artificers. The Lex Agraria and the legislation it superseded are discussed in E. G. Hardy, *Roman Laws and Charters* (1912; reprinted New York, 1975), pp. 35-92. The Statute of Artificers is the subject of Margaret Gay Davies, *The Enforcement of English Apprenticeship: A Study in Applied Mercantilism, 1563-1642* (Cambridge, Mass., 1956), esp. pp. 1-14; William Cunningham, *The Growth of English Industry and Commerce*, 6th ed., 2 vols. (Cambridge, 1919), 2:25 ff.; and Heckscher, *Mercantilism*, 1:224-32.

50. Leon Radzinowicz, *A History of English Criminal Law and Its Administration from 1750* (New York, 1948), p. 77. The most thorough account of the law is E. P. Thompson, *Whigs and Hunters: The Origin of the Black Act* (New York, 1975). On the use of mantraps and spring guns, see E. S. Turner, *Roads to Ruin: The Shocking History of Social Reform* (1950; reprinted

London, 1966), pp. 17–36. Douglas Hay provides an acute conspectus of how criminal law was used for social ends in his essay "Property, Authority and the Criminal Law," in Douglas Hay, Peter Linebaugh, John G. Rule, E. P. Thompson, and Cal Winslow, *Albion's Fatal Tree: Crime and Society in Eighteenth-Century England* (New York, 1975), pp. 17–63.

51. Baldwin, *Sumptuary Legislation,* pp. 186–91, 196–208, 229, and passim. Cf. John Martin Vincent, *Costume and Conduct in the Laws of Basel, Bern, and Zurich, 1370–1800* (Baltimore, 1935), pp. 42–95; and K. R. Greenfield, *Sumptuary Laws in Nürnberg* (Baltimore, 1918), passim.

52. Sarah B. Pomeroy, *Goddesses, Whores, Wives, and Slaves: Women in Classical Antiquity* (New York, 1975), pp. 46, 57, 178–82; Brunt, *Italian Manpower,* pp. 558–66.

53. Quoted in Chilton Latham Powell, *English Domestic Relations, 1487–1653* (New York, 1917), pp. 149–50, 147; see also Doris Mary Stenton, *The English Women in History* (London, 1957), pp. 29–74. For the rights of women in marriage, see George E. Howard, *A History of Matrimonial Institutions,* 3 vols. (Chicago, 1904); Gellert S. Alleman, *Matrimonial Law and the Materials of Restoration Comedy* (Wallingford, Pa., 1942); and Francis Lee Utley, *The Crooked Rib: An Analytical Index to the Argument about Women in English and Scots Literature to the End of the Year 1568* (Columbus, 1944).

54. I draw these instances from W. Warde Fowler, *The Religious Experience of the Roman People* (London, 1922); H. J. Rose, *Ancient Roman Religion* (London, 1949); and M. I. Finley, *Democracy Ancient and Modern* (New Brunswick, 1973).

55. The expedient equation of station with virtue was certain to catch Gibbon's sensitive eye. His fifteenth chapter (1776) explains:

> In their censures of luxury, the fathers are extremely minute and circumstantial; and among the various articles which excite their pious indignation, we may enumerate false hair, garments of any colour except white, instruments of music, vases of gold or silver, downy pillows (as Jacob reposed his head on a stone), white bread, foreign wines, public salutations, the use of warm baths, and the practice of shaving the beard. . . . When Christianity was introduced among the rich and the polite, the observation of these singular laws was left, as it would be at present, to the few who were ambitious of superior sanctity.

Horace Walpole, it will be recalled, said he went to church merely to set a good example to the servants.

56. In book 5 of the *City of God* Augustine holds that the cycle of fortune besets all nations, as luxury and pride lead to the downfall of even the most mighty. In Boethius, Boccaccio, Petrarch, and others the wheel of fortune usually rotates from peace to wealth to luxury to pride to war to poverty to humility to patience and back to peace. A literary gloss is Howard R. Patch, *The Goddess Fortuna in Medieval Literature* (Cambridge, Mass., 1927), pp. 170–71. A vivid illustration is the painting "The Dance of Life" by Nicolas Poussin.

57. Huizinga, Weber, Troeltsch, Schlatter, and Brinton all draw this conclusion in a general way. Stressing it specifically are Carlyle and Carlyle, *Medieval Political Thought,* 3:92–114; and Davis, *Problem of Slavery,* pp. 88–89.

58. Vincent, *Costume and Conduct,* pp. 3–11.

59. Quinlan, *Victorian Prelude,* pp. 9–22.

60. Contemporary accounts appear in London corporation records, Stow, and Cecil's memoirs: Corporation of the City of London, *Remembrancia,* 1:62; John Stow, *Annales of England* (1605); and Robert Cecil, first Earl of Salisbury, *Calendar of the MSS . . . Hatfield House, Hertfordshire,* ed. R. A. Roberts (London, 1883), 5:249–50.

CHAPTER TWO

1. *Gentleman's Magazine,* 27 (Supplement, 1757): 591. For further comments and reports during 1757–58, see the weekly columns headed "Colliers," "Mob," "Corn," "Wheat," and "Riots." For discussion of the riots see Robert B. Rose, "Eighteenth-Century Price Riots and Public Policy in England," *International Review of Social History* 6 (1961): 277–92; and James

E. T. Rogers, *A History of Agriculture and Prices in England,* 7 Vols. (Oxford, 1866-1902), vols. 6 and 7.

2. See the *Journals* of the House of Commons, especially for 1751-55 and 1757-60.

3. See also *London Magazine* 38 (April 1768): 683-84; 41 (November 1772): 539; 42 (February 1773): 68-70; 43 (October 1774): 481; 48 (December 1779): 537-39. Lois Whitney called attention to the controversy in the periodicals in *Primitivism and the Idea of Progress* (1934, reprinted New York, 1965), p. 46.

4. *Fable of the Bees,* Kaye ed., 1:108, 115.

5. J. G. A. Pocock, *The Machiavellian Moment: Florentine Political Thought and the Atlantaic Republican Tradition* (Princeton, 1975), pp. 401-2. No one has treated the complex interrelations of history, language, and political theory during the period with more subtlety than Pocock. A beginning point for any serious study of the age is his "Machiavelli, Harrington and English Political Ideologies in the Eighteenth Century," in *Politics, Language and Time: Essays on Political Thought and History* (New York, 1971), pp. 104-47. He is concerned not with any particular idea or theory, but with the ways various theories collide and converge. In a general way he accounts not only for the presence of the attack upon luxury, but also for the decline of the attack later in the century:

> The language of politics is obviously not the language of a single disciplined mode of intellectual inquiry. It is rhetoric, the language in which men speak for all the purposes and in all the ways in which men may be found articulating and communicating as part of the activity and the culture of politics. Political speech can easily be shown to include statements, propositions and incantations of virtually every kind distinguished by logicians, grammarians, rhetoricians and other students of language, utterance and meaning; even disciplined modes of inquiry will be found there, but coexisting with utterances of very different kinds. It is of the nature of rhetoric and above all of political rhetoric— which is designed to reconcile men pursuing different activities and a diversity of goals and values—that the same utterance will simultaneously perform a diversity of linguistic functions. What is a statement of fact to some will symbolically evoke certain values to others; what evokes a certain cluster of factual assertions, and value judgments concerning them, to one set of hearers will simultaneously evoke another cluster and recommend another resolution of conduct in the ears of another set. Because factual and evaluative statements are inextricably combined in political speech, and because it is intended to reconcile and coordinate different groups pursuing different values, its inherent ambiguity and its cryptic content are invariably high. [*Politics, Language and Time,* p. 17]

6. Peter G. M. Dickson, *The Financial Revolution in England: A Study of the Development of Public Credit, 1688-1756* (London, 1967). For the context out of which this revolution grew, see L. A. Clarkson, *The Pre-Industrial Economy in England, 1500-1750* (London, 1971). The economic historian F. J. Fisher notes that the century was "the first period in which inventions played a significant part in the economic development of England." From the inventions came innovations in banking and agriculture and then a remodeled economic policy and new manufacturing practices. See *Augustans and Romantics, 1689-1830,* ed. H. V. D. Dyson and John Butt (London, 1961), p. 139. Fisher supposes that the new social structure that resulted from such changes was not visible as a whole until mid-century—the time of Smollett's historical and journalistic writing.

7. Isaac Kramnick, *Bolingbroke and His Circle: The Politics of Nostalgia in the Age of Walpole* (Cambridge, Mass., 1968), p. 4; see also pp. 30-55. William Pulteney expressed the situation more crassly and probably more accurately when he said that in an age of luxury the great families are at a disadvantage: they possess great wealth, but not ready cash. Cf. Peter Marris, *Loss and Change* (London, 1974), which studies in modern psychological terms the crisis of social change, entailing "the irretrievable loss of the familiar."

8. George Rudé, *Hanoverian London 1714-1808* (Berkeley and Los Angeles, 1971), pp. ix-x.

9. Carl J. Friedrich has said, "If Hobbes retained the verbiage of natural law while draining it of its substance, David Hume . . . is generally credited with its destruction" (*The Philosophy of Law in Historical Perspective,* 2d ed. [Chicago, 1963], p. 91). Both parts of Friedrich's statement are pertinent to the eighteenth-century situation.

10. The latter group is cited in Heckscher, *Mercantilism,* 2:290, the former in Johnson, *Predecessors of Adam Smith,* pp. 281–94; Buck, *Politics of Mercantilism,* pp. 14–20; Viner, *Studies,* pp. 6–51; and George, *London Life,* pp. 23–24. A partial list of the writers involved would include Petty, Grew, Davenant, Hale, Sheridan, Coke, Cary, Bellers, Yarranton, Firmin, Fortrey, Mun, Fauquier, and Gee. Those who attack luxury saw it as: (1) a pernicious example of bourgeois emulation of the nobility, (2) a temptation to the wealthy to squander their patrimonies, and (3) a waste of precious metals, through exports for payment and the manufacture of jewelry. Beneath and beyond these practical considerations lay the assumptions that the threat of bankruptcy was ever present and that an unequal distribution of wealth was necessary within Europe as well as within England. Since misfortune was a constant threat, economic activity became a desperate attempt to preserve the present. Accepting the axiom that one nation can prosper only at the expense of all others, these opponents interpreted luxury within their own country as a sign of national decadence and a spur to the economies of their competitors. They tended to see an economic structure at once predetermined and fraught with uncertainty. Calls for stronger control over trade and labor were a common attempt to resolve the paradox. Unregulated trade, they held, would permit consumption of useless, transient, or precious goods and thereby upset the balance of trade, squander gold and silver supplies, cause unemployment, and reduce the value of land. If the passion for French lace of women like Swift's female Yahoos and Smollett's Tabby was to be gratified, then England would be forced to increase imports. The transaction would require the loss of gold or needed raw materials to its traditional enemy. The next steps would involve natives left without work because of lost capital and the diversion of effort from agriculture to competing luxuries. Having been economically depleted, the nation would then be physically exhausted. Depopulation would follow from poverty, the abandonment of the land, the flight to the cities, and the neglect of subsistence farming. A proliferation of tariffs, prohibitions, and duties—many not removed until Gladstone's ministry—testify to the intensity of such fears.

11. Mandeville's own position will be discussed further in the following chapter. Here should be noted those studies that remark upon his significance as a bridge figure: Jacob Viner, *The Long View and the Short* (Glencoe, Ill., 1958), pp. 332–42; Kramnick, *Bolingbroke and His Circle,* pp. 201–4; and Hector Munro, *The Ambivalence of Bernard Mandeville* (Oxford, 1975).

12. [Nathaniel Forster], *An Inquiry into the Causes of the Present High Price of Provisions* (1767), pp. 47–48; Walpole's letters to Horace Mann, 1 July 1761 and 9 April 1772, in *Correspondence,* ed. W. S. Lewis (New Haven, 1937–), 22:49, 455; 23:400.

13. In *Consent and Consensus* (London, 1971), P. H. Partridge argues that consent of the governed is agreed to be the first characteristic of democratic government, but that modern use of the term "consent" is so vague that it can be employed to justify almost any regime. And while we are not disturbed, readers two centuries hence may wonder what is being requested when, say, Leon Radzinowicz and the London *Daily Mail,* Spiro Agnew and Jesse Jackson, all call for "law and order."

Of course many writers of historical or literary inclination continued through the nineteenth and even into the twentieth century to identify luxury with lechery. While economists like Veblen and Henry George were giving luxury a thoroughly modern cast, bookish and nostalgic critics like Saintsbury and Chesterton retained the older vocabulary. In his collection of *Miscellaneous Essays* (New York, 1892), Saintsbury writes disapprovingly of those who would introduce questions of morality into literature and observes that "you may write about murder all you like, and no one will accuse you of having committed that crime. You may depict an interesting brigand without being considered a thief. But so soon as you approach the other deadly sin of Luxury in any of its forms, instantly it appears self-evident that you not only take pleasure in those who do these things but also do them yourself" (p. 248).

14. Caroline A. Robbins, *The Eighteenth-Century Commonwealthman: Studies in the Transmission, Development and Circumstances of English Liberal Thought from the Restoration of Charles II until the War with the Thirteen Colonies* (Cambridge, Mass., 1959), esp. pp. 103–5; Lois F. Schwoerer, "The Literature of the Standing Army Controversy," *HLQ* 28 (1964–65): 187–212; Pocock, *Machiavellian Moment,* pp. 427–46; Kramnick, *Bolingbroke and His Circle,* pp. 236–60.

15. Charles Davenant, *The Political and Commerical Works of Dr. Charles D'Avenant,* ed.

Charles Whitworth, 6 vols. (London, 1771), 1:319. All other quotation from Davenant will be from this edition and cited in the text.

16. French theories of progress, some dating from the sixteenth century, are discussed in George Huppert, *The Idea of Perfect History* (Urbana, Ill., 1970). For English conceptions, see —in addition to the standard works on historiography and those by Pocock and Kramnick already cited—J. G. A. Pocock, *The Ancient Constitution and the Feudal Law: A Study of English Historical Thought in the Seventeenth Century* (Cambridge, 1957); G. H. Nadel, "Philosophy of History before Historicism," in *Studies in the Philosophy of History*, ed. G. H. Nadel (New York, 1965); and Isaac Kramnick, Introduction to Bolingbroke, *Historical Writings* (Chicago, 1972).

17. For the political quarrels of Anne's reign and documentation of the division of legislators, there are two excellent books of readings and two essential studies. The former are Geoffrey Holmes and W. A. Speck, eds., *The Divided Society: Party Conflict in England 1694-1716* (London, 1967); and J. A. W. Gunn, *Factions No More: Attitudes to Party and Opposition in Eighteenth-Century England* (London, 1972). The latter are Geoffrey Holmes, *British Politics in the Age of Anne* (London, 1967); and W. A. Speck, *Tory and Whig: The Struggle in the Constituencies 1701-1715* (London, 1970). For the influence of the Revolution of 1688 on the age of Anne, see Stuart Prall, *The Bloodless Revolution: England, 1688* (New York, 1972), pp. 21-39, 55-57, 245-93. Perhaps the best description of Anne's reign as an era of new peace, harmony, and prosperity appears in Pope's *Windsor Forest* (1713):

Oh Fact accurst? What Tears has *Albion* shed,
Heav'ns! what new Wounds, and how her old have bled?
She saw her Sons with purple Deaths expire,
Her sacred Domes involv'd in rolling Fire,
A dreadful Series of Intestine Wars,
Inglorious Triumphs, and dishonest Scars.
At length great ANNA said—Let Discord cease!
She said, the World obey'd, and all was *Peace*! [11.321-28]

18. *Works* (London, 1844), 1:115.

19. Addison notes the social distinctions within London in *Spectator* no. 403, for 12 June 1712:

When I consider this great City in its several Quarters and Divisions, I look upon it as an Aggregate of various Nations distinguished from each other by their respective Customs, Manners and Interests. The Courts of two Countries do not so much differ from one another, as the Court and City in their peculiar ways of Life and Conversation. In short, the Inhabitants of St. James's, notwithstanding they live under the same Laws, and speak the same Language, are a distinct People from those of *Cheapside*, who are likewise removed from those of the *Temple* on the one side, and those of *Smithfield* on the other, by several Climates and Degrees in their ways of Thinking and Conversing together. [Bond ed., 3:506]

20. *Gulliver's Travels*, ed. Herbert Davis (rev. ed. Oxford, 1959), p. 201. The two following long quotations appear on pp. 199 and 201-2 respectively of the Davis edition.

21. Cf. part 4 generally and the remarks on the frugal diet of the Houyhnhnms and the luxury of the female Yahoos particularly.

22. Pocock, "Machiavelli, Harrington and English Political Ideologies," pp. 124-47; Kramnick, *Bolingbroke and His Circle*, pp. 76-83.

23. In at least four pamphlets Pulteney argues that the constitution is safe only when it is under the direct protection of "the Great and Rich Families in the several counties, Cities, and Boroughs." Such protection insures not only the safety of the constitution, but also the just administration of the crown. Pulteney's tracts are valuable as bills of particulars in the indictment of Walpole during the early 1730s. See especially *A Proper Reply to a late Scurrilous Libel* (1731); *The Politics on Both Sides* (1734); *An Humble Address to the Knights, Citizens, and Burgesses* (1734); and *An Enquiry into the Conduct of Our Domestick Affairs* (1734).

24. The *Craftsman* serialized Bolingbroke's "Remarks on the History of England" between September 1730 and June 1731, "A Dissertation upon Parties" from October 1733 through June 1734, and the briefer essays, "On Luxury" and "On the Policy of the Athenians." Most of his attacks upon luxury were reprinted in the *Collection of Political Tracts* of 1748. Pocock examines the shades of meaning within the term "corruption" in *Machiavellian Moment*, pp. 402, 477–86.

25. No. 59 (19 August 1727), 2:104. See also nos. 166, 178, 291, 312, 320. The argument dismissing party labels and attachments was a critical one for the Opposition and is the subject of Caroline Robbins, "Discordant Parties—A Study of the Acceptance of Party by English-men," *Political Science Quarterly* 73 (1958): 505–29; H. N. Fieldhouse, "Bolingbroke and the Idea of Non-Party Government," *History* 23 (1938): 41–56; and Norman Baker, "Changing Attitudes towards Government in Eighteenth-Century Britain," in *Statesmen, Scholars and Merchants: Essays in Eighteenth-Century History Presented to Dame Lucy Sutherland*, ed. Anne Whiteman, J. S. Bromley, and P. G. M. Dickson (Oxford, 1973), pp. 202–19.

26. Perhaps as many as half of the numbers of the *Craftsman* urge some version of this point. See for instance nos. 5, 9, 12, 19, 47, 56, 57, 71, 114, 127, 134, 151, 166, and 184. This model had much appeal to aggrieved landowners, the smaller squires anxious lest they be driven out entirely, the larger anxious that they would find as neighbors such of the new rich as lawyers, doctors, goldsmiths, and tradesmen. Their anxieties over taxes are reported in William Kennedy, *English Taxation 1640–1799* (London, 1913), pp. 64–100; over the movement of landholdings in H. J. Habakkuk, "English Landownership 1680–1740," *Economic History Review* 10 (1940): 2–17, and G. E. Mingay, *English Landed Society in the Eighteenth Century* (London, 1963), pp. 50–130. The more general changes in the quality of gentry life are considered in Edward Hughes, *North Country Life in the Eighteenth Century* (Oxford, 1952). Their hatred of stock-jobbers is caught in the second of *Cato's Letters* (12 November 1720), occasioned by the Bubble: "The Resurrection of Honesty and Industry can never be hoped for, while this Sort of Vermin is suffered to crawl about, tainting our Air, and putting every thing out of Course; subsisting by Lies, and practicing vile tricks, low in their Nature, and mischievous in their Consequences" (3d ed., 1:8). What should be done about them? To Trenchard and Gordon, "The Answer is Short and at Hand, Hang Them!"

27. In "On Luxury" Bolingbroke writes, "They are puny politicians, who attack a people's liberty directly. The means are dangerous, and the success precarious. . . . But he is a statesman formed for ruin and destruction, whose wily head knows how to disguise the fatal hook with the baits of pleasure, which his artful ambition dispenses with a lavish hand, and makes himself popular in undoing."

28. *Works*, ed. David Mallet, 7 vols. (London, 1754–98), 3:299–300. See also 1:474 ff.; 2:65, 234, 333, 355–56, 373–74. One other essay of the 1730s merits brief attention because of a parallel with Smollett. In his letter from London of May 29, Bramble complains that "the capital is become an overgrown monster; which, like a dropsical head, will in time leave the body and extremities without nourishment and support." The metaphor of London as a dropsical head was used at least as early as the opening years of the seventeenth century, but its earliest occurrence within the controversy over luxury, so far as I have discovered, is in Erasmus Jones's *Luxury, Pride, and Vanity* (n.d. [BM catalog suggests 1735]), which went through at least five editions. Jones's concerns include the size and squalor of London and the consequent depopulation of the rest of the country: "It is not an ungrateful Spectacle . . . to behold the prodigious Growth and Encrease of this unwieldy *City*. . . . Who can reflect upon this, but must necessarily believe that the Head, in a very little time longer, will grow so much too big for the Body, that it must consequently tumble down at last and ruin the whole" (4th ed., p. 2).

29. William Wood, *A Survey of Trade* (1718), p. 158. See also Nicholas Barbon, *A Discourse on Trade* (1690); John Bellers, *An Essay for Imploying the Able Poor* (1714); and *Some Considerations on the National Debts* (1729). The most valuable account of the relation between economic hardship and political unrest in the 1760s is Walter James Shelton, *English Hunger and Industrial Disorders* (London, 1974).

30. See also Henry Knight Miller, *Essays on Fielding's Miscellanies* (Princeton, 1961), pp. 94–103; and Malvin R. Zirker, Jr., "Fielding and Reform in the 1750s," *SEL* 7 (1967): 453–56. A useful compilation of attacks upon the luxury of the poor from contemporary books, news-

papers, and documents is J. P. Malcolm, *Anecdotes of the Manners and Customs of London during the Eighteenth Century* (London, 1808).

31. John Fielding, *An Account of the Origins and Effects of a Police* . . . (1758), p. 8.

32. William Horsley, *The Universal Merchant* (1753), p. xv. For similar views, see John Campbell, *The Present State of Europe* (1750), esp. p. 22; Duncan Forbes, *Reflections on the Sources of Incredulity, with Regard to Religion* (Edinburgh, 1750); Matthew Decker, *An Essay on the Causes of the Decline of the Foreign Trade* (1744); and *Sixteen Discourses upon Doctrines and Duties* (1754).

33. See for example *Critical Review* 2 (August 1756): 2.

34. John Brown, *Estimates of the Manners and Principles of the Times* (1757), 1:35-38, 42-49, 58-59, 85-93, 201.

35. Brown's tirade contains several literary echoes, perhaps recalling for his readers the wit and learning of the natural leader. His description of England racked by luxury uses the language applied to an Antony ruined by luxury in speeches of Philo and Octavius in the opening act of *Antony and Cleopatra*. His account of the psychology of luxury recalls, from *Paradise Lost*, the dream Satan forces upon Eve: "distemper'd, discontented thoughts, / Vain hopes, vain aims, inordinate desires / Blown up with high conceits ingend'ring pride."

36. Why Bolingbroke should lead this group is not clear. Brown had attacked Mandeville and luxury earlier, in the second of his *Essays on the Characteristics of the Earl of Shaftesbury* (1751), where he calls the *Fable of the Bees* an "immense *Labyrinth* of Falsehood." Mandeville is termed "this coarse Writer" and "a dishonest Mind" whose appeal is to "our modish Coffee-house philosophers" and to "a Set of Wrong-headed Enthusiasts." Nevertheless, Brown says little about the nature of luxury in the earlier work, except to note that it amounts to "un-profitable *Riot* and *Excess*." Volume 2 of the *Estimate* was published in 1758. For Brown's other comments on the consequences of luxury see 1:193-96; 2:26-27, 33, 49, 95-96, 105-7, 189-90, 194-95.

37. *London Magazine* 27 (May 1758): 223. For earlier comments in the periodical see 25 (January 1756): 15-17; 25 (October 1756): 473-76; and 26 (December 1756): 576. See also *World*, no. 157 (1 January 1756), pp. 116 ff.; no. 167 (11 March 1756), pp. 173; and no. 171 (8 April 1756), pp. 195; *Grand* 1 (February 1758): 68, 73; 1 (September 1758): 450; 1 (October 1758): 514; 2 (June 1759): 298-99. For the *Universal*, see 20 (supplement 1757): 308; 24 (January 1759): 4; 25 (August 1759): 70, 73-74. *The New Royal's* views are contained in the issues for October (p. 152) and November (pp. 218-19) 1759. For the comparable opinions of the lesser periodicals, see the *Old Maid*, no. 31 (12 June 1756), p. 256; *Connoisseur*, no. 107 (12 February 1756), p. 71; no. 118 (29 April 1756), p. 128, and the *Prater*, no. 14 (12 June 1756), p. 79. The *Universal Visiter's* comments appear in no. 6 (June 1756), pp. 264-65; and no. 8 (August 1756), pp. 353-54. For the background of this reception see Stephen, *History of English Thought*, chap. 10, pp. 67-70; and Robert Donald Spector, *English Literary Periodicals* (The Hague, 1966), pp. 63-66.

38. Quoted in *Critical Review* 6 (October 1758): 350. See also George M. Kahrl, *Tobias Smollett, Traveler-Novelist* (Chicago, 1945), p. 127, n. 21.

39. Quoted in *Monthly Review* 23 (July 1760): 26.

40. See also Henry Stebbing's *Sermons on Practical Christianity* (1759) and Dr. Bolton's *Letters and Tracts on the Choice of Company, and other Subjects* (1761).

41. Pocock, *Politics, Language and Time*, pp. 286-87.

42. Among other attacks set in the traditional vein after 1763 are Young's *Farmer's Letters to the People of England* (1767), letter 7; and the anonymous *Political Speculations* (1767), *An Infallible Remedy for the High Price of Provisions* (1768), and *The Present State of Great Britain and North America* (1767). The most influential of these latter attacks appears to have been William Paley's *Principles of Moral and Political Philosophy* (1785), which was used as a textbook well into the nineteenth century and saw fifteen editions by 1805. Paley, archdeacon of Carlisle from 1782, traces the degradation of the poor to their luxury and laziness; he notes that the rich, too, engage in luxury but defends them as elevated beings to whom common regulations do not apply.

43. *Collected Works*, ed. Arthur Friedman (London, 1966), 4:286. References to luxury appear in the poem in 11.295-314, 385-94. Goldsmith's other comments on luxury are to be

found in *The Roman History* (2 vols., 1769); the *Citizen of the World,* letter 25; and "The Revolution in Low Life" from *Lloyd's Evening Post,* 14–16 June 1762. Scholarly commentary includes Howard J. Bell, Jr., "The Deserted Village and Goldsmith's Social Doctrines," *PMLA* 59 (1944): 747–72; and Friedman's notes, 2:50 ff.

44. *Critical Review* 20 (October 1765): 315–16. But this is the only such "moderate" comment to appear during Smollett's lifetime.

45. *Monthly Review* 47 (Appendix 1773): 508.

46. Ronald L. Meek, *Social Science and the Ignoble Savage* (Cambridge, 1976), pp. 99–130, 150–76.

47. *Wealth of Nations,* ed. William R. Scott, 6th ed. (London, 1921), 1:79–80. The whole of this chapter is apposite; it is chap. 8 of book 1, "On the Wages of Labour." See also D. P. O'Brien, *The Classical Economists* (London, 1975).

48. Chapter 19 of *The Vicar of Wakefield,* in *Collected Works,* ed. Friedman. See also J. Trusler, *Luxury no political evil, but . . . proved to be necessary to the preservation and prosperity of States. Addressed to the British Senate* (c. 1780).

49. Stephen, *History of English Thought,* chap. 10, 68; Ian R. Christie, *Crisis of Empire* (New York, 1967), p. 113. Full accounts of commercial expansion after 1763 are contained in V. T. Harlow, *The Founding of the Second British Empire 1763–1793,* 2 vols. (London, 1952, 1964); and Judith Blow Williams, *British Commercial Policy and Trade Expansion 1750–1850* (Oxford, 1972). The growing awareness of new forces in the political economy is traced in M. Blaug, "Economic Theory and Economic History in Great Britain, 1650–1776," *Past & Present* 28 (1964): 111–16. Several times in his *Europe in the Eighteenth Century: Aristocracy and the Bourgeois Challenge* (New York, 1973), George Rudé comments upon a change in English attitudes visible after 1763.

50. M. Dorothy George, *Hogarth to Cruikshank: Social Change in Graphic Satire* (New York, 1967), p. 13 n.

51. From early in the century American abolitionists had argued that an unnatural desire for luxury was responsible for slavery. John Hepburn, in *The American Defence of the Christian Rule* (Philadelphia, 1715), charged that the inordinate thirst for wealth brought men, even once-pious Quakers, to enslave other men for profit and to ensnare themselves in idleness and sexual debauchery. Hepburn's position was approved and reiterated by Elihu Coleman in *A Testimony Against that Antichristian Practice of Making Slaves of Man* (1733), the first abolitionist tract to receive official acceptance by a Quaker meeting. The identification of luxury with slavery was to be a consistent part of Quaker polemics during the first half of the century and was elaborated by Ralph Sandiford in *A Brief Examination of the Practice of the Times* (1729) and by Benjamin Lay in *All Slave-keepers Apostates* (1735). Probably the most important statements of the Quaker position appear in the works of John Woolman, whose *Some Considerations on the Keeping of Negroes* (2 parts, 1754, 1762) and *Journal* (1774) argue that slave owners had passed on the corruption of luxury to their children and their children's children. Instead of the "inheritance incorruptible" of God's word, they had brought to the New World a succession of wars and calamities that was but a sign of the awful retribution of God's justice. In his *Letters from an American Farmer* (1782), Crèvecoeur pursues a theme from Woolman, the contrast between the potential vitality of America and a Europe "fatigued with luxury, riches, and pleasures" (letter 3). Benjamin Franklin later returns to the portrait of a luxurious, dissipated Old World.

52. Henry Mackenzie, chap. 21 of *The Man of Feeling,* ed. Brian Vickers (London, 1967)— the Oxford English Novels edition. Another sign of the declining force of traditional slogans against luxury is the humorous appearance of one of these in the mouth of the pompous Mr. Sneer in act 1 of Sheridan's *The Critic* (1779).

53. J. W. Archenholtz, *A Picture of London* (London, 1797), p. 122. See also Charles Morazé, *The Triumph of the Middle Classes,* trans. anon. (London, 1966), esp. chap. 1, "London-Berlin: A Contrast." For a fascinating account of economic change described through family history, see T. W. Beastall, *A North Country Estate: The Lumleys and Sandersons as Landowners, 1600–1900* (Chichester, 1975). Although Smollett might have been shocked at the idea of a citizen expressing contempt for his betters, he saw clearly that the "cits" would gain an even greater ascendency. He would have appreciated the irony of a nineteenth-century

descendant of Charles James Fox, and a fervent Whig, leaving in his journal this account of an annual dinner to honor Fox's birthday:

> Mr. Fox's birthday. I went with Lord Thanet to the Fox dinner. We sat for ever and I was bored. Lord Erskine, Mr. Lens, Mr. Scarlett, Mr. Dennison and many dirty, violent little black people, who talked about taxes, poverty, funds, war, peace, the wickedness of ministers generally, for they had no particular fact or person in view, and the usual prophecies of ruin, tyranny and revolution which wind up the sentences of speculative politicians. Good dinner at Grillon's Hotel.

The Journal of the Rt. Hon. Henry Edward Fox, ed. the Earl of Ilchester (London, 1923), p. 153; quoted by Archibald Foord, *His Majesty's Opposition 1714-1830* (Oxford, 1964), p. 460.

CHAPTER THREE

1. The new collection of 1760 was *Essays and Treatises on several Subjects,* published in London in four volumes. During the 1770s the word *refinement* served as a partial but convenient circumlocution for *luxury,* then the two were used in conjunction, and by the early nineteenth century *refinement* had completely supplanted *luxury* when progress was meant. See, for example, Adam Sibbit, *A Dissertation, Moral and Political, On the Influence of Luxury and Refinement on Nations* (1800).

2. In this and later chapters I associate Smollett with the views of anonymous reviewers for the *Critical* without identifying the two. Grounds for this association are given in chapter 5.

3. According to Joan Robinson, *Economic Philosophy* (London, 1962), chap. 1, Mandeville has never been successfully refuted. He was certainly not alone in his defense of luxury. A few other writers anticipated or repeated many of his ideas, among them: Dudley North, *Discourses upon Trade* (1691); *An Essay on Money and Bullion* (1718); *Some Considerations on the Nature and Importance of the East-India Trade* (1728); [Patrick Lindsay], *The Interest of Scotland considered* (1733); and Jacob Vanderlint, *Money answers all Things* (1734). See Viner, *Studies in the Theory of International Trade,* pp. 90-91. Although bound to Veblen's sense of luxury, Gordon Vichert has useful things to say about Mandeville's satire in "The Theory of Conspicuous Consumption in the Eighteenth Century," in *The Varied Pattern: Studies in the Eighteenth Century,* ed. Peter Hughes and David Williams (Toronto, 1971), pp. 253-67. See also Philip Harth's fine introduction to the Penguin edition of the *Fable* (1970).

4. Mandeville's conservatism is apparent in the full title of the 1714 edition, which holds that the work will "demonstrate, That Human Frailties, during the degeneracy of Mankind, may be turn'd to the Advantage of the Civil Society, and made to supply the Place of the Moral Virtues." That he wishes to benefit traditional, hierarchical English society is made explicit in his contempt for women and the "Essay on Charity and Charity Schools" included in the edition of 1723. See also Viner, "Satire and Economics," p. 95. Quotations from the *Fable* are taken from the edition by Kaye.

5. See, e.g., *The Miracles Performed by Money* (1695); *The Character of a Covetous Citizen* (1702); *The Cheating Age Found Out* (1705); *To that Celebrated Idol Mammon, Chief Governor of Men's Consciences and Both Spiritual and Temporal Lord of all Christendom* (1709); John Dennis, *An Essay upon Public Spirit* (1711); Swift's essays in the *Examiner* and his *History of the Last Four Years of the Queen;* and Kramnick, *Bolingbroke and His Circle,* pp. 201-4.

6. He also wrote, "What Men have learnt from their Infancy enslaves them, and the Force of Custom warps Nature, and at the same Time imitates her in such a Manner, that it is often difficult to know, which of them we are influenced by."

7. Pocock, *Machiavellian Moment,* p. 461.

8. See, e.g., the *Review,* no. 18 (14 April 1705); *Complete English Tradesman,* 2d ed. (1727), pp. 318-19; *The Great Law of Subordination Consider'd; or, The Insolence, and Unsufferable Behavior of Servants in England duly enquired into* (1724); *The Behavior of Servants* (1726); and *Street-Robberies, Consider'd* (1728).

9. Defoe, *A Plan of the English Commerce* (1727; reprinted Oxford, 1927), p. 5. Further

citations in the text are to this edition. Among his innumerable other statements on the subject, see esp. *The Consolidator* (1705); *Whigs turned Tories and Hanoverian Tories from their avowed Principles proved Whigs; or, Each side in the other Mistaken* (1713); *Torism and Trade can never Agree* (1713); and *A True State of Publick Credit* (1721).

10. *London Journal*, nos. 689 (9 September 1732), 706 (6 January 1733), and 605 (6 March 1731); Thomas Gordon, *Essay on Government* (1747); Robbins, *Eighteenth-Century Commonwealthman*, p. 5; and Kramnick, *Bolingbroke and His Circle*, pp. 117-19. In this and the following paragraph I draw heavily from Robbins's book, her article, "Discordant Parties," and from Kramnick, *Bolingbroke and His Circle*, pp. 117-36.

11. *London Journal*, nos. 575 (8 August 1730), 740 (1 September 1733), 768 (16 March 1734), and 769 (23 March 1734); John, Lord Hervey, *Ancient and Modern Liberty Stated and Compared* (1734).

12. *London Journal*, nos. 592 (5 December 1730) and 777 (18 May 1734); *Daily Courant*, 28 August 1731; *A Full and True Account of the Strange and Miraculous Conversion of the Tories in Great Britain by the Preaching of Caleb d'Anvers, Prophet and Apostle to these Nations* (1734). The subject is treated in depth in J. H. Plumb's *The Growth of Political Stability in England 1675-1725* (Boston, 1967).

13. *London Journal*, no. 571 (11 July 1730); *Daily Gazetteer*, nos. 72 (20 September 1735), and 120 (15 November 1735).

14. *London Journal*, nos. 558 (11 April 1730), 606 (13 March 1731), 770 (30 March 1734), 783 (29 June 1734), and 799 (19 October 1734); *Free Briton*, no. 128 (11 May 1731); *The Case of the Opposition Stated Between the Craftsman and the People* (1731).

15. *The Letters of Tobias Smollett*, ed. Knapp, p. 136.

16. I have been unable to locate a copy of the original edition of this pamphlet. Here I rely upon the nine pages of extracts printed by the *Monthly Review* 9 (March 1753): 191-99. Page numbers following quotations from the work refer to this issue of the *Monthly*.

17. Like the *Critical*, Smollett in his histories generally denies that the lower orders suffer demonstrably in periods of shortage. The contrary position is to be found in most of the studies of the period: David Davies, *The Case of the Labourers in Husbandry* (1795); Frederic Eden, *The State of the Poor* (3 vols., 1797); W. J. Ashley, *The Bread of Our Forefathers* (London, 1930); J. D. Chambers and G. E. Mingay, *The Agricultural Revolution, 1750-1880* (London, 1966); and John Burnett, *A History of the Cost of Living* (London, 1969).

18. W. Hazeland, *A View of the Manner in which Trade and Civil Liberty Support each Other* (1756); Malachy Postlethwayt, *Great Britain's True System* (1756), and *Britain's Commercial Interest Explained and Improved* (1757); William Mildmay, *The Laws and Policy of England, relating to Trade Examined . . .* (1765); *Observations on the Number and Misery of the Poor* (1765); [Nathaniel Forster], *An Enquiry into the Causes of the Present High Price of Provisions* (1767); James Steuart, *An Inquiry into the Principles of Political Economy* (2 vols., 1767); *Considerations on the Effects which the Bounties, Granted on Exported Corn, Malt and Flour, have on the Manufactures of the Kingdom* (1768); [Soame Jenyns], *Thoughts on the Causes and Consequences of the Present High Price of Provisions* (Dublin and London, 1767); *An Answer to a Pamphlet entitled Thoughts . . .* (1768); *Considerations on the Exportation of Corn . . .* (1770); *An Inquiry into the Connection between the present Price of Provisions and the Size of Farms . . .* (1773); *An Inquiry into the Late Mercantile Distresses in Scotland and England . . .* (1772); and Francis Moore, *Considerations on the Exorbitant Price of Provisions* (1773).

19. In 1795-96, when there was another great outcry against the cost of corn, wheat, and bread, at least seven pamphlets appeared that repeated or extended Forster's argument. See the British Museum catalog under "Price of Provisions" for a convenient listing.

20. Trade is discussed in chapters 19 and 20 of book 2; the status of laborers in chapters 11, 17, and 18 of the same book.

21. The *Critical's* bias becomes plainer when such reviews as the above are compared with those of the *Monthly Review*. See the *Monthly* 2:326; 6:22; 8:197; 11:137; 19:104; 23:25; 25:342; 30:168; 33:48; 36:279-84, 365-78, 469, 518; 37:470-73.

CHAPTER FOUR

1. A likely explanation of Smollett's interest in politics and social theory comes from J. H. Plumb. During the earlier portion of the century the powerholders, the dominant oligarchical wing of the Whigs, were for the most part interested only in technique; they became managers, technicians, and pragmatists. Theory was left largely to the political "outs." Plumb writes: "In a world of political stability, intellectual inquiry into the nature of politics and rational criticism of institutions is unlikely to be encouraged. After 1720 it was to be found only in important circles of opposition, amongst the dissenters and, above all, across the border in Edinburgh and Glasgow." Smollett, it will be recalled, was born the year after Walpole assumed control of the Treasury (Plumb, *In the Light of History* [Boston, 1973], p. 8). On what Smollett would have considered working-class insubordination, a useful study of the later part of the century but with application for the earlier is John Foster, *Class Struggle and the Industrial Revolution: Early Industrial Capitalism in Three Industrial Towns* (London, 1974).

2. For Pope, as for Smollett, the bubble could not be forgotten, for it marked the moment when:

> At length corruption, like a general flood
> (So long by watchful Ministers withstood)
> Shall deluge all; and Avarice, creeping on,
> Spread like a lowborn mist, and blot the sun;
> Statesmen and Patriot ply alike the stocks,
> Peer and butler share alike the Box,
> And Judges job and Bishops bite the Town,
> And mighty Dukes pack cards for half-a-crown
> See Britain sunk in lucre's sordid charms.   [*Moral Essays*, epistle 3, 11.135–43]

3. In many places, though not in the narrative of events of 1720, Smollett seems to associate the Whigs and especially Walpole with the whole career of the Bubble, and not simply with its resolution. The *Critical* did this openly, and this transfer of blame had been practiced by Tory political figures throughout the 1720s. Smollett's acceptance of the maneuver thirty years later is perhaps a measure of his willingness to condemn Walpole. Modern accounts nevertheless establish that the stock operation was a Tory affair: W. R. Scott, *Joint Stock Companies to 1720* (London, 1955); Eric Wagstaff, "Political Aspects of the South Sea Bubble," diss., London 1934; and John Carswell, *The South Sea Bubble* (London, 1961). Carswell (p. 190) notes that whatever Blunt, Hungerford, and Aislabie were, they were certainly not Whigs; the early support of Harley and Bolingbroke, moreover, was of great value to the scheme.

4. After discussing Johnson's moderate attitudes toward the Puritans and the civil war, Donald J. Greene comments, "Yet those things never become to Johnson as they do to, say, Thomas Hearne and Thomas Carte, Shebbeare and Smollett (to whose writings one may turn for examples of genuine Tory prejudice) matters calling for direct personal resentment" (*The Politics of Samuel Johnson* [New Haven, 1960], p. 33). The *Monthly Review* often challenged the authority of Smollett's histories; see 18:293–302; 19:249; 34:421; and 12:535. With the *Craftsman*, the *Complete History* is probably the source of the stereotype of Walpole as archdemon of political events, the cynical corrupter of all that was good in English life. Cf. Savage's *Epistle to Walpole* (1732).

5. Smollett's views of the ravages of Whig rule under George II are contained in volume 3 of the *Continuation*, published in 1763.

6. The consistent villain and source of calamity in the *Atom*, it will be recalled, is not any single political figure or group, but the mob, the Legion.

7. A similar passage occurs a few pages later in the *Continuation*, in which Smollett drops all attempts to confine his remarks to the subject at hand—parliamentary discussion of the poor laws—in favor of open partisanship upon a contemporary issue. While he had been writing, Parliament had been debating the licensing and control of those chief resorts of working-class recreation, the public houses. The proper decision, he holds, would be total suppression of these

"receptacles of vice" and "infamous recesses of intemperance" which are "the bane of industry, as well as population." Such places sap the wealth of the country by creating "the diminution of hands, the neglect of labour." Paradoxically, however, he concludes by arguing for both abolition and control, calling for legislation,

> that would abolish those infamous places of entertainment, which swarm in every corner of the metropolis, seducing people of all ranks to extravagance, profligacy, and ruin; that would restrict within due bounds the number of public houses, which are augmented to an enormous degree, affording so many asylums for riot and debauchery, and corrupting the morals of the common people to such a pitch of licentious indecency as must be a reproach to every civilized nation. [3:63]

Throughout the *Continuation* Smollett takes note of the "riotous and turbulent spirit" of the common people. Describing a grain shortage in the northern counties in 1753, he writes:

> At Leeds, a detachment of the King's troops were obliged in their own defence to fire upon the rioters, eight or nine of whom were killed on the spot; and, indeed, so little care had been taken to restrain the licentious insolence of the vulgar by proper laws and regulations, duly executed under the eye of the civil magistracy, that a military power was found absolutely necessary to maintain the peace of the kingdom. [3:71]

8. In the Admiral Byng affair, Smollett saw a fierce, clamorous, licentious, and intractable mob roused by a greedy faction to condemn the unfortunate officer. See the *Continuation,* 1:322, 479.

9. The most important work on this major aspect of social history has been done by George Rudé: "'Mother Gin' and the London Riots of 1736," *Guildhall Miscellany,* no. 10 (September 1959); "The London 'Mob' of the Eighteenth Century," *Historical Journal* 2 (1959): 1–18; "The Gordon Riots: A Study of the Rioters and Their Victims," *Trans. Royal Hist. Soc.,* 5th ser., 6 (1956): 93–114; *Wilkes and Liberty* (London, 1962); and *Hanoverian London* (Berkeley and Los Angeles, 1971). A useful summary of Rudé's earlier research is contained in chapters 1 and 9 of *Wilkes and Liberty.* See also Jack Lindsay, *1764* (London, 1959).

10. Martz discusses Smollett's contribution to the *Present State* in *Later Career,* pp. 104–23.

11. See 1:406, 431, 451, 464–65, 474, 480, 490–92; 2:30, 148–49.

12. Smollett's other comments on the lower orders appear in 1:406, 431, 441, 464–65, 474, 480, 490–502; 2:11–13.

CHAPTER FIVE

1. I do not wish to suggest that Smollett's journalistic campaign was hackneyed, at least any more so than the earlier ones of, say, Addison and Fielding or the different ones of economists and clergymen. Rather, all attacks upon luxury tend to fall within familiar patterns, and journalistic attacks are usually more enlightening than others. With a minimum of philosophizing, they reveal specifically what is disturbing the writers or their patrons. A visual analogue to the novelist's work in the *Critical* and the *Briton* would be the *Election* series that Hogarth painted in 1753 and 1754.

2. For this comparison I have retraced ground already covered for different purposes in several studies, most recently and thoroughly in Robert Donald Spector's *English Literary Periodicals* (The Hague, 1966), a valuable guide to journalistic vagaries of the period. Of the twenty-five or so periodicals publishing in the 1750s, none was so consistently conservative as Smollett's. The *Critical* anticipated by months the pessimism that became widespread in reviews of Brown's *Estimate.* As early as April 1756 the review was arguing against luxury in the context of immediate political, economic, and social issues.

3. During two lengthy periods, however, he probably did little direct writing or editing for the review. He spent the winter of 1759–60 in prison. And in a letter to Garrick dated 5 April 1761 (*Letters,* p. 98), he states that during the past six months he had written only one article for the *Critical* and might not do more during the next six. In a later letter (p. 125) he wrote that he gave up all connection with the periodical before leaving England in June 1763.

4. For attacks directed at Smollett as "Mr. Critical," see Knapp, *Tobias Smollett,* pp. 176–81; Claude E. Jones, *Smollett Studies,* University of California Publications in English, vol. 9, no. 2 (Berkeley, 1942), pp. 107 ff; and six notes by Robert D. Spector: "Attacks on the *Critical Review," Periodical Post Boy* (June 1955), pp. 7–8; "Further Attacks on the *Critical Review," N & Q* 200 (1955): 535; "Additional Attacks on the *Critical Review," N & Q* 201 (1956): 425; "Attacks on the *Critical Review* in the *Court Magazine," N & Q* 202 (1958): 308; "Attacks on the *Critical Review* in the *Literary Magazine," N & Q* 205 (1960): 300–301; and "Attacks on the *Critical Review* (1764–1765)," *N & Q* (1957): 121.

5. See the *Letters,* pp. 40, 81, 152–53; and Edward S. Noyes, "Another Smollett Letter," *MLN* 42 (1927): 232, 234.

6. See Derek Roper, "Smollett's 'Four Gentlemen': The First Contributors to the *Critical Review," RES* 10 (1959): 38–44; and Knapp, *Tobias Smollett,* pp. 176–77.

7. Reflecting upon the war in the *Continuation,* Smollett was most critical of the continental campaign. See 1:423–24; 2:391–92, 426–27; 3:254–55, 293–95, 352; 4:15–16, 421–22; 5:160–65, 293–94. After remarking at one point upon the prudence of the king of Denmark for remaining apart from the European conflict, he wrote:

> It was reserved for another nation [England] to adopt the pernicious absurdity of wasting its blood and treasure, exhausting its revenues, loading its own back with the most grievous impositions, incurring an enormous debt big with bankruptcy and ruin; in a word, of expending above an hundred and fifty millions sterling in fruitless efforts to defend a distant country, the intire property of which was never valued at one twentieth of that sum; a country with which it had no natural connection, but a common alliance arising from accident. [2:391–92]

Compare Bolingbroke's remark on the necessity to end "Marlborough's war": "Whenever we shall have got rid of our war, the landed interest will then rise, and the moneyed interest, which is the great support of Whiggism, must of course decline."

8. Such prosperity was of course literary, not financial. The review demanded attention and received it, as countless numbers of contemporary comments attest. In the most famous, Johnson suggested to George III in February 1767 that of the literary journals "the *Monthly Review* was done with the most care, the *Critical* upon the best principles."

9. All identifications of authorship are from the article by Roper, "Smollett's 'Four Gentlemen.'" While it has become a historical truism to note that the English were not prepared for either the prosecution or the consequences of the war, that fact has much bearing upon the *Critical's* editorial positions. Smollett, Griffiths, and Beckford saw different events and saw events differently. The *Critical, Monthly,* and *Monitor* not only disagreed about the importance of various issues and goals of the war, they also disagreed about what those issues and goals were. Even distance from those events did not modify the discrepancies, as a comparison of Smollett's histories with, say, Walpole's memoirs reveals. It must suffice here to remark that, normally acting as partisans, Smollett and the other writers for the *Critical* had a highly selective view of what was happening during the course of the conflict.

Among secondary works, I draw upon: J. S. Corbett, *England in the Seven Years' War* (London, 1907); O. A. Sherrard, *Lord Chatham: Pitt and the Seven Years' War* (London, 1955); Bernard Schilling, *Conservative England and the Case against Voltaire* (New York, 1950); and Keith Feiling, *The Second Tory Party, 1714–1832* (London, 1938).

10. The reviews attributed to Smollett are 2 (August 1756): 35–44; 2 (October 1756): 251–52, 257, 278–79, 285–86. The others are 2 (October 1756): 281, 284; 3 (February 1757): 185; 3 (March 1757): 283. Over sixteen months, the *Critical* published at least twenty-three reviews on the subject of Byng. On the validity of the charges against the ministry, see James A. Henretta, *"Salutary Neglect": Colonial Administration under the Duke of Newcastle* (Princeton, 1972).

11. In the *Continuation,* Smollett implies that Byng was innocent of wrongdoing. Spector has examined the more important passages of that work in "Smollett and Admiral Byng," *N & Q* 200 (1955): 66–67.

12. *Critical* 4 (October 1757): 371. See also 4 (November 1757): 468; and 4 (December 1757): 550–52.

13. The extent to which Pitt's conduct was supported by Tory leaders is explored by Romney Sedgwick in "Letters from William Pitt to Lord Bute, 1755–1758," in *Essays Presented to Sir Lewis Namier,* ed. Richard Pares and A. J. P. Taylor (London, 1856), especially pp. 121–22.

14. *Critical* 15 (February 1763): 150. Knapp's "Smollett and the Elder Pitt," *MLN* 59 (1944): 250–57, brings together the novelist's major comments on Pitt, but without placing them in political context. Arnold Whitridge remarks briefly in passing upon the relationship between the two men in his *Tobias Smollett: A Study of His Miscellaneous Works* (Brooklyn, 1925), pp. 23–52.

15. There is perhaps one exception to this generalization during Smollett's tenure as editor. In the January 1759 issue (7:48–49), the reviewer of the work by Rousseau seems to repeat an argument from Hume, but his point is quite muddled and applied only to conditions in *France.*

16. For a few examples see the *Critical* 2 (August 1756): 95–96; 2 (December 1756): 460; 3 (May 1757): 451–52; 4 (September 1757): 219–20; 5 (April 1758): 290; 9 (April 1760): 263; 10 (July 1760): 42; and 14 (May 1765): 395.

17. *Critical* 3 (May 1757): 478.

18. For examples of such chiding see *Critical* 1 (April 1756): 257; and 2 (October 1756): 259–60. For its generosity see 2 (December 1756): 460; 11 (June 1761): 435–39; 13 (January 1762): 80; 15 (March 1753): 161; 16 (November 1763): 378–81; 17 (January 1764): 31–36; 17 (April 1764): 304–5; 20 (July 1765): 25–35.

19. See also 5 (1758): 72–75, 443–45.

20. See also 17 (January 1764): 55–58.

21. For Smollett's role in the enterprise see Martz, "Tobias Smollett and the *Universal History,*" *MLN* 56 (1941): 1–14.

22. See, for example, *Critical* 8 (October 1759): 267; 9 (March 1761): 173–74; 12 (November 1761): 323–24; and 13 (February 1762): 109.

23. The exchange between Bramble and Lismahago, for comparison, is as follows.

> I allowed the truth of this remark, adding, that by their industry, oeconomy, and circumspection, many of them in England, as well as in her colonies, amassed large fortunes, with which they returned to their own country, and this was so much lost to South Britain.—"Give me leave, sir, (said he) to assure you, that in your fact you are mistaken, and in your deduction, erroneous.—Not one in two hundred that leave Scotland ever returns to settle in his own country; and the few that do return, carry thither nothing that can possibly diminish the stock of South-Britain; for none of their treasure stagnates in Scotland—There is a continual circulation, like that of the blood in the human body, and England is the heart, to which all the streams which it distributes are refunded and returned: nay, in consequence of that luxury which our connection with England hath greatly encouraged, if not introduced, all the produce of our lands, and all the profits of our trade, are engrossed by the natives of South-Britain; for you will find that the exchange between the two kingdoms is always against Scotland; and that she retains neither gold nor silver sufficient for her own circulation.—The Scots, not content with their own manufactures and produce, which would very well answer all necessary occasions, seem to vie with each other in purchasing superfluities from England; such as broad-cloth, velvets, stuffs, silks, lace, furs, jewels, furniture of all sorts, sugar, rum, tea, chocolate, and coffee; in a word, not only every mode of the most extravagant luxury, but even many articles of convenience, which they might find as good, and much cheaper, in their own country. For all these particulars, I conceive, England may touch about one million sterling a-year.—I don't pretend to make an exact calculation; perhaps, it may be something less, and, perhaps, a great deal more.—The annual revenue arising from all the private estates of Scotland cannot fall short of a million sterling; and, I should imagine, their trade will amount to as much more.—I know, the linen manufacture alone returns near half a million, exclusive of the home-consumption of that article.—If, therefore, North-Britain pays a balance of a million annually to England, I insist upon it, that country is more valuable to her in the way of commerce, than any colony in her possession, over and above the other advantages which I have

specified: therefore, they are no friends, either to England or to truth, who affect to depreciate the northern part of the united kingdom."

I must own, I was at first a little nettled to find myself schooled in so many particulars.—Though I did not receive all his assertions as gospel, I was not prepared to refute them; and I cannot help now acquiescing in his remarks so far as to think, that the contempt for Scotland, which prevails too much on this side the Tweed, is founded on prejudice and error. [MB, September 20]

Martz discusses a further pair of parallel passages, from the *Briton* and *Humphry Clinker*, in *Later Career*, pp. 171-73. A. J. Youngson provides a valuable historical gloss on the situation in his *After the Forty-Five: The Economic Impact on the Scottish Highlands* (Edinburgh, 1973).

24. See especially *Critical* 1 (March 1756): 97 (Smollett); 2 (August 1756): 48; 2 (September 1756): 121 (Smollett); 3 (March 1757): 238; 4 (July 1757): 46; 7 (April 1759): 375; 8 (October 1759): 271-72.

25. See, for example, *Critical* 5 (April 1758): 292, and the review's prefatory remarks to its extracts of the *Complete History* and *Continuation*.

26. See the previous section on luxury in the *Critical*, and 5 (April 1758): 285-319. In the preface to the opening volume (1758) of the *Grand Magazine of Magazines*, the editors criticized the bias of both the *Critical* and the *Monthly*: "The managers of the *Reviews* are not, perhaps, incompetent judges, but they are too slovenly or too remiss: too partial or too much interested in the characters they give; too much bigotted, or too free thinkers; too zealous Tories or too rigid Whigs, to judge with candour of the labours of their contemporaries; hence it is, that the characters they give, often stand in contrast to each other." Cited by Spector, *English Literary Periodicals*, pp. 190-91, n. 121.

27. Since the *Monitor* was a *political* and not a trade periodical, the call for reform amounted to its "platform," as it did with the allied periodicals the *Con-Test*, *Patriot*, and *North Briton*.

28. See *Critical* 2 (August 1756): 10-11, 44; 5 (January 1758): 1; and 7 (April 1759): 292.

29. *Critical* 9 (June 1760): 466-67.

30. Occupying the broad middle ground of Smollett's political vision was the companion of luxury, commerce itself, which the novelist came to distrust as later writers did industrialization and technology. Severely controlled, as it would be under the administration of a natural legislator, commerce would not disrupt the process of civil government and would surely not precipitate a costly war; rather, it would have a beneficent, consolidating effect upon the whole of English society. Under the Whigs, however, the meddling arrogance of mere merchants and tradesmen was tolerated, sometimes even encouraged, and commerce was permitted to assume unprecedented importance. Thus unrestrained, it upset the social order, threatened the constitution with sedition, and engendered "tumult, riot, and insurrection." During the last years of the reign of George II the *Critical* gave considerable, normally pejorative, attention to the effects of commerce, much of it in connection with the war and the price of food. Smollett was meanwhile also composing his acerbic remarks on the influence of commerce for the concluding volume of the *Complete History* and then resuming the theme in the initial volume of the *Continuation* (1760). Of the effects of the cessation of war in 1748, he writes in the *Continuation*:

Commerce and manufacture flourished again, to such a degree of encrease as had never been known in the island: but this advantage was attended with an irresistible tide of luxury and excess, which flowed through all degrees of the people, breaking down all the mounds of civil polity, and opening a way for licence and immorality. The highways were infested with rapine and assassination; the cities teemed with the brutal votaries of lewdness, intemperance, and profligacy. The whole land was overspread with a succession of tumult, riot, and insurrection. [1:56]

Four years later, unregulated commerce still threatened the kingdom.

The tide of luxury still flowed with an impetuous current, bearing down all the mounds of temperance and decorum; while fraud and profligacy struck out new channels, through which they eluded the restrictions of the law, and all the vigilance of civil polity. New arts of deception were invented, in order to ensnare and ruin the unwary; and some infamous practices, in the way of commerce, were countenanced by persons of rank and importance in the commonwealth. [1:128]

In the *Present State* (7:64), he equates "trade and commerce" with "cheating and over-reaching."

31. The greatest source of information about the City is contemporary periodicals themselves. Of secondary sources the most important are four studies by Lucy B. Sutherland: *A London Merchant* (London, 1933), *The East India Company in Eighteenth-Century Politics* (Oxford, 1952), *The City of London and the Opposition to Government, 1768–1774* (London, 1959), and the article "The City in Eighteenth-Century Politics," in *Essays Presented to Sir Lewis Namier,* ed. Richard Pares and A. J. P. Taylor (London, 1956), pp. 49–74. The strength of Whig sentiment in the City can be gauged by the entries in *The Diary of Sylas Neville,* ed. Basil Cozens-Hardy (London, 1950). Neville regarded himself as a staunch republican and was a friend of Wilkes. For another contemporary view, see *The Diary of the Late George Bubb Dodington . . . March 8, 1749 to February 6, 1761,* ed. Henry P. Wyndham (London, 1784); and *The Political Journal of George Bubb Dodington,* ed. John Carswell and Lewis A. Dralle (Oxford, 1965). Dodington may have been the man who recommended Smollett to Bute's attention as editor of the pro-administration paper that was to become the *Briton.*

Important specialized studies include A. H. John, "War and the English Economy, 1700–1763," *Economic History Review,* 2d ser., 7 (1954–55): 329–44; Walter E. Minchinton, "The Merchants in England in the Eighteenth Century," in *The Entrepreneur: Papers Presented at the Annual Conference of the Economic History Society at Cambridge, England April 1957* (Cambridge, Mass., 1957), pp. 22–31; and W. P. Treloar, *Wilkes and the City* (London, 1917).

An instance of City independence that Whigs of Smollett's age were proud to recall occurred in 1688, when in contravention of James II's "reforms" the lord mayor and aldermen continued to apply the Test Act, ordered that the Guy Fawkes Day celebration be maintained, declined to invite the new papal nuncio to dinner though ordered to do so at royal command, and did continue Anglican services in the Guildhall chapel.

32. On the political friction created by the City Whigs, within and without London, see the studies by Sutherland cited in note 31; Robbins, *Eighteenth-Century Commonwealthman,* pp. 9, 16, 228; Treloar, *Wilkes and the City,* pp. 126–36; Rudé, *Wilkes and Liberty,* chap. 9. An attempt to explain the friction in social terms appears in the second half of Anthony Giddens, *The Class Structure of Advanced Societies* (London, 1973).

33. *Memoirs of William Beckford of Fonthill* (London, 1859), 1:33. Beckford was apparently the principal financial backer of the *Monitor* when it was founded in 1755 and continued to be a major contributor. He was thus at the hub of reform politics, opposition journalism, and City commerce. The interrelationships among City figures were various. The main editor of the *Monitor,* Arthur Beardmore, was Temple's lawyer and a successful businessman. Richard Grenville, Lord Temple, was of course the brother of George Grenville and the brother-in-law of Pitt. The scholarly work of first resort, and the one I usually follow in this and the following chapter for information regarding important political figures and movements, is Lewis Namier and John Brooke, *The History of Parliament: The House of Commons, 1754–1790,* 3 vols. (London, 1964). Beckford's career is discussed in 1:329–30.

34. Cited by Sutherland, "The City in Eighteenth-Century Politics," p. 66. The City stressed electoral reform both because of its intrinsic merit as a political issue and because its success would lead, it was argued, to further acceptance of "the sense of the people." Until 1832 the City sent only four members to Parliament, with two additional supporters of metropolitan causes coming from Southwark and, on occasion, two more from Westminster. Meanwhile, as Defoe noted repeatedly in his *Tour* (1724–26), "barren villages" like Old Sarum and "miserable, dirty, decayed, poor, and pitiful towns" each sent half that number. Yet the disproportion was actually not as great as it at first appears, as was shown by Namier in his *England in the Age of the American Revolution,* 2d ed. (London, 1961), pp. 223–24. Forty-eight other members returned for the Parliament of 1761 provided latent support for City interests, since, whatever their nominal constituencies, they were London merchants. These forty-eight did not normally

share the political attitudes of the City Radicals, but they did to a large extent share their commerical views. In any case, City parliamentary strength taken at its highest numerical figure of fifty-six remained a paltry thing, for in 1761 Devon and Cornwall together returned seventy members. The theme was repeated widely outside of Parliament and the periodicals by scores of pamphlet-writers. For one example, the anonymous author of *Political Disquisions* (1763) contended that the present British constitution represented interests no longer predominant and that the merchant class must now obtain a greater share of governmental influence. The best recent account of the agitation is John Cannon, *Parliamentary Reform 1640–1832* (Cambridge, 1973).

35. Valuable contemporary accounts of this movement, from the point of view of a supporter, are contained in three works by John Almon: *A Review of Mr. Pitt's Administration* (1762), *A Review of Lord Bute's Administration* (1763), and *The History of the Late Minority* (1766). There is a copy of the last of these with marginal comments by Wilkes in the British Museum. Secondary discussions are Rudé, *Wilkes and Liberty;* Robert R. Rea, *The English Press in Politics, 1760–1774* (Lincoln, Neb., 1963); George Nobbe, *The North Briton* (New York, 1939); and James T. Boulton, *The Language of Politics in the Age of Wilkes and Burke* (London, 1963).

36. Spector makes this point briefly in his *"The Monthly* and Its Rival," *Bulletin of the New York Public Library* 71 (1960): 159-61. A thorough comparison would include discussion of the following comments from the *Monthly.* On political representation and commentary: 15 (July 1756): 1-2; 15 (September 1756): 233; 15 (October 1756): 408; 15 (November 1756): 518-21, 526-29; 17 (October 1757): 291; 17 (November 1757): 467; 18 (May 1758): 401. On progress in commerce and trade: 14 (January 1756): 37; 14 (February 1756): 81; 15 (September 1756): 217; 16 (February 1757): 163; 16 (April 1757): 302-3, 349-52; 18 (May 1758): 465.

37. See the attacks upon Smollett cited in note 4. Horace Walpole provided a sample in his *Memoirs of . . . the Reign of King George the Third:*

> Smollett was a worthless man, and only mentioned here because author of a History of England, of the errors in which posterity ought to be warned. Smollett was bred a seasurgeon, and turned author. He wrote a tragedy, and sent it to Lord Lyttelton, with whom he was not acquainted. . . . Smollett's return was drawing an abusive portrait of Lord Lyttelton in Roderick Random, a novel; of which sort he published two or three. His next attempt was on the History of England; a work in which he engaged for booksellers, and finished, though four volumes in quarto, in two years; yet an easy task, as being pilfered from other histories. Accordingly it was little noticed till it came down to the present times; then, though compiled from the libels of the age and the most paltry materials, yet being heightened by personal invectives, strong Jacobitism, and the worst representation of the Duke of Cumberland's conduct in Scotland, the sale was prodigious. [Ed. H. R. V. Fox (London, 1822), pp. 419-20]

Political and social divisions were also geographical divisions, there being great areas where no member of the London mob would be tolerated. Bramble, it will be remembered, wished to confine the vulgar who resorted to Bath to the lower town. Contemporary pamphleteers often referred, in a kind of shorthand, to the contests of "Soho vs. Wapping" or "St. Marylebone vs. St. George-in-the-East."

38. *The Adventures of an Atom,* in *Miscellaneous Works,* ed. Robert Anderson, 2d ed. (Edinburgh, 1800), 6:415. Further citations to the *Atom* are to this edition and will be given in the text.

39. For Murphy's political character and abilities, see Almon, *History of the Late Minority;* Spector, *English Literary Periodicals,* pp. 68-72: Nobbe, *North Briton,* p. 33; and *DNB.*

40. Those identified as Smollett's are: *Critical* 1 (January-February 1756): 88, 89; 1 (April 1756): 258-59, 259-60, 263-64; 2 (September 1756): 121 ff.; 2 (December 1756): 471-72. See also his related review, 2 (August 1756): 38-39. Those by other writers are: 2 (September 1756): 188; 3 (January 1757): 83; 3 (February 1757): 179-82; 4 (October 1757): 369-70; 5 (February 1758): 101; 6 (July 1758): 81-83; 6 (August 1758): 170-71; 6 (November 1758):

438. Related reviews are 5 (January 1758): 9-10; 5 (April 1758): 284; and 6 (September 1758), 228-39.

41. See for example *Critical* 11 (May 1761): 363-69, 389-90; 15 (January 1763): 68-69.

42. See for example *Critical* 2 (December 1756): 343-48; and 4 (November 1757): 379, 385.

43. Representative examples are *Critical* 9 (June 1760): 465-67; 12 (August 1761): 108-9, 13 (January 1762): 1-4; and 15 (June 1763): 449-67.

44. The *Critical* was far from being alone in raising this specter. See, for example, George Watson, *The Scripture Doctrine of Obedience to Government* . . . (1763); and John Brown, *Thoughts on Civil Liberty, on Licentiousness, and Faction* (1765). See also Rudé, "The London 'Mob' of the Eighteenth Century," *Historical Journal* 2 (1959): 1-18.

45. See *Critical* 10 (July 1760): 43. In the *Continuation* Smollett seems to suggest that crowds of common people gather for political meetings only when hired by sinister agents of faction. See, for example, 4:334.

46. See *Critical* 5 (April 1758): 312; and 9 (February 1760): 89-90. See also *Travels*, letter 9, for Smollett's comments on Joseph, his postilion.

47. See *Critical* 2 (November 1756): 348-50; 7 (May 1759): 427-28; 10 (October 1760): 290-91; and 18 (June 1764): 467. See also Schilling, *Conservative England and the Case against Voltaire,* pp. 23 ff., 69-83. In *English Literary Periodicals,* Spector draws this conclusion: "Yet in no periodical was the relationship of Church and state more emphatically argued than in the *Critical.* For its reviewers, religion and morality were interdependent, and the social order itself depended upon the perpetuation of traditional religious belief. Without religious morality to enforce civil duty, preservation of justice and mercy would rest upon 'the written laws of men; and . . . the unwritten laws of reason and conscience—both which [are] totally insufficient'" (p. 193). In *Humphry Clinker,* Bramble writes ironically (July 4) that a friend of his, George Hewitt, returns to Italy by way of Geneva "that he may have a conference with his friend Voltaire, about giving the last blow to the Christian superstition."

48. *Critical* 11 (January 1761): 40; and 8 (November 1759): 419.

49. *Critical* 16 (December 1763): 456.

50. The declaration that the enthusiast "is hardly known in England" is of course inconsistent with many of his other writings, but it is in keeping with his plan for the *Travels.* As noted in connection with his remarks on luxury, Smollett is here minimizing English vices while emphasizing those of the French and the Italians.

CHAPTER SIX

1. The diplomatic maneuvers of the period are discussed in Zenab Esmat Rashed, *The Peace of Paris 1763* (Liverpool, 1951). The terms of the alliance between Bute and George III are clarified in *Letters from George III to Lord Bute, 1756-1766,* ed. Romney Sedgwick (London, 1939), and in James Lee McKelvey, *George III and Lord Bute: The Leicester House Years* (Durham, N.C., 1973). One of the best running commentaries on the war of the weekly papers is volume 1 of *The Correspondence of the Late John Wilkes,* ed. John Almon (London, 1805). Almon includes three letters Smollett wrote to Wilkes before the paper war began, in one of which he addresses Wilkes as "my friend."

2. Besides the intervention and support of the *Auditor,* there are three items of evidence to indicate that the *Briton* fell short of the administration's purpose. (1) John Almon, whose *History of the Late Minority* is the only source for this kind of information, recorded at the time that "the number [of copies of the *Briton*] printed was but 250," implying further that not even this small number was completely distributed. The Whiggish *St. James's Chronicle* on 5 June 1762 noted the appearance of the new sheet with these remarks: "The late Revolution in the Ministry having again set the numerous Tribe of Pamphleteers, Politicians, periodical Paper-Writers, and others of the Machiavellian Class to work, the Public was presented last Saturday with a new Paper entitled the *Briton,* professedly written in Opposition to the *Monitor*: Of this Paper it was our Intention, agreeably to our accustomed Impartiality, to have laid an Abstract before our Readers; but on examining it, we found the Execution, besides

some very exceptionable Points in the *real* Intent of the Piece, to be infinitely beneath either our Notice or Criticism" (quoted in Nobbe, *North Briton,* p. 38). (2) After its first three issues, the *North Briton* largely ignored Smollett and the *Briton;* when it attacked the pro-administration press, it cited the *Auditor.* (3) If Smollett had succeeded in increasing the administration's popularity, Bute would probably have continued to finance the *Briton* beyond the peace treaty. As it happened, the treaty was signed 10 February 1763, and the *Briton* issued its last number 12 February.

3. Defending Smollett against numerous misconceptions, Knapp is eloquent in his biography on the novelist's behalf, citing as evidence, usually, his own answers to his detractors. This method—and the important research that permitted it—is an immeasurable improvement over nineteenth-century studies. When it involves issues of contemporary controversy, however, it is not always adequate. In addition to *Tobias Smollett,* see Knapp's "Rex versus Smollett: More Data on the Smollett-Knowles Libel Case," *MP* 41 (1944): 221–27; "Smollett's Early Years in London," *JEGP* 31 (1932): 220–27; "Ralph Griffiths, Author and Publisher, 1746–1750," *Library* 20 (1939): 197–213; "Smollett and the Elder Pitt," *MLN* 59 (1944): 250–57; and the introduction and notes to Knapp's edition of *Humphry Clinker.*

Gassman extended this method into areas of social and intellectual background in his "The Background of *Humphry Clinker,*" diss., University of Chicago 1960; "*The Briton* and *Humphry Clinker,*" *SEL* 31 (1963): 397–414; and "Religious Attitudes in the World of *Humphry Clinker,*" *Brigham Young University Studies* 6 (Winter 1965): 65–72. Other studies approaching the novelist in much the same way include Whitridge, *Tobias Smollett;* Goldberg, *Smollett and the Scottish School;* and Bruce, *Radical Dr. Smollett.* The most recent example is Robin Fabel, "The Patriotic Briton: Tobias Smollett and English Politics, 1756–1771," *ECS* 8 (1974): 100–114. Fabel regards Smollett as "the nonpolitical doctor" who transcended political disputes and who dismissed political groups of all types.

4. See Namier, *The Structure of Politics,* 2d ed. (London, 1957), pp. 99–100, 117, 210, 268–70, 280–82; and J. Steven Watson, *The Reign of George III* (Oxford, 1960), pp. 81–91.

5. In the third issue Smollett explained that the Briton was "Printed for J. Coote, at the King's Arms, in Paternoster Row."

6. *The Grenville Papers,* 1:457, cited by Nobbe, *North Briton,* p. 32.

7. As part of his political housecleaning, Bute upon becoming first lord began removing Whigs from office. Between October 1760 and February 1762, he expunged nearly all of the Whiggish country lords-lieutenant and justices of the peace, created seventeen new Tory peers and nine Tory lords, and in the largest category, many new Tory grooms of the bedchamber, part of which purge has been called "the massacre of the Pelhamite Innocents."

8. See the *Briton,* nos. 2 (5 June 1762), 7 (10 July 1762), 8 (18 July 1762), 11 (7 August 1762), 35 (22 January 1763). See also the *Continuation* 1:424; 2:4, 6, 18, 196, 261, 306, 381 ff., 426–27; 4:116, 327 ff.

9. See also *Continuation* 5:211–19.

10. See *Critical* 14 (September 1762): 238; 18 (August 1764): 150; and *Auditor,* no. 31 (18 December 1762).

11. In the *Auditor,* Murphy called Wilkes Colonel Squintum and Colonel Cataline. Temple was Lord Gawkee, and Beckford Alderman Sugarcane. See, for example, no. 16 (23 September 1762).

12. *Boswell's London Journal, 1762–1763,* ed. F. A. Pottle (New York, 1950), contains the two standard, but antithetical, views of this charge. On one side, Boswell—who was then reading regularly the *Briton, Auditor, Monitor,* and *North Briton*—found the *North Briton* a polished and witty journal of debate and discovered "a poignant acrimony in it that is very relishing." He records his admiration for Wilkes and even sends him an essay for publication (that was never used). On the other side, Pottle in his introduction calls Wilkes an "unscrupulous demogogue" who "roused the anger of the mob" and "played upon the fears of the mob." Nobbe's book *The North Briton* examines the traditional charges against Wilkes.

13. Smollett's argument here echoes the attacks of the *Critical* upon Rousseau's political teachings. While generally favorable to his style and imagination, the review objected strongly to his political theories. See 7 (January 1759): 48–59; 11 (January 1761): 65–66; 12 (September 1761): 203–11; 13 (February 1762): 101–7; 14 (October 1762): 250–70; 14

(November 1762): 336–46; 14 (December 1762), 426–40; 15 (January 1763): 21–34.

14. This argument provides further evidence of the political nature of his attacks upon luxury. For seven years, since 1756, Smollett had been arguing that such enervation, destruction, and depopulation *had already* ruined Old England, for in no other way could he explain the influence of such unworthy men as the City Whigs.

When reprinting the *Briton* for the *Political Controversy* collection, Wilkes appended the following note to Smollett's statement: "I never yet heard that wealth was the occasion of the ruin of any kingdom.—It must be allowed, indeed, that it introduces luxury, and enervates the disposition in impolitic governments, and so far may be reckoned a misfortune.—But in trading nations industry always keeps us active, tho affluence should render us extravagant . . . we have nothing to fear from our riches while we pay a proper attention to our laws. . . . Upon the whole, the Briton's arguments are calculated for the primitive ages of the world, when a king would feast upon a bit of bread and milk, and an Emperor was unacquainted with the luxury of a mutton chop or a decent pair of breeches" (2:28).

15. Upon hearing of the signing of the preliminary articles, Wilkes is alleged to have said that "it was certainly the peace of God which passeth all understanding."

16. In many ways the rival political sheets determined each other's contents. Whom the *Briton* would damn the *North Briton* must praise, and vice versa. Since Murphy and Smollett regularly denounced Beckford, Wilkes often lauded the lord mayor. In no. 39, for example, published on 26 February 1763, Wilkes reports Beckford's "*elegant* and *masterly* speech" in which he stated "*that the present Peace was in every respect more infamous than that of Utrecht.*" He continues:

> He did accordingly, from the duty he owed to his fellow-citizens, and from his steady, admirable uniformity of conduct, summon a common-council expressly on that great occasion, to explain and enforce with patriotic zeal the important cause of their meeting, and propose an address to the Legislature, to stop in time the progress of so alarming a negociation, founded on the strong evidence of the *preliminaries*. This was his clear duty, and this he nobly discharged. . . . He will therefore, never lend himself to *prop* the minister who made this *infamous peace* as he terms it; but will, I am persuaded, continue steady, indefatigable and animated in an opposition to him.

17. Edward S. Noyes, "Another Smollett Letter," *MLN* 42 (1927): 232.

18. In addition to the works previously cited on this point, see Carl B. Cone, *The English Jacobins* (New York, 1968).

19. *Miscellaneous Works,* ed. Anderson, 6:390. Further citations from the *Atom* will be to this edition and volume, and will be given in the text. The political analogies with Japan are discussed in James R. Foster, "Smollett and the *Atom,*" *PMLA* 68 (1953): 1032–46; and Knapp, "The Keys to Smollett's *Atom,*" *ELN* 2 (1964): 100–102. Hereafter I take the liberty to use the "translated" English names in the text.

20. The famous allegation that Newcastle did not know Britain to be an island is mentioned as fact twice in the *Atom*, pp. 398, 417.

CHAPTER SEVEN

1. E. D. Hirsch, *Validity in Interpretation* (New Haven, 1967), p. 74.

2. The essay is Trilling's "Art and Fortune" in *The Liberal Imagination* (1950; reprinted New York, 1953), pp. 247–71. The approach suggested here could be used with several early fictional narratives. In *Tom Jones,* for example, Fielding uses luxury as concept and as characteristic in the middle and latter portions of the novel. When Tom enters the inn at Hambrook or Upton, he is beholding a world of perfervid pretense as repellent as that Bramble found in the Pump Room at Bath, and the degeneracy he finds in London has the same roots as that Bramble found.

3. A comparable but more recent reading of the novel is John M. Warner's "Smollett's Development as a Novelist," *Novel* 5 (Winter 1972): 148–61. Warner's essay is a well-written and (in its own terms) closely argued exposition of what he considers to be Smollett's movement away

from satire and toward irony. It contains direct or tacit evaluations of all the important elements of *Humphry Clinker,* but without a single reference to the literary history of its own time. From his own perspective Warner can discover Smollett to be much closer as a novelist to Henry James and Lawrence Durrell than to Henry Fielding.

In what might become a similar situation, readers a century or so from now may wonder at the sudden and ambiguous appearance in the later 1960s of black characters in novels by white American authors who had previously left untouched all aspects of black life—for example, John Updike's *Rabbit Redux,* Bernard Malamud's *The Tenants,* Walker Percy's *Love in the Ruins,* and especially Saul Bellow's *Mr. Sammler's Planet.*

4. In his preface to the opening volume of the *Continuation* (1760), Smollett professes that,

> he will carefully avoid the imputation of enthusiasm. In the midst of his transports he hopes to remember his duty, and check the exuberance of zeal with the rigid severity of historical truth.
>
> This is the guiding star by which he hath hitherto steered his dangerous course; the star whose chearing radiance has conducted him safe through the rocks of prejudice and the tides of faction. Guiltless of all connexions that might be supposed to affect his candour, and endanger his integrity, he is determined to proceed with that fearless spirit of independence, by which he flatters himself the former part of the work hath been remarkably distinguished. [1:v]

5. I have not tried to demonstrate further the working of this pattern, for it will be taken up in following chapters. Nor have I attempted to encompass all the political issues touched upon in the novel, but have restricted myself here to the most prominent.

6. Compare the nobleman's lecture to Harrison on the effects of luxury upon a nation in book 11, chapter 2 ("Matters Political") of *Amelia.*

7. This passage has troubled several critics, who have wondered why on this issue alone Smollett should be challenging the government of George III. But as discussion of the *Complete History* has shown, Lismahago is here recalling the practices of Walpole under George II. The review of *An Additional Dialogue of the Dead* in the *Critical Review* for June 1760, cited in chapter 5, calls elections the chance politicians have for "soothing, cajoling, corrupting and destroying the morals of their constituents" (9:466). Its conclusion merits repeating: "Consult history, consult your own mind . . . there can [never] be a dependence on the integrity of the people, where luxury and interest contribute in rendering corrupt, those on whom they have devolved their rights, and constituted their representatives" (9:467).

8. These identifications are explained, and several others for pseudonymous characters attempted, in a forthcoming note in *Notes & Queries* (1977).

9. In the *Continuation,* Smollett interrupts his narrative to praise Heathcote and to apologize for an "injury done him in an earlier volume [*Complete History,* 4:575] in classing him with partisans of the ministry."

> We think it our duty to declare, upon better information, that alderman Heathcote, far from being a partisan of any ministry, always distinguished himself in parliament by a constant and uniform opposition to all ministerial measures, which tended to the prejudice or dishonour of the nation; and ever approved himself an honest, resolute, and zealous assertor of the rights and liberties of the people. [3:442]

Further information on Heathcote is contained in the *DNB;* Sutherland, *The East India Company in Eighteenth-Century Politics;* and Namier and Brooke, *History of Parliament.*

10. Byron Gassman takes a different approach to Methodism in the novel in his "Religious Values in the World of *Humphry Clinker,*" *Brigham Young University Studies* 6 (Winter 1965): 65–72. A valuable study of attacks on the sect is Albert M. Lyles, *Methodism Mocked* (London, 1961). In a letter to John Chute, 10 October 1766, Horace Walpole describes a Methodist chapel he visited at Bath and concludes that luxury can be found even here.

11. Repeatedly through the 1760s Smollett identified himself as a sturdy warrior on behalf of the king's causes. The recurring praise of the young monarch in the *Briton* had been preceded by the encomiums of the *Critical* and was followed by yet stronger advocacy in the *Continuation* and the *Atom.* In the *Continuation* he wrote:

[The people's] love was heightened to rapture and admiration . . . when they were made acquainted with the transcendent virtues of his heart, and the uncommon extent of his understanding; when they knew he was mild, affable, social, and sympathizing; suscepti-ble of all the emotions which private friendship inspires; kind and generous to his dependents, liberal to merit . . . when they knew his heart was intirely British; warmed with the most cordial love of his native country, and animated with plans of the most genuine patriotism; when they learned . . . that he possessed almost every accomplish-ment that art could communicate, or application acquire. [4:151-52]

CHAPTER EIGHT

1. During the last thirty years or so, most of the critical commentary on Smollett's handling of character has emphasized the novelist's irony. Warner, in the article on Smollett's develop-ment cited above, says that no character is reliable of himself, since all are treated ironically; truth is found by splicing together the comments of all five letter-writers: "The scene of life . . . as the diversified points of view indicate . . . is approached from many angles and is seen to reflect truth not just from one of these but from all" (p. 159). A similar conclusion, making Smollett an early romantic in his vision of truth, is drawn by William A. West in "Matt Bramble's Journey to Health," *Texas Studies in Literature and Language* 11 (1969): 1207. More recent and elaborate examples of this approach (in studies otherwise quite different) are John Valdimir Price, *Tobias Smollett: The Expedition of Humphry Clinker,* Studies in English Literature, no. 51 (London, 1973); and Eric Rothstein, *Systems of Order and Inquiry in Later Eighteenth-Century Fiction* (Berkeley and Los Angeles, 1975), pp. 109-53, esp. pp. 100-21. Among the studies that relate Smollett's characters, especially Bramble, to contemporary fic-tional types, two of the best are Thomas R. Preston, "Smollett and the Benevolent Misanthrope Type," *PMLA* 79 (1964): 51-57; and John Sena, "Smollett's Persona and the Melancholic Traveler: An Hypothesis," *ECS* 1 (1968): 353-69.

2. In an instance of plebeian luxury, I take the liberty once more to separate that which is inseparable. Only for convenience of discussion can the characters of *Humphry Clinker* be divided from its politics or its structure.

3. According to long-standing Welsh and English beliefs, the bramble plant is curative as well as prickly. In one version, its leaves in solution were used to heal burns, infections, and diseases. In another, a plant that had rooted at both ends to form an arch was regarded as beneficent to all sickly persons and animals that passed under it. See E. M. Leather, *The Folk-Lore of Herefordshire* (London, 1912); and Edwin and Mona Radford, *Encyclopedia of Super-stitions,* 2d ed., rev. Christina Hole (London, 1961).

4. In the preface to *Ferdinand Count Fathom,* Smollett speaks of the need for contrasting incidents and characters: "That the mind might not be fatigued, nor the imagination disgusted, by a succession of vicious objects, I have endeavoured to refresh the attention with occasional incidents of a different nature; and raised up a virtuous character, in opposition to the adven-turer, with a view to amuse the fancy, engage the affection, and form a striking contrast which might heighten the expression, and give a *relief* to the moral of the whole."

5. This criterion seems to hold with even those figures who do not appear in his letters. Cer-tain characters like Mr. S— and Squire Prankley we encounter only through Jery; yet it is a nephew who is exercising those methods of assessment he has recently learned from his uncle.

6. Martz in *The Later Career,* pp. 170-75, describes Lismahago's role in the novel as essentially didactic. For an account of the effect of English prejudice upon Scots, see George M. Kahrl, *Tobias Smollett: Traveler-Novelist* (Chicago, 1945), pp. 65-79.

7. Goldberg, *Smollett and the Scottish School,* pp. 169-75, builds his argument for the novelist's primitivism on the character of Clinker. Although he does not note that Clinker is not a hard primitivist (and Bramble is not a primitivist at all), he is perceptive on Clinker's moral function.

8. See for example *Spectator* no. 55, Pope's "Of the Characters of Women," William White-head's "Song for Ranelagh," and Chesterfield's famous "Women . . . are only children of a larger growth" letter, 5 September 1748. Patricia Meyer Spacks presents an interesting review

of the position of women, from the viewpoint of women writers, in "Ev'ry Woman Is at Heart a Rake," *ECS* 8 (1974): 27–46. One might say that for traditional critics of luxury, there lingered a Miltonic image, not of that "fair defect of nature" alone, but of Eve joined by Sin, half graceful woman and half loathsome serpent. In her *Marriage: Fielding's Mirror of Morality* (University, Ala., 1973), pp. 122–43, Murial Brittain Williams includes useful appendixes on marriage and divorce laws and popular attitudes toward women. Jean H. Hagstrum's forthcoming book on changing conceptions of love will trace the theme through eighteenth- and early nineteenth-century literature.

9. See also her letter of June 14, Jery's of May 29, Liddy's of April 26 and June 10, and Bramble's of June 12.

10. On many occasions from the *Critical Review* of 1756 to the *Atom* of 1769 Smollett was to remark what he considered criminal conspiracies among the working poor. Bramble's comments on the servants of Squire Burdock are anticipated in many places, particularly in the closing letter of the *Travels,* which is devoted to methods of extortion and advises weary travelers to oblige the "confederacy" lest their journeys be made intolerable. Apropos the delight Win and Dutton take in dressing like their betters, at least six times during Smollett's editorship the *Critical* attacked the dress of servants as indicative of the luxury of the laboring population. The strictures upon women's dress and habits in Smollett and the *Critical* should be compared with those found in *The Lady's Magazine; or, Polite Companion for the Fair Sex* (September 1759–).

CHAPTER NINE

1. My sense of the structure of *Humphry Clinker* is close to that Malcolm Bradbury finds in most fiction; see his "Towards a Poetics of Fiction: 1. An Approach through Structure," *Novel* 1 (1967): 51. There is a further parallel in Henry Knight Miller's excellent analysis "Some Functions of Rhetoric in *Tom Jones,*" *PQ* 45 (1966): 209–35. Miller demonstrates in Fielding's rhetoric an attempt to reach "every Reader in the world." Smollett's ambition was no less; he would have his work appeal to the reason, to the senses, and to all shadings of the two.

2. In stressing Smollett's attack upon luxury, let me repeat, I do not wish to be seen as neglecting or minimizing the novelist's relationship to his contemporaries. His indebtedness to earlier epistolary fiction, to Anstey's *New Bath Guide,* and to Fielding has been well treated before. Yet if one were to search out specific parallels, one would still be obliged to go to antiquity: to the attack on juries in the *Wasps* and on the comprehensive franchise in the *Knights,* for example, or to the dialectic of character and action in the Platonic dialogues, where a figure of known background and temperament enters with a question to be answered or a dilemma to be resolved and is guided to his own enlightenment. In any case, my argument here is concerned with uses, not sources.

3. Byron Gassman first noted the change in Jery's attitude in "The Background of . . . *Humphry Clinker,*" p. 61. Bramble's charge that the common people defile a spa has a historically familiar ring. For three centuries the authorities of Zurich ordained by law who was permitted to travel to the mineral springs at Baden, fourteen miles away.

4. See Louis A. Landa, "London Observed: The Progress of a Simile," *PQ* 54 (1975): 275–88.

5. Scotland, Dennison's small part of England, and Bramble's small part of Wales all offer a way of life that is providential as well as arcadian. To meet as many of the good people of North Britain as he wishes, Bramble must be vigorous in his pursuits. In London he was, it seems, content to spend the time writing long letters. (He also discovered there that the only decent food to be had was eggs "imported from France and Scotland.") In Scotland he is apparently too busy to write, and his letters are relatively few for the length of time he spends in the country. As he is vigorously exercised, he loses all signs of gout and constipation, incidently following Chowder's example of a healing regimen.

In Dennison's estate a few acres of Scotland seem to be transplanted, and in their descriptions of the two places Jery and Bramble provide what amount to Smollett's Discourses—offering the proper subjects, methods, and ideals for Imitation in Excellence. Like the typical Scotsman, Dennison is in features "hale, robust, and florid." Yet because he resides below the Tweed, he like Baynard requires a fortunate death in the family before he can be his own man. He inherited the estate when his elder brother "was happily carried off by a fever, the immediate consequence of a debauch" (MB, October 8).

CONCLUSION

1. Christopher Hill, "The Norman Yoke," *Puritanism and Revolution* (London, 1958), pp. 50-122.

2. In our day this mode of thought would be called an ideology, pertinently defined by Karl Mannheim as a pattern of thought characteristic of ruling groups who "in their thinking become so intensely interest-bound to a situation that they are simply no longer able to see certain facts which would undermine their sense of dominance" (*Ideology and Utopia,* trans. Louis Wirth and Edward Shils [New York, n.d.], p. 40). Yet perhaps the best gloss is also the most famous. When Alice questions his arbitrary use of words, Humpty Dumpty replies that only one issue is involved, "which is to be *master*—that's all."

3. To this myth Johnson is said to have replied: "Sir, it is not so much to be lamented that Old England is lost as that the Scotch have found it."

4. See his *Emblem and Expression: Meaning in English Art of the Eighteenth Century* (Cambridge, Mass., 1975), pp. 9-10 and passim.

5. When a new anti-Jacobin newspaper appeared in Edinburgh in 1819, Scott wrote to Lord Melville that the present discontent of the common people could "be easily extinguished if men of property will be true to themselves and use their power." He then identifies men of property. "It is the middle class which requires to be put on the guard—every man who has or cultivates a furrow of land or has a guinea in the funds or vested in stock, in trade or in mortgage or in any other way whatsoever" (*Letters,* ed. H. J. C. Grierson, 12 vols. [London, 1932-37], 6:31, punctuation supplied). Smollett was alarmed over the agitation of the City Whigs because, he said, they possessed no muniments—no titles, rights, or deeds. There is an important parallel in the rise of the City Whigs and the coming to power of the "country men" of the Roman Senate. For the latter see T. P. Wiseman, *New Men in the Roman Senate B.C. 139–A.D. 14* (Oxford, 1971). There is also a family resemblance among Smollett's vulgar plebeians, Cato's barbarians, and Hobbes's natural men.

INDEX

Periodicals and anonymous works are cited under titles; all other works are included in entries under authors. Two abbreviations have been used: S for Smollett, *HC* for *Humphry Clinker*.

Library of Congress Cataloging in Publication Data

Sekora, John.
  Luxury.

  Includes index.
    1. Smollett, Tobias George, 1721–1771 –Criticism and
interpretation. 2. Luxury. 3. Smollett, Tobias George,
1721–1771. The expedition of Humphry Clinker.
I. Title
PR3698.L88S4   823'.6   77–4545
ISBN 0–8018–1972–5

t